Prakaraṇapañcikā

Prakaraṇapañcikā

of Śālikanātha

With an Exposition in English

K.T. Pandurangi

Indian Council of
Philosophical Research
New Delhi

D.K. Printworld (P) Ltd.
Publishers of Indian Traditions
New Delhi

Cataloging in Publication Data — DK

[Courtesy: D.K. Agencies (P) Ltd. <docinfo@dkagencies.com>]

Śālikanāthamiśra, fl. 780-825.

Prakaraṇapañcikā of Śālikanātha : with an exposition in English / K.T. Pandurangi.

p. cm.

In Sanskrit; exposition and introductory matter in English.

Reprint.

Includes bibliographical references (p.).

ISBN 13: 9788124605844

1. Mimamsa — Early works to 1800. I. Pandurangi, Krishnacharya Tamanacharya, 1918- II. Title.

DDC 181.42 22

First published in 2004

Reprinted in 2011

ISBN 13: 978-81-246-0584-4 ISBN 10: 81-246-0584-X

Published by:

INDIAN COUNCIL OF PHILOSOPHICAL RESEARCH
Darshan Bhawan, 36 Tughlakabad Institutional Area
Mehrauli Badarpur Road, New Delhi - 110 062

and

D.K. PRINTWORLD (P) LTD.
Regd. Office: 'Srikunj', F-52, Bali Nagar
Ramesh Nagar Metro Station
New Delhi-110 015
Phones: (011) 2545 3975; 2546 6019; *Fax*: (011) 2546 5926
E-mail: indology@dkprintworld.com, *Website*: www.dkprintworld.com

Printed by: D.K. Printworld (P) Ltd., New Delhi

CONTENTS

Preface

In Indian Philosophy Vedānta and Nyāya have received greater attention than Pūrvamīmāṃsā both in the traditional and modern circles of scholars. Within Pūrvamīmāṃsā the Bhāṭṭa texts are widely studied than the Prābhākara. The credit of drawing the attention to the Prābhākara school goes to two distinguished modern scholars viz., Dr. Ganganath Jha and Dr. Kunhan Raja.

The publication of *Bṛhati,* a commentary by Prabhākara on *Śābarabhāṣya,* and Ṛjuvimalā a sub-commentary by Śālikanātha on *Bṛhati* provided the source books for the Prābhākara study. A presentation of the Prābhākara thought in English by Dr. Ganganath Jha in his work Prābhākara school of Pūrvamīmāṃsā enabled the modern scholars to get acquainted with Prābhākara. The publication of *Prakaraṇapañcikā* of Śālikanātha edited by Subrahmaṇya Śāstry further augmented the source works. This work was published long back from Vārāṇasi. However, Subrahmaṇya Śāstry's edition has a commentary i.e., Nyāyaśuddhi of Nārāyaṇa which is very helpful to comprehend the text. Śāstriji has also added a detailed introduction, brief notes all along the text, and a summary of the main points at the end of each chapter. This edition is very useful to undertake research in the Prābhākara system.

After a careful reading of this text I felt that it has rich material for research. However, its language and style are very terse. The Prābhākara terminology is also quite unfamiliar to modern scholars. The use of the same terms by the Bhāṭṭas and the Prābhākaras with different implications also requires clarification. Most of the Pūrvamīmāṃsā scholars are greatly influenced by the Bhāṭṭa approach and the Bhāṭṭa interpretation. This comes in the way of comprehending the subtle distinction between the Bhāṭṭa approach and the Prābhākara approach.

I felt that it will be a help to younger scholars, if an exposition in English of this valuable text is prepared.

A sentence by sentence translation of such highly technical works is not possible. Even if such a translation is prepared taking pains, it will not be intelligible unless one goes back again to the text and traces the contents.

Therefore, in this exposition a simple and direct summary of the content closely following the text is given. The plan of presentation of the main point, the arguments to support it, the objections and answers given in the text is followed. The ritual details incidently mentioned and the laboured supplementary arguments are avoided to maintain the clarity of the central point.

The title and subtitles are given under each chapter. Detailed extracts are also given for ready reference. This will also help the learned readers to check the authenticity of the English presentation.

The Prābhākara's approach is novel and unusual in many respects. There is a good deal of scope for research and giving a new orientation to some of the issues of Indian Philosophy. It is hoped that this English exposition will give deeper insight into the Prābhākara thought and inspire further research.

I take this opportunity to thank the authorities of Indian Council of Philosophical Research for publishing this work.

K.T. Pandurangi

Introduction

The two schools of Pūrvamīmāṃsā *viz.*, the Bhāṭṭa and the Prābhākaras are well-known. Both claim *Jaimini sūtras* and *Śābarabhāṣya* as their sources. Some scholars have tried to trace some of the concepts of the Prābhākaras to Bādari whose views are quoted in *Jaimini sūtras*. Attempts are also made to identify Bhavadāsa and Bhartṛmitra as the precursors of the Prābhākara view. References are also found to some old Prābhākaras as Cirantana Prābhākara and Jarat Prābhākara. Their views are quoted on two important topics *viz.*, on the number of categories and the nature of *akhyāti*. 'Prameya Pārāyaṇa portion of *Prakaraṇapañcikā* is not available. However, its commentator Nārāyaṇa lists the eight categories mentioning *sāṃkhya* and *sādṛśya* as the seventh and the eighth. However, the view of the old Prābhākaras quoted by Vidyāraṇya in *Vivaraṇaprameya Saṅgraha* mentions *viśeṣa* and *niyoga* in place of *sāṃkhya* and *sādṛśya*. In respect of *akhyāti* also the old Prābhākaras had slightly a different explanation from the one commonly given. Their view is quoted in *Isṭasiddhi* of Vimuktātman. From this it is clear that the Prābhākara's thought had an early base and Prabhākara only rejuvenated it.

It is difficult to ascertain whether *Śābarabhāṣya* mainly supports the Bhāṭṭas or the Prābhākaras. The most important *sūtra tadbhūtānām kriyārthena samāṃnāyaḥ* etc. and Śabara's remarks on it seem to support *anvitābhidhāna* theory of sentence meaning. Śālikanātha quotes half a dozen *adhikaraṇas* to establish *kāryānvita* procedure. All these seem to support this theory. However, a detailed scrutiny of the entire *bhāṣya* with the help of a computer has to be made to find out Śabara's support to one of them entirely or partially. Prabhākara was an younger contemporary of Kumārila. He quotes

Kumārila's views in a number of *adhikaraṇas*, such as *guṇakāmādhikaraṇa, abhikramaṇādhikaraṇa, balābalādhikaraṇa*. His only one work i.e., *Bṛhatī*, a detailed commentary on *Śābarabhāṣya* is available.

The literature of the *Bhāṭṭa* school is quite large. There are only seven works of the Prābhākara school. *Bṛhatī* of Prābhākara, *Ṛjuvimalā*, *Prakaraṇapañcikā*, and *Bhāṣyadīpa* of Śālikanātha, *Nayaviveka* of *Bhavanātha*, *Tantrarahasya* of Rāmānuja and *Prabhākara Vijaya* of *Nandīśvara*. Among these Śālikanātha's *Prakaraṇapañcikā* is the central text. It discusses all important issues and concepts of the Prābhākara school in detail. Two *vārtikakāras* are quoted in it. One is in support of the Prābhākara view, the other is against the Prābhākara view. The latter is Kumārila Bhāṭṭa. The first one seems to be an old Prābhākara writer.

Apart from the seven works of Prābhākara school, there is another source to know the Prābhākara thought. The works that criticize the Prābhākara thought constitute this source. The earliest among these are the three important works of Mandana Mishra. His *Vidhiviveka*, *Vibhramaviveka* and *Bhāvanāviveka* examine the Prābhākara concept of *kārya* and their *akhyāti* theory in detail. These were composed before Śālikanātha. He answers the objections raised in these works. Vachaspati Mishra's commentary on *Vidhiviveka* quotes Śālikanātha's answers and shows the drawbacks from Mandana's point of view. Pārthasārathi Mishra's *Śāstradīpikā*, particularly, *Tarkapāda* portion and his *Nyāyaratnamālā* review the important issues of the Prābhākara system. This tradition of reviewing Prābhākara thought is continued in the later Bhāṭṭa Mīmāṃsā works.

Important writers of Nyāyavaiśeṣika and the Vedānta schools also quote the Prābhākara's theories and criticize. The *Kāryatāvāda*, *anvitābhidhānavāda*, and the *akhyātivāda* are particularly criticized. Nyāya works like *Nyāyamañjari* of Jayanta, Kusumāñjali of Udayana, *Tatvacintāmaṇi* of Gaṅgeśa review the Prābhākaras views. These works give a clearer picture of the Prābhākara thought and constitute an important source. Modern scholars also have written good many works in English on Bhāṭṭa school by way of translations, studies and research papers. There are very few on the Prābhākara system. Prābhākara Mīmāṃsā by Ganganatha Jha and by Paśupatinātha Shastry are two important works of Prābhākara Mīmāṃsā. The long introduction to *Tantrarahasya* by K.S. Ramaswamy is quite informative. The papers on *Niyoga*, and Prābhākaras the old and new by M. Hiriyanna and on *Karma* by Halbfass give an insight into Prābhākara thought. Professor Kuppuswamy Shastry's two papers on the old Prābhākaras give valuable information about the early Prābhākaras.

The criticism of Prābhākara views is two-fold: (i) criticism of the import of the injunction and the issues connected with the organization of the sacrifice. (ii) The issues connected with the epistemology and the theory of knowledge. In the first area it is mainly a fight between the Bhāṭṭas and the Prābhākaras. In the second area, all other systems of Indian Philosophy, particularly Nyāya and Vedānta participate and confront the Prābhākaras.

Among the Vedānta schools, Viśiṣṭādvaita and Dvaita are a little friendly. Both these have accepted *anvitābhidhāna* theory with some modifications. Viśiṣṭādvaita theory of *yathārthakhyāti* is closer to *akhyāti*. The concept of difference being an internal attribute of the object is acceptable to Dvaita. In this way the Prābhākara thought is preserved more by its opponents than by its own literature.

Prakaraṇapañcikā gives a detailed account of the Prābhākara system in all aspects. These are given in the exposition along with the relevant portions of text in this study. Here the main issues are presented by way of recapitulation of the exposition of the text. There are eight main issues that require special attention. These are: (i) The concept of *kārya* or *niyoga* is the import of Vedic injunction, (ii) The theory of *anvitābhidhāna*, (iii) *Akhyāti* theory of perceptual error, (iv) Rejection of *abhāva*, (v) Non-Vedic statements communicate through inference, (vi) The concept of *tripuṭīkaraṇa*, (vii) The nature of *savikalpaka, nirvikalpaka*, (viii) The categories.

The other systems of Indian Philosophy do not agree with the Prābhākaras on these issues and have bitterly criticized them. A proper understanding of the Prābhākara point of view on these issues will help to meet these criticisms and understand the Prābhākara thought more clearly. This is attempted here.

1. The Concept of Kārya

The Prābhākaras state that *kārya* is the import of Vedic injunction. This *kārya* has three dimensions: (i) It is conveyed only by *śabdapramāṇa* i.e., Vedic injunction, but not by any other *pramāṇa*. To convey this aspect it is designated as *apūrva* i.e., *mānāntara apūrva*. (ii) It elicits an agent who has the entitlement to undertake the *kārya*. Therefore, it is called *niyoga* i.e., direction or command. The person elicited is called *niyojya*, i.e., the person directed to accomplish *kārya*. (iii) It inculcates a sense of accomplishing a task as 'this is my task'. Therefore, it is called *kārya*. It is this *kārya* that is conveyed by the Vedic injunction. Its designation *apūrva* conveys its epistemological status as conveyed by *śabdapramāṇa* only. Its designation *niyoga* conveys the fact that it motivates the person who has the entitlement to undertake the task, and its designation as *kārya* conveys that it is of the nature of the accomplishment of a task. The task to be accomplished by it i.e., *yāga*, is conveyed by the root of the verb *yajeta*. This *yāgakriyā* is the subject-matter of *kārya*. It is also the instrument i.e., *karaṇa*. *Yāga* is both the subject and instrument of *kārya*.

The injunctive suffix conveys *kṛti* i.e., initiative also. No *kārya* can be accomplished without initiative. Therefore, *kṛti* i.e., initiative, is also conveyed by the injunctive suffix. The initiative has to operate through an activity. Such an activity, in the present context, is *yāgakriyā*. This *yāgakriyā* gives a form to kārya conveyed by the Vedic injunction. Therefore, it is its content or *viṣaya*. It is also *karaṇa*, not in the sense that it produces *kārya* but in the sense that it gives a form to it. The *kṛti* is called *bhāvanā* as it leads to *kārya* i.e., *bhāvya* i.e., the goal. Keeping this role of *kṛti* in mind *kārya* is defined as *kṛtyuddeśyam kṛtipradhānaṃ kāryaṃ*. This *kārya* is distinct from *kriyā* so far as the Vedic injunctions are concerned. In the case of ordinary injunctions *kriyā* is called *kārya* in the secondary sense. It is already stated that this *kārya* is designated as *apūrva* taking into account the fact that it is conveyed by *śabdapramāṇa* only. For another reason also it is called *apūrva*. When *yāgakriyā* is duly performed, *kārya* is accomplished. In this accomplished state it is something unique. Therefore, it is called *apūrva*. To distinguish the two usages of *apūrva* it is called *pandāpūrva* at that stage. It is with this *kārya* that all other items get connected. *Niyojya*, the *yāga*, and *aṅgas* i.e., auxiliaries, get connected with it. The *kārya* connected with all these constitutes *vākyārtha* and *vedārtha* for Prābhākaras. In this context it should be noted that the terms *bhāvanā* and *apūrva* are used in the Prābhākara system in altogether different senses than the Bhāṭṭas system. Bhāṭṭas use the term *bhāvanā* in the sense of two *bhāvanās viz., śābdībhāvanā* and *ārthībhāvanā* envisaged by them. The Prābhākaras use it in the sense of *kṛti*. The Prābhākaras do not accept the scheme of *śābdibhāvanā* and *ārthībhāvānā* as conveyed by the injunctive suffix. The term *apūrva* is used in the sense of a concept that serves as a link between *yāga* and *svarga* by the Bhāṭṭas while the Prābhākaras have made it a designation of *kārya* to indicate its unique nature. It is not a link between *yāga* and *svarga*. It is the goal of the performance of *yāga*.

Now, we have to find out the role of *svargakāmanā*, and the position of *svarga* in this scheme. *Svargakāmanā* is a qualification that entitles a person to undertake such sacrifices that provide him *svarga*. He is *adhikārī* i.e., a person entitled for these *kāmya* sacrifices. The injunctions of these sacrifices elicit only such persons as *niyojya* who have a desire for *svarga*. When he is elicited as *niyojya* he comprehends it as his *kārya* and proceeds to perform the sacrifice. It is *kāryatājñāna* that motivates him. *Iṣṭakāmanā* only provides him the entitlement i.e., *adhikāra*, of course, he obtains *svarga*, not as a primary result but as a secondary result. The primay result is the accomplishment of *kārya* itself. This *kārya* provides the secondary result since, this secondary result viz., *svarga*, had provided entitlement to the *niyojya* who accomplished *kārya*. It is something like a master providing maintenance to his servant to serve his own purpose. *Iṣṭasādhanatā* is not the import of the injunction. It is only a ground to acquire entitlement.

This *kāryatā* theory of the import of Vedic injunction is criticized by almost every other system of Indian Philosophy. It is criticized on two grounds: (i) The very nature of kārya cannot be satisfactorily explained (ii) As it is not of the nature of happiness or means of happiness it cannot motivate and generate initiative to undertake any activity.

The earliest criticism of the concept of *kārya* is found in *Vidhiviveka* of Mandana Mishra. He neatly sums up the concept of *kārya* or *niyoga* as proposed by the Prābhākaras and examines it clause by clause.

यदपि दर्शनम्-प्रमाणान्तरागोचरः शब्दमात्रावलम्बनः नियुक्तोऽस्मीति प्रत्यात्मवेदनीयः सुखादिवत् अपरामृष्टकालत्रयः लिङादीनामर्थो विधिरिति। (वि०वि० पृ० ३५)

Two important clauses in this explanation of *kārya* or *niyoga* are: (i) That which is not conveyed by any other *pramāṇa* but conveyed only by *Śabdapramāṇa* (ii) That which has no reference to particular time. Mandana Mishra argues that since the so-called *kārya* or *niyoga* is not conveyed by any *pramāṇa* the very *vācya-vācakabhāva* relation between the injunctive suffix and *kārya* cannot be ascertained. Therefore, *śabda* also cannot convey *kārya* or *niyoga*. Śālikanātha notices this objection as under:

ननु व्युत्पत्त्यपेक्षेषु शब्देष्वर्थाभिधायिषु ।
कथं मानान्तरावेद्यं कार्यमाहुः लिङादयः ॥

Śālikanātha answers this objection by pointing out that the *vāchya vāchaka bhāva* relation between the injunctive suffix and *kārya* is comprehended through elders' conversation as in the case of other words. Vāchaspati Mishra elaborates this answer in his *Tattvakaṇikā*, a commentory on *Vidhiviveka* as under:

इदमत्र आकूतम्-कार्याभिधायिता तावत् लिङादीनामवगता आचार्यवाक्येषु 'माणवक! समिधमाहर' इत्यादिषु । एतद्वाक्यश्रवणानन्तरं प्रवर्तमानं समिदाहरणे माणवकमुपलभ्य पार्श्वस्थो व्युत्पित्सुः एवमवधारयति । बुद्धिपूर्वेयमस्य प्रवृत्तिः स्वतन्त्रप्रवृत्तित्वात् मदीयप्रवृत्तिवत् । अहं च न क्रियामात्रावगमात् नापि फलमात्रवगमात् नापि फलसाधनत्वावगमात् किन्तु कार्यतावगमात् प्रवृत्तः । न खलु अन्ततः अर्भकः स्तनपानादिकमपि क्रियां कार्यतया यावन्नावगतवान् तावत् न प्रवृत्तः । (त०क० पृ० ३८)

Both Mandana Mishra and Vāchaspati Mishra are not satisfied with this reply and the debate is going on.

The second clause viz., that which has no reference to time is also questioned by Mandana Mishra. He argues that if it has no reference to time, it cannot be an entity. It will be a non-entity i.e., '*asat*' like a barren woman's son. It will have no *sattā* i.e., existence. However, Prābhākaras define '*sat*' in a different way. They define '*sat*' as that which is conveyed by a *pramāṇa.* They do not accept *sattā jāti. Sattva* is *svarūpasattva* for them. Even the *Nyāya-Vaiśeṣikas* talk of *sattā jāti* for first three categories viz., *dravya, guṇa* and *karma* only. The other categories viz., *sāmānya, viśeṣa* etc. do not have *sattājāti.* These have only *svarūpa sattā. Niyoga* or *kārya* has such *svarūpasattā.* We may note here that even *Nyāya-Vaiśeṣikas* define a category as *prameya.*

The main objection raised against *kārya* or *niyoga* by its critics is that it cannot motivate to undertake the task. To motivate for undertaking activity, the object concerned should enkindle desire. Happiness or the means of the happiness only enkindle the desire to undertake an activity. *Kārya* is neither of the nature of happiness nor it is a means of happiness. Mere *kāryatā-jñāna* does not motivate the activity. It is *iṣṭasādhanatā-jñāna* that motivates the activity.

This contention is not acceptable to the Prābhākaras. They argue that by an analysis of the experience it is found that it is *kāryatā-*

jñāna that prompts a person to undertake a task but not mere *iṣṭasādhanatā-jñāna.* The latter is only a step to comprehend *kāryatā.* One will not proceed to act only by the knowledge that something is the means of happiness. He has to consider it as a task to be undertaken by him. The expectation of the desired result only creates interest in the task but the actual undertaking of the task has to be prompted by the sense that now it is my task. That is to say, he has to realize that he is the *niyojya* for that *kārya.*

Inculcating such a sense of *kārya* is much more evident in the case of Vedic injunction. Accomplishing *kārya* conveyed by a Vedic injunction is an end by itself. It is not a means to happiness. In the case of *kāmyakarma*, the happiness is only a by-product. In the case of *nitya* i.e., obligatory rites, it is not there even as a by-product.

This position of the Prābhākaras has a historical background in the Indian cultural tradition. In the Vedic period the rituals were considered as having their own efficacy. The performance of the rituals itself was a holy act and a value. It gave a satisfaction to the performer. The idea of obtaining any outside happiness is only a later development. Even the *kāmyakarmas* were performed as if they were *nityakarmas.* This can be made out by the fact that *agnihotra* originally was a *nityakarma* and later was made a *kāmyakarma* also. *Nityakarmas* were always considered as superior to *kāmyakarmas.* The concept of *niṣkāmakarma* developed later is a rejuvenation of the early concept of *karma* being a task to be accomplished for its own sake but not for any outside result. This tradition of performance of *karma* for its own sake is upheld by the Prābhākaras. The Bhāṭṭas were of the view that the rituals and other activities are meant for deriving happiness. This is the basis of the controversy whether *iṣṭasādhanatā-jñāna* prompts activity or *kāryatā-jñāna.* The clause *sukhādivat* in the explanation of the nature of *niyoga* or *kārya* brings out this aspect. The accomplishment of *kārya* is as much an end as deriving happiness. It is not an instrumental value, but it is an intrinsic value.

The *kārya* is more an ethical concept than a ritualistic concept. Even if it is taken as a ritualistic concept, it has to be taken out of empirical level and has to be looked upon as a mystical or transcendental value. Achieving such a mystical efficacy of Vedic rituals is the goal of performing Vedic rituals. The other benefits are by-products.

The criticism of *kāryatā* theory has a linguistic dimension also. Whether the language is learnt through the conversation of elders by observing their activities or it is learnt by introducing the objects as they are, is an old controversy. These two approaches are designated as *kārye vyutpatti* and *siddhe vyutpatti.* The former makes the action conveyed by the verb the focal point and the centre of semantic organization in a sentence, and the latter makes the noun as the centre of semantic organization. The latter, naturally opposes the *kāyatā* theory of linguistic communication.

Another aspect of linguistic communication is that whether the linguistic communication is meant just to give the knowledge or to prompt action also. For those who hold the first view, it is sufficient if the injunction informs that the sacrifice leads to the desired result. It need not specifically command to accomplish the task. The criticism of the theory of *kāryatā* is based on these controversies.

Further, informing something as the means of happiness is taken for granted as a sure means of prompting an activity and the other nature of the man acting on the urge to accomplish a task is completely ignored.

The critics have also failed to understand the difference between *kriyā*—a physical event, and *kārya*—to which an ethical or transcendental status is given. To convey this aspect of *kārya*, it is designated as *apūrva.* A modern scholar has remarked that the Prābhākaras have carefully avoided mentioning the ontological status of *kārya.* However, it may be pointed out that they have stated *kriyā* as its content. That is its status at empirical level. At ethical and transcendental level the question of its ontological status in the manner of an empirical entity does not arise. It may be noted that the old Prābhākaras had given the status of a separate category to *niyoga.*

2. The Anvitābhidhāna Atheory of Sentence-meaning

It is noticed above that *niyoga* or *kārya* elicits the agent as *niyojya* and *yāga* as *viṣaya*. It also elicits aṅgas and other requirements to accomplish *kārya*. By eliciting all these, *kāryānvita vākyārtha* takes its full shape as the import of Vedic injunction. This means that all the requirements for the accomplishment of *kārya* are organized into a unit and *kārya* is accomplished. These do not serve any purpose individually in isolation. These serve the purpose of accomplishing *kārya* by being connected with *kārya*. This process has to be reflected in the language that conveys *kārya* as connected with these. Therefore, individual terms conveying different items of this programme have to reflect this connection as a part of their meaning. For this purpose, the Prābhākaras have evolved the *anvitābhidhāna* theory of sentence-meaning. This theory of *anvitābhidhāna* is intimately connected with the concept of *kārya* centered organization of sacrificial programme. Śālikanātha clearly states this purpose at the commencement of the exposition of *anvitābhidhāna* theory.

अपूर्वमेव वाक्यार्थ इति साधनीयम् । तस्य मूलं पदानामन्विता-भिधायितेति तामेव तावदादौ परिशोधयति । (प्र०पं० ३७६)

According to *anvitābhidhāna* theory of sentence-meaning a word conveys its meaning as connected with the meaning of the other relevant word. Subordinate words convey their meanings as connected with the meaning of the main word. Such connected meanings of the words is the sentence-meaning. Contributing to the evolution of the prominent meaning is the purpose of all other words. This is the import of the whole sentence. Neither the individual words are the means of communication separately, nor the meanings of the individual words are intended to be communicated.

प्रधानगुणभावेन लब्धान्योन्यसमन्वयान् ।
पदार्थानेव वाक्यार्थान् सङ्गिरन्ते विपश्चितः ॥ (प्रं०पं० ३७७)

On this theory of *anvitābhidhāna* two objections are raised by the critics of this theory *viz*., **आनन्त्य** and **अन्योन्याश्रय**.

(i) According to this theory each word is expected to convey its meaning as connected with the meaning of the other relevant word in the sentence. This connection is included in the scope of the meaning of the word. The other word will be different in different sentences. Consequently the meaning of a word has to be connected with the meanings of those many words. This means each word will have an unlimited number of connections as its meanings. To have *śaktigraha* of a word with such a large number of meanings of other words is impossible.

(ii) The second objection is that when it is considered that a word conveys its meaning as connected with the meaning of other relevant word, is the other word also to be taken as conveying its meaning as connected with the meaning of this word or not? In the first alternative it will result in reciprocal dependency i.e., *anyonyāśraya.*

The first objection does not hold good if the way in which the connection is effected and ascertained are examined. The connection envisaged among the word-meanings in a sentence is based on three criteria *viz., ākāṅkṣā, sannidhi* and *yogyatā.* Among the three, *ākāṅkṣā* is very important. A word conveys the meaning connected with the meaning of the other relevant word that has the *ākāṅkṣā.* This *ākāṅkṣā* in respect of different words in a sentence does not arise simultaneously or in a disorderly way. The import of the injunction viz., *kārya* i.e., *apūrva,* is the central meaning of a Vedic injunctive sentence. This needs *viṣaya* i.e., *yāga.* It also needs a *niyojya* to perform *yāga.* Then *karaṇopakāras* are needed. All these have an *ākānkṣā* with the central meaning i.e., *kārya,* and are conveyed as connected with that meaning in the respective order. In view of this orderly connection there is no room for any reciprocal dependency. Nor there is any need to envisage innumerable denotative powers to each word to account for its occurrence in different sentences.

The answers to these objections are succinctly put forth by Pārthasārathi Mishra himself while summarising the Prābhākara point of view.

सन्निध्यपेक्षायोग्यत्वैरुपलक्षणलाभतः ।
आनन्त्येप्यन्वितानां स्यात् सम्बन्धग्रहणं मम ॥ ६ ॥

न च सन्निध्यपेक्षत्वे भवेदन्योन्यसंश्रयः ॥ ९ ॥
(न्या०र०मा० ९८-९९)

These objections are answered by Śālikanātha in detail in *Prakaraṇapañcikā*. The main points of the answer are summarized in the above verses. Pārthasārathi does not rake up these objections further. He has a different objection against *anvitābhidhānavāda*. He argues that if the word has to convey connected word meaning, then, it has to have two denotative powers *viz.*, one denotative power to convey the word meaning and another to convey the connection.

अन्विताभिधायित्वे हि पदानामवश्यमेव विशेषणभूतोप्यन्वयोऽभिधातव्यः । अन्यथा अन्वितप्रतीतेरुत्पत्त्ययोगात् । ततश्चान्वयान्वित-विषयशक्तिद्वयकल्पनात् अदृष्टकल्पना गुरुतरा स्यात् ।

This is merely a procedural point. The substantial issue is whether the words are capable of communicating individually in an isolated way or only as a part of a syntactically knit unit. In other words, whether word is a unit of communication or a sentence is a unit of communication, particularly, in the context of communicating the organization of a sacrificial programme through the Vedic injunction. To protect the unity of the programme, the unity of its communication is essential. This point seems to have been ignored by *abhihitānvayavādins*.

3. Akhyāti Theory of Perceptual Error

In Indian Philosophy the theories of perceptual error have played an important role. There are five dimensions of these theories: (i) optical (ii) psychological (iii) epistemological (iv) logical and (v) metaphysical

The process of error starts at optical level. The psychological level adds to it. It takes epistemological shape. These three aspects have to be taken into account while analysing the nature of error. The analysis has to satisfy the logical requirements. Different schools of Indian Philosophy have different metaphysical views. They have worked out their theories of perceptual error within the framework of their metaphysical systems. Consequently every school has its own theory. These theories are known as *khyāti* theories. These could be broadly grouped into (i) Idealists (ii) Realists. Within the realists *anyathākhyātivādins* and *yathārthakhyātivādins.*

Ātmakhyāti and *asatkhyāti* come under the idealist group. The *anyathākhyāti* of *Nyāyavaśeṣikas, viparītakhyāti* of the Bhāṭṭas and *abhinava-anyathākhyāti* of Davita Vedānta come under *anyathākhyāti* group. *Akhyāti* of the Prābhākaras, *yathārthakhyāti* of *Rāmānujas* and *satkhyāti* of *Sāṃkhyas* come under the *yathārtha* group. The Advaita theory of *anirvacanīyakhyāti* is a class by itself. It is based on the Advaita concept of *sad-asad vilakṣaṇa* metaphysics. The basic concept of the idealists is that there are no objects outside knowledge. The concept of the *anyathākhyātivādin* is that one entity is comprehended as another. The *yathārthakhyātivādins* hold that the cognition agrees with the entities cognized. There is a good deal of debate on this theory in the major works of these schools. But the chief opponent for the realists is the idealist. Among the realists the Prābhākaras have been targetted by all. It is surprising to find that the *anyathākhyātivādins* have made room for *asat* element in their explanation which cuts the very ground of realism. Their criticism of *akhyāti* is more in procedural aspect of their explanation of error than on any substantial issues. The *akhyāti* theory is narrated below.

The Prābhākaras have adopted *akhyāti* theory. According to this theory all cognitions are true i.e., *Yathārtham sarvavijñānaṃ*. Prābhākaras explain this position as under:

Whatever is presented in a cognition that is its object. That which is presented in the cognition is termed as *bhāsamāna* and the object is termed as *vedya.* These two always agree. In other words, the content of the cognition and the fact conveyed by it always agree.

The knowledge communicated by the statement *idam rajatam* on seeing *śukti* is the usual example of perceptual error. According to *anyathākhyāti* theory of perceptual error *śukti* is the object of this knowledge. However, it is presented as *rajata.* In other words one is presented as another. 'A' is presented as 'B'. Therefore, it is *anyathākhyāti.*

The Prābhākaras do not agree to this analysis. According to them the statement *idam rajatam* represents two cognitions i.e., perception and memory. One who observes *śukti* present before him cognizes it as *idam* i.e., this, in a general way without the comprehension of its special features which distinguish it from *rajata* i.e., silver. Due to the similarity between *śukti* and *rajata* he remembers *rajata.* The cognition of *śukti* and the memory of *rajata* occur in such quick sequence that he does not realize the difference between the two cognitions and the objects conveyed by them.

The contents of both these cognitions agree with the facts conveyed by them. There is no disagreement between the contents of these two cognitions and the objects conveyed by them.

Though the two cognitions *idam* and *rajatam* are true and distinct, an erroneous statement is made as *idam rajatam* due to the non-realization of the difference between the two cognitions and their objects. For the non-realization of the difference the following factors are responsible:

(i) The absence of the comprehension of the distinct features of *śukti* and its comprehension merely as *idam* in a general way.
(ii) Remembering *rajata* due to the similarity between *śukti* and *rajata.*
(iii) Absence of the reference to the past time in the memory of *rajata.*
(iv) Occurrence of the two cognitions in quick succession.

These circumstances lead to the non-realization of the distinction between the two cognitions and their objects. This leads to the statement i.e., vyāvahāra, as *idam rajatam*. It is this *vyāvahāra* that is repudiated later.

The non-realization of the distinction is termed as *viveka-agraha* and the absence of the reference to the past time in the memory is termed as *tattāpramoṣa*. *Tattā* means reference to the past time and *pramoṣa* means the deletion of it. This analysis of *idam rajatam* offered by the Prābhākaras is termed as *akhyātivāda*.

Śālikanātha himself mentions some of the objections raised against *akhyātivāda* and answers. These are as under:

(i) The so-called memory of *rajata* cannot be classed as memory as it lacks the main feature of the memory viz., reference to the past time.

(ii) *Idam* and *rajatam* are stated with *sāmānādhikaraṇya*. Therefore, the two refer to one and the same. *Idam* refers to something that is presently observed before. Therefore, *rajata* also should refer to the same.

(iii) *Pravṛtti* i.e., initiative to fetch the object seen cannot be properly explained in the *ākhyāti* theory. The mere occurrence of the cognitions of *idam* and *rajatam* in quick succession and the non-realization of the difference between the two cannot motivate the observer to proceed to fetch *rajata*. Non-realization of the difference is a negative factor. It cannot motivate *pravṛtti* i.e., initiative. The initiative is possible only if the *sāmānādhikaraṇya* between *idam* and *rajatam* is realized. This means *śukti* has to be comprehended as *rajata*. This is exactly *anyathākhyāti*. In the analysis of this cognition by *akḥyātivādin sāmānādhikaraṇya* is not worked out.

(iv) If the knowledge represented by the statement *idam rajatam* is true, then, how is it that it is repudiated later as *na idam rajatam*. What is it that is repudiated? Mere realization of the difference that was not comprehended earlier is not a repudiation.

Śālikanātha Answers these Objections as Follows:

(i) The *rajata* cognition is considered as memory since it is caused by the impressions of the earlier cognition of *rajata*. These impressions are roused by the similarity between *śukti* and *rajata*. However, the reference to the past time is not roused due to inadequate attention. Being produced by the impressions of the past experience is the chief feature of memory. Reference to the past time is incidental.

(ii) The purpose of *sāmānādhikaraṇya* is served by the *samāna rūpatā* here. Not only the difference between the cognitions *idam* and *rajatam* is not realized but also the difference between the earlier cognition of *rajata* and these two cognitions is not realized. Therefore, there is *samāna rūpatā* here. This serves the purpose of *sāmānādhikaraṇya*.

(iii) This *samāna rūpatā* supported by the non-realization of the difference facilitates the statement i.e., *vyavahāra*, as '*idam rajatam*' and motivates the initiative i.e., *pravṛtti*, to proceed to fetch the object.

(iv) As regards the *bādha* i.e., repudiation, it has to be clarified that by the realization of the difference between the object of the cognition *idam* i.e., *śukti*, and *rajatam* i.e., silver, the observer gets correct knowledge of *śukti*. This enables him to discover that the statement i.e., *vyavahāra* '*idam* rajatam' was not bonafide. It is this statement that is repudiated. It is more a discovery of *śukti* than the repudiation of *rajata*.

In spite of these clarifications, the same objections are raised again and again in the works of other schools. While the works of the other schools are produced century after century, there were no works on Prābhākaras side. However, it should be said to the credit of these opponents that they kept the Prābhākara theory alive and analysed it more and more to find faults in it. Some of the new objections not mentioned by Śālikanātha are given below:

(i) According to the Prābhākaras the difference is an integral attribute of the object concerned, that is to say, it is *dharmi-svarūpa.* When an object is cognized its attribute i.e., the difference, is also cognized. In the present case, the cognition '*idam*' has to be cognized along with the difference it has from the other cognitions and the cognition '*rajatam*' has to be cognized along with its difference from the other cognitions. Thus, the cognition of the difference between these two cognitions is a part and parcel of the these two cognitions. Therefore, the Prābhākaras cannot talk of the non-realization of the difference between the two cognitions.

This objection can be answered as follows: Though the difference is an integral attribute of the object and can be comprehended in a general way as this object is different from all others, to comprehend the difference from a specific object, the presentation of that object as *pratiyogin* is necessary. In the present case, the cognitions *idam* and *rajatam* are not presented as *pratiyogins* for each other since these have occurred in quick succession. Hence, their difference is not comprehended.

(ii) Non-realization of the difference is of the nature of *abhāva.* Prābhākaras do not accept *abhāva.* Therefore, they cannot make it a ground to explain the error.

This can be answered as follows. Though the Prābhākaras do not accept the category of *abhāva,* they have their own explanation to the situations wherein the cognition of *abhāva* is claimed by *abhāvavādins.* The cognition of the object and its attribute i.e., difference is *sansṛṣta viṣaya buddhi,* and cognising the object alone is *ekaviṣaya buddhi.* Such *ekaviṣaya buddhi* is found here in respect of these two cognitions in view of quick succession so for as the attribute difference is concerned. The difference is *dṛṣya pratiyogin* here.

4. The Rejection of *Abhāva* and *Abhāvapramāṇa*

The Prābhākaras do not accept the category of *abhāva.* Consequently, they do not accept *abhāvapramāṇa* also.

To understand the Prābhākara's stand that the *abhāva* is not a separate category their concepts of *sansṛṣṭaviṣaya buddhi* and *ekaviṣaya buddhi* need to be analysed. When two positive entities are cognized together it is *sansṛṣṭaviṣaya buddhi* while cognising only one of them is *ekaviṣaya buddhi.* The latter serves the purpose of *abhāva.*

For instance, cognizing the ground and jar together is *sansṛṣṭaviṣaya buddhi* while cognising ground alone is *ekaviṣaya buddhi.* In the latter case, *abhāvavādins* claim that there is the *abhāva* of jar. What has really happened is that *ekaviṣaya buddhi* has taken place instead of *sansṛṣṭaviṣaya buddhi.* The absence of jar is not a separate fact. Therefore, no separate *pramāṇa* is necessary to cognize it.

It cannot be argued that how can *ekaviṣaya buddhi* arise in respect of the same ground about which there was *sansṛṣṭaviṣaya buddhi* without the cognition of the *abhāva* of the jar. This is answered by a counter question that how can *abhāva buddhi* arise with reference to the same place wherein there was *bhāva buddhi* of a jar earlier? If the withdrawal of the jar is stated as the ground for *abhāva buddhi*, then, the same may be taken as the ground for *ekaviṣaya buddhi.*

The jar is designated as *dṛśya pratiyogin* i.e., an object that could be cognized if it were present. When one cognizes the ground without the jar he reflects on the *dṛśyapratiyogin* i.e., jar, that was present earlier and realizes that he is cognizing the ground alone. No additional factor i.e., *abhāva* is cognized. The statement that 'there is no jar' only means that the *sansṛṣṭa viṣaya buddhi* of the ground and the jar is replaced by the *ekaviṣaya buddhi* of the ground.

Even in the case of *pradhvansābhāva,* on the destruction of jar the cognition of jar is replaced by the cognition of its pieces. No additional factor like *pradhvansābhāva* is cognized. The statements like *ghaṭābhāva, paṭābhāva* also mean that the respective *sansṛṣṭa viṣaya buddhi* is replaced by *ekaviṣaya buddhi*. The reference to the *pratiyogins* is a reference to the respective *dṛśya pratiyogins* i.e., the objects that could be cognized if these were present as a part of the content of the respective *sansṛṣṭaviṣaya buddhi*.

Those who accept *abhāva* as a separate category accept *anupalabdhi* i.e., *pramāṇābhāva*, as the means to comprehend *abhāva*. This is also not acceptable to the Prābhākaras. *Anupalabdhi* i.e., the absence of cognition by the appropriate *pramāṇa* cannot be the means of cognition by its very presence as in the case of the eye being the means of cognition by its very nature. One has to have the knowledge of the absence of *pramāṇa* as in the case of the knowledge of liṅga for *anumāna*. If it is accepted that *pramāṇābhāva* is *pramāṇa* only when it is known, then, for the knowledge of *abhāvapramāṇa* another *abhāvapramāṇa* will be required and so on. This leads to inifinite regress.

Finally, the Prābhākaras explain the Śabara's remark **'अभावोऽपि प्रमाणाभाव: नास्ति इत्यस्य अर्थस्य असन्निकृष्टस्य'** as supporting the rejection of *abhāva*. This very remark is interpreted by the Bhāṭṭas as the definition of *abhāvapramāṇa*. Śālikanātha takes pains to interpret it in support of the rejection of *abhāvapramāṇa*. However, his explanation is laboured and not convincing. This is explained in the *Amṛtakalā* section of this text. The question of *abhāvapramāṇa* is discussed in detail both in *Amṛtakalā* chapter and *pramāṇa Pārāyaṇa* under *abhāva*.

5. Non-Vedic Statements Communicate through the Inference of the Speaker's Knowledge

According to the Prābhākaras the *pauruṣeya* statements are not *śabdapramāṇa*. These help to infer the speaker's knowledge and communicate the same. By the statement of a speaker his knowledge of the facts represented by his statement is inferred. His statement plays the double role of serving as a means to infer his knowledge and to communicate it to the listeners. In the first role it is a *liṅga* i.e., the means or the ground of the inference. Its second role is verbal communication. If the meaning communicated by the statement does not represent the knowledge of the speaker of the facts mentioned in the statement it is a defect of its role as a *liṅga*, that is to say, the speaker has not invested it with the knowledge which the statement is expected to communicate. This may be due to the defect or inadequacy of the speaker's knowledge itself or his intention not to communicate his knowledge truly. In any case, it is a case of a defective *liṅga*. This naturally makes the second role of the statement viz., verbal communication defective. That is to say, it disagrees with the facts supposed to have been communicated by that statement. In this process, though there may not be any *śabda doṣa, puruṣa doṣa* is responsible for the disagreement between the statement and the facts.

It is found that the statements that do not agree with the facts are made for the following reasons:

(i) The speaker's knowledge itself is erroneous.

(ii) He has no intention to speak truly.

(iii) He is out of his mind.

(iv) He formulates the statement defectively as a result of which something different than what he intends is presented in the statement.

In all these instances, the relation between the knowledge supposed to have been communicated and the statement which is expected to represent is violated. That is to say, the *vyāpti* relation between the knowledge to be communicated and the statement is broken. Therefore, the statement fails to play its first role of being the *liṅga* to infer the knowledge that the speaker intends to communicate. Consequently it fails in its second role of valid communication.

There seems to be some difficulty in working out the process of the inference of the knowledge of the speaker by his statement. In order to proceed to infer the knowledge of the speaker from his statement the listener has to understand the meaning of the statement. This means that the statement has already communicated to him what it is expected to communicate. Then, the listener need not take the trouble to infer the knowledge through the statement and get it communicated by the same statement.

To solve this difficulty one has to understand the process of the inference in a little more detail.

When a statement is heard the facts referred to by the words are brought to the mind of the listener. Then, he proceeds to sort out as to how these could be meaningfully organized. This process is termed *vimarśa*. Then, he arrives at an organized sense. From this he infers the knowledge of the speaker and finally infers the position of the facts. This crystallized position is finally communicated by the statement.

The first stage viz., reminding of the facts by the meaning of the words and their organization is only a step towards inference of the knowledge of the speaker. It is not a crystallized final communication. The listener has to go through the process of inference to arrive at the final verbal communication.

The advantage of making the inference of the knowledge of the speaker the ground for the verbal communication in non-Vedic speech is to provide a ground for sorting out the true statements and false statements. In Vedic speech there is no question of false statement.

6. The Formula of Triputīkaraṇa

An important contribution of the Prābhākaras to the concept of *pratyakṣa* is extending its scope beyond the sense-perception. So far as the external objects are concerned the perception is through the senses. However, there are two other items that are directly cognized. These are the knower and the knowledge.

The knowledge produced by senses, inference, *saṃskāra* etc., is of the nature of perception in respect of the knower and the knowledge itself. All cognitions in which some or other object is presented, the knower is also presented. The objects are not comprehended without the comprehension of the knower also along with them. It is clear from the statement 'I know this', otherwise the statement would have been as 'He knows this'..In case the knower is not comprehended there would not have been any difference between one's own knowledge and the knowledge of someone else.

The knowledge is self revealing. It does not require another knowledge to reveal it. It is well-known that according to the Nyāyavaiśeṣikas the knowledge of the objects is known as *vyavasāya* and the knowledge of this *vyavasāya* is *anuvyavasāya*. The Prābhākaras do not agree with this arrangement. According to the Prābhākaras every knowledge conveys three entities viz., the knower, the object known, and the knowledge. No knowledge arises without a reference to the knower and the object known. These three are always conveyed together. This procedure is designated as *triputīkaraṇa*.

This formula is evolved to rule out the Buddhist's contention that there are no objects outside the knowledge. According to this formula, if there were no objects outside, then, the knowledge itself would not have arisen. It is not the knowledge that is to be utilized to ascertain the existence of the objects, but it is the object that gives rise to the knowledge. One cannot think of the existence of knowledge without the existence of the object to be known, and the knower.

According to this formula of *triputīkaraṇa* the ascertainment of the existence of the object and the knowledge does not depend upon either knowledge alone or the object alone. But the two help to ascertain the presence of both jointly.

7. Nirvikalpaka and Savikalpaka Perceptions

The explanation of the Prābhākaras in these two stages of perception is quite different from that of Nyāyavaiśeṣikas.

In *nirvikalpaka pratyakṣa* mere *svalakṣaṇa* is not presented as contended by the Buddhists. Both the substance and attributes are presented in *nirvikalpaka.*

The general and the particular features of the objects are presented. But these are not so realized until some more objects in which general aspect is observed or from which particular aspects are contrasted and compared. In the *savikalpaka-pratyakṣa* these aspects are realized.

In the *nirvikalpaka,* though the attributes are comprehended, these are not comprehended as qualifying the object. At that stage the difference between the substance and the attributes is not grasped. The difference could be grasped only through *anvaya* and *vyatireka.* This *anvaya* and *vyatireka* verification does not take place at the *nirvikalpaka* stage. Consequently these are not organized as the qualifications and the qualified. Therefore, there is no *viśiṣṭapratyaya* at the *nirvikalpaka* stage. In *savikalpaka* as already stated these are organized.

Now, a question may be raised here. The perception is caused by sense-contact. The sense is in contact with only that object which is actually perceived. It is not in contact with other objects either of the same class or any other. Therefore, it is difficult to agree with the contention that the general and the special aspects are cognized involving a reference to other objects in the *savikalpaka* stage.

This difficulty is solved by pointing out that the *Ātman* who is to comprehend the object presented in his perception does comprehend the general and particular aspects with the aid of *saṃskāra* i.e., the impressions of the cognitions of the other object cognized earlier.

According to the Prābhākaras, to have *viśiṣṭapratyaya,* it is not necessary that *viśeṣaṇa* also must be presented by the perception only. In the case of *savikalpaka* perception when the *viśeṣaṇas* are perceived in the cognition of the object concerned, the corresponding *viśeṣaṇas* of the object seen earlier are brought to the observer's mind by *saṃskāra.*

8. Number and the Nature of Categories According to the Prābhākaras

While explaining the objects that are cognized by the perception Śālikanātha mentions three categories viz., *dravya, jāti,* and *guṇa* and gives the details of four *dravyas* viz., *prithvi, ap, tejas* and *vāyu.* He also mentions colour, taste etc., sixteen *guṇas.* The commentator gives full details of the categories.

(i) Substance, qualities, motion, universal, inherence, poteney, number and similarity are the eight categories.

It may be noted here that *abhāva* is dropped and *śakti, sādṛśya* are added.

(ii) The nine substances are the same as those of the Nyāyavaiśeṣikas. Twenty-two qualities are common to the Nyāyavaiśeṣikas and the Prābhākaras. *Saṃkhyā* and *laghutva* are dropped.

(iii) Motion i.e., *karma,* represents both ordinary motion and ritual activities. Motion is not perceived. It is inferred.

(iv) Śakti is present in all positive entities. *Saṃkhyā* cannot be considered as a substance as it is found in qualities. It cannot be considered as a quality as it is found in many. *Sadṛśya* is a distinct category distinct from the substance, qualities etc.

(v) In respect of the concepts of *jāti* i.e., universal, and *samavāya* the Prābhākaras have made some improvements in the Nyāyavaiśeṣika position. These answer some of the objections raised against these concepts.

This brief sketch of the major theories and concepts of the Prābhākaras will give an idea of the distinct contribution made by the Prābhākaras to Indian Philosophical thought. *Prakaraṇapañcikā* gives a detailed exposition of these issues. This text is very terse. The terminology of the Prābhākara system is quite different from other systems with which a student of Indian philosophy is familiar. Therefore, an exposition of this text in English is attempted here.

Extracts of the relevant portions of the text are given for ready reference. It also helps to check the exposition with reference to the original text. The entire text is covered. However, ritualistic details and laboured arguments supplemented to the main arguments are avoided to maintain the clarity of the presentation.

CHAPTER I

Śāstramukha

Justification for the Undertaking of *Mīmāṃsā* i.e., Enquiry into *Vedārtha*

It is usual for the writers on the systems of Indian Philosophy to raise the question of justification for undertaking an investigation into the area of the knowledge with which that system is concerned. Accordingly, the writers on *Pūrvamīmāṃsā* also raise the question as to what is the justification to investigate the purport of Veda. This question is raised in the form of analyzing the nature of the injunction *Svādhyāyo Adhyetavyaḥ*

स्वाध्यायविधिवाक्यार्थविचारे प्रयतामहे ।
प्रभाकरगुरोर्दृष्ट्या मीमांसारम्भसिद्धये ॥ (प्र०पं०१)

Both the Bhāṭṭa and the Prābhākara schools of Pūrvamīmāṃsā examine this injunction for this purpose. However, there is a vital difference in their approach in respect of the status of this injunction. The Prābhākara's contention is that it is not an independent injunction. It is only consequential. It is consequential to the injunction of *adhyāpana* viz. *Vedam Adhyāpayīta.* On the other hand the Bhāṭṭas hold that *Svādhyāyo Adhyetavyaḥ* is an independent injunction. Both the Prābhākaras and the Bhāṭṭas do utilize this injunction to justify the undertaking an investigation into *Vedārtha.* However, the Bhāṭṭas consider it as a primary injunction while the Prābhākaras treat it as consequential of adhyāpanavidhi. This difference is not a superficial difference of choosing one or the other view to justify the investigation of *Vedārtha* or granting the primary or consequential status to an injunction. It is due to the very basic difference of fixing the meaning and the scope of an injunction in the two schools of the Mīmāṃsā and the whole fabric of their analysis of the Vedic language, ritual programmes, and the ritual ethics. A detailed analysis of the arguments, for and against, in support of their respective contentions will reveal this basic difference.

Śālikanātha takes up this issue under the head Śāstramukha in his *Prakaraṇapañcikā*. He first narrates the Bhāṭṭa view giving the *pūrvapakṣa* and *siddhānta* of this topic according to the Bhāṭṭas.

Pūrvapakṣa View According to the *Bhāṭṭas*

The contention of pūrvapakṣa is as follows:

In the injunction *svādhyayo adhyetavyaḥ* the *bhāvanā* which is of the nature of direction to undertake an activity needs three requirements to be effective. These are *bhāvya* i.e., *sādhya*, something to be achieved, *karaṇa* an instrument to achieve it, and the *itikartavyatā* i.e., certain aids to help the process. Here, *adhyayana* i.e. the study of the Vedas itself cannot be *bhāvya* i.e., the thing to be achieved as it does not serve any purpose of the person who undertakes it. It is not *puruṣārtha*. The *svādhyāya* i.e., Veda itself cannot also be the *bhāvya* i.e., the object to be achieved, since even without an injunction one can obtain it by the study. It is also not possible to make it a *niyamavidhi* i.e., a mandatory injunction by stipulating that one has to obtain the Veda by duly studying it. Only such items that are meant for a sacrifice could be covered by a *niyamavidhi* i.e., a mandatory injunction.

(i) स्वाध्यायोऽध्येतव्यः इत्यत्र परप्रेरणात्मकविध्यवरुद्धा भावना तव्यप्रत्यय वाच्या प्रतीयते । सा च स्वभावतः भाव्यं करणम् इतिकर्तव्यतां च अपेक्षते ।

(ii) तत्र न तावत् अध्ययनमेव समानपदोपात्तं भाव्यतया सम्बन्धमर्हति अपुरुषार्थत्वात् ।

(iii) नापि स्वाध्यायस्य भाव्यतया सम्बन्धः अवकल्पते । विध्यानर्थक्यप्रसङ्गात् । अन्तरेणापि विधिं प्रतीयते एव अध्ययनेन स्वाध्यायः अवाप्यते इति ।

(iv) न च व्रीहिनवहन्तीतिवत् नियमार्थो विधिरिति शक्यते वक्तुम् । अक्रत्वर्थत्वात् अध्ययनस्य । अक्रत्वर्थश्च न नियमविषयः । अवधातादयो हि क्रतावेव नियम्यन्ते न तुण्डुलादिस्वरूपे । (प्र०पं० ३४)

The comprehension of the purport of the Veda also cannot be considered as *bhāvya* i.e., the object to be achieved, since even without any injunction, the comprehension of the purport of Veda could be obtained in the natural course. In this respect also the injunction cannot be made a *niyamavidhi* i.e., a mandatory injunction. Therefore, following the ruling given in the case of *viśvajit* sacrifice, *svarga* has to be considered as *bhāvya* i.e., the objective to be achieved. There is another way out also. Following the ruling given in *rātrisatra* the benefit mentioned in the *arthavāda* passages may be considered as *bhāvya.* In either case the comprehension of the purport of the Veda becomes irrelevant in carrying out this injunction. To achieve the *svarga* or to obtain the benefits mentioned in *arthavāda* passages, the *adhyayana* i.e., study of the Vedas is *karaṇa* i.e., instrument. The study is nothing but acquiring the mastery over the recitation of Vedas. The scope of the injunction to study the Veda need not extend to the comprehension of the purport. This means that no investigation into the purport of Veda is warranted by this injunction. Therefore, no such investigation i.e., mīmāṃsā be undertaken.

(i) एतेनैव अर्थावबोधस्यापि भाव्यतया सम्बन्धो निरस्तो वेदितव्यः । तथाहि यद्यपि अधीतात् स्वाध्यायात् फलवत्कर्मावबोधो दृश्यते इति तस्यैव भाव्यता अवसीयते । तथापि विनापि विधिना अन्वयव्यतिरेकाभ्यामध्ययनस्य अर्थावबोधसाधनत्वात् विधिः अनर्थक एव ।

(ii) न च अध्ययनेनैव अर्थमवबुद्ध्य, अनुतिष्ठतां क्रतुफलभावनासिद्धिरिति नियमः सम्भवति । अक्रत्वर्थत्वादध्ययनस्य ।

(iii) तस्माद्विश्वजिन्न्यायेन स्वर्गे एव भाव्यतया कल्पयितव्ये प्राप्ते फलमात्रेयो निर्देशादित्यार्थवादिक पित्रादिप्रसादलभ्यसर्वकामफलावाप्तिरेव भाव्यतया अवसीयते । (प्र०पं० ५)

Pūrvapakṣin clarifies that though there is no *ārthavādika phala* in respect of *adhyayana* for the first time, there is *ārthavādika phala* in respect of retaining the *svādhyāya* studied, its *japa* i.e., repeated recitation, and *yajña.* i.e., utilising it for the sacrifice. This *ārthavādika phala* has to be taken for the *adhyayana* as a whole and *rātrisatranyāya* has to be applied here.

ननु आद्याध्ययने न किञ्चिदार्थवादिकं फलं श्रूयते । तत्र एषामर्थवादानामश्रवणात् । धारणजपयज्ञविध्यर्थवादाः हि एते । तदाहुः वार्तिककारमिश्राः

आद्येत्वध्ययने नैव काचिदास्ति फलश्रुतिः ।
धारणे जपयज्ञे च या साप्येवं निवारिता ॥

सत्यमेवं तथापि तेषामतिदेशतोऽपि लब्धेः युक्तैव तदीयफलस्य भाव्यता (प्र०पं० ६)

While explaining the application of *rātrisatranyāya* to *adhyayana* the very procedure of the development of the import of the injunction is explained as under:

The Process of the Development of the Import of the Injunction

An injunctive suffix conveys two *bhāvanās* viz., *śābdībhāvanā* and *ārthībhāvanā.* The *sābdībhāvanā* is of the nature of direction to undertake an activity. The actual undertaking of an activity i.e., *pravṛtti* i.e., *ārthībhāvanā* is its result i.e., the *bhāvya.* The injunctive suffix is *karaṇa.* To be more specific the *vācya-vācaka bhāva* relation between the injunctive suffix and its meaning is *karaṇa.* The glorification of the activity by the *arthavāda* is *itikartavyatā.* In the present context of adhyayanavidhi, as the *śābdībhāvanā* needs *arthavāda* by way of *itikartavyatā* and as it is not actually found in the context of first *adhyayana*, it has to be brought by way of *atideśa* from the context of *dhāraṇa*, *japa*, and *yajña* wherein an *arthavāda* is found and *rātrisatranyāya* is applied.

The *ārthavādika phala* brought in here by applying *rātrisatranyāya* is *bhāvya* and the *adhyayana* is *karaṇa*. The *svādhyāya* is meant for *adhyayana*. The *svadhyāya* is nothing but *akṣararāśi grahaṇa*.

Since, the mere *akṣararāśi grahaṇa* leads to *ārthavādika phala*, there is no need of the comprehension of the import of Veda. In fact, since the purpose of *adhyayana* is served by *ārthavādika phala* the *akṣararāśi grahaṇa* is *anyapara*, that is to say, it is meant for something other than the *arthāvabodha*. Hence there is no need of the comprehension of the import, nor any *need of vyutpatti* to yield the comprehension. Since there is no possibility of comprehension of the meaning no investigation of the import is needed, nor there is any benefit for it.

(i) लिङादियुक्तेषु वाक्येषु द्वे भावने अवगम्येते - शाब्दीभावना आर्थीभावनाचेति । तत्र शब्दीभावना परप्रेरणात्मिका । तस्याः पुरुषप्रवृत्तिः भाव्यम् । तथा च प्रेरणया सह यो लिङादीनां वाच्यवाचकभावः सम्बन्धः सः तत्र योग्यतया करणम् । तदाहुः वार्तिककारमिश्राः । लिङादयो हि प्रेरणां कुर्वन्ति अभिदधति च । प्रवर्त्यरुच्युत्पादनयोग्यतया च आर्थवादिकी स्तुतिः इतिकर्तव्यता । तदेवमध्ययनविधौ साक्षादश्रुतार्थवादके शब्दभावनायां इति कर्तव्यतार्थवादाकाङ्क्षिण्यां जपयज्ञाध्ययनादतिदेशेन अर्थवादाः स्वीक्रियन्ते । तदाहुः वार्तिककारमिश्राः 'अनुषङ्गानुमानाद्यैः लभ्यन्तेऽन्येऽतिदेशतः' । ते च अतिदिष्टाः अर्थवादाः अर्थभावनायां फलं समर्पयन्ति रात्रिसत्रवत् ।

(ii) एवं च यदा एकस्मात् अपूर्वं तदा इतरत् तदर्थमिति न्यायेन स्वाध्यायशब्दवाच्यो अक्षरराशिरपि अध्ययननिवृत्त्यर्थ एव अवसीयते ।

एवं च अन्यपरत्वादक्षराणां तेभ्यो अर्थप्रतिपत्तिरेव अनुपपन्ना । व्युत्पत्तिविरहात् । वृद्धव्यवहारे हि अनन्यपराण्येव अक्षराणि अर्थावबोधकतया व्युत्पन्नानि व्युत्पत्त्यपेक्षश्च शब्दोऽर्थावबोधकः । अप्रतीयमानश्च अर्थः न विचारविषयः । नापि प्रयोजनमिति विचारस्तावन्नारब्धव्यः । तदनारम्भे च तदुपायभूतन्यायपरिज्ञानमपि अनुपयोगि । तदनुपयोगे तन्निबन्धनं मीमांसाशास्त्रमनारम्भणीयमिति पूर्वः पक्षः । (प्र०पं० ६)

The whole of this discussion is briefly summarized at the commencement of this discussion as under:

अत्र केचिदाचक्षते । न मीमांसाशास्त्रमारम्भणीयमिति । तद्धि वेदवाक्यार्थविचारोपायभूतन्यायनिबन्धनम् । न च वेदवाक्यार्थो विचार्योऽस्ति यो विचारस्य विषयभूतः । नाप्यसौ विचार्य निर्णीतः प्रयोजनमवकल्पते । अपुरुषार्थत्वात् । पुरुषार्थत्वे तस्य चोदनैव प्रमाणं स्यात् । न च अविवक्षितार्था सा प्रमाणं भवितुमर्हति । (प्र०पं० १-२)

The *Siddhānta* View According to the Bhāṭṭas:

The above contention of *pūrvapakṣin* is rejected by the *siddhāntin*. In the statement of injunction viz., *svādhyāyo adhyetavyaḥ*, *svādhyāya* i.e., Veda, is mentioned as the *karma* i.e., the object. Therefore, that is *bhāvya* i.e., the object to be achieved. Though Vedas are already there, these have to be acquired by the study. This is a kind of *saṃ skāra* for the Vedas. This *saṃskāra* has to be effected keeping in view, their future use to comprehend their meaning which will be useful for the performance of the sacrifices. The objection that the *svādhyāya* cannot be *śeṣī* i.e., *aṅgī*, as in the case of *Saktu* is not valid since, *svādhyāya* serves the purpose of *arthāvabodha*. Though *arthāvabodha* occurs later, there is no difficulty in treating it as *śeṣin*.

(4) राद्धान्तस्तु

(i) 'स्वाध्यायोऽध्येतव्यः' इति स्वाध्यायस्य कर्मत्वावगमात् स एव भाव्यतया अवसीयते ।

(ii) यद्यपि नित्यत्वात् निर्वर्त्यकर्मता नास्ति स्वाध्यायस्य, विकार्यकर्मता वा अध्ययनेन तस्य विकारानुपपत्तेः तथापि प्राप्यतया तस्य कर्मता न अनुपपन्ना । अत एव प्राप्यकर्मोदाहरणं वृत्तिकारस्य अध्ययनम् । यच्च कर्म तदर्थैव क्रिया युक्ता । सोऽयं श्रौतो विनियोगः ।

(iii) न च स्वाध्यायस्य सक्तुवत् शेषित्वमनुपपन्नम् । फलवदर्थाव-बोधोपयोगित्वात् ।

(iv) यद्यपि च अर्थावबोधोपयोगित्वमध्ययनात् प्राक् नावगम्यते तथापि पश्चाद् भाव्यपि भवत्येव प्रयोजनम् । भाविनापि च उपयोगेन शेषित्वं न अनुपपन्नं अग्निवत् ।

(v) उत्पन्नानां हि अग्नीनां विनियोगावगमः । न अवगतविनियोगानां उत्पत्तिः । आहवनीयादिशब्दानामलौकिकार्थपरतया प्राग् व्युत्पत्त्यवागमादर्थानवगतेः होमादिषु विनियोगासम्भवात् । तथा चोक्तं 'भूतभाव्युपयोगं हि द्रव्यं संस्करमर्हति' । (प्र०पं० ७)

Effecting this *saṃskāra* of study is a mandatory injunction. The Vedas have their natural meaning. The purport arising out of these meanings has close association with the sacrifices. Therefore, the study of the Veda is meant for the sacrifices through the meanings conveyed by the Veda. Therefore, this study is *kṛtvartha* i.e., meant for the sacrifices. Hence, the injunction for the study of Veda is a *niyamavidhi* i.e., a mandatory injunction.

(i) ननु च अर्थावबोधोपयोगितया संस्कारविधिरनर्थक ऐवत्युक्तमिति । नानर्थकः नियमार्थतया अर्थवत्त्वात् ।

(ii) ननु च नियमो न सम्भवति अक्रतुसंस्पर्शित्वादित्युक्तम् । तन्न सम्भवति । स्वाभाविकार्थपरत्वानुसारेण क्रत्वनुप्रवेशो क्रतुसंस्पर्शितायाः ऐवोचितत्त्वात् । यदि खलु अध्ययनविधेः क्रत्वनुप्रवेशिता नाश्रीयते तदा शब्दानां वृद्धव्यवहारव्युत्पन्नानां स्वाभाविकार्थपरता हीयेत । (प्र०पं० ७)

The mandatory nature of this injunction with reference to the various forms of Vedic statements viz., *vidhi, arthavāda* and *mantra* can be explained as under:

1. One will obtain the benefits of the performance of the sacrifices only when he performs them by knowing the meaning of the injunction through the study of Veda.
2. One will obtain the benefits of the performance of sacrifices only when he performs them by knowing their importance from the *arthavādas* studied by him through the study of Vedas.
3. One will obtain the benefits of the performance of the sacrifices only when he is reminded of the meaning of the *mantras* studied by him through the study of Vedas.

In this way the injunction *svādhyāyo adhyetavyaḥ* is stated to be a *niyamavidhi* i.e., a mandatory injunction. Its mandatory nature is justified by showing its connection with the sacrifices i.e., its *kṛtvartha* nature.

तत्र कर्म विधिषु एवं नियमवर्णना। अध्ययनाविर्भावितैरेव कर्मविधिभिः अर्थमवबुद्ध्य अनुतिष्ठतां क्रतुफलभावनासिद्धिरिति। अर्थवादेषु अध्ययनाविर्भावितार्थवादप्ररोचिताः क्रियमाणाः क्रतवः फलभावनाय अलमिति। मन्त्रेषु पुनः अध्ययनपरिगृहीतैरेव मन्त्रैः क्रतुषु पदार्थस्मरणं फलं भावनाङ्गमिति। (प्र०पं० ८)

As per this explanation, the study of Veda is not for *svarga* nor for the benefits mentioned in *arthavāda* passages but it is for the comprehension of the purport of the Veda which is required for the performance of sacrifices. In view of this the comprehension of the purport is relevant and an investigation into the purport of the Veda has to be undertaken. This is the *siddānta* view of the Bhāṭṭa school.

एवं च अनन्यपरत्वादक्षराणां फलवत्कर्मावबोधोत्पत्तेः विचारस्य विषयप्रयोजनलाभात् शास्त्रस्य आरम्भणीयत्वम्।

Since it is established that the *vicāra* i.e., investigation into the import of Veda has *viṣaya* and *prayojana* it follows that such a *vicāra* has to be undertaken after the study of Veda. Hence, the *smṛti* statement that the student should leave the *gurukula* after the study of Veda has to be held in abeyance. Keeping this in mind the *sūtrakāra* commends the *vicāra* as *athāto dharmajijñāsā.*

विषयप्रयोजनलाभे च विचारस्य अध्ययनानन्तरमुपनिपातित्वात् गुरुकुलस्थितेरर्थवत्त्वात् तन्निवृत्तिमध्यनानन्तरप्राप्तां स्मरद् वेदमधीत्य स्नायादिति स्मृतिवचनमन्यायमूलं दर्शयन् अर्थावबोधपरतया स्वाध्यायस्य विवक्षितार्थतां मन्यमानः सूत्रकारः विचारस्य विषयं चाह 'अथातो धर्मजिज्ञासा' इति । (प्र०पं० ८)

Prābhākara's Criticism of the Bhāṭṭa View

The Prābhākaras totally differ from this way of the presentation of *the pūrvapakṣa* and the *siddhānta* in respect of the injunction.

The *pūrvapakṣa* and the *siddhānta* stated by the Bhāṭṭa centre round the question of *bhāvya* i.e., the objective to be achieved.

The *pūrvapakṣin* contends that the objective to be achieved is *svarga* or the benefits stated in the *arthavāda* passages and the *siddhāntin* states that it is acquiring the Veda through the study leading to the comprehension of its purport. From this it is clear that both the *pūrvapakṣin* and the *siddhāntin* are seeking the *bhāvya* outside the purview of the meaning of the injunction. Therefore, the *Prābhākaras* reject the contentions of both the *pūrvapakṣa* and the *siddhānta* proposed by the Bhāṭṭas.

Prābhākara's Concept of Bhāvya i.e., The Objective to be Achieved:

According to the *Prābhākaras* the import of an injunction is *kārya* and that itself is bhāvya i.e., the objective to be achieved. It is not the result that is to be achieved but it is *kārya* that is to be accomplished. Therefore, neither *svarga* is *bhāvya* nor *svādhyāya* is *bhāvya.* It is always *kārya* that is the *bhāvya* for an injunction. The *kārya* is conveyed by the very injunction. *Bhāvanā* i.e., *kṛti* is also conveyed by the injunctive suffix as subordinate to *kārya*. Therefore, *kārya* is *bhāvya* for it. This is also called *niyoga* i.e., command, and *apūrva* i.e., something that is conveyed only by a Vedic injunction but not by any other *pramāṇa* i.e., *mānāntarāpūrva*.

नहि लिङादिवाक्येषु भावना भाव्यान्तरमपेक्षेते । अपूर्वस्य भाव्यस्य स्वशब्देन अभिहितत्वात् । लिङादयोहि भाव्यकोटिनिविष्टप्रधान-भूतापूर्वोपसर्जनतापन्नामेव भावनामभिदधतीति विषयकरणीये निपुणतरमुपपादितम् । अतो न पूर्वपक्षे भाव्याकांक्षायामार्थवादिकफलसम्बन्धः । नापि सिद्धान्ते स्वाध्यायस्य साध्यतया अन्वयः । (प्रं०पं० ११)

This *kārya* conveyed by an injunction could be accomplished by performing a sacrifice that is stated as a subject-matter of the injunction concerned. This needs an agent. To act as an agent one needs entitlement i.e., *adhikāra*. To be an agent one has to be brought under the scope of a *niyoga*, that is to say, he has to be a *niyojya*. Now, in the instance of *svādhyāyo adhyetavyaḥ* the student who is expected to study the Veda cannot be independently a *niyojya*. Therefore, this injunction cannot be considered as an independent injunction.

(i) **यदपूर्वं कार्यभूतं प्रतीयते तत् विषयत्वेन सम्बद्धकरणीभूत यागाद्यनुष्ठनाधीनात्मलाभम् । न च विना कर्त्रा तदनुष्ठानोपपत्तिः । न च अधिकारं विना कर्तृत्वलाभः । न च नियोज्यमन्तरेण कर्तृत्व सिद्धिः । (प्र०पं० ११)**

The study of Vedas enjoined by *svādhyāyo adhyetavyaḥ* is a consequential injunction of another injunction viz., *vedam adhyāpayet* the vedas be taught. The injunction conveys 'Accomplish the duty of a teacher'. This is the *kārya* or *niyoga* conveyed by this injunction. One who desires to be a teacher is *adhikāri* and *niyojya* here. In order to accomplish the duty of teaching he has to obtain a pupil, perform the *saṃskāra* of *upanayana* for him, and make him to study the Veda.

Thus, the study of the Veda enjoined for a student is consequential of the injunction to teach Veda. *Adhyayanvidhi* is *adhyāpanavidhi prayuktavidhi.*

(i) अन्यतोऽनुष्ठानसिद्धेः । कुतोऽन्यतः? आचार्यकरणविधिप्रयुक्तेः ।

(ii) कः पुनः आचार्यकरणविधिः?

उपनीय तु यः शिष्यं वेदमध्यापयेत् द्विजः ।
सकल्पं सरहस्यं च तमाचार्यं प्रचक्षते ।।

इति स्मरणानुमितः शिष्यमुपनीय वेदाध्ययनेन आचार्यकं भावयेदित्येवंरूपः । अलौकिकं च आचार्यकं आहवनीयादिवदिति तन्निष्पत्त्युपायविधानं युक्तमेव । तत्र अर्थादाचार्यीबुभूषत एव अधिकारः धनार्जननियमवत् । तत्र शिष्यं प्रति विहिततद्धिताचरणदक्षिणादानदर्शनात् तल्लिप्सोरेव आचार्यभवनेच्छा । (प्र०पं० १२-१४)

(iii) यथा दीक्षाणीयया दीक्षितत्वसिद्धिः तथा वेदाध्यायनेन आचार्यत्वसिद्धिः । (प्र०पं० १४)

As per this position of the *adhyayanavidhi* i.e., the injunction to study the Vedas, the question whether comprehending the purport of the Veda is relevant or not has to be examined. *Prima facie* it appears that since the student is made to study the Veda by the teacher to accomplish his *niyoga* of acquiring teachership, the comprehension of the purport of the Veda by the student is not relevant. Consequently an investigation into the purport of Veda is not warranted. Hence, there is no need of *dharmajijañāsā* i.e., an investigation into purport of Vedas. It is with this background that the Prābhākaras formulate the *pūrvapakṣa* and *siddhānta* of these two injunctions.

Adhyayana is Consequential of *Adhyāpanavidhi*

The process by which the Prābhākaras have arrived at the conclusion that the *adhyayana* is consequential of *adhyāpanavidhi* is explained as under:

In the statement *upaniya tu yaḥ śiṣyaṃ vedam adhyāpayet dvijaḥ* the suffix *ktvā* is used. This means that the agent who teaches and who performs the *upanayana* is one and the same. This means the two i.e., *upanayana* and *adhyāpana* have to have *aṅga-aṅgī bhāva* relation, that is to say, *upanayana* has to be taken as *aṅga* of *adhyāpana*. This *upanayana* is intended to procure the boy for the teaching. Therefore, it is *aṅga* of *adhyāpana* through him only. The boy so procured will be useful for accomplishing the teaching only. It is exactly for this reason that the statement *svādhyāyo adhyetavyaḥ* occurs in the context of prescribing *upanayana*. In this way, the injunction of *adhyāpana* necessitates *upanayana* which in its turn necessitates *adhyayana* since the need of *adhyayana* is brought about in this way, no separate *adhikāra* i.e., *kāmanā* is necessary to accomplish *adhyayanavidhi*. Hence there is no need of resorting to either *viśvajinyāya* or *rātrisatranyāya* to bring about *svarga rūpa phala* or *ārthavādika phala*.

उपनयनं च क्त्वाप्रत्ययेन अध्यापनसमानकर्तृकमवगम्यमानमेकप्रयोगतया विना समानकर्तृत्वासम्भवात् अङ्गाङ्गिभावेन विना एकप्रयोगत्वानुपपत्तेः आचार्यकभावनाकरणीभूतमध्यापनं प्रति अङ्गत्वेन अवतिष्ठते। एतदाश्रितश्च 'अष्टवर्षं ब्राह्मणमुपनयीत' इत्यादिनियमः। उपनयनं च स्वभावतः उपनेयासत्तिप्रयोजनकमिति तद्वारेणैव तस्याङ्गम्। न च अध्यापनं प्रत्यनुपयोगिनः उपनेयस्य आसत्तिः अध्यापनोपयोगिनीत्युपनेयस्य कर्मापेक्षायामुपनयनं प्रक्रम्य स्वाध्यायोऽध्येतव्य इत्यध्ययनं विधीयमानं उपनेयस्य कर्मेत्यवगम्यते। अध्ययनं च अध्यापनोपयोगीति सिद्धमेतत्। तेन स्वाध्यायमध्येष्यमाणस्य माणवकस्य उपनयनमध्यापनाङ्गमिति अध्यापनविधिः स्वाङ्गभूतमुपनयनं प्रयुञ्जानः तस्य अन्यत्र अनुपपत्त्या अध्ययनमपि प्रयुङ्क्ते।

तत्प्रयुक्ताध्ययननिष्पत्त्या लब्धसिद्धिः स्वाध्यायाध्ययननियोगः न अधिकारान्तरमपेक्षते। अतः न अयं विश्वजिन्न्यायस्य विषयः नापि रात्रिसत्रन्यायस्य। अनन्यप्रयुक्तविषयनियोगगोचरत्वात् तयोः। (प्र०पं० १६)

Further, if *adhyayana* is made to be undertaken on account of some or the other result, then, it will have to be open to the *śūdras* also who desire to have these results. This will be the consequence if the entitlement i.e., *adhikāra*, for the *adhyayana* is based on the desire for the results of the *adhyayana*. On the other hand, if the *adhyayana* is made dependent on the requirement of *upanayana*, and the *upanayana* the requirement of teaching, only those who are selected for the *upanayana* will be eligible for the *adhyayana*. The teacher will naturally select only those for *upanayana* who belong to first three *varṇas* since for them only the *upanayana* is prescribed.

अन्यथा सिद्धान्तेपि कामश्रुतिप्रयुक्तमध्ययनमिति विद्यासाध्येष्वपि कर्मसु शूद्रादीनामधिकारः स्यात् । अतो अध्यापनविधिप्रयुक्तत्वादध्ययनस्य येषामेव उपनयनं तेषामेव तत्प्रयुक्तमन्त्रलाभात् शूद्रादीनामनधिकारः । (प्रं०पं० १६)

Śālikanātha Rejects the *Bhāṭṭa's* Contention that the *Svādhyāyavidhi* can be a *Niyamavidhi*

The *svādhyāyavidhi* is intended to accomplish the *niyoga* i.e. the duty of the study of Veda. This is clear from *tavya* suffix. It cannot be treated as *niyamavidhi* either on the lines of *avahananavidhi* or on the lines of *yasya parṇamayi juhūḥ bhavati.* In the first case, the *avahanana* i.e., pounding the rice, is stated in the context of *Darśapūrṇamāsa* and therefore, it is *kṛtuviṣaya niyogānuvāda*, that is to say, it is *kṛtvartha.* In the second case of *parṇamayi juhu bhavati*, *parṇamayitva* is connected with an *yajñapātra* i.e., *juhu*. Therefore, it is also *kṛtvartha.* It is already stated that the ground for the *niyamavidhi* is *kṛtvarthatva.* The entire *svādhyāya* cannot be considered as *kṛtvartha*, since *hum*, *phat* etc. are not connected with the *kṛtu*. Hence, the *svadhyāya* is not *kṛtvartha.*

The very *svādhyāya* cannot be considered as *sādhya* i.e., *bhāvya* since, it is intended to accomplish *niyoga* and therefore, *niyoga* is *bhāvya*. Two *sadhyās* i.e., *bhāvyas* cannot be conveyed by one statement.

Svādhyāya cannot also be taken as *niyojya viśeṣaṇa* as it is not the outcome of *niyoga.* It is only the outcome of *niyogānuṣṭhāna* that can be the *sādhya* as in the case of *svarga.*

The final outcome of the above discussion is that the *adhyayanavidhi* conveys the *niyoga* of the *adhyayana* only, that is to say, it only conveys that the duty of the study of *svādhyāya* be accomplished. It is not connected with any particular sacrifice and therefore, it cannot be treated as *niyamavidhi.*

यच्चोक्तं नियमार्थो विधिरिति तदयुक्तम् । स्वाध्यायाध्ययनस्य नियोगनिष्पत्त्यर्थतया विधानेन वचनस्य अर्थवत्त्वात् । स्वाध्यायोऽध्येतव्य इति तव्यप्रत्ययेन विधिरभिधीयने । न च अवहन्त्यादिषु इव क्रतुविषयनियोगानुवादोऽयमवकल्पते । असन्निधानात् क्रतुनियोगानाम् । सन्निधानवशेनैव हि क्रतुनियोगप्रत्यभिज्ञानात् तत्र क्रतुनियोगानुवादोपगमः । न चेह सन्निधानमस्ति ।

नापि पर्णमयीजुहूर्भवति इतिवत् पदार्थसम्बन्धमुखेन क्रतुनियोग-प्रत्यभिज्ञानम् । स्वाध्यायस्य व्यभिचरितक्रतुसम्बन्धत्वात् । हुमित्येवमादीनामनर्थकानां स्वाध्यायान्तर्गतिदर्शनात् । अत एवात्र नियोगः साध्यतया अवगम्यते । अत एव स्वाध्यायस्य नेप्सितकर्मतया सम्बन्धोऽवकल्पते । एकस्मिन् वाक्ये साध्यद्वयविरोधात् ।

न च स्वर्गादिवत् स्वाध्यायस्य नियोज्यविशेषणतया अन्वयादविरोधः । अनियोगफलत्वात् स्वाध्यायग्रहणस्य । यदेव हि नैयोगिकं फलं तदेव साध्यतया नियोज्यविशेषणं नान्यदिति तृतीये दर्शितम् । अतो अध्ययनविषयनियोगप्रतिपादनेनैव तस्य अर्थवत्वात् न क्रतुप्रवेशकल्पनया नियमार्थता । (प्र०पं० १८)

Adhyayana is not an *Aṅga* of *Adhyāpana*

Before the presentation of the *pūrvapakṣa* and the *siddhañta* view of *the Prābhākaras*, Śālikanātha quotes the views of some earlier *Prāhākaras* and discusses the question whether *adhyayana* is the *aṅga* of *adhyāpana* or merely a *prayojya*. These early *Prābhākaras* considered *adhyayana* as the aṅga of *adhyāpana* and formulated the *pūrvapakṣa* as under:

The *adhyayana* which is consequential of *adhyāpanavidhi* is the *aṅga* of *adhyāpana*. It is meant for accomplishing *adhyāpana* and hence, it is *anyārtha* i.e., meant for something else. Consequently the comprehension of the import of *svādhyāya* is not required. This means no investigation into the import of *svādhyāya* is needed. Therefore, *vicāra* i.e. *mīmāṃsā* need not be undertaken.

अन्ये पुनरेवं पूर्वपक्षयन्ति अध्यापनविधिप्रयुक्तममध्ययनमध्यापना-पनाङ्गभूतम् । तन्निष्पत्त्यर्थतया च स्वाध्यायस्य अन्यपरत्वादविवक्षितार्थता इति ।

This *pūrvapakṣa* is based on the assumption that *adhyayana* is the *aṅga* of *adhyāpana*. Śālikanātha discusses this question in detail and rejects *aṅgatva* of *adhyayana*. In the course of this discussion the following points are presented:

(i) It is true that the *adhyayana* is *adhyāpana prayukta*. But that is not sufficient ground to treat it as its *aṅga*. For *aṅgatva*, *viniyoga* is necessary. Mere *prayuktatva* is not the ground.

प्रयुक्तिमात्रेण तादर्थ्यानुपपत्तेः । (प्र०पं० १८)

(ii) *Prayuktatva* does not necessarily lead to *tādarthya* i.e., *aṅgatva*. For instance, *agni-ādhāna* is *kṛtuvidhi prayukta* but it is not *kṛtu aṅga*

प्रयुक्तेः तादर्थ्यव्यभिचारात् । असत्यपि तादर्थ्ये केवलोपकारता-मात्रेण आधानस्य क्रतुविधिभिः प्रयुज्यमानत्वात् । (प्र०पं० १९)

आहवनीयाद्यङ्गभूतस्य आधानस्य क्रत्वनङ्गत्वेपि क्रतुविधिभिः प्रयुज्मानत्व-दर्शनात् । (न्या०सि० १९)

(iii) In the instance of *paśunā yajeta* the *ekatva* is *aṅga* by *viniyoga*. Its *aṅgatva* is not *aupādānika* but it is *laiṅgika* only. Therefore, this instance cannot be cited as an instance of *aṅgatva* by *prayukti*.

कथं तर्हि पश्वेकत्वादेः अङ्गत्वम्? तत्रापि शेषत्वं न औपादानिकं किन्तु लैङ्गिकमेव । (प्र०पं० १९)

The technicality of *saṃkhyā* i.e., *ekatva* being *laiṅgika* but not *aupādānika* is explained as under:

वस्तु सामर्थ्यमेव लिङ्गमुच्यते संख्या च स्वभावत एव संख्येयावच्छेदिका इति सङ्ख्येयार्थैव, किन्तुसङ्ख्येयभूतप्रातिपदिकार्थमात्रसम्बन्धे ग्राहकान्वयव्याघातापत्तेः ग्राहकीयभूतपश्वादिसम्बन्धः औपादानिकः । सन्निधि समाम्नातमात्रेणैव हि विभक्त्यर्थस्यापि ग्राहकं प्रति ऐदमर्थ्येन अन्वितस्यैव अभिधानम् । तदन्यथानुपपत्त्या च केवलाभिधाननिबन्धनं स्वरूपसम्बन्धमतिलङ्घ्य साधनीभूतसङ्ख्येयसम्बन्धावसानमिति न औपादानिकं तत्रापि शेषत्वम् । (प्र०पं० १९)

4. While raising the point that *paśunā yajeta* is an instance of *aṅgatva* by *prayukti* but not by *viniyoga*, similarly *adhyayana* also can be treated as *aṅga* by *prayukti* but not necessarily by *viniyoga*, two interesting points are made.

(i) *Vibhakti* i.e. case suffix, does not convey *kṛtusambandha* of ekatva. If this were so *ekatva anvaya* could have been treated as *anvaya* by *vākya* as in the case of *aruṇayā ekahāyanyā*. However, *vibhakti* conveys the connection of its meaning with the meaning of *prātipādika*. Therefore, *aṅgatva* of *ekatva* in the instance of *paśuna yajeta* is not conveyed by *vibhakti*.

कथं तर्हि पश्वेकत्वादेः अङ्गत्वम् । न तावद् विभक्तिरेव क्रतुसम्बन्धितया एकत्वादिकमभिधत्ते येन आरुण्यादिवत् वाक्येन विनियोगः स्यात् । विभक्तयो हि प्रातिपादिकार्थगतमेव स्वार्थं श्रुत्या अभिदधति ।

(ii) The second point is that the *saṃkhyā* i.e., *ekatva* is not stated as that of *karaṇa*, nor the *karaṇa* is stated as qualified by the *saṃkhyā*. This is because, *karaṇatva* and *ekatva* are stated simultaneously. Therefore, the *aṅgatva* of *saṃkhyā* conveyed by *vibhakti* is not by way *viniyoga* but it is only due to *prayukti*.

This claim of *prayukti* being the base of *aṅgatva* is already rejected as stated above.

(i) नापि करणभूतस्य एकत्वमुच्यते सङ्ख्यान्वितस्य वा करणत्वम् करणैकत्वयोः युगपदभिधानात् । अतो न वैनियोगिकं शेषत्वं विभक्त्याभिहितायाः सङ्ख्यायाः । इष्यते च शेषत्वम्, तच्च प्रयुक्तिकृतमेव ।

(ii) मैवम् । न तत्रापि शेषत्वमौपादानिकं किन्तु लैङ्गिकमेव ।

(प्र०पं० १९)

5. The early *Prābhākaras* who have formulated the *pūrvapakṣa* on the basis of *aṅgatva* of *adhyayana*, having failed to establish *aṅgatva* on the ground of *prayukti* try to establish *aṅgatva* by *viniyoga* only. They claim that *liṅga* itself is *viniyojaka*. However, this claim cannot be granted. To have *viniyoga* by *liṅga Sāmānya Sambandha* is necessary. Such *Sāmānya Sambandha* is not found in the case of *Adhyayana*. In the case of *ekatva* of *paśu* there is *sannidhi samāmnāna* while in the case of *adhyayana* no such *sannidhi samāmnāna* is found.

(i) भवतु तर्हि लिङ्गादेव अध्ययनस्यापि अध्यापने विनियोगः । नैवं भवितुमर्हति, सामान्यसम्बन्धबोधकप्रमाणसापेक्षत्वात् लिङ्गविनियोगस्य । न चास्य सामान्यसम्बन्धबोधकं किञ्चदस्ति प्रमाणम् । (प्र०पं० २०)

(ii) सन्निधिसमाम्नानमात्रेण सामान्येन ग्राहकसम्बन्धे सति पश्चात् पश्वेकत्वादीनां लिङ्गेन विनियोगः । अत्र सामान्यसम्बन्धापादकं सन्निधिसमाम्नानं नास्ति । (प्र०पं० २०)

6. The **णिच्** suffix, i.e., causal suffix in the expression **अध्यापयति** also cannot convey the *aṅgatva* of *adhyayana*. *Adhyāpana* is *prayojaka vyāpāra* while *adhyayana* is *prayojya vyāpāra*. Therefore, if at all *aṅgatva* is to be indicated, then, it will be the *aṅgatva of adhyāpana*.

(i) ननु च णिच् श्रुतिः प्रकृत्यर्थभूतस्य अध्ययनस्य शेषतामापादयतीति । तन्न । प्रयोजकव्यापारस्य प्रयोज्यव्यापारोत्पत्तिहेतुत्वात् विपरीतशेषत्वापत्तेः । (प्र०पं० २०)

(ii) प्रयोजकव्यापारः आचार्यव्यापारभूतमध्यापनम् । प्रयोज्यव्यापरः माणवकव्यापरभूतमध्ययनम् । प्रयोज्यव्यापरोत्पत्तिहेतुत्वात् विपरीतशेषत्वापत्तेः ।

7. *Vākya, prakaraṇa* and other *pramāṇas* are not at all available for conveying the *aṅgatva* of *adhyayana* to *adhyāpana*. Moreover, to consider *adhyayana* as the *aṅga* of *adhyāpana* is against the *Tikāgrantha*. Therefore, the formulation of *pūrvapakṣa* on the basis of the *aṅgatva* of *adhyayana* is not a correct approach.

वाक्यप्रकरणस्थानसमाख्यानानि तु अध्ययनस्य अध्यापनं प्रति विनियोजकतया नाशङ्कनीयान्येव । किञ्च टीकाग्रन्थविरोधश्च अङ्गत्ववादिनाम् । यत एवमाह भगवान् प्रयोज्यत्वात् अनङ्गत्वात् भवति संशयः । इति तस्मादनङ्गतयैव पूर्वपक्षणीयम् । (प्र०पं० २१)

Pūrvapakṣa View According to the *Prābhākaras*

Every injunction needs an *adhikārin*. No *adhikārin* is found for *adhyayanavidhi* since no *prayojana* is mentioned for it. No *prayojana* can be assumed also as *adhyayana* is only consequential to *adhyāpana*. Therefore, whatever is the *prayojana* for *adhyāpanavidhi* the same has to be considered as *prayojana* for the *adhyayana*. In fact the *prayojana* of *adhyāpanavidhi* occurs first. The *prayojana* of *adhyāpana vidhi* can be the *prayojana* of *adhyayana* though it is not an *aṅga* of it as in the case of *agni ādhāna* and *homa*.

सर्वोहि विधिः अधिकारपर्यवसायी । न च अध्ययनविधौ कस्याचिदधिकारोऽस्तीत्युक्तमेव । साक्षादश्रवणात् । अध्यापनविधिप्रयोज्यतया कल्पनानुपपत्तेः । तत्र य एवासौ प्रयोजकविधावधिकारः स एव प्रयोजनमिति

युक्तम् । प्रथमोपनिपातित्वात् यदपि यस्य अनङ्गं तदपि प्रयोजनं भवत्येव आधानस्येव होमादयः इति । (प्र०पं० २२)

It is argued that since the comprehension of the import of the Veda is the *prayojana* for *adhyayana*, he who studies it has his own *adhikāra* and that is the *prayojana* for *adhyayana*. This *prayojana* is *antaraṅga* since both *adhikāra* and *prayojana* belong to one and the same person.

However, this argument cannot be accepted. *Antaraṅga* can decide the priority only when the two alternatives are on equal footing. Here the *adhikāra* of *prayojakavidhi* i.e., *adhyāpanavidhi* occurs first, and that of *prayojyavidhi* i.e., *adhyayanavidhi* occurs later. Therefore, there is no separate *prayojana* for *adhyayanavidhi*. *Adhyayana* is meant only to accomplish *adhyāpana*.

ननु च अनन्तरभाविकर्मावबोधफलकतया अध्ययनस्य अध्येतुरेव अधिकारः अध्ययने प्रतीयते इति तत्प्रयोजनतैव स्वाध्यायविधेर्युक्ता अन्तरङ्गत्वात् । न । तस्योत्तरकालभावित्वात् । तुल्यायां हि प्राप्तौ अन्तरङ्गता बलीयसी । न च अनयोरधिकारयोः तुल्या प्राप्तिः । प्रथमोपनिपातित्वात् प्रयोजकविध्यधिकारस्य । उत्तरकालभावित्वाच्च अर्थावबोधनिबन्धनस्य अधिकारस्य । (प्र०पं० २२)

Once it is granted that the *adhyayana* is meant for accomplishing *adhyāpana*, the comprehension of the import of *svādhyāya* becomes unnecessary. Consequently undertaking an investigation into the import of Veda also becomes unnecessary. This means that the pupil's stay at the *gurukula* is no longer needed. The purpose of staying at *gurukula* and observing the code of conduct prescribed to a student is served by the very study of Veda and he can now return home and give up the rigourous discipline prescribed to a student. This is stated by the Smṛti *vedam adhitya snāyāt*. Hence, there is no scope for *Mīmāṃsā śāstrārambha*.

(i) यदा च अध्यापनविध्यधिकारसिद्धिः अध्ययनस्य प्रयोजनमित्यध्ययन-विधिना बोधितं तदा अध्ययननिष्पत्त्यर्थत्वात् स्वाध्यायस्य अन्यपरत्वात्

अविवक्षितार्थत्वम् । अविवतक्षितश्चार्थो न विचारणीय इति वेदाध्ययनमात्रेणैव गुरुकुलस्थितेः कृतार्थत्वात् अध्ययनोत्तरकालं गुरुकुल-निवृत्तिरेव युक्ता इति स्मृतम् 'वेदमधीत्य स्नायात्' ।

(ii) गुरुकुलवासादीनामपि निवृत्तिः प्राप्तैवेति सकल ब्रह्मचारिधर्मनिवृत्तिरेव अध्ययनानन्तरमुच्यते । एवं च अध्ययनविधिना विचारस्य अनाक्षिप्तत्वात् तदुपायभूतन्यायनिबन्धनं मीमांसाशास्त्रमनारम्भणीयमिति पूर्वः पक्षः । (प्र०पं० २२)

Siddhānta View According to the *Prābhākaras*

Though the *adhikāra* of *prayojaka vidhi* i.e., *adhyāpanavidhi* occurs earlier, the accomplishment of this is not the *prayojana* of *adhyayana* so far as the student is concerned. The *prayojana* should be such that accrues to him only. The benefit of an activity should accrue to the agent of that activity. It is *antaranga* to him. The benefit to be provided by an injunction need not be comprehended immediately. It is intened to enkindle the interest to undertake that activity. If that activity could be undertaken on account of some other activity, the benefit need not be comprehended immediately. Only in such cases wherein the comprehension of the benefit is necessary to undertake an activity, its understanding beforehand is necessary. In the present case, the undertaking of the *adhyayana* i.e., the study of Veda is brought about by the injunction of *adhyāpana* i.e., acquiring teachership. Therefore, there has been no need of the comprehension of *prayojana* i.e., comprehension of the import of Veda before. As already stated the *prayojana* i.e., comprehension of the meaning is *antaraṅga* i.e., accrues to the same person who undertakes the study. Therefore, comprehending the import of the Veda is necessary.

(i) राद्धान्तस्तु यद्यपि प्रयोजकविध्यधिकारः प्रथमभावी तथापि तन्निष्पत्तिः प्रयोजनमिति न युक्तम् । किन्तु दृष्टार्थावबोधफलकतया अध्ययनोत्तरकालभाव्यपि अध्येतुरेव अधिकारः प्रयोजनतया युक्त आश्रयितुम् । कर्तृसमवायित्वात् । यत्कर्तृकं यत् कर्म तस्यैव तत्रैश्वर्यं युक्तम् अन्तरङ्गत्वात् ।

(ii) न च सहसैव विधिदर्शनात् अत्र अधिकारपर्यवसानकल्पना कारणमस्ति। परप्रयुक्त्यैव अनुष्ठानस्य सिद्धत्वात् । यत्र खलु अधिकार-पर्यवसानकल्पनामन्तरेण प्रागनुष्ठानं न लभ्यते तत्र अनुष्ठानात् प्रागनवगतोऽधिकारः तदनुप्रवेशात् साध्यः । इह तु अध्यापन-विधिप्रयुक्तैव अधिकारपर्यवसानकल्पनामन्तरेण अनुष्ठानं लब्धमिति प्राथम्यमकिञ्चित्करम् । अन्तरङ्गत्वात् अध्येतुरेव अधिकारः युक्तः इति । (प्र०पं० २३)

From the above analysis it is clear that the *adhyayanavidhi* has an *adhikārin*. However, no *niyojya* is required since the *adhyayana* will be undertaken consequent on *adhyāpanavidhi*. He for whose benefit an activity is to be undertaken is the *adhikārin* for that activity. The *adhyayana* is beneficial to a student as it enables him to comprehend the import of *svādhyāya* i.e., *Veda*. Therefore, he is the *adhikārin*. However, he does not comprehend before taking *adhyayana*. He will realize later. After he studies *Vedas* with the *Vedāṅgas* he comprehends that the *Vedas* convey the sacrifices that are beneficial to him. This happens in between his mere study of *Veda* by way of recitation and his full investigation into the import of *Veda*. Taking this future benefit into account the parents of the student persuade the teacher to teach him the *Vedas*. In some cases the students themselve approach the teachers. In view of the interest of the students and the necessity of the comprehension of the import of the *Veda*, *vicāra* i.e., an investigation into the import of *Veda*, has to be undertaken. Hence *Mīmāṃsa śāstra* is *ārambhaṇīya*.

(i) तदेवमध्ययनविधेः अन्यप्रयुक्त्यैव अनुष्ठानसिद्धेः नियोज्यो नास्ति । अधिकारी तु विद्यत एव । यदर्थं हि यत् स तत्र अधिकारी । अर्थावबोधोपयोगेन च अध्येत्रर्थता अध्ययनस्येति स तत्र अधिकारी । स चायमधिकारः प्रागध्ययनात् नावगम्यते । (प्र०पं० २३)

(ii) इत्थं अध्ययने क्रियमाणे अङ्गाध्ययनसंस्कृतस्य वेदवाक्यादर्थावगमो जायते । स चायमध्येता मन्यते मदुपयोगिकर्मावबोधकतया मदर्थमध्ययनमिति । योऽयं वेदाध्ययनमीमांसाश्रवणयोः मध्ये अधिकारः सोऽयं मौलिकः शास्त्रार्थः । (प्र०पं० २४)

(iii) इममेव तावदधिकारमालोच्य पित्रादयो अर्थदानादिना कांश्चिदानमय्य पुत्रादीनुपनाययन्ति । प्रबुद्धाश्च केचन स्वयमेवात्मानम् । अन्यथा अध्यनासम्भवात् । (प्र०पं० २५)

Formulation of the *Pūrvapakṣa* and the *Siddhānta* on the Basis of *Śruti*

The above presentation of the *pūrvapakṣa* and the *siddhānta* given by Śālikanātha is based on the *smṛti* statement *upaniya tu yaḥ śiṣyam* etc. However, Prabhākara himself has formulated the *pūrvapakṣa* and *siddhānta* in his Bṛhati on the basis of a *śruti* statement viz. *aṣṭavarṣam brahmaṇam upanayita, tam adhyāpayita.* Śālikanātha briefly mentions these also as under:

The expression *svadhyāya* means *svaśākhā Veda.* The *adhyāpana vidhi* found in *śruti* does belong to some *śākhā.* If the import of *svādhyāya* is not taken into account, then, the import of *adhyāpana śruti* passage also is not to be taken into account. In the absence of the comprehension of its import, *adhyayana* cannot be consequential of the *adhyāpanavidhi.* Therefore, instead of making the accomplishment of *adhyāpana* the *prayojana* of *adhyayana,* the comprehension of the import of *svādhyāya* has to be made the *prayojana* i.e., the ground of *adhikāra.* This requires the comprehension of the import which necessitates an investigation into the import.

(i) अन्ये तु साक्षात् श्रुताध्यापनानुसारेण एवमाहुः । यदि अध्यापनविध्यधिकारप्रयोजनता स्वाध्यायाध्ययनविधेः स्यात् तदा अध्यापनविधेरपि स्वाध्यायान्तर्गतत्वाद् अविवक्षितार्थत्वेन तत्प्रयुक्ततापि न सम्भवति ।

(ii) स्वाशाखा हि स्वाध्यायशब्देन उच्यते । साक्षादधीतश्च अध्यापनविधिः नूनं केषाञ्चित् शाखिनां स्वशाखान्तर्गतो भवेत् इति स्वाध्यायस्य अविवक्षितार्थत्वेन तस्यापि अविवक्षितार्थत्वात् न प्रयोजकत्वमवकल्पते इति पश्चाद् भाव्यर्थावबोधोपयोगितया अध्येतुरेव अधिकारः अध्ययनविधेः प्रयोजनम् । (प्र०पं० २६)

The Basic Doctrinal Difference is the Ground for this Debate

As already stated at the commencement, the whole debate involves certain basic doctrinal differences between the Bhāṭṭas and the Prābhākaras. These doctrines can be identified by identifying the focal points of this debate. The Prābhākaras harp on the points that the *adhyayanavidhi* cannot be considered as *niyamavidhi* because *adhyayana* is not *kṛtvartha* i.e., not directly connected with the performance of the sacrifice. They also insist that initially *adhikāra* i.e., *arthajñāna kāmanā* is not present in the pupil and therefore this injunction cannot attract him. Therefore, this injunction has to be made operative only on the basis of *niyoga* conveyed by *tavya* suffix in *adhyetavyaḥ*. For this purpose this *niyoga* has to have a *niyojya*. Such a *niyojya* is provided by another injunction viz., *adhyāpanavidhi*. This injunction for teaching necessitates securing a pupil and the *adhyayana* by that pupil. From this line of argument of the *Prābhākaras* it is clear that their interest is to remove the *phalakāmana* from the primary position and make it only secondary. They are interested in making the *niyoga* the main driving point. They do not want to loose their *niyogavākyārthavāda* i.e. *niyoga-vidhyarthavāda* in the very first injunction that initiates *pūrvamīmāṃsā śāstra.*

On the other hand the Bhāṭṭas struggle to defend the *kṛtvarthatva* of *ādhyanavidhi* through the *arthajñana* i.e., comprehension of the meaning, and insist that the pupil has *adhikāra* i.e., *phalakamanā.* The benefit i.e., *arthajñāna* is set before as the driving point by the import of the injunction viz., the two *bhāvanas* viz., *śābdībhāvana* and *ārthībhāvanā.* These make the injunction operative. This is actually in the defence of *bhāvanāvākyārtha vāda* i.e., *bhāvanāvidhyarthavāda.* Therefore, the debate is not merely about the choice of an injunction of teaching or of study to provide a ground for *dharmajijñāsā* and *mīmāṃsā śāstra,* but it is a contest between *niyogavākyārtha* and *bhāvanāvākyārtha.*

It is interesting to note that the *adhyayanavidhi* could have been treated on par with *nityavidhi* and the question of *phalakāmanā* could have been avoided by both the *Prābhākaras* and the Bhāṭṭas. But this would not have served the purpose of initiating *Vedārtha vicāra.* This would have made the study of the *Veda* mandatory and the comprehension of the meaning would not have come into the picture. Therefore, both the Prābhākaras and the Bhāṭṭas do not raise this point at all.

Prayuktatva of Adhyayana cannot be Avoided by the Bhāṭṭas

Finally, it may be stated that treating the injunction of *adhyayana* as consequential in some way, cannot be avoided by the Bhāṭṭas also. Either they have to make it a requirement consequent to the need for comprehending the import of Veda to perform sacrifice or an activity undertaken consequent to the advice of the elders who know that an understanding of the import of it will be useful to the pupil for performing the sacrifice. This is because, initially, the pupil himself is not aware of its benefit and knowing the benefit and desiring to have it is an essential requirement for undertaking an activity. Therefore, the choice boils down to two alternatives viz.,

(1) *Adhyayanavidhi* is *kṛtuvidhi prayukta* or *pitrādi hitapodeśa-prayukta.*

(2) *Adhyāpanavidhi prayukta.*

The Bhāṭṭas go by the former while the Prābhākaras go by the latter.

The entire debate is not merely for settling this choice but to affirm their respective theories on the import of an injunction viz. whether *bhāvanā* is the import of an injunction or *niyoga* i.e., *kārya* is the import.

CHAPTER II

Nītipatha

Non-vedic Speech Communicates through the Inference of the Speaker's Knowledge

The Comprehension of the purport of the Veda is stated as the aim of *Pūrvamīmāṃsā* in the earlier section. This will be possible and purposeful only if the words are reliable and independent means of knowledge. Therefore, the question arises whether the words are invariably associated with the meanings conveyed by them and validly communicate the facts referred to through the meaning. The invariable and valid association is termed as *arthasamsparśa* and the absence of it as *artha asamsparśa.* This question is raised in the second chapter viz., Nītipatha.

The Words Do not Communicate Valid Meaning

In the case of *pratyakṣa* there is a definiteness of the association between the knowledge and the object referred to. Wherever there is no such agreement the defects in the means of perception could be identified and the error could be traced. But in the case of verbal communication we have instances of verbal communication even in the absence of the corresponding facts. For instance, the statement 'There is a herd of elephants on the tip of a finger' communicates its meaning but does not agree with the facts. These instances take away the confidence of the words being invariably associated with the facts conveyed through the meaning.

अथ लौकिकवाक्यानां व्यभिचाराभिमानतः ।
अर्थासंस्पर्शितां केचिदाहुः शब्दस्य वादिनः ।
निश्चयोऽर्थस्य संस्पर्शः सचार्थाव्यभिचारिणः ।
प्रत्यक्षादेरेव भवेत् शब्दस्य व्यभिचारवान् ॥
विनाप्यर्थं हि शब्देन प्रतीतिरुपजायते ।
अङ्गुल्यग्रेऽस्ति करिणां यूथमित्येवमादिना ॥

(प्र०पं० II-२-४)

Now, verbal communication cannot be sorted out as fallacious or true as in the case of perception. In the case of perception the inadequacy or the distortion of the means of perception could be identified and the knowledge obtained could be sorted out as fallacious or true as in the case of *śūktirajatajñāna.* In the case of verbal communication the words are the means. No defect in the words or in a properly formulated statement is to be found irrespective of whether there is agreement with the facts communicated or not. The statement 'There is a herd of elephants on the tip of a finger' is a defectless statement though it does not agree with the fact. Therefore, there is no guarantee that the sentences that are linguistically flawless will communicate valid knowledge. Therefore, the *Pūrvamīmāṃsā* investigation into the language of the Veda and the purport arrived at by such an investigation may not necessarily constitute the valid knowledge. The linguistic structure of a sentence whether it agrees with the fact or not will be intact if it is properly formulated. Therefore, one cannot distinguish true or false statement merely on the basis of a defectless statement. Therefore, the best course to assume is, there is no connection between the linguistic communication and the fact. This position is termed here as *artha asamsparśa.*

न चात्र शक्यते वक्तुं शुक्तौ रजतबोधवत् ।
अग्रहात् भ्रान्तिरेवेति कारणस्याविशेषतः ।
दुष्टा हि हेतवः कार्यं सम्पूर्णं कर्तुमक्षमाः ।
तेन भेदाग्रहो शुक्तिकारजतादिषु ।

इह तु ज्ञानहेतुर्यः शब्दः स न विशिष्यते ।
विशिष्यते यस्तु वक्ता सः ज्ञानस्य न कारणम् ।

(प्र०पं० II-७)

The Speaker has no Role in Verbal Communication

Now, one may try to say that the criterion to verify the truth or falsity of a statement is not the linguistic purity or the defect of the structure of the sentence but it is the capacity or the intention of the speaker. If the speaker's knowledge is inadequate or defective, if the speaker wants only to communicate something that does not agree with the fact, then, the statement will be false and will not communicate valid knowledge. On the other hand if his knowledge of what he communicates through his statement is valid and he has the intention to communicate it truly, the statement is valid and communicates valid knowledge.

This claim is not sound. The speaker's job is only to make the statement. He gives expression to the verbal form of the statement. The knowledge arises from the statement irrespective of the speaker's intention or his knowledge. Therefore, so long as the statement is linguistically defectless, it leads to the communication. However, there is no guarantee that these statements actually agree with the facts. Hence, no valid knowledge is communicated by the language—Vedic or non-Vedic.

वक्ता तु केवलं शब्दव्यक्तावेवोपयुज्यते ।
ज्ञानं तु शब्दमात्रेण निरपेक्षेण जन्यते ॥

न च तस्येह दुष्टत्वं किञ्चदप्युपलक्ष्यते ।

दोषश्चाग्रहणे हेतुः तदभावे स्फुटो ग्रहः ॥

तेन शब्दोपजनितं ज्ञानमेवेदमीदृशम् ।
अर्थं व्यतिक्रामतीति कुतस्तेनार्थनिश्चयः ।

(प्र०पं० II९-११)

It is true that we utilize the statements of reliable persons to obtain the knowledge of things and carry on with our activities in the daily life. But his reliability and the reliability of his statements are constantly checked through the other means of knowledge. From this it is clear that mere verbal communication itself is not trusted as a valid means of knowledge. In the case of non-Vedic language the reliability of the speaker at least creates a semblance of validity of verbal communication but in the case of the Veda since there is no speaker reliable or otherwise, even that advantage is not available.

नन्वेवमाप्तवाक्येभ्यः कथं व्यवहृतिः भवेत् ।
व्यवहारो हि लोकस्य कथं स्यान्निश्चयं विना ।
उच्यते व्यवहारोहि सन्देहादपि लौकिकः ।
प्रायशो घटते तेन न किञ्चिदपि दुष्यति ।
अपि चाप्तत्वमालोच्य वक्तुस्तत्रार्थनिश्चयः ।
मानान्तरवशेनापि कथञ्चिदुपपद्यते ॥
वेदस्यत्वलौकिकार्थत्वादभावाद्वक्तुरेवच ।
अहो बत दशां कष्टामुपनीतोहि पण्डितैः ॥

(प्र०पं० II१३-१६)

II

Non-vedic Speech is not Independent of the Speaker

The above contention of *pūrvapakṣa* is met without sacrificing the validity of verbal communication and *arthasamsparśa* position of words.

So far as non-vedic language is concerned, it is not independent of the speaker. It only represents the speaker's knowledge. On hearing a statement made by a person the meaning conveyed is only a means to infer the knowledge of the speaker intended to be conveyed. By the inference of his knowledge the facts of his knowledge are comprehended from the statement made by him. His statement plays the double role of serving as a means to infer the speaker's knowledge and communicate it to the listeners. In the first role it is a *liṅga* i.e., the means or the ground of the inference, and its second role is verbal communication. If the meaning presented by the statement does not represent the knowledge of the speaker of the facts mentioned in the statement it is a defect of its role as a *liṅga,* that is to say, the speaker has not invested it with the knowwldge which the statement is expected to communicate. This may be due to the defect or inadequacy of the speaker's knowledge itself or his intention not to communicate his knowledge truly. In any case, it is a case of a defective *liṅga* i.e., defective *hetu,* for the inference. This naturally makes the second role of the statement viz., verbal communication defective, that is to say, disagrees with the facts supposed to have been communicated by the statement. In this process, though there is no *śabdadoṣa*, the *puruṣa-doṣa* is responsible for the disagreement between the statement and the facts. Since, such an explanation is available in respect of a false statement, one need not jump to the conclusion that in all cases of statements there is *artha asamsparśa* i.e., disagreement between the statement and the facts conveyed. The statement which is expected to be a *liṅga* i.e., the ground of the inference of the knowledge of the speaker is either a defective *liṅga* or no *liṅga* at all in such instances in which it desagrees with the facts.

श्रूयतामवधानेन गतिर्नरगिरामपि ।
अनुमानात् पृथग्भावं तासां नेच्छन्ति सूरयः

विवक्षितार्थविषयमिन्द्रियार्थनिबन्धनम् ।
तस्य ज्ञानं च वाक्येन लिङ्गभूतेन गम्यते ।
ज्ञात्वैवार्थं ब्रवीतीति य एवमवधारितः ।
तस्य ज्ञानेन नियतं वाक्यं ज्ञानानुमापकम् ।
ज्ञानं चार्थाविनाभावि तेनार्थेऽपि विनिश्चयः ॥

तत्रार्थे निश्चिते पश्चात् सोऽर्थो वाक्येन गम्यते ।
तस्यां दशायां वाक्यस्य तस्य स्यादनुवादता ।

पूर्वं तु लिङ्गभूतं तत् वक्तुर्ज्ञानावधारणे ।
वक्तृज्ञानप्रसूतं हि वाक्यं तत्कार्यमिष्यते ॥

कार्यात् कारणसिद्धिश्च सर्वेषामनुमानतः ।
पौरुषेयमतो वाक्यं न शास्त्रमभिधीयते ॥ (प्र०पं० II२७-३०)

The Grounds of the Invalid Statements

It is found that the statements that do not agree with the facts are made for the following reasons:

(i) The speaker's knowledge itself is erroneous

(ii) He has no intention to speak truly

(iii) He is out of his mind

(iv) He formulates the statements defectively as a result of which something different than what he intends is presented in the statement.

In all these instances, the relation between the knowledge supposed to have been communicated and the statement which is expected to represent it is violated. That is to say the *vyāpti* relation between the knowledge to be communicated and the statement is broken. Therefore, the statement fails to play its first role of being the *liṅga* to infer the knowledge that the speaker intends to communicate. Consequently it fails in its second role of valid verbal communication.

वाक्यं हि पुरुषाधीनरचनं लौकिकं सदा ।
शङ्क्यमानायथार्थत्वं नार्थनिश्चयकं स्वतः ॥
अन्योन्यानन्वितार्थानि पदान्यपि हि मानवः ।
रचयन्तो विलोक्यन्ते तेन नान्वयनिश्चयः ।

केचित् तावत् भ्रमेणैव केचिदाशयदोषतः ।
प्रमादात् केप्यशत्केश्च केप्यनन्वितवादिनः ।
तदुक्तानां पदार्थानां यद्यप्यन्वययोग्यता ।
तथाप्यनन्वयस्यापि दृष्टेः नान्वयनिश्चयः ॥

तत्र निश्चयशब्देन ज्ञानमेवाभिधीयते ।
अन्वयानिश्चये तेन ज्ञानमेवास्ति नान्वये ।

शङ्क्यमानायथार्थत्वरचनं तेन पुंवचः ॥
श्रुतमात्रकमेवार्थे न तावन्निश्चयावहम् ॥
यावद्वक्तुरविज्ञातं पूर्वभाविप्रमान्तरम् ।
विवक्षितार्थविषयमिन्द्रियार्थनिबन्धनम् ॥ (प्र०पं० II२१-२५)

III

The Process of the Inference of the Speaker's Knowledge

There appears to be some difficulties in working out the process of inference of the knowledge of the speaker by his statement. The listener, in order to proceed to infer the knowledge of the speaker presented in the statement has to know the meaning of the statement. The listener cannot infer the knowledge just as knowledge in a general way. He has to infer it in the form in which it is presented in the statement. This means that he has to understand the meaning of the statement and then proceed to infer the knowledge presented through it. This means that the statement has already communicated to him what it is expected to communicate. Then the listener need not take the trouble to infer the knowledge through the statement and get it communicated by the same statement.

नन्वर्थ एव प्रथमं पुंवाक्येभ्योऽवगम्यते
अन्यथा हि कथं वक्तुर्धीर्विशिष्टानुमीयते ।

अर्थेनैव विशेषो हि निराकारतया धियाम् ।
न चाप्रतीतेनार्थेन विशेषश्चावकल्पते ॥ (प्र०पं० ३४-३५)

To solve this difficulty one has to understand the process of the inference in a little more detail. When a statement is heard, even before the organized communication of the meaning of the statement, the facts referred to by the words are brought to the mind of the listener. Then, he proceeds to sort out as to how these could be meaningfully organized. This process is termed as *vimarśa*. Then, he arrives at an organized sense. From this he infers the knowledge of these facts on the part of the speaker and finally infers the position of the facts, This crystallized position is communicated by the statement finally. In the first stage the reminding of the sense by the words and their organization corresponding to their position in the statement is only a step towards the inference of the knowledge of the speaker. It is not a crystallized final communication. Therefore, the listener has to go through the process of the inference to arrive at the verbal communication. The first stage is a surmise but not a definite communication. That is why the final communication is not a repetition of the first impact. The advantage of making the inference of the knowledge of the speaker the ground for the verbal communication in non-Vedic speech is, it provides a ground for sorting out the true statements and the false statements. In Vedic speech there is no question of a false statement.

अत्र ब्रूमोऽयथार्थत्वशङ्क्याऽर्थो न निश्चितः ।
अनिश्चितश्च न ज्ञात इति तावद् व्यवस्थितम् ॥
किन्तु अज्ञातेऽपि हि वाक्यार्थे पदजाते श्रुते सति
विमर्शो जायते श्रोतुरीदृशो मतिशालिनः ॥
अन्योन्यान्वययोग्यार्थं पदजातं ब्रवीत्ययम् ।
आप्तस्तेनामुना नूनं ज्ञातस्तेषां समन्वयः ॥
न कदाचिदसमबद्धानर्थानेष विवक्षति ।
न वा अप्रतीतसम्बन्धानिति दोषो न कश्चन ॥

(प्र०पं० II३८-४०)

CHAPTER III

Nayavīthī
Akhyāti theory

The *akhyāti* theory of the Prābhākaras is a distinct contribution to the theories of the truth and the falsity of cognition in Indian Epistemology.

The Prābhākaras take the firm stand that all knowledge is true—*yathārtham sarvavijñānam.*

यथार्थं सर्वमेवेह विज्ञानमिति सिद्धये ।
प्रभाकरगुरोर्भावः समीचीनः प्रकाश्यते ।। (प्र०पं० III-१)

Whatever is presented in a knowledge that is its object. Nothing else is the object. That which is presented in the knowledge, is termed as *bhāsamāna.* The object is termed as *vedya.* These two always agree. In other words, the content of the knowledge and the fact conveyed by it always agree.

अत्र ब्रूमो य एवार्थः यस्यां संविदि भासते ।
वेद्यः स एव नान्यद्धि विद्यात् वेद्यस्य लक्षणम् ।।
(प्र०पं० III-२३)

Even in the instances of *bhrama* i.e., error, and *sandeha* i.e., the doubt, the content of the cognition agrees with the fact conveyed by it.

स्वाणुर्वा पुरुषो वेति सन्देहेऽपि यदा द्वयम् ।।
स्मर्यतेऽन्योन्यनिर्मुक्तं तदार्थविरहः कुतः ।। (प्र०पं० s-६५)

In case, it is conceeded, even in a single instance, that the knowledge conveys something other than what is presented in it, then, there can be no confidence in knowledge conveying its object validly in any instance.

यदि चार्थं परित्यज्य क्वचिद्बुद्धिः प्रवर्तते ।
व्यभिचारवती स्वार्थे कथं विश्वासकारणम् ॥
(प्र० पं० III-६६)

Therefore, the Prābhākaras insist that whatever is presented in a knowledge the same is the object conveyed by that knowledge. The knowledge communicated by the statement *idam rajatam* on seeing *śukti* is the usual example of false knowledge i.e., *bhrama.* According to *anyathākhyāti* theory of false cognition, *śukti* is the object of this knowledge. However, it is presented as *rajatam* in the knowledge. In other words one is presented as another. Therefore, it is a case of *anyathākhyāti.*

Akhyāti Theory of the Prābhākaras

The Prābhākaras do not agree with such an analysis of this knowledge. According to them the statement *idam rajatam* represents two pieces of knowledge i.e., perception and memory. One who sees the *śukti* i.e., shell, present before him, sees it as *idam* i.e., 'this', in a general way without the comprehension of its special features which distinguishes it from *rajata* i.e., silver. Due to the similarity between *śukti* and *rajata* he remembers *rajata.* The knowledge of *sukti* as *idam* and the memory of *rajata* as *rajata* occur in such quick sequence that he does not realize the difference between the two cognitions or the objects conveyed by these two cognitions.

उच्यते शुक्तिशकलं गृहीतं भेदवर्जितम् ।
शुक्तिकाया विशेषा ये रजताद् भेदहेतवः ॥
न ते ज्ञाता अभिभवात् ज्ञाता सामान्यरूपता ।
अनन्तरं च रजते स्मृतिर्जाता तथापि च ॥

मनोदोषात् तदित्यंशपरामर्शविवर्जितम् ।
रजतं विषयीकृत्य नैव शुक्तेर्विवेचितम् ।
स्मृत्यातो रजताभास उपपन्नो भविष्यति ॥ (प्र०पं० III -२६-२९)

The contents of both these cognitions agree with the facts conveyed by them. *Idam* refers to *śukti* that is present before, and *rajatam* refers to *rajata* that is remembered. Therefore, there is no disagreement between the contents of these two cognitions and the objects of these two cognitions. On the contrary *śukti* is not the content of the cognition *'idam'* since it is not presented in this cognition as *śukti*. Therefore, it cannot be the object of this cognition. *Rajata* is the content of the cognition i.e., memory, since it is presented as *rajata* in it. Therefore, it is the object of the cognition i.e., memory.

इदं रजतमित्यत्र रजतं चावभासते ।
तदेव तत्र वेद्यं स्यान्नतु शुक्तिरवेदनात् ॥ (प्र०पं० III-२४)

That only is the object of the knowledge which is presented in the knowledge. Therefore, the question of the presentation of one object as another does not arise. It is against the experience. One object is never presented as another.

तेनान्यस्यान्यथाभानं प्रतीत्यैव पराहतम् ।
परस्मिन् भासमानेहि न परं भासते यतः ॥ (प्र०पं० III-२५)

Though the two pieces of knowledge viz. *idam* and *rajatam* are true and distinct, an erroneous statement is made as *idam rajatam* due to the non-realization of the difference between the two cognitions and their objects. For the non-realization of the difference of these the following factors are responsible. (i) The absence of the comprehension of the distinct features of *śukti* and its comprehension merely as *idam* in a general way. (ii) Remembering of *rajata* on account of the similarity between *śukti* and *rajata*. (iii) Absence of the reference to the past time in the memory of *rajata*. (iv) Occurrence of the perception of the *śukti* as *idam* and the memory of *rajata* in quick succession. These circumstances lead to the non-realization of the distinction between the two cognitions and their objects. This leads to the statement i.e., *vyavahār 'idam rajatam'*. It is this statement that is *bhrama*. It is this that is repudiated later. The fact of the cognition of *śukti* in a general way as *idam* or the memory of *rajata* are not repudiated. The non-realization of the distinction is termed as *viveka-agraha* and the absence of the reference to the past time in the memory is termed as *tattā pramoṣa. Tattā* means reference to the past time, and *pramoṣa* means the deletion of it. In the memory of *rajata* the reference to the past time is deleted.

नन्वेवं रजताभासः कथमेष घटिष्यति ।
उच्यते शुक्तिशकलं गृहीतं भेदवर्जितम् ॥
शुक्तिकायाः विशेषा ये रजताद् भेदहेतवः ।
ते न ज्ञाता अभिभवाद् ज्ञाता सामान्यरूपता ॥
अनन्तरं च रजते स्मृतिर्जाता तथापि च ।
मनोदोषात् तदित्यंशपरामर्शविवर्जितम् ॥
रजतं विषयीकृत्य नैव शुक्तेर्विवेचितम् ।
स्मृत्यातो रजताभासः उपपन्नो भविष्यति ॥

(प्र०पं० III-२६-२९)

This analysis of *idam rajatam* offered by the Prābhākaras is termed as *akhyātivāda*.

Objections against Akhyāti Theory

A number of objections are raised by *anyathākhyātivādins* against this analysis of the Prābhākaras:

(i) The so called memory of *rajata* cannot be classed as memory as it lacks the main feature of the memory viz., reference to the past time.

(ii) *idam* and *rajatam* are stated with *sāmānādhikaraṇya*. Therefore, the two refer to one and the same. *Idam* refers to something that is present before. Therefore, *rajata* also should refer to the same. Hence, it cannot be the remembered *rajata*. Further without *sāmānādhikaraṇya*, there cannot be *pravṛtti*.

(i) अनुभूतेऽपि विषये तत्परामर्शवर्जितम् ।
न बोधं स्मृतिमिच्छन्ति धारावाहिकबोधवत् ।। (प्र०पं० III-१७)

(ii) अपरोक्षपुरोवर्तिसामनाधिकरण्यतः ।
नेयं स्मृतिः किन्तु शुक्तौ भ्रान्तोऽयं रजतग्रहः ।। (प्र०पं० III-१८)

The first objection is answered by giving the reasons to class it as 'memory'. Firstly, it is caused by the impressions of the past knowledge of the *rajata*. These impressions are roused by the similarity between the *śukti* and the *rajata*. However, the reference to the past time is not roused due to the inadequate attention of the mind.

Secondly, it cannot be classed under *pratyakṣa*, *anumiti*, or any other form of knowledge. It cannot be classed as *pratyakṣa* since the *rajata* is not actually present before. It cannot be classed as *anumiti*, since the *liṅga* i.e., *hetu* etc. which are means of *anumiti* are not available. Hence, by *pariśeṣa* i.e., by the process of elimination, it has to be classed as memory only.

(i) उच्यतेऽनन्यगतितः स्मृतिरत्रावगम्यते
नह्यसन्निहितं तावत् प्रत्यक्षं रजतं भवेत् ।
लिङ्गाद्यभावाच्चान्यस्य प्रमाणस्य न गोचरः ।।
परिशेषात् स्मृतिरिति निश्चयो जायते यतः
तस्याः कारणसद्भावात् । (प्र०पं० III-३०-३२)

(ii) तस्याः कारणसद्भावात्
स्मृतिकारणभूतसदृशदर्शनोद्भूतसंस्कारजन्यत्वसम्भवात् स्मरणमेव
(न्या०सि०)

The suggestion that it may be treated on par with *dhārāvāhikajñāna* i.e. the recurring series of the cognitions, cannot be accepted.

In *dhārāvāhikajñāna* the senses are in touch with the object in each occurrence of the cognition and produce a series of cognitions of the same object. Here, the sense is not in touch with the *rajata*.

धारावाहिकेषु प्रत्युत्पन्नेन्द्रियग्रामसामग्रीकारणम् । (न्या०सि०)

(2) The second objection against the *akhyāti* theory is that the *pravṛtti* i.e., the initiative to fetch the object seen cannot be properly explained in the *akhyāti* theory. The mere occurrence of the knowledge of *idam* and *rajatam* in quick succession and the non-realization of the difference between the two cannot motivate the observer to proceed to fetch the *rajata*. Non-realization of the difference is only a negative factor. It cannot motivate *pravṛtti* i.e., initiative, to fetch the object. The initiative to fetch the object is possible only if it is comprehended as *rajata*. Comprehending it merely as *idam* is not sufficient to motivate nor the non-realization of the difference between *idam* and *rajatam* is sufficient to motivate the initiative. The initiative is possible only if the *sāmānādhikaraṇya* between *idam* and *rajatam* is positively realized. The *sāmānādhikaraṇya* between the *dharmi* and *dharma* i.e., object and attribute, has to be brought about. This means *idam* i.e., *śukti*, has to be comprehended as *rajata*. This is exactly *anyathākhyāti*. In the analysis of *idam rajatam* by *akhyātivādin* no such *sāmānādhikaraṇya* is worked out. Therefore, no *pravṛtti* could be justified as per *akhyāti* analysis.

अभेदं रजतत्वेन न शुक्तिमवलम्बते ।
सामानाधिकरण्येन प्रतिपत्तिर्विरुध्यते ।।
रूप्यार्थिनः प्रवृत्तिश्च शुक्तौ स्यान्निर्निबन्धना ।
अग्रहोपि न भेदस्य प्रवृत्तौ कारणं यतः ।

(प्र०पं० III-११-१२)

This objection can be answered by a closer examination of the circumstances of the occurrence of the *idam* and *rajatam* cognitions. Not only the difference between these two cognitions and the objects conveyed by these is not realized, but the difference between the cognition of a true *rajata* and these two cognitions is also not realized. In the cognition of true *rajata*, the *dharmi* and *dharma* are cognized with *sāmānādhikaraṇya* i.e., with reference to the same entity. Since the difference between the cognition of true *rajata* and these two cognitions is not realized, these two are also taken on par with the cognition of true *rajata*. The difference between the cognition of a true *rajata* and these two cognitions is not realized for two reasons: (1) One of these cognitions is also perceptual. (2) The same object i.e., *rajata* is presented in the true cognition and in one of these cognitions.

The fact of the cognition of true *rajata* and these two cognitions being on par in the above respects supported by the fact of non-realization of the difference between the cognitions of *idam* and *rajatam* facilitates the statement *idam rajatam* and motivates the initiative i.e., *pravṛtti*, to proceed to fetch the object present before. The purpose served by *sāmānādhikaraṇya* in the case of true *rajata* is served by *samāna rūpatā* here.

(i) ग्रहणस्मरणे चेमे विवेकानवभासिनि ।
सम्यग्रजतबोधात्तु भिन्ने यद्यपि तत्त्वतः ।
तथापि भिन्ने नाभातो भेदाग्रहसमत्वतः ॥
सम्यग्रजतबोधश्च समक्षैकार्थगोचरः ।
ततो भिन्ने अबुध्वा तु स्मरणग्रहणे इमे ।
समानेनैव रूपेण केवलं मन्यते जनः ।
अपरोक्षार्थबोधेन समानार्थग्रहेण च ।
अवैलक्षण्यसंवित्तिरिति तावत् समर्थितम् ।
समत्वेन च संवित्तेः भेदस्याग्रहणेन च । (प्र०पं० ३३-३७)

(ii) सन्निहितरजतशकले रजतमतिर्या भवति यादृशी सत्या ।
भेदानध्यवसायादियमपि तादृक् परिस्फुरति ।
साधारणं हि रूपं तस्या अस्याश्च विद्यते तेन ।
तन्मात्रप्रतिभानात् समानतामेव मन्यन्ते । (प्र०पं०III-४१-४२)

(3) The third objection is that if the knowledge represented by the statement *idam rajatam* is true, then how is it that it is repudiated as *na idam rajatam* later. What is it that is repudiated? Mere realization of the difference that was not comprehended earlier is not repudiated.

यथार्थदर्शनत्वे च बाधकोऽपि न युज्यते ।
अज्ञातभेदग्रहणैः न बाधकमतिर्भवेत् । (प्र०पं० III-१७)

This objection also does not stand. By the realization of the difference between the object of the knowledge *idam* i.e., *śukti*, and that of *rajatam* i.e., silver, the observer gets the correct knowledge of *śukti*. This enables him to discover that the statement i.e., *vyavahāra* '*idam rajatam* was not bonafide'. It is this statement that is repudiated. It is the correct knowledge of *śukti* that dissuades him from such *vyavahāra*.

(i) रजतप्रत्ययांशो विसंवादयतो नरान् ।
बाधकप्रत्ययस्यापि बाधकत्वमतो मतम् ॥
प्रसज्यमानरजतव्यवहारनिवारणात् । (प्र०पं० III-३९-४०)

(ii) इयं शुक्तिकेतिस्वरूपज्ञानस्य स्वविषयविरुद्धरजतोचित-
व्यवहारनिवारणरूपत्वात् बाधकत्वमनेनोक्तम् (न्या०सि० ५३)

Analysis of the Dream, the Doubt and the Instances of Bhrama

After explaining the process of *vyavahāra*, *pravṛtti*, and *bādha* as per the *akhyāti* theory, Śālikanātha proceeds to explain the dream, doubt, and certain other instances of error to show that none of them is *ayathārtha*. All these are true. His explanations are briefly narrated below.

(1) The objects cognized in the dream are also true. The dream cognition is memory. No dream arises in respect of the matters that are not experienced earlier. The fact of these having been experienced earlier is not realized in the dream.

Therefore, the dreamer feels that he is cognising them for the first time. However, these are only remembered. The impressions of the earlier cognitions are aroused by *adṛṣṭa.* Since dream cognitions convey the objects that have been there when these were cognised earlier, the dream cognitions also are true i.e., *yathārtha.*

एवं स्वप्नेऽपि वस्तूनि स्मर्यमाणानि सन्त्यपि ।
अनुभूतांशमोषेण भासन्ते गृह्यमाणवत् ।
ग्रहणस्य विशेषोहि गृहीतग्रहणं स्मृतिः ।
सा गृहीतांशमोषेण गृहीतिरिव तिष्ठति ।
संस्कारोद्बोधहेतुश्च तत्राद्दष्टं प्रकल्प्यते । (प्र०पं० III-४४,४६)

(2) The doubt is also *yathārtha.* The doubt consists of two memories of two items on seeing an object that has common characteristics. For instance, on seeing a tall object from a distance, the observer remembers a pole and a man. Since the objects of these two memories have been there when these were cognised these are *yathārtha.*

स्थाणुर्वा पुरुषो वेति सन्देहेपि यदा द्वयम् ।
स्मर्यतेऽन्योन्यनिर्मुक्तं तदार्थविरहः कुतः ॥

(प्र०पं० III-६५)

The cognition whether it is a pole or a man is not one cognition. These two cognitions refer to two different attributes. Since the observer is not able to fix one of the attributes with reference to the object observed by him, his cognition is not of the nature of certainty. However, the attributes remembered by him have been there when he had cognized the respective objects.

यौहि धर्मौ संशय्येते तयोरेकमिदं ज्ञानं नोदीयते । किन्तु द्वे एते ज्ञाने विशेषणस्मरणे । तयोश्च विशेषणयोः एकस्यापि तस्मिन् धर्मिणि निश्चयो नास्तीति एकान्ततो व्यवहारं प्रतिपत्ता प्रवर्तयितुमशक्नुवन् संशेते इव भवति (प्र०पं० १२१)

Though these two are memories, the reference to the past time is deleted. There is *smṛtipramoṣa.* Therefore, it is not stated as: **'सः स्थाणुः सः पुरुषः'** Since the observer is not able to fix either **स्थाणुत्व** or **पुरुषत्व** remembered by him with reference to the object observed by him, he states as: **स्थाणुर्वा पुरुषो वा ।**

(i) **ननु स्मृतिद्वयपक्षे सः स्थाणुः स पुरुषः इति स्यात् न तु स्थाणुर्वा पुरुषो वेति । मैवं स्मृतिप्रमोषात् ।**

(ii) **स्मर्यमाणस्थाणुत्वपुरुषत्वयोरेकस्यापि पुरोवर्तिन्यनिर्धारणात् तथात्वम् । (न्या०सि० १२१)**

(3) In the instance *pītaḥ śaṅkhaḥ* i.e., the conch is yellow, the yellow colour of *pitta dravya* i.e., the bile, settled on the eye is seen. The conch that is present before is seen without seeing its white colour. The yellow colour seen needs an object as its base while the object *śaṅkha* i.e., conch, needs a colour to be present in it. The observer does not realize that the objects of these two cognitions are not related with each other. These are taken on par with a real yellow object. Consequently, the observer makes the statement 'the conch is yellow'.

There is no *viśiṣṭabuddhi* here. There is only *viśiṣṭa vyavahāra.* So far as the two cognitions are concerned they agree with the facts presented in them. Bhāsamāna i.e., presented, in the two cognitions and *vedya* i.e., the objects, of the two cognitions agree. Therefore, these are *yathārtha* i.e., true. The two cognitions viz., 'yellow' and 'conch' are taken on par with the cognition of a true yellow object. Therefore, the statement *pītaḥ śaṅkhaḥ* is made. In this instance, the two cognitions are of the nature of *grahaṇa* i.e., the first experience, while in the case of doubt both were of the nature of *smaraṇa* i.e., memory.

पीतशङ्खावबोधेच पित्तस्येन्द्रियवर्तिनः ।
पीतिमा गृह्यते द्रव्यरहितोऽप्स्विव तिग्मता ॥

शङ्खस्येन्द्रियदोषेण शुल्किमा च न गृह्यते ।
केवलं द्रव्यमात्रं तु प्रथते रूपवर्जितम् ॥
गुणे द्रव्यव्यपेक्षे च द्रव्ये च गुणकांक्षिणि ।
भासमाने तयोर्बुद्धिरसम्बन्धं न बुद्ध्यते ॥
सत्यपीतावभासेन समे भातो मती इमे ।
व्यवहारोऽपि तत्तुल्यः एवमत्रापि युज्यते ॥

(प्र०पं० III-४८-५१)

(4) In the instance of *tikto guḍaḥ* i.e., the jaggery is bitter, the bitter taste of *pittadrayva* only is cognized without the cognition of *pittadravya.* The jaggery only is cognized without its sweet taste. The difference between these two cognitions is not realized. Therefore, the statement *tiktaḥ guḍaḥ* is made. So far as the two cognitions are concerned, these agree with the facts conveyed by them. Therefore, these are *yathārtha.*

मधुरे तिक्तधीरेवं व्याख्याता तिक्तवर्तिनः ।
तैक्त्यस्य रसहीनस्य गुडस्य च परिग्रहात् ॥

(प्र०पं० III-५७)

(5) In the instance of two moons, the rays proceeding from the eyes of the observer are split into two paths and the observer sees the moon through each set of the rays. The observer does not realize that the one and the same moon is presented in two cognitions. He does not realize the difference between the two cognitions and takes the moon as two moons on the model of a cognition in which two objects are really seen. However, so far as the two cognitions are concerned, one moon is presented in each and this agrees with the fact. Therefore, these two cognitions are also *yathārtha.* In this case he remembers that the moon is one but still when his vision provides the same moon twice in two cognitions he feels that he is seeing two moons. *Smṛti pramoṣa* is not necessarily found in all cases.

तथा द्विचन्द्रबोधेऽपि भिन्नं द्वेधेन्द्रियं महः ।
भिन्ने जनयति प्रख्ये एकस्मिन्नेव शीतगौ ।।
संवित्ती ते न भिद्येते तद्द्वित्वे सति मन्यते ।
भिन्नार्थबुद्धितुल्यत्वमत्रापि खलु पूर्ववत् ।
स्मरतोप्येकतां तेन भ्रमोऽयमुपपद्यते ।
नहि स्मृतिप्रमोषेण सर्वत्रैव भ्रमो मतः ।। (प्र० पं० III-५८-६०)

(6) In the instance of *diṅmoha* i.e., wrong identification of the quarters viz. East as West, the correct quarter is not comprehended. Some other quarter is remembered and the statement is made as West pointing to the East. Here also, so far as the memory is concerned it agrees with the fact conveyed by it and it is *yathārtha*. The error lies in pointing to the East.

दिङ्मोहेऽदृष्टसामर्थ्यात् दिक्स्वरूपानवग्रहात् ।
दिगन्तरस्वरूपस्य स्मरणाच्च भ्रमो मतः ।।

(प्र० पं० III-६२)

(7) In the instance of *alātacakra* i.e., circularly moving torch, there arise a series of cognitions of the torch light that moves in quick succession. The fact that the movements of the torch take place in different parts of the space and at different moments is not realized. Therefore, the observer feels that there is one circular movement, and one cognition of this movement. However, the actual fact is that there are different movements in successive different spaces and at different seconds. The cognitions comprehending these are also different. There is a perfect agreement between the cognitions and the movements of the torch. Hence, all these are *yathārtha*.

अलातचक्रेऽलातस्य भ्रमतः सर्वतो द्रुतम् ।
निरन्तरं धियो जाताः चक्रबुद्धिसमा मताः ।

कालभेदस्तु शीघ्रत्वात् धियां तासां न लक्ष्यते ।
चक्रधीव्यवहारश्च तेनास्मिन्नपि युज्यते ॥

(प्र० पं० III-६२-६३)

Śālikanātha concludes this discussion with the remark that all instances of *bhrama* could be analysed in this way, the ground of the error could be identified and *yathārthatva* could be established.

अनेनैव प्रकारेण सर्वभ्रान्तिषु पण्डितैः ।
ऊहनीयाः हेतुभेदाः यथार्थज्ञानसिद्धये ॥ (प्र० पं० III-६४)

A close review of these instances will reveal the following facts.

(i) In all cases there is the absence of the realization of difference between two cognitions. This is termed as *viveka agraha.*

(ii) The two cognitions are of the nature of *grahaṇa* and *smaraṇa* in some cases, both are *grahaṇa* in some cases, and both are *smaraṇa* in some cases.

(iii) The two cognitions agree with the facts conveyed by them. Hence, these are *yathārtha.*

(iv) These very cognitions are not repudiated. The non-realization of the difference is resolved and the objects of the two cognitions are correctly comprehended.

(v) In the instances wherein there is *smaraṇa*, the reference to the past time is not cognized. This is called *tattā pramoṣa.*

(vi) The nature of *vyavahāra*, *pravṛtti*, and *bādha* are already explained.

(vii) In no instance, one is comprehended as another, that is to say, there is no *anyathākhyāti.*

(viii) In no instance there is *sāmānādhikaraṇya* with a *vyadhikaraṇa dharma*, that is to say, no attribute of one is comprehended in another.

Defending the *akhyāti* theory as narrated above, *Śālikanātha* points out the drawbacks of *anyathākhyāti* theory in four important respects:

The Drawbacks of Anyathākhyāti

(1) If the cognition has no corresponding object, that is to say, if it is not *yathārtha*, then, what is presented in the cognition will be merely a form of the cognition. This form belongs to cognition only. There will be no object outside. This amounts to *bāhyārtha apalāpa* i.e., total denial of the outside objects. It also amounts to the cognition of the non-existent. If it is contended that the object exists elsewhere but its contact is wrongly presented here, then, the so-called contact is non-existent. Hence, this also amounts to the cognition of the non-existent.

(i) **अयथार्थत्वपक्षे च ज्ञानं साकारमापतेत् ।**
आकारो भासते योहि ज्ञान एवावतिष्ठति । (प्र० पं० III-७२)

(ii) **''रजताकारस्य स्वरूपेण भानात् न असत्यता । नापि शुक्तिरूपता'' इति धीरेव साकारा स्यादिति बाह्यार्थापलापो दुर्निवारः । ज्ञानरूपत्वासम्भवे असतः ख्यातिप्रसङ्गः । अन्यथा सतः एव रजतस्य अत्र दोषवशात् संसर्ग इति तर्हि संसर्गांशे असतः ख्यातिप्रसङ्गः । (न्या० सि० ६०)**

(2) There is no cause for the production of the *ayathārtha* cognition. The defects cannot be the causes. The defects can only prevent the effect. These cannot give rise to a different effect.

अयथार्थस्य बोधस्य नोत्पत्तावस्ति कारणम् ।
दोषाश्चेन्नहि दोषाणां कार्यशक्तिविघातिता ।।

(प्र०पं०III-६३)

The defects can only obstruct the comprehension of the object. Therefore, it is more proper to say that the *viveka agraha* leads to the error.

विद्यमानवस्तुरूपग्रहणे प्रतिबन्धृता ।
दोषाणामुपपन्नेति भ्रान्तिरग्रहबन्धना । (प्र० पं० III-७५)

The main purpose of the Prābhākara's theory of *akhyāti* is to firmly support their realistic metaphysics. Even if one cognition is permitted to arise without the corresponding object outside, then, the Buddhists will jump with their idea of all cognitions being without the corresponding objects outside. This will cut the very roots of the realistic metaphysics. It is difficult to get such a firm base for realism in *anyathākhyāti* theory. Something that is really not present outside is considered as cognized in *anyathākhyāthi* theory. This will make room for the total elimination of the outside objects.

Though the Prābhākaras have laid such a strong ground for defending realism almost all other systems of Indian Philosophy including the Bhāṭṭa *mīmāṃsakas* have criticized this theory. Their criticism is merely on the ground of some procedural difficulties such as *sāmānādhikaraṇya* in explaining the epistemological process. Procedural difficulties are found in *anyathākhyāti* theory also. It seems better to make some compromises in the procedure than to sacrifice the very roots of realism.

CHAPTER IV

Jātinirṇaya
Universal

Different Views on the Concept of Jāti i.e. Universal

Śālikanātha commences his discussion on *jāti* i.e., universal, by stating different views held by the different schools of philosophy. These are: (1) The concept of *jāti* is merely a *vikalpa* i.e., a mental construction. (2) *Jāti* exists but it is not different from the *vyaktis* in which it subsists. (3) It exists and distinct from the *vyaktis* to which it belongs but it is not perceptible. It could only be inferred. (4) It exists and it is both different and non-different from the *vyaktis* to which it belongs. (5) Some consider certain characteristics that are not *jāti* as *jāti*.

बहुधा जातिविषये विवदन्ते विपश्चितः ।
प्रभाकरमतेनायं तेषां प्रत्यास उच्यते ।।

केचिदाचक्षते जातिरिति विकल्पविलसितम् इति । एके तु सतीमपि जातिमाश्रयेभ्योऽभिन्नामनुमन्यन्ते । अन्ये तु भिन्नामप्यनुमेयामाहुः। अपरे च भिन्नाभिन्नामिच्छन्ति । तथा अजातावपि जातिव्यवहारो बहुलमुपलभ्यते केषांचिदिति तन्निराकरणायेदमारभ्यते । (प्र०पं० ६३)

Śālikanātha rejects all these views and states the Prābhākara's view as follows. Jāti exists. It is distinct from the *vyaktis* to which it belongs, and it is perceived on reflecting its continuity.

(i) **जातिराश्रयतो भिन्ना प्रत्यक्षज्ञानगोचरा ।**
पूर्वाकारावमर्शेन प्रभाकरगुरोर्मता ।। (प्र०पं० ४)

(ii) पूर्वाकारावमर्शेनित्यनेन अजातावपि जातिव्यवहार: इति पक्षं व्युदस्ति। पूर्वाकारावमर्शनाभावात् सत्तादौ सामान्यं नामान्यं नास्तीत्यर्थ:। (न्या०सि० ६४)

Buddhists' Arguments against the Concept of Jāti

The Buddhists who state that *Jāti* is merely a *vikalpa,* not only deny the *jāti* but also the *vyaktis* in which it is supposed to subsist.

There is No Jāti at Paramāṇu Level

First, the case of *paramāṇus* is taken. In the case of *paramāṇus* of *pṛthvi, ap, tejas, and vāyu,* there is no comprehension of a continuing characteristic commonly present in all *paramāṇus* of these. For envisaging a *jāti* i.e., universal characteristic, comprehension of the continuity of a characteristic commonly present is the ground. Such a characteristic is not found is these *paramāṇus*. In fact these *paramāṇus* themselves are not comprehended. The *paramāṇus* are stated to have been conceived by the inference and the inference grasps them as *sat* only. Therefore, there is no question of any common characteristic being found in them. The common name *paramāṇu* is given to all these simply because these have the attribute of *pārimāṇḍalya.*

The grouping of these as *pṛthvi paramāṇu, jala paramāṇu* etc., also does not warrant the acceptance of *pṛthvitva* etc. as *jātis,* because these groupings can be explained on the basis of the odour, cold, touch etc., which are the attributes of these *paramāṇus*. Thus there is no need of any *jāti* concept at *paramāṇu* level.

(i) ननु आश्रय एव द्रव्यं जातिरसदिति सौगता: । तथाहि न परमाणुषु चतुर्विधेषु पार्थिवाप्यतैजसवायवीयेषु जातिराश्रिता अभिमता अनुवृत्ताकारप्रत्ययवियोगात् । भिन्नेषु यदभिन्ना जातिरुच्यते तत्रानुवृत्ताकारावभासिनी बुद्धिरेव निबन्धनम् । न कस्यचित् जन्तो: परमाणुषु करणपथविदूरवर्तिषु निपुणमपि निरूपयत: अनुवृत्ताकारावभासिनी मतिराविर्भवति । (प्र०पं० ६४)

(ii) **यापि चेयं परमाणुरिति मतिः सापि पारिमण्डल्यलक्षणगुणकारणिका मीमांसकैरपि अङ्गीक्रियते । पृथिवीत्वादिकमपि न तत्तदसाधारण-गन्धादिगुणसमवायमात्रलब्धात्मलाभायां पृथिव्यादिबुद्धौ निबन्धनम् । (प्र०पं० ६५)**

There are no Gross Objects

The question of *jāti* does not arise at the gross object level also, because, the very idea of the formation of gross objects cannot be logically established.

Each *paramāṇu* by itself cannot give rise to a gross object. By the conjunction of the two or more *paramāṇus* also a gross object cannot be brought about. This conjunction cannot be stated as inhering in each *paramāṇu* or in more than one. By the inherence in each *paramāṇu* separately no gross object of two or more *paramāṇus* can arise. There are no two or more *paramāṇus* brought together before the inherence of conjunction in them to bring them together.

In addition to the concept of each *paramāṇu*, there is no concept of two or more *paramāṇus.* Therefore, if the conjunction cannot inhere in each *paramāṇu*, there is no question of its inherence in many. Therefore, the formation of even a *dvyanuka* i.e., a two *paramāṇu* unit is not possible. Further, *paramāṇu* has no parts. It has no sides at which another *paramāṇu* can join it and produce the dimension of length and breadth. For the same reason a third *paramāṇu* also cannot be joined to it. Therefore, the formation of a *dvyaṇuka* is impossible. Consequently the formation of a *tryaṇuka* and so on is also not possible, since the formation of a gross object itself is not possible, the possibility of a *jāti* present in it is ruled out.

(i) **न च स्थूलेषु द्रव्येषु जातिः समवेयात् । तेषामेव दुरुपगमत्वात् । (प्र०पं० ६५)**

(ii) न खलु द्रव्यारम्भो घटते । तथाहि द्व्यणुकादिक्रमेण स्थूलद्रव्यारम्भोऽभिधीयते । तत्र तावद् द्रव्यारम्भ एव न साधीयानिति मन्यामहे । न खलु तथैवैकः परमाणुः द्रव्यस्यैकाकिनः स्थूलद्रव्यान्तरारम्भकत्वानुपपत्तेः । नचैकैकद्रव्यतिरिक्तमपरमारम्भकमस्ति । संयोगोपि च तयोरनुपपन्न एव । सहि नैकैकद्रव्यसमवेतः नाप्यनेकद्रव्यसमवेतः । एकैकातिरेकेण अनेकस्य अभावात् । एवं च प्रत्येकमेकद्रव्य-समवेतत्त्वाभावे न अनेकद्रव्यसमवेतत्वमपि सम्भवति । अनेनैव मार्गेण त्र्यणुकस्य त्रिभि:व्द्यणुकैः आरम्भणीयस्य महिमगुणशलिनः सम्भवो निरस्तः । तदेवं दूरभूतः स्थवीयसामवयविनामारम्भसंकथा । (प्र०पं० ६६-६७)

The Problem of the Whole and the Parts

Further, even if it is granted that the formation of a gross object is possible, the problem of explaining as to how the gross object which is constituted of so many constituents is located in its constituent parts, how the *avayavin* i.e., the whole, is located in *avayavas* i.e., its parts, has to be explained.

(i) It cannot be said that the whole is located in each constituent separately as a whole. In this case one would have observed it in each constituent separately. If it were in each constituent separately, then, when some motion takes place in one constituent the whole would have been observed as moving. When a colour is given to one constituent the whole would have been observed with that colour, since, the whole is located in that constituent. Similarly, since the motion or colour is not present in the other constituent, the whole would have been observed as without motion or colour. This means that one and the same gross object i.e., *avayavin*, will have moton and its absence, colour and its absence and so on, because, in its presence in another constituent it has no motion and no colour. This is an absurd position.

अपि च अवयविनः किमवयवेषु प्रत्येकं कार्त्स्न्येन वृत्तिः? व्यासङ्गेन वा? इति चिन्तनीयम् । न तावत् कार्त्स्न्येन वृत्तिमुपलभामहे । एकैकावयवगतस्य तस्य अप्रतिपत्तेः । एकैकावगते च कम्पे रागे वा सकलस्य अवयविनः कम्परागप्रतीतिप्रसङ्गात् । तथा अवयवान्तरे च कम्परागविरहे कम्परागविरहसमासक्तेः अवयवी कम्पेत न कम्पेत रज्येत न रज्येत चेति विषमां दशामाविशेत् । (प्र०पं० ६७)

(ii) It cannot also be said that the gross object i.e., the whole, is located in its constituents in a spreading way. That is to say, one and the same whole is spread over all its constituents. To be spread over all its constituents it has to have parts, apart from its constituent parts, so that each part can occupy a constituent part. No such parts in addition to the constituent parts could be envisaged.

Further, since the whole is not present in each part separately, and since there are no separate parts, apart from the whole, to occupy part by part, it would lead to the position that the whole is not present anywhere. Therefore, the idea of spreading over is nothing but the total absence of the whole in the parts.

नापि व्यासङ्गेन अवयविनः वृत्तिः अवयवान्तरविरहात् । अवयवान्तरशालिनो हि केनचिदवयवेन क्वचन केनचिदवयवेन क्वचन इति व्यासङ्गिनी वृत्तिः उपपत्तिमती । किञ्च एकैकत्रावृत्तेरवृत्तिरेव । एकैकातिरिक्तानेकाभावात् । किञ्च सकलावयग्रहणे एव नियमेन अवयवी ज्ञायेत । न च तथा सम्भवति अवयवान्तरेण अवयवान्तरतिरस्कारात् । न च प्रकारान्तरेण वृत्तिरिति वदितुं शक्यम् । अनुपपत्तेः प्रकारान्तरस्य । (प्र०पं० ६७-६८)

The problem whether the whole is different from the parts or identical with the parts also remains unsolved. If the whole and the parts are different from each other, then one would have been comprehended without the other at least for some time.

The objects that are different are not always comprehended together as in the instance of a jar and a cloth. No one comprehends the whole without comprehending the parts. To avoid this difficulty if it is stated that the whole and the parts are one, it amounts to saying that there is no such thing such as a whole. Thus, the concept of a gross object is not logically tenable.

अवयवेभ्यश्च अवयवी व्यतिरिच्यमानः अव्यतिरिच्यमानो वा न प्रमाणेन सङ्गच्छते । व्यतिरिक्तो हि तदग्रहेपि ग्रहणं कदाचिदनुभवेत् । न खलु भिन्नयोः सहोपलम्भनियमः घटपटयोरिव । तद्वदवयव्यपि भिद्यमानो नावयवैरेव सह उपलभ्येत । कस्याञ्चिदपि दशायाननुभूयमानेष्ववयवेषु अनुभूयेत । न च अवयविनमवयवानुभवमन्तरेण केचिदुपलभन्ते । अव्यतिरिच्यमानस्तु नास्त्येवेति वचनभङ्गिमात्रेणोक्तं भवति । तदेवमवयविद्रव्यमुपपत्तिभिः अनुसन्धीयमानमेकान्ततो लीयते । (प्र०पं० ६८)

Now, the common notion of a gross object can be explained as follows: The *paramāṇus* that occur in a continuous flux are observed in continuity. This creates a mental image of a gross object. When one observes a group of trees from a distance, a mental image of a forest is created. Similarly, the mental image of a gross object i.e., a whole, is projected on observing a series of *paramāṇus* in a continuous flux. Therefore, there is no such thing such as a gross object in which *jāti* can subsist and hence the concept of *jāti* is not justified.

कथं तर्हि स्थूलावयवभासिनी मनीषा समर्थनीया? इत्थम् उत्तराधरभावेन निरन्तरमुत्पन्नाः परमाणवः एव समधिगतैन्द्रियकज्ञानजननयोग्यदशाविशेषाः प्रत्यक्षमीक्ष्यन्ते । तान् तथाभूताननुसन्दधतः तद्बलभावी मानस एव स्थूलविकल्पो विजृम्भते दूरादिव तरुषु निरन्तरेषु समनुभूयमानेषु वनमिति मतिः । अतः स्थवीयसां द्रव्याणामश्रयत्वेन अभिमतानामयोगात् जातिरपि तदाश्रया नाभ्युपगममर्हति । (प्र०पं० ६८)

Jāti is not Comprehended by any Pramāṇa

Apart from the impossibility of a locus for *jāti*, it cannot be ascertained also by any *pramāṇa*. It cannot be perceived by the senses. It is considered as *nitya* i.e., eternal. No eternal entity can produce any effect. An eternal object, if it has the capacity to produce any effect, will have to produce it all the time. If it has no capacity it can never produce any effect. Nothing new can be expected from an eternal entity. That which cannot produce any effect cannot be the object of knowledge. Therefore, the so-called *jāti* which is claimed to be eternal cannot be comprehended by *pratyakṣa.*

This is the Buddhists' criticism of the concept of *jāti.* According to the Buddhists, producing means presenting the object in the knowledge. They define the *hetu* i.e., the cause, as that which is capable of presenting itself in the knowledge. Therefore, an eternal entity, that is not capable of producing anything cannot present itself in the knowledge. Hence, it cannot be ascertained by *pratyakṣa.*

The Buddhists argue that even if the *mīmāṃsā* concept of *pratyakṣa* viz., the knowledge produced by the contact between the senses and the objects is accepted, it is found that no one perceives *jāti* as he perceives a cow or any such object even if he attentively observes an object. Therefore, even the contact between the senses and the object cannot help one to ascertain *jāti* by *pratyakṣa.*

(i) **अपि च जातिरपि नेन्द्रियज्ञानविषया प्रतीयते । तस्या नित्यत्वेन अभ्युपगमात् । नहि नित्यं कस्मैचित् कार्याय पर्याप्तम् । तद्धि न शक्तस्वभावं नित्यं कार्योदयप्रसङ्गात् । अशक्तस्वभावं तु नित्यत्वात् अविचिकित्सया अशक्तिकं नित्यं न किञ्चित् कुर्यात् । न च अजनक-मिन्द्रियज्ञानविषयतामनुभवति । योहि विषयः स्वस्य अन्वयवयतिरेकज्ञानमनुकारयति स प्रत्यक्षः ।**

(ii) **किञ्च समुन्मिषितचक्षुषः चिराय विषयान्तरानुसन्धानव्यावृत्तचित्तस्य पुरोवर्तिनीं कालाक्षीं वा साक्षात् कुर्वाणस्यैव न जातिरपरा अवभासते । (प्र०पं० ६९)**

Jāti cannot be Either Eternal or Produced

Further, the *jāti* cannot be stated as produced along with the *vyakti* and perishes when the *vyakti* perishes. If such a position is accepted, then, the very essential nature of *jāti* viz., it being one and eternal will be destroyed. It is held that *jāti* is one and is present in many. If it is now stated that it is produced along with the *vyakti* and perishes along with it, then, it amounts to saying that there is a separate *jāti* in each *vyakti*.

अन्यच्च न जातिरसौ पिण्डैः सह उत्पद्यते विनश्यति वा । तथोपगमे स्वरूपहानिप्रसङ्गात् । एका च जातिः अनेकाधिष्ठाना प्रतिज्ञायते । उत्पत्तिमती विनाशिनी च अन्या अन्या स्यात् विरुद्धधर्माध्यासस्य भेदापादकत्वात् । (प्र०पं० ६९)

If *jāti* is eternal, then, the questions where it was before the production of *vyakti*, and how it came to *vyakti* when the *vyakti* was produced have to be answered. It cannot remain in *ākāśa* since *vyakti* alone is its locus. Nor does it move into the *vyakti* since it is motionless. As it is observed as soon as the *vyakti* is produced one has to say that it was already there. Since there is no locus other than the *vyakti* concerned for the *jāti* one has to say that it was not there before the production of *vyakti*. This will lead to a contradictory position viz., it was there, and it was not there. Therefore, the concept of *jāti*, cannot be justified.

सेयं नित्या जातिः उदितवत्यां व्यक्तौ प्रतीयमाना नान्यतः आगता निष्क्रियत्वात् । न च तत्रैवासीत् प्रागप्रतीतेः । न च स्थितिरपि युक्तिमती व्यक्तिरेव हि तस्याः देशो नाकाशादिः । अनुत्पन्ना च क्व अवतिष्ठातामाकृतिः । न चोत्पाद्येप्यवतिष्ठते । तदेषा जातिः अवतिष्ठते नावतिष्ठते च इति सङ्कटमापतितम् । (प्र०पं० ६९-७०)

Jāti is Neither Different nor Identical with the Vyakti

The problem whether the *Jāti* is different from the *vyakti* or non-different from it or both different and non-different has also to be faced.

It cannot be considered as non-different from *vyakti*, because, in that case it has to arise and perish along with the *vyakti*.

This will destroy its very nature of being one and eternal. Further, if it is identical with the *vyakti,* then, it amounts to saying that there is no *jāti,* there is *vyakti* only. This is exactly our view.

If the *jāti* is different from the *vyakti,* then, it should have been possible to comprehend *Jāti* separately without comprehending *vyakti.* If the two were to be comprehended together, then, the relation of *ādhāra-ādheya bhāva* also should have been comprehended. However, on seeing a cow nobody will say he is comprehending cowness in the cow.

(i) **किञ्च व्यक्तेः अभिन्ना भिन्ना वा उभयरूपा वा जातिरास्थेया । तत्र न अभिन्ना तथाभावे व्यक्त्या सहोत्पादे विनाशे वा स्वरूपहानिप्रसङ्गः इति पुरस्तादुपन्यस्तम् । व्यक्तिमात्राङ्गीकारे कोऽस्मत्पक्षस्य अस्य च भेदः इत्यपि चिन्तयन्तः सीदन्तु भवतः । अतो व्यक्तिमात्रमेव तत्त्वमिति वदतां साहाय्यमेव आचरितमनतिरेकिणीं जातिमुररीकुर्वाणैः ।**

(ii) **भिन्नत्वेपि पिण्डग्रहणमन्तरेण ग्रहणापत्तिः उभयप्रतीतौ च सम्बन्धप्रतीतिसमापत्तिः । अस्त्येवेति चेत् महदिदं वैयात्यम् । कः खलु इह गवि गोत्वमिति मतिमभ्युपगच्छेत् अन्यत्र निरस्तत्रपायन्त्रणात् भवतः । (प्र०पं० ७०-७१)**

In case the *jāti* is stated as located in the *vyakti,* the question again arises whether it is located in all *vyaktis* in a spreading manner or it is located in each *vyakti* separately. It cannot be said that it is located in all in a spreading manner, because, it cannot do so with reference to the *vyaktis* that were in the past and that will be in the future. It cannot also be said that it is located in each *vyakti* separately, because, it will result in a situation 'where and when it is present in one *vyakti* it is not present in other *vyaktis.'*

भिन्नत्वे च वृत्तिप्रकारो दुर्निरूप एव । किं व्यासङ्गिनी वृत्तिः उत प्रत्येकपरिसमाप्तिमतीति । एकत्र च परिसमाप्तौ अन्यत्र न वर्तेत इति पुनरपि स्वरूपहानिप्रसङ्गः । व्यासङ्गोपि कालत्रयवर्तिनीषु व्यक्तिषु अनुपपन्न

एव । प्रत्येकं च गौः गौः इति प्रत्ययः विकल्पमात्रमित्यङ्गीकृतं स्यात् । (प्र०पं० ७१)

It also cannot be said that the *jāti* is both different and non-different from the *vyakti.* This will be a contradiction. It cannot be insisted that since there is the comprehension of both the difference and non-difference, there is no contradiction. No such comprehension is found. That which is presented alone in the knowledge, is comprehended as identical with it and those that are presented in the knowledge as two are comprehended as different.

For instance, a jar presented alone in the knowledge is comprehended as identical with itself, and a jar and a cloth presented in the knowledge are comprehended as distinct. The comprehension of the distinction takes place when something is presented along with another. Now, in the case of *jāti* and *vyakti*, these have to be presented as two in the knowledge in respect of their difference, and as one in respect of their identity. In the latter case, it is either *jāti* or *vyakti.* In either case there will be the presentation of one of them twice but not their identity. Now, in respect of these being different each one of them is already presented in the knowledge. Now, in respect of their identity one of them is presented again. This means that the identity between the *jāti* and *vyakti* is not presented but only one of them is presented twice. Thus, the presentation of *bhedābheda* in the knowledge is not possible. Therefore, it cannot be said that *bhedābheda* has to be accepted on the ground of experience.

(i) न च उभयरूपता विरोधात् । न च उपलम्भबलेन विरोध एव नास्तीति चतुरस्रम् । तथाविधस्य उपलम्भस्यैव असम्भावनीयत्वात् ।

(ii) अभिन्नाकारबुद्धिबोध्यं हि वस्तु अभिन्नमिति लौकिकाः मन्यन्ते । विलक्षणाकारबोधविषयश्च भिन्नमिति । तत्र यदि विलक्षणाकारप्रतीतिसमये द्वे वस्तुनी विलक्षणेन आकारेण प्रतिभातः तदा अभेदप्रतीतिदशायामेक आकारो अनुभवनीयः । स जातिभागस्य पिण्डभागस्य वा । तत्र एकस्य द्विरवभासोऽयं स्यान्नतु जातिजातिमतोरभेदावभासः । (प्र०पं० ७२)

It cannot be contended that even though *jāti* and *vyakti* are two, these are presented as one because of the *tādātmya* of the two. What is this *tādātmya*? If it is a presentation of the two as one in the knowledge, it is already stated that such a presentation is not possible. It also cannot be contended that a common reference by two words as *gauh ayam* is *tādātmya,* because, in the instance of *gauh vāhikaḥ* a common reference by two words is found but there is no *tādātmya.*

Those who claim *tādātmya* on the basis of the usages like *gauh ayam* argue that in the usage like jar and cloth there is no *sāmānādhikaraṇya* i.e., common reference by two words, since these two referred to are different. There is also no *sāmānādhikaraṇya* in the usages like *hastaḥ* and *karaḥ* since the two words are synonyms and refer to an identical entity. However, the usage of *gauh ayam* is different from the above two. *Jāti* and *vyakti* are neither different as in the usage of jar and cloth nor identical as in the usage of *hastaḥ and karaḥ.* Therefore, as a third alternative the concept of *tādātmya* has to be accepted. This plea is rejected by pointing out that in the usage of *gauh vāhikaḥ* a common reference is found but no *tādātmya* is found. If it is contended that the usage is a secondary or a loose usage, then, those who accept the difference between *jāti* and *vyakti* also say that the usage *gauḥ ayam* is also of the same type. So far as the Buddhists are concerned the words do not affirm any corresponding entities at all. These are mere expressions of our own notion.

अथ विलक्षणावप्याकारौ तादात्म्येनावसीयेते इति मतम् । तत्रापि पर्यनुयोजनीयः किमिदं तादात्म्यं नामेति? यद्येकाकारतेति ब्रूयात् तर्हि पूर्वोक्तमेव दूषणमात्मसात् कृतम् । शब्दयोः सामानाधिकरण्यं तादात्म्यमिति चेत् अयुक्तमिदं गौर्वाहीक इत्यादौ अतादात्म्येपि सामानाधिकरण्यदर्शनात् । उपचारस्तत्रेति चेत् अत्रापि भिन्नजातिवादिनः उपचारमेव मन्यन्ते । वयं तु विवक्षामात्रपरतन्त्राः शब्दाः न वस्तुव्यवस्थापनाय ईशते इति सर्वत्र मन्यामहे । (प्र०पं० ७२-७३)

Now, *jātivādin* contends that we have the cognition as *gauḥ gauḥ* with reference to many cows. This is a cognition of reference to a continuity in respect of different individual cows. To account for this reference to the continuity some qualifying characteristic of all these individual cows has to be accepted. This is *jāti* i.e., universal.

कथं तर्हि गौः गौः इति नानाभूतासु व्यक्तिषु बुद्धिरनुवृत्ताकार-मुल्लिखन्ती समुपजायते? तेन अस्या एव बुद्धेः दृढिम्नः कारणमनुमास्यामहे । अस्ति तद्विशेषणं यदुपरागवशेन इयं भिन्नेषु अभिन्नाकारानुसन्धायिनी धीः उदीयते इति । (प्र०पं० ७३)

This line of argument of *Vaiśeṣikas* is not acceptable to the Buddhists. The Buddhists' explanation for this continuity of reference in the cognition *gauḥ gauḥ* etc., is as under:

The comprehension of cow as 'cow' 'cow' is an effect. Therefore, its cause has to be traced. That following which a comprehension arises is the cause of the comprehension. It is found that after observing a series of cows this comprehension arises. Therefore, it is better to hold that these very objects cause their comprehension, as well as the comprehension of a kind of continuity of them, without involving an additional entity called 'cowness'. Just as the contact of the eye, the light and the mind together give rise to one knowledge, though these are different. Similarly many cows give rise to the comprehension of a continuity of a form of them without involving any additional entity continuously present in them. In this process the difference among the cows is concealed and a continuity of form is projected. This is called *samvṛti*. In such comprehensions the pure form of the objects is not comprehended. But, that form which projects a relation and a reference is comprehended.

(i) **तदपि न जातिसाधनसमर्थम् । कार्यभूता हि बुद्धिरेषा कारणमाक्षिपन्ती यदनन्तरमेवोपजायते तदेव कारणं कल्पयति । न पुनरप्रतीतं अपरमपि किञ्चिदुपस्थापयति । सा चेयं स्वलक्षणविषयदर्शन समनन्तरभाविनीति**

ता एव व्यक्तयः स्वनिर्भासा बुद्धीरुपजनय्य तन्मुखेन तामेकाकारानुभासिनीं धियमविर्भावयन्ति । नितान्तभेदवतीनां च व्यक्तीनां कासाञ्चिदेव न सर्वासामिति किमनुपपन्नम् । यथा अत्यन्तभिन्ना अपि चक्षुरालोकमनस्संयोगाः एकसामग्रीसमुपनिपतिताः एकविज्ञानलक्षणं कार्यमारभन्ते तथा व्यक्तयोपि किं नारभन्ते इति नेदं प्रतिपत्तिकठिनम् ।

(ii) सा चेयं स्वाकारेण अभेदेन आत्यन्तिकभेदयोगिनामपि व्यक्तीनां भेदं संवृणोतीति संवृतिरित्युच्यते । (प्र०पं० ७३-७४)

Buddhists' Way of Cognition

In this connection, the Buddhist approach to the comprehension of the objects is clarified as follows: Buddhists make a distinction in the comprehension of an object as that of *svalakṣana* aspect and the *vikalpa* aspect. The *svalakṣana* aspect is *niyatākāra* i.e., that of pure and constant nature, and *vikalpa is aniyatākāra* i.e., that of changing and qualified nature. In every comprehension both are presented. The presentation of *svalakṣaṇa* is *viśada*, that is to say, it is *nirvikalpaka* i.e., without any *vikalpa* i.e., qualifications or variety, and the presentation of *vikalpa* is *aviśada* i.e., with qualification and variety. These two are distinct in nature. However, since the comprehension of *vikalpa* arises out of the comprehension of *svalakśaṇa* the observer takes them as one and proceeds to deal with them on that basis. This comprehension is like that of the rays of a gem being taken as gem. Keeping this process of the cognition in mind the Buddhists argue that *jāti* is only a *vikalpa.*

(i) नियताकारश्च स्वलक्षणम् । अनियताकारश्च अस्यां बुद्धौ चकास्ति । तदेवं विशदाविशदतया नियतानियततयाच स्वलक्षणस्य विकल्पाकारस्य च भेदे सत्यपि विकल्पाः साक्षात् परम्परया वा स्वलक्षणविषयदर्शनप्रभवतया स्वलक्षणग्रहणाभिमानिनो जायन्ते । तत एव तत्र प्रवर्तयन्तः पुरुषं व्यवहाराङ्गभावमनुभवन्ति । पारम्पर्येण वस्तुनि प्रतिबन्धात् अवस्त्वपि प्रतिबद्धं भवति मणिप्रभायां मणिबुद्धिवत् ।

यथा हि खलु मणिप्रभायां मणिदीप्तायां मणिकिरणविषयिणी मणिबुद्धिः अयथार्थतया भेदमजुषमाणापि मणिमनुप्रबुद्धेति मणिसमधिगमनिमित्तं भवेत् । तथा इयमपि वस्तुतः स्वलक्षणमगृहणत्यापि स्वलक्षणाद् दर्शनं दर्शनतो विकल्प इति स्वलक्षणप्रतिबद्धा सती तत्प्राप्तये भवति ।

(ii) तस्मात् जातिप्रत्ययः विकल्पमात्रम् । परमार्थतस्तु न जातिर्नाम किञ्चित् । (प्र०पं० ७५-७७)

The process of *viśadāvabhāsa* and *aviśadāvabhāsa* are further explained as under:

In *aviśadāvabhāsa* the objects are presented with appropriate relations and the name. Therefore, it is not a pure presentation of the *svalakṣaṇa.* It is true that in the cognition *gauḥ ayam,* there is *viśadāvabhāsa*, that is to say, there is the cognition of mere object but this is due to the *svalakṣaṇa* at the basis of it. Here is an interesting position of *viśadāvabhāsa* in the perception of the object and *aviśadāvabhāsa* when it is described in words and named. Technically the *viśadāvabhāsa* is always only in respect of *svalakṣaṇa* only. However, because of the proximity of the *svalakṣaṇa* aspect and the *vikalpa* aspect the *viśadāvabhāsa* is also taken for granted for *vikalpa* for practical purposes.

(i) एषा च मनीषा संवृतिः न स्वलक्षणं विषयीकरोति । तस्य विशदावभासित्वात् । अस्याश्च अभिलापसंसर्गयोग्यार्थप्रतिभासात् । अभिलापानां च विशदाकारमवभासितुमशक्तेः । अभिलापमात्रेण तथाविधप्रतीत्यभावात् । तेन एषा न स्वच्छाकारावभासिनी ।

(ii) ननु एतत् प्रतीतिविरुद्धमुदितम् । अयं गौरितिबुद्धौ विशादावभासात् । उच्यते । न विशदावभासित्वमावजानीमहे । तत्तु समानकालभाविनः निर्विकल्पप्रत्ययस्य स्वलक्षणावलम्बिनः प्रसादात् । तदभावे तथात्वानुपलम्भात् ।

(iii) न चैतद्वाच्यं कथमेकमेव वस्तु इन्द्रियैः विशदावभासमनुभूयते शब्दैश्च अविशदाभासमिति । भिद्यमानेपि बोधोपाये बोध्याभेदे बोधवैलक्षण्यानुपपत्तेः ।

(iv) विशदाविशदतया नियतानियततया च स्वलक्षणस्य विकल्पाकारस्य च भेदे सत्यपि विकल्पाः साक्षात् परम्परया वा स्वलक्षणविषय-दर्शनप्रभवतया स्वलक्षणग्रहणाभिमानिनो जायन्ते । ततः तत्र प्रवर्तयन्तः पुरुषाः व्यवहाराङ्गभावमनुभवन्ति । (प्र०पं० ७४-७५)

Conclusion of the Buddhists' Arguments against Jāti

In the course of the above *pūrvapakṣa* that denies *jāti* the following points are made:

(1) There is no *dravya* i.e. substance, that can be the locus of *jāti.*

(2) There is no *avayavin* apart from *avayavas.*

(3) The so-called *jāti* is not the object of any cognition.

(4) The *jāti* cannot be considered either as *nitya* or *anitya.*

(5) The *jāti* cannot be considered as different, or identical or both different and non-different from the *vyakti.*

(6) The so-called *jāti* is merely a *vikalpa.*

All these arguments are advanced by the Buddhists. These arguments of the Buddhists are mostly drawn from the Buddhists' work i.e., *Pramāna vārtika.* These arguments are primarily directed against the *vaiśeṣika* concept of *jāti.* Śālikanātha replies all these points and presents the Prābhākara concept of *jāti.*

II

Śālikanātha's Defence of the Concept of Avayavin

Śālikanātha commences the presentation of the *Siddhānta* view with a remark of a fundamental nature that, it is the experience that is the final authority to affirm the objects. It is the experience of all that, the experiences as 'cow' etc., relate to the corresponding objects. It is already explained in the *Nayavīthi* chapter that all experiences have corresponding facts and are true i.e., *yathārtham sarvavijñānam.* Therefore, the very existence of *dravya* cannot be denied.

अत्रोच्यते । संविदेवहि भगवती विषयसत्त्वोपगमे शरणम् । गवादिषु स्थूलाकारावलम्बिनी संविदुदेतीति निर्विवादम् । नयवीथ्यां निर्णीतं प्रमाणं स्मृतिश्च नः प्रत्ययः इति । (प्र०पं० ७७)

The arguments advanced by the Buddhists for establishing that the very concept of *avayavin* is not tenable are not valid arguments. When an effect is observed a cause has to be envisaged for it. A clearly observed effect cannot be denied merely on the ground that the process of its production cannot be plausibly explained. Therefore, one has to envisage that the *avayavas* brought together by the relation of conjunction produce the *avayavin.* The relation of conjunction operates when one *avayava* is brought together with other *avayavas.* This results in an *avayavin.* The conjunction between the *avayavas* is *asamavāyi-kāraṇa* while the very *avayavas* are *smavāyi kāraṇa.*

(i) ननु तदेव असदिति मन्यते । अवयव्यादीनामेकान्ततो अनुपपन्नत्वात् । उच्यते । न दृष्टे काचिदनुपपत्तिः । ननु उक्ता अवयविनः अनुपपत्तिः । आरम्भकाभावात् । अनुपपन्ना इयमनुपपत्तिः । कार्यं प्रतीतं कारणकल्पनायां प्रमाणम् । न पुनः स्फुटावभासिकार्यं कारणानिरूपणे अपह्नवमर्हति । तेन अवयवाः एव समासादितसंयोगलक्षण-साधारणगुणाः अवयविनः उत्पादकाः भविष्यन्ति । (प्र०पं० ७७-७८)

(ii) संयोगलक्षणासाधारणगुणासमवायिकारणोपगृहीताः अवयवाः एव समवायिकारणमवयविनः उपपद्यन्ते । (प्र०पं० ८३)

The contention of the Buddhists that the conjunction cannot be only in one *avayava*, nor it can be among more than one, since every *avayava* is isolated and no second *avayava* can be thought of or brought about for the conjunction, is not correct. One and the same conjunction can be in many. Though each *avayava* is one only, it can be the locus of the conjunction with another *avayava*.

(i) ननु संयोगः किमेकत्र वर्तते? अनेकत्र वा? एकैकत्र संयुक्तप्रत्ययाभावादेकत्र न वर्तते । एकातिरिक्तानेकाभावादनेकत्रापि न वर्तते इत्युक्तमित्यत्राह संयोगश्चेति । (न्या०सि० ७८)

(ii) संयोगश्चैक एवानेकत्र वर्तते एकैकत्र संयुक्तप्रत्ययानुदयात् । एकातिरिक्तानेकाभावेऽपि एकैकसद्वितीयः आश्रयः संयोगस्येति न दोषः । (प्र०पं० ७८)

The Buddhists contention that the conjunction is only a *vikalpa* arising after the cognition of the object arises. There is no such thing such as conjunction apart from the object is also not correct. The occurrence of more than one object is cognized. Sometimes these are cognized in a special position as conjuncted. Therefore, the conjunction is distinct from the objects conjuncted.

(i) ननु द्रव्ये एव तथा उत्पन्ने संयोगविकल्पमाविर्भावयतः न तदतिरेकी संयोगो नाम कश्चिद् गुणविशेषः । (प्र०पं० ८२)

(ii) चोदयति ननु द्रव्य एवेति । उत्तराधरभावेन निरन्तरोत्पन्नो द्रव्यक्षण एव संयोगक्षणमुत्पादयतीति द्रव्यव्यतिरेकी संयोगो नाम न कश्चित् गुणविशेषः अस्माकमभिमतः इति शङ्कां परिहरति । तन्नेति । (न्या०सि० ८२)

(iii) तन्न । प्रत्यभिज्ञायेते हि द्रव्ये अनुवृत्ते । कदाचित्की च तयोः अपरा इयं दशा इति भवत्येव भेदसिद्धिः । स्थापिता च मीमांसाजीवरक्षायां प्रत्यभिज्ञा । (प्र०पं० ८२)

The Location of Avayavin

As regards the objections raised in respect of the location of *avayavin* on *avayavas*, the position is that the *avayavin* is spread over all the *avayavas*. It is not separately present in each like *jāti*. Though it has not another set of *avayavas* to occupy each *avayava* by them, it can occupy all *avayavas* by itself. This is because the *avayavas* that produce the *avayavin* with the aid of *samyoga* also serve as its location. The *avayavas* are *samavāyikāraṇa*. These produce the *avayavin* and also serve as the locus of *avayavin*.

> यश्चायमवयविनः वृत्तिविकल्पेन दोषः उक्तः सोऽपि अवयविनः प्रतीतौ स्थितायामुपपन्नः। व्यासक्त एव अवयवेषु अवयवी। नैकत्र जातिवत् परिसमाप्तः। अवयवान्तरैरपि च विना स तस्य कोपि महिमा य एक एव अनेकावयवानुस्यूत इति किं न कल्प्यते। यद्यपि अवयविनः एकैकत्रावृत्तिः तथापि नावृत्तिदोषः। संयोगसचिवा एवावयवाः जनकाः आश्रयभूताः यतः जनकतयैव आश्रयत्वात् समवायकारणानाम्। अत एव संयोगः सद्वितीयाश्रयः इति न दोषः। (प्र०पं० ८३-८४)

The Cognition of Avayavin

It is also not correct to raise the objection as to whether the *avayavin* is cognized, when all *avayavas* are cognized, or even one *avayava* is cognized. The *avayavin* is different from the *avayavas*. Its cognition has to be stated as possible by the cognition of those many *avayavas* that are sufficient for the purpose on the basis of the experience. Neither the cognition of all *avayavas* is required nor the cognition of only one is sufficient.

Though *avayavas* and *avayavin* are different these are comprehended together, because, these have the relation of the cause and effect.

(i) न च सकलावयवोपलम्भसापेक्षा तदुपलब्धिः तेभ्यः भिन्नत्वात् । न चैतावता एकावयवग्रहणेपि ग्रहणपर्यनुयोगो युक्तः । कार्यानुगुणत्वात् कारणकल्पनायाः । कार्यसिद्ध्यर्थं हि कारणं परिकल्प्यते न कार्यविनाशाय । तेन यावतामवयवानां ग्रहणे तदुपलम्भः तावतामेव अवगमः तदवगमनिबन्धनमिति दर्शनबलेन अभ्युपेयते ।

(ii) भिन्नत्वेपि सहोपलम्भनियमः उपेयोपायभावात् । उपेयभूतोऽवयवी उपायपदवर्तिनश्च अवयवाः । प्रत्येकं तु तेषां शक्यत एव असहोपलम्भनियमोपि वक्तुम् । अवयवान्तरयोगिनो अवयविनोपि परिग्रहे इतरावयवव्यतिरेकोपि सुदर्शएव । (प्र०पं० ८४-८५)

When *avayavin* is observed, it is found to be distinct from *avayavas* in respect of its dimension. The *avayavin* has a larger dimension than the *avayavas.* The *avayavins* of the earth, water, and fire could be cognized by the eye and the touch, while the *avayavas* of these at the *dvyaṇuka* level cannot be seen by the eye. On these grounds, it can be established that the *avayavas* and the *avayavin* are different.

इयञ्च भेदसाधने युक्तिः । अन्वयव्यतिरेकाभ्यां हि वस्त्वन्तरत्वमवसीयते । अवगम्यमानोपि च अवयवी विलक्षणबुद्धिगोचरतामावहत्येव । अवयवो हि स्थवीयान् एको हृदयमागच्छति अवयवास्तु क्षोदीयांसः भूयांसश्च । सचायमवयवी महत्त्वात् रूपवत्त्वाच्च चाक्षुषः स्पार्शनोवा, पार्थिवो वा आम्भसो वा तैजसो वा । वायवीयस्तु महत्त्वात् स्पर्शवत्त्वाच्च स्पार्शन एव । द्व्यणुकस्तु चातुर्भौतिकोऽपि अमहत्त्वादप्रत्यक्ष एव । तस्य च अमहत्त्वम् अवयवबहुत्वमहत्त्वप्रचयविशेषाणां महत्त्वगुणाकारणनामभावात् । गगनादीनां तु महतामपि रूपस्पर्शविधुरतया न प्रत्यक्षगोचरतेत्यलमतिविस्तरेण । (प्र०पं० ८५-८६)

Substance and the Qualities are Distinct

The objection that there is no *dravya* i.e., substance, apart from the qualities, the colour, odour, touch etc., is also not valid. One and the same object is cognized by seeing, touching etc. This means that the object as such must be distinct from these qualities. The distinction of the object and the qualities may also be made out by the instances of the *sphaṭika* and the red flower. Though the red colour reflected in it conceals its true colour the object as such is recognized. This clearly shows that the object is different from the qualities.

In the instance of the trees and the forest, since the fact of the trees being separated, is realized on a closer observation the two are not treated as *avayavas* and *avayavin.*

ननु उक्तं रूपादिव्यतिरेकि द्रव्यं नोपलभ्यत इति । किमिदं पश्यतोहरत्वम् । प्रतीयतेहि महानवयवी रूपादिव्यतिरेकी । अत एव जपाकुसुमसन्निधानाभिभूतरूपमपि स्फटिकद्रव्यं प्रत्यभिज्ञायते । कथं नाम अगृहीतं प्रत्यभिज्ञायेत । अपि च दर्शनस्पर्शनाभ्यामेकार्थग्रहणात् रूपस्पर्शव्यतिरेकिद्रव्यं स्फुटतरप्रतीतं तत् नापह्नोतुमुचितम् । अत एव वनादिषु बाधकप्रत्ययबलेन तत्कल्पना न प्रसरतीति दूरतया अन्तरालाग्रहणनिबन्धोऽयमभेदव्यवहार: प्रवर्तते इति । अवयविनि तु बाधकज्ञानं नास्तीति पुरस्तादावेदितम् । तेन आश्रयद्रव्याभावाद् जातेरपलाप: प्रलापमात्रमिति स्थितम् । (प्र०पं० ८६-८७)

The objection 'that if the *jāti* is eternal it cannot give rise to its cognition, since no eternal entity can produce any effect. If it is capable of producing any effect it should produce it all the time. If it is not capable, it should never be able to produce any effect', is also not valid. It will be answered later while refuting *kṣaṇabhaṇga vāda.* Further, even if *jāti* is not the cause of its knowledge, it can be cognized. To be cognized it is not necessary to be the cause. It is sufficient if it is the object of the cognition.

यच्चोक्तं नित्यतया जाते: आत्मविज्ञानजननेपि न शक्तता इति तदपि क्षणभङ्गनिराकरणप्रकरणे विस्तरेण नित्यानामर्थक्रियाकारित्वसमर्थनेन प्रत्युक्तम् । मा वा स्वविज्ञानमपि जातिरजीजनत् । तथापि कथं कारमसौ अप्रत्यक्षा । काममप्रत्यक्षा । अथवा न खलु इयमाज्ञा राज्ञ: कारणभूतस्यैव

प्रत्यक्षेण भवितव्यमिति । यस्तु यतः प्रतीयते सः तस्य विषयः इति सार्वलौकिकम् । (प्र०पं० ८८)

Criterion for the Validity of Knowledge

The Buddhist further argues that a perceptual knowledge is valid only when it does not disagree with that from which it arises. Agreement between the knowledge and fact is possible only when that knowledge is produced by that fact. If it has not arisen from the fact concerned, and arises from other factors or without any fact, no agreement between the knowledge and the fact referred to by it is possible. Therefore, one is forced to accept that whatever is the cause of the knowledge that only is the object of the knowledge. For this very reason, only *pratyakṣa* and *anumāna* are considered as *pramāṇa*. These do not disagree with that which is referred to by them. The *pratyakṣa* is directly connected with its content while *anumāna* is connected through the *hetu*. That knowledge which is not connected with that which is referred to by it either directly or through *hetu* is not dependable. Therefore, there is no certainty about its validity.

ननु प्रत्यक्षमपि अविसंवाद्येव प्रमाणम् । अविसंवादश्च तस्मादात्मलाभात् अन्यतस्तु भवतो अतथाभूतस्य वा अभावेपि भावसम्भवात् नियमेन संवादायोगादिति बलादभ्युपेयं प्रत्यक्षस्य कारणमेव विषय इति । अत एव च प्रत्यक्षं अनुमानं च द्वे एव प्रमाणे । तयोरेव अर्थाविसंवादकत्वात् । प्रत्यक्षं साक्षादर्थेन प्रतिबद्धम् अनुमानं तु अर्थप्रतिबद्धलिङ्गजन्यतया पारम्पर्येण प्रतिबद्धम् । यस्य तु न साक्षात् नापि परम्परया अर्थप्रतिबन्धः न तस्य प्रामाण्यमुचितम् । तस्य तदविसंवादनियमाभावात् । अर्थाविसंवादि च प्रमाणं व्यवजिहीर्षमाणाः लौकिकाः आद्रियन्ते । (प्र०पं० ८८)

This line of approach in respect of the validity of knowledge is not sound. It is based on the presumption that the validity of the knowledge depends upon the verification by another knowledge. This is not the position. The object of the knowledge is identified by the knowledge itself and no verification by another knowledge is necessary. The knowledge conveys the agreement with the facts referred to by it in its own right. Knowledge depends upon something else in respect of its production but in respect of its validity it is self-sufficient. From this it is clear that *śāstra* etc., are also *pramāṇa* though these are not directly connected with the facts. It is already stated in *Nayavīthi* that all knowledge agrees with the facts referred to by it. Therefore, *jāti* can be the object of perception even though it is eternal.

सिद्धेयदयं मनोरथः यदि ज्ञानान्तरनिबन्धनः अविसंवादः प्रार्थनीयः । यद्विषयमेव यज्ज्ञानं तेनैव तस्मिन् विषये प्रत्युपस्थापिते नास्ति प्रत्ययान्तरनिबन्धना अविसंवादप्रार्थना । अर्थेनाप्रतिबद्धमपि ज्ञानं स्वमहिमपर्युपस्थापितार्थमविसंवादकमेव सम्प्रवर्तते । तेन उत्पत्तिमात्र एव विज्ञानस्य परापेक्षा न प्रामाण्ये अर्थाव्यभिचारलक्षणे । अतः सिद्धं शास्त्रादीनामपि अर्थप्रतिबन्धविरहिणां प्रामाण्यम् । एतदर्थमेव नयवीथ्यां सर्वं ज्ञानं विषयाव्यभिचारि इति प्रतिपादितम् । अतः नित्यायामपि जातौ भवत्येव प्रत्यक्षस्य प्रामाण्यम् । (प्र०पं० ८९)

The Cognition of Jāti i.e., Universal

The contention that the *jāti* is not perceived even when one observes a *vyakti* intently is not correct. When one observes a *vyakti* he also observes *jāti*. However, on seeing the first object, though he cognizes the *jāti* he does not comprehend the continuity of it in the next *vyakti* until he cognizes the second *vyakti*. One can cognize the *dharmi* i.e., *jāti* without cognizing its *dharma* i.e., the continuity in the next *vyakti* until he cognizes the next *vyakti*. When he cognizes the next *vyakti* he recognizes the *jāti* seen earlier.

यदुक्तम् एकभावेन मनसा समाकलयतः कालाक्षीं स्वस्तिमतीं वा नास्ति जातिप्रतीतिः इति । तदसिद्धम् । आकारो हि सा । प्रतीते चाकारे यदि परमर्थान्तरानुसन्धानविकलतया तस्यानुवृत्तिर्नावसीयते । अनुवृत्ता हि

जातिः नानुवृत्तिः । अग्रहणेपि च धर्मस्य धर्मिणां ग्रहणं नानुपपन्नम् । अत एव पिण्डान्तरसमधिगमे पूर्वाकारपरामर्शिनी मनीषा प्रत्यभिज्ञा समाख्याता उदीयते । (प्र०पं० ८९-९०)

The Location of Jāti

The objections raised in respect of the location of *jāti* are also not difficult to be solved. The objections raised were: *jāti* cannot be stated as present in the *vyakti* before its production, as there is nothing to remain on, nor it can be stated as coming to *vyakti* after the *vyakti* is produced, since it has no motion to move from one place to another. It also cannot be stated as simultaneously produced along with the *vyakti* since it is eternal. Therefore, it is difficult to explain as to how and when the *jāti* got connected with the *vyakti.*

यच्चोक्तम् अनाश्रयतया तत्रैव प्रागनवस्थिता निष्क्रियतया अन्यस्मादनागच्छन्ती स्वरूपहानिप्रसङ्गेन व्यक्त्या सह अनुपजायमाना कथं सम्बन्धमनुभवति जातिः इति । तदिदं मायामोहजननं यथाजात-जनमनोद्वेजनमात्रम् । (प्र०पं० ९०)

These objections are not applicable for the connection to be developed between *jāti* and *vyakti.* If this connection were to be *samyoga* i.e., cornjunction, then, that would have required motion and bringing together. However, the relation between the *jāti* and the *vyakti* is *samavāya.* This *samavāya* relation is altogether different in nature from *samyoga.* It does not require any motion or prior existence. Out of the *very samavāyikāraṇa* from which the *vyakti* arises, the *samavaya* of *jāti* also arises.

संयोगो हि उभयकर्मजो भवति मल्लयोरिव, अन्यतरकर्मजो वा स्थाणुश्येनयोरिव संयोगजो व यथा तन्तुतुरीसंयोगादुत्पन्नस्य पटस्य तुरीसंयोगः। संयोगश्च कर्म प्राक् सन्निधानं वा अपेक्षते । समवायस्तु

संयोगाद् विभिन्नः न कर्म प्राक् सत्तां वा अपेक्षते । यत एव तु पिण्डस्य उदयः समवायिकारणात् तत एव जातिसमवायोपि उत्पद्यते । (प्र०पं० १०, १२)

The Concept of Samavāya

The *samavāya* is not eternal. When the *vyakti* perishes the *jāti* does not move to some other place, nor remains in the same place. It does not perish also. Only its association by *samavāya* with that *vyakti* is withdrawn. *Jāti* does not move out of that *vyakti* as it has no motion, nor does it remain since its abode i.e., *vyakti* is no longer present. It does not perish also as it is recognized in other *vyaktis*. Only that which is totally destroyed is to be considered as perished.

(i) समवायं च न वयं काश्यपीया इव नित्यमङ्गीकुर्मः ।

(ii) समवायं च वैशेषिकादय इव न वयं नित्यमुपयेमः । समवायः आकाशमहत्त्वयोः नित्यः अनित्ययोः अवयवावयिनोः अनित्यः । अनित्ययोः अन्यतरोत्पत्तिकारणादुत्पद्यते । तस्मात् प्रतिसम्बन्धि समवायो भिन्नः । सम्बन्धरूपत्वात् संयोगवत् । (न्या०सि० १२)

(iii) विनष्टायामपि व्यक्तौ न जातिः अन्यत्र याति, न च तत्र अवतिष्टते, न विनश्यति । केवलं तद्व्यक्तिसमवायः तस्याः निवर्तते । तेन तस्यानुपलम्भनम् । तथापि न याति निष्क्रियत्वात् नावतिष्ठते व्यक्तिमात्राश्रयत्वात् तदभावे अवस्थानासम्भवात् न च विनश्यति पिण्डान्तरे प्रत्यभिज्ञायमानत्वात् । विनाशो नाम आत्यन्तिकोऽनुपलम्भः इत्यमृतकलायां वक्ष्यते । अतो न सङ्कटं किञ्चित् । (प्र०पं० १३)

Jāti is Eternal and Pervasive

These observations of *Śālikanātha* will be clear if we grasp the concept of *jāti* as conceived by the *Prābhākaras*. According to *the Prābhākaras* the *jāti* is eternal and all-pervasive. Its all-pervasiveness is of the nature of its being present all over. However, this need not lead to the absurd position that the space itself has to be considered as 'cow' etc., since the *jāti* i.e., cowness etc., are present in it. The *jātis* 'cowness' etc., are not connected with the space by *samavāya.* Just as *kāla* is not cognized as possessing colour, since the colour is not connected with the *kāla* by *samavāya* relation though the colour is present in *kāla,* the space need not be cognized as possessing *jāti* since it is not connected with the space by *samavāya* relation though it is present in the space. Whenever the *vyakti* is produced the *jāti* gets connected with it in the same place. The production of the *vyakti* and the connection with the *jāti* are simultaneous.

जातिः नित्या व्यापिका च । व्यापकत्वं स्वरूपतः सर्वदेशसम्बद्धत्वम् । न देशानां गोव्यवहारापत्तिः शङ्कनीया । समवायेन तद्व्यवहारस्य अभ्युपगमात् । यथा काले रूपस्य सत्त्वेपि कालो रूपवानिति प्रतीतिः न भवति न वा व्यवहारः । तथा यत्र पिण्डः उत्पद्यते तत्रस्थमेव सामान्यं तेन सम्बध्यते । जातः सम्बद्धश्च एकः कालः इत्यभ्युपगमात् । एतेन कीदृशाश्रये वर्तते इत्यस्य यत्र प्रतीयते इत्युत्तरम् । कुत्र प्रतीयते इति प्रश्नस्य यत्र वर्तते इति बोध्यम् । गोत्ववृत्तेः प्राक् सः पिण्डः कीदृशः आसीदित्यस्य नासीदित्येव उत्तरम् । 'नायाति' 'न च तत्राऽसीत्' इत्यादिवचनं गगनरोमन्थायितमिति ज्ञेयम् । (वि०टि० १४)

Jāti is Different from Vyakti

To the question whether *jāti* is different, non-different, or both different and non-different, the *Prābhākaras* answer is, it is different. But still it is not cognized as 'here it is' that is to say, *jāti* is not cognized as present in *vyakti.* Both the *vyakti* and *jāti* are cognized together. No attribute can be cognized without the cognition of the entity of which it is an attribute. Both the entity and its attribute viz., the *vyakti* and *jāti* are cognized simultaneously. The cognition of the *jāti* is included in the cognition of *vyakti.*

(i) यच्च पिण्डेभ्यः जातेः अभिन्नत्वम् उभयरूपत्वं च दूषितं तदस्माकं सहायकमेव आचरितम् । कोहि नाम सचेतनः पदार्थान्तर-प्रत्यभिज्ञामभेदाश्रयेण साधयेत् । को वा परस्परविरोधिनी द्वे रूपे एकस्य प्रतिजानीते । भेदवादः पुनः अस्माकमपि सम्मत एव ।

(ii) न च तत्र इह प्रत्ययापत्तिः दोषः । प्रतीत्य हि आधारं आधेयं च सम्बन्धं प्रतीयात् । सर्वं च रूपं रूपिग्रहणमन्तरेण न प्रतीयते । अतः समानेन्द्रियग्राह्यतया जातिरपि व्यक्तिप्रत्ययानुप्रवेशिनीति न इह प्रत्ययसम्भवः ॥ (प्र०पं० १३-१४)

The Location of Jāti

As regards the question whether the *jāti* occupies the *vyakti* as a whole or is spread over all the *vyaktis*, the answer is, it occupies the *vyakti* as a whole. However, this does not result in the absence of the *jāti* on the other *vyaktis* of the same class, since the presence of the same is recognized in other *vyaktis* also. It is already stated that *jāti* is not separately cognized from *vyakti* and the two are cognized together. When the *jāti* is cognized in the second and the next *vyaktis*, it is cognized in them only excluding the *vyaktis* cognized earlier. The *jāti* is cognized by the perception only, since its cognition arises following the contact of senses by *samyukta-samavāya* relation. The cognition as *gauḥ* which clearly presents the *vyakti* and *jāti* cannot be ignored.

वृत्तिविकल्पे तु कृत्स्नसमाप्तिरेव अङ्गीकरणीया । न च अन्यत्र अवृत्तिदोषः । प्रत्यक्षावगमाद् वृत्तेः । प्रत्यभिज्ञायाः स्थापितत्वात् । पृथग ग्रहणं तु जातेः असिद्धमेव । व्यक्त्यन्तरे हि जातिः प्रतीयमाना प्राच्यपिण्डपरिहारेण प्रकाशते । उदीच्यपिण्डपरिहारस्तु प्राक्तनपिण्ड-समधिगमसमये सिद्ध एवेति परिहृतनिखिलानुपपत्तिकमुपपादितं गवादिषु साधारणाकारानुभवसिद्धं जातितत्त्वम् । उपपन्नं च जातेः प्रत्यक्षवेद्यत्वम् । जातेः इन्द्रियव्यापारानुविधानेन प्रतीतेः । संयुक्तसमवायलक्षणश्च सन्निकर्षोऽपि नानुपपन्नः । (प्र०प० १४-१५)

The Buddhists' contention that it is the uninterrupted presentation of a series of *nirvikalpaka* i.e., *svalakṣaṇa* that projects the notion of a continuity is already rejected.

The Buddhists argue that the *viśada* cognition is always about *svalakṣaṇa* only. The outside objects are not cognized by *pratyakṣa.* Since the *vikalpa* of *jāti* etc., arise simultaneously with the *nirvikalpaka* it is felt as if it is also *viśada* i.e., *pratyakṣa.* Therefore, the *jāti* is not *pratyakṣa.* This contention of the Buddhists is not correct. It is already pointed out that this *viśada-aviśada* scheme has no support of any *pramāṇa.* In the case of verbal communication there may not be *vaiśdya.* However, in the case of *pratyakṣa* there is *vaiśadya*, that is to say there is the cognition of *jāti*, attributes etc.

गौरयमिति मतिः विशदतरार्थावभासिनी न शक्यते अपवदितुम् । समसमयसम्भवनिर्विकल्पक बलेनेत्त्थमियं प्रथते इति चेत् । तन्न । तथाभावे प्रमाणाभावात् । शब्दमात्रेण तु केवलाकारपरिगृहीताकारप्रतीतेः रूपान्तरावभासाच्च अविशदावभास एव । ऐन्द्रियकेतु संवेदने प्रचुरतरावयवरूपावभासात् विशदावभासः इति न बाह्यविषयत्वापत्तिः (प्र०पं० ९६)

It is contended that the *jāti* is only to be inferred. It is not *pratyakṣa.* When one observes an object, the *jāti* present in it is comprehended as if it is identical with the *vyakti* though it is different. This comprehension is an error. No error takes place without a basis for it. Therefore, *jāti* has to be inferred as the basis for this error. Such an error can be found in the instance of hot iron ball. The particles of heat enveloping the ball are taken as identical with the ball.

This contention is already rejected. It is already stated that the object and its attribute are not identical though these are comprehended together. Reference to these as if these are identical is only a secondary usage.

ननु एषा जातिप्रतीतिः भिन्नामेव व्यक्तिमभेदेन अवगमयन्ती जायत इति भ्रान्तिरेषा न प्रत्यक्षं प्रमाणम् । इयं तु भ्रान्तिः निर्बीजा न युज्यते इति बीजभावेन जातिः अनुमीयते । तत्समवायश्च । दृष्टा हि सन्तापसञ्चारितदहन-परमाणुसंवलितायोगोलके दहनाकारानुकारिणी प्रतीतिरिति । तदिदमुक्तोत्तरमपि पुनः पर्यनुयोज्यामहे विस्मरणापराधादिति मन्यामहे । भिन्ना हि जातिरवगम्यते । न खलु आकारमाकारिणं च एकमेव मन्यन्ते । केवलं शब्दप्रयोगे एव समाधिः वक्तव्या । तत्र लौकिकः प्रयोग एव शरणम् । प्रयोगश्च श्रुत्या लक्षणया गौण्या वा वृत्त्या नानुपपन्नः । (प्र०पं० ९६)

III

The Refutation of Sattā Jāti

At the close of this Section, Śālikanātha takes up the question of *sattā jāti* accepted by the *Nyāyavaiśeṣikas* and rejects the same.

The *Nyāyavaiśeṣikas* have envisaged a *jāti* called *sattā* as present in the first three categories viz. *dravya, guṇa* and *karma.* This is not acceptable to the *Prābhākaras.* The ground for accepting *sattā jāti* is stated to be the cognition as '*sat*' '*sat*' with reference to the objects of these three categories. According to the *Prābhākaras* this cognition only refers to the existence aspect of the entitites and the fact that they could be cognized. The very essential nature of these entitites capable of being cognized as 'is', is conveyed by the cognition *sat.* This cognition does not refer to any separate common characteristic called *sattā-jāti.* It is true that for the use of a common word with reference to more than one entity, a common ground is necessary. But such a common ground need not necessarily be a *jāti.* Even an *upādhi* can be the common ground. Here *pramāṇa sambandha yogyatva* is the *upādhi.*

(i) अत्र केचित् गवादितुल्यतया द्रव्यगुणकर्मस्वपि सत्ताजातिमङ्गीकुर्वन्ति 'भवति हि सर्वेष्वपि सत् सदिति प्रत्ययानुवृत्तिरिति' ति संवदन्तः ।

(ii) तदिदमपरामृष्टजातितत्त्वानामुपर्युपरि जल्पितम् । पूर्वरूपानुकारिणी यदि धीरुदीयते ततो उपेयत एव जातिः । न च नानाजातियेषु द्रव्येषु सर्पमहीधरादिषु, गुणेषु गन्धरसादिषु वा समानाकारानुभवो भवति । केवलं तु सत् सदिति शब्दमात्रं प्रयुज्यते । भवति च विनापि जात्या पाचकमीमांसकादिशब्दप्रवृत्तिः ।

(iii) ननु एवं शब्दप्रवृत्तिरपि नैकनिबन्धनमन्तरेण उपपद्यते । सत्यम्, अस्त्येव उपाधिरेका प्रमाणसम्बन्धयोग्यता नाम ।

The entities coming under *dravya, guṇa* and *karma* have an essential nature 'to be' 'to exist'. This is termed as *svarūpasatva.* This *svarūpasatva* could be ascertained by their being cognized. This is termed *pramāṇa sambandha yogyatva.* Only that entity which is capable of being cognized exists and only that which exists could be cognized. Therefore, the cognition *sat* sat with reference to *dravya, guṇa* and *karma* conveys that these are the entities whose essential nature is 'to be' i.e., 'to exist'. Thus the cognition as *'sat'* does not refer to any *jāti* such as *sattā jāti* but to the very core nature i.e., *svarūpasatva* of *dravya, guṇa* and *karma.* Such a position is accepted by *Nyāyavaiśeṣikas* in respect of the other three categories viz. *Samānya, viśeṣa* and *samavāya.* These are stated to have *svarūpasatva* but not *sattājāti.* This can hold good even in the case of the first three categories viz., *dravya, guṇa* and *karma.*

Those who accept *sattājāti* try to argue that *pramāṇa sambandha sattā* cannot serve as *upādhi* and cannot help the use of the common word as *sat sat* for the following reasons:

(1) For conveying an object by using a word that is based on an *upādhi*, the knowledge of *upādhi* is a pre-requisite. For instance, to use the word *pācaka* i.e., a cook with reference to a person, the knowledge of *pacanakriyā* as *upādhi* is necessary. Otherwise, one cannot use this word based on this *upādhi* with reference to that person. In the present case, the *upādhi ie pramāṇa sambandha* itself is equated with the cognition of *sat.* It is not prior to the cognition of *sat.* Therefore, it cannot be an *upādhi.*

(2) *Pramāṇa sambandha* is always at the present time. But the cognition of the *sat* may arise with reference to the past and the future also. This means that the *pramāṇa sambandha* cannot be an *upādhi* i.e., a common ground for the cognition of *sat.*

(3) People entertain the possibility of *sattva* of such entities that are hidden underground long back, that have no indications, the persons who knew about them have disappeared long back. This belief about the possibility of the presence of the underground deposits by itself cannot be treated as *pramāṇa sambandha* and the *sattva* of these deposits cannot be affirmed or denied. Therefore, the *sattva* is something different from the *pramāṇa sambandha.*

(i) (a) तत्रान्यः पण्डितंमन्यो मन्यते । ननु इदमसञ्जसमुच्यते सर्वत्र हि उपाधिभेदमवगम्य औपाधिकशब्दानुविद्धः प्रत्ययो भवति न पुनः प्रागेव, सह वा । इह च प्रमाणमेव जायमानमस्तीत्येव जायते । प्रमाणोदयोत्तरकालमनया भवितव्यम् । (प्र०पं० ९८)

(b) पाचकादिषु पचनक्रियायोगमवगतस्यैव पाचक इति औपाधिकशब्दानुविद्धो बोधो भवति । (न्या०सि० ९८)

(ii) किञ्च सत्यपि प्रमाणयोगे किञ्चिदस्तीति गम्यते किञ्चिदासीदिति तथा अन्यद् भविष्यति । तत्र प्रमाणसम्बन्धस्य वर्तमानत्वात् सर्वत्रमानसत्ताप्रत्ययेन भवितव्यम् । तदतिरेकिणि तु सत्त्वे तस्य त्रेधा व्यवस्थानात् युक्तः त्रिधा अवभासः ।

(iii) अपि च भूमितलनिखातेषु चिरतरकालवर्तिषु प्रलीनज्ञातृपुरुषेषु लिङ्गादिरहितेषु सकलप्रमाणप्रत्यस्तमयेपि वर्तमानसत्तासन्देहः । स च प्रमाणसम्बन्धातिरेकिणीं सत्तामन्तरेण अनुपपन्नः इति । (प्र०पं० ९८)

Śālikanātha rejects the above objection with a simple remark that it is not *pramāṇa sambandha* that is *upādhi* but it is *pramāṇa sambandha yogyatā.* This satisfies the three requirements.

(i) prior presence of *upādhi* (ii) connection of *upādhi* with the object of past, present and future (iii) making room for the possibility of the existence of the object that cannot be reached by *pramāṇa* presently.

तदिदमनाकलितपरवचनस्य केवलं गलगर्जितम् । उक्तमस्माभिः प्रमाणसम्बन्धयोग्यता उपाधिरिति । यदि हि प्रमाणसम्बन्धः उपाधिरिति वदेम तत इत्थमुपालभ्येमह्यपि । योग्यता तु प्रमाणसम्बन्धातिरिक्ता प्रमाणेनावसीयते इति युक्त एवास्तीति प्रमाणोदयः । तस्याश्च त्रैकाल्यात् त्रैकाल्यावगमोपि समर्थित एव । तस्याश्च संशयिततापि युक्तैव । (प्र०पं० ९८)

It is not correct to say that *pramāṇa sambandha yogyatā* is only another name for *sattā jāti* i.e., *mahāsāmānya.* Those who talk of *mahāsāmānya* or *sattā jāti* have to accept *svarūpa sattā* also. The entities that are not yet produced, that have perished and that are totally non-existent like *śaśa viṣāṇa* do not have *sattā jāti*, simply because these have no *svarūpa sattā.* Therefore, *svarūpasattā* has to be accepted even by those who talk of *sattājāti.* Therefore, these two are not one and the same. *Svarūpasattā* itself is *pramāṇa yogyatā.* Only such entities that have *svarūpasattā* can be cognized by *pramāṇas.* Presence in past, present and future is possible only to *svarūpasattā.* The *sattā jāti* is stated to be eternal. By itself it cannot have the past, present and the future. It depends upon the presence of the very *svarūpa* of the entities concerned at three times. Therefore, the expression *sat* is used with reference to *dravya, guṇa,* and *karma* on account of their *svarūpa sattā* and there is no such thing such as *sattā jāti.* It is already stated that even those who accept *sattā jāti* accept *svarūpasattā* in the case of *jāti, viśeṣa* and *samavāya* to describe them as *sat.*

(i) **का पुनरियं प्रमाणसम्बन्धयोग्यता नाम । ननु नामान्तरेण सामान्यमेव इदम् उररीकृतम् । नैतदेवम् । यो हि महासामान्यं सत्तां सङ्गिरते**

सोऽपि स्वरुपसत्तां पदार्थनां मन्यत एव । अन्यथा शशशृङ्गादीना- मुत्पन्नातिवृत्तानाञ्च किमिति महासामान्येन सम्बन्धः एव न स्यात् इति पर्यनुयोगे कः परिहारः? तेन स्वरूपसत्तैव प्रमाणसम्बन्धयोग्यता । यस्य हि स्वरूपमस्ति तत् प्रमाणेन परिच्छिद्यते। त्रैकाल्यमपि स्वरूपसत्तैव युक्तम् न च महासामान्यस्य नित्यत्वात्। तथा संशयिततापि तस्यैव न परमसंशयिते स्वरूपे अपरः सत्तासन्देहः भवति । अथ नित्यायाः अपि सत्तायाः कः सम्बन्धः यः त्रिकालः । तस्यैव त्रैकाल्यं कुतः? नान्यदत्रोत्तरं स्वरूपत्रैकाल्यादित्यतः । तस्मात् स्वरूपसत्तोपाधिकः सच्छब्दः न पुनरेक आकारः सत्ता नाम द्रव्यगुणकर्मणाम् ।

(ii) अपि च काश्यपीयानां जातिसमवायविशेषेषु स्वरूपसत्तोपाधिक एव सच्छब्दः इत्यभ्युगमः । तस्य च द्रव्यगुणकर्मस्वपि तथाभावोऽस्तु इति । तदेवमपाकृते पदार्थस्वरूपातिरेकिणि सत्ताख्ये महासामान्ये यत् स्वमनीषानिर्मितकुतर्कबलेन सन्मात्रविषयं प्रत्यक्षमिति साधितम् । तदतिदूरोत्सारितम् । (प्र०पं० १००)

Śālikanātha also rejects the status of *jāti* to *śabdatva.* He also rejects the status of *jātitva* to *brāhmaṇatva, kṣatriyatva* etc. These are *upādhis* that are indicated by the respective parentage. Similarly, *jvālātva* the characteristic of being a flame is also not a *jāti.*

In this connection it may be noted that in Avesti *adhikaraṇa* and *Rathakāra adhikaraṇa,* the mention of *kṣatriyatva jāti* and *rathakāratva jāti* be taken as referring to the respective *upādhis.*

CHAPTER V

Amṛtakalā
A brief account of pramāṇas

Definition and Classification of Pramāṇa

Anubhūti i.e., direct cognition is *pramāṇa.* This is distinct from *smṛti.* The cognition that arises from the impressions of a previous cognition is *smṛti.* The *smṛti* is not a *pramāṇa* as it depends upon a previous cognition.

अनुभूतिः प्रमाणं सा स्मृतेरन्या स्मृतिः पुनः ।
पूर्वविज्ञानसंस्कारमात्रजं ज्ञानमुच्यते
न प्रमाणं स्मृतिः पूर्वप्रतिपत्तिव्यपेक्षणात् । [प्र०पं०(१-४)(V-१)]

In the case of *dhāravāhikajñāna* i.e., a series of the occurrence of a cognition, each one is directly generated by the sense contact and does not depend upon the earlier occurrence. Therefore, it is *pramāṇa.*

अन्योन्यनिरपेक्षास्तु धारावाहिकबुद्धयः ॥ (V-२)

According to the Prābhākaras there are five *pramāṇas* viz. *pratyakṣa, anumāṇa, śāstra, upamāṇa* and *arthāpatti.*

तत्र पञ्चविधं मानं प्रत्यक्षमनुमा तथा ।
शास्त्रं तथोपमानार्थापत्ती इति गुरोर्मतम् । (V-३)

Pratyakṣa

The direct cognition is perception. The object, the knower and the knowledge are cognized by the preception. In respect of the objects viz., *dravya, guṇa,* and *jāti,* the perception is generated by the senses.

साक्षात् प्रतीतिः प्रत्यक्षं मेयमातृप्रमासु सा ।
मेयेषु इन्द्रिययोगोत्था द्रव्यजातिगुणेषु सा (V-४)

The *pratyakṣa* is at two levels viz., *nirvikalpa* and *savikalpa.* At *nirvikalpa* level mere *svarūpa* of the object and the attributes are cognized, while at the *savikalpa* level the object as qualified by the attributes is cognized.

सविकल्पाऽविकल्पा च प्रत्यक्षा बुद्धिरिष्यते ।
आद्या विशिष्टविषया स्वरूपविषयेतरा ॥ (V-५)

The cognition of the knower and the knowledge is of the nature of perception in all cognitions since these two are directly cognized in all cognitions.

सर्वविज्ञानहेतूत्था मितौ मातरि च प्रमा ।
साक्षात् कर्तृत्वसामान्यात् प्रत्यक्षत्वेन सम्मता ॥ (V-६)

When the expression *pramāṇa* is taken in the sense of *pramiti* i.e., *saṃvit,* that is to say, when it is taken as *bhāva sādhana,* then, outside activities in the form of *hāna, upādāna* and *upekṣā* i.e., rejection, acceptance and indifference are the result of it. But when the expression *pramāṇa* is taken in the sense of *pramāsādhana,* that is to say, it is taken as *karaṇa sādhana,* thereby meaning the senses, *manas,* or the contact of the senses with the object, then, the *saṃvit* itself is the result.

मानत्वं संविदां बाह्यं हानादानादिकं फलम् ।
ज्ञानस्य तु फलं सैव व्यवहारोपयोगिनी ।
अपेक्षिकं च करणं मन इन्द्रियमेव वा ।
तदर्थसन्निकर्षो मानं चेत् पूर्वकं फलम् ।

[(प्र०पं०१०५)(V-७, ८)]

The Definition of Anumāna

The cognition of *ekadeśāntara* i.e., *sādhya,* by the cognition of *ekadeśa* i.e., *hetu,* when the certainty of its relation with the *sādhya* is known, is the inference.

The Prābhākaras use the expression *ekadeśa* for the *hetu* and *ekadeśāntara* for the *sādhya*. By *sambandhaniyama* they refer to *avyabhicarita sambandha*. They do not spell out any particular relation such as the cause and the effect. A relation between *hetu* and *sādhya* that is *avyabhicarita* will satisfy the requirement of *sambandhaniyama*. But it should be so known at the time of the cognition of the *hetu*. Then only that *hetu* will lead to the inference of the concerned *sādhya*. Further, there should not be any *bādha* from any other *parmāṇa* including another *anumāna*.

ज्ञातसम्बन्धनियमस्यैकदेशस्य दर्शनात्
एकदेशान्तरे बुद्धिरनुमानमबाधिते ।। (V-९)

A *hetu* that has a relation with *sādhya* free from *upādhi* and duly established by *pratyakṣa* etc. *pramāṇas* will be a valid *hetu* to infer the *sādhya* concerned.

यः कश्चिद् येन यस्येह सम्बन्धो निरुपाधिकः ।
प्रत्यक्षादिप्रमासिद्धः स तस्य गमको भवेत् ।।

There are two types of objects of the inference viz. those that can be seen and those that can not be seen but are inferred on certain general grounds. These are called *dṛṣṭasvalakṣaṇa* and *adṛṣtasvalakṣaṇa* respectively. For instance, the fire inferred from the smoke is *dṛstasvalakṣaṇa* while the motion inferred from the conjunction and the disjunction of an object with the different points of space is *adṛṣṭasvalakṣana*. The motion i.e., *karma*, is never actually seen. It is always inferred.

प्रमेयमनुमानस्य दृष्टादृष्टस्वलक्षणम् । (V-१०)

A syllogism that is formulated to convey an inference to others is *parāthānumāna*.

परप्रत्ययनेच्छूनामनुमोदयसाधनम् वचनम् । (V-११)

The various clauses of the definition of *anumāna* given here ward off the various fallacies of *anumāna.*

वचनं दूषणैः सार्धमर्थादेतेन वर्णितम् ।

Śāstrapramāṇa

The knowledge of an object that is not known by any other *pramaṇa* and known through the knowledge of the scriptural injunction is *śāstrapramāṇa.*

शास्त्रं शब्दविज्ञानाद् यदसन्निकृष्टार्थविज्ञानम् ।

The Definition of Upamāna

The knowledge of similarity in an object arising from the observation of similarity in another object is *upamāna.*

साद्दश्यदर्शनोत्थं ज्ञानं साद्दश्यविषयमुपमानम् ।
साद्दश्याद् द्दश्यमानाद् यत् प्रतियोगिनि जायते ।
साद्दश्यविषयं ज्ञानमुपमानं तदुच्यते ॥ (V-१५)

The object to be cognized by *upamāna pramāṇa* viz., *sādṛśya* i.e., similarity, is established by the very cognition of it. It is a distinct category from other categories—*dravya, guṇa* etc.

विषयोऽस्य वित्तिसिद्धो भिन्नो द्रव्यादिभावेभ्यः । (V-१४)

Arthāpatti

An observed fact leading to the envisaging of an unobserved fact in order to avoid the incompatibility with a known fact is *arthāpatti.*

विना कल्पनयाऽर्थेन द्दष्टेन अनुपपन्नताम् ।
नयता द्दष्टमर्थं या साऽर्थापत्तिस्तु कल्पना ॥
[(प्र० पं० १०६) (V-१६)]

The absence of a person at his residence makes his very existence incompatible unless his presence outside is envisaged.

अभावेन गृहे भावो बहिष्कल्पनया विना ।
नयताऽनुपपन्नत्वं कल्प्यमानो बहिर्यथा ॥ (V-१७)

If the outside presence of the person is not envisaged, then, his very existence becomes doubtful. His existence itself cannot be denied as it is indicated by another *pramāṇa.*

गम्यस्य अनुपपन्नत्वमिह कल्पनया विना
मानान्तरविरोधेन सन्देहापत्तिलक्षणम् ॥ (V-१८)

Normally the person is never found absent at home. However, his absence now makes his very existence doubtful though it is indicated by the other *pramāṇa* i.e., *jyotiṣya.*

The envisaging of a fact that can remove this doubt is *arthāpatti.* The absence at the home causes the doubt about the existence. Envisaging the presence outside removes this doubt.

देशेन हि विनाभावो न कदाचन दृश्यते
विनाभावेन सिद्धोपि तेन सन्देहमृच्छति ।
तत्सन्देहव्युदासाय कल्पना या प्रवर्तते ।
सन्देहापादकादर्थादर्थापत्तिरसौ स्मृता । (V-१९,२०)

Arthāpatti is defined in another way also. That which becomes incompatible without envisaging something leads to the envisaging of the same by way of *arthāpatti.* The existence of the person becomes incompatible if his presence outside is not envisaged. Therefore, the same has to be envisaged by way of *arthāpatti.*

यत्कल्पनां विना योऽर्थः प्रतीतोप्येति संशयम् ।
तेन तत्कल्पनामेके त्वर्थापत्तिं प्रचक्षते ॥ (V-२१)

In the case of *anumāna,* if the *gamya* i.e., the fire, is not there, it will result in the incompatibility of the *gamaka* i.e., smoke, not being absent in the place where the fire is not present.

गमकस्य अनुमाने तु विपक्षासत्त्वलक्षणम् ।
गम्यतेऽनुपपन्नत्वं विना गम्येन वस्तुना ॥ (V-२२)

Since the procedure of *arthāpatti* and *anumāna* are quite different, these two are distinct *pramāṇas.*

तत्सामाग्रीविभेदेन भिन्ने एते परस्परम् ।
अर्थापत्त्यनुमानाख्ये प्रमाणे इति निश्चितम् ॥ (V-२३)

Rejection of Anupalabdhi Pramāṇa i.e., Abhāva Pramāṇa

Some thinkers say that *abhāva* is the sixth *pramāṇa.* The Prābhākaras reject this contention. A *pramāṇa* is meant to convey a *prameya.* Therefore, it has to be thought out as to what is the *prameya* of *abhāva.*

अभावाख्यं प्रमाणं ये षष्ठमाहुर्मनीषिणः
तेषां प्राभाकरैरेवं प्रत्यादेशोऽयमुच्यते ।
प्रमाणं खलु कस्यापि प्रमेयस्यावबोधकम् ।
तत्राभावस्य किं तावत् प्रमेयमिति चिन्त्यताम् ।
[(प्र०पं० १०७) (V-२४-२५)]

The *abhāvavādin's* claim that the cognition *na asti* conveys the *abhāva.* This is the *prameya* for the *abhāva pramāṇa.* The cognition that there is no jar on the ground is not about the ground. In that case, even when there is a jar on the ground such a cognition would be permissible. If it is stated that this cognition conveys the ground alone, the question has to be answered as to what is conveyed by the expression alone i.e., *kevala.* It can't refer to the ground only. It has to refer to some attribute. This attribute is 'absence' of the jar. This amounts to the acceptance of *abhāva.*

ननु नास्तीति बुद्ध्या बोध्यं यदुपकल्पितम् ।
अभावस्य प्रमाणस्य प्रमेयं तद् भविष्यति ।
भूतलेऽत्र घटो नास्तीत्येषा या जायते मतिः ।
सा न भूतलमात्रे स्यात् प्रसक्तेः घटवत्यपि ।
केवले भूतले स्यात् चेत् कैवल्यं तत्र कीदृशम् ।
स्वरूपमात्रं नो तावत् धर्मान्तरमथोच्यते ।
प्रमेयान्तरमेवात्र तावताङ्गीकृतो भवेत् । (V-२६, २८)

This absence conveyed by 'alone' is not cognized by the eye since the eye is not employed at this. There are instances where in the ground is cognized without reflecting on any absence and later on the absence of this or that is realized. This means that when the eye was employed at the ground, it cognized only the ground and the absence was cognized by some other means.

तच्च नेन्द्रियविज्ञेयं तद्व्यापारानपेक्षणात् ।
स्वरूपमात्रे दृष्टेऽपि भावे दूरगतोपि सन् ।
कथञ्चित् जातजिज्ञासो नास्तित्वं प्रतिपद्यते ॥
तेन यत्रापि नास्तित्वं बुद्ध्यते व्यापृतेंद्रियः
भावांशमात्रे तत्रापि प्रत्यक्षस्य प्रमाणता ॥

The absence is cognized by the very absence of the cognition by other *pramāṇas*. Therefore , the very absence of the operation of the other *pramāṇas* that are capable of cognizing an entity if it were present is the means to cognize the absence of that entity. This will avoid the contingency of the ground alone being seen even when there is. a jar on it.

नास्तित्वं च प्रमाणानामनुत्पत्त्यैव गम्यते ।
नास्तित्वप्रतिपत्तिर्हि तां विना नास्ति कुत्रचित् ।
योग्यप्रमाणानुत्पत्तेः कारणत्वपरिग्रहात् ।
अतिप्रसङ्गदोषो हि नावकाशमुपाश्नुते । (V-३२-३३)

The absence of the cognition of the entity even when the appropriate *pramāṇa* is employed is the *pramāṇa* for the cognition of the absence of that entity by its very nature. It is not the cause as known but it is the cause just by itself. This distinguishes it from the *liṅga* of an *anumāna*. The *liṅga* is the cause only when it is known while the absence of the cognition of an entity by appropriate *pramāṇas* is the cause of the cognition of the absence by its very nature. It is like the eye. The eye need not be known to generate the knowledge of the object seen. If it were the cause of the absence of the cognition, when known only, then, it would have needed another cause to know it which should be of the nature of the absence of *pramāṇa*. That also would similarly need one more. This would lead to the infinite regress.

अनुत्पत्तिश्च न ज्ञाता सती कारणमक्षवत् ।
तेन लिङ्गत्वशङ्कापि दूरादेव निराकृता ।
अनुत्पत्तिश्च विज्ञाता हेतुश्चेद् लिङ्गवद्भवेत् ।
अनवस्था प्रसज्येत नास्तित्वं च न सिद्ध्यति ॥ (V-३४-३५)

The free movement on the ground cannot take place by the cognition of the mere ground. In that case one would have freely moved even on such ground that has thorn etc. The cognition of the ground alone, without the verification of the absence of the thorn etc. will not enable one to move freely. One moves duly checking the absence of the thorns etc. that would have become known if these were present. This also establishes that it is the absence of the cognition of an entity by the appropriate *pramāṇas* that enables one to cognize the absence of the entity concerned. This establishes *abhāvapramāṇa* as well as *abhāvaprameya.*

किञ्च पादविहारादिव्यवहारश्च भूतले ।
न भूतलपरिच्छेदमात्रेणैव प्रवर्तते ।
प्रसङ्गस्तत्र दुर्वारः कण्टकाद्यन्वितेपि हि ।
अथ केवलभूभागपरिच्छेदात् प्रवर्तते ।

विकल्प्यं तत्र कैवल्यं ग्राह्यस्य ग्रहणस्य वा ।
ग्राह्यस्य चेत् पुरैवोक्तो दोषस्तत्र प्रवर्तते ।
ग्रहस्य चेत् तदा सूक्ष्मजिज्ञासा विफला भवेत् ।
जाता हि केवला संवित् व्यवहारस्य कारणम् ।
तेन भावं परिच्छिद्य व्यवहारे चिकीर्षति ।
दृश्यादर्शनसिद्ध्यर्थं युक्तं सूक्ष्मनिरीक्षणम् ।
(V-३६-४०)

Refutation of Abhāvapramāṇavāda

Objects like ground are cognized in two ways viz. (i) *Sansṛsta viṣaya* i.e., an object along with another object (ii) *tanmātraviṣaya* i.e., *tadekaviṣaya* i.e., the object alone. In the second way also the object is cognized in two conditions viz., (i) when there is an observable *dṛśya pratiyogin* elsewhere (ii) when there is no such *pratiyogin*. It is only when there is a *tanmātraviṣaya* cognition and *a dṛśya pratiyogin*, then the *abhāva* is claimed to be present. What has really happened is that only *tanmātraviṣayabuddhi* i.e., *ekaviṣayabudhi,* has taken place. To give a concrete example, when there is cognition of a jar on the ground it is *sansṛṣtaviṣayabuddhi* i.e., the cognition of two objects together. When the jar is removed it is *ekaviṣayabuddhi* i.e., the cognition of the ground only. The jar which is observable elsewhere is *dṛśyapratiyogin*. Such a situation is claimed to be a situation of *abhāva* by *abhāvavādin*. The Prābhākaras consider it as *tanmātraviṣayabuddhi* i.e., *tadekaviṣayabuddhi,* i.e., the cognition of the ground alone.

अत्रोच्यते द्वयी संवित् वस्तुनो भूतलात्मनः ।
एका संसृष्टविषया तन्मात्रविषयाऽपरा ।
तन्मात्रविषया या च द्विधा सा च प्रसज्यते ।
प्रतियोगिन्यदृश्ये च दृश्ये च प्रतियोगिनि ।
तत्र तन्मात्रधीर्येयं दृश्ये च प्रतियोगिनि ।
नास्तित्वं सैव भूभागे घटादिप्रतियोगिनः । (V-४१-४३)

It cannot be argued that 'how can *tanmātrabuddhi* arise in respect of the same ground about which there was *sanṣṛṣtabuddhi* earlier without the cognition of the *abhāva* of the jar?' A counter question can be asked that how can *abhāvabuddhi* arise in the same place with reference to which there was *bhāvabuddhi* of the jar earlier. Whatever the reason given to *abhāvabuddhi* in the place of *bhāvabuddhi* the same reason is the ground for *ekaviṣayabuddhi* in the place of *sansṛṣtaviṣyabuddhi.* Withdrawal of the jar is stated as the ground for *abhāvabuddhi* and the same may be taken as the ground for the *ekaviṣayabuddhi.*

ननु संसृष्टबुद्ध्या यः पुरस्तादवधारितः ।
कथं तन्मात्रधीस्तत्र जाताऽभावो न तत्र चेत् ।
शक्यते तदभावेऽपि वक्तुं यो यत्र सन्नभूत् ।
तस्याभावः कथं तत्र ब्रूयाच्चेत् तत्र कारणम् ।
तन्मात्रधिय एवास्तु वरं तत्कारणं ततः ।
तस्याः सम्प्रतिपन्नत्वाद्वादिनोरुभयोरपि ।। (V-४४-४६)

The Absence of Cognition i.e., Anupalabdhi, can be a Pramāṇa only as known

The absence of the cognition by the appropriate *pramāṇa* cannot be the means of the cognition of *abhāva* by its very nature as in the case of the eye being the means of the cognition by its very nature. One has to have the knowledge of the absence of *pramāṇa* as in the case of the knowledge of *linga* for *anumāna,* otherwise even the dream cognitions would become *pramāṇa.*

चक्षुर्वदपरामृष्टं न कारणमदर्शनम् ।
स्वप्नावस्थागतस्यापि प्रमाणत्वप्रसङ्गतः ।। (V-४७)

Cognizability cannot be an attribute of *abhāva.* A positive attribute cannot be an attribute of a negative entity.

विशेषापादिका तस्य न निषेधस्य दृश्यता ।
भावरूपो निषेधोहि नाभावस्योपपद्यते । (V-४८)

The absence of the cognition by the appropriate *pramāṇa* will be the *pramāṇa* for the cognition of *abhāva* only when it is known. This is clear from the fact that when an object is brought back to a place and its absence is no more, the statement is made 'There was no jar here earlier'.

अदर्शने निवृत्तेपि पुनर्भावस्य कस्यचित् ।
प्राङ् नास्तित्वं व्यपदिशन्त्यदृष्टस्य पुरा क्वचित् ।
दृश्यस्यादर्शनं तेन ज्ञातं सदवबोधकम् । (V-४९)

If it is accepted, that the *abhāva* is *pramāṇa* when it is known only, then, for the knowledge of this *abhāva pramāṇa* another *abhāva pramāṇa* is required and so on. This leads to infinite regress. On the other hand, if *tanmātrabuddhi* is accepted instead of *abhāva* there is no room for any *anavasthā.*

When one observes the ground without a jar he reflects on the *dṛśya pratiyogin* that was present earlier and realises that he is cognizing the ground only. Therefore, the so-called *abhāva* is nothing more than cognizing the ground alone.

दृश्यादर्शनतस्तस्य ज्ञानं चेदनवस्थितिः ।
यदि तन्मात्रसंवित्तिरूपं स्यात् तददर्शनम् ।
तदा तस्याः स्वसंवित्तेरनवस्था निवर्तते ।
तेनावश्याभ्युपेतव्यो विमर्शो दृश्यगोचरः ॥
अदर्शनमभावो हि तन्मात्रानुभवात्मकम् ।
तन्मात्रानुभवश्चायं यददर्शनरूपितः ।
विमृश्यते भूतलादौ तदभावोऽपदिश्यते ॥

(V-५०-५३)

The *tanmātrānubhava* i.e., *ekaviṣayabuddhi,* is self revealing. It is not an object of the cognition. It is the cognition itself. It is this situation that is referred to as '*na asti*'. The correct statement should be that the existence of the jar is not found. But not that the non-existence of the jar is found. Hence, there is no *prameya* called *abhāva*. Consequently there is no separate *pramāṇa* called *abhāvapramāṇa*.

तन्मात्रानुभवश्चायं न मेयः फलभावतः ।
किञ्च स्वयं प्रकाशोऽसाविति न्यायविदो विदुः ॥
नास्तीति शब्दः तत्रैव स्वसंवेद्ये प्रवर्तते ।
तेन नास्तीति विज्ञानन्यायेन न समगतम् ।
मेयाभावे ततो मानमभावाख्यं कथं भवेत् ।
घटसत्ता न लभ्याहि नासत्ता चोदितात् क्रमात् । (V-५४-५६)

The free movement etc. on the ground also takes place by *tanmātrānubhava* only. When the *dṛśyapratiyogin* i.e., thorn etc. is not cognized along with the ground, that is sufficient for the free movement. The effort to verify the thorn etc., is intended to verify the *dṛśyapratiyogin*. It is not a case of cognizing the absence of the thorns etc., but it is the case of affirming the cognition of the ground alone. This is the implication of *tanmātra viṣayabuddhi*.

अभावव्यवहारो हि निश्शङ्कगमनादिकः ।
तन्मात्रानुभवेनैव यथोक्तेन प्रवर्तते ।
यदा यस्य च दृश्यत्वे सत्यप्यनुपलम्भनम् ।
तदभावव्यवहृतिः तदानीं सम्प्रवर्तते ।
सूक्ष्मकण्टकजिज्ञासाप्यतः सार्थकतां गता ।
तां विना नहि दृश्यत्वं सूक्ष्मसत्ताऽधिरोहति ।
व्यवहारप्रवृत्तिश्च दृश्यादृष्टिनिबन्धना
तेन दृश्यत्वसिद्ध्यर्थं युक्तं तस्य निरीक्षणम् । (V-५७-६०)

The Implications of Bhāṣyakāras' Remark on Abhāva

In the *Śabarabhāṣya* it is stated that **'अभावोपि प्रमाणाभावः नास्ति इत्यस्य अर्थस्य असन्निकृष्टस्य'** This remark is interpreted by the Bhāṭṭas as a definition of *abhāvapramāṇa*. The Prābhākaras do not agree with this interpretation. According to the Prābhākaras it is not a definition of *abhāvapramāṇa*, but actually a rejection of *abhāvapramāṇa*.

नन्वेवं लक्षणग्रन्थस्यार्थस्तर्ह्यस्य कीदृशः ।
मीमांसार्णवसम्भूतं पीयतां समयामृतम् ।
प्रत्यक्षाद्यपरिच्छेद्यमभावाख्यं चतुर्विधम् ।
प्रमेयं साधयत् मानमभावाख्यं वदन्ति ये
तन्निराकरणार्थोऽयं यत्नो भाष्यकृता कृतः ॥

(V-६१-६३)

The expression *abhāva* in this *bhāṣya* conveys that there is no *prameya* to be cognized. This is expressed by *nāsti*, since it conveys the absence of *prameya*, it cannot have the status of *pramāṇa*. Only that which conveys a *prameya* can be *pramāṇa*.

अभावोऽसन्निकृष्टस्य नास्तीत्यस्यावबोधकः ।
प्रमाणं न भवतीति प्रमाणाभाव उच्यते । (V-६३-६४)

Now, a question arises as to why *Bhāṣyakāra* indulges in rejecting a *pramāṇa* while the context is that of stating *pramāṇas*. Śālikanātha replies that it is not merely the rejection of *abhāvapramāṇa*, that is the purpose of this *bhāṣya* remark but it is to affirm the *pramāṇas pratyakṣa* etc. stated earlier. This remark is *vākya śeṣa* i.e., a supplementary statement of the definitions of *pratyakṣa* etc., given earlier. The affirmation made here is as under:

The role of a *pramāṇa* has to be ascertained by its result. The result of a *pramāṇa* is to give firm knowledge. The firm knowledge has two aspects viz., 'it is this' and 'it is not any other'. To ascertain the latter aspect of the firm knowledge, the absence of the other *prameya* consequent on the absence of *pramāṇa* for it has to be checked up. *Bhāṣyakāra* conveys this requirement by his remark **'अभावोपि प्रमाणाभावः नास्तीत्यस्य अर्थस्य'** The expression **नास्ति** conveys *prameyābhāva* and the expression *abhāva* conveys *pramāṇabhāva*.

This verification of the absence of any other is necessary to have the firm knowledge 'it is this' conveyed by each of the five *pramāṇas* described earlier. This is the purpose of the *bhāṣya* remark. The so-called sixth *parmāṇa* i.e. *abhāva pramāṇa* is not at all stated here.

किं निराकरणस्येह फलमित्यथ चेन्मतम् ।
उच्यते लक्षणग्रन्थः प्रत्यक्षादेः समर्थ्यते
प्रमाणं कार्यगम्यं हि सर्वत्रेति विनिश्चितम् ।
निश्चयश्च प्रमाणस्य कार्यमित्यपि सम्मतम् ।
निश्चयश्चायमेवेति संवित्तिः सर्ववस्तुषु ।
सा च वस्त्वन्तराभावसंवित्त्यनुगमे सति
प्रमाणानुदयस्तत्र यत्राभावोऽवसीयते ।
तदा तेन सहैव स्यात् प्रत्यक्षादेः प्रमाणता
लक्षणं क्रियमाणं च तथाभूतस्य युज्यते ।
न कृतं च तथा तेन न कृतं साधुलक्षणम् ।
इमां शङ्कां निराकर्तुं निराकरणमुच्यते ॥ (V-६४-६९)

There is no *prameya* called *abhāva*. Consequently no *parmāṇas* proceeds to cognize it. All *parmāṇas* cognize their respective *prameyas* and affirm it by not proceeding to grasp anything more and thereby indicate the unambiguity of the respective *prameyas*.

कथं पुनरियं शङ्का भवत्यत्र निराकृता ।
अभावाख्यो न मेयोऽस्ति यदर्थं प्रार्थ्यते पुनः ।
प्रमाणानामनुत्पादः साधु तल्लक्षणं कृतम् ।
इति पूर्वप्रमाणानां लक्षणानि समादधत् ।
भाष्यकार इमं ग्रन्थं चक्रे नाभावलक्षणम् । (V-७०-७२)

In the context of answering **चित्राक्षेप** *Bhāṣyakāra* states that there are five *pramāṇas* in addition to *Sāstrapramāṇa*. This gives an impression that he holds that there are six *pramāṇas*. This will be possible if *abhāva* also is taken into account. However, the

Prābhākaras explain this remark of *bhāṣya* without accepting *abhāvapramāṇa.* They explain that the *pramāṇas* are meant for *vyavahāra.* Five *pramāṇas* lead to positive *vyavahāra* while the sixth one which is of the nature of reflecting on *dṛśyapratiyogin* helps negative *vyavahāra.* This is the implication of *Bhāṣyakāras'* remark.

नन्वेवमपि पञ्चाह शब्दं हित्वा कथं पुनः ।
भाष्यकारः प्रमाणानि चित्राक्षेपं समादधत् ।
उच्यते व्यवहारस्य हेतुभूतप्रसिद्धये ।
एवमाहोभयात्मापि व्यवहारः प्रतिष्ठितः ।
तत्र भावव्यवहृतिः पञ्चस्वेवोपलभ्यते
अभावव्यवहारस्तु दृश्यादृष्टिविमर्शजः ।
सा हि भूभागसद्भावमात्रावच्छेदबन्धना
तदभावव्यवहृतिरिति प्रागेव दर्शितम् । (V-७२-७६)

CHAPTER VI

Pramāṇa Pārāyaṇa

The Exposition of Pramāṇas

Śālikanātha commences this topic with the remark that there is difference of opinion among the philosophers in respect of the nature of valid cognition, the number of the means of valid cognition, the nature of the objects conveyed by the cognition, and the result of the cognition.

स्वरूपसङ्ख्यार्थफलेषु वादिभिः
यतो विवादाः बहुधा वितेनिरे ।
ततो वयं तत्प्रतिबोधसिद्धये
प्रमाणपारायणमारभामहे ॥ (प्र० पं० ११२)

Review of the Buddhists' Definition of Pramāṇa

He commences his exposition with the examination of the Buddhists' definition of *pramāṇa* viz., *avisamvādijñānam pramāṇam*. The cognition that does not disagree with the facts conveyed by it is a valid cognition.

This Definition Suffers from the Ativyāpti in Smṛti, and Avyāpti in Anumāna

There is no disagreement between the cognition and the facts conveyed by it in the case of *smṛti* i.e., memory. *Smṛti* is not considered as a valid cognition as it does not convey anything new.

However, this definition of valid cognition given by the Buddhist applies to it. Therefore, this definition suffers from *ativyāpti* in respect of *smṛti*. A definition that goes wider than its scope suffers from *ativyāpti.*

किं पुनरिदं प्रमाणं नाम । न तावदविसंवादिज्ञानम् । स्मृतेरपि तथाभावप्रसक्तेः । (प्र०पं० ११३)

To overcome the contingency of *ativyāpti* in *smṛti,* it is argued that *smṛti* does not comprehend the *svalakṣaṇa* which is the real object of the cognition. It only comprehends *vikalpa* which is not real. Therefore, it is not *avisaṃvādi.* Hence, the definition of *pramāṇa* given above does not apply to *smṛti.* Therefore, there is no *ativyāpti.* In Buddhist terminology it is *svalakṣaṇa* only that is, *vastu* i.e., a real entity, the *vikalpa* is *avastu* i.e., not a real entity. *Svalakṣaṇa* is *paramārtha sat* while *vikalpa* is *samvṛtisat.*

अथ स्मृतिः विकल्परूपतया परमार्थसत् स्वलक्षणम् अगृण्हन्ती संवृतिसन्तमाकारम् अवस्तुभूतम् उल्लिखन्ती द्विचन्द्रादिबोधवत् न अविसंवादिनी । (प्र०पं० ११३)

This argument does not solve the problem. It only results in *avyāpti* in *anumāna.* In *anumāna* also *vikalpa* is comprehended. If *smṛti* is ruled out from the scope of *pramāṇa* on the ground that *vikalpa* is comprehended in *smṛti,* then, *anumāna* also has to be ruled out. This results in *avyāpti* in *anumāna.* A definition that is narrow suffers from *avyāpti.*

एवमपि नानुमानं प्रमाणं स्यात् । तस्यापि विकल्परूपत्वात् । (प्र०पं० ११४)

The Import of the Terms Svalakṣaṇa and Vikalpa

The term *svalakṣaṇa* is explained as **स्वलक्षणशब्देन स्वम् असाधारणं तत्त्वं यस्यात्मानो लक्षणं नान्यत् तदेव उच्यते । तदेव परमार्थसत् ।**

The terms *vikalpa* and *samvṛtisat* are explained as:

यत् अभिलापसंसर्गनिमित्तमनुवृत्तं जातिगुणादिरूपं स्वलक्षणे योजितमिव भाति तत् कृत्रिमत्वेन संवृतिसत् इत्युच्यते । यद्यपि तस्य स्वारसिको बाधो नास्ति तथापि यौक्तिकबाधो ज्यालायामिव अस्त्येवेति विचार्यमाणशून्यत्वम् । तदुक्तम्—

सत्याभासः परं तत्र न सत्यं परमार्थतः
विचार्यमाणशून्यत्वे संवृतिश्चेति गीयते ।। (प्र०पं० ११४)

To overcome this difficulty the Buddhists try to distinguish the cases of *smṛti* and *anumāna* on the ground that though *anumāna* also comprehends *vikalpa* which is *avastu,* it comprehends it as *vastu* through *adhyavasāya.* Therefore, it is in agreement with *svalakṣaṇa* i.e., *vastu,* through its *adhyavasāya.* Hence *anumāna* is *pramāṇa* while *smṛti* is not so.

विकल्परूपमनुमानमवस्तुविषयमपि वस्तुविषयमिव अध्यवसीयते इति अध्यवसीयमानवस्तुभूतस्वलक्षणाविसंवादितया तत् प्रमाणम् । (प्र०पं० ११४)

In Buddhistic terminology *svalakṣaṇa* is *vastu* while *vikalpa* is *avastu.* The *svalakṣaṇa* is comprehended at two levels viz., *grahaṇa* and *adhyavasāya.* It is *grāhya* for *nirvikalpaka jañāna* and *adhyavasēya* for *vikalpajñāna.* The distinction between *svalakṣaṇa* and *vikalpa* is not realized at the *adhyavasāya* level. Therefore, *vikalpa* is taken to be *svalakṣaṇa.* Therefore, *anumāna,* though comprehends *vikalpa,* it is in agreement with *svalakṣaṇa* through *adhyavasāya.* Hence, it is *pramāṇa.*

द्विविधो हि ज्ञानानां विषयः ग्राह्यः अध्यवसेयश्च । निर्विकल्पकज्ञानस्य स्वलक्षणं ग्राह्यं विकल्पज्ञानानामध्यवसेयः । अध्यवसायो नाम व्यक्त्या तद्व्यावृत्तिसाम्येन भेदाग्रहः । एवमगृहीतभेदो विकल्पः स्वलक्षणत्वेन अध्यवसीयते इति स्वलक्षणमेवाध्यवसितमनुमानस्येति अध्यवसितस्वलक्षणाविसंवादात् प्रामाण्यमनुमानस्येति नाव्याप्तिः । (न्या०सि० ११४)

The above ground to distinguish the cases of *anumāna* and *smṛti* does not help. *Smṛti* is also related with the *svalakṣaṇa* in the same way.

स्मृतिरपि तथा स्यात् । सापि हि स्वलणाध्यवसायिन्येव जायते । (प्र०पं० ११४)

This explanation not only does not serve the purpose of distinguishing the cases of *anumāna* and *smṛti* but also results in making *anumāna* itself *apramāṇa.* The object of *anumāna* is *vikalpa* which is *avastu.* If there is an *adhyavasāya* of this *avastu* as *vastu* i.e., *svalakṣāṇa*, then, this comprehension will be on par with *śuktirajata* comprehension and *apramāṇa.*

अपि च अवस्तुभूतं स्वविषयं वस्तुतया अध्यवस्यत् शुक्तिकार-जतबोधवत् कथम् अनुमानम् अविसंवादि? (प्र०पं० ११४)

Further, *grahaṇa* and *adhyavasāya* cannot be strictly demarcated. If there is no *grahaṇa* of *svalakṣaṇa* as *vikalpa,* there cannot be any *adhyavasāya* of it as *vikalpa.* The form of *grahaṇa* and *adhyavasāya* cannot be different.

किञ्च यदि अनुमानं विकल्परूपतया स्वलक्षणं न गृहणाति कथं तर्हि अध्यवस्यत्यपि । न हि ग्रहणादन्यः अध्यवसायो नाम यो हि आकारः न गृह्यते कथं सः अध्यवसीयेतापि ।

The very concepts of *grahaṇa* and *adhyavasāya* cannot be properly explained. Therefore, *ativyāpti* and *avyāpti* in respect of *smṛti* and *anumāna* cannot be avoided.

Expansion of the Scope of Avisamvāda

(i) To overcome the *ativyāpti* and *avyāpti* the Buddhists expand the definition given above by explaining the implication of the expression *avisaṃvādi.*

न वयं यथावस्थितार्थग्राहकम् अविसंवादकमभिदध्महे । किन्तु अर्थक्रियासमर्थवस्तुपरिप्रापकम् । यथाभूतं हि वस्तु येन उपदर्शितं प्रवृत्तोऽपि यदि तथाभूतमेव प्रतिलभते । तदा तदविसंवादिज्ञानं प्रमाणमुच्यते । (प्र०पं० ११५)

The cognition which enables the observer to obtain the object in the same form in which it is presented in the cognition is *avisamvādi jñānam.* If it fails to do so then, it is *visaṃvādi.* For instance, the cognition of water as water is *avisaṃvādi.* One who has this cognition can obtain water. But the cognition of mirage as water is *not avisaṃvādi*, since the observer cannot obtain it on proceeding to fetch it.

प्रमाणमविसंवादिज्ञानमर्थक्रियास्थितिः ।
अविसंवादनं शब्देप्यभिप्रायनिवेदनात् ॥ (प्र०पं० ११६)

It is अर्थक्रियास्थिति i.e. obtaining the object that is *avisaṃvāda* but not the mere agreement between what is given in the cognition and comprehended by the cognition. In the case of *smṛti*, the object remembered cannot be obtained. स्मृत्वा अर्थं प्रवर्तमानो नियमेन अर्थं न लभते (प्र०पं० ११६)

This explanation of *avisaṃvāda* also does not help. This again results in *avyāpti* in the case of the *anumāna* of past events or entities. These also cannot be obtained.

एवमपि भूतार्थविषयम् अनुमानम् अप्रमाणं स्यात् । न हि तदुपदर्शितार्थस्य प्रतिलम्भोऽस्ति ।

(ii) The Buddhists make an attempt to distinguish the cases of *smṛti* and *bhūtānumāna*. In the case of the inference relating to the past object, though the past object cannot be obtained, it is capable of being obtained as it is connected with the *liṅga* i.e., probane which has given rise to its inference. There is *prāptiyogyatā* in this case. That is sufficient for *avisaṃvāda*. Therefore, the cognition of *bhūtānumāna* is *pramāṇa*.

यद्यपि अनुमानप्रतीतस्य भूतस्य वस्तुनः प्राप्तिः नास्ति तथापि तत्प्रतिबद्धलिङ्ग जन्मतया तस्य प्राप्तियोग्यता तावदस्त्येव । तावताच तस्य प्रामाण्यम् । (प्र०पं० ११६)

This explanation also does not help to distinguish the cases of *bhūtānumāna* and *smṛti*. Just as the cognition of *bhūtānumāna* is related to the object by *paraṃparā* the *smṛti* is also related to its object by *paraṃparā*.

एवमपि स्मृतिः प्रमाणमापद्यते । स्मृतिरपि हि अनुमानवदर्थे पारम्पर्येण प्रतिबद्धैव ।

The manner in which the *anumāna* and *smṛti* are connected with the respective objects is worked out as follows:

(a) From *vahnisvalakṣaṇa, dhūmasvalakṣaṇa* arises. This *dhūma* is observed, *dhūmavikalpa* is cognised. From this *vahni* is inferred. In this way the inferential cognition is connected with the object inferred. This makes it *artha avisaṃvādi* and *arthaprāpaṇa-samartha.*

वह्निस्वलक्षणात् धूमस्वलक्षणं, ततश्च धूमदर्शनं, ततश्च धूमविकल्पः तस्माच्चानुमानमिति अनुमानमर्थेन पारम्पर्येण प्रतिबद्धत्वात् अर्थाविसंवादि अर्थप्रापणसमर्थम् ।

(b) In the case of *smṛti*, there is the cognition of the object, its impressions, and its memory. In this way *smṛti* is also related to its object and capable of obtaining the object.

स्मृतिरपि अर्थादनुभवः, ततः संस्कारः, संस्काराच्च स्मृतिरिति अर्थप्रतिबद्धैव इति तत्प्राप्तियोग्यतया प्रमाणमापद्येत । (प्र०पं० ११७)

Introduction of Two more Clauses viz., Aprāpta Prāpakatva and Pravartakatva

The Buddhists may try to rule out *smṛti* from the scope of *pramāṇa* by introducing an additional clause viz., *aprāpta prāpakatva* i.e., cognising the object that is already not cognised. *Smṛti* cognises that which is already cognised by *anubhava* while *anumāna* cognises for the first time.

यदि मन्वीत सत्यामपि प्राप्तियोग्यतायां स्मृतेर्यत् तया प्रापितव्यं स्वलक्षणं तदनुभवेनैव प्रापितमिति न प्रमाणं स्मृतिः । अनुमानं तु अप्राप्तस्वलक्षणप्रापकतया प्रमाणमिति ।

अर्थक्रियासमर्थवस्तुपरिपाकतामात्रं न प्रमाणलक्षणम् । किन्तु विशेषणमुपादेयम् । अप्राप्तप्रापकमविसंवादि ज्ञानं प्रमाणमिति ।

This distinction between *smṛti* and *anumāna* also does not hold good. In the Buddhists' terminology *prāpakatā* i.e., obtaining, is explained as *artha pratibaddhatā* i.e., being connected with the object. Such a connection with *svalakṣaṇa* is found in the case of *smṛti* also. *Smṛti* is as much related with its object as *anubhava.*

अर्थप्रापकताहि प्रतिबद्धता सा च ज्ञानान्तरस्यापि न अनुपपन्ना (प्र०पं० ११७)

Buddhist further tries to say that mere *prāpakatā* i.e., obtaining, is not sufficient but *pravartakatā* i.e., providing initiative is also to be added. This also does not help him. He explains *pravartakatā* as *pravṛttiyogya arthapradarśakatva* i.e., presenting an object which is capable of causing initiative. This is as much provided by *smṛti* as by *anumāna.*

यद्युच्येत न प्रापकतामात्रेण प्रामाण्यम् । अपितु प्रवर्तकतयापि । तथा सति यत् प्रापयति प्रवर्तयति च तत् प्रमाणम् । एतदपि न किञ्चित् । प्रवर्तकतापि ज्ञानान्तरस्यापि घटत एव । प्रवृत्तियोग्यार्थोऽपदर्शकत्वमेव प्रवर्तकत्वम् । तच्च भूतार्थविषयानुमानस्येव स्मरणस्यापि अस्ति ।

(iv) The introduction of this clause viz., *pravartakatva* in the definition of *pramāṇa* will create a new problem. The cognition of *svalakṣaṇa* is *nirvikalpaka*. Therefore, it is not *pravartaka*. Therefore, if the clause *pravartaka* is introduced in the definition of *pramāṇa* the cognition of *svalakṣaṇa* will cease to be *pramāṇa*. On the other hand the cognition of *vikalpa* is *pravartaka*. There will be the contingency of considering that as *pramāṇa*. This will upset the whole scheme of Buddhistic epistemology.

प्रवर्तकत्वे च प्रमाणलक्षणानुप्रवेशिनि निर्विकल्पकज्ञानानामप्रमाणता स्यात् । स्वयं व्यवहारप्रवर्तकत्वाभावात् । तदुत्त्थास्तु विकल्पा एव प्रापकतया प्रमाणभूताः स्यु ।

(v) The introduction of the clause *aprāptaprāpakatva* will also result in ruling out the *dhārāvāhikajñāna* i.e., recurring cognitions, from the scope of *pramāṇa*, since the object of these cognitions is the same. It cannot be argued that since each *kṣaṇa* is distinct, there is *aprāptaprāpakatva* in each case, therefore, these can be treated as *pramāṇa*, since the distinction of these *kṣaṇas* is not cognised. Moreover, the very concept of *kṣaṇa* will be rejected in the section of *Mīmāṃsā Jivarakṣā*.

धारावाहिकज्ञानेषु च पूर्वज्ञानविषयार्थत्वादुत्तरेषां प्रमितत्वं न स्यात् अथ उच्येत । इष्यते एव तेषामप्रमाणता इति तदयुक्तम् । लोके तेषु पूर्वस्मादविशिष्टत्वात् प्रमाणभावस्य ।

अथ भिन्नत्वादर्थक्षणानां सर्वेषामप्राप्तप्रापकत्वमस्तीति । तदसत् क्षणभेदस्य अपरामर्शात् न तदपेक्षा प्रमाणता । क्षणिकता च मीमांसाजीवरक्षायां प्रतिक्षिप्तैवेति कृतमति विस्तरेण । (प्र०पं० ११८)

(vi) The commentator brings out the implication of the closing remark **कृतमतिविस्तरेण** in an interesting way. The Buddhists talk of *avisamvāda* i.e., agreement of the fact with the cognition that has conveyed it. However, all perceptual cognitions are of *sthūla* form i.e., *vikalpa* form. The *sthūla* form is not considered as *vastu* i.e., real entity, by the Buddhists. Therefore, the perceptual cogniton of it is *apramāṇa*. Since, *pratyakṣa* is *apramāṇa, anumāna* based on this is also *apramāṇa*. Therefore, the whole exercise of defining *pramāṇa* and identifying *pramāṇa* is a futile exercise.

किञ्च यदाकारं विज्ञानं तेन अविसंवादः त्वया अविसंवादः इष्यते। स्थूलाकारं च सर्वं प्रत्यक्षज्ञानम्। न च स्थूलस्य वस्तुत्वं त्वया अङ्गीकृतम्। न च स्थूलाकारं मुक्त्वा अन्यत् प्रत्यक्षमस्ति। तस्मात् प्रत्यक्षस्यापि अप्रमाणत्वमेव। प्रत्यक्षमूलत्वादेव अनुमानादीनामपि अप्रमाणत्वमेवेति एतदभिप्रेत्य कृतमतिविस्तरेण इति उपेक्षितम्। (न्या०सि० ११८)

The Review of the Bhāṭṭamīmāmsaka's Definition of Pramāṇa

After reviewing the Buddhists' definition of *pramāṇa*, Śalikanātha takes up the Bhāṭṭa *mīmāmsaka's* definition of *pramāṇa* for examination. The Bhāṭṭas define *pramāṇa* as *dṛdham avisamvādi agṛhītārtha grāhakam pramāṇam* i.e., the cognition that is not doubtful, that does not disagree with the fact conveyed by it, and that comprehends an object that is not already comprehended is *pramāṇa*.

Avyāpti in Dhārāvāhikajñāna

This definition is not acceptable to the Prābhākaras. Firstly, it excludes *dhārāvāhikajñāna* i.e., a recurring series of cognitions, from the scope of *pramāṇa*. In *dhārāvāhikajñāna* the second occurrence of the cognition onwards, all cognitions in the series comprehend the same object. Therefore, these are not *agṛhītagrāhārthaka*. Hence the above definition of *pramāṇa* does not apply to it. Consequently, it is excluded from the scope of *pramāṇa*. The *Bhāṭṭas* offer the explanation that 'though the same object is comprehended in each cognition of the series, the moments of its occurrence differ. This time factor is an additional aspect of the object. Therefore, it is not *gṛhītagrāhi*.

This explanation is not convincing. The difference in the moments is so subtle that it is not comprehended.

धारावाहिकज्ञानानामुत्तरेषां पुरस्तात्तनप्रतीतिविषयतया प्रामाण्यापाकरणात् । न च कालभेदावसायितया प्रामाण्योपपत्तिः । सतोऽपि कालभेदस्य अति सौक्ष्म्यादनवग्रहात् । (प्र०पं० ११९)

The commentator explains the Bhāṭṭa's explanation based on the time factor as under:

पूर्वज्ञानगृहीतकालव्यतिरिक्तकालविशिष्टार्थग्रहणादुत्तरेषामपि प्रामाण्यं युक्तमेव । (न्या०सि० ११९)

The rejection of this claim is made on two grounds (i) there is no **कालभेद** (ii) even if there is **कालभेद** it is not perceived.

कालस्य एकत्वादेव भेदाभावात् । एकः कालः अनात्मत्वे सति विभुद्रव्यत्वात् आकाशवत् । परमार्थतः कालभेदो नास्ति ।

कौमारिलमतानुसारेण कालभेदमभ्युपेत्याह । सतोपीति । द्रव्येषु रूपवत् स्पर्शवत् महत्त्ववत् वा प्रत्यक्षम् । न च कालः तथाविधः अरूपत्वात् अस्पर्शत्वाच्च । तस्मात् कालभेदः न प्रत्यक्षः । (न्या०सि० ११९)

Since *agṛhītagrāhitva* cannot be managed for *dhārāvāhikajñāna* in this way the Bhāṭṭa' definition of *pramāṇa* fails in the case of *dhārāvāhikajñāna.*

The Prābhākaras who accept *pramāṇya* for *dhārāvāhikajñāna* explain its *agṛhītagrāhitva* differently. In each occurrence of the cognition in a series of the cognitions of the same object, there is contact between the sense and the object in each occurrence. Each cognition is produced by this contact without depending upon the impressions of the previous cognition. Therefore, there is no *gṛhītagrāhitva*. This explanation is offered in the context of distinguishing it from *smṛti*.

न चैवं धारावाहिक ज्ञानानां स्मृतित्वम् । इन्द्रियार्थसन्निकर्षजत्वात् पूर्ववत् । (प्र०पं० १२५)

The later occurrence of the cognition in the series is perfectly produced by the sense contact with the object as the earlier occurrence. Therefore, there is no *gṛhītagrāhitva.*

The Clause Dṛidham is Superfluous

The clause *dṛdham* is introduced in the definition by the Bhāṭṭas to exclude the doubt from the scope of *pramāṇa.* The Prābhākaras explain the instances of the doubt also as *yathārtha* and consider them as *pramāṇa.* Therefore, Śālikanātha says it is not necessary to include the clause *dṛdham* in the definition.

He quotes three varieties of doubts mentioned by the logicians and points out that these are *yathārthajñāna* i.e., valid cognitions.

The three varieties are

(i) The doubt arising out of seeing a common feature. For instance, on seeing a pole by observing its tallness and not observing its special feature the observer gets the doubt whether it is a pole or a person.

(ii) The doubt arising by the comprehension of more than one characteristic. For instance, the air is perceptible as it has the attribute of touch, the air is not perceptible as it is colourless.

(iii) The doubt arising out of the dispute among the philosophers. For instance, some philosophers say that *śabda* is eternal while others say that it is perishable. In all these instances, the cognition is not a single cognition involving a reference of two attributes with reference to one entity as contended by the logicians. There are two cognitions of memory type in each instance. In the first instance, the observer remembers both the pole and the person on observing a tall object. As he is not able to fix one of them with reference to the object observed by him he has a doubt. So far as his memories of the two objects are concerned his cognitions agree with the facts conveyed by the cognitions. Similarly, in the other two instances also he has two different comprehensions of perceptibility and non-perceptibility, eternity and perishability. He is not able to fix one of them with the entity concerned. Therefore, he has a doubt. However, his comprehensions agree with the facts conveyed and therefore, are *yathārtha*. **यौ हि धर्मौ संशय्येते तयोरेकमिदं ज्ञानं नोदीयते। किन्तु द्वे एते विज्ञाने विशेषणस्मरणे। तयोश्चविशेषणयोः एकस्यापि तस्मिन् धार्मिणि निश्चयो नास्तीति एकान्ततो व्यवहारं प्रतिपत्ता प्रवर्तयितुमशक्नुवन् संशेत इव भवतीति भवति संशयव्यवहारः। (प्र०पं० १२१)**

The Clause Avisamvādi is also Unnecessary

All cognitions agree with the facts conveyed by them. Therefore, there is no room for *visamvāda.* All cognitions are *artha avyabhichāri.* This is already established while discussing *akhyāti.*

अविसंवादिग्रहणमपि सर्वज्ञानानामर्थाव्यभिचारित्वादविशेषकम्। (प्र०पं० १२२)

In this respect the cognitions *'idam' 'rajatam'* are already examined. Here, it is further examined to show that *śukti* cannot be the object of this cognition. According to the Prābhākaras *rajata* is the object of the cognition *rajatam.* This cognition, of course, is of the nature of memory. This cognition agrees with the fact conveyed by it i.e., *rajata.* Therefore, there is no *visamvāda* i.e., *arthavyabhichāra.* However, the *anyathākhyātivādins* who take *idam rajatam* as a single cognition do not take *rajata* as its object but take *śukti* itself as the object.

ननु नेदं ज्ञानं रजतविषयं किन्तु शुक्तिकाविषयमेव। (प्र०पं० १२२)

This claim is examined and rejected. When *śukti* is stated as the object, whether it is the *śuktivyakti* that is claimed to be the object or the attribute *śuktitva* that is considered as the object? It cannot be *śuktivyakti*. The cognition is of the form of *rajata* that is to say the *ākāra* of the cognition is *rajatākāra* since, *rajata* is *bhāsamāna* in this cognition. If *śukti* is taken as the object i.e., *viṣaya*, then, *śukti* will be *ākārin*. This will result in the difference between *ākāra* and *ākārin*. The *ākāra* is *rajatākāra* while *ākārin* is *śukti*. This is not desirable. So far as *śuktitva* is concerned it cannot be the object of this cognition since it is not at all presented in it.

शुक्तिकाविषयमित्यस्य कोऽर्थः? यासौ शुक्तिकाव्यक्तिः तामेव विषयीकरोति उत शुक्तिकात्वमेव । न तावत् शुक्तिव्यक्तिरनेन विषयीकर्तुं शक्या । भिन्नात्वादाकारस्य आकारिणश्च । शुक्तिकात्वं पुनरभासमानवमेव विषय इति नोपपद्यते ।

The criterion for *viṣayatva* is *bhāsamānatva* but not *vyāvahārayogyatāpatti*. Even if the latter is taken as the criterion *śuktitva* does not fulfil this requirement to be considered as *viṣaya*. Without bhāsamānatva there cannot be any *vyāvahārayogyatāpatti*.

अथ उच्येत व्यवहारयोग्यतापत्तिर्विषयत्वमिति तथापि शुक्तिकात्वमविषय एव । न हि तद् व्यवहारयोग्यतामापाद्यते । अवभासमानतैव विषयत्वम् । अतः रजतत्वमेव विषयः । तच्च पुरोवर्तिनि न सम्भवतीति तद्विषयिणी स्मृतिरेव इयम् । (प्र०पं० १२३)

The term avabhāsamāna is explained as **अवभासमानत्वमपि न अर्थगतं किञ्चित् । किन्तु अर्थव्यवहारानुगुणायाः प्रतितेः पुरुषे वर्तमानत्वम् । (न्या०सि० १२३)**

Avabhāsamānatva is not an attribute of the object. It is the cognition obtained by the observer that can produce initiative to fetch that object or make a statement about that object.

In the instance of *pratibiṃba* i.e., the reflection of the face in the mirror what one cognizes is the face itself. The rays from the eye move towards the mirror, return to the face and cognise it. The cognition of the right and left sides in a reverse way is due to the returning of the rays. The place of the face and that of the mirror are not cognised as distinct. Therefore, the face is taken as present in the place of the mirror. The smallness of the face in the reflection is also the result of the obstruction and the limitedness of the rays from the eye. In this way *yāthārthya* of the cognition of a reflection is also explained.

प्रतिबिम्बज्ञानं तु मुखाद्यवभासं मुखादिविषयमेव। भास्वरे हि दर्पणादौ नयनरश्मिः निपतितः प्रतिहतः परावृत्तः मुखादिना संयुक्तः तदेव मुखादि गृह्णाति । ननु एवमपि सव्यदक्षिणविपर्यासः देशविशेषान्यत्वमहत्त्व-प्रतिभासश्च निर्निबन्धनः। अत्राभिधीयते। मुखादेर्देशो न गृह्यते दर्पणादीनां तु अग्रहणमिति मुखादयः तद्देशाः भवन्ति। अभिमुखेन मुखादिना नयनरश्मिः संयुक्त इति तथैव तदवगमात् सव्यदक्षिणविपर्यासो युक्त एव। अल्पत्वमहत्वे च दर्पणादेः रश्मिप्रतिघातहेतोः अल्पतया महत्तया च दोषभूतया मुखादिपरिमाणाग्रहात् दर्पणादिपरिमाणग्रहणाच्च मुखादिष्ववभासेते। तेन नास्ति व्यभिचारः ।

Prābhākara's Definition of Pramāṇa

After reviewing the definition of *pramāṇa* given by the *Bhāṭṭamīmāmsakas*, Śālikanātha states the definition given by the Prābhākaras as *anubhūtiḥ pramāṇam.* Direct cognition is *pramāṇa.* The expression *anubhūti* is explained as **स्वरूपपरिच्छित्तिः अनुभूतिः उच्यते (न्या०सि०** 124) A cognition that enables to directly comprehend the object concerned is *anubhūti.* Only such *anubhūti* is *pramāṇa.* This excludes *smṛti* from the scope of *pramāṇa.* In *smṛti* the object concerned is cognised through the impressions of its earlier cognition. Therefore, *smṛti* is distinct from *anubhūti* and is not *pramāṇa.*

अनुभूतिः प्रमाणम्, सा स्मृतेरन्या, स्मृतिः पुनः ।
पूर्वविज्ञानसंस्कारमात्रजं ज्ञानमुच्यते ।
न प्रमाणं स्मृतिः पूर्वप्रतिपत्तेरपेक्षणात् ॥ (प्र०पं० १२४)

The Prābhākaras consider *dhārāvāhikajñāna* as *pramāṇa*. It is produced by the contact between the sense and the object. It is not produced by the impressions of previous cognition. Therefore, it is distinct from *smṛti*. *Pratyabhijñāna* is also distinct form *smṛti* as it is produced not merely by the impressions of the previous cognitions but also by the contact between the sense and the object.

धारावाहिकज्ञानानां न स्मृतित्वम् । इन्द्रियार्थसंनिकर्षजत्वात् पूर्ववत् । प्रत्यभिज्ञानस्य न स्मृतित्वम् । इन्द्रियसचिवसंस्कारजत्वात् । (प्र०पं० १२५)

Smṛtipramoṣa i.e., mutilated memory in which the reference to the past time is not cognised is also on par with *smṛti*. The content retained in this mutilated memory is produced by the impressions of the previous cognitions. Therefore, *smṛtipramoṣa* is also *apramāṇa*.

स्मृतिप्रमोषः तर्हि प्रमाणम् । न । सोऽपि पूर्वप्रतीतिसव्यपेक्ष एव । तज्जन्यसंस्कारमात्राधीनजन्यत्वात् । (प्र०पं० १२६)

Dhārāvāhikajñāna cannot be treated on par with *smṛti*. In the series of cognitions that constitute *dhārāvāhikajñāna* each is independent of the other. The sense that is employed to produce the first cognition is repeatedly employed to produce subsequent cognitions. Therefore, these cognitions do not depend upon each other either for being produced or for comprehending. Therefore, these are distinct from *smṛti pramoṣa* and *smṛti*. Hence, these are *pramāṇa*.

धारावाहिकज्ञानेषु तर्हि उत्तरविज्ञानानि स्मृतिप्रमोषादविशिष्टानि कथं प्रमाणानि इत्यत्राह अन्योन्यनिरपेक्षास्तु धारावाहिकबुद्धयः ।

व्याप्रियमाणे हि पूर्वविज्ञानकारणकलापे उत्तरेषामपि उत्पत्तिरिति न उत्पत्तितः प्रतीतितो व धारावाहिकविज्ञानानि परस्परमतिशेरते इति युक्ता सर्वेषामपि प्रमाणता । (प्र०पं० १२६)

The Import of the Expressions Pramāṇa, Yathartha and Bhrama in Prābhākara School

The implications of the terms *pramāṇa* and *yathārtha* in the Prābhākara tradition have to be clearly understood. All cognitions that are *pramāṇa* are *yathārtha*. But all cognitions that are *yathārtha* are not necessarily *pramāṇa*. For instance, *smṛti* is *yathārtha* but not *pramāṇa*. For a cognition to be *pramāṇa*, its *yathārthatva* only is not sufficient. It should be also *agṛhītarthagrāhaka*. *smṛti* does not fulfil this requirement. Similarly, the implications of *pramā* and *bhrama* have also to be clearly understood. Most of the instances of *bhrama* consist of two cognitions. In some of them, one is *grahaṇa* and the other is *smaraṇa*. Out of these two, *grahaṇa* type of cognition is *pramāṇa* while *smaraṇa* type is *apramāṇa*. Both are *yathārtha*. In the instance wherein both are *grahana* both are *pramāṇa*. However, all these are *yathārtha*. What makes these the instances of *bhrama* is *vyavahāravisamvāda*. The *vyavahāra* undertaken on the basis of these cognitions fails. Therefore, these are called *bhrama*. It is already explained as to how *vyavahāra*, *pravṛtti* and *bādha* take place on the basis of these two cognitions. The *akhyāti* theory of error has found out suitable explanations for all these.

Śālikanātha explains the implications of *pramāṇa*, *apramāṇa*, and *bhrama* by analysing the cognition *idam rajatam* again here.

(i) The cognition *idam rajatam* is not a single cognition. This statement represents two cognitions viz., *grahaṇa* and *smaraṇa*. Here *idam* is *grahaṇa* i.e., *anubhava*. Therefore, it is *pramāṇa*. *rajatam* is *smaraṇa*. Therefore, it is *apramāṇa*. Since *rajatasmaraṇa* has led to the *vyavahāra* which should have been led by *rajata grahaṇa*, it has resulted in *vyavahāravisamvāda*. This is *bhrama*.

इदम रजतमिति न एकं विज्ञानम् । किन्तु द्वे एते विज्ञाने ग्रहणस्मरणरूपे । तत्र रजतमिति स्मरणम् । तस्य अनुभवरूपत्वाभावात् न प्रमाणयप्रसङ्गः । इदमिति विज्ञानमनुभवरूपं प्रमाणमिष्यते एव । भ्रान्तिरूपता रजतज्ञानस्य स्मरणरूपस्यैव ग्रहणव्यवहारप्रवर्तकतया व्यवहारे विसंवादकत्वात् । (प्र०पं० १२६)

Śālikanātha further points out that even those who consider *idam rajatam* as a single cognition and not valid, cannot brand *'idam'* part of its content as not valid, since it is not repudiated later. One and the same cognition may be *pramāṇa* and *apramāṇa* depending upon the aspects of the objects referred to.

येपि च एकमिदं ज्ञानं मिथ्याभूतमास्थिषत तेपि बाधकप्रत्ययाधीनं मिथ्यात्वमभ्युपगच्छन्तो न इदमंशस्य मिथ्याभावं वदितुमीशते । तत्र बाधकप्रत्ययाभावात् । बाधकप्रत्ययदशायामपि इदमंशस्य अनुवृत्तेः एकमपि विज्ञानम् अर्थावच्छेदमाश्रितभेदं प्रमाणमप्रमाणं च युक्तमेव । (प्र०पं० १२६)

(ii) In the instance of *pītaḥ śaṅkhaḥ* both the cognitions i.e., *pitaḥ* and *śaṅkhaḥ* are of *grahaṇa* type i.e., *anubhava* type. Therefore, both are *pramāṇa.* However, these two cognitions are on par with a single cognition of a yellow object. It is this which makes the observer to undertake the *vyavahāra.* This *vyavahāra* fails. Therefore, it is considered as *bhrama.*

को नाम पीतशङ्खज्ञानमप्रमाणमाह । प्रमाणमेव तत् यथार्थविषयत्वात् । विज्ञानद्वयं तु एतत् एकविज्ञानसाधारणरूपम् । तत्र एकविज्ञानसाधारणरूपावमर्शादेकविज्ञानसदृशव्यवहारप्रवर्तकतया व्यवहारदशायां विसंवादमावहत् प्रमाणमपि सत् भ्रान्तमित्युच्यते । (प्र०पं० १२७)

(iii) In the instance of the heat of the water the heat belongs to the fire particles interspersed with water particles. No heat is caused in the water particles. When the fire particles cease to be present the heat is not cognised. No heat is caused in the water particles by the process of *pāka,* i.e., *agnisamyoga* i.e., contact with fire. However, there is no *vyavahāra visamvāda* here. Therefore, it is not considered as *bhrama.*

यत्र तु व्यवहारविसंवादो नास्ति तत्र भ्रान्तिरपि न व्यपदिश्यते यथा उष्णजलज्ञाने । तत्रापि न जलगतमौष्ण्यमनुभूयते । किन्तु वह्न्यवयवगतमेव । जलगतस्य औष्ण्यस्य च वह्न्यसंयोगेन उत्पादनानभ्युपगमात् । गत्वराः हि तत्र तेजोवयवाः सञ्चारिताः तेषु अन्यत्र गतेषु अपरतेजोवयवसञ्चारणविच्छेदे युक्तैव औष्ण्यस्य निवृत्तिः । (प्र०पं० १२७)

The Number of Pramāṇas

The Prābhākaras accept five *pramāṇas* viz., *pratyakṣa* i.e., perception, *anumāṇa* i.e., inference, *śāstra* i.e., vedic injunction, *upamāna* i.e., anology, *arthāpatti* i.e., presumption. They do not accept *anupalabdhi* i.e., *abhāva*. The very category of *abhāva* is not accepted. Non-Vedic *śabda* is included under *anumāṇa*.

तत्र पञ्चविधं मानं प्रत्यक्षमनुमा तथा ।
शास्त्रं तथोपमानार्थापत्ती इति गुरोर्मतम् ॥

Pratyakṣa

Perception

Definition of Pratyakṣa

Now, Śālikanātha proceeds to review the definition of *pratyakṣa* given in different systems. Firstly he reviews the definition of *pratyakṣa* given in the *Gautama Sūtra*. This definition reads as follows:

इन्द्रियार्थसन्निकर्षोत्पन्नं ज्ञानं अव्यपदेश्यं अव्यभिचारि व्यवसायात्मकं प्रत्यक्षम् ।

The cognition that is produced by the contact between the sense and the object is *pratyakṣa* i.e., perception. This is the main clause of this definition. To explain the nature of the contact, six types of contacts are worked out in Nyāya system. These are **संयोगः, संयुक्तसमवायः, संयुक्तसमवेतसमवायः, समवायः, समवेतसमवायः, संयुक्तविशेषणता ।**

Though these are well-known, these are narrated by Śālikanātha as he differs in certain respects in working out these contacts.

The Six Relations that Establish Contact between the Sense and the Object

A clear statement of the six types of the contact accepted in Nyāya will help to present the differences between the Nyāya and the Prābhākara approach more clearly. The six types of contacts are as under:

(1) *samyoga* i.e., conjunction

(2) *samyukta samavāya* i.e., conjunction and inherence, that is to say, conjunction with the object and the inherence with the attributes through the object conjuncted.

(3) *samyukta samavēta samavāya* i.e., conjunction-inherence--inherence i.e., conjunction with the object—Inherence with the attributes of the object conjuncted, and Inherence again with the attributes of the attributes through the object and the attribute.

The first three substances are perceived by the sight and the touch by conjunction. The attributes of these such as colour, taste etc., are perceived by the contact of conjunction with the object and the inherence through the object conjuncted. The attributes of these attributes viz., *rūpatva, rasatva* etc., are perceived by the contact of conjunction with the object and inherence with the attributes through the object conjuncted, and again by the inherence with the attributes of the attributes.

It may be noted that in working out these three levels of relations the first one i.e., conjunction, is actually brought about at the time of the perception. The other two levels viz., Inherence, and Inherence-inherence are naturally existing relations between the object and the attributes, and the attributes of the attributes. Therefore, the narration of the other two levels as a part of the contact required for the perception is more a statement of the ontological and the technical position than a relation to be actually developed for the contact with the concerned attribute for the purpose of perception.

The next three viz., (4) *samavāya* (5) *samavēta samavāya* and (6) *samyukta-viśeṣaṇatā* are also of the nature of the natural positions but not the relations brought about for the purpose of establishing the contact for the perception.

Samavāya is conceived as a relation between the ear and *śabda* to perceive *śabda*. The ear is *ākāsa* i.e., space, present in the ear cavity. *Śabda* is the quality of *ākāśa*. Therefore, the two are already related with each other by *samavāya*. Therefore, it is not a new relation brought about for the purpose of perceiving the *śabda* by the ear. The same is the case with *samavēta-samavāya* which is a natural relation between the *śabda* and *śabdatva.* In the case of the last viz., *samyuktaviśeṣaṇàtā* which is conceived as a relation to perceive *abhāva* i.e., negation, the contact is between the place on which the negation of the jar etc. is perceived. This contact is achieved by the conjunction of the sense with the place. No conjunction is possible with the *abhāva* which is stated as perceived. Nor there is the relation of inherence between the negation of the *jār* and the place. Therefore, the negation is considered as an attribute of the place and a relation viz., *viśeṣaṇatā* is conceived. A relation called *svarūpasambandha* is also envisaged by some. In any case what is actually brought about for the purpose of the contact to perceive the negation is only the conjunction between the sense and the place on which the negation is stated to be perceived. The other part of the relation viz., *viśeṣaṇatā* or *svarūpa* is merely the narration of the position of a technical nature.

Criticism of the Scheme of Six Relations

This scheme of the relations for the contact between the senses and the objects for the purpose of perception is not accepted by the Prābhākaras in all details. They differ in many respects. The *abhāva* is not accepted as a separate category by the Prābhākaras. Therefore, there is no need to conceive a relation called *samyukta viśeṣaṇatā* to perceive *abhāva.* Similarly, *guṇatva, rūpatva* etc., are not acceptable as *jāti* to the Prābhākaras. Therefore, there is no need of the relation *samyukta samavēta-samavāya* to account for their perception. The relation *samavēta-samavāya* is also not necessary to perceive *śabdatva.* In this way three relations are eliminated. The Prābhākaras accept only the remaining three, viz., (i) *saṃyoga* (ii) *samyukta samavāya* and *samavāya.*

To point out that the *Nyāya* scheme has unnecessarily multiplied the relations, Śālikanātha says that you have to accept *samavāya-viśeṣaṇatā* also. Not only this, you may have to accept such *viśeṣaṇatā* with reference to all other relations resulting in twelve relations in all.

अन्यच्च समवायविशेषणता नाम सन्निकर्षान्तरं किमिति नेष्यते। यथा गोरश्वस्य च अन्योन्याभावप्रतीतये संयुक्तविशेषणता नाम सन्निकर्षान्तरमाश्रीयते तथा ककारखकारयोः अपि इतरेतराभावावगमाय समवेतविशेषणतालक्षणं सन्निकर्षान्तरमभ्युपगन्तुमुचितम्। (प्र०पं० १३४)

Regarding the perception of the number, similarity etc., present in the attributes, the substance that is the locus of the attributes itself is the locus for these, viz., number, similarity etc., of these attributes. It has to be managed as the Nyāya manages the statement *ekam rūpam rasāt pṛthak.* The *ekatva* and *pṛthaktva,* though talked of with reference to the *guṇas* these really belong to the substances to which these *guṇas* belong. Therefore, there is no need to accept the *samyukta samavēta samavāya* relation to account for the perception of number, similarity etc., of *guṇas.*

While discussing the contact between the senses and the object the question whether the eye actually reaches the object or comprehends it without actually reaching it, that is to say, whether it is *prāpyakāri* or *aprāpyakāri* is raised and certain difficulties are pointed out if it is taken as *prāpyakāri* through the rays of the eye.

The eye comprehends the object by actually reaching it. It is made of *tejas* as it comprehends the colour.

१. चक्षुः प्राप्यकारि बहिरिन्द्रियत्वात् त्वगिन्द्रियवत् । चक्षुः तैजसं रूपप्रतीतिहेतुत्वात् दीपवत् ।

Rays of the eye spread towards the object and get connected with it. These can spread widely and these can develop contact with the large objects also.

२. तस्य रश्मयः प्रसरन्तो द्रव्येण संयुज्यन्ते । ते च पृथ्वग्रा इति पृथून्यपि द्रव्याणि प्राप्नुवन्ति । (प्र०पं० १२९)

On this position, two objections are raised (i) If the rays from the eye actually reach the object, the gap between the eye and the object is eliminated. Therefore, there should not be the comprehension of the gap i.e., the distance between the eye and the object.

३. ननु एवं दूरे अर्थ इति सान्तरालग्रहणं न स्यात् । प्राप्तौ सत्यां दूरत्वासम्भवात् । प्राप्यकारित्वात् स्पर्शनवत् ।

Further, the contact of the eye-rays with the object depends upon the movement of the rays. The movement towards near and far objects has to be in a sequence, therefore, simultaneous comprehension of the near and far objects is not possible.

किञ्च संयोगस्य गतिनिबन्धनत्वात् गतिमतां च क्रमेण आसन्नदूरगमनात् समकालमासेदुषां दवीयसां च अर्थानां ग्रहणं नोपपद्यते (प्र०पं० १२९)

Śālikanātha quotes the answers given by others for these objections and finally gives his own answers.

Some answer the objection as follows. The eye-rays mingle with the light that has spread all over and comprehend the objects simultaneously. This explanation is rejected by others on the ground that this would have led to the comprehension of the objects closed by the wall etc., and also far off objects, since the outside light is spread in all these places.

४. समसमयवेदने तु केचित् परिहारमेवं वर्णयन्ति । सकलानर्थान् प्राप्य युगपदुपस्थितेन बाहयेन तेजसा सह एकीभूतास्ते चाक्षुषाः रश्मयः युगपद् ग्रहणहेतवः ।

तदन्ये दूषयन्ति एवं प्राप्तावभ्युपगम्यमानायां अतिदूर-व्यवहितानामपि अर्थानां ग्रहणं दुर्निवारम् । (प्र०पं० १३०)

Some answer this objection in a different way. The rays from the eye move so quickly that the difference in time in comprehending the objects that are close and that are away is not realized. This creates the impression that one is seeing these simultaneously. This explanation is rejected by others. They point out that it may not be possible to realize the difference in time, in the case of the comprehension of the objects that are close by as in the instance of piercing a needle into a bundle of a hundred petals of a lotus but it is difficult to accept that the difference of time will not be realized in perceiving the objects that are placed beyond thousands of miles like *dhruva* star which is far away.

५. अन्ये तु आहुः क्षेपीयस्तया तेषां रश्मीनां कालभेदानवग्रहात् यौगपद्याभिमानः इति ।

तदपरे नानुमन्यन्ते अतिसन्निकृष्टवस्तुनः गतिकालभेदः पद्मपत्रशत भेदवत् मा नाम अवसायि । अनेकयोजनसहस्रान्तरितेषु भूमिष्ठेषु अर्थेषु ध्रुवे च सदैव कालभेदानवसायो न बुद्धिमनुरञ्जयति ।

Another objection is that when the eye is separated by the glass etc., how can its rays reach the objects. This objection is brushed aside with the remark that these do not prevent the rays from the eye.

६. ननु प्राप्यकारिणि नायने तेजसि काचाभ्रपटलतिमिरान्तरितेषु कथमुपलब्धिः? तैः नयनरश्मेः अप्रतिघातात् ।

Those who state that the eye perceives the object without actually reaching it cannot avoid the contingency of its seeing the close and distant objects simultaneously, since, no actual contact is necessary. The eye also should have been able to see the distant objects and the minute objects as clearly as the nearby objects and large objects.

७. ये पुनः अप्राप्यकारि चक्षुः आहुः तेषां व्यवहितविप्रकृष्टार्थग्रहणं दुर्निवारम् । सन्निधान इव विप्रकर्षेऽपि स्फुटतरमणीयांसोऽपि अर्थाः गृह्येरन् ।

After quoting the explanations of others and noting the drawbacks in the same, Śālikanātha offers his own explanation.

The range of the vision, and the simultaneity or otherwise of the perceptions of the objects, cannot be fixed merely on the consideration of the empirical factors. Whatever an observer is destined to see that much only he will be able to see, though the rays from the eye mingle with the outside light that has spread all over. His seeing the distant objects on the ground and also *dhruva* star etc., simultaneously is also has to be explained in the same way. Here Śālikanātha has introduced the destiny as a factor which may not be acceptable to modern mind.

८. वयं तु वदामः । अदृष्टसापेक्षत्वाददोषः । नयनरश्मिभिरेकीभूतेपि बाह्ये तेजसि यावानेव तस्य भागोऽदृष्टवशेन उपलब्धिहेतुतया उपात्तः तावानेव उपलब्धये प्रभवति, न सर्वं, इति न सर्वोपलम्भो युगपत् भौमध्रौवादिसिद्धिश्च । (प्र०पं० १२०)

Such a contingency will not arise in the case of the eye-rays actually reaching the object. Due to the dimness of the light the distant objects are not clearly seen and the minute objects are also not seen.

९. प्राप्य ग्रहणे तु तेजोऽवयवानामप्रचुरतया युक्तमस्फुटदर्शनं दवीयसाम्, क्षोदिष्ठानामदर्शनम् ।

The other Requirements for the Perception

For the purpose of perception, in addition to the relations explained above, the *Nyāya* has also laid down certain other requirements viz., *mahatva* i.e., the dimension of at least of three atom-unit, *anekadravyatva*, constituted of more than one unit of the substance, and possessing colour. An atom i.e., *paramāṇu* is not perceived, because, it is only one. *Dvyaṇuka* is not perceived, because it has no *mahat* dimension. *Ākāśa* etc. are not perceived, because these have neither colour nor have constituent parts.

महत्त्वम्, अनेकद्रव्यत्वम्, रूपविशेषश्च सन्निकर्ष इव प्रत्यक्षहेतुः । अनेकद्रव्याभावात् परमाणोरदर्शनम् । अमहत्त्वात् द्व्यणुकस्य । आकाशदीनां तु अरूपत्वात् । (प्र०पं० १३१)

The Vāyu is Cognized by Pratyakṣa

The Prābhākaras object for *rūpavatva* alone being made a criterion in addition to the other two. They say that the air i.e. *vāyu* that has no colour is also perceived. Therefore, *sparśavatva* i.e., possessing touch must be taken as an alternate requirement for *rūpavatva.*

१०. रूपवत्त्वमिव स्पर्शवत्तापि प्रत्यक्षे हेतुरिति उपसंख्यानं कर्तव्यम् (प्र०पं० १३३)

In support of *pratyakṣatva* of *vāyu*, it is stated that the perception of *vāyu* could be established by *pratyabhijñāna.* One comprehends hot touch of *tejas,* cool touch of water and neither hot nor cool touch of the air when the air breezes. In all these cases it is not merely the touch that is perceived, but the substance that possesses the touch is also perceived.

११. न च वायोः अप्रत्यक्षता इष्यते एवेति वाच्यं। स्पर्शनेन तदुपलम्भात्। स्पर्शमात्रं तेन उपलभ्यते न वायुद्रव्यमितिचेत्। शीतोष्णानुष्ण-शीतस्पर्शेषु उपलभ्यमानेषु प्रत्यभिज्ञायमानत्वात् द्रव्यस्य। यदा हि तैजसमुष्णत्वं जलगतं च शीतत्वं वायोश्च अनुष्णाशीतत्वं स्पर्शनेन वायौ वाति सति प्रतीयते, तदा प्रत्यभिज्ञायते द्रव्यं तदेवेदमिति। तेन न स्पर्शमात्रप्रतीतिः। (प्र०पं० १३३)

Karma i.e., Motion is Cognized by the Inference

The Prābhākaras reject the *Nyāya* contention that the *karma* i.e., motion, is perceived by *samyukta samavēta* relation. According to the Prābhākaras the *karma* is inferred.

यच्च संयुक्तसमवेतत्वात् कर्मणां प्रत्यक्षत्वमुक्तम्, तदपि अयुक्तम्। तस्य संयोगविभागलक्षणफलानुमेयत्वात्। (प्र०पं० १३५)

The Review of the other Clauses of the Definition of Pratyakṣa

After examining the first clause viz., *indriyārthasannikarṣotpannam* of the definition of *pratyakṣa*, Śālikanātha reviews the other clauses. The clause *avyapadeśyam* is included to remove the impression that the statements 'This is colour' 'This is taste' etc., made after perceiving the colour, taste, etc., are the perceptions couched in words. This knowledge is verbal. *Avyapadeśya* means not stated in words. These statements are the results of the perception of the colour, taste etc., couched in words but not the very perceptions. This is made clear by including the clause *avyapadeśya* in the definition. Perception is the knowledge produced by the contact between the senses and the objects. The statement of this knowledge is not the perception.

Reviewing this clause, Śālikanātha states that there is no need to add this clause. The very first clause i.e., *indriyārtha sannikarṣajanya* excludes such statements from the scope of the perception. Further, if there is any overlapping of verbal nature and the nature of the perception in these statements, it should be examined while discussing *śabdapramāṇa*, but not here.

अव्यपदेश्यमिति किमर्थम्? इन्द्रियार्थसन्निकर्षोत्पन्नस्य शाब्दताशङ्कानिराकरणार्थम्। यदा 'रूपम्' रूपमिति जानाति, 'रसम्' रस इति जानाति तदा शब्दसञ्जल्पसम्भवात् शब्दताशङ्का कदाचित् स्यात्। तन्निराकरणाय अव्यपदेश्यमित्युक्तम्। नहीन्द्रियार्थसन्निकर्षजे ज्ञाने शब्दस्य व्यापृतिरस्ति यतः शाब्दता स्यादिति। तदिदमसङ्गतम्। लक्षणं हि प्रत्यक्षस्य वक्तव्यम्। येन रूपेण सजातीयविजातीयेभ्यो भेदः तदेव लक्षणम्। तत्र तावत् भेदः इन्द्रियार्थ सन्निकर्ष जन्यत्वेन सिद्धः। शब्दसञ्जल्पनानुविद्धस्य प्रत्यक्षस्य शाब्दत्वशङ्का शाब्दपरीक्षापर्वणि निराकर्तृमुचिता। (प्र०पं० १३६)

The next clause *avyabhicāri* is included in the definition to exclude the false knowledge. However, according to the Prābhākaras there is no false knowledge. All knowledge is true. Therefore, this clause is also not necessary. The clause *vyavasāyātmakam* is included in the definition to exclude the 'doubt'. However, according to the Prābhākaras the doubt consists of two memories and it is not perception at all. Further, the earlier clause viz., *avyabhicāri* excludes the doubt also. It may also be pointed out that *avyabhicārita* and *vyavasāyātmaka* are the criteria of a *pramāṇa* in general and therefore, are not required to be specially mentioned in the definition of *pratyakṣa.*

In view of the above clause by clause review, what remains as the definition of *pratyakṣa* is only this viz., *indriyārtha sannikarṣotpannam pratyakṣam.* This definition is inadequate since it does not cover the direct cognition of the inferential knowledge and the knower.

(i) **अव्यभिचारिपदं च विपर्ययनिराकरणाय यदुक्तम् तत् सर्वज्ञानानामव्यभिचारित्वादविशेषकमित्युक्तम् । व्यवसायात्मकतापि संशयनिवृत्त्यर्थं न वक्तव्या । स्थाणुर्वा पुरुषोवेति स्मृतिज्ञानद्वयम् । (प्र०पं० १३६)**

(ii) **अपि च अव्यभिचारिता व्यवसायात्मकता च न प्रत्यक्षलक्षणं किन्तु प्रमाणलक्षणम् । प्रत्यक्षस्य प्रातिस्विकं सजातीयविजातीयव्यावृत्तिसमर्थं लक्षणं वाच्यम् । इन्द्रियार्थसन्निकर्षोत्पन्नं प्रमातरिच प्रत्यक्षमिति । अस्मिन्नपि लक्षणे अनुमानादिप्रमितिः स्वात्मनि प्रत्यक्षा न स्यात् । अनिन्द्रियजत्वात् । (प्र०पं० १३७)**

The above review of the definition of *pratyakṣa* of *Nyāya* does not merely involve a difference in respect of the procedure of the contacts. It reveals the differences in some important metaphysical concepts and the epistemological concepts. We may note the following differences in this connection:

(i) The Prābhākaras do not accept any false knowledge while *Nyāyavaiśeṣikas* consider *samśaya* and *viparyaya* as false knowledge.

(ii) The Prābhākaras do not accept *guṇatva, rūpatva* etc., as *jāti.*

(iii) The Prābhākaras do not take colour only as one of the three requirements of perception. They take touch also as one of the grounds. This will enable them to say that *vāyu* is also perceived.

(iv) The Prābhākaras reduce the relations required for the contact in connection with the perception to three only.

Criticism of the Buddhists' Definition of Pratyakṣa

After reviewing the *Nyāya* definition of *pratyakṣa* Śālikanātha takes up Buddhists' definition of *pratyakṣa.* Their definition reads as *kalpanāpodham abhrāntam pratyakṣam.* This is given as stated by Dharmakīrti. This is an improvement over *Diṅnāga's* definition merely as *kalpanāpodham pratyakṣam. Kalpanā* means reference to the *jāti* etc., characteristics. *Apodha* is deviod of that. Thus *pratyakṣa* is that kind of knowledge wherein no reference is made to any characteristics or features. In other words, it is mere *svalakṣanajñāna* not involving any *vikalpas. Abhrānta* means that which does not go wrong in communicating the *vastu* that is capable of *arthakriyā.* This clause is added to avoid the claim of the perception for the vision of a colour patch on rubbing the half closed eye. The vision of a moving tree when one travels on a speedy vehicle is another stock example of *bhrānti.*

अपरे पुनः आहुः । कल्पनापोढं अभ्रान्तं प्रत्यक्षमिति । कल्पना जात्यादियोजना तया रहितं यद् विज्ञानं तत् प्रत्यक्षम् । तथाभूतमेव तैमिरिकादीनां केशोण्ड्रकादिज्ञानं प्रत्यक्षं मा प्रसांक्षीदिति उक्तम् अभ्रान्तमिति । (प्र०पं० १३८)

अभिलापसंसर्गयोग्यप्रतिभासप्रतीतिः कल्पना तया रहितम् । तिमिराशुभ्रमणनौयानसंक्षोभाद्यनाहितविभ्रमं ज्ञानं प्रत्यक्षम् । (न्या०सि० ११३-१६)

The Buddhists classify the perception into four groups viz., (i) *indriyajñāna* (ii) *svasamvedana* (iii) *mānasa*, and (iv) *yogijñāna*.

The comprehension of colour, taste etc., is *indriyajñāna*. Self revelation of all knowledge is *svasamvedana*. Sukha, duhkha etc., are also comprehended by *svasamvedana*. Comprehension of the continuity of *kṣaṇa* in a series is *mānasajñāna*. The knowledge of *dharma, adharma* etc., is *yogijñāna*.

तच्चतुर्विधम् इन्द्रियज्ञानम्, सर्वचित्तचैत्तानां स्वसंवेदनम्, मानसम्, योगिज्ञानं चेति । यदिन्द्रियाणामर्थेन सन्निकर्षादुपजायते तदिन्द्रियज्ञानं पञ्चसु रूपादिषु पञ्चविधम् । सर्वज्ञानानां संवेदनं विकल्पविरहात् प्रत्यक्षम् । सुखादयस्तु विज्ञानाभिन्नहेतुकतया न तस्मात् भिद्यन्ते इति तेपि स्वसंविदिता एव । मानसं तु इन्द्रियज्ञानेन स्वविज्ञेयक्षणान्तरक्षणसहकारिणा जन्यते । तस्य च इन्द्रियग्राह्यस्य अनन्तरक्षण एव ग्राह्यः । (प्र०पं० १३८-३९)

The term *citta* refers to *jñāna* while the term *caitta* refers to *sukha* etc., special forms of *jñāna*. चित्तशब्देन अर्थग्राहिज्ञानमुच्यते । चैत्ताः तद्विशेषावस्थाग्राहिणः सुखादयः । सर्वेच चित्तचैत्ताः स्फुटानुभवत्वात् स्वसंविदिता इति प्रत्यक्षभूताः । (न्या०सि० १३८)

Every *arthakṣana* is comprehended when it arises and leads to next *arthakṣaṇa*. Therefore, there is no room for the objection that how can there be the knowledge of *arthakṣaṇa* as it vanishes before it could produce the knowledge of it. It becomes the object of knowledge during the very moment when it arises. The perceptual knowledge is of the form of its object. There can be no formless knowledge. This accounts for the knowledge of colour, taste etc. The validity of the knowledge consists in its being of the form of the object. It is the form of the knowledge that demarcates the cognition of different objects.

१. ननु जन्यज्ञानसमये जनकस्य अर्थक्षणस्य अतीतत्वात् कथमर्थस्य प्रत्यक्षग्राह्यता । उच्यते । एतदेव ग्राह्यत्वमर्थानां यत् उत्पादकत्वं

स्वरूपार्पकत्वं चेति । अर्थाकारं प्रत्यक्षं ज्ञानम् । अन्यथा निराकारा संवित्तिः कथं रूपादिसंवित्तिव्यवस्थां लभते । अत एव अर्थसारूप्यं प्रमाणम् । तस्यैव व्यवस्था हेतुत्वात् । (प्र०पं० १३९)

An objection is raised that so called form of the knowledge is found in the knowledge itself. Therefore, how can this be considered as perception of the object. This objection is answered by pointing out that the object whose presence leads to certain form of the knowledge and in whose absence such form of the knowledge is absent is stated to be perceived in that knowledge.

२. ननु एकस्य आकारस्य प्रतीतेः तस्य च ज्ञान एव अवस्थिततत्वात् कथमर्थस्य प्रत्यक्षता । उच्यते । योऽर्थो ज्ञानस्य आकारम् आत्मनः अन्वयव्यतिरेकौ अनुकारयति स प्रत्यक्षः इति न दोषः । (प्र०पं० १३९)

Knowledge has to be accepted as having its own form. Otherwise it will be difficult to explain the form of dream cognitions as there are no external objects to give it a form. Further, the form of the object which is outside the knowledge cannot be revealed into the knowledge since the objects are *jada*. It is only the knowledge that is self revealing.

३. किञ्च ज्ञानस्य साकारता आश्रयणीया । अन्यथा स्वप्नादिषु असति बहिरर्थे कस्य आकारः प्रकाशेत । प्रकाशात्मकज्ञानात् बहिर्भूतस्य आकारः कथं प्रकाशेत । जडस्य प्रकाशायोगात् । (प्र०पं० १४०)

Further, the knowledge and the object are always found together. Therefore, the two are one. The impression that these are two is erroneous like that of a vision of two moons.

४. अपि च अर्थस्य वित्तेश्च सहोपालम्भः नियतः । भेदावभासस्तु द्विचन्द्रादिप्रतीतिवदनादिवासनानिबन्धन इति परिकल्पनीयम् । (प्र०पं० १४०)

Śālikanātha refutes the above contention of the Buddhists. He argues that it is not correct to reject *pratyakṣatva* of *savikalpakajñāna.* The knowledge obtained by the senses necessarily refers to *jāti, guṇa* etc., attributes of the objects. These attributes are as much perceived as the objects are perceived. It is not correct to say that since *jāti* etc., are not separately comprehended these are not separate entities at all. These are separate since these are observed as recurring in each *dravyavyakti.* Similarly, the concept of a substance is also valid since we have the perception such as a 'person with a stick in his hand' 'an animal with the horns' etc. These cognitions take place following the contact of the senses with the relevant objects.

५. एतदनुपपन्नम् । सविकल्पकविज्ञानानां जात्यादियोजनया उदीयमानानामिन्द्रियज्ञानानां प्रत्यक्षातापकरणात् । अथोच्येत जातिगुणयोः द्रव्यात् पृथक्त्वेन अग्रहणात् भेद एव नास्ति । तेन ताभ्यामविद्यमानाभ्यां योजयित्वा जायमानं ज्ञानं न प्रत्यक्षमिति । तदप्यसत् । एकैकद्रव्यव्यतिरेकेण द्रव्यान्तरे ग्रहणात् पृथक्त्वेन अग्रहणस्य असिद्धेः । एकस्मिन्नपि द्रव्ये द्रव्यान्तराद् व्यावर्तमाने अनुवर्तमानयोः जातिगुणयोः भेदावगमादिति जातिनिर्णये निर्णीतम् ।

द्रव्यकल्पना तु विषाणी दण्डीति च न प्रत्यक्षतामतिवर्तते । इन्द्रियव्यापारानुविधायित्वात् । (प्र०पं० १४१)

Identifying the objects by their names also is a result of the perception of these objects as this takes place following the contact of the senses with these objects. In this respect it may be noted that the name which is verbal is remembered. The denotation of that object or person by that name is also remembered. But so far as the very cognition of that object or person is concerned it is a perception.

६. नामकल्पनापि देवदत्तोऽयमिति प्रत्यक्षा । इन्द्रियव्यापारानुविधायित्वात् । तत्र यद्यपि वर्णात्मकं नाम स्मरणनिविष्टम्, तेन सह वाच्यवाचक-भावोऽपि स्मृतिसमारूढ एव तथापि संज्ञी प्रत्यक्षतां न मुञ्चति ।

नहि संज्ञा तत्सम्बन्धो वा तदानीमेकविज्ञाने विशेषणत्वेन प्रतिभातः । किन्तु एतौ स्मृतिसमारूढावेव । संज्ञिनि दृश्यमाने प्रागनुभूतौ तौ स्मृतिमारोहतः ।

संज्ञा हि स्मर्यमाणापि प्रत्यक्षत्वं न बाधते । संज्ञिना सा तटस्थाहि रूपाच्छादनक्षमा । (प्र०पं० १४२)

Further, if *jāti, guṇa* etc., attributes are not perceived, then, nothing can be perceived. No object can be perceived without the perception of its characteristics. All objects are comprehended as 'it is of this characteristic'. No perception without a reference to the characteristics is possible. Therefore, the clause *kalpanāpodham* in the definition of *pratyakṣa* does not serve any purpose.

७. अपि च जातिगुणयोः अप्रत्यक्षत्वमिच्छन्तो न किञ्चित् प्रत्यक्षमवकल्पते । नहि रूपशून्या काचित् रूपिबुद्धिरस्ति । जातिगुणौ च रूपिणां रूपे । सर्वा हि प्रतीतिः एवमित्युपजायते । प्रकारश्च एवंशब्दार्थः । जातिगुणौ च अर्थानां प्रकारभूतौ । अतस्ताभ्यां योजयन्त्येव सर्वा इन्द्रियप्रतीतिः समुत्पद्यते इति निर्विषयं कल्पनापोढपदम् । (प्र०पं० १४२)

The clause *abhrānta* is also not necessary. All cognitions present the gross objects and also involve the demarcation of the knower, known and the knowledge. Therefore, there is no *bhrama* i.e., error, involved in these cognitions. Therefore, the clause *abhrānta* is also not necessary in the definition of *pratyakṣa.*

अभ्रान्तपदमपि सर्वज्ञानानां स्थूलावभासित्वात् ग्राह्यग्राहकसंवित्ति भेदयोगित्वात् सौगतानां निर्विषयमेव ।

The so called *mānasa pratyakṣa* of the Buddhists' is nothing different from *dhārāvāhikajñāna.* It is not correct to argue that in the case of *mānasajñāna* the contact of the senses is withdrawn while in the *dhārāvāhikajñāna* the contacts of the senses continue. Even, in so called *mānasajñāna* of Buddhist the contact of the senses continues. It is also not correct to say that the *mānasajñāna* refers to the past objects, since, according to the Buddhists it is always the present object that is cognised. It is also not correct to say that the so called object is the very form of the knowledge, since, the object and the knowledge are presented clearly as distinct. It is also not correct to say the distinction felt is *bhrama* i.e., error, since, no valid reason could be deduced to prove it.

यच्च मानसं नाम प्रत्यक्षमुक्तम् । तत् धारावाहिकज्ञानात् न अतिरिक्तं मन्यामहे । स्यान्मतम् । अनुपरते इन्द्रियव्यापारे इन्द्रियज्ञानम्, उपरते तु अनन्तरक्षणप्रभवं मानसमिति । इन्द्रियव्यापारोपरमस्यापि अपरोक्षार्थप्रतीतिफलसम्भवे सति असिद्धत्वात् ।

यच्च अतीतार्थविषयं मानसमित्युक्तम् । तदयुक्तम् । वर्तमानस्य आकारस्य प्रतीतेः । न च अयमाकार । वित्तेरेव वेद्यतया वित्तेः पृथगवभासनात् । वित्तिर्हि वित्तितया वेद्यश्च आकारः वेद्यतया अवभाति इति न तयोः तदात्मकता उपपद्यते । (प्र०पं० १४३)

The contention that it is the correspondence with the *arthakṣaṇa* that is the ground of the demarcation of different objects is also not correct. Because, according to Buddhists, the form of the knowledge is of gross form while *arthakṣaṇa* is subtle. Considering an object as an object of a cognition on the two grounds that there is *sārūpya* i.e., similarity in the form of the two, and *tadutpattī* i.e., the cognition concerned has arisen from that object i.e., *arthakṣaṇa* is also not correct. In this case, the next *arthakṣaṇa*, which is similar to it will also have to be treated as its object.

१०. अर्थसारूप्यं यद् व्यवस्थाकारणमुक्तम् । तदसिद्धम् । स्थूलावभासित्वात् ज्ञानानाम् अणुरूपत्वाच्च अर्थस्य ।

किञ्च यदि तत्सारूप्यतदुत्पत्ती संवेद्यतालक्षणं ततः समानाकारस्य समनन्तरप्रत्ययस्यापि वेद्यता स्यात् । (प्र०पं० १४३)

So far as the dream cognition is concerned, it is already pointed out in *Nayavīthi* that it is the form of the outside object that is presented through the memory in the dream cognition.

११. स्वप्नादिषु अपि बाह्यस्यैव अर्थस्य आकारः स्मृतौ प्रथते इति नयवीथ्यां साधितम् ।

It is stated earlier by the Buddhists that a *jada* object cannot reveal itself in the knowledge. Therefore, what is revealed as a form of the knowledge is not different from the knowledge. This contention also cannot be accepted. A *jada* object can be revealed by the knowledge. It is only not self revealing, but not that it is not revealed at all.

१२. यच्च जडस्य प्रकाशायोगादित्यभेदकारणमुक्तम् । तदपि अयुक्तम् । जडस्यैव प्रकाशसम्बन्धो घटते । तदात्मकता नेष्यत एव ।

अपि च यदि ज्ञानातिरिक्तस्यैव प्रकाशः तदा ग्राह्यग्राहकवित्तीनां भेदस्य कथं प्रकाशः । तस्य अलीकस्य ज्ञानस्वरूपाननुप्रविष्टत्वात् ॥ (प्र०पं० १४४)

The contention that since the knowledge and the object are necessarily comprehended together these are not different, is also not correct. The two can be different but still could be comprehended together.

१३. यच्च सहोपलम्भनियमात् अभिन्नत्वमाकारस्य वित्तेश्चोक्तम् । तदपि असारम् । वित्तेर्भेदेऽपि अर्थस्य नियमोपपत्तेः । यैव हि संवित्तिः सैवहि तस्य अर्थस्य उपलब्धिरिति कथमसौ तां विना प्रकाशेत । (प्र०पं० १४४)

The tenet that all knowledge is self revealing is acceptable. However, the contention that the bliss is also self revealing is not acceptable. The contention that the knowledge of *yogins* is *pratyakṣa* is also not acceptable. It is a kind of special memory since it relates to the past events and the past objects.

Criticism of Vṛttikāra's Interpretation of the Pratyakṣa Sūtra of Jaimini

The *pratyakṣa-sūtra* of Jaimini reads as *satsamprayoge puruṣasya indriyāṇām buddhijanma tat pratyakṣam.* The cognition that arises by the contact of senses with the object is perception. *Vṛttikāra* explains this *sūtra* by interchanging the expressions, *sat* and *tat* in the *sūtra.* He reads it as *tat samprayoge puruṣasya, indriyāṇām buddhijanma sat pratyakṣam.* As a result of this interchange, the *sūtra* means 'the cognition that arises by the contact of senses with that very object which is conveyed by the cognition is a valid perception.

Śālikanātha says this *sūtra* is not intended to be a definition of *pratyakṣa.* The scope of *pratyakṣa* is not confined to the cognition that arises by the contact of the senses and the object only. The knower is cognized by perception, the knowledge obtained by the inference is also cognised by the perception. In fact all knowledge is cognised by the perception.

१४. यदपि केचित् मन्यन्ते तत्सम्प्रयोगे पुरुषस्य इन्द्रियाणां बुद्धिजन्म सत् प्रत्यक्षम् । तदपि अव्यापकत्वात् अलक्षणम् । स्वात्मनि, लिङ्गादिजापि प्रतीतिः, प्रत्यक्षत्वेन इष्यते, सकलप्रतीतीनां च स्वरूपं प्रति प्रत्यक्षता अभिमता इति । (प्र०पं० १४५)

If this *sūtra* does not give the definition, then, what is the purpose served by it?

Śālikanātha answers that by this *sūtra* the cognition of *śuktirajata* is excluded from the scope of *pratyakṣa.*

The cognition that conveys an object with which the senses are in contact is the perception. *Śuktirajatajñāna* does not fulfil this requirement. In the case of this cognition the eye is not in contact with the *rajata.* It is in contact with the *śukti* only. Therefore, this *rajatajñāna* is not *pratyakṣa.* It is only a memory. This *sūtra* is intended to convey this fact.

उच्यते । ये शुक्तिकारजतादिज्ञानादिष्वपि प्रत्यक्षतामाहुः ते निराक्रियन्ते ।

The Prābhākara's Definition of Pratyakṣa

The Prābhākaras define *pratyakṣa* as *sākṣat pratitiḥ pratyakṣam* i.e. direct cognition is perception.

The expression *sākṣāt* i.e., direct, could be understood in three ways viz., (i) *svarūpa pratīti* i.e., the cognition of the object concerned through its very nature but not by its capacity such as its being *vyāpaka* to something that is *vyāpya* to it. This happens in the case of inference. (ii) *avyavahita pratīti* i.e., the cognition that is not dependent upon any other intervening cognition of some other object other than what is to be cognised by the cognition concerned. (s*vaviṣaya-anantargata-arthāntarajñāna-anapekṣa svabhāvajñānam).* (iii) cognition that cognises an object that is present when that cognition arises.

(i) साक्षात्त्वमपि स्वेन रूपेण वस्तुभानम् । लिङ्गादिभिः न स्वेन रूपेण वस्तु प्रतीयते । किन्तु परसम्बन्धिरूपेण । (न्या०सि० १४६)

(ii) स्वोत्पत्तौ स्वविषयानन्तर्गतार्थान्तरज्ञानानपेक्षस्वभावज्ञानं साक्षात् ज्ञानम् । सविकल्पकज्ञानस्य निर्विकल्पकापेक्षत्वेपि स्वविषयानन्तर्गत-विषयत्वाभावात् नास्ति व्यभिचारः । (न्या०सि० १४६)

(iii) स्वकाले विद्यमानवस्तुसत्तावबोधस्वभावं साक्षात् ज्ञानम् । अनुमानादि तु व्याप्तिकालावच्छिन्नवस्तुसत्तावबोधस्वभवमिति न प्रत्यक्षम् । (न्या०सि० १४६)

Among these three explanations, the first one gives the correct picture of *sākṣāt* i.e., direct. As per this explanation the object is directly comprehended in the perception. This is certainly the position in *nirvikalpaka pratyakṣa.* However, in *savikalpaka* the object is cognised as having *jāti, nāma* etc. attributes. But still the fact that the object is cognised in its very nature stands. In any case to make the position more clear the second explanation is given.

Referring to something more than the very nature of the object concerned does not affect *sākṣāt* i.e., directness. But what affects is, dependence on some other cognition of an object which is outside the scope of the present object. The *jāti, nāma* etc., are part and parcel of the object concerned in *savikalpakajñāna.* These are not outside the object. Hence *sākṣāt* i.e., directness of the cognition is not affected in the case of *savikalpakajñāna* also.

The contention that the cognition of *sādṛśya* i.e., similarity, depends upon the comprehension of its *pratiyogin* i.e., counter entity and therefore, ceases to be *sākṣāt* as per this explanation is not correct. Because the cognition of similarity by itself does not require the comprehension of *pratiyogin.* But only when one desires to know with reference to what other object the similarity is comprehended, then, the comprehension of *pratiyogin* is necessary. Therefore, the cognition of the similarity as such does not depend upon any other cognition and its directness is not affected. iii) The third explanation is intended to exclude *anumāna* from the scope of this definition.

ननु साद्दश्यज्ञानस्य स्वविषयानन्तर्गतार्थान्तरभूतप्रतियोगिज्ञानापेक्षत्वात् न प्रत्यक्षत्वम् । मैवम् । तत्रापि भेदादिव्यवहार एव प्रतियोगिज्ञानापेक्षा न ग्रहणे इत्युक्तत्वात् । (न्या०सि० १४६)

Smṛti i.e., memory is already excluded from the scope of *pramāṇa.* Therefore, its claim to be *pratyakṣa* on the ground of *sākṣāt* need not be examined.

The Scope of Pratyakṣa is Wider than the Sense Perception

After giving the definition of the perception Śālikanātha explains its scope. According to the Prābhākaras the scope of the perception is not confined to the cognition generated by the senses only. So far as the perception of the external objects is concerned it is generated by the contact of the senses. But in the case of the knower and the knowledge the direct cognition of these is explained by the process of *triputīkaraṇa.* This is a very important epistemological concept formulated by the Prābhākaras. The *sākṣāt pratīti* i.e., direct cognition, covers the three areas viz., *meya* i.e., the objects known, *mātā* i.e., the knower, and *pramā* i.e., the knowledge.

Mēya i.e., the objects known consist of substance, universal, qualities etc. The perception of this is generated by the contact of the senses with the objects by the relations of *samyoga, samyukta-samavāya* and *samavāya* as already stated. The five external senses and the *manas* i.e., the internal sense, are well-known.

प्रत्यक्षस्य विषयमाह मेयमातृ प्रमासु सा । तत्र विभागमाह मेयेषु इन्द्रिययोगोत्त्था । द्रव्यजातिगुणेषु इन्द्रियसंयोगोत्था सा प्रत्यक्षा प्रतीतिः । (प्र०पं० १४७)

The Concept of the *Manas* and the other Senses

Śālikanātha gives detailed arguments to establish *manas* as a separate substance and as an *indriya.* The points made by him may be briefly stated as follows. The cognition of the objects is a product. *Ātman* itself is its *samvāyi kārana.* To produce the cognition for *ātman,* some *asamvāyi kāraṇa* is required. This is the *samyoga* of *manas.* For this purpose *manas* has to be accepted. This *manas* cannot be envisaged to be *vibhu* i.e. all pervasive. If both the *ātman* and *manas* are *vibhu,* then, there can be no conjunction between the two. This will defeat the very purpose of accepting *manas* as a separate substance to provide its conjunction as *asamvāyi kārana.* Therefore, *manas* is *aṇu* i.e., atomic. When one is destined to have the knowledge, the cognition of joy, sorrow etc., the motion sets in the *manas* and it gets conjuncted with the *ātman.* This leads to the knowledge. The first motion in the *manas* takes place by the destiny of the *ātman* concerned. It may be noted that for the motion in *aṇu,* and the upward movement of the fire and the circular movement of the air destiny is stated to be the cause.

अग्नेः ऊर्ध्वज्वलनं वायोः तिर्यक् गमनं अणूनां मनसश्च आद्यं कर्म अदृष्टकारितमिति । (प्र०पं० १५१)

Buddhists also accept *manas.* However, they consider it as sixth *vijñāna* arising after the five *vijñānas* caused by the senses. Since the *manas* is established as a separate category of substance there is no need to go by the Buddhists view of *manas.*

The nature of the sense organs is explained by the Prābhākaras in the same way as *Nyāyavaiśeṣika.* They also consider *śrotrendriya* as *ākāśa* while the Bhāṭṭas consider it as *diksvarūpa.* The nature of the contact between the senses and the object is already explained above. In this context the contact between the *ātman* and *manas*, the *manas* and *indriyās* also has to be taken into account.

'षण्णामनन्तरातीतं विज्ञानं यद्धि तन्मनः' इति बौद्धग्रन्थस्य अयमर्थः— रूपादिविज्ञानानि ऐन्द्रियकाणि पञ्च । तज्जन्यं मानसमेकमित्यर्थः । षण्णां मध्ये यदनन्तरातीतं विज्ञानं ऐन्द्रियकं तन्मनः इति । (न्या०सि० १५१)

The Number and the Nature of the Categories According to the Prābhākaras

While explaining the objects that are cognized by the perception Śālikanātha mentions the three categories viz., *dravya*, *jāti*, and *guṇa* and gives the details of four *dravyas* viz., *pṛthivi*, *ap*, *tejas* and *vāyu* that are perceived. He also mentions the *guṇās*, colour, taste etc., sixteen *guṇas* that are perceived as per the Prābhākaras definition of the perception.

The commentator gives full details of the categories and their sub-divisions. The nature and the number of these are discussed in different contexts in *Prakaraṇapañcikā* and the other Prābhākara works. It will be helpful if these are mentioned in a consolidated way in one place. Therefore, a detailed account of the categories and the sub-categories according to the Prābhākaras is given below.

(1) ***The Categories i.e., Padārthas***

Substance, qualities, motion, universal, inherence, potency, number and similarity are the eight categories:

Dravya, guṇa, karma, sāmānya, samavāya, śakti, samkhyā, sādṛśya iti aṣṭau padarthāḥ.

It may be noted that the *viśeṣa* and *abhāva* are dropped and *śakti, samkhyā* and *sādṛśya* are added compared to the categories of *Nyāyavaiśeṣikas.* The Bhāṭṭas on the other hand retain only the first four and *abhāva.* They enumerate only five categories.

(2) ***Dravya i.e., Substances***

Earth, water, fire (light), air, space, time, quarters, *ātman* and the manas are the nine substances.

Pṛthivi, ap, tejas, vāyu, ākāśa, kāla, dik, ātma, manaḥ iti nava dravyāṇi.

This list of substances of the Prābhākaras is the same as that of *Nyāyavaiśeṣika.* However, the Bhāṭṭas add two more viz., *tamas,* i.e. darkness and *śabda.*

(3) ***Guṇas i.e., Qualities***

Rūpa, rasa etc., twenty-two qualities are common to *the Nyāyavaiśeṣikas* and *the Prābhākaras. Samkhyā* i.e., number, *laghutva* i.e., lightness, are dropped from *the Nyāyavaiśeṣika* list of twenty-four qualities.

The Bhāṭṭas drop the three viz., *laghutva, śabda* and *dharma,* and add the three viz., *dhvani, prākaṭya* and *śakti.*

(4) ***Karma i.e., Motion, Activity***

This category represents both the ordinary motion and also the ritual activity enjoined by the scripture.

(5) *Sāmanya or Jāti i.e., Universal*

(6) *Samavāya i.e., Inherence*

The nature and the function of these two categories are already discussed in '*Jātinirṇaya*' chapter.

(7) *Śakti i.e., Potency or Capacity*

This is present in all positive entities. It has to be inferred by its functions.

(8) *Samkhyā i.e., Number*

This is considered as a separate category by the Prābhākaras. It cannot be considered as a substance, since it is found in the qualities also. It cannot be considered as a quality as it is found in many.

(9) Sādriśya *i.e., Similarity*

This is a distinct category, distinct from the substance, qualities etc.

Coming back to the discussion of *pratyakṣa,* Śālikanātha, informs that it is not necessary that the substance and the attributes be perceived simultaneously. Sometimes the substance is perceived and sometimes the attributes only are perceived.

The Nirvikalpaka and Savikalpaka Perceptions

The perception of the substances etc., is of two types viz., *savikalpaka* and *nirvikalpaka.* In the *savikalpaka* perception the object is perceived as qualified by the *jāti, guṇa* etc. In the *nirvikalpaka* perception the substance, the attributes i.e. *jāti, guṇa* etc., are presented as they are. This does not mean that in the *nirvikalpaka* mere *svalakṣaṇa* is presented as stated by the Buddhists. This is because, the *jāti, guṇa* etc., are also presented in the *nirvikalpaka.*

(i) **द्विविधा च इयं द्रव्यादिप्रतीतिः 'सविकल्पा अविकल्पा च प्रत्यक्षा बुद्धिरिष्यते' इति । विभजति 'आद्या विशिष्टविषया**

स्वरूपविषयेतरा' प्रथमं हि स्वरूपमात्रग्रहणं द्रव्यजातिगुणेषु उपपद्यते । (प्र०पं० १६१)

(ii) निर्विकल्पकस्य स्वलक्षणमात्रं न विषयः । जात्याद्याकारावभासस्य स्पष्टत्वात् । नापि सामान्यमात्रं विषयः भेदग्रहणस्य प्रतीतिसिद्धत्वात् । (प्र०पं० १६१)

(iii) प्रथममक्षसन्निपातोत्पन्नमापातजं वस्तुमात्रग्राहकं विकल्पावस्थात्प्रागवस्थं निर्विकल्पकम् ।

(iv) तत्र विकल्पो नाम भेदको धर्मः जात्यादिः तैः सह वर्तते इति सविकल्पकम् । तच्च जात्यादिभिः व्यावृत्तं शब्दोल्लेखि पञ्चधा । यथा घटोऽयम्, शुकलोऽयम् । गच्छति गौतमः, देवदत्तोऽयं दण्डीति विशिष्टप्रत्ययः । (न्या०सि० १६१)

(v) सविकल्पकं हि अनुवृत्तिव्यावृत्ति विशिष्टार्थविषयम्, शब्दसञ्जल्पनानुविद्धं च जायते । तत्र न इन्द्रियं केवलं समर्थमिति संस्कारसहायस्य एकत्र व्यापारो वक्तव्यः । सति चैवं संस्कारोद्बोधसिद्ध्यर्थं पूर्वं पदार्थग्रहणमवश्यं आश्रयणीयम् । तेन विशिष्टप्रत्ययान्यथानुपपत्त्या सविकल्पात् पूर्वं स्वरूपग्राहि ज्ञानमवश्यमाश्रयणीयम् । (न्या०सि० १६२)

Both the general nature and the particular nature of the object are presented in the *nirvikalpaka*, but these general and the particular aspects are not so realized until the other objects in which this general aspect is observed or from which the special aspect is contrasted. In the *savikalpaka pratyakṣa* these aspects are realized. In both *pratyakṣa*, the presentation of the substance and the attributes is found. However, in *nirvikalpaka* these are isolated while in *savikalpaka* these are organized.

In the *nirvikalpaka* perception though both the substance and the attributes are grasped and the general and particular aspects of these objects are perceived, the difference between the two is not realized. This will be possible only when the continuity of the general aspect in the other objects and the absence of the particular aspect in the other objects is realized. This happens only at the *savikalpaka* stage.

तस्मात् सामान्यविशेषौ द्वे वस्तुनी प्रतिद्यमानं प्रत्यक्षं प्रथममुत्पद्यते । किन्तु वस्त्वन्तरानुसन्धानशून्यतया सामान्यविशेषतया न प्रतीयते । अनुगतं हि सामान्यमुच्यते व्यावृत्तिश्च विशेषः । न च वस्त्वन्तरानुसन्धानमन्तरेण अनुगतिव्यावृत्ती प्रत्येतुं शक्येते । अप्रतिपद्यमानोऽपि च ते, शक्नोत्येव स्वरूपं तयोः प्रतिपत्तुमिति निर्विकल्पकमसामान्यविशेषविषयम् । (प्र०पं० १६३-१६४)

Now a question may be raised here. The perception is to be caused by the sense contact. The sense is in contact with only that object which is actually perceived. It is not in contact with the other objects that belong to the same class or any other. Therefore, it is difficult to agree with the contention that the general and special aspects of the object are comprehended involving a reference to other objects in the *savikalpaka* stage, since the sense is not in contact with the other objects.

This is solved by pointing out that the *ātman* who is to comprehend the object presented in his perception does comprehend the general and particular aspects with the aid of the *samskāra* i.e., impressions, of the cognitions of the other objects cognised earlier.

सविकल्पकं तु तत्पृष्ठाभावि त एव वस्तुनी सामान्यविशेषात्मना प्रतिपद्यते । न नु वस्त्वन्तरानुसन्धाने नेन्द्रियं समर्थम् । इन्द्रियसामर्थ्यसमुत्त्थं च प्रत्यक्षमिति कथं सामान्यविशेषात्मकं प्रत्यक्षस्य विषयः । उच्यतेभवेदेतदेवं यदि इन्द्रियाण्येव चेतनानि स्युः, ज्ञानानि वा । आत्मा तु एकः सर्वानुभवितव्यानुभविता संस्कारवशेन वस्त्वन्तरमनुसन्दधदिन्द्रियेण सामान्यविशेषात्मना वस्तु शक्नोत्येव प्रत्येतुम् । (प्र०पं० १६५)

In the *nirvikalpaka*, though the attributes are comprehended these are not comprehended as qualifying the object. At that stage the difference between the substance and the attributes is not grasped. The difference between the two could be grasped only through the *anvaya* and *vyatirēka*. This *anvaya* and *vaytirēka* verification does not take place at the *nirvikalpaka* stage. Hence the difference between the substance and the attributes is not grasped though both of these are comprehended. Consequently, these two are not organized as the qualifications and the qualified. Therefore, there is no *viśiṣṭapratyaya* at the *nirvikalpaka* stage. In *savikalpaka* as already stated these are organized as *viśeṣaṇa* and *viśeṣya* and there is *viśiṣṭapratyaya.*

(2)(i) निर्विकल्पकेन सामान्यविशेषौ द्वे वस्तुनी प्रतिपाद्यमानेनापि तयोः भेदो गृहीतुं न शक्यते । नहि वस्तुभेदमात्रेण भेदबुद्धिः किन्तु धर्मान्तरग्रहोपि भेदबुद्धौ सहकारी । तेन अनुगतिव्यावृत्ती धर्मान्तरभूते अगृह्णतः सत्यपि सामान्यविशेषयोः भेदे भेदबुद्धिर्नासीत् । उत्तरकाले च वस्त्वन्तरानुसन्धानेन ते प्रतिपद्य भिन्नत्वमवसीयते । भेदे सति विशेषणविशेष्यभावावसाय इति न निर्विकल्पकदशायां विशिष्टबुद्धिः । सविकल्पकदशायां तु विशेषणविशेष्यभावमवगच्छति ।

(ii) गुणप्रतीतावपि निर्विकल्पकं न विशिष्टतया द्रव्यमवच्छिनत्ति । द्रव्यगुणयोः भेदानवगमात् । अन्वयव्यतिरेकाभ्यां हि गुणजात्योः द्रव्यात् भेदः अवगम्यते । न च निर्विकल्पके अन्वयव्यतिरेकाद्यनुसन्धा-नमस्तीति तेन न भेदग्रहः । अगृहीतभेदं च तत् न विशिष्टतां गृहीतुमीष्टे इति सविकल्पक एव विशिष्टप्रत्ययः । (प्र० पं० १६५)

The Nature of Viśiṣṭapratyaya

In this connection some special points of the Prābhākaras have to be noted. These are: (i) To have *viśiṣṭapratyaya*, it is not necessary that the *viśēṣaṇa* also must be presented by the perception only. This can be supplied by the memory also. For instance, the name is supplied by the memory and *viśiṣṭapratyaya* of the person or the object by qualifying with the name is achieved as a perceptual knowledge. Similarly, in the case of *karma* i.e., motion also, it is inferred and utilized to qualify the object perceived leading to *karma-viśiṣṭavastu pratyaya.*

(1)(i) नामकल्पनायामपि शब्दवाच्यतायाः स्मर्यमाणायाः एव विशेषणत्वम् । कर्मकल्पनाप्येवमेव व्याख्येया । प्रत्ययान्तरोपस्थापितेपि विशेषणे विशिष्टप्रत्ययो भवत्येव । (प्र०पं० १६६)

(ii) ननु भिन्नविषययोः संस्कारेन्द्रिययोः नैकज्ञानजनकत्वं दृष्टम् । सत्यम् । संज्ञि प्रत्यक्षं संज्ञा च स्मर्यते तयोः भेदाग्रहात् विशिष्टज्ञानकरत्वात् ज्ञानैक्यमपि युज्यते एव । तदुक्तम्-

संज्ञा हि स्मर्यमाणापि प्रत्यक्षत्वं न बाधते ।
संज्ञिनः प्रागवस्थानात् न रूपाच्छदनक्षमा ।।

(iii) प्रत्ययान्तरेण विजातीयेन उपस्थापितस्यापि विशेणत्वाविरोधात् बुद्धिस्थत्वमेव विशेषणप्रयोजकम् । न एकजातीयप्रत्ययो-पस्थापितत्वमपि इति अनुमेये कर्मणि 'गच्छति अयम्' इति विशिष्टप्रत्ययो भवत्येव । (न्या०सि० १६६)

(iv) ननु एकज्ञाने भासमानः अर्थः ज्ञानान्तरार्थे कथं विशेषणं भवतीत्यत्राह आत्मनः प्रमातृत्वात् । (न्या०सि० १६६)

(2) This way of obtaining the attributes by some other *pramāṇa* and making it a part of the content of *savikalpaka pratyakṣa* does not affect the *prāmāṇya* of this knowledge. It should be treated on par with the *dhārāvāhikajñāna.* The organization of the *viśeṣaṇa* and *viśeṣya* is an additional factor in *savikalpaka.* Therefore, it is not *gṛhītagrāhi.* Moreover it is directly produced

by the sense. Therefore, it is not on par with mere *smṛti*. Therefore, its *prāmāṇya* is not affected.

(i) निर्विकल्पकपृष्ठभाविनश्च सविकल्पकस्य गृहीतग्राहित्वेपि धारावाहिकन्यायेन प्रमाणत्वं वेदितव्यम् ।

(ii) विशेष्यविशेषणभावातिरेकेण अगृहीतग्राहकतापि सम्भवत्येव सविकल्पकस्य । (प्र०पं० १६६)

(iii) न च इदम् अनिन्द्रियजं ज्ञानम् । इन्द्रियाधीनप्रवृत्तित्वात् । अपरोक्षावभासोहि अयं सविकल्पकप्रत्ययः । न तादृशो इन्द्रियव्यापारमन्तरेण अस्ति । (प्र०पं० १६७)

The Formula of Tripuṭikaraṇa

The most important contribution of the Prābhākaras to the concept of *pratyakṣa* is extending its scope beyond the sense perception. So far as the external objects are concerned the perception is through the senses. However, there are two other items that are directly cognised. These are the knower and the knowledge.

सर्वविज्ञानहेतूत्था मितौ मातरि च प्रमा ।
साक्षात्कर्तृत्वसामान्यात् प्रत्यक्षत्वेन सम्मता ।

सम्प्रति मितौ मातरि च प्रत्यक्षं व्याख्यातुमाह ।

The knowledge produced by senses, inference, and *samskāra* etc., means is of the nature of perception in respect the knowledge itself.

इन्द्रियसम्प्रयोगपूर्वानुभवजनितसंस्कारव्याप्तिलिङ्गमित्येवमादि सर्वविज्ञानहेतूत्था जायामाना संवित्तिः साक्षात्कर्तृत्वसामान्यात् प्रत्यक्षत्वेन सम्मता । (न्या०सि० १६७)

In all cognitions in which some or the other object is presented, the knower is also presented. The objects are not comprehended without the comprehension of the knower also along with them. It is clear from the statement 'I know this.' Otherwise, the statement would have been 'He knows this'. In case the knower is not comprehended in the cognition, there would not have been any difference between one's own knowledge and someone else's knowledge.

या काचित् ग्रहणस्मरणरूपा अर्थप्रतीतिः, तत्र साक्षादात्मा भाति । न हि अर्थावभासिनि आत्मनि अनवभासमाने विषया भासन्ते । सर्वा हि प्रतीतिः एवमुपजायते 'अहमिदं जानामी' ति न पुनः 'जानाति' इति एवं काचिद् बुद्धिरस्ति । तदा च स्वपरसंवेद्ययोः अनतिशयप्रसङ्गात् । (प्र०पं० १६८)

It cannot be argued that the reference to 'I' in the statement 'I know' is brought about by another cognition. In the cognition represented by the statement 'I know this' 'I' and 'this' are comprehended simultaneously. Therefore, 'I' is not provided in this cognition by another cognition.

(i) न च प्रत्ययान्तरविषयत्वेन नियमः सम्भवति । एकप्रतीतिविषयत्वे युक्त एव सहोपलम्भनियमः । (प्र०पं० १६९)

(ii) ननु यथा चाक्षुषं रूपम्, श्रावणः शब्दः, इत्यत्र चक्षुःश्रौत्रयोः अप्रत्यक्षत्वेऽपि ज्ञानान्तराधीन एव तद्गोचरव्यवहारः तथा अत्र अहमादिशब्दप्रयोगो ज्ञानान्तराधीनः एव भविष्यति इत्यत्राह— न च प्रत्ययान्तरेति । प्रत्ययान्तरनिबन्धनत्वे प्रमेये सहोपलम्भनियमो नोपपद्यते । (न्या०सि० १६९)

The Knower cannot also be Considered as Mānasa Pratyakṣavedya

ननु आत्मा मानसप्रत्यक्षवेद्यः सुखसम्बन्धाश्रयत्वात् सुखवत् इति चेत् । मैवम् । मानसत्वे सुखादिवत् अविभुत्वं ग्राह्यत्वं च स्यात् । (न्या०सि० १६९)

Śālikanātha concludes this discussion with the remark that तस्मात् सर्वैरेव ज्ञानहेतुभिः आत्मनि साक्षात्कारवती धीः उत्पद्यते ।

The Knower is Directly Cognized in all Cognitions

An important point to be noted in this context is that it is only the knower who is perceived directly in all cognitions. In the case of the objects, these are cognised by the other means also such as smṛti and inference. The other *pramāṇas* are meant for the cognition of objects only when these are not cognised by the sense contact. So far as the knower is concerned, he is always directly perceived. The same is the case with the knowledge. The knowledge is self-revealing.

ननु एवं तर्हि सर्वं प्रत्यक्षं प्रसक्तम्? यदि मात्रभिप्रायम् । इष्टमेव । प्रमेयाभिप्रायमितिचेत् । सर्वत्र प्रमेयस्य अपरोक्षत्वनियमाभावात् । स्मृतिषु अनुमानादिषु च न प्रमेयमपरोक्षम् । तेन प्रमेयापेक्षयैव प्रमाणान्तरत्वव्यपदेशः इति मन्तव्यम् । सर्वाश्च प्रतीतयः स्वयं प्रत्यक्षाः प्रतीयन्ते । तेन तासां स्वात्मनि युक्तमेव प्रत्यक्षत्वम् । (प्र०पं० १७०)

The knowledge is self-revealing. It does not require another knowledge to reveal itself. It is well-known that according to *Nyāyavaiśeṣikas* the knowledge of the objects is known as *vyavasāya* and the knowledge of this knowledge is called *anuyavasāya*. The Prābhākaras do not agree with this arrangement. The knowledge does not require another knowledge. It is *svaprakāśa*. Every knowledge conveys three entities viz., the knower, the object known and the knowledge. While the knower and the object known are conveyed by the knowledge, the knowledge conveys itself. However, no knowledge arises without a reference to the knower and the object known. These three are always conveyed together. This procedure is designated as *tripuṭīkaraṇa*.

मेय-मातृप्रमेयानां विशेषः कः? उच्यते मेये मातरिच व्यतिरिक्ता प्रतीतिः साक्षात्कारवती, मितौ च अव्यतिरिक्ता । 'इदमहं गृह्णामि'

इति वा 'इदमहं स्मरामि' इति वा त्रितयमेव अवभासते । मेयमात्रावभासरूपा संविदेका । न च सा नावभाति तदनवभाने सर्वानवभासप्रसङ्गात् ।

The objects and the knower are not of the nature of self-revealing. Therefore, these require the knowledge to reveal them. During the deep sleep, these are not known. If these were self-revealing, then, these would have been known during the deep sleep. Therefore, these are not of self-revealing nature. So far as the knowledge is concerned it has no existence at all without its revelation. Therefore, it is self-revealing. It also reveals the objects and the knower.

किञ्च अप्रकाशस्वभावानि मेयानि माता च प्रकाशमपेक्षन्ताम् । प्रकाशस्तु प्रकाशात्मकत्वात् न अन्यमपेक्षते । जाग्रतो हि मेयानि माता च प्रकाशन्ते । सुषुप्तस्य तदा न तत् द्वयमपि प्रकाशते । न च तदानीं तद्द्वयमपि नास्त्येव, प्रबोधे प्रत्यभिज्ञानात् । तत्र प्रकाशात्मकत्वे तु सुषुप्तिदशायामपि तद्द्वयं प्रकाशेत् । तस्मादप्रकाशात्मकं तद्द्वयमङ्गीक्रियते । प्रकाशस्य तु अप्रकाशमानस्य सत्तैव नाभ्युपेयते । तस्मात् स्वयंप्रकाशसमय एव मातृमेयप्रकाशः । (प्र०पं० १७३)

In this procedure the knowledge conveys itself by *tādātmya*, the knower, is *āśraya* and the object as *viṣaya*. This fact viz., the knower, is conveyed as *āśraya* but not as *viṣaya* has to be especially noted, because, it refutes the Bhāṭṭa view that the knower is also *viṣaya* i.e., the object of the knowledge.

तच्च ज्ञानं आश्रयविधया आत्मानम्, विषयविधया घटादिकं प्रकाशयति, तादात्म्येन स्वस्मिन् व्यवहारं प्रयोजयति । (वि०टि० १६७)

In Indian Philosophy, *svaprakāśatva* of the knowledge is accepted by *Vijñānavādins* and the *Advaitins* also. But the *svaprakāśatva* concept of the Prābhākaras is altogether different from that of *Vijñānavādins* and *Advaita*. According to the *Vijñānavādins* there are no external objects. The knowledge itself is projected as the object. It is this projection that is termed as *svaprakāśatva* in *Vijñānavāda*.

In *Advaita* two types of the knowledge viz., *svarūpajñāna* and *vṛttijñāna* are accepted. It is only *svarūpajñāna* of *Brahman* that is stated to be *svaprakāśa*. According to *Advaita* all empirical knowledge is *vṛttijñāna*. This is of the nature of the modification of *antaḥkaraṇa* and hence *jada*. Therefore, it is not *svaprakāśa*.

The Prābhākaras consider the very empirical knowledge as *svaprakāśa*. It is like a lamp that reveals itself along with the revealing of the objects. No lamp requires another lamp.

The *tripuṭīkaraṇa* concept has two important features viz., (i) the knowledge reveals itself, the knower, the known, together. There is no knowledge without a reference to the knower, and known. (ii) The knowledge is of the nature of self-revealing.

The Purpose Served by the Tripuṭīkaraṇa Formula

This formula is evolved to rule out the Buddhists' contention that there are no objects outside the knowledge. According to this formula, if there were no objects, then, the knowledge itself would not have arisen. It is not the knowledge that is to be utilized to ascertain the existence of the object, but it is the object that gives rise to the knowledge. One cannot think of the existence of the knowledge without the existence of the objects to be known and the knower. No knowledge can take its shape without these two.

Once it takes a shape nothing more is required to reveal it. According to this formula of *tripuṭīkaraṇa* the ascertainment of the existence of the object and the knowledge does not depend upon either knowledge alone or the object alone, but the two help to ascertain the presence of both jointly. This will prevent the Buddhists' attempt of ruling out of the objects outside the knowledge.

To achieve the same objective, the Bhāṭṭas have thought of *prākatya.* According to the *prākatya* formula it is the knowledge that has to be inferred by the fact of the revelation of the objects. The objects are invested with a special quality called *prākatya* when the knowledge arises. This reveals the object. It is by this revelation of the objects that the presence of the knowledge has to be ascertained. Thus the ascertainment of the knowledge is made dependent upon the objects, but not the ascertainment of the objects dependent upon the knowledge.

The objective of both the *tripuṭīkaraṇa* formula and the *prākatyānumēyatva* formula is the same. The objective is, not to make the ascertinment of the objects exclusively dependent upon the knowledge. Such a dependence will give scope for the total elimination of outside objects. According to the *prākatyānumeya* formula the ascertainment of the knowledge is made dependent upon the objects. According to the *tripuṭīkaraṇa* formula the ascertainment of the object is made an integral part of the ascertainment of the knowledge. In both the formulas the exclusive dependence of the ascertainment of the object on the knowledge is avoided.

Criticism of the Buddhists' Concept of Svaprakāśatva

In the context of explaining the *svaprakāśatva* concept of the Prābhākaras, Śālikanātha reviews the *Sautrāntika* Buddhists' concept of *svaprakāśatva* which claims the necessity of the acceptance of a form for the knowledge. Their line of argument is as follows:

If the knowledge has no form, then, one cannot talk of as: 'this is blue', 'this is yellow'. If the knowledge has the form, then, such bifurcation is possible.

तत्राहु:— स्वयं प्रकाशा चेत् मतिरभ्युपेयते, तदा निराकरस्य प्रकाशायोगात् अवश्यमाकारोऽभ्युपगमनीयः । एकश्च अयमाकारः अवभासते। तेन प्रकाश एव तदाकार इति युक्तम् ।

किञ्च निराकारत्वे प्रकाशस्य प्रतिकर्मव्यवस्था न उपपद्यते । नहि तस्य सर्वार्थेषु कश्चिद् विशेषः । अर्थाकारत्वे तु यस्याकारोऽसौ तस्येति घटते प्रतिकर्मव्यवस्था ।

Mere presence of the cognition does not lead to its comprehension. If it assumes a form, then, it is comprehended in that way.

(i) **तदाहुः— न हि संवित्ति सत्तयैव तद्वेदना युक्ता । तस्याः सर्वत्र अविशेषप्रसङ्गात् । तां तु सारूप्यमाविशत् तत्सरूपयद् घटयेत् । अत एव अर्थसारूप्यमेव प्रमाणमिति युक्तम् । (प्र०पं० १७४)**

The two viz., the knowledge and the known are not different. This is because, the two are always comprehended together. No two entities that are always comprehended together are different. On the same line the knower i.e., *ālayavijñāna,* and the knowledge are also identical. The notion of the difference among the knower, the known and the knowledge is an erroneous notion. This notion of the difference is due to *anādivāsanā* that has been all along. The *grāhaka* i.e., the knower within, and *grāhya* i.e., the objects are one. The notion of their difference is an error like that of the cognition of two moons.

(i) **किञ्च वित्तिसंवेद्ययोः सहोपालम्भः नियतः उपलभ्यते । 'सहोपालम्भनियमादभेदो नीलतद्धियोः' । एतेनैव न्यायेन अहमित्याकारकस्य आलयविज्ञानस्य वित्तेश्च अभेदः समर्थनीयः ।**

(ii) **कथं तर्हि ग्राह्य-ग्राहकाकारबुद्धयः परस्परं भिन्नाः प्रतिभासन्ते । भेदश्च भ्रान्ति विज्ञानैः दृश्यतेन्दाविवाद्वये । भेदभ्रान्तौ च अनादिभेदवासनैव निमित्तम् । (प्र०पं० १७६)**

The question to be examined here is, whether the form of the knowledge is caused by the objects present outside or by an earlier occurrence of such a knowledge i.e., *samanantara partyaya.* The *Sautrāntikas* take the view that it is not caused by the mere occurrence of such knowledge earlier but it is caused by the object present outside. If it were a mere repetition of an earlier knowledge, then, the variations in respect of the content, time, place etc., cannot be accounted for. On the other hand if it is caused by the objects present outside, since, these are differently present at different places and different times, the variations of different knowledges could be explained on these grounds. In the instance of *maru marīcikā* i.e., mirage, we find that one who proceeds to fetch the water does not get it. But in the instance of water one who proceeds to fetch it, finds it. If the outside objects are totally absent in all knowledge, then, difference between the two ceases. Therefore, external objects have to be accepted. These provide the respective forms to the knowledge.

(i) **एतद्विचारणीयम् । येयमाकारविशेषयोगिनी प्रतीतिः, सा किं बाह्यार्थादुपजायते किं वा समनन्तरप्रत्ययादिति ।**

(ii) **अत्र सौत्रान्तिका मन्यन्ते समनन्तरप्रत्ययमात्रादाकारविशेष इति न घटते । देशकालप्रतिनियमायोगात् घटज्ञानानन्तरमपि पटज्ञानं जायेत । यत्र यदा बहिर्देशे घटोऽस्ति तत्र यदि घटज्ञानमात्रमेव पटज्ञानोत्पत्तौ हेतुः, तर्हि यदा यत्र पटो नास्ति तत्र तदज्ञानं स्यात् । न चैवमस्ति अतः अस्ति समनन्तरप्रत्ययादधिकः अर्थः ज्ञानाकारोत्पत्तिहेतुः ।**

(iii) **किञ्च यथा मरीचिकाजलज्ञाने जलार्थिनः प्रवृत्तस्य अर्थक्रिया न सम्भवति तथा सम्यग् जलज्ञानेऽपि न स्यात् । नहि अर्थशून्यत्वाविशेषे सम्यग् ज्ञानमिदम्, इदं न, इति विभागः अवकल्पते । तस्मात् बाह्यः अर्थः अङ्गीकार्यः । (प्र० पं० १७७)**

This approach of the *Sautrāntika* is not accepted by the *Vijñānavādin.* He argues that there is no need to accept the outside objects. The knowledge occurred earlier causes the next knowledge. For the variation among different knowledges, the variation of the knowledge occurring earlier itself is the ground. Each knowledge is preceded by an occurrence of a similar knowledge earlier. This accounts for the variation among the different knowledges. Since the variation could be explained in this way, there is no need to posit the outside objects. In the instance of mirage and the water also the fetching of water or not getting the water, are also mere knowledges. These are prompted by the respective earlier knowledges. The absence of the outside object is common to both. The so-called fetching of water is as much mental as that of not getting the water.

The occurrence of the various forms of the knowledge without the corresponding objects outside has to be accepted, since such a situation is clearly found in dream experiences. If it is argued that though there are no corresponding objects actually present outside during the dream, the impressions left by the earlier experiences provide the form to the dream knowledge, then, one can as well say that the knowledge occurred earlier can give rise to its next occurrence without the presence of the objects outside even in the waking stage. This is a beginningless process due to *anādivāsanā.*

(i) तदपरे भ्रान्तमिति मन्यन्ते । तथाहि न तावत् क्वचित् अर्थस्य आकारविशेषाधायकत्वं साक्षादवगतम्, कल्पनीयं तु तत् । तच्च दृष्टे समनन्तरप्रत्यय एव वरं कल्प्यम् ।

(ii) कार्यभूतज्ञानानां वैलक्षण्ये समनन्तरप्रत्ययवैलक्षण्यं हेतुरस्तु ।

(iii) विज्ञानवादी च अर्थक्रियामपि ज्ञानरूपां मन्यते । तेन किञ्चदेव जलज्ञानं अर्थक्रियाजननसमर्थं किञ्चिच्च न इत्यापि प्रतिनियमसिद्धिः ।

(iv) अवश्यं च अर्थमन्तरेण विशिष्टाकारज्ञानौत्पत्तौ समनन्तरप्रत्ययस्य सामर्थ्यमास्थेयम् । अन्यथा स्वप्नादिषु आकारप्रतिभासनियमो न स्यात् ।

(v) अथ अनुभवजनितसंस्कारात् तत्र आकारप्रतिभासनियम इति चेत् । योऽसौ अनुभवः सोऽपि तर्हि अनुभवान्तरजनितसंस्कारादेव अस्तु अनया दिशा किमर्थाभ्युपगमेन ।

(vi) अनुभवपूर्वकमेव विज्ञानं कार्यकारणभावेन प्रवर्तते । तेन अर्थानुभवाकारात् ज्ञानात् यदपरं विज्ञानं जायते तत् विशिष्टस्वभावम्, ततोऽपि यदपरं तदपि विज्ञानं विशिष्टस्वभावमेवेति विज्ञानस्वभावविशेष एव भावना, वासना, संस्कारः इत्यादिशब्दैः गीयते । तस्मात् विज्ञानानि आकारविशेषयोगीनि हेतुफलभावेन अनादिसन्तानवाहीनि सन्तु । तदतिरेकी न कश्चिदर्थो नाम । (प्र०पं० १७९)

Presenting the views of the Sautrāntika and the Vijñānavādins as stated above, Śālikanātha proceeds to refute the same.

The contention of the Buddhists that 'the knowledge should have a form and it should be like the object so that different knowledges could be demarcated' is not correct, because, according to *Sākāra Vijñānavādi Buddhists* no object is ever experienced. Without the experience of the object how can a form similar to that of an object could be envisaged to the knowledge. It cannot be urged that on the basis of the form of the knowledge itself the object of that form could be envisaged. It is not always certain that the form of the knowledge and the form of the object are the same.

(i) यत्तावदुक्तं ज्ञानस्य साकारत्वसिद्धये 'न अर्थसारूप्यमन्तरेण प्रतिकर्मव्यस्थासिद्धि' रिति तदयुक्तम् । नहि कस्यचिदपि अर्थस्य स्वरूपमनुभूतं साकारविज्ञानवादिना । ज्ञानाकारपर्यवसितवृत्तित्वात् सर्वज्ञानानाम् । यस्य च स्वरूपमेव नावसितं न तेन सह कस्यचित् सारूप्यपरिकल्पनम् ।

(ii) न चापि ज्ञानाकारोदयवशेन अर्थः व्यवस्थाप्यमानः सरूपतया परिकल्पयितुं शक्यते । असरूपादपि कार्यगताकारोपपत्तेः । लाक्षारक्तबीजाङ्कुरावस्थायाः विशेषानवगमेपि रक्तकार्यस्य उत्पत्तिः दृश्यते । (प्र०पं० १८०)

According to the Buddhists the knowledge is of gross form and the object i.e., *arthakṣana,* that causes the knowledge is atomic. The knowledge has a common form while the object i.e., *arthakṣana,* is unique in its nature. Further, mere sameness of the form of the knowledge and the object cannot be the ground to consider them as known and the knowledge. The recurring series of the same knowledge cannot be considered as known and the knowledge.

(i) नहि यदाकारं ज्ञानमुत्पद्यते तदाकार एव अर्थः ज्ञानस्योत्पत्तौ निमित्तमित्यत्र किञ्चित् प्रमाणं प्रक्रमते ।

(ii) अपि च स्थूलाकारं ज्ञानमुत्पद्यते परमाण्वाकारश्च अर्थः । साधारणाकारा बुद्धिः असाधारणाकारश्च अर्थः इति किं सारूप्यं भवति? किञ्च सारूप्यमात्रस्य वेद्यत्वे वेद्यवेदकभावव्यवस्था नोपपद्यते । एकार्थविषयाणां सन्तत्यन्तरविज्ञानानां वेद्यवेदकत्वानुपपत्तेः । (प्र०पं० १८०)

The known also cannot be defined as that which causes the knowledge and provides a form for it. In this case in the *dhāravāhikajñāna* the earlier will be the known to the later. The known also cannot be defined as that which provides the particular form to the knowledge. In this case the earlier occurrence of the knowledge would have to be considered as known to its next occurrence.

अथ उत्पादकं स्वरूपार्पकं च वेद्यम्, तथापि धारावाहिकं पूर्वं पूर्वं उत्तरस्य उत्तरस्य वेद्यं स्यात् । अथ आकारविशेषाधायकं वेद्यम्, एवमपि पूर्वपूर्वविज्ञानमात्रं वेद्यमापद्यते । पूर्वं पूर्वं हि विज्ञानम् आकारविशेषोदयकारणमित्युक्तम् । (प्र०पं० १८०)

The contention of the Buddhists that if the knowledge has no form, it will not be possible to bifurcate different knowledges is also not correct. Knowledge is an attribute of the knower that helps to know the object conveyed by it. It is self-revealing. It reveals itself along with its objects. This results in the knowledge of the object concerned. Therefore, no separate form corresponding to the form of the object is necessary for the knowledge.

अपि च निराकारत्वे संविदां प्रतिकर्मव्यवस्था न अनुपपन्ना । अर्थप्रतिबद्धव्यवहारविशेषप्रवृत्त्यनुगुणः पुरुषस्य धर्मविशेषः संवेदनम् । तच्च स्वयंप्रकाशम् ।

यत् यदर्थप्रतिबद्धव्यवहारानुगुणतया प्रकाशते तत् तदर्थ संवेदनमिति व्याचक्षते । (प्र०पं० १८०)

The contention that the object and the knowledge are always comprehended together and therefore these are not different, is also not correct. The expression *saha* i.e., together, requires the two different parties to be together. No knowledge is possible without the presence of that which is to be known. Therefore, these are together. However, these are different. If the two are identical, then, they cannot be differently described as the knowledge and the known. Even he who talks of the identity between the knowledge and the known has to say that the known is presented in the knowledge. This implies the difference between the two.

(i) **सहोपलम्भनियमश्च भेदेपि उपपद्यते । यैवहि नीलधीः सैव नीलस्य उपलम्भः । उपलभ्यमन्तरेण उपलम्भासम्भवात् । तेन तयोः भेदेपि सहोपलम्भनियमो दृष्टो न अभेदं साधयितुं क्षमः ।**

(ii) **योऽपि वित्तेः वेद्यस्य च अभेदमाह, सोऽपि तावत् वेद्यप्रतिभासं नावजानीते । (प्र०पं० १८२)**

(iii) **यदपि ज्वालादिषु अभेदानुमानं तदपि न प्रतीतिं स्वार्थात् प्रच्यावयति । किन्तु सैवेयं ज्वालेति ग्रहणस्मरणरूपे द्वे प्रतीती व्यवस्थितविषये दर्शयति । (प्र०पं० १८२)**

(iv) **'भेदश्च भ्रान्तिविज्ञानैः दृश्यते इन्दाविवाद्वये' इति च अनुपपन्नम् । न हि तत्र भेदो दृश्यते । किन्तु एकस्मिन्नेव चन्द्रमसि नेत्रवृत्तिभेदेन**

द्वे प्रतीती जायेते । तयोः इन्द्रियवृत्तिभेदात् अभिन्नेपि चन्द्रमसि अर्थद्वयविषयं व्यवहारविमूढाः प्रवर्तयन्ति । (प्र०पं० १८३)

The contention of the Buddhists that the knowledge cannot be without a form and formless knowledge cannot be self-revealing is also not tenable. What is meant by 'formless'? If it is meant as *nisvabhāva* i.e., not of any nature, then, we will say that the knowledge is of the nature of knowledge. If it is meant that, it has to be of the form of 'blue, yellow' etc., we say that these are not the forms of the knowledge but the objects presented in the knowledge.

(i) यच्चेदमुक्तम् स्वयंप्रकाशायाः संविदोऽभ्युगतायाः नीलाद्याकारोऽस्तीति । तदप्ययुक्तम् । संविदभिन्नतया अवभासमानस्य आकारस्य संविद्रूपाश्रयणानुपपत्तेः ।

(ii) निराकारा संवित् कथं प्रकाशेत इति चेत् । निराकारेति किमुक्तम्? निस्स्वभावेति चेत् । तदसत् । संविदः संवित्स्वभावत्वाभ्युपगमात् ।

The contention that in the dream cognitions, the forms of the knowledge only occur without any corresponding objects outside is also not correct. It is already pointed out that the outside objects experienced earlier are presented in the dream through the *samskāras* i.e., impressions. Therefore, the dream cognitions are not merely the forms of the knowledge.

Now, a question may be raised as to how the impressions of the objects only are revived but not the fact of their experience earlier, and how is it that the dream cognition is felt as if it is an experience but not as memory? The answer given is that, it is *adṛṣṭa* i.e., destiny that determines the portion of the impressions to be revived. The impressions of the objects are revived since these lead to the joy and sorrow. The fact that it is an earlier experience is not realized since this is not relevant for the experience of the joy or sorrow in the dream. Therefore, the dream cognitions are felt as if these are the first experiences.

(i) यच्चोक्तम् स्वप्ने ज्ञानस्य आकारः अवभासते इति तदप्ययुक्तम् । तत्रापि बहिरवभासित्वात् संविदः । न च सा बहिर्विषया न भवति । तस्याः पूर्वानुभवाहितसंस्कारोद्बोधवशेन पूर्वानुभूतवस्तुविषयत्वात् ।

(ii) कथं तर्हि पुनः पूर्वानुभूतत्वं नानुसन्धीयते । कथं वा अनुभूयमानत्वाध्यवसानम्? उच्यते । संस्कारोद्बोधनिमित्ता इयं स्मृतिः इष्यते । संस्कारोद्बोधश्च अदृष्टनिबन्धनः । तस्य सुखदुःखहेतुत्वात् । स्वप्नेऽपि सुखदुःखानुभवात् । तेन तावत्येव अंशे तददृष्टं संस्कारमुद्बोधयति यावत्येव सुखं दुःखं वा उपपद्यते । न च अनुभूतांशानवधारणे सुखदुःखोदयः इति न तत्र संस्कारोदयः । नापि स्मृतिः । अत एव च गृहीतांशानवधारणे अनुभवमात्रमेवावशिष्यते इति अनुभवाध्यवसायोऽपि समर्थितः । (प्र०पं० १८४)

The contention that the *jaḍa* objects cannot be revealed is answered by pointing out that these are revealed by the knowledge along with itself. The Buddhists tenet that it is only the form of the knowledge that is revealed is given up by the Buddhist himself in the instance of an object of variegated colours.

यत्पुनः आहुः— जडस्य प्रकाशायोगात् प्रकाशात्मक एव आकारः इति । तदपि न चतुरस्रम् । जड इति किमुक्तम्? अप्रकाशात्मक इति चेत् न । अप्रकाशात्मकस्यैव प्रकाशाद् व्यतिरिक्तस्य एष प्रकाश इति प्रकाशादेव सिद्धम् । (प्र०पं० १८४)

The knowledge of a variegated coloured object has no particular form. As one goes on analysing no form can be taken as the form of the knowledge. Many forms cannot be the forms of one knowledge, according to the Buddhists' analysis in this instance. This is an instance of a formless knowledge that reveals itself. This cuts their arguments that only the knowledge with a form can reveal itself. Similarly, the difference among the known and the knowledge, which does not exist and therefore, not a part of the form of the knowledge is also revealed. This also disproves the Buddhists' contention that only such knowledge that has a form is self-revealing.

(1) किञ्च चित्रतुरगज्ञाने नानाभूतानामाकाराणां एकप्रकाशात्मकत्वविरोधात् असद्भूतत्वमेव अभ्युपगतम् ।

चित्रावभासाद्यर्थेषु यद्येकत्वं न युज्यते । सैव तावत् कथं बुद्धिरेका चित्रावभासिनी । (प्र०वा०द्वि०प० १८०)

इदं वस्तु बलायातं यद् वदन्ति विपश्चितः ।
यथा यथा अर्थाश्चिन्त्यन्ते विविच्यन्ते तथा तथा ॥
(प्र०वा०द्वि०प० २०५)

यथा यथा आकाराः विचार्यन्ते तथा तथा अघटमाना विविच्यन्ते । शून्याः भवन्ति, असद्भूताः भवन्ति इत्यर्थः ।

एवं च ते तावदाकाराः असद्भूताः प्रकाशात्मानो न भवन्तीति कथं प्रकाशन्ते । (प्र०पं० १८५)

(2) तथा ग्राह्यग्राहक संवित्तीनां भेदः अत्यन्तासद्भूतः प्रकाशाननुप्रवेशी कथं प्रकाशेत? (प्र०पं० १८६)

The attempt to prove the absence of the outside objects experienced during the waking state on the analogy of the dream state stands rejected as it is already pointed out that even in the case of dream experiences there have been corresponding outside objects.

(3) ये पुनः जाग्रत्प्रत्ययानां स्वप्नप्रत्ययदृष्टान्तेन प्रत्ययत्वादित्यनेन हेतुना बाह्यार्थशून्यत्वं प्रतिपादयन्ति तेषां बाह्यविषयसकलप्रतीतिविरुद्धः पक्षः । दृष्टान्तीकृतस्यापि स्वप्नदिप्रत्ययस्य बाह्यग्राह्यसमर्थनेन हेतोः विरुद्धत्वं दोषः ।

तस्मात् स्वयंप्रकाशत्वेपि संविदः न बाह्यग्राह्यापह्नवः । (प्र०पं० १८६)

The Prābhākaras reject the Buddhists' contention of the absence of the outside objects by examining the question both from *pramāṇa* point of view and *pramēya* point of view. Śālikanātha examined it from *pramēya* point of view in the *'Jātinirṇaya'* section and examines here from *pramāṇa* point of view.

(4) प्रमेयविमर्शोत्त्थास्तु बाह्यार्थापह्नवप्रकाराः जातिनिर्णय एव प्रायशो निराकृताः इति ते नेह प्रस्तूयन्ते । (प्र०पं० १८६)

In respect of the *svaprakāśatva* of the knowledge, a clarification is necessary. Just as the tip of a finger cannot touch itself the knowledge cannot be both the agent and the object, that is to say, it cannot be both the revealer and the revealed. Therefore, it seems *svaprakāśatva* which assigns both the status of the revealer and revealed to the knowledge, is not justified. This objection is answered by pointing out that *kartṛtva* and *karmatva* conflict only in the case of *kāraka* but not in the case of *jñāpaka*. Further, both the *kartṛtva* and *karmatva* are accepted in the case of *ātman* on the ground of the actual experience, the same is the case here also.

ये तु आहुः—

(5)(i) अङ्गुल्यग्रं यथात्मानं नात्मना स्पृष्टुमर्हति ।
स्वांशेन ज्ञानमप्येवं नात्मना ज्ञातुमर्हति ॥

तत्र यदि कर्मकर्तृत्वानुपपत्तिः उच्यते । ततो न किञ्चिदवहीयते । नहि वयं कर्मकर्तृभावमभ्युपेमः ।

(ii) अथ अर्थप्रकाशरूपायाः स्वयं प्रकाशता विनिवार्यते ततः प्रतीतिविरोधः । किञ्च प्रतीतिबलेन यैः आत्मनः कर्तृकर्मभावः अभ्युपगम्यते कथमिव ते संविदो अपह्नुवीरन् । (प्र०पं० १८८)

The theory that the knowledge is inferred but not self-revealing is also not tenable. What is the *liṅga* i.e., the ground, to infer the knowledge. It cannot be the mere presence of the object. There is no invariable relation between the presence of the object and the knowledge. It is also not the knowledge of the object. The mere fact of arising of the knowledge cannot be the ground for the inference. It cannot also be stated that the awareness of it is the ground to infer it. Because, the awareness also being the knowledge requires one more step of the knowledge to play its role. The next step of the knowledge requires one more step of the knowledge and so on. Thus, it leads to the infinite regress. Therefore, the knowledge has to be considered as self-revealing.

(i) अपि च ज्ञानमनुमेयमिष्यते । तदनुमाने न अर्थसत्तामात्रं लिङ्गम् । तस्य तदविनाभावानियमात् । अथ अर्थज्ञानमित्युच्यते तदपि न उत्पत्तिमात्रेण लिङ्गम् । नहि अनवभासमानं लिङ्गं लिङ्गिनमनुमापयति । न च ज्ञानान्तरादवगमः । ज्ञानान्तरादवगमेन अवगमे अनवस्थाप्रसङ्गात् । तस्मात् अर्थज्ञानं स्वयं प्रकाशमेव अभ्युपेतव्यम् ।

(ii) एतेन ये सुखादिवत् मानसप्रत्यक्षं ज्ञानान्तरमेव ज्ञानसद्भावे प्रमाणमित्याहुः तेपि निराकृताः । स्वयंप्रकाशत्वेनापि उपपत्तौ पराधीनत्वकल्पना अनुपपन्ना इत्युक्तमेव ।। (प्र० पं० १८९)

Before closing the section, Śālikanātha raises a ticklish question arising out of a remark in *Śabara Bhāṣya*. In the *Bhāṣya* it is remarked that *'Jñānam anumeyam'* this gives the impression that the knowledge is to be inferred. This goes against the Prābhākara's view of the *svaprakāśatva* of the knowledge. Therefore, Śālikanātha, raises this question to clarify his position. He appears to distinguish between *jñāna* and *samvit.* The latter means the knowledge proper and the former refers to the means of the knowledge. The Sanskrit expression *pramāṇa* means both the knowledge and the instruments of the knowledge. The instruments of the knowledge are the *manas*, the senses, and the contact between the senses and the objects. These are called *jñāna* in the sense of *jñānasādhana.* These are not self-revealing. The operation of these has to be inferred. However, the knowledge generated by these is self-revealing. Keeping this position in the mind, the *Śabara Bhāṣya* remark *'jñānam anumīyate'* has to be understood.

(1)(i) यदि स्वयंप्रकाशा संवित्, भाष्यकारेण ज्ञानमनुमेयमिष्यते इति किमुच्यते इति पृच्छति 'किं तर्हि अनुमीयते' इति । परिहरति ज्ञानमिति ।

(ii) ननु तत् ज्ञानं स्वयंप्रकाशायाः संविदः भिन्नं नोपलभामहे इति चोदयति– ननु न तत् संविदः इति । परिहरति – सत्यम्, अत एव अनुमीयते ।

(iii) प्रतिवादिरूपं विहाय शिष्यभावेन पृच्छति-ननु किं तदिति न विद्मः । सौहार्देन उत्तरमाह संविदुत्पत्तिकारणम् आत्ममनःसन्निकर्षाख्यं तदित्यवगम्य परितुष्यतामायुष्मता । (न्या०सि० १९०)

The expression *pramāṇa* refers to *samvit* when it is taken as *bhāvasādhana*, and it refers to the *manas*, the senses, and the contact with the object if it is taken as *karaṇa sādhana*. In the first alternative *hāna-upādāna* will be the result of the *pramāṇa* and in the second alternative the *samvit* itself is the result of *pramāṇa*. The contention of those who talk of the identity of *pramāṇa* and *phala* has to be rejected, since, the cause and the effect cannot be identical.

(2)(i) यदा प्रमितिः प्रमाणमिति भावसाधनमाश्रियते तदा संविदेव प्रमाणम् । तस्याश्च व्यवहारानुगुणस्वभावत्वात् हानोपादानोपेक्षाः फलम् ।

(ii) प्रमीयते अनेनेति करणसाधने प्रमाणशब्दे आत्ममनःसन्निकर्षात्मनो ज्ञानस्य प्रमाणत्वे तद्बलभाविनी संविदेव बाह्यव्यवहारोपयोगिनी सती फलम् । (प्र०पं० १९२)

The following epistemological issues and concepts are highlighted by Śālikanātha in the course of his exposition of *pramāṇa* and *pratyakṣa* narrated above.

1. *Anubhava* only is *pramāṇa, smṛti* is not *pramāṇa.*
2. Not only the objects, but even the knower and the knowledge are comprehended by *pratyakṣa.*
3. The knowledge reveals itself, its object, and its agent. This formula is called *triputīkaraṇa.*
4. The knowledge is *svaprakāśa.* There is no need of *anuvyavasāya* or *mānasapratyakṣa* to comprehend the knowledge.
5. The substances and the attributes are comprehended in an isolated way at the *nirvikalpaka* stage and cognised as *viśeṣaṇa-viśeṣya* at the *savikalpaka* stage. For the latter a reference to the other objects of the same class and also of different class is necessary through the *samskāra* of the previous experiences of these objects. This will enable one to comprehend the common aspect and the particular aspect of the object cognised at the *savikalpaka* stage.
6. All knowledge agree with the facts presented in it. Even the doubt and the error agree with the facts presented in them.

The most important contributions of the Prābhākaras to the Indian Epistemology are:

(i) *Yathārtham sarva vijñānam* i.e., all knowledge is true.

(ii) *Tripuṭīkaraṇa* formula i.e., the formula that every knowledge contains a reference to the knower, known and the knowledge.

Anumāna

Inference

Śabarabhāṣya defines *anumāna* as *jnātasambandhasya ekadeśa darśanāt ekadeśantare buddhiḥ*. The cognition of the *sādhya* which is presently not in contact with the senses, by means of the cognition of *hetu* which is known as related with the *sādhya* is *anumāna*. In this definition the term ekadeśa refers to hetu while the term *ekadeśantara* refers to *sādhya*, *Sālikanātha* states this very definition with the addition of two more significant expressions viz., *niyama* and *abādhita*. These two expressions are added to avoid certain fallacies.

(१) अनुमानं ज्ञातसम्बन्धस्य एकदेशदर्शनात् एकदेशान्तरे असन्निकृष्टे अर्थे बुद्धिः । (शा०भा०)

**(२) ज्ञातसम्बन्धनियमस्यैकदेशस्य दर्शनात् ।
एकदेशान्तरे बुद्धिरनुमानमबाधिते ॥ (प्र०पं० १९६)**

Before elaborating the definition given by him, Śālikanātha reviews the definitions given by the Buddhists and the Vaiśeṣikas.

The Buddhists' View of Anumāna

The Buddhists claim that *avinābhāva* i.e., not being without each other, is the ground for inferring the *sādhya* from the *hetu*. This *avinābhāva* is based on two grounds viz., (i) *tādātmya* i.e., identity (ii) *tadutpatti* i.e., the cause and the effect status. Ordinarily an object gives rise to its cognition. This confirms its existence. When there is no cognition, then, naturally it has to be taken as non-existent. The object and its cognition have *avinābhāva* i.e., these are not without each other. This could be ascertained by *pratyakṣa pramāṇa.*

However, there is another set of objects which also have *avinābhāva* relation. These are the objects connected with each other through a suitable relation. For instance, the smoke has *avinābhāva* relation with the fire. Consequently, the cognition of the fire produced by the cognition of the smoke has *avinābhāva* relation. The ground for the *avinābhāva* here is the fact that the smoke is the effect of the fire. The *kārya-kāraṇabhāva* relation between these could be ascertained by *anvaya* and *vyatirēka.* The smoke arises only when there is fire. This is *anvaya.* When the fire is absent, then, the smoke is also absent. This is *vyatirēka.* This two way verification helps to ascertain its *avinābhāva.* Similarly, *tādātmya* i.e., identity is another ground to ascertain *avinābhāva.*

(१) कः पुनः अयं सम्बन्धनियमः । अविनाभावः । स च तादात्म्यतदुत्पत्तिनिबन्धनः इति केचित् । (प्र० पं० १९७)

(२) पारम्पर्येणापि यत् यत्प्रतिबद्धम् तत् तदविसंवादि भवत्येव । धूमादिजन्यं पावकादिविज्ञानं धूमाद्यविनाभावि धूमादिकमपि पावकाद्यविनाभावि इति तदविसंवादिनियमोपपत्तिः । अविनाभावनियमश्च न अप्रतिबद्धस्य उपपद्यते । प्रतिबन्धश्च तादात्म्येन तदुत्पत्या सम्भवेत् नान्यथा ।

कार्यकारणभावाद्वा स्वभावाद्वा नियामाकात् ।
अविनाभावनियमोऽदर्शनात् न, न दर्शनात् ॥

विपक्षे अदर्शनमात्रात् न अविनाभावः । नापि सपक्षे दर्शनमात्रात् ।

(३) कार्यकारणभावावगमः प्रत्यक्षानुपलम्भाभ्यां सर्वत्र सम्भवति सत्येव अग्नौ धूमः उपलभ्यते असति अग्नौ सत्स्वपि तदितरकारणेषु नोपलभ्यत इति (प्र० पं० १९९)

As stated above *tādātmya* i.e., identity, is another ground of *avinābhāva.* The *tādātmya* could be ascertained from the fact that the two are interknit. If this was not so, one of them would have been separately available. However, it is not separately available. Hence it is identical.

तन्मात्रानुबन्धसिद्धा च तादात्म्यसिद्धिः । तन्मात्रानुबन्धासिद्धिरपि विपक्षे बाधकप्रमाणप्रवृत्त्यायत्ता । बाधकं च प्रमाणं अनुपलब्धिरूपमेव । (प्र०पं० १९९)

Refutation of Buddhists View

Śālikanātha develops his argument against the *karya-kāraṇa- bhāva* ground of *avinābhāva* as under:

1 (i) The fact that the smoke is present when the fire is present may be ascertained by the perception. But there is no evidence to ascertain the other fact that when there is no fire, there is no smoke. It cannot be argued that this negative position could be ascertained from the *anupalabdhi* i.e., non-availability of them (non-cognition of them). In that case *avinābhāva* has to be worked out between the absence of the fire and the absence of smoke, and their *anupalabdhi.* This cannot be ascertained by claiming *tādātmya* between the absence of the two and their *anupalabdhi. Tādātmya* needs to be verified by *tanmātrā-nubandha* and this needs to be verified by *anupalabdhi.* Now this *anupalabdhi* has to be verified by *another anupalabdhi.* This *anupalabdhi* has to be ascertained by a further *anupalabdhi.* This leads to infinite regress.

अग्नौ सति धूम इति तावत् प्रत्यक्षेण अवगतम् । असति तु अग्नौ धूमो नास्तीति किं प्रमाणम्? ननु अनुपलब्धिलिङ्गकानुमानमेव । अनुपलब्धावपि तर्हि अविनाभावः पर्येषितव्यः । स तावत् न तादात्म्येन । तन्मात्रानुबन्धसिद्धौ हि तादात्म्यं सिद्ध्यति । तन्मात्रानुबन्धसिद्धिरपि विपक्षे बाधकप्रमाणप्रवृत्त्यायत्ता । अनुपलब्धिरेव बाधकं प्रमाणम् । सर्वत्र निषेधानामनुपलब्धिसाधनकत्वात् । बाधकभूतप्रमाणानुपलब्धावपि च उक्तेन न्यायेन अनुपलब्ध्यन्तरा-पेक्षायामनवस्था प्रसङ्गात् । (प्र०पं० १९९)

(ii) The *avinābhāva* between the absence of the fire and absence of smoke, and their *anupalabdhi* cannot be ascertained by *taduptatti* i.e., the *kārya-kāraṇabhāva* between these. Since, the *kārya-kāraṇabhāva* itself depends upon the *anupalabdhi* of *vipakṣa* and leads to the infinite regress as already pointed out. In this way either by *tādāmya* or by *tadutpatti* the *avinābhāva* between *anupalabdhi* and the absence of the fire and the smoke cannot be established. Therefore, though *anvaya* condition is fulfilled, the *vyatirēka* condition cannot be fulfilled. Therefore, *kārya-kāraṇabhāva* does not determine the *avinābhāva* between *sādhya* and *hetu*.

नापि तदुत्पत्त्या अनुपलब्धौ अविनाभावसिद्धिः ।

कार्यकारणभावस्य विपक्षानुपलब्धिसापेक्षत्वेन अनवस्थाप्रसङ्गादेव । तदेवं तदुत्पत्तेः अविनाभावावसायो दुर्लभः । (प्र०पं० २००)

(iii) *Tādātmya* also does not help to determine *avinābhāva* between the *sādhya* and *hetu* since this also depends upon the ascertainment by *anupalabdhi* and leads to infinite regress.

तादात्म्यस्य अनुपलब्धिनिबन्धनतया तन्मात्रानुबन्धसिद्ध्यधीनत्वात् अनवस्थाप्रसङ्गादेव तादात्म्येनापि अविनाभावः दुरवसायः (प्र०पं० २००)

After pointing out the *vyatireka* i.e., when the fire is absent the smoke is also absent, cannot be ascertained by the *anupalabdhi* i.e., non-cognition, either on the ground of *tādātmya* or *taduptatti*, Śālikanātha goes to the very root of it viz., *avinābhāva* between the cause and the effect and questions it:

किञ्च यदपि यस्य कार्यं तदपि तेन विना किं न भवति?

The Buddhist answers that in the absence of the cause, the effect cannot take place. Then, the next question arises that why should it be held that the effect will not arise if the cause is absent? This question is answered by pointing out that the effect is found to arise at a certain time only. This could be explained by holding that it arises only when the cause is present. If the effect could arise without the cause, then, either it should arise all the time or it should not arise at all.

कारणाभावादिति चेत् । कारणाभावे कार्यं न भवतीत्येतदेव कुतः? अकारणस्य नित्यं सत्त्वं असत्त्वं स्यादिति कादाचित्कत्वात् कार्यस्य कारणेन विना कार्यं न भवतीति निश्चीयते । तदुक्तम्—

नित्यं सत्त्वमसत्त्वं वा हेतोरन्यानपेक्षणात् ।
अपेक्षातो हि भावनां कादाचित्कत्वसम्भवः ॥

It cannot be argued that even if one cause is absent, the effect may arise from another cause. In such a case both will cease to be the causes. Since, when, one cause operates, the other is not the cause. When the other cause operates the first one is not the cause.

अत एव कारणान्तरादपि कार्यस्य सम्भवः निरस्तो वेदितव्यः । कारणान्तरजन्मनो हि कार्यस्य द्वयमपि कारणं न स्यात् । एकत्र भवतः अन्यत्र अभावेपि भावात् । ततश्च अकारणत्वापत्तेः ।

The fact of the effect arising only at a certain time cannot establish the need of a cause, since the very contention that 'if the effect does not need the cause, either it has to exist all the time or it has to be non-existent' has no basis. The contention that 'whatever is only at a certain time that needs some cause' and 'whatever does not need a cause is either always present or non-existent' is also not correct. This is based on the maxim wherever, there is no *vyāpaka*, there is no *vyāpya*. Such a maxim itself has no basis.

कादाचित्कत्वविरोध इति चेत् न । अनपेक्षितस्य नित्यं सत्त्वम् असत्त्वं वा इत्यस्य नियमस्य प्रमाणाभावेन अनवल्कृप्तेः । सापेक्षत्वं हि कादाचित्कत्वस्य व्यापकमुपलब्धम् । व्यापकाभावे व्याप्यं न भवतीति अनपेक्षस्य कदाचित्कत्वानुपपत्तेः नित्यं सत्त्वम् असत्त्वं वा स्यादिति निश्चीयत इति चेत् न । व्यापकाभावे व्याप्यं न भवतीति नियमस्यैव अनवकल्पनात् । (प्र०पं० २००)

Further, when the effect is inferred from the cause, then the effect is not the *hetu*, nor there is any *tādātmya* between the two. Therefore no *avinābhāvaniyama* can be worked out on these grounds.

In the instances of the inference of the spate in the sea from the rising of the moon, and the inference of the proximity of the Rohini star from the rising of the *Kṛttikā* star, *kārya-kāraṇabhāva* is not the ground.

The very idea of the inference on the ground of *tādātmya* is not valid. The *liṅga* i.e., *hetu,* is *siddha.* Therefore, there cannot be any identity between the *siddha* i.e., *hetu,* and the *sādhya.* It cannot be said that there is no real difference between *vṛkṣatva* and *Simśupātva.* According to those who hold that the *sāmānya* i.e., characteristics are real, there is real difference between *vṛkṣatva* and *simśupātva.* According to those who consider that the characteristics are projected, there is no identity also. The difference and the identity are the features of real entities only.

There cannot be any inference on the basis of the projected characteristics and the entity in which these are projected. In that case, the difference also will be projected. If it is argued that even though there is projected difference, since *vṛkṣatva* is interknit with *Simśupātva* there is *avinābhāva* between the two. In this case, *avinābhāvatva* will depend upon the *sādhāraṇa dharma.* Such *avinābhāva* is possible without *kārya-kāraṇābhāva* status or *tādātmya.*

Refutation of the Vaiśeṣika View

The Vaiśeṣikas hold that the five relations viz., cause and effect relation, conjunction, inherence, presence by the relation of inherence in a common object, opposition are the grounds for the inference, Śālikanātha rejects this view.

> **एतेनैव न्यायेन येऽपि कार्यकारणभावसंयोगसमवायैकार्थसमवायविरोधाख्यान् पञ्च सम्बन्धान् 'अस्येदं कार्यं, कारणं, संयोगि, समवायि, एकार्थसमवायि विरोधि चेति लैङ्गिकमित्यनुमानकारणमाहुः तेऽपि निराकृताः ।**

In the instance of the spate in the sea by the moon rise, none of these relations is present. The relation viz., conjunction, inherence, and the presence by the inherence in a common object are not the causes of the inference. The umbrella cannot be inferred by the *kamaṇḍalu* merely on the ground of conjunction, the earth cannot be inferred by the colour on the ground of the relation of inherence between the two. The *rasa* i.e., taste, cannot be inferred by the colour on the ground that the two are present by the relation of inherence in the same object.

समुद्रवृद्ध्यादौ यथोचितसम्बन्धाभावेऽपि अनुमानदर्शनात् । संयोगसमवायैकार्थीभावास्तु नानुमानोत्पत्तौ कारणम् । न हि कमण्डलुना छत्रानुमानम् । नापि रूपादेः पृथिव्यनुमानम् । नापि रूपाद्रसानुमानम् ।

The instance given for the inference of the opposite viz., the inference of the absence of pushing away of the clouds by the wind by the presence of the rain, and the presence of the same by the absence of the rain is an instance of the presence and the absence causing the inference but not the opposite. *Anugamana* i.e., following, *niyamana* i.e., regulating, *vyāpti* i.e., pervasion are not the relations at all. The relations involve motion. No *anugamana* etc., involve any motion. No such relation is possible between the fire and the smoke.

यच्च विरुद्धस्य अनुमापकत्वोदाहरणम् । 'यथा भूतं वर्षणकर्म अभूतस्य वाय्वभ्रसंयोगस्य अनुमापकम्, तथा अभूतं वर्षणकर्म भूतस्य वाय्वभ्रसंयोगस्य अनुमापकमिति' । तदनुपपन्नम् । भावाभावयोर्हि अत्र गम्यगमकता । न च तयोः विरोधोऽस्ति । अनुगमननियमनव्याप्तिरूपास्तु सम्बन्धा एव अयुक्ताः । क्रियागर्भत्वात् सम्बन्धस्य अग्न्यादीनां धूमादीन् प्रति अनुगमननियमनव्यापनक्रियासम्भवात् । (प्र०पं० २०२)

Prābhākara's View of Anumāna

Prābhākara's definition of *anumāna* is already given at the commencement of *anumāna* chapter. It reads as:

ज्ञातसम्बन्धनियमस्य एकदेशस्य दर्शनात् एकदेशान्तरे बुद्धिः ।

In this definition, the clause *jñātāsambandha niyama* distinguishes Prābhākaras' definition from the other definitions. Mere *kāryā-kāraṇabhāva* etc., relations are not the grounds of the inference but the *niyama* is the ground. When these relations between the *hetu* and *sādhya* are such that these do not fail, then only, there is *sambandhaniyama.* A *hetu* that has such *sambandhaniyama* is capable of establishing the *sādhya* concerned.

कार्यकारणभावादयः एव सम्बन्धाः यस्य येन नियताः स हेतुरिति दर्शयितुं ज्ञातसम्बन्धनियमस्येत्युक्तम् । (प्र०पं० २०२)

For instance, the smoke as the effect of the fire has *niyatasambandha* with it. Therefore, the fire could be inferred by it. But the fire as the cause has no such *niyatasambandha.* There are instances wherein the fire is present without the smoke. Similarly, where *rasa* i.e., taste, is present, the *rūpa* i.e., the colour is present. Therefore, *rasa* has *niyatasambandha* with *rūpa. But rūpa* is present in certain objects where *rasa* is not necessarily present. Therefore, *rūpa* has no *niyatasambandha.* In this way *sambandhaniyama* has to be ascertained. It is not merely the relation that is the ground for the inference, but it is *sambandhaniyama* that is the ground. Such a *sambandhaniyama* on the part of *hetu* has to be known to infer the *sādhya.* This is the implication of the clause *jñātāsambandhaniyamasya.*

धूमस्य कार्यस्य कारणसम्बन्धः नियतः । अग्नेस्तु अनियतः । तथा रसस्य रूपेण सह एकार्थसमवायलक्षणः सम्बन्धः नियतः । न रूपस्य रसेन । अनया दिशा सर्वहेतुषु सम्बन्धनियमः अनुसरणीयः (प्र०पं० २०२)

An observer observes the *ekadeśa* i.e., *hetu,* remembers its *sambandhaniyama* with *ekadeśāntara* i.e., *sādhya,* and then infers it. These two are *āśrita* i.e.; located in the same thing that is a common *āśraya* for these two. For instance, an observer observes the smoke on the hill, he remembers the *sambandhayaniyama* between the smoke and the fire grasped by him in the kitchen and then infers the fire on the hill. Here the smoke and the fire are *āśritas,* while the hill is *āśraya* for both. Though the fire is present on a spot of the hill and the smoke is above it, since the hill as such is one *avayavi,* it is a common *āśraya* for both.

(i) **ज्ञातसम्बन्धनियमत्वं च एकदेशस्य स्मरणेन उपकारकम् । लैङ्गिकैकदेशसम्बन्धनियमं स्मरतः पुरुषस्य नियतसम्बन्धस्य एकदेशान्तरे या बुद्धिः सा अनुमानम् । एकदेशश्च आश्रितः उच्यते । एकदेशान्तरे इत्यत्रापि एकदेशशब्दः आश्रितवचनः एव । न च आश्रितस्य आश्रयमन्तरेण सम्भवोऽस्तीति आश्रयापेक्षायां न भिन्नस्य आश्रयस्य आक्षेपः । एकदेशाक्षेपेणैवोपपत्तेः । (प्र०पं० २०६)**

How to Ascertain Sambandhaniyama

Since the *sambandhaniyama* plays a vital role in the inference, the question as to how this *niyama* is ascertained arises. Śālikanātha discusses this question in detail.

Sambandhaniyama cannot be ascertained by *pratyakṣa.* The *pratyakṣa* enables to comprehend only those items that are present before. By observing an item in some places and at some time only *sambandhaniyama* cannot be established. It cannot be established by inference also, since, to ascertain the *sambandhaniyama* of *hetu* and *sādhya* of that inference, another inference is needed and so on. Thus it leads to infinite regress. *Śāstra* conveys only *apūrva* and has nothing to do with *sambandhaniyama* of the *hetu* and *sādhya. Upamāna* is also concerned with *sādṛṣya* only.

(i) **किं पुनः सम्बन्धनियमे प्रमाणम् ? न तावत् प्रत्यक्षम्, तस्य सन्निहितदेश वर्तमानकालविषयत्वात् । येन हि प्रमाणेन सर्वदेशेषु सर्वकालेषु च धूमादीनां वह्न्यादिसम्बन्धः अवसीयते तेन तेषां सम्बन्धनियमः अवसीयते । न च प्रत्यक्षं तत्र समर्थम् । (प्र०पं० २०२)**

(ii) नापि अनुमानेन सम्बन्धनियमावसायः अनवस्थाप्रसङ्गात् ।

(iii) शास्त्रं तु अपूर्वकार्यार्थविषयनियतप्रामाण्यमत्र शङ्कापि न याति । तथा उपमानमपि नात्र प्रमाणं सादृश्यमात्रविषयत्वात् । (प्र०पं० २०३)

Sambandhaniyama cannot be determined by *arthāpatti* also. The very *arthāpatti* needs *sambandhaniyama* to determine its own ground viz., *anupapatti*. For instance, the *anupapatti* of the fact of Devadatta being alive unless his presence somewhere outside home is assumed is dependent upon the *sambandhaniyama* between being alive and being present somewhere. If *arthāpatti* is to be utilized to determine the *sambandhaniyama*, it needs another *arthāpatti* to determine its own ground viz., *anupapatti*. That needs one more *arthāpatti* and so on. This leads to the infinite regress. No *anupapatti* can be worked out without assuming *sambandhaniyama*.

The argument that the fact of smoke etc., being the effect of the fire can be the ground of *anupapatti* is not a valid argument, since, it may be claimed that the smoke may be the effect of something else also. It is true that such a contingency is not found, but still the doubt of such a possibility cannot be ruled out. Ordinarily, it is found that different effects arise form different causes but there is no certainty about it. Though the smoke is found to be the effect of the fire, it is quite likely that it might arise from something else in some remote place and remote time. It is true that in a large number of cases the smoke is found when the fire is present and the smoke is not found when the fire is not present. However, this only proves that in these cases, the two were related with each other. It does not follow that in all cases this will be so. Therefore, such a presence in many cases does not prove *sambandhaniyama* between the two, that is to say, the mere fact of being *kārya* and *kāraṇa* in certain instances does not prove *sambandhaniyama*. Therefore, *arthāpatti* also does not help to determine the *sambandhaniyama*.

अर्थापत्तिरपि सम्बन्धनियमसापेक्षा अनवस्थाप्रसङ्गादेव न प्रमाणम् ।

सम्बन्धनियमकल्पनया च विना कस्यानुपपत्तिः । धूमादीनामग्न्यादिकार्यत्वस्य चेत् न । वह्निकार्यस्यापि धूमस्य अन्यकार्यत्वसम्भवात् । न दृश्यते तावदन्यकार्येतेति चेत् । सत्यम् । तथापि शङ्कानिराकरणमशक्यम् । कारणभेदे कार्यभेदादेकस्यानेकस्मादुद्भवो नोपपद्यते इति चेत् न । यद्यपि क्वचित् कारणभेदात् कार्यभेदो दृश्यते तथापि सर्वत्र तथैवेति न शक्यमवधारयितुम् । अतः अग्निकार्यस्यापि धूमस्य देशान्तरे कालान्तरे वा कारणान्तरादपि सम्भवशङ्कया न सम्बन्धनियमाध्यवसानं युक्तम् । (प्र० पं० २०३)

The Rejection of Mānasapratyakṣatva

The view that the *sambandhaniyama* is comprehended by *mānasapratyakṣa* is also not correct. If *manas* comprehends the outside objects without the aid of some other *kāraṇa*, then, it should have been possible to comprehend all outside objects by all. It cannot be argued that the *manas* can comprehend the outside objects assisted by the impressions of frequent observations. The impressions produce only the memory of what is observed but nothing more. *Sambandhaniyama* is an additional factor. It is true that the *manas* is a common factor for all cognitions but still all cognitions are not of the nature of *mānasapratyakṣa*. If it is claimed that by the addition of a special means it functions as a different *pramāṇa*, therefore, it comprehends something that is outside with the assistance of the impressions of frequent observations, then, it will be a separate *pramāṇa*.

(i) कश्चित् मानसं प्रत्यक्षमत्र प्रमाणमित्याह । तदयुक्तम् । मनश्चेत् बहिर्विषये कारणान्तरनिरपेक्षं प्रवर्तेत तदा सर्वः सर्वदर्शी स्यात् अविशेषात् ।

(ii) अथ भूयोदर्शनसंस्कारसचिवं मनःबहिरपि प्रवर्तते इत्युच्यते । तन्न । संस्कारस्य स्मृतिमात्रहेतुत्वात्, अधिकार्थपरिच्छेदासम्भवात् ।

(iii) यद्यपि सर्वप्रमाणसाधारणं मनः तथापि सर्वं न मानसप्रत्यक्षम्, किन्तु असाधारणकारणानुप्रवेशेन प्रमाणान्तरत्वव्यवहारः । एवं चेदसाधारणभूतभूयोदर्शनसंस्कारानुप्रवेशात् प्रमाणान्तरमिदमापतति । (प्र०पं० २०४)

Prābhākaras' View on the Ascertainment of Sambandha Niyama

The conjunction of the fire and the smoke is comprehended by the perception. In this comprehension the conjunction is presented as an adjective, fire and smoke as substantives. The comprehension is stated as *imau samyuktau* i.e., these two are conjuncted but not as there is a conjunction between these two. At first, the conjunction between the fire and the smoke is comprehended without any reference to the space and time. However, in the case of fire, since sometimes it is found without the conjunction of the smoke, the time factor also has to be taken into account, that is to say, the fire has conjunction with the smoke at a certain time only has to be realized. But in the case of smoke, since it is never comprehended without the conjunction with the fire, no time factor comes into the picture. This enables the observer to comprehend the fact that the conjunction of the smoke with the fire is a certainty. This exactly is the comprehension of *sambandhaniyama.* Once this is comprehended, the presence of the smoke is sufficient to infer the fire. No observation of the specific conjunction with the fire is necessary.

(i) अत्रोच्यते । अग्निधूमादीनां तावत् संयोगसम्बन्धः प्रत्याक्षादिभिः अवसीयते । तत्रसंयोगो विशेषेणत्वेन गुणानां द्रव्यपरतन्त्र स्वभावात्वात् । विशेष्यतया स्वतन्त्रभूतं द्रव्यं प्रकाशते । (प्र०पं० २०३)

(ii) देशकालानवच्छिन्नः प्रथमम् अग्निधूमयोः संयोगलक्षणः सम्बन्धः द्वयोरपि अवगम्यते । तत्रापि अग्नेः कदाचित् धूमासंयुक्तस्यापि अवगमात् संयोगासंयोगायोश्च परस्परं विरोधात् कालभेदमाश्रित्य अविरोधः परिकल्प्यते । तेन अग्नेः धूमसम्बन्धस्य कालावच्छेदोऽनुप्रवेश्यते । धूमस्य कदाचिदपि अग्निसंयोगरहितस्य सम्बन्धो नास्ति । तस्य अग्निसम्बन्धः धूमामात्रानुबन्धी नियतः इति निश्चीयते । तथा च धूमसत्तैव कालान्तरे देशान्तरे प्रमाणमपेक्षते । न तु तस्यां सत्यामग्निसंयोगः । तस्य धूममात्रानुबन्धित्वेनावगमात् । (प्र०पं० २०४)

It cannot be argued that since the fire is found in some instances without the conjunction of the smoke, one can think of the possibility of the presence of the smoke also without the conjunction of the fire, because, the conjunction of the fire with the smoke is due to a condition viz., the contact with the wet fire wood, while the conjunction of the smoke with the fire has no such condition. This could be made out by the fact that even on a careful examination of a number of examples it is found that for the conjunction of the smoke with the fire, there is no other condition. That is why careful observation in a number of instances is considered as an aid to detect the absence of the condition.

ननु अग्नौ असंयोगस्यापि दर्शनात् अदृष्टोपि अस्य असंयोगो धूमं प्रति आशङ्कामावहति उच्यते । वह्नेः आर्द्रेन्धनसंयोगोपाधिकः धूमसंयोगः इति तदभावे भवेत् वह्नेः धूमसंयोगाभावः । धूमस्य वह्निसंयोगः न औपाधिकः । कथमसौ न सम्भवतीत्याशङ्क्येत ।

कथमनौपाधिकत्वावगमः । प्रयत्नेन अन्विष्यमाणे औपाधिकत्वानवगमात् । तच्चैतत् भूयोदर्शनायत्तमिति मन्वानाः आचार्याः भूयोदर्शनमाद्यतवन्तः । (प्र०पं० २०५)

An objection may be raised here that since, at the time of the comprehension of *sambandhaniyama* itself it is settled that in all instances of the presence of smoke there is the conjunction with the fire, nothing remains to be inferred. This means that the inference is not a separate means of the cognition.

ननु एवं सम्बन्धनियमावसानसमये एव यावद्धूमादिभावितया अग्न्यादिसम्बन्धस्यावगमात् धूमादिसत्तानिश्चयादधिकं निश्चेतव्यं नावशिष्यते इति अनुमानं न प्रमाणं स्यात् । (प्र०पं० २०५)

The above objection would have some justification if the *pramāṇa* was defined as that which conveys the knowledge of that which is not already known. However, the Prābhākaras have defined *pramāṇa* as *anubhutiḥ pramāṇam.* The cognition of the fire produced on seeing the smoke is of *anubhūti* type. It is not a recollection. Here, *sambandhaniyama smaraṇa* and *ekadeśa darśana* produce the cognition of the fire which is a direct cognition. Hence, *anumāna* is a distinct *pramāṇa.*

स्यादेतत् यदि अनधिगतार्थगन्तृ भवेत् प्रमाणलक्षणम् । अनुभूतिस्तु प्रमाणमित्युक्तम् । धूमाच्च अग्निज्ञानं अनुभवाकारं जायते धारावाहिकवत् । नात्र स्मृतिप्रमोषकल्पना प्रत्युत्पन्नकरणसम्भवात् । इह तु सम्बन्धनियमस्मरणम् एकदेशदर्शनं च प्रतीतिकारणमस्तीति यथाप्रतीति अनुभूतिरूपतैव आश्रयितुमुचितेति युक्तमेव अनुमानस्य प्रामाण्यम् । (प्र०पं० २०५)

The Purpose Served by the Various Clauses in the Definition of Anumāna

The adjective *jñāta* i.e., comprehended, is intended to exclude the fallacy *asādhāraṇa* i.e., exclusive. For instance, in the syllogism, *prthivī rasavatī gandhavatvāt,* the *hetu* i.e., *gandha,* has *niyatasmabandha* with the *sādhya* i.e., *rasa.* However, the relation is not known since *gandha* is not present in anything else other than *pṛthivi.*

अत्र च ज्ञातसम्बन्धनियमस्येत्यनेन ज्ञातशब्देन असाधारणस्य अहेतुत्वमुक्तम् । यथा पृथिवी रसवती गन्धवत्त्वात् । अस्त्येव हि गन्धाख्यस्य

एकदेशस्य रसाख्येन एकदेशान्तरेण एकार्थसमवायलक्षणः सम्बन्धः नियतः । स तु सम्बन्धनियमः न प्रतीतपूर्वः । पृथ्वीव्यतिरेकेण गन्धस्य अन्यत्र अवर्तमानत्वात् । पृथिव्याश्च जिज्ञासितधर्मत्वात् । (प्र०पं० २०७)

Some state that *asādhāraṇa* leads to the doubt. This is not correct. An attribute related to an object can cause the memory of that object. An attribute that is related with two objects causes the memory of both. Since one and the same cannot be both, it leads to the doubt. In the case of an attribute the relation of which is not comprehended with any other, it is not able to cause the memory of any other. Therefore, how can it lead to any doubt? Just as an attribute that is *dharmi svarūpa* does not cause any doubt, an attribute that is *asādhāraṇa* i.e., exclusive to an object, does not cause any doubt.

स चायमसाधारणः संशयहेतुरिति केचित् । तदयुक्तम् । योहि येन सह सम्बद्धः सः तत्र स्मृतिमुत्पादयितुमलम् । यश्चोभयधर्मसम्बद्धः प्रतीतः उभयोः स्मृतिं जनयन् एकस्योभयात्मकत्वविरोधात् सन्देहमापादयति । यस्य तु केनचिदपि न सम्बन्धः अवधारितः सः क्वचिदपि स्मृतिं जनयितुं न समर्थः इति कथं संशयं प्रसुवीत । तस्मात् धर्मिस्वरूपवत् असाधारणोऽपि न संशयहेतुः । (प्र०पं० २०८)

The clause *sambandha* is intended to exclude the fallacy of *bādha*. For instance in the syllogism *śabdaḥ nityaḥ kṛtakatvāt*. The *hetu kṛtakatvāt* has no relation with *nityatva*. On the contrary, it has *niyatasambandha* with *anityatva*. Consequently, it brings *anityatva* to the mind and disproves the *nityatva* proposed to be proved. This results in the fallacy of *bādha*. The clause *sambandha* in the definition wards off such a contingency.

सम्बन्धग्रहणेन च बाधकस्य हेत्वाभासत्वमुक्तम् । यथा शब्दः नित्यः कृतकत्वात् । कृतकत्वस्य नित्यत्वेन सम्बन्ध एव नास्ति । किन्तु अनित्यत्वेनैवायं प्रतीतसम्बन्धनियमः स्वासामर्थ्येन अनित्यत्वमुपस्थापयन् नित्यत्वं बाधते इति सिषाधयिषितधर्मबाधात् बाधको हेत्वाभासः । (प्र०पं० २०८)

The clause *niyama* is intended to exclude the fallacy *sādhāraṇa* i.e., *anaikāntika*. For instance, *śabdaḥ nityaḥ prameyatvāt*. Here, the *hetu prameyatva* has the relation with *nityatva*. However, the relation is not *niyata*, since, it has the relation with *anityatva* also. Therefore, it suffers from the fallacy of *anaikāntika*. The clause *niyama* excludes such cases.

नियमग्रहणेन च साधारणस्य निरासः । यथा शब्दः नित्यः प्रमेयत्वात् । प्रमेयत्वस्य नित्यत्वेन सम्बन्धः अस्ति ज्ञातश्च किन्तु अनियतः । अनित्येष्वपि प्रमेयत्वदर्शनात् । स चायम् अनैकान्तिकः इति गीयते । (प्र०पं० २०८)

The clause *ekadeśadarśana* is intended to exclude such *hetus* that are not *ekadeśa*. For instance, *vyoma* i.e., *ākāśaḥ na pratyakṣam rūpavatvāt*. Here, *rūpavatva* is not *ekadeśa* of *ākāśa* since it is not present in *ākāśa*. It will be established later in the 'Tatvāloka' Chapter that the *rūpa* i.e., colour, felt in respect of *ākāśa* does not belong to *ākāśa*. It belongs to the water or light present in it.

Such *hetus* that have both *ekadeśatva* and *anekadeśatva* are also excluded by this clause. For instance, *Vedāḥ kṛtakāḥ upākhyānātmakatvāt*. In this instance, *upākhyānātmakatva* is not found in the '*Vidhi*' portion of *Veda*. Therefore, the *hetu* is *anekadeśa* also. In the case of smoke the entire hill is a unit. Therefore, there is no *anekadeśatva* while in the case *of upākyānatva* it is in a different part of the *Veda*.

(i) **तथा एकदेशदर्शनादित्यनेकदेशभूतस्य हेत्वाभासत्वमुक्तम् । यथा व्योम प्रत्यक्षं रूपवत्त्वात् । रूपवत्त्वं व्योमैकदेशत्वेन असिद्धम् । उन्मीलिते चक्षुषि गृहोदरादिषु यद्रूपमुलभ्यते तत् तैजसम् औदकं वा इत्युक्तं तत्त्वालोके । (प्र०पं० २०८)**

(ii) **यस्य पक्षं प्रति एकदेशत्वम् अनेकदेशत्वंच तस्यापिअत एव निरासः । यथा वेदः कृतकः उपाख्यानात्मकत्वात् । विधिभागे तु उपाख्यानात्मकता न व्याप्नोति । ननु धूमोऽपि न हेतुः स्यात् । कृत्स्नपर्वतव्यापकत्वाभावात् । मैवम् । तत्र अवयवी पर्वतः एकः, तस्यैकदेश एव धूमः । (प्र०पं० २०८)**

The clause *darśana* excludes the fallacy *svarūpā siddha*. For instance, *Buddhaḥ dharmādharmau pratyakṣam īkṣatē sarvajñātvāt.* The fact of Buddha perceiving *dharma* and *adharma* cannot be ascertained by any *pramāṇa*. Similarly, the smoke in a dark place also cannot be the *hetu* since it is not seen. The clause *darśana* excludes such instances wherein *hetusvarūpa* itself is *asiddha*.

The clause *ekadeśāntara* excludes the fire present in some other place from the scope of *sādhya*. The expression *antara* excludes the possibility of *gamya-gamakabhāva* between the two that are in different locus.

(i) **दर्शनग्रहणेन स्वरूपासिद्धं हेत्वाभासं दर्शयति । यथा बुद्धः धर्माधर्मौ प्रत्यक्षमीक्षते सर्वज्ञत्वात् । न हि बुद्धस्य सर्वज्ञत्वं केनचित् प्रमाणेन अवगन्तुं शक्यते ।**

(ii) **तथा विद्यमानस्यापि एकदेशस्य यावद् दर्शनं नास्ति तावदहेतुत्वम् । यथा अन्धकारे धूमस्य । (प्र०पं० २०९)**

(iii) **अन्तरग्रहणेन च भिन्नाधारयोः गम्यगमकभावो निराकृतः । (प्र०पं० २०९)**

In the instance of the inference of the spate in the sea by the moon rise, the same time is the common locus, since these two take place at the same time. In the instance of the rise of *Kṛttikā* star and the proximity of *Rohiṇī* star, the same day and night unit is the common locus. In the instance of spate at the lower level of a river and the rain at the higher level, one and the same river is the common locus.

(i) **ननु चन्द्रोदयात् समुद्रवृद्ध्यनुमाने कृत्तिकोदयाच्च रोहिणी सन्निधानानुमाने कथं समानाश्रयत्वम्? उच्यते । एककालवर्तित्वं चन्द्रोदयसमुद्रवृद्ध्योः सम्बन्धः । तत्र काल एव एकः आश्रयः ।**

(ii) **तथा कृत्तिकोदयरोहिण्यासत्त्योरपि अहोरात्रिवर्तित्वमेव सम्बन्धः । तेन कृत्तिकोदयादहोरात्र एव आसन्नरोहिण्युदयो अनुमीयते ।**

(iii) अधोनदीपूराच्च उपरिवर्षणानुमानमप्येवं वर्णयितव्यम् । एका हि नदी तत्राप्याश्रयः । (प्र०पं० २०९)

Comprehension of *brāhmaṇya* of the son from the *brāhmaṇya* of his parents is not an instance of inference according to the Prābhākaras. The fact of the birth from the *brāhmaṇa* parents is *brāhmaṇya*. There is nothing to be inferred here. *Brāhmaṇatva* is not a *jāti*. It is only *'upādhi'*.

पित्रोस्तु ब्राह्मणतया यत् पुत्रस्य ब्राह्मण्यज्ञानं तदपि अनुमानमिति केचिदिच्छन्ति । तत् प्राभाकराः नानुमन्यन्ते । ब्राह्मणभूताभ्यां पितृभ्यामुत्पत्तिरेव ब्राह्मणता, नान्या । तेन ब्राह्मणशब्दवाच्यस्त्रीपुंस प्रसूतत्वादन्यत् ब्राह्मण्यं नास्ति इति अनुमानस्य अवकाशः नास्ति। (प्र०पं० २०९)

The clause *abādhita* is intended to exclude *pramāṇāntara bādhita* instances. In the syllogism *vanhiḥ anuṣṇaḥ dravyatvāt*, the *sādhya* is *pratyakṣa bādhita*. Therefore, it has to be excluded from the scope of right *anumāna*.

Here a question is raised. Whether it is a case of *bādhita viṣaya* or *sambandhaniyama abhāva*. It seems that as there is no *sambandhaniyama* between *anuṣṇatva* and *dravyatva*, this *anumāna* can be treated as fallacious on that ground only. There is no need to find *pratyakṣa bādha*. Śālikanātha rejects this contention. He explains the need of *bādhita viṣayatva* as under:

In the process of *anumāna* the ascertainment of *sambandhaniyama* has to be without depending upon the present *sādhya* proposed to be inferred. The *sambandhaniyamāvadhāraṇa* between *anuṣṇatva* and *dravyatva* excepting the case of *vanhi* has already taken place. If the inference of *anuṣṇatva* of *vanhi* also is made on this basis, then, there will be no breakdown of *sambandhaniyama*. Therefore, this *anumāna* has to be treated as fallacious only on the ground of *pratyakṣabādha* and consequently the *sambandhaniyamabhanga*.

'अबाधिते' इत्यनेन प्रमाणान्तरबाधिते विषये नानुमानमुत्पद्यत इति दर्शयति । यथा वह्निः अनुष्णः द्रव्यत्वात् । ननु द्रव्यत्वस्य अनुष्णत्वेन सम्बन्धनियम एव नास्ति । तेन सम्बन्धनियमाभावात् अनुमानानुदयः न पुनः बाधितविषयत्वात् । उच्यते । सर्वत्र हि अनुमाने अनुमित्सितविषयनिरपेक्षमेव सम्बन्ध नियमावधारणमुपयोगि । द्रव्यत्वस्य च वह्निनिरपेक्षं सर्वत्र अनुष्णत्वेन सह सम्बन्धनियमावधारणं जातमिति तद्बलेनानुमानोदये पाश्चात्योपि सम्बन्धनियमभङ्गो नात्मानं लभते । तस्मात् बाधितविषयत्वादेव अनुमानानुदयात् सम्बन्धनियमोऽपि भज्यत इत्यबाधितविषयत्वमप्यनुमानस्य कारणम् । अतो द्रव्यत्वं वह्नौ प्रत्यक्षबाधितविषयं नानुमानमुत्पादयति । (प्र०पं० २१०)

There are instances of the *anumāna* that is invalidated by another *anumāna*. For instance, the syllogism *śabdaḥ śrotragrahyaḥ na bhavati guṇatvāt* is invalidated by the syllogism *śabda pratītiḥ śrotrakaraṇikā śrotrānvaya vyatirekānuvidhāyitvāt*. The fact that the *śabda* is comprehended by *śrotra* is established by *anvaya* and *vyatireka*. When *śrotrendrīya* operates the *śabda* is comprehended. This is *anvaya*. When *śrotrendriya* does not operate then *śabda* is not comprehended is *vyatirēka*. By these the *kārya-kāraṇabhāva* between the *śrotrendriya* and the comprehension of *śabda* is established.

शब्दः श्रोत्रग्राह्यः न भवति गुणत्वादित्यनुमानस्य विषयोऽनुमानेन बाधितः । शब्दप्रतीतिः श्रोत्रकारणिका श्रोत्रान्वयव्यतिरेकित्वादित्यनुमानेन श्रोत्रग्राह्यत्वमवधृतम् । तद् यो हि वादी नास्तीति आह तस्य अनुमानमनुमानेन बाध्यते । (प्र०पं० २१०)

Some people say that one *anumāna* cannot invalidate another. This is not correct. An *anumāna* that occurs earlier and negates the subject of another *anumāna* does invalidate that *anumāna*. Similarly an *anumāna* whose constituents are well established does invalidate another *anumāna*, the constituents of which are yet to be established.

शीघ्रभावि अनुमानम् अनुमानान्तरस्य विषयमपाहरद् बाधकतां प्रतिपद्यते। प्रसिद्धाङ्गकमनुमानं प्रसाध्याङ्गकादनुमानादशुतरभावि। (प्र० पं० २११)

The *śruti* also invalidates *anumāna* in certain cases. For example, the inference that there will be no results for the rituals is invalidated by the *śruti* that prescribes the result for the rituals.

The Condition Asādhitaviṣayatva is not Necessary

Some hold that just as *abādhitaviṣayatva* i.e., non-invalidation by another *pramāṇa*, is a requirement of inference, *asādhitaviṣayatva* i.e., not being already established is also a requirement for the inference. If the *sādhya* is already established by some other *pramāṇa* there is no need of establishing it by inference. For instance, the fact of the fire being hot is known by *pratyakṣa*. Therefore, *anumāna* has no room here.

The Prābhākaras do not agree with this view. If *sambandhaniyama* is brought to the mind on seeing *ekadeśa* i.e., *hetu*, the inference will take place. However, those who already know the *sādhya* will not be interested in bringing *sambandhaniyama* of *ekadeśa* to the mind. Therefore inference does not take place. It is left to the choice of the knower whether he should proceed to know the *sādhya* by inference also or he need not proceed to infer since he already knows the *sādhya*.

The Condition of Abādhitaviṣayatva is Necessary

In respect of *abādhitaviṣayatva* a doubt is raised. In the instance of *jvālā* i.e., the flame, there is a comprehension by the perception that it is one and the same flame. The cognition of oneness is later repudiated. Therefore, it is *bādhitaviṣaya*. However, the inference of the difference of the flames is made. Therefore, this is an instance of the inference even though there is *bādhitaviṣayatva*.

यद्यबाधितविषयत्वमप्यनुमानकारणं कथं तर्हि ज्वालाभेदग्राहिणोऽनु-मानस्योदयः? प्रत्यक्षेण सैवेयं ज्वाला इत्यभेदे प्रतीतेऽपि पश्चात् गृहोदरवर्ति प्रभामण्डलदर्शनात् भेदोऽनुमीयते। पूर्वज्वाला विनष्टा विशीर्णावयवत्वात् घटवत्। दृश्यमाना ज्वाला विनष्टाया भिन्ना। तस्यां विनष्टायामपि उपलक्ष्यमानत्वात्। पटविनाशे पटान्तरवत्।

The process of the inference of difference among the flames is as follows: The withdrawal of flames is not possible until the fire particles drop out one by one. When one set of the particles constituting the flame drops out the flame consisting of another set continues. From this the difference between the two flames is inferred. However, before such an inference, a perceptual cognition of an identical flame had taken place. This is repudiated later. Therefore, it is an instance of the inference that has taken place inspite of *bādhitaviṣayatva.*

The above line of argument is rejected by the Prābhākaras. Here, the *bādhitaviṣayatva* is not definitely known in advance. The comprehension of one and the same flame suggests identity.

But the likelihood of such a comprehension on the ground of similarity also cannot be ruled out at that stage. Therefore, there is no *niścitabādhaviṣayatva* here. It is only a case of *sandigdha bādhaviṣayatva. Abādhitaviṣayatva* is made a condition of *anumāna,* keeping in mind only *niścitabādhaviṣayatva.* In the instance of *vanhi anuṣṇaḥ* there is *niścitabādha.*

उच्यते बाधितविषयत्वं यत्र निश्चितं तत्र अनुमानं नोत्पद्यते। यत्र तु विषयबाधा सन्दिग्धा तत्र अनुमानमुत्पद्यते एव। इह तु सैवेयं ज्वाला इति प्रतितौ जातायामपि शङ्का अवतरत्येव। सादृश्येन शुक्तिरजतयोरिव भेदानवसायादेवंविधा प्रतीतिः भेदेऽपि दृष्टा। तेन किं भेदेऽपि सादृश्येन भदाग्रहणादेवंविधा प्रतीतिः उत अभेदे वा इति शङ्कोदयात् बाधितविषयत्वं सन्दिग्धमिति नानुमानोत्पत्तिप्रतिबन्धः।

वह्नौ उष्णत्वप्रतीतिः अन्यथा सम्भावयितुमशक्येति निश्चितं बाधितविषयत्वम् । अतः तत्र युक्त एवानुमानोदयविरोधः । (प्र०पं० २१३)

The Condition of Asatpratipakṣatva is not Necessary

Some propose one more condition for *anumāna* viz., *asatpratipakṣatva* i.e., the absence of a *satpratipakṣa*. If there is a *satpratipakṣa*, it will lead to a doubt in respect of the *sādhya*. Consequently, there will be no valid inference. For instance, the syllogism *vāyuḥ pratyakṣaḥ mahatvē sati sparśavatvāt* i.e., *vāyu* is perceptible since it has *mahat* dimension and has the attribute of touch, has a *satpratipakṣa* syllogism viz., *vāyuḥ apratyakṣaḥ dravyatvē sati arūpatvāt* i.e., *vāyu* is not perceptible since it is a *dravya* and has no attribute of colour. Since these two syllogisms are opposed to each other these lead only to a doubt in respect of *sādhya* but not any valid inference. Therefore, the condition *asatpratipakṣatva* is also necessary.

अन्ये पुनः असत्प्रतिपक्षत्वमपि अनुमानकारणमाहुः । यथोदितलक्षणो हि हेतुः यथोदितलक्षणहेत्वन्तरप्रतिबद्धो न अनुमानं जनयति किन्तु संशयम् । यथा वायुः अप्रत्यक्षः द्रव्यत्वे सति अरूपत्वादित्यनेन प्रतिपक्षेण हेत्वन्तरेण प्रतिबद्धः 'वायुः प्रत्यक्षः महत्त्वे सति स्पर्शवत्त्वादित्ययं हेतुः' वायौ प्रत्यक्षत्वाप्रत्यक्षत्वसंशयमापादयति । न तु अनुमानं जनयितुमलम् । (प्र०पं० २१३)

The Prābhākaras do not accept the above contention. The *sādhya apratyakṣatva* proposed to be proved by *arūpatva* suffers from *bādha* by the *anumāna* that has established *pratyakṣatva* by the *hetu* of *sparśavata*. *Vāyu* is cognized by the *sparśa* and it is not cognized when its *sparśa* is absent. This *anvayavyatireka* establishes *pratyakṣatva* of *vāyu* even before one tries to infer *apratyakṣatva* by the absence of *rūpa* i.e., colour. Consequently, *apratyakṣatva* is repudiated by the earlier syllogism. Thus it is an instance of *anumānabādha*. Since one of the alternative viz., *apratyakṣatva* is *bādhita* there is no room for any doubt in the instance of *satpratipakṣa*. Hence, the condition *asatpratipakṣatva* is not necessary.

तदनुपपन्नम् । यथोदितयोः हेत्वोः एकत्र समवायाभावात् । भावे वा नित्यं संशयितधर्मत्वापत्तेः । अरूपत्वादिति हेतुः स्पर्शनेन्द्रियान्वय-व्यतिरेकानुविधायितया वायुप्रतीतेरनुमानबाधितविषयः । इदं च अनुमानं यथा शीघ्रभावि तथा उदितमेव प्राक् ।

It cannot be argued that the object *vāyu* is not cognised by *sparśa*, but only the attribute is cognised. When different *sparśas* are cognised and there is a recognition of the object cognised, the cognition is not merely that of the *sparśa* but of an object that has the attribute of *sparśa*. Therefore, *vāyu* the object is perceived through the sense of touch. Though *vāyu* has only one kind of *sparaśa* i.e., *anuṣṇaśīta* as its natural attribute, it will have the other two *sparśas* viz., *uṣṇa* and *śīta* when the water and the fire dominate its *sparśa*.

(i) **ननु न स्पर्शनेन वायुः प्रतीयते किन्तु स्पर्शमात्रमेव । नेत्युच्यते । स्पर्शान्तरप्रत्ययेऽपि द्रव्यप्रत्यभिज्ञानात् । यदि स्पर्शमात्रमेव स्पार्शनं भवेत् तदा स्पर्शभेदे किं प्रत्यभिज्ञायेत ।**

(ii) **ननु न वायोः स्पर्शभेदः सम्भवति । अनुष्णाशीतस्पर्श एव वायुः । तस्य तोयसम्पर्कात् तोयगः शीतस्पर्शः प्रतिभाति । एवं तेजः संयोगादुष्णास्पर्शः इति । उच्यते सत्यं वायोरनुष्णाशीत एव स्पर्शः तोयतेजोगतौ च शीतोष्णस्पर्शौ । तथापि ताभ्यामभिभूते अनुष्णाशीतस्पर्शे शीतोष्णस्पर्शावपि प्रतीयेते । तदन्वयिनी प्रतिपत्तिश्च स्पर्शमात्रप्रत्यये नोपपद्यते इति वदामः । तस्मादनुमानबाधितविषयत्वात् 'अरूपत्वात्' इति हेतुः अप्रत्यक्षत्वं नोत्थापयति । स्पर्शवत्त्वादित्येव निष्प्रतिपक्षमनुमानं जनयति । (प्र०पं० २१८)**

Two Kinds of the Objects of Anumāna

There are two kinds of objects *of anumāna* viz., (i) *dṛṣṭasvalakṣaṇa* i.e., the inference in which the *sādhya* is perceivable such as the fire

(ii) *adṛṣṭa-svalakṣaṇa* i.e., the inference in which the *sādhya* is not perceivable such as *karma* i.e., motion.

'प्रमेयमनुमानस्य दृष्टादृष्टस्वलक्षणम्' इति द्विविधं हि अनुमानस्य प्रमेयम् । किञ्चिद् दृष्टस्वलक्षणं वह्न्यादि । किञ्चिच्च अदृष्टस्वलक्षणं कर्मादि ।

It is argued that the *sambandhaniyama* is possible only with such objects that are perceivable. The same cannot be ascertained in the case of the objects that are not perceivable. Therefore, the inference of *adṛṣṭasvalakṣaṇa* is not possible.

कथं पुनः यस्य स्वलक्षणं न प्रतीतं तदनुमातुं शक्यते । येन सह हेतोः सम्बन्धनियमः प्रतिपन्नः सः तस्माद् हेतोः अनुमातुं शक्यते । न च अदृष्टस्वलक्षणेन सह सम्बन्धनियमावधारणं कस्यचित् सम्भवतीति न अदृष्टस्वलणमनुमातुं शक्यते । (प्र०पं० २१८)

However, this argument is not valid. *Sambandhaniyama* is possible in a general way even with such objects that are not perceivable. Therefore, an inference can be made on the basis of such *sambandhaniyama* also. For instance, that which arises at sometimes has a cause to produce it at that time. For instance, a piece of cloth arises when its cause viz., joining of the threads takes place. Now, conjunction and disjunction take place only at a certain time. Therefore, a cause to produce these has to be inferred. This cause is motion. Here, the *sambandhaniyama* between the motion, and the conjunction and disjunction is ascertained on the basis of a general rule that whatever arises at sometime that has a cause. Only eternal objects that are always present have no cause.

उच्यते । सामान्यतोऽपि सम्बन्धनियमावगमो भवत्येव अनुमानोत्पत्तौ निमित्तम् । यथा यत् कादाचित्कं तदागन्तुकात् जायमानं दृष्टम्, यथा तन्तुसंयोगेभ्यः पटः । कादाचित्कौ हि द्रव्यस्य संयोगविभागौ इति ताभ्याम् आगन्तुकं किञ्चिद् वस्तु प्रतीयते ।

It is argued that why not take the very object as the cause of the conjunction and disjunction. Though the object is constant, it is different when it plays different roles, that it to say, it is different when it plays the role of a cause for the conjunction and disjunction. It appears as identical due to the similarity as in the case of a flame.

The above argument is not valid. There is no ground to treat the very object as different when it plays different roles. In the case of the flame it is validly established. In the present case the object may be taken as the same and a cause viz., motion, can be envisaged in the object to explain the conjunction and the disjunction.

न च द्रव्यमेव आगन्तुकम् । तस्य प्रत्यभिज्ञानेन स्थिरत्वावगमात् । न च शक्यं वक्तुं भिन्नानि एव द्रव्याणि अत्यन्तसादृश्येन अप्रतीयमानभेदानि तत्प्रत्यक्षविषयाणीव भासन्ते ज्वालादिवदिति । द्रव्यभेदे प्रमाणाभावात् । ज्वालादिभेदे प्रमाणमुपन्यस्तमेव । संयोगविभागादिकार्योत्पत्तिस्तु यथा प्रतीते द्रव्यस्थैर्ये सत्यपि आगन्तुककर्माभ्युपगमेनापि उपपद्यत इति न द्रव्यभेदे प्रमाणमस्ति ।

The Criticism of the Prābhākara's Theory of Anumeyatva *of* Karma *i.e., Motion, by Maṇḍanamiśra.*

1. The cognition that arises on seeing a moving object as 'It moves' arises only when the eye is employed and it does not arise when the eye is not employed. This is a clear evidence to say that the motion is comprehended by perception.

2. It cannot be claimed that this cognition arises by observing the conjunction and the disjunction that are the results of the motion. Such an explanation involves the following difficulties:

   (i) If the conjunction and the disjunction enable to infer the motion, then, when one *śyena* bird leaves the tree and another sits on the tree, the conjunction and the disjunction of these two should result in the cognition of motion in the tree.

(ii) It will also result in the cognition of motion in an object that has stopped after moving for sometime, since, this object also had conjunction and disjunction.

(iii) It will also result in the absence of the cognition of the coming down of a bird, since the conjunction and the disjunction of it with the sky cannot be seen as the sky itself is not perceptible.

Further the motion cannot be the object of inference. If the motion is eternal, then, the conjunction and the disjunction due to it should always go on. If it is non-eternal i.e., if it is caused, then, some *asamavāyikāraṇa* has to be envisaged for it. It is better to envisage such *asamavāyikāraṇa* for the conjunction and the disjunction rather than for the motion.

(i) अत्र कश्चिदाह — न कर्म अदृष्टस्वलक्षणम् । प्रत्यक्षत्वात् कर्मणः । तथा हि—या 'गच्छति अयमिति' प्रतीतिः सा इन्द्रियान्वयव्यतिरेकानुकारिणी । तदेव कर्मणः प्रत्यक्षत्वे प्रमाणम् ।

(ii) न च वाच्यं कर्मफलभूतसंयोगविभागविशेषबलेनैव इयं प्रतीतिरिति । तन्निबन्धनत्वे स्थाणावपि एकश्येनवियुक्ते श्येनान्तरसंयुक्तेचापत्तेः । चलित्वा स्थिते न चलतीति वर्तमानावभासप्रसक्तेः विभागसंयोगयोः वर्तमानत्वात् । अतीन्द्रियस्य व्योम्नः संयोगविभागयोरपि अतीन्द्रियत्वात् पतति पतत्रिणि पततीति प्रत्ययानुत्पत्तिप्रसङ्गात् ।

(iii) न च कर्म अनुमातुं शक्यते । तद्धि न नित्यम्, संयोगविभागयोः सर्वदा उदयप्रसक्तेः । अनित्यत्वे तस्यापि अवश्यं समवायिकारममाश्रयणीयम् । तद्वरं संयोगविभागयोरेव अस्तु इति न कर्मानुमाने किञ्चिदपि लिङ्गं समर्थम् ।

तदुक्तम् —

नित्यत्वे सर्वदा जन्म स्यात् संयोगविभागयोः ।

अनित्यत्वेऽस्य यो हेतुः तयोरेवास्तु तेन किम् ॥

(भा०वि०२०, प्र०पं० २१६)

Śālikanātha's Defence of the Anumeyatva of Karma

The contention that when an object moves the motion is perceived is not correct. Only the conjunction and the disjunction of the object with the different points of the place is seen. Nothing more than that is perceived. By the perception of these conjunction and disjunction motion is inferred. Śālikanātha answers the objections raised by *Maṇḍana* as under:

(i) When a *śyena* bird leaves the tree and another comes and sits, the motion takes place in these two birds, but not in the tree. Therefore, there is no question of inferring motion in the tree on the ground of the conjunction and the disjunction of different birds with the tree.

(ii) In the case of an object that has stopped after moving for some time, the motion ceases when it comes to the stopping point. Therefore, there is no question of the cognition of the motion in the object at that time.

(iii) Though the *ākāśa* is not perceptible, the light will have spread all over *ākāśa*. The conjunction and the disjunction of the bird that is coming down with the parts of this light helps to infer the motion.

Therefore, none of the above difficulties can come in the way of considering the motion as inferred.

(i) तदिदमसारम् । प्रत्यक्षेण गच्छति द्रव्ये संयोगविभागातिरिक्त-विशेषानुपलब्धेः । यस्यत्वयं गच्छतीति प्रत्ययः सः संयोगविभागा-नुमितक्रियावलम्बनः । सा क्रिया न स्थाणावनुमीयते । श्येनगतयोः कर्मणोः अनुमितयोः उपपद्येते । तयोः देशान्तरसंयोगविभागौ तस्मात् स्थाणुः चलतीति न युज्यते ।

(ii) चलित्वा स्थितस्यापि देशान्तरसंयोगेन क्रियाविनाशात् वर्तमानक्रियाप्रत्ययानुत्पादः ।

(iii) अतीन्द्रियत्वेपि व्योम्नः वियति विततालोकावयवसंयोगविभागनिबन्धनात् पतति पतत्रिणि पततीति विशिष्टबुद्धिः । तद्वशेन क्रियानुमानमपि तत्र सुकरमेव । (प्र०पं० २१७)

Envisaging the motion as the cause of the conjunction and disjunction is quite reasonable. The cause of the motion itself cannot be the cause of the conjunction and the disjunction. The motion is caused in the body by the contact of the body and the self by the initiative of the self. By this very contact of the body and the self the conjunction and the disjunction of the body with the outside objects is not possible. The conjunction between the self and the body is present in them by the relation of *samavāya* i.e., inherence. It is not present in the object outside. The motion in the body can cause the conjunction and the disjunction with the outside objects. But the very cause of the motion in the body viz., the contact between the self and the body, cannot generate the conjunction and the disjunction with the objects outside. Therefore, the motion has to be envisaged as a cause of the conjunction and disjunction. It has to be inferred by the cognition of these.

न च कर्मानवकल्पनमपि दोषः । कर्महेतोः संयोगविभागोत्पत्त्यसम्भवात् । तथाहि शरीरे तावत् प्रयत्नापेक्षादात्मशरीरसंयोगात् कर्मोत्पत्तिरवकल्पते । न च ततः शरीरदेशसंयोगविभागयोः उत्पत्तिः अवकल्पते । संयोगो हि स्वाश्रये स्वाश्रयसमवेते वा द्रव्यान्तरे कार्यमारभते इति नियतम् । आत्मशरीरसंयोगश्च आत्मनि शरीरे च समवेतः । स कथं शरीरदेशे कार्यमारभेत । तत्र असमवेतत्वात् । तेन सह एकार्थसमवायाभावाच्च। कर्म तु स्वाश्रये शरीरे जनयितुं शक्नुयादेवेति कर्महेतोः संयोगविभागावनुत्पद्यमानौ ततोऽन्यत् कारणं कल्पयन्तौ कर्म अनुमापयतः । (प्र०पं० २१७)

Similarly, the conjunction and the disjunction between the arrow and *ākāśa* are not caused by the conjunction between the bow and the string. It is the motion generated by this conjunction that produces the conjunction between the arrow and the sky. In the same way the conjunction and the disjunction between *musala* and *ākāśa* is not caused by the hammering of *musala* and *ulūkhala*. It is caused by the motion generated by the hammering. From these two instances it is clear that the cause of the motion is not the cause of the conjunction and the disjunction but it is the very motion that is the cause of these.

(i) एतेन नोदनाभिधातात्मकौ कर्महेतू संयोगविभागौ व्याख्यातौ । नोदनाख्यो हि शरज्यासंयोगः तयो : तत्समवेते वा कार्यमारभितु-मलमिति न ततः शरीराकाशगतौ संयोगविभागौ उत्पत्तिं लभेयाताम् ।

(ii) तथा अभिघातात्मकोपि वेगवन्मुसलोलूखलसंयोगो मुसलोलूखसमवेतः कथमूर्ध्वमुत्पततः मुसलस्य आकाशस्य च संयोगविभागावारभेत । (प्र०पं० २१८)

Vega i.e., the speed, which is considered as the cause of the motion also cannot be the cause of the conjunction and the disjunction. *Vega* i.e., the speed is a *samskāra*. Therefore, it can generate an effect in its locus only. The *bhāvanā* which is also a *samskāra* is known to generate its effect *smṛti* i.e., memory. Its locus is the self only. Therefore, how can the speed that is located in the bow generate the conjunction and the disjunction between the string and the *ākāśa*. From this also it is clear that the cause of motion cannot be the cause of the conjunction and the disjunction. It is the motion that is the cause of these and inferred by these.

यश्च वेगाख्यः संस्कारः कर्महेतुरिष्यते, न ततोऽपि संयोगविभागावुपपन्नौ। संस्कारस्य स्वाश्रय एव कार्यारम्भनियमात्। भावनाख्यो हि संस्कारः आत्मनि समवेतः आत्मन्येव स्मृतिलक्षणं कार्यं

जनयन् दृष्टः इति कथं वेगात्मा संस्कारः शरवर्ती ज्याकाशेन तेजोऽवयवैश्च स्तिमितैः वायुभिः सह संयोगविभागावारभते इति शक्यमाश्रयितुम् । अतो न कर्महेत्वाभिमतादेव संयोगविभागावुत्पद्येते इति युक्तमेव ताभ्यां कर्मानुमानम् । (प्र०पं० २१८)

No rule to the effect that the motion generates the effect in a close by object could be laid down. The nature of the cause has to be inferred by the nature of the effect. If a locus is fixed for an effect, then an effect arising from itself becomes difficult to be explained.

All motions generate conjunction with the later by generating the disjunction with the earlier. The *vega* i.e., speed, which is a *samskāra* is also generated. This ceases when there is the conjunction with the later. The concrete objects are locus of the motion.

(i) न च कर्मणः प्रत्यासन्नद्रव्यवर्तिकार्यारम्भनियमः अवधारितः । तस्य कार्यगम्यत्वात् । यादृशेन हि कार्येण यदनुमीयते तादृशमेव तस्य कारणम् । यदि च तस्य आश्रयनियमः स्यात् तदा कार्यमेव ततो नोपपद्येत ।

(ii) तच्च कर्म सर्वमेव विभागपूर्वकं संयोगमारभते । किञ्चित्तु वेगाख्यं संस्कारमपि । अस्ति वेगाख्यः संस्कारः संयोगाच्च तस्योपरतिः मूर्तानिच तस्याश्रयभूतानीत्यादि प्रमेयपारायणे प्रपञ्चितम् । (प्र०पं० २१८)

Acceptance of Śakti as a Separate Category

The Prābhākaras accept *śakti* as a separate category. It is established by the following arguments:

1. The fire produces heat. The same fire does not produce heat when *mantra* i.e., hymn of charm, *auṣadhi* i.e., medicinal plant etc., are present. In both cases the fire is present but the result is different. This means that mere fire is not sufficient to produce the heat. Therefore, a potency i.e., *śakti* to produce the heat has

to be inferred in the fire. What is actually seen is the fire. That alone is not capable of producing heat. Therefore, something unseen viz., a potency i.e., *śakti* which is not seen i.e., *adṛṣṭasvalakṣaṇa* has to be inferred. When *mantra, auṣadhi* etc., are present, this power is obstructed by them. Consequently, the fire does not produce the heat.

सर्वभावानां शक्तिः अदृष्टस्वलक्षणापि कार्येण अनुमीयते । अग्नेः यथाभूतादेव दाहो दृष्टः तथाभूतादेव अग्नेः मन्त्रौषधिप्रणिधाने कार्यं न दृश्यते । विलक्षणं न कार्योदयसमये प्रत्यक्षदृश्यं रूपमुपलभ्यते । भवितव्यं च वैलक्षण्येन अन्यथा कार्यानुत्पत्तिप्रसङ्गादिति कार्योत्पत्तेः अतीन्द्रियं किञ्चिद्रूपं वह्नेरनुमीयते । (प्र०पं० २१८-२१९)

2. It cannot be argued that *mantra, auṣadhi* etc., do not obstruct any unseen power. Their very presence is sufficient to prevent the production of the heat. This argument is not valid. When the cause i.e., the fire, is intact, the production of the heat cannot be prevented by the presence of the other factors.

न च वाच्यं मन्त्रौषधिभिः अतीन्द्रियं रूपं न किञ्चिद्विनाश्यते किन्तु मन्त्रौषधिसन्निधानेनैव कार्यानुदयः इति । कारणावैगुण्ये कार्योदयविधातासम्भवात् । (प्र०पं० २१९)

3. It is argued that the absence of the *mantra, auṣadhi* etc., is also the cause. When these are present, the cause of the heat viz., the absence of these, is lacking. Therefore, the heat is not produced.

This argument is also not valid since all positive effects are caused by the positive conditions only. The heat is a positive entity. It is to be produced by a positive cause only. Therefore, the absence of *mantra, auṣadhi* etc., cannot be the cause.

Therefore, instead of considering mere fire as the cause of the heat and the absence of *mantra* etc., also as the cause, it is better to consider the potency in the fire as the cause. This potency produces the heat. However, when *mantra* etc., prevent it, the heat is not produced.

अथोच्यते मन्त्राद्यप्रयोगोऽपि कार्योत्पत्तिनिमित्तम् । सम्प्रयोगे च अप्रयोगौ निवर्तेते इति अस्ति कारणवैगुण्यमिति । तन्न । अप्रयोगस्य प्रयोगाभावरूपत्वात् सर्वभावकार्याणां च भावकारणनियतत्वदर्शनात् । अभावस्य क्वचिदपि कार्ये जनकत्वाश्रयणानुपपत्तेः ।

यच्च तदतीन्द्रियं अग्नेः स्वरूपं तत् शक्तिसामर्थ्यादिशब्दवाच्यतया लोके प्रतीतम् । (प्र०पं० २१८)

Such a potency has to be in all positive entities. This *śakti* is eternal in the eternal objects and non-eternal in non-eternal objects. In the case of non-eternal it is produced along with the object concerned.

There is an important difference between *samskāra* and *śakti*. The *śakti* arises by the very cause of the object concerned while *samskāra* is invested by some other means.

(i) एवं वह्न्यादौ प्रसिद्धस्य सर्वभावेषु कार्योदयानुकूलं कार्योत्पादकत्वादेव अनुमानेन कल्पनीयम् ।

(ii) संस्काराच्च अस्य अयमेव विशेषः । संस्कारो हि नित्येषु नित्यः अनित्येषु कारणान्तरायत्तः । (प्र०पं० २१८)

Explanation of Pratijñā etc., Steps of Anumāna

Anumāna arises in two ways: (i) By comprehending the requirements of *anumāna* by oneself and (ii) by the statement of these to enable the others to comprehend these requirements. The first approach is known as *svārthanumāna* and the second as *parārthānumāna.*

In *parārthānumāna* the various steps are specifically stated. Śālikanātha states that these steps are suggested by the very clauses of the definition. These are stated as follows:

(i) The clause *abādhita* suggests *pratijñā* (ii) *jñātasambandhaniyama* suggests *dṛṣṭānta*, (iii) *ekadeśadarśanāt* suggests the *hetu*. These three are the means to the inference. These are further explained below.

तत्र अनुमानोत्पत्तिसामाग्रीप्रतिपादनेनैव तत्प्रतिपादकवाक्यस्वरूपमपि सूचितमेव । तत्र 'अबाधित' इति प्रतिज्ञा । ज्ञातसम्बन्धनियमस्येत्यनेन दृष्टान्तवचनम् । एकदेशदर्शनादिति हेत्वभिधानम् । तदेवं त्र्यवयवं साधनम् । (प्र०पं० २२०)

(1) (a) *Pratijñā* is the statement of *sādhya*. For instance *śabda* is *nitya*. The subject of the inference is stated in *pratijñā*. Only after the subject is stated it can be verified whether it is repudiated by any other *pramāṇa* or not.

The clause *ekadeśāntara* also suggests the subject of the inference. This is also conveyed in the statement of *pratijñā*. From this it is also suggested that the statement of a *pakṣa* that is repudiated by *pratyakṣa* etc., is *pakṣābhāsa*. The instances of *pratyakṣabādha* etc., are already given.

(i) **साध्यनिर्देशः प्रतिज्ञा । यथा 'शब्दः नित्यः' इति । अनेन च अनुमानस्य विषयो निर्दिश्यते । निर्दिष्टे च विषये तस्य अबाधितत्वं शक्यतेऽवगन्तुम् । तथा एकदेशान्तरे इत्यनेनापि एकादेशान्तरभूतस्य अनुमानविषयत्वमित्युक्तम् । तदपि प्रतिज्ञावचनेन गम्यते । एतेनैव प्रत्यक्षादिबाधितपक्षादिनिर्देशः पक्षाभासः इत्युक्तो भवति ।**

(ii) **अप्रसिद्धविशेष्यकः पक्षाभासः । यथा सर्वज्ञो वीतरागः इति । (प्र०पं० २२१)**

(b) *Pratijñābhāsa*: The statement 'my mother is a barren woman' is an instance of *pratijñābhāsa*. The term barren cannot be the predicate of the term 'mother'. The two cannot be syntactically connected.

The statement 'I have been a dumb person by birth is not an instance of the contradiction of one's own statement. It is an instance of *anumānabādha* i.e., invalidation by the inference. From hearing his statement his ability to speak is inferred. From this the fact of his being a dumb person is invalidated. His statement conveys that he is a dumb person. His not being a dumb person is not conveyed by it. Therefore, it is not an instance of contradiction of one's own statement.

यावज्जीवमहं मौनीत्यत्र अनुमानबाध एव न स्ववचनबाधः । शब्दश्रवणात् कार्यात् शब्दोच्चारयितृत्वमनुमीयते । शब्दानुच्चारकत्वं च मौनित्वमिति अनुमानबाध एव । स्ववचनं तु मौनितामाह न पुनः अमौनितामिति न तेन बाधः । (प्र०पं० २२१)

(ii) (a) Dṛṣṭānta

A *dṛṣṭānta* i.e., example, is that in which *sambandhaniyama* with the *dharmi* i.e., *sādhya*, is demonstrated. For instance, *sambandhaniyama* of the smoke with the fire is demonstrated in the kitchen i.e., *mahānasa.* Therefore, it is a *dṛṣṭānta.* A *dṛṣṭānta* is quoted to demonstrate the *sambandha* between the *gamya ekadeśa* i.e., the *sādhya* to be inferred, and the *gamaka ekadesa* i.e., the *hetu* i.e., the ground of the inference. Until this is done no inference is possible.

(b) *Dṛṣṭāntabhāsa* is that which lacks *sādhana* or *sādhya*, both these, or *sambandhaniyama.*

यस्तु साध्यविकलः, साधनविकलः तदुभयविकलः सम्बन्धनियमविकलः स दृष्टान्ताभासः । (प्र०पं० २२२)

The following instances are cited in this connection:

(i) In the instance *śabdaḥ prayatnotthaḥ tadanantaram utpatteḥ mulodakādivat'* i.e., the word is produced by efforts, since it is found arising after the efforts as in the instance of ground water.

The ground water itself is not produced by the effort. Therefore, the *sambandhaniyama* of *hetu* cannot be demonstrated in that example. Hence, it is an instance of *dṛṣṭāntābhāsa* of *sādhyavikala* type.

(ii) In the instance *śabdaḥ nityaḥ amūrtatvāt ghaṭavat* i.e., the word is eternal since it is non-corporal like jar. The jar is corporal. Therefore, the *sambandhaniyama* between the non-corporal and the eternal cannot be demonstrated in the example i.e., jar. Therefore, this is a case of *dṛṣṭāntabhāsa* of *sādhanavikala* type.

(iii) In the instance *śabdaḥ anityaḥ kṛtakatvāt gaganavat* the *kṛtakatva* and *anityatva* are not found in the *gagana* i.e., sky. Therefore, the *sambandhaniyama* between these two cannot be demonstrated in the example i.e., *gagana*. Hence, this is an instance of *dṛṣṭantābhāsa* of *ubhayavikala* type.

(iv) In the instance, *śabdaḥ nityaḥ prameyatvāt dravyavat* the *sambandhaniyama* between the *prameyatva* and *nityatva* cannot be demonstrated in *dravya* as a whole, since some *dravyas* like *kāla*, *ākāśa* are eternal while the others like *dveṇuka* are non-eternal. Hence, this as an example of *dṛṣṭāntabhāsa* of *sambandhaniyama vikala* type.

Not mentioning *ekadeśaniyama* or mentioning *viparīta sambandhaniyama* is also an *ābhāsa* i.e., fallacy. If one simply states *parvataḥ vahnimān dhūmavatvāt mahānasa*vat and does not state *sambandhaniyama* as *yo yo dhūmavān sa sa agnimān* then it does not lead to any inference. On the other hand if one wrongly states the *sambandhaniyama* as 'yo yo *agnimān sa sa dhūmavān*' then also no inference arises.

Anumāna arises on seeing *ekadeśa* and remembering *sambandhaniyama*. Therefore, the *hetu* should be stated to present *ekadeśa*. That is to say, the *hetu* should be stated in its capacity as *ekadeśa*. If it is not *ekadeśa* i.e., not *samānāśrayāśrita*, then, it is fallacious.

सम्बन्धनियमं स्मरतः एकदेशदर्शनात् अनुमानमुत्पद्यते इति एकदेशं दर्शयितुं हेतुवचनं प्रयोक्तव्यम् । यथा अग्निमत्त्वे साध्ये धूमवानयमिति । तेन यस्य एकदेशत्वं नास्ति तस्य आभासत्त्वमुक्तमेव । (प्र०पं० २१८)

After explaining the above instances of fallacies, Śālikanātha remarks that *asādhāraṇa* etc., all other fallacies could be brought into the above varieties.

There is no rigidity in the order of stating the *hetu* and *dṛṣṭānta*. There are two possibilities of the procedure: (i) First *ekadeśadarśaṇa*, then, *sambandhaniyama smaraṇa* and the *sādhyajñāna* (ii) First *sambandhaniyama smaraṇa*, then, *ekadeśa darśana* and then *anumāna*. In the first alternative, first *pratijñā* is to be stated, then, *hetu* and then *dṛṣṭānta*. In the second alternative, first *pratijñā*, then *dṛṣṭānta*, and then *hetu*.

Upanaya and Nigamana are not Necessary

Some logicians hold that first *pratijñā*, then, *hetu* and *dṛṣṭānta*, and then *upanaya* have be stated. However, since, the statement either of *hetu* or *upanaya* is sufficient, both need not be stated. Similarly, *nigamana* is also not necessary. The conclusion will be automatically clear by the statement of *hetu*.

Sādharmya Dṛṣṭānta is Sufficient for the Inference

Some logicians rely upon *vaidharmya dṛṣṭānta* also for the inference. For instance, a lake is *vaidharmya dṛṣṭānta* for the inference of the fire from the smoke. It is demonstrated as 'wherever there is no fire there is no smoke'. According to them this negative verification is necessary. The *sādharmya dṛṣṭānta*, only conveys that wherever there is smoke there is fire. But it is equally necessary to comprehend that where the fire is absent, there the smoke is also absent. Unless this negative aspect is comprehended *sambandhaniyama* cannot be comprehended.

This argument is not acceptable to the Prābhākaras. The above purpose is served by the *sādharmyadṛṣṭānta* itself. From the *sādharmyadṛṣṭānta* not only the presence of the fire in the place where there is the presence of the smoke is comprehended with reference to a *dṛṣṭānta* but it is comprehended with reference to all the places where the smoke is found. This excludes the possibility of the presence of the smoke where there is the absence of fire. Therefore, no negative verification is necessary. Hence, no *vaidharmyadṛṣṭānta* is necessary.

वैधर्म्यदृष्टान्तोपादानं केचित् साधनवाक्ये कुर्वन्ति । यथा 'यत्र अग्निर्नास्ति तत्र धूमोऽपि नास्ति' । यथा जलह्रद इति । तदनुपपन्नम् । साध्यधर्मसम्बन्धबलेन हेतोः गमकत्वम् । तच्च साधर्म्यदृष्टान्तेनैव समर्थितम् ।

अथोच्येत साधर्म्यदृष्टान्तमात्रेण साध्यधर्मवति हेतोः वृत्तिः अवगम्यते । न तद्विरहिणो निवृत्तिः । न च तया विना हेतोः साध्यसम्बन्धनियमोवकल्पते अतः तदर्थं वैधर्म्यदृष्टान्तः अभ्युपेयः इति । तन्न । नहि साध्यधर्मवति हेतोः वृत्तिमात्रं साधर्म्यदृष्टान्तेन उच्यते । किन्तु नियत एव साध्यधर्मसम्बन्धः निर्दिश्यते । तथाहि साधनधर्मोद्देशेन साध्यधर्मविधिः साधर्म्यदृष्टान्तेन क्रियते । तत्र धूमवत्तया उपलक्षणेन सर्वधूमवतामुद्दिष्टत्वात् प्रत्युद्देशं वाक्यपरिसमाप्तेः सर्वेषां धूमवतामग्निमत्ता विहितेति नास्ति सम्भावना विनापि अग्निना धूमो भवेदिति । तस्मात् सम्यक् साधर्म्यदृष्टान्तप्रयोगेणैव सम्बन्धनियमावगतेः अनर्थकं वैधर्म्यदृष्टान्तोपादानम् । (प्र०पं० २२४)

It is claimed that *vaidharmyadṛṣṭānta* can serve as an alternate reference for the verification of *sambandhaniyama* on the ground that it can as much help the comprehension of *sambandhaniyama* as *sādharmyadṛṣṭānta*. By the *vaidharmyadṛṣṭānta* it is comprehended that wherever there is the absence of the fire there is the absence of smoke. This enables us to conclude that the smoke is found only in those places where the fire is found. In this way the *vaidharmyadṛṣṭānta* also helps to comprehend the *sambandhaniyama* and therefore, it can be an alternate means for the inference.

This claim involves a round about procedure. Since, the *sādharmyadṛṣṭānta* serves both the purposes of positively ascertaining the *sambandhaniyama* and excluding the possibility of a negative position, there is no need to refer to a *vaidharmyadṛṣṭānta.*

In this connection, it may be noted that the procedure laid down by the Prābhākaras for ascertaining *sambandḥaniyama* strongly supports the reliance only on *sārdharmyadṛṣṭānta.*

Śālikanātha also briefly discusses *pratijñāhāni, pratijñāsanyāsa* etc., *nigrahasthānas.* In the course of this discussion the following points are made:

(i) *Pratijñāsanyāsa* i.e., giving up the statement made is not different from *pratijñāhāni* i.e., defective *pratijñā,* since the *pratijñā* is given up on account of some defect only. The *pratijñā* is given up only when some defect is pointed out in it.

(ii) For the same reason *pratijñāntara* is also not a separate defect. One makes a different *pratijñā* only when some defect is pointed out in his earlier *pratijñā.*

(iii) *Hetupratijñāvirodha* is also not a separate defect. If the *hetu* is not known, then, it comes under *asiddhatā.* If it is known, since the *pramāṇa* that comprehends is invalidated, it comes under the defect of *pakṣa.*

(iv) *Aprasiddhaviśeṣaṇatā* is not a defect since *adṛṣṭasvalakṣaṇa* type of inference is accepted by the Prābhākaras.

The Nature of Pramāṇa and Phala in Respect of Anumāna

The expressions *pramāṇa* and *anumāṇa* could be derived in two ways:

(i) *bhāvavyutpatti* as *pramitiḥ pramāṇam* i.e., the knowledge *is pramāṇa,* and *anumitiḥ anumānām* i.e., the inferential cognition is inference.

(ii) *Karaṇavyutpatti* as *pramīyate anena iti pramāṇa* i.e., that by which the knowledge is obtained and *anumīyate iti anumānam* i.e., that by which an inferential cognition is obtained.

In the first explanation, inferential cognition itself is *anumāna*. This is obtained by the contact between the self and the *manas* arising from the cognition of the *liṅga* i.e., *hetu*. Proceeding to act on the basis of this inferential cognition positively or negatively is the result of this cognition.

In the second explanation, the very contact between the self and *manas* is *anumāna*. *Sambandhaniyama smaraṇa* and *ekadeśa darśana* are the aids. The inferential cognition is the result.

(i) यदा 'अनुमितिः अनुमानम् इति' प्रमितिः प्रमाणमिति भावव्युत्पत्तिः आश्रियते तदा अग्न्यादिविषया लिङ्गदर्शनसापेक्षादात्ममनः सन्निकर्षादुत्पन्ना अधिगतिरेव अनुमानं प्रमाणम् । फलं च उपादानादिक्रिया ।

(ii) यदा 'अनुमीयते अनेन' इति अनुमानम् प्रमीयते अनेनेति प्रमाणमिति करणव्युत्पत्त्याश्रयणम् । तदा आत्ममनसन्निकर्षोऽनुमानम्, सम्बन्धनियमस्मरणम् एकदेशदर्शनं च इतिकर्तव्यता । फलं च लैङ्गिकविषया प्रतीतिः ।

(iii) साधकतमस्य करणत्वात् तमर्थस्य च अतिशयरूपत्वात् व्यवहितापेक्षया च सन्निहितस्य अतिशययोगात् लिङ्गदर्शनादीनां प्रमाणत्वम् । (प्र०पं० २२८)

Śāstra Pramāṇa

It is interesting to note that Śālikanātha designates *śabda pramāṇa* as *śastra pramāṇa.* This is intended to indicate that it is the only Veda that constitutes *śabdapramāṇa.* According to the Prābhākaras the *laukika śabda* is not an independent *pramāṇa.* It is only *anuvāda* i.e., a restatement of what the speaker knows. It is a means to infer the knowledge of the speaker. In other words, it is *vaktṛjñāṇa anumāpaka* and *vaktṛjñāna anuvāda.* Keeping this position in mind Śālikanātha designates it as *śāstrapramāṇa* instead of *śabdapramāṇa.* It may also be noted that *Śābarabhāṣya* also mentions this *pramāṇa* as *śāstra.*

Śāstrapramāṇa is defined as 'The knowledge of an entity that is not known by any other *pramāṇa* and known through the contact of the self and the mind arising out of the knowledge of a scriptural injunction.'

'शास्त्रं नाम शब्दविज्ञानात् यदसन्निकृष्टार्थविज्ञानम्' शब्दविज्ञानापेक्षादात्ममनःसन्निकर्षात् यददृष्टार्थविषयं विज्ञानं तत् शास्त्रं नाम प्रमाणम् । (प्र०पं० २२९)

The expression *asannikṛṣṭa* conveys that it is a knowledge of that which is not conveyed by any other *pramāṇa.* It will be explained a little later, that this knowledge is that of *niyoga* which is also designated as *kārya, apūrva.*

(i) असन्निकृष्ट इति किमिदम्? प्रमाणान्तरेण अप्रतीत इति । यद्येवं कथमसौ शब्दैः अवबोध्यते? उक्तम्-वृद्धव्यवहारावगतसम्बन्धः शब्दः अर्थस्य अवबोधकः इति । (प्र०प० २३४)

(ii) स पुनः असन्निकृष्टः अर्थः नियोगः एव । (प्र०पं० २३५)

Prābhākara's Definition of Word i.e., Pada

Before explaining the concept of *niyoga,* Śālikanātha discusses the nature of *śabda* and refutes the view of *Sphoṭavādin.* According to the Prābhākaras the *varṇas* i.e., the syllables, that convey a unit of meaning constitute a word. Though a word is constituted of many syllables and these syllables disappear one after the other, the cognition of these leaves an impression. The last syllable supported by this impression ie *samskāra* conveys a unit of meaning. A group of syllables that convey such a unit of meaning constitute a word. There is no separate entity as word apart from the syllables that convey a unit of meaning as stated above. The impression stated above is not the same as the impression that causes memory. It is a different kind of impression. If it were the same as that which causes the memory, then, it would have led to the memory of the isolated syllables only. It is the fact of conveying a unit of meaning that is the ground for considering these syllables as a word.

It is only varṇa i.e., syllable, that is comprehended by the ear. Neither *śabdatva* nor *sattājāti* in general can be claimed to be comprehended by the ear since the concepts of *sattā* and *śabdatva* are not acceptable to the Prābhākaras.

(i) कः शब्दोऽभिमतः? वर्णाः तेषामेव श्रोत्रग्राह्यत्वात् । श्रोत्रग्राह्ये हि वस्तुनि शब्दपदं वर्तते । (प्र०पं० २३०)

(ii) एकपदबुद्धिस्तु एकार्थप्रतिपत्तिनिबन्धना । (प्र०पं० २३१)

The Sphoṭavāda View of the Śabda

The *Sphoṭavādins* accept the word as distinct from the syllables. They argue as under:

1. The words: *vana, nava, nadī-dīna* etc., contain the same syllables. However these are different words.

It cannot be stated that these appear to be different words because of the different order of syllables. The *varṇas* i.e., syllables are eternal and all-pervasive. Therefore, there cannot be any temporal and spacial order for the syllables. There can be only an order in their comprehension. Due to the sequence in the comprehension, the syllables are heard as in a sequence. But so far as the word is concerned, since the duration of the comprehension is momentary, no sequence in respect of comprehension is possible.

2. The syllables are many, the comprehension of a word is one. Therefore, the word is distinct from the syllables.

3. If the word is not a distinct entity from the syllables, then, comprehension of its meaning will not be possible. The meaning is not comprehended when the syllables are grasped individually. All the syllables of a word are not grasped together. The syllables are pronounced one after the other and grasped one after the other.

If the syllables were to convey the meaning, then, these would have conveyed different meanings with different order and different speakers. Since, the syllables are not capable of conveying the meaning, a distinct entity viz., *pada* i.e., the word, has to be accepted. This is *padasphoṭa.* The concept of *vākyāsphoṭa* is also justified on the same lines.

(i) **ननु वर्णातिरिक्तं पदमपि श्रौत्रमेव । तथा हि- वन-नव नदी-दीनेत्यादिषु वर्णभेदेपि पदान्यत्वं प्रतीयते । न च वाच्यं वर्णा एव पदम् । वन-नव-नदी-दीनेत्यादिषु क्रमभेदेन पदभेदबुद्धिरिति वर्णानामक्रमिकत्वात् । देशनिबन्धनो वा क्रमो भवेत् । कालनिबन्धनो वा । उभयविधोपि न वर्णेषु आस्पदं लभते । तेषां सर्वगतत्वात् नित्यत्त्वाच्च । बुद्धिस्तु तेषां क्रमवती । तदनुरोधेन वर्णा अपि क्रमवन्तः इति प्रत्येकं श्रवणेषु अवभासन्ते । एकक्षणवृत्त्यान्तु पदबुद्धौ एकस्यां बुद्धिनिबन्धनोपि क्रमो नोपपद्यते इति कुतः तद्भेदेनापि भेदप्रतिभासोपपत्तिः ।**

(ii) किञ्च वर्णाः बहवः, एकविषया च पदबुद्धि इति वर्णेभ्यः भिन्नं पदम् ।

(iii) किञ्च यदि वर्णेभ्यः भिन्नं पदं नावभासते ततः तेभ्यः अर्थप्रत्यय एव नोपपद्यते । एकैकवर्णप्रतीतौ तावत् अर्थस्य नावगमः । न च सकलवर्णोपलम्भो युगपत् सम्भवति । वर्णानां क्रमोच्चारणात् । उच्चारणानुसारित्वाच्च उपलब्धेः ।

(iv) वर्णानां वाचकत्वे क्रमभेदे वक्तृभेदे च अर्थप्रत्ययः स्यात् । तस्मात् वर्णेभ्यः असम्भवन् अर्थप्रत्ययः तदतिरेकिस्वनिमित्तपदप्रतीतिं प्रसाधय । (प्र०पं० २३१)

The Refutation of Sphoṭavāda

These arguments of *Sphoṭavādins* are not acceptable to *Varṇavādins.* It is already stated above that the *varṇas* give rise to the concept of *pada* i.e., word, on the ground of conveying a unit of meaning. There is no separate entity as *pada* i.e., the word. This point is elaborated as follows:

1. The expressions *vana-nava, nadī-dīna* etc., do not represent a separate entity called *pada* i.e., word, in addition to the syllables. The syllables *na, va* etc., only are grasped. The difference in the comprehension of these expressions is due to the difference in the order. The comprehension of these expressions is not one unit of comprehension together. The comprehension of each syllable is a unit. Different order of syllables arises by the order in the comprehension of these. These different comprehensions of different syllables give the impression of one expression as these occur in continuity. The comprehension of the syllables follow the order of the pronunciation of the same that are heard. The memory of this comprehension also arises in the same way.

These expressions are taken as one word on the ground that these convey one unit of meaning. There is no separate phonetic unit such as word as the ground for the meaning. It is the meaning that is the ground to consider a group of syllables as a word. Apart from the syllables, there is no separate phonetic entity that is the ground for a unit of meaning.

It is already stated above that the last syllable supported by the impression of the cognitions of previous syllables serves as the basis to convey a unit of meaning which is the ground for the concept of a word. It is also stated that this impression is different from the impression that leads to memory. The impression that leads to the memory is capable or reviving the cognition as it occurred. In the present case the cognitions of syllables occur as separate units and merely reviving these cognitions will not help to form a unit on the basis of a unit of meaning.

Therefore, the Prābhākaras conceive a unique kind of impression that enables the last syllable to be the basis for a unit of meaning which will serve as a ground for the concept of a word. Since this unique impression is conceived to serve a definite purpose, its capacity has to be conceived in such a way that it serves the purpose. Its purpose is to give rise to a unit of meaning. This will happen when the syllables are pronounced and comprehended in a certain order. Therefore, the unique impression operates only when such an order is found. It does not arise or operate when such an order is not found. In this way the Prābhākaras explain the nature and the rise of a word without accepting a separate phonetic entity as word apart from the syllables.

(i) उच्यते । वन-नव-नदी-दीनेत्यत्रापि वर्णातिरिक्त वस्त्वन्तरावभासो नास्ति । नकारादय एव प्रतीयन्ते । बुद्धिभेदस्तु क्रमभेदनिबन्धनः । न चेयमेका बुद्धिः यतो वर्णानां बुद्धिभेद निबन्धनोपि क्रमो न स्यात् । भिन्नवर्णविषयाः भिन्नाः एव हि बुद्धयः निरन्तरतया एकतामिव आपद्यन्ते । तथाहि । श्रवणेन्द्रियनिबन्धनास्तावत् वर्णोच्चारणानुबन्धिन्यो बुद्धयः उच्चारण भेदेन भिद्यन्ते । एवं स्मृतिरपि प्रत्येकवर्णोपलम्भप्रभावितभावनावशेन भवन्ती सर्वविषया

एका अवकल्पते । भावनानां भेदात् । एकपदबुद्धिस्तु एकार्थप्रतिपत्त्युपाधित्वनिबन्धना ।

(ii) एकार्थप्रतिपत्तिस्तु प्रत्यक्षं तावत् निमित्तं न शक्नोति कल्पयितुम् । प्रत्यक्षं वर्णेभ्यः भिन्नपदावभासि न भवतीत्युक्तमेव । तेन वर्णेष्वेव प्रत्यक्षेषु अर्थप्रतिपत्त्युपपत्तये कश्चिद् विशेषः आश्रयितुं युक्तः । स च पूर्वपूर्ववर्णसापेक्षत्वादन्त्यवर्णस्य उपलम्भस्य च क्षणिकतया स्वतो विशेष्टुमशक्यत्वात् पूर्वपूर्ववर्णोपलम्भजन्यः संस्कारः एव आश्रियते ।

(iii) स च स्मृतिहेतोः संस्काराद् भिन्नः एव । स्मृतिहेतुः संस्कारः यदुपलम्भप्रभावितः तत्रैव उपलम्भान्तरं जनयितुमलं नार्थान्तरे इति अर्थविषया ततः प्रतीतिः अनुपपन्नेति तदतिरेकिणः संस्कारस्य आश्रयणम् । तस्य च कार्यकल्प्यत्वात् यथाभावे अर्थप्रतीतिरूपकार्यदर्शनं तथाभाव एव उत्पत्तिरनुमीयते । तेन क्रमविपर्यये वक्तृभेदे व्यवधाने च कार्यादर्शनात् तत्र संस्कारस्यादर्शनात् अर्थप्रत्ययाभावः । (प्र०पं० २३१-२३२)

The Nature of the Meaning and the Relation between the Word and the Meaning

After discussing the nature of the word, Śālikāntha, discusses the nature of the meaning and the relation between the word and the meaning. He states that *pratyāya-pratyāyakabhāva* is the relation between the word and the meaning.

This relation is natural and permanent. It is not conventional i.e., *saṅketa.*

कः पुनः अर्थः? अभिधेयः । अभिधेय एव कः? येन सह शब्दस्य अपौरुषेयः सम्बन्धः । अथ कः सम्बन्धः? प्रत्यायप्रत्यायकभावः । (प्र०पं० २३२)

The fact that this relation is natural is clear from the very process of learning the language.

A boy who watches two elders in conversation, observes that on hearing the statement of one elder, the other elder proceeds to act. Since the other elder proceeds to act after hearing the statement, the boy infers that the other elder understood the meaning of the statement and acted accordingly. He further infers that the statement conveyed its meaning to the elder in a natural way. In this process, no fixing of meaning by convention i.e., *saṅketa*, is involved. A meaning that is fixed by convention could be understood only by those who know the meaning of the other words in the context. This is a later process in the case of such words such as the name *Devadatta.* This word is fixed as a name of a certain person by convention, and therefore, it conveys him as its meaning. However, it is not a general rule, nor, it is a general procedure in respect of the meaning of a word. The words naturally convey their meanings and the relation between the word and the meaning is natural and permanent. Though it is natural, one has to learn it through the elders' conversation. The elders do not fix it by any convention. They have learnt it from their elders, these elders have learnt from their elders. At no stage the meaning is fixed by any convention. It is only learnt from generation after generation. Therefore, it is *apauruṣeya.*

(i) **स्वाभाविकमेव शब्दस्य अर्थप्रत्यायकत्वं न सङ्केतापेक्षम् । तथाहि-वृद्धयोः व्यवहरतोः एकस्य वाक्यं श्रुत्वा परस्य प्रवर्तमानस्य प्रवृत्त्या बुद्धिमनुमाय तस्याः शब्दश्रवणानन्तरभावित्वात् शब्दस्य तद्धेतुतां तावदवधारयति ।**

(ii) **शब्दश्रवणे वृद्धव्यवहारावगतार्थप्रत्यायकत्वमात्रेण स्वयमर्थावगमदर्शनात् अर्थप्रत्यायकत्वावगम एव विशेष इति निर्धारणा जायते । न पुनः सङ्केतविशेषप्रतीतिः वृद्धस्य विशेषः इति कल्पना शक्या । सङ्केतस्यैव तदानीमप्रतीतेः । व्युत्पन्नेतरशब्दार्थो हि सङ्केतादर्थमवबुध्यमानः सङ्केतं प्रतिपद्यते नान्यथा ।**

(iii) **ननु एवं सति देवदत्तादिपदेष्वपि कथं सङ्केतस्य कारणत्वम्? उच्यते-प्रत्यक्षपरिदृष्टः तत्र सङ्केतः । न तु कल्पयितव्यः । तेन देवदत्तादिपदेषु**

तस्यैव अर्थप्रतीतिकारणत्वम् । गवादिपदेषु तु केवलकार्यदर्शनमात्रकल्पनीयो नावकाशं लभते इति अपौरुषेयः शब्दानामर्थेन सह प्रत्याय्य प्रत्यायकभावः सम्बन्धः । (प्र०पं० २३३-२३४)

Niyoga i.e., Kārya is the Import of the Entire Veda

The nature of meaning of Veda is set in the *Jaiminīya Sūtra codanā lakṣaṇo artho dharmaḥ.* Here *niyoga* i.e., injunction is stated as the meaning of Veda. This is not conveyed by any other *pramāṇa.* The *niyoga* i.e., injunction, cannot be understood without the subject-matter. The other words in an injunctive statement convey their meanings as connected with the *niyoga* only. Hence, the full import *of niyoga* is conveyed by an injunctive statement only. The detailed procedure of the conveying of *niyoga* is as under.

The injunctive suffix liṅ conveys the *niyoga.* The *prakṛtī* the root of the verb, conveys the subject-matter. The other words i.e., convey the adjectives, the root meaning, the name of the sacrifice, and *niyojya* i.e., the performer etc. and get connected with *niyoga.* In this way all words contribute to convey the full *niyoga.*

(i) स पुनः असन्निकृष्टः अर्थः नियोगार्थ एव । नियोगो हि प्रमाणान्तरानवगतमपूर्वमर्थमवबोधयतीति वाक्यार्थमातृकायामुकम् । न च नियोग एव एकः तस्यावबोधकः। विषयव्यतिरेकेण तदप्रतीतेः । पदानामपि तदन्वितस्वार्थपरतयैव व्युत्पत्तेः । तेन वाक्येनैव नियोगार्थः प्रतीयते ।

(ii) तत्र लिङादिप्रत्ययः नियोगार्थमेव अभिदधाति । प्रकृतिस्तावद् विषयं, पदान्तराणि च विषयविशेषणं नामधेयं, नियोज्यञ्च अभिदधति सन्ति नियोगार्थप्रतीतौ व्याप्रियन्ते । (प्र०पं०२३६)

The statements that state *sannipatya upakāraka aṅgas* do not have their own *niyoga.* Therefore, these convey their meanings as connected with the main *niyoga* and contribute to convey the main *niyoga.* The *mantras* play the role of the *aṅgas* of *niyoga* by reminding the ritual programme and its means. The *arthavāda* passage are also connected with the *niyoga* by way of glorifying the sacrifice. In this way the entire Veda conveys *kārya* i..e, *apūrva* i.e., *niyoga*. This is stated in *Codanāsūtra*. The summum bonum of the import of Veda is *kāryātmā vedārthaḥ*.

सन्निपत्योपकारकाङ्गानि यद्यपि नियोगशून्यानि तथापि प्रधाननियोगान्वितस्वार्थाभिधायकया प्रधाननियोग प्रतिपत्तावेव पदान्तरवत् व्याप्रियन्ते । विनियुक्तमन्त्रसमाम्नायोऽपि द्रव्यभूतं मन्त्रजातं नियोगाङ्गतया समर्पयन् तद्विशिष्टविनियोगावगतावेव उपक्षीयते । नियोगाङ्गत्ता तु योग्यतया प्रयोगकाले नैयोगिककर्मतत्साधनस्मारणेन मन्त्रजातस्य । अर्थवादा अपि विधेयस्तुतिमुत्पादयन्तः स्तुतिविषयविधेयान्वित नियोग प्रतिपत्तिपराए वेतिकृत्स्न एव वेदो अपूर्वे कार्यात्मनि प्रमाणम् । अत एव को वेदार्थः इति जिज्ञासमानेभ्यः 'चोदनालक्षणोऽर्थो धर्मः' इति सूत्रेण कार्यात्मा धर्मः इत्युक्तम् । (प्र०पं० २३६)

The Criticism of Siddha Vyutpatti Theory

Stating the import of Veda as *kārya* and pointing out that all other expressions get connected with *kārya* i.e., *niyoga*, and unfolding the full implications of *niyoga*, Śālikanātha reviews the view of those who take the stand that even the *siddha* i.e., something that is already there, and that is not an activity can also be the import of a statement. This view is advanced, particularly, to justify the statement about the Brahman in the Upaniṣads. There is no reference to any activity in these statements. The *siddha vyupatti-vādins* argue that the elders' conversation is not the only source of understanding the import of a statement. There are statements like 'A son is born to you' which do not contain any reference to the activity. From the facial expression of the pleasure it can be made out that the listener understood the import of this statement. The birth of a child is conveyed by this statement. This is the statement of a fact. Therefore, it is *siddhaviṣayaka*. Similarly, from the statement *kāṣṭhaiḥ pacati* one understands the meaning of the word *Kāṣṭha* from the fact that it is used with an instrumental case suffix and is an instrument. This understanding has no reference to its connection with the activity.

Even those who say that *kārya* is conveyed, have to say that it is conveyed as connected with the meaning of the other words. Therefore, there is no reason to give particular emphasis on the connection with the *kārya* only. Further, *kārya* is that which is a means for a desired result. As such it is *siddha*. Therefore, *siddha* is the import of Veda.

(i) ननु कथं पुनः कार्यरूपः एव वेदार्थः? यावता वेदान्तानां सिद्ध एवार्थो ब्रह्मात्मकः विज्ञानमानन्दं ब्रह्मेति प्रतीयते ।

(ii) विनापि व्यवहारं सिद्धार्थप्रतिपत्तिपरादपि लौकिकवचनात् सम्भवत्येव व्युत्पत्तिः । यथा पुत्रस्ते जातः इत्यादिषु कार्यान्वयरहितेषु शब्देषु । प्रतिपदमावापोद्धाराभ्यां व्यवहार इव स्वार्थविशेषसम्बन्धाध्यवसायः ।

(iii) तथा व्युत्पन्नेतरपदविभक्तयर्थाः काष्ठैः पचतीति वर्तमानापदेशेपि यत् पाके करणं तत् काष्ठशब्देन प्रतिपाद्यते इत्यवगम्य प्रत्यक्षेण काष्ठानां करणभावमवगच्छन्तः काष्ठशब्दार्थे कार्यान्वयरहिते एव व्युत्पद्यन्ते ।

(iv) अपि च येन नाम कार्याभिधायित्वमभ्युपगम्यते तेनापि तावत् अर्थान्तरान्विताभिधायित्वमभ्युपगतमेव । तावता च कार्यान्विताभिधानस्याप्युपपत्तेः न शक्यते विशेषान्विताभिधानशक्तिः कल्पयितुम् ।

(v) किञ्च कार्यमपि तदुच्यते यत् अपेक्षितोपायः । तेनैव सिद्धैव कर्मणामपेक्षितोपायता कार्यपरेषु गम्यते । अतः सिद्धः एव वेदार्थः इति । (प्र०पं० २३९-२४०)

The Prābhākaras do not agree with the above line of argument. They insist that the elders' conversation is the only source of learning the import of the statement. The facial expression of the joy on hearing the statement 'A son is born to you' does not necessarily indicate that the listener understood the import of the statement viz., birth of a son, is the base of his joy. There are many other factors that could be the base for this joy. Therefore, one cannot be sure that he understood the import of that statement and the facial expression of pleasure is due to that only. Therefore, this statement cannot establish *siddha vyutpatti.*

The *siddha viṣayaka* statements in day to day language are secondary usages. In *kāryavāda*, there is necessarily *padārthānvaya* also. Therefore, people make *siddha* statement without particularly drawing attention to *kārya.* However, such statements are only *lākṣaṇika* i.e., secondary usages. So far as Vedic statements are concerned, there is no room for *lakṣaṇā.*

The contention that the *kārya* is a means for the desired result and this is a *siddha* fact is also not correct. *Kārya* is accomplished by *kṛti.* Therefore, it is *sādhya.* However, the activities need a lot of efforts. To undertake these difficult activities, *kārya* is considered as a motivating factor. Therefore, it is confused to be the means by ordinary persons.

(i) सर्वपुरुषाणां तावत् वृद्धव्यवहारे एव प्रथमं शब्दानां व्युत्पत्तिरङ्गीकरणीया । न खलु व्यवहारमन्तरेण सिद्धार्थान्व्याख्याने व्युत्पत्तिरवकल्पते । यद्यपि मुखप्रसादादिभिः हर्षोत्पत्तिः अनुमीयते । हर्षोत्पत्त्या च हर्षहेत्ववगमः । तन्निमित्तता च शब्दस्य । तथापि पुत्रस्ते जातः इति वाक्यस्य पुत्र जन्माख्यहर्ष हेतुप्रतिपादकता हर्षहेतूनामानन्त्यात् दुरनुमाना । व्यवहारः पुनः प्रत्यक्षः विशिष्टार्थविषय एवोपलभ्यमानः तद्बुद्ध्यनुसारेण तद्धेतुतामेव वाचकताम्नायासेन आपादयन् व्युत्पत्तौ उपायतां गन्तुमलम् ।

(ii) व्यवहारश्चेत् व्युत्पत्त्युपायः कः कार्यान्विताभिधानं शब्दानामपहरेत् । नहि कार्यावगमं विना व्यवहारोऽवकल्पत इत्युक्तं वाक्यार्थमातृकायाम् ।

(iii) एवं च लोके यः सिद्धार्थपरतया पदानां प्रयोगः सः लाक्षणिको भविष्यति । वेदेतु लक्षणानिमित्तं किञ्चिन्नास्तीति स्वाभाविककार्यत्वं नापहर्तुं शक्यते ।

(iv) न अपेक्षितोपायतैव कार्यता । कृतिसाध्यं हि कार्यम् । साधनमुपायः । साध्यत्वोपायत्वेच भिन्ने किन्तु क्लेशात्मकं कर्म अपेक्षितोपायतया कार्यं प्रतीयते इति कार्यता साधनतां न व्यभिचरतीति तादात्म्यश्रमो मन्दधियाम् । (प्र०पं० २४०-४१)

The *Vedānta* statements have to be connected with the injunctives like *'ātmā jñātavyaḥ'* and have to be taken as conveying *kārya* only.

The *Vedānta* statements cannot convey Brahman as *paramānandasvarūpa*. To convey this the Brahman has to be known from some other *pramāṇa* and be stated here. The Brahman has to be taken as *Ātman* that is known to us through our experience. In all our cognition the *Ātman* is revealed. However, in these cognitions it is not revealed as possessing *paramānanda*. This means that the *Vedānta* statements that describe Brahman as *paramānanda* are not valid. It cannot be argued that this *paramānanda* is concealed during *samsāra*. The suffering in *samsāra* is limited while *ānanda* that is intrinsic is unlimited. The unlimited cannot be concealed by the limited. The theory of identity between *Ātman* and Brahman is also not acceptable. The concept of the absence of change is also not acceptable *Vijñāna* and *ānanda* etc., also cannot be connected with each other. In this way the acceptance of *siddha Brahman* as the import of *Vedānta* statements leads to many difficulties in understanding these statements. Hence, these also should be taken as conveying *kārya* only.

(i) वेदान्तानामपि 'आत्मा ज्ञातव्यः' इति अपुनरावृत्तये समाम्नातेन विधिना एकवाक्यतामाश्रित्य कार्यपरत्वमेव वर्णनीयम् ।

(ii) अपि च सिद्धार्थपरत्वेपि वेदस्य न वेदान्तानां परमानन्दादिरूपत्वे ब्रह्मणः प्रामाण्यमवकल्पते । तत्रहि ब्रह्म स्वरूपानुवादेन आनन्दादिविधिः आस्थेयः । ब्रह्मस्वरूपञ्च प्रमाणान्तरसिद्धमेव आश्रयणीयम् ब्रह्म शब्दस्य च लोके प्रमाणान्तरसिद्धात्मवाचित्वेन

प्रसिद्धेः वेदेऽपि स एवार्थः । तथा सति नित्यप्रकाशपरमानन्दरूपविधिः सकलप्रतीतिविरूद्धः ।

(iii) सर्वप्रतीपत्तिषु हि प्रमाणस्मृतिभूतासु आत्मा प्रकाशते । न च तत्र परमानन्दः संवेद्यते ।

(iv) अभिन्नैकात्मतत्त्वप्रतिपादनमपि प्रमाणान्तरविरूद्धमेवेति वक्ष्यते तत्त्वालोके । (प्र०पं० २४२)

Non Vedic Statements are not Śabdapramāṇa

The Prābhākaras consider only the Vedic statements as *śabda pramāṇa*. That is why it is designated as *śāstra*. In the case of *laukika śabda* there is a possibility of falsity and the absence of agreement with the fact. This does not happen in the case of Vedic statements. These are authentic by their very nature. Therefore, there is no room for any doubt.

Their authenticity does not need the ascertainment of the absence of disagreement. These give firm knowledge as in the case of sense-perception.

(i) न शास्त्रव्यतिरिक्तं शाब्दमस्ति । यद् विज्ञानमसन्निकृष्टे अर्थे तत् शास्त्रं स्यात् । न च वेदव्यतिरेकेण तत् सम्भवति । लौकिकं वाक्यं नार्थे स्वयं निश्चयमुत्पादयति लौकिकवचसामनृतभूयिष्ठत्वात् अर्थव्यभिचारस्य शङ्कितत्वात् ।

(ii) ननु एवं वैदिकमपि वचो नार्थनिश्चायकं स्यात् । शब्दोत्त्थापितस्य अर्थज्ञानस्य लोकेऽर्थव्यभिचारित्वात् । अथोच्येत वैदिकात् वचनात् स्वतः तावत् निश्चयो ज्ञायते । पश्चात्तनस्तु संशयः तद्विरोधादात्मानं न लभते । यदा च निश्चितोऽर्थः तदा उपलब्धिः व्यवस्थितेति संशयो न युक्तः । न च अव्यभिचारनिश्चयपूर्वकं शब्दस्य निश्चायकत्वम् । किन्तु स्वभावतः इन्द्रियवत् शब्दो निश्चयहेतुः । (प्र०पं० २४३)

On this position it is argued that when the very statement gives room for the doubt, it cannot lead to firm knowledge. The firm knowledge can prevent only such doubts that arise from external circumstances. In response to this argument it may be conceded that such a doubt is possible in the case of *laukika* statements. People are found to make incoherent statements by ignorance or incapacity. However, day to day activities go on the basis of the statements since people proceed to act without waiting to verify the authenticity.

(i) शब्दजनितं निश्चयमेव उभयथा दृष्ट्वा यः संशयः स निश्चयेनैव न शक्यते निरोद्धुं बाह्यहेत्वन्तरो हि निश्चयेन विरुध्यते । यः पुनः तत्प्रभवः एव नासौ तेन विरुध्यते ।

उच्यते । युक्तः तावत् लौकिके वचसि सन्देहः । पुरुषा हि प्रायेण अनन्विितार्थान्येव पदानि आशयदोषेण भ्रमेण प्रमादेन अशक्त्या वा प्रयुञ्जानाः दृश्यन्ते । ततश्च यद्यपि तदुक्तानामन्विताभिधानसामर्थ्यमस्ति तथापि अनन्वितार्थत्वशङ्कया अन्वयो न निश्चीयते । कथं तर्हि लौकिकवाक्येभ्यः प्रवृत्तिः । उच्यते । अर्थसंशयेनापि लोको व्यवहरति । सन्दिग्धायामपि वृष्टौ वृष्ट्यायत्तफले कृष्यादिषु प्रवर्तन्ते । (प्र॰पं॰ २४३)

(ii) ननु वेदेपि शङ्कया भवितव्यमित्युक्तम् । सत्यमुक्तमयुक्तं तत् । न तावदन्वयनिश्चायानुपपत्तिः वेदे भवति । अशत्क्यादिवक्तृदोषवशेन हि अनन्वितार्थप्रयोगो लोके दृष्टः न च वेदे कर्ता पुरुषोऽस्ति । तेन तदाश्रिताः दोषा अनन्वितार्थपदरचनादिहेतवः वेदे शङ्कामपि नावतरन्तीति अन्वयनिश्चयस्तावत् जायते । न च पौरुषेयवाक्यजन्यनिश्चयस्य व्यभिचारदर्शनात् वैदिकेपि निश्चये व्यभिचारशङ्का शाब्दस्य क्वचिदपि व्यभिचारादर्शनात् । (पृ॰ २४५-४६)

The fact of people proceeding on the basis of such statements is explained in another way also. They do ascertain the authenticity of these statements as follows:

First, they will ascertain the fact that the person who has made the statement is a reliable person, he is careful, he has the capacity to state accurately, he has the knowledge of what he says and no intention to mislead. Though this appears to be an elaborate process, this takes place spontaneously and quickly in day-to-day dealings. In this way, the statement is found consistent. From this, the correct knowledge of the person who made the statement and its agreement with the facts is ascertained. Thus, his statement serves as a *liṅga* to infer his knowledge and ascertain the facts. The statement, which initially serves as a *liṅga* and enables to infer the knowledge of the speaker, finally serves as *anuvāda* ie restatement of that which is known through the inference.

अथवा अस्त्येव निश्चयोपाय: । यो हि पुरुष: एवमवधारित: 'नायमशक्त:, न प्रमादी, सम्भवदेतदर्थप्रमाण: सकलाशयदोषरहित:, नायमविज्ञाय अन्वयमर्थानामन्वितार्थानि प्रयुङ्क्ते' इति तद्वाक्यप्रयोगस्यान्वयज्ञानपूर्वकत्वात् । अन्वयज्ञानं तावदनुमीयते । अन्वयज्ञानाच्च अन्वयोपि अनुमीयते । ज्ञानं हि ज्ञेयाविनाभावि ज्ञेयानुमाने भवत्येव लिङ्गम् । तदेवं लौकिकाद्वचस: लिङ्गभूतात् वक्तृज्ञानमनुमीयते । ततो । अर्थं निश्चित्य व्यवहार: प्रवर्तते । एवं च निश्चिते अन्वये निवृत्तान्वयशङ्काद् वाक्यादपि अर्थनिश्चयो जायते । किन्तु तस्यां दशायां तद्वाक्यस्य अनुवादकतैव । अत एव लौकिकं वचनं न शब्दं प्रमाणम् । अभिप्राये शब्द: लिङ्गम्, अभिप्रायोप्यर्थे लिङ्गम् । शब्दस्तु पश्चादर्थे निश्चयं जनयन्नपि अनुवादकत्वात् न प्रमाणम् । (प्र०पं० २४३)

Here, an interesting question is raised viz., whether the ascertainment of the absence of the capacity to make correct statement, the absence of carelessness etc., on the part of the speaker helps only to remove the doubt in respect of the *ananvitārthatva* of the statement made by him or determine the very authenticity of the facts conveyed by the statement. In the latter case there is no need to make any further inference about the knowledge of the facts conveyed by the statement and treat the statement merely as a means of such an inference and a re-statement of that which is inferred from the statement. Śālikanātha answers this question by affirming that the statement restates the facts conveyed by it by going through the process of inference of the knowledge of the speaker and the facts conveyed by it. Ascertainment of the absence of the incapacity, the absence of carelessness etc., merely remove the doubt. In this connection he also explains the implication of the expression *abhrāntatva, aprmāda, aśaktatva* etc.

ननु अशक्तप्रमादिभ्रान्तदुष्टाशयपुरुषप्रयुक्तानां पदानामनन्वितार्थत्वदर्शनात् या पुरुषान्तर वचनेषु अनन्वितार्थत्वशङ्का जायते तन्निवृत्तिमात्र एव पुरुषस्य वक्तुः शक्तत्वाप्रमादित्वाभ्रान्तत्व शुद्धाशयत्वज्ञानं व्याप्रियताम् । अर्थनिश्चयस्तु वाक्यादेव अपास्तसन्देहादस्तु । मा भूत् वक्तृज्ञानादनुमितार्थनिश्चये जाते वाक्यस्य अनुवादकत्वमिति । उच्यते अभ्रान्तत्वं नाम पुरुषस्य यथार्थज्ञानयोगित्वम् । आशयदोषविरहश्च यथाविदितार्थ विवक्षायोगः । शक्तत्वञ्च यथा विवक्षित-पदप्रयोगसमर्थत्वम् । शक्तस्यापि यथाविवक्षितार्थाविक्षेपः अप्रमादः । यस्य एतच्चतुष्टयमस्ति सः प्रत्ययितः । यस्य एतदवगतं सम्यग् ज्ञाननियतः अस्य वाक्यप्रयोगः इति । तेन तस्य तदीयवाक्यश्रवणे तद्गतसम्यग् ज्ञाननिश्चयो जायत एव । समीचीनं तज्ज्ञानमुच्यते यत् विसंवादि । तच्च अविसंवादि यस्य यथा प्रतीयमानो अर्थोस्ति । तेन समीचीनज्ञाननिश्चयः अन्तर्भावितार्थनिश्चय एवेति न संशयनिवारणमात्रे पुरुषविशेषविज्ञानं व्याप्रियते । किन्तु अर्थनिश्चय एवेति, निश्चिते अर्थे । निवृत्ते च संशये वाक्यमर्थनिश्चयं कुर्वदपि अनुवादकत्वात् न प्रमाणम् । (प्र०पं० २४४)

Śālikanātha also rejects the plea that let the *laukika* statement be *pramāṇa* in such cases wherein the knowledge of the speaker is not derived from any other *pramāṇa*. Such a contingency is not possible since the possession of the required knowledge and making a statement about the facts conveyed by it are two essential aspects of the speaker who makes the statement.

ननु तर्हि यत्र वक्तृज्ञानस्य अन्यतोऽनवगतस्य अवगमकं पौरुषेयं वाक्यम्, तत्रैव शब्दं प्रमाणमस्तु । न । तत्र अनुमानत्वात् । वक्तृज्ञानेन हि निश्चतसम्बन्धं प्रत्ययितवचनम् । वक्ता तु धर्मी ज्ञानविशेषयोगिता वाक्यप्रतियोगिते तस्य एकदेशौ इति ।। (प्र० पं० २४४)

Śālikanātha quotes the *Vaiśeṣika Sūtra* in support of his theory that the *laukika* statements only help us to infer the knowledge of the speaker and the facts conveyed by it.

An important point to be noted here is that the statement by itself is never false. The inference drawn through it, is sometimes false. Here, the listener fails to distinguish between a statement that correctly represents the fact and that which does not correctly represent. Consequently, his action on the basis of such a statement fails and thinks that the statement was wrong. In the course of the above discussion, the following points are made:

1. The Vedic statements are intrinsically authentic.
2. The *laukika* statement serves as a *liṇga* to infer the knowledge of the speaker and ascertain the facts conveyed by him through the statement. The statement recounts the facts inferred through it.
3. Whenever, a statement is found wrong, it is the inference drawn through it that is wrong. The statement by itself is not wrong. It is a case of the inability to distinguish between a statement that infers correctly and that which does not do so.

Apauruṣeyatva of Vedas

Vedāpauruṣeyatva is the corner stone of *Mímāmsā*. Therefore, they refute the views of those who try to say that the Vedas are *pauruṣeya. Paurusyatva* for Vedas is claimed mainly on two grounds. (i) Vedas consist of the arrangement of words. Therefore, someone must have arranged them like *Bhārata* etc., the other literature. (ii) *Kaṭha* etc., names of certain persons are associated with the Vedas. Therefore, these must be the authors of the respective hymns. These names cannot be taken as the names of those who taught the Vedas. A large number of teachers have been teaching the Vedas and there is no special reason to select only a few as teachers and associate their names with the hymns. Therefore, these must be considered as the authors only.

ननु पदसङ्घातात्मकतया वेदा अपि पौरुषेयाः एव भारतदिवत् । तथा काठकादिसमाख्या प्रवर्तते न चेयं प्रवचननिमित्ता समाख्या इति कल्पयितुं युक्तम् । साधारणत्वात् प्रवचनस्य । बहवोपि प्रब्रूयुः । कर्ता पुनः असाधारणो भवति । असाधारण्येन व्यपदेशाः भवन्ति । (प्र०पं० २४६)

Śālikanātha answers these points suitably (i) There is no tradition that holds *Kaṭha* etc., as the authors of Vedic hymns. In the case of *Bhārata* there is tradition that *Vedavyāsa* is the author. Mere mention of the names cannot be the evidence for their authorship. This requires some other evidence. No other evidence is available. Therefore, these persons have to be taken as the teachers of Vedas only. Though there have been many such teachers, the names of some distinguished teachers could be associated.

उच्यते । पुरुषकृतत्वं तावत् वेदानां साक्षात् भारतादाविव न स्मर्यते । समाख्या तु पौरुषेयी प्रमाणान्तरानुसारिणी न शक्नोति स्वयमर्थव्यवस्थां कर्तुम् । यदि विचारयन्तः कृतकतामेव निर्णेष्यामः ततः करणनिबन्धना समाख्येत्यध्यवस्यामः । अथ तु यत्नेन अन्विष्यन्तोऽपि पौरुषेयतां नोपलप्स्यामहे ततः प्रवचननिबन्धनेति वक्ष्यामः । यदपि असाधारणं स्यात् । प्रकृष्टं हि वचनं कस्यचिदेव । कुत्र चिदेव । (प्र०पं० २४७)

(ii) The fact of Vedas consisting of the arrangement of the words also cannot be the base for *pauruṣyatva*. Men are not capable of composing Vedic sentences. They are not able to comprehend the import of the Veda by another *pramāṇa* and formulate sentences to state it. *Apūrva* is the import of the Veda. This cannot be comprehended by any other *pramāṇa*. It is conveyed only by Vedas. Therefore, no one is able to comprehend before studying Vedas and put it in the form of Vedic sentences.

It is not necessary that the arrangement of words is to be effected by the men only. The arrangement of the words is found in two ways: (i) someone intentionally arranging the words. (ii) The tradition of reciting the words in a certain order by the teacher after teacher. Only in such cases wherein a person is traced to be the first arranger, the arrangement is *pauruṣeya.* Where no such person is traced it is *apauruṣeya.* Recitation in the same order generation after generation is found in the case *Bhārata* also. In the case of *Bhārata* it is second generation onwards while in the case of Vedas it is all along.

Such a privilege of *apauruṣeyatva* cannot be extended to Buddha's statements. In the case of Buddha's statements, it is known that he had made these statements, even though his statements also contain certain injunctions, the *apūrva* is not conveyed by them. These statements only indicate that certain practices are the means of certain benefits. These statements are only modelled on Vedic injunction but these are not injunctions. The *apūrva* is not conveyed by them. Therefore, these are not *apauruṣeya.*

(i) **न तावत् पदसङ्घातात्मकत्वं पौरुषेयतामनुमातुमलम् । वेदार्थविषये पुरुषाणां वाक्यविरचना सामर्थ्यानुपपत्तेः । प्रमाणान्तराविषयो हि अपूर्वात्मा वेदार्थः । स च प्राग् वेदवचनेभ्यः बुद्धिस्थतामापादयितुमशक्यः । (प्र०पं० २४७)**

(ii) **न च पौरुषेयत्वं विना सङ्घातात्मकतैव नोपपद्यते । उच्चारणवशेन हि पदानि संहततामापाद्यन्ते । तच्च उच्चारणम् उच्चारणान्तरपूर्वकं वा स्यात् स्वबुद्धिप्रभवं वा । दृश्यते हि अन्येनापि प्रयुक्तमन्येनाधीयमानं भारतादिवत् । यथा अद्यतनाः पुरुषाः भारतादिकमुच्चारणनन्तरदर्शनपूर्वकमधीयते तथा वेदानपि सर्वपुरुषा एवेति किमनुपपन्नम् । अतः सिद्धमपौरुषया वेदा इति । अपौरुषेयाश्चेत् नास्ति प्रमाणान्तरापेक्षा प्रत्यक्षवत् । (प्र०पं० २४८)**

(iii) ननु बुद्धादिवचनान्यपि एवमेव अपौरुषेयाणि स्युः । न । तेषां साध्यसाधनभावस्य कल्पयित्वापि बुद्धौ आरोपयितुं शक्यत्वात् । ज्योतिष्टोमादिषु दृष्टं स्वर्गादिसाधनत्वं चैत्यवन्दनादौ आरोपयितुं शक्यते । अपूर्वं तु अपूर्वत्वादेव आरोपेणापि नावतरति । (प्र०पं० २४७)

(iv) अथ कथं तुल्येपि लिङादिप्रयोगे बुद्धादिवचनानि साध्यसाधन-भावमात्रपराणि । न वेदवाक्यानि । उच्यते बुद्धादिवचनानि तावत् साक्षात् दृष्टकर्तृपुरुषाणि । तेन यदेव पुरुषाः प्रमाणान्तरेण बुद्धिस्थीकर्तुमीशते तद्विवक्षा प्रयुक्तान्येवेति निश्चीयते । पुरुषाश्च नापूर्वं बुद्धौ निवेशयितुमलम् । साध्यसाधनभावं तु अन्यत्र दृष्टं बुद्धिस्थीकृत्य वाक्यं विरचितुम् क्षमन्ते । (प्र०पं० २४७)

The Apūrva Provides the Results of the Kāmya Sacrifices

After establishing the *apauruṣeyatva* and *prāmāṇya* of the Vedas on the ground that its import is *apūrva*, Śālikanātha mentions an objection raised against the *prāmāṇya* of the Vedas and clarifies the position. In the Vedic injunctions *citrayā yajeta paśukāmaḥ* etc., certain results are mentioned. These are not obtained immediately after the sacrifice. Later, when these results are supposed to accrue their cause i.e., sacrifice, is not present. Since, the cause and effect relation cannot be established here, these Vedic injunctions are not valid. This objection does not hold good. It is not stated in the Vedic injunction that the result is obtained immediately. Though the sacrifice is not there at the time of the result, the *apūrva* accomplished by the sacrifice is present. This enables to get the result. The sacrificer is also able to enjoy the result later as he is distinct from his body and senses and is permanent as *Ātman.*

ननु चित्रया यजेत पशुकामः इत्यादिचोदनाः पश्वादिफलानुबद्धस्वार्थं बोधयन्ति । न च कर्मानन्तरं फलमुपलभ्यते । न च कालान्तरे फलं भविष्यतीति शक्यं वक्तुम् । तदानीं कर्माभावात् । अतः

प्रमाणान्तरबाधादप्रमाणामिदं शास्त्रंम् उच्यते । न तावत् शास्त्रेण अनन्तरभावितया फलं श्राव्यते ।

(i) येन अनन्तरफलादर्शनेन बाधः स्यात् । न च कालान्तरे कर्माभावात् फलोत्पादासम्भवः । कालान्तरस्थायिनोऽपूर्वादेव फलोत्पत्त्यवगमात् ।

(ii) न च कालान्तरभाविनि फले कर्तुः भोक्तृत्वमनुपपन्नम्, नित्यत्वात् पुरुषस्य । नित्यतया कालान्तरभावीन्यपि फलानि भोक्तुमलम् । (प्र०पं० २४६)

The Authenticity of Smṛti

Śālikanātha next takes up the topic of *smṛti*. *Śabda* is of two types: (i) actually available, (ii) inferred. The Vedic statements that are not actually available are to be inferred from the corresponding *smṛti* statements. Such as *aṣṭakāḥ kartavyāḥ*. The injunctions contained in these *smṛti* passages are followed by all. That which is not based on an authentic source is not followed by any. Since these *smṛti* injunctions convey *apūrva* i.e., *kārya*, *pratyakṣa* etc., cannot be the source of these. *Śāstra* is the only source.

Though the Vedic passages corresponding to these are not available now, and these were not available even to Manu etc., early *smṛti* writers, there has been a continuous tradition of *smṛtis*. Through these, Manu etc., also inferred the corresponding Vedic passages. The *smṛtis* have recorded the injunctions contained in these inferred source passages of Veda and therefore are authoritative.

The continuous tradition of *smṛti* is something like the continuous tradition of elders' use of language and the comprehension of the same by the new generation. These inferred passages also can convey their import like the written alphabets helping to infer. These inferred Vedic passages were not actually heard, because, these were not actually recited by the earlier generation all along. Though these were never recited, these do constitute *śabda* and Veda since these consist of syllables. These are *apauruṣeya* statements and hence consistute Veda.

(i) अत्रापि शिष्टः शास्त्रमिति ज्ञानम् । शास्त्रं शिष्यते अनेनेति तु शब्दः । स च द्विविधः प्रत्यक्षः अनुमेयः । किं पुनः शब्दानुमाने लिङ्गम्? 'अष्टकाः कर्तव्याः' इति स्मृतिवचनम् । कथम्? इयं तावत् स्मृतिः त्रैवर्णिकैः अविगानेन परिगृहीता । न च निर्मूलायाः परिग्रहः उपपद्यते । मूलं च प्रत्यक्षादि न सम्भवति । तस्य कार्यविषयत्वाभावात् । स्मृतौ च अपूर्वकार्यावगमात् शास्त्रं सम्भवति मूलम् । (प्र०पं० २४९)

(ii) वयमिव मन्वादयोपि तच्छास्त्रं प्रत्यक्षं नोपलभन्ते । अनुमानं तु अस्माकमिव तेषाम् सम्भवति म्मृत्यन्तरं हि महाजनपरिगृहीतं दृष्ट्वा तेपि तत्कर्तुः स्मृत्यन्तरानुमितं शास्त्रं मूलभूतमनुमातुं शक्नुवन्तीत्येवमनादित्वात् स्मृतिपरम्पराया लिङ्गभूतयाः सम्भवात् नानुमानविघातः । शब्दार्थसम्बन्धवत् ।

(iii) ममेव वृद्धान्तरस्यापि अपरवृद्धव्यवहारदर्शनमेवेत्यनादि वृद्धव्यवहाररूपलिङ्गपरम्परां परिकल्प्य लोको व्युत्पाद्यते । तथा स्मृतिपरम्परामनादिमेव कल्पयित्वा शास्त्रानुमानमपि कुर्वन्ति । न च अनुमित्सया शास्त्रस्य अर्थप्रतिपादकत्वमनुपपन्नम् । लिप्यनुमितिवत् । सर्वदा च तस्य अश्रवणम् अनाम्नातत्वात् । अनाम्नानमेव कस्मादिति चेत् । आचार्यैः अनाम्नानात् । (प्र०पं० २९१)

The Need of Adhyāhāra

An important point to be noted in connection with the import of *niyoga* is that when it is not complete, it has to be completed by *adhyāhāra* of that which is not expressly stated in the injunctive statement. For instance, in the passage that enjoins *piṇḍapitṛyajñā*, the *niyojya* is not mentioned. Therefore, the *niyojya* has to be brought in by way of *adhyāhāra*.

In that passage *kārya* is stated. That has to be accomplished by the performance of the sacrifice. Without an agent, no sacrifice can be performed. One will act as agent, only when he knows that he is *adhikārin*. He will be *adhikārin* only if he is *niyojya*. He who knows that performing a particular sacrifice is his *kārya* is *niyojya* for that *kārya* i.e., *niyoga*. If a *niyojya* is not stated in connection with an injunction, there is no *adhikārin* and no agent. Without an agent there will not be *karmānuṣṭhāna*. Consequently, the *kārya* i.e., *niyoga* of that injunction remains unaccomplished. Therefore, for this reason such an injunction is incomplete. It has to be made complete by the *adhyāhāra* of *niyojya*. *Adhyāhāra* means bringing to the mind the left out element. The expressed part of the injunctive statement gets connected with this expressly not stated element that is now brought to the mind. The particular items that have to be presented by *adhyāhāra* should be decided by the requirements and the consideration of economy in each such instance. In the present instance of *piṇḍapitryajña niyojya* has to be brought in by way of *adhyāhāra*.

प्रत्यक्षमपि शास्त्रं किञ्चिदध्याहारापेक्षम् । यथा अमावास्यायामपराण्हे पिण्डपितृयज्ञेन चरन्तीति पिण्डपितृयज्ञादिशास्त्रम् । पिण्डपितृयज्ञादौ हि नियोज्याश्रवणात् अपरिपूर्णं वाक्यम् ।

ननु पदानामन्विताभिधायित्वेन व्युत्पत्तेः भवतु एकपदप्रयोगे अन्वितार्थान्तरापेक्षत्वादन्विताभिधानस्य तदसिद्धौ अपूर्णता । अनेकपदप्रयोगेतु अन्विताभिधानस्य सिद्धत्वात् किं निबन्धनमपरिपूर्णत्वम्? उच्यते-अत्रापि अभिहितार्थस्य अनुपपत्त्या भवत्येव अपरिपूर्णता । अत्रापि लिङ्गादिभिः अपूर्वं कार्यरूपमभिधीयते । न च अनुष्ठानमन्तरेण कार्यरूपता निर्वहति । न च कर्तारमन्तरेण अनुष्ठानोपपत्तिः न च अधिकारमप्रतीत्य कर्मणि कर्तृतां प्रतीपद्यन्ते । कर्मणि च अधिकारः नियोगार्थे नियोज्यस्य अवकल्पते । यो हि ममेदं कार्यमितिप्रतिपद्यते सः स्वकीयकार्यसाधनं कर्म स्वार्थतया प्रतिपद्यमानो अधिकारी स्यादिति । नियोज्याश्रवणे कार्यत्वानिर्वाहात् उपपन्नमपरिपूर्णत्वम् । अतो लोके अपरिपूर्णवाक्यपूरकतया अवधारितः वेदेऽपि आश्रयते । (प्र० पं० २५२)

कः पुनः अध्याहारो नाम । अधिकस्य अर्थस्य बुद्धौ निवेशनम् । बुद्धौ सन्निहितेन तेन श्रूयमाणः शब्दः स्वार्थमन्वितमभिधत्ते । तस्य च विशेषावगतौ योग्यत्वं लाघवं च कारणम् । (प्र०पं० २५२)

The Grounds of Niyojyatva in Nitya and Kāmya

The ground of *niyojyatva* is *jīvana* itself in the case of obligatory sacrifices like *agnihotra* enjoined by the injunction *yavajjīvam agnihotram juhoti.*

In the case of *kāmya* sacrifices, the desired result itself is the ground for *adhikāra* and *niyojyatva.* Such *adhikārin* proceeds to perform the sacrifices on that ground only. The desired result is *svarga.* This term *svarga* refers to the happiness not mixed with the sorrow. *Duritakṣaya* is not the ground for *niyojyatva* since the presence of *durita* has to be envisaged for this purpose. This is an unnecessary extra consideration. Resorting to *sāmānyato dṛṣta* type of inference for setting *niyojya* is also not warranted. In the case of *adhyayana,* no *niyojya* is necessary. The injunction of *adhyayana* is managed by the injunction of *adhyāpana.* Therefore, no separate *niyojya* is necessary for *adhyayana vidhi.*

(i) यद्यपि जीवनमन्तरङ्गं नित्यं च । तथापि तस्मिन् नियोज्यविशेषणे आश्रियमाणे विधेरपरमनुष्ठानाक्षेपकत्वं कल्पनीयम् ।

(ii) काम्ये तु अधिकरविशेषणे तदर्थितयैव विधेरनुष्ठानापेक्षकत्वकल्पना न कर्तव्या । यद्यपि चोपात्तदुरितक्षयोपि पुरुषैरिष्यते शङ्कित्वा दुःखहेतुत्वं दुरितस्य तथापि तस्य उपात्तदुरितक्षयसापेक्षत्वात् गौरवम् । तस्मात् सकलपुरुषाभिलषणीयं सकलदुःखसम्भेदरहितं सुखं स्वर्गपदाभिधेयं नियोज्यविशेषणं कल्प्यते । (प्र०पं० २५२)

(iii) सामान्यतो दृष्टानुमानं तु न नियोज्यकल्पनायां प्रमाणम् । अध्ययनविध्यादौ व्यभिचारदर्शनात् । विध्यन्तरप्रयुक्ततया च अनुष्ठानलाभात् अपरिपूर्णतापि नास्ति । (प्र०पं० २५४)

The Procedure of Karaṇopakāra in Vikṛti

In the case of *vikṛti yāgas*, since *karanopakārakapadārthas* are not stated, these have to be brought in by *adhyāhāra*. In this *adhyāhāra*, *karaṇopakāra* is brought in by *upadeśa* only, while the *padārthas* are brought in by *atideśa*. It should be noted here that the *karaṇopakāra* brought in here is not new. It is *prākṛta karaṇopakāra* that is brought in by *adhyāhāra*. Similarly, the *padārthas* brought in are also not new. The *prākṛta padārthas* only are brought in here by way of *adhyāhāra*. Earlier these were connected with *prākṛtāpūrva*. Now these get connected with *vaikṛtapūrva*.

विकृतिषु करणोपकारजनकपदार्थवर्गाणामनाम्नानात् तद्व्यतिरेकेण उपकारासम्भवात् तदभावे करणस्य कार्यसाधनासमर्थत्वात् कार्यस्य कार्यत्वानिर्ह्लादपरिपूर्णत्वे सति परिपूर्णर्थमध्याहार: कर्तव्य: । तत्र यावत् स्वतन्त्रपदार्थाध्याहारो नोपपद्यते । विशेषावगमे कारणाभावात् । करणोपकाराध्याहारेपि प्रकृतिवदपरिक्लृप्ताध्याहारे पुनरपि पदार्थानामभावे निर्वाहासम्भवात् प्राकृतोपकाराध्याहार: कर्तव्य: । तत्रापि प्रकृतीनां बहुत्वात् चोदनालिङ्गसामान्यात् यद् बुद्धौ सन्निधीयते तदीयोपकाराध्याहार: युक्त: । तदध्याहारे तथैवापरिपूर्तेः पदार्थाकाङ्क्षायां तदुपकारोपस्थापितै: पदार्थै: अन्विताभिधानम् ।

यद्यपि चासौ उपकार: प्राकृत: तत्तत्पदार्थजन्यतया निर्ज्ञात: । तथापि अपूर्वप्रयुक्तत्त्वात् पदार्थानां प्राकृतापूर्वसम्बद्धस्यैव सत: तस्योपकारस्यैते पदार्था: जनका: न अपूर्वान्तरसम्बद्धस्येति सम्प्रति वैकृतापूर्वसम्बन्धमुपगत: करणोपकारो न तत्पदार्थजन्यतया अवसीयते इति अस्ति तज्जनकपदार्थापेक्षा इति पूर्वप्रतीतसम्बन्धेन उपकारेण उपस्थापितै: पदार्थै: अन्वित: वैकृतो विध्यर्थ: स्वशब्देनाभिधीयते । (प्र०पं० २५४-५५)

Upamāna is not the Ground for the Atideśa

The Prābhākaras do not consider the *upamāna* i.e., *sādṛśya* as a ground for *atideśa* while the Bhāṭṭas do consider it. For instance, the similarity between *āgenya* and *saurya* is the ground for the *atideśa* of *padārthas* from *āgenya* to *saurya* according to Bhāṭṭas.

उपमानं तु प्राकृतोपकारपदार्थसम्बन्धेन प्रमाणम् । सादृश्यमात्रविषयत्वात् । अतो अध्याहारापेक्षमपि प्रत्यक्षशास्त्रम् । (प्र०पं० २५५)

The Role of Propriety in Comprehending the Vedas

The import of the expressed statements of the Vedas should be understood in the light of general guidelines of propriety. For instance, whether the statement *udbhidā yajeta paśukāmaḥ* enjoins a *guṇa* i.e., a subordinate item or *udbhid* is the ṇame of the sacrifice, has to be decided by the guidelines of propriety in favour of the name. It is to help in such contexts that the *Mīmāmsā* plays the role of *itikartvyatā.*

(i) प्रत्यक्षमपि शास्त्रं वचनव्यक्त्यवधारणाय न्यायसापेक्षम् । यावत् हि न्यायानुसारेण वचनव्यक्त्यवधारणं न क्रियते न तावत् समीचीनार्थबोधोत्पादनक्षमं शास्त्रम् ।

(ii) अत एव स्वार्थमवबोधयतो वेदस्य मीमांसा इतिकर्तव्यताभूता धर्मे प्रमीयमाणे हि वेदेन करणात्मना ।
इतिकर्तव्यताभागं मीमांसा पूरयिष्यति ।। बृहट्टीका (प्र०पं० २५५)

The Criteria of Śāstrabheda

After discussing the different aspects of *śāstrapramāṇa* Śālikanātha discusses the question of *śāstrabheda.* In this context *śāstrabheda* means *vidhibheda* i.e., demarcations of injunctions resulting in the demarcations of the ritual. This is also known as *karmabheda.* For this purpose the scope of a *śāstra* i.e., an injunction, is explained as a group of words that convey one ritual. This explanation is on the same line as in the case of a *mantra.* A *mantra* is also explained as 'A group of words that convey one subject-matter. It is true in the case of a *mantra* its subject-matter is known through some other *pramāṇa* and it is described in the *mantra.* However, in the case of an injunction about the ritual it is conveyed for the first time. The scope of an injunctive sentence is also explained as a group of words that enjoin one ritual. The units of a word and a sentence are determined on the basis of the units of the meaning only.

The subject-matter of an injunction that demarcates the scope of an injunction is comprehended through the injunction only.

(i) कियत् पुनः पदजातमेकं शास्त्रमितिचेत् । उच्यते यावतां पदानामेकार्थत्वं तावदेकं शास्त्रम् । अर्थभेदे तु शास्त्रभेदः । यथा-मन्त्रेषु यावता पदजातेन एकोऽर्थः प्रतीयते तावदेकं वाक्यमित्यवगम्यते तथा शास्त्रमपीति ।

(ii) ननु मन्त्रेषु प्रमाणान्तरप्रमितेषु तत्त्वम् अन्यथात्वं वा अर्थस्य अन्यतोऽवधारयितुं शक्यते । शास्त्रं तु प्रमाणान्तराप्रतीतार्थावबोधकम् । अतस्तदर्थस्य तत्त्वमन्यथात्वं वा नान्यतः शक्यतेऽवसातुम् । उच्यते शब्दानामर्थावच्छेदेनैव सर्वत्र एकता प्रतिपत्तिः । पदतापि वर्णानामेकार्थावच्छेदेनैव । (प्र०पं० २५५-५६) सतु अर्थः अवच्छेदेकः शास्त्रस्य शास्त्रादेव अवगम्यते ।

The import of an injunction is *kārya.* The *kārya* can be accomplished by *kṛti.* The *kṛti* is always in respect of an activity. Therefore, an activity i.e., a ritual programme, connected with the *kārya* through *kṛti* is the subject-matter of an injunction. The group of words that convey such an activity as connected with an injunction constitute the import of that injunction and that is a unit of *śāstra.* The individuality of an injunction is determined by the individuality of its subject-matter.

कः पुनः विषयो नाम । डच्यते कार्यमेव विध्यर्थः । कार्यं च कृतिसाध्यम् । कृतिश्च प्रयत्नः । स च सर्व एव भावार्थसमम्बद्धः । तेन कार्यं प्रतीयमानं कृतिविशिष्टं प्रतीयते नान्यथा । कृतिरपि भावार्थेन विशेष्यते । तेन भावार्थः कृतिं विशिंषन् कार्यं विशिनष्टीति विषयः उच्यते । यो हि यत्र विधीयते स तस्य विषयः । अतश्च यावति पदसङ्घे एको विषयः तावत्येको नियोगार्थः । तदैक्याच्च एकं शास्त्रम् । तत्र नियोगाभेदस्यापि

विषयाभेदोन्नेयत्वात् विषयाभेदादेव शास्त्रमेकमिति व्यवस्थाप्यते । तद्भेदाच्च भिन्नम् । (प्र०पं० २५६-५७)

For the demarcation of the sacrifices and consequently considering the concerned injunctions as separate injunctions five guidelines are laid down. These are: *śabdāntara, abhyāsa, guṇa, sanjñā* and *prakaraṇāntara*. Śālikanātha discusses these guidelines. In the course of this discussion he also clarifies certain connected matters:

śabdāntara: The expressions *yajeta, juhoti* and *dadāti* occur in the same context. These are not synonyms. Therefore, these enjoin different rituals.

In this context, the meaning of the expressions *yāga, homa* and *dāna* are also explained. Offering the sacrificial offering to the deity is *yāga*. He for whom the sacrificial offering is made is the deity. The deity is also explained as 'he whose qualities are described in the hymns recited at the sacrifice is the deity'. Withdrawing the ownership of the offering made at the sacrifice is *tyāga*.

In *yāga* the transfer of the ownership of the offering to the others is not particularly brought to the mind. While in *dāna* the same is brought to the mind. In the *homa* the dropping of the special offering in the sacrificial fire is a special feature. On account of the differences in the implications of these expressions viz., *yāga, homa* and *dāna* the verbs *yajeta, juhoti* and *dedāti* are to be taken as enjoining different ritual items.

(i) **पञ्चधा विषयभेदोऽवसीयते । तत्र 'ज्योतिष्टोमेन स्वर्गकामो यजेत' 'जुहोति' 'हिरण्यमात्रेयाय ददाति' इत्येकप्रकरणगतानि अपर्यायधातुभेदानि आख्यातानि उदाहरणम् ।**

(ii) **देवतोद्देशेन द्रव्यत्यागो यागः । कापुनर्देवता? कश्चत्यागः । उच्यते स्तोत्रं शस्त्रं वा यद्गुणवचनम् । यदुद्देशेन हविषां त्यागः चोद्यते सा देवता । तत्रैव याज्ञिकवृद्धानां देवताशब्दप्रयोगात् । तत्र हि आग्नेयाद्युद्देशेन अर्थानुष्ठाने प्रवृत्तः अग्निमुद्दिश्य हविस्त्यजति । तत्रैवमाहुः अग्निदैवतेति ।**

उद्देशश्च चतुर्थ्यन्ततद्वाचकपदप्रयोगः । त्यागश्च आत्मसम्बन्धिनि स्वे औदासीन्यसङ्कल्पः । स चानभिसंहितपरस्वत्त्वापत्तिफलको यागः । देशविशेषगतद्रव्यप्रक्षेपोपाधिकश्च स एव होमः । अभिसंहितपरस्वत्त्वापत्तिफलं च दानमिति । अभिधानभेदात् यजत्याद्यनुबन्धभेदावगमः ।

Abhyāsa: when the same injunctive expression such as *yajati* is repeated, then, also it has to be taken as enjoining more than one ritual. For instance, the injunctions *somidho yajati, tanūnapātam yajati* etc., five have to be taken as five different rituals though the same expression *yajati* is repeated and no different injunctive expressions are found as in the instance of *śabdāntara.* The purpose of an injunction is to convey an item that is not conveyed by any other *pramāṇa.* Here, since different such five items are conveyed these have to be taken as different rituals though the expression *yajati* is common to all. This is supported by the repetition of *yajati.*

तथा विध्युच्चारणाभ्यासात् असति अभिधानभेदे भावार्थभेदोऽवगम्यते। असन्निकृष्टार्थावबोधस्वरसं हि सर्वमेव विध्याम्नानम् । तदर्थबोधेनैवमवसीयते । नूनं भिन्ना इमे धात्वार्थाः इति । (प्र०पं० २५८)

In this connection two interesting points are raised viz., (i) whether an injunctive expression repeated by men leads to two different rituals (ii) whether an injunctive statement repeated in another *śākha* of Veda leads to two different rituals. Śālikanātha replies both these questions negatively. In the first case it is clarified that it is only the repetition in the Veda that is the ground for considering the possibility of two rituals but not voluntary repetition by the persons engaged in the rituals. In the second case also since the subject-matter in the other *śākha* is also the same, it does not lead to two different rituals.

(i) ननु तर्हि यदा पुरुषः स्वेच्छया विधिमामनति तदापि तर्हि विषयभेदः स्यात् । न । स्वतन्त्रत्वादुच्चारणस्य । यद्धि न पूर्वोच्चारणदर्शनपूर्वकमुच्चारणं तदपौरुषेयं स्वातन्त्र्येणार्थपरिच्छेदकम् । यत्पुनरस्वतन्त्रम्

तत्पौरुषेयं प्रमाणान्तरोपात्तार्थावबोधकम् । न च तत्र भेदे प्रमाणोऽस्तीति । न भेदो विषयस्य ।

(ii) शाखान्तरगतस्तर्हि विध्याम्नानाभ्यासो भेदकः स्यात् । नेत्युच्यते । अभ्यासाभावात् । यत्र हि एक एव हि वक्ता पुनः पुनः तदेव शब्दमुच्चारयति तत्राभ्यासो व्यपदिश्यते । शाखान्तरगतं विधिं पुरुषान्तरं पठतीति नाभ्यासः शक्यते वक्तुम् । (प्र०पं० २५८)

In the case of *Darśapūrṇamāsa,* though there is the repetition of *yajate* there is no *karmabheda.* To work out *karmabheda yāgarūpabheda* is necessary. *Dravya* and *devatā* constitute *yāgarūpa.* Here, *dravya* can be some how managed either by taking *dhruvyaājya* expressly stated in the context or any other. However, there is no *devatā* here. Neither by the occurrence of the very *yajate* nor by the mention of the *vārtaghni hymn devatā* can be envisaged here. Mere occurrence of *yajate* is not a sufficient ground to envisage any special *devatā.* The *vartaghni* relates to *ājyabhāga* as indicated by the use of the dual number. Therefore, there is no *karmabheda* here on the ground of *abhyāsa.*

यद्येवं तर्हि 'य एवं विद्वान् पौर्णमासीं यजते' इत्यत्रापि तद्भेदः स्यात् । न अभ्यासकल्प्यस्य भेदस्य अनिर्वाहात् । रूपभेदेन हि भेदो निर्वहति । यागस्य द्रव्यदेवते रूपम् । ताभ्यां स रूप्यते । नर्ते ताभ्यां स भवति । यद्यपि अत्र द्रव्यमविहितमपि यत्किञ्चिदुपादाय क्रिया सिद्ध्यति । यद्यपि वाचनिकमपि ध्रौवमाज्यं गम्यते तथापि देवता अविहिता भवतीति विधानमन्तरेण तदलाभः । न च यजिरेव तदन्वितस्वार्थमाचक्षाणो देवतां विधातुमलम् । विशेषावगमे कारणाभावात् । नापि वार्तघ्नी पौर्णमास्यामनूच्यते इति मन्त्रविधानात् मान्त्रवर्णिकदेवताश्रवणं सम्भवति । मन्त्रविधेरभावात् । आज्यभागयोरयं मन्त्रविधिः द्विवचनानुरोधादिति स्थितम् । तस्मादनुवादमन्तरेण रूपालाभात् अनुवादोऽयं नाभ्यासात् कर्मभेदः ।

In this context an interesting question is raised viz., whether *āgneyaghāra* etc., also be taken as *pradhānakarma* or *aṅgakarma.* It is argued that just as in the case of *rajasūya yāga, iṣṭi, paśu* and *soma yāgas* are taken on par with each and are taken as *pradhāna yāga,* why not take *āgneyaghara* etc., also as *pradhāna yāgas* in the context of *Darśapūrṇamāsa*? This argument cannot be accepted since the expression *darśapūrṇamāsabhyām* is used in dual and envisages two groups of three rituals. Therefore, all cannot be taken on equal footing. The expressions *darśa* and *pūrṇamāsa* refer to the time. Therefore, the rituals have to be organized on that basis and the *aṅgapradhānabhāva* has to be worked out accordingly.

नन्वेवं तर्हि प्रकृतसर्वरूपवद्यागानुवादः किमिति न स्यात् । ततश्च अनूदितानां 'दर्शपूर्णमासाभ्यां स्वर्गकामो यजेत इत्यधिकारसम्बन्धात् राजसूयवत् सर्व यजीनां प्राधान्यं स्यात् अङ्गत्वं चाधारादीनां न स्यात् । उच्यते । सर्वानुवादाश्रयणे दर्शपूर्णभासाभ्यामिति द्विवचनं नोपपद्यते । समुदायद्वयानुवादकत्वेन सर्वेषामेव दर्शशब्दवाच्यता पूर्णमासशब्दवाच्यता अवगम्यते । ततश्च दर्शाः पूर्णमासाश्चेति कर्मधारयसमासः । तत्र यजीनां विशेष्याणां बहुत्वात् बहुवचनं स्यात् । न द्विवचनम् । अतः तदनुरोधेन केषाञ्चिदेव तावत् 'य एवं विद्वान् पौर्णमासीं यजते' इत्यानुवादः । न सर्वेषाम् । तथा 'य एव विद्वानमावास्यां यजत' इति केषाञ्चिदेव अनुवादः । तेन अनुवादेन समुदायद्वयापत्तेः द्विवचनान्तोपपदवशेन तेषामेवा-धिकारसम्बन्धः । तत्र केषां पौर्णमासीकालयुक्तानुवादः केषाञ्चामावास्यायुक्तः इत्यपेक्षायां कालनिमित्तोपपदानुसारेण उत्पत्तिकालयोगिनामेवानुवादः इति निश्चयो जायते । अन्यथा विशेषाग्रणादिति न सर्वानुवादः । न वा सर्वेषां प्राधान्यम् । (प्र०पं० २६०)

Guṇāt karmabheda: The mention of an additional *guṇa* is another ground for *anubandhabheda* i.e., *viṣayabheda,* and consequently for *karmabheda.* In the instance of *tapte payasi dadhi anayati sā vaiṣvadevi āmikṣa vājibhyo vājinam.* The *āmikṣā guṇa* is mentioned first and then *vajina* is also mentioned. When *dadhi* i.e., curd, is mixed with the hot milk it will be split into a hard portion i.e., *āmikṣā,* and water i.e., *vājina.* These two cannot be taken as *guṇa* for one and the same ritual. One *guṇa* i.e., *āmikṣā* is *utpatti śiṣṭa* i.e., stated along with the statement of the ritual, and the other *utpannaśiṣṭa* stated later. Therefore, two rituals have to be envisaged to account for these two *guṇas.*

(i) गुणान्तरयोगादपि अनुबन्धभेदोऽवगम्यते । उत्पत्तौ यत्कारकानुविद्धं कर्म प्रतीयते ततो अन्येन कारकेण अनुबद्धं तत् न शक्यते अवगन्तुमित्यनुबन्धभेदावगमः । (प्र०पं० २६०-६१)

(ii) तप्ते पयसि दध्यानयति सा वैश्वदेव्यामिहथा वाजिभ्यो वाजिनमिति श्रूयते । अस्यायमर्थः:- तप्ते पयसि दध्नि आसिक्ते तत्पयो द्वेधा सम्पद्यते । घनीभूतत्वेन द्रवीभूतत्त्वेन च । घनीभूतं पयः आमिक्षापदेन व्यपदिश्यते द्रवीभूतं च वाजिनमिति । तत्र आमिक्षावरुद्धे वैश्वदेवयागे वाजिनस्य उत्पन्नशिष्टस्य निवेशायोगेन अनुबन्धभेदमवगमयतीति वाच्यम् । (प्र०पं० २६०)

Sanjñayā karmabhedaḥ: The *anubandhabheda* i.e., *viṣayabheda* is found on the ground of *sanjñābheda* also. Consequently different rituals have to be envisaged to account for different *sanjñās* i.e., names. For instance, *atha esaḥ jyotiṇ atḥa eṣaḥ viśvajyoti atḥa sarva jyotiḥ etena sahasra dakṣiṇena yajeta.* Here, since different names are given, these have to be considered as different rituals from *jyotiṣṭoma* though these are stated in the context of *jyotiṣṭoma.*

संज्ञान्तरादपि अनुबन्धभेदोऽवगम्यते । अन्याय्यं हि एकस्य अर्थस्य अनेकशब्दत्वमिति भेदस्तावदौत्सर्गिकः । यत्र तु बलीयसा प्रमाणेन अनेकशब्दत्वमपि गम्यते । भवति तत्रैक्यम् । (प्र०पं० २६१)

Vidhānāntareṇa karmabheda: Śālikanātha does not take *prakaraṇāntara* as a ground for *karmabheda.* He considers the instances of *prakaraṇāntara* as *vidhānāntara.* The instance *māsam agnihotram juhoti* given for *prakaraṇāntara* is treated as *vidhānāntara.* In the instance, *upasadbhiḥ caritvā māsam agnihotram juhoti* it cannot be taken as *guṇavidhi* in respect of *nitya agnihotra. Anantarya, māsa,* etc. many *guṇas* cannot be enjoined with reference to *nitya agnihotra* which is already enjoined. This will result in *vākyabheda.* Therefore, this has to be treated as enjoining a separate *karma* i.e., *māsagnihotra* with many *guṇas* being stated at the very start. Since another *karma* is enjoined it is a case of *vidhānāntara. Prakaraṇāntara* is the same as *vidhānāntara.*

विधानान्तरादपि कर्मान्यत्वावगमः । विधानान्तरं च संयुक्ते कर्मणि अनेकगुणसंयुक्तकर्मग्रहणात्, तत्र हि गुणविधिः तावत् न सम्भवति । अनेकगुणश्रवणात् अनेकगुणविधाने वाक्यभेदप्रसङ्गात् । गुणविशिष्टकर्मविधौ तु तस्यैव एकस्य विधानादेवाक्यत्वनिर्वाहात् । कर्मैव विधेयम् । विधीयते चेत् कर्म ततः प्रकृतादन्यत्वम् । प्रकरणान्तरमपि कर्मणः प्रक्रियान्तरं विधानान्तरमेव ।

Śālikanātha does not take *samkhyā* i.e., number, as a ground for *karmābheda.* In the instance of *saptadaśa prājāpatyān* the *dravya* and *devatā* that are conveyed by the expression *prājāpatya* get connected with the *niyoga* only once, since these are stated only once. The number *saptadaśa* does not convey any multiplication of the ritual programme itself. It indicates only the number of *paśu.* Therefore, *samkhyā* is not a ground for *karmabheda.*

सङ्ख्या तु भावार्थमात्रभेदे प्रभवति न विषयभेदे । यथा 'सप्तदशप्राजापत्यान्' इति प्राजापत्यप्रातिपदिकोपात्तानां द्रव्यदेवतासम्बन्धानां नियोगविषयत्वम् । ते च सकृदेव अभिहिताः सकृदेव सम्बध्यन्ते । 'दर्शपूर्णमासाभ्यां स्वर्गकामो यजेत' इतिवत् न भेदेन विषयभावं भजन्ते । (प्र०पं० २६२)

Before the discussion on *sāstrapramāṇa* is closed Śālikanātha discusses whether the *darśapūrṇamāsa* enjoined by *darśapūrṇa māsābhyām svargakamo yajeta* and *yavajjīvam darśapūrṇa-māsābhyām yajeta* are one and the same sacrifice or different. The first one is *kāmya* since a *phala* is stated for it. The second if treated as distinct will be *nitya.* Śālikanātha points out that the two cannot be treated as one. To treat the second statement also as dealing with the same sacrifice that is enjoined by the first, it has to be taken as enjoining the time viz., the duration of the whole life, as the time for the *darśapūrṇa* sacrifice. This means that *lakṣaṇā* has to be made for the second statement in this sense. Secondly, to perform the *darśapūrṇamāsa* throughout the life, it has to be repeated. This also means that *yajeta* has to be taken in the sense *yagam abhyaset*. In this way indulgence in *lakṣaṇā* in two respects will be necessary. This is not desirable. Therefore, the second has to be treated as a separate injunction enjoining a separate sacrifice of the same name. Since no *phala* is stated for it, it is nitya sacrifice, *Svargakāmanā* is the ground for *adhikāra* for the first while *jīvana* is the ground for *adhikāra* for the second. This is *sādhyabheda*. This leads to *śāstrabheda* i.e., *vidhibheda*, and consequently leads to *karmabheda*.

साध्यभेदादपि शास्त्रभेदोऽवसीयते । यथा 'दर्शपूर्णमासाभ्यां स्वर्गकामो यजेत' 'यावज्जीवं दर्शपूर्णमासाभ्यां यजेत' इति ।

(i) **नहि यावज्जीवचोदना कामाधिकारे कालविधानार्था लक्षणाप्रसङ्गात् ।**

(ii) **किञ्च जीवनकाले एव प्रयोगस्य प्राप्तत्वात् यावदर्थसम्बन्धेन विधेयत्वं तावांश्च कालः न अनभ्यस्तेन प्रयोगेण शक्यत व्याप्तुमिति यजेतेत्यपि यागमभ्यसेदिति वर्णनीयम् । (प्र०पं० २६२-६३)**

Therefore, it is better to take *jīvana* as a separate ground of *adhikāra* and consider the second statement as a separate injunction. This means that the *niyojya* for the two are distinct and consequently the *niyogas* and *śāstra* i.e., *vidhivākyas* are distinct.

जीवतोऽधिकारान्तरमेतदाश्रयणीयम् । जीवने हि अधिकारिविशेषणे सति जीवतोऽवश्यं यागेन भवितव्यमिति शब्दाद् गम्यते । ततश्च नियोज्यभेदात् नियोगस्यापि भेदोऽवश्यंभावी । तद्भेदाच्च शास्त्रभेद एव । (प्र०पं० २६३-६४)

The *niyojya* comprehends the *niyoga* as his *kārya*. By this he comprehends that the *apūrva* is to be realized by his *kṛti*. The *kṛti* of each *niyojya* is distinct from the other. The distinct *kṛti* makes *kārya* also distinct. In this way the distinct *niyoga* that leads to distinct *śāstra* has to be envisaged by the distinction of the *niyojya*. The distinction of *niyojya* naturally suggests the distinction of *adhikāra* also. The process of the comprehension of the *śāstrabheda* from *sādhyabheda* may be stated as under:

(i) *sādhyabheda* i.e., *adhikārabheda*, (ii) *niyojya bheda*, (iii) *niyogabheda*, (iv) *kṛtibheda*, (v) *kārybheda*, (vi) *śāstrabheda* i.e., *vidhibheda*.

In the case of *kārya* of *darśapūrṇamāsa* the *adhikāra* is *svargakāmanā* while in the case of *nitya darśapūrṇamāsa* the ground of *adhikāra* is *jīvana*. This distinction at the *sādhya* i.e., *adhikāra*, level leads to the distinction at *śāstra* level i.e., *vidhi* level through the steps indicated above.

नियोज्यभेदात् नियोगस्यापि भेदोऽवश्यंभावी । तद्भेदाच्च शास्त्रभेद एव । नियोज्यो हि स्वसम्बन्धितया ममेदं कार्यमिति नियोगमवबुद्ध्यते । तेन स्वकृतिसाध्यमपूर्वमवबुद्ध्यते । यदीया च या कृतिः सा तद्भेदेन भिद्यते । कृतिभेदेन च कार्यस्यापि भेदः । तेन नियोज्यः कृतिं भिन्दन् कार्यमपि भिनत्ति । अतो नियोगभेदस्यापि शास्त्रभेदहेतोः नियोज्यभेदोन्नेयत्वात् तद्भेदेनैव शास्त्रभेदो व्यपदिश्यते । नियोज्यभेदेन अवश्यं साध्यभूतस्य ऐश्वर्यलक्षणस्याधिकारस्य भेद इति साध्यभेदोऽपलक्षणीयोऽयं शास्त्रभेदः । (प्र०पं० २६४)

Finally Śālikanātha explains the purpose served by each clause in the definition of *śāstra*.

The expression *artha* which means conveyed by the word, excludes the speaker's knowledge conveyed by *liṅga* from the scope of *śāstra pramāṇa*. The expression *asannikṛṣṭa* i.e., not known through any other *pramāṇa*, excludes the knowledge conveyed by the *laukika* statements which restate the knowledge of the speaker gathered from some other *pramāṇa*. It also excludes the knowledge conveyed by *arthavāda* statement that could be ascertained from the other *pramāṇas*.

That is why *arthavādas* are considered as *pramāṇa* only as connected with the injunction by conveying *prāśastya*. The expression *śabda* excludes such items from the scope of *śāstrapramāṇa* that are conveyed by way *of ārthika* process. For instance, in the instance of *vāsasi minoti* the same cloth is to be used for the *māna* and also *upaharaṇa* at the *prakṛti yāga*. Here, using the same cloth for both is *ārthika*. Therefore, it is not *śāstra*. In this way *Śālikanātha* has given a detailed account of *śāstra pramāṇa* according to Prābhākara's approach.

किं पुनरत्र व्यावर्तितमर्थादिग्रहणेन । उच्यते ।

(i) **अर्थग्रहणेन अभिधेयवचनेन लैङ्गिकं वस्तु अभिप्रायज्ञानम् अशास्त्रमित्युक्तम् ।**

(ii) **असन्निकृष्ट ग्रहणेन पौरुषेय वाक्याभिधेयस्य अर्थस्य वक्त्रभिप्राय-निश्चयपुरस्सरं यद्विज्ञानम् तन्न शास्त्रमिति दर्शितम् ।**

(iii) **तथा वेदेति अर्थवादानां न स्वतन्त्राणां सन्निकृष्टार्थपराणां शास्त्रत्वम् किन्तु अर्थवादानां विध्यन्तरप्रवेशेनेति ।**

(iv) **शब्दग्रहणेनैव अर्थस्य (आर्थिकस्य) अशास्त्रत्वमुक्तम् ।**

(v) **विज्ञानादिति न्यायाभासाद् वाक्यस्य वचनव्यक्तिमवधार्य यत् तदर्थज्ञानं तन्न शास्त्रमिति प्रकटितम् । यादृशं सम्यग् न्यायावधार्य वचनव्यक्तिकं तदेव शास्त्रम् ।**

Upamāna

Śālikanātha defines *upamāna* as 'the knowledge of similarity in an object arising from the observation of the similarity in another object is *upamāna.'*

For instance, a person who has seen a village cow later sees a forest cow similar to it, and gets the knowledge of its similarity present in the village cow.

(i) साद्दश्यदर्शनोत्थं ज्ञानं साद्दश्यविषयमुपमानम् ।

(ii) द्दष्टगोः पुरुषस्य तत्सद्दशं गवयं पश्यतः यद्गोविषयकं गवयगतसाद्दश्यज्ञानं तदुपमानम् । (प्र०पं० २७६)

Sādṛśya is a Separate Category

In the context of the explanation of the nature and the role of *upamāṇa pramāṇa*, Śālikanātha raises two important questions viz., (i) The status of *śādṛśya* as a separate category (ii) The grounds to consider *upamāna* as a separate *pramāṇa.*

On the first question, Śālikanātha states that the concept of *śādṛśya* is vouchsafed by its cognition. That which is the content of a cognition cannot be rejected. This concept of *śādṛśya* cannot be included under the categories *dravya, guṇa* etc., for the following reasons:

(1) It cannot be considered as *dravya*, since it is found in *guṇa* and *karma* also.

(2) It cannot be considered as *guṇa* or *karma* for the same reason.

(3) It cannot also be considered as *sāmānya* since it is not a ground for the notion of continuity.

(4) It cannot be included under the catagory *samavāya* since it is not a relation.

(i) सर्ववस्तूनि संविदेकशरणानि । अस्ति च अयं सदृशः इति संवित्। सा च सर्वैव विषयाव्यभिचारिणी इति दर्शितं नयवीथ्याम्। अतः संवित्स्वभावसिद्धं सादृश्यम्।

(ii) तच्च न द्रव्यं गुणकर्मणोरपि आश्रितत्वात् । अत एव न गुणत्वं नापि कर्मत्वम् । अनुवृत्तप्रत्ययनिमित्तत्वाभावाच्च न सामान्यम्। समवायस्तु संबन्धरुप इति न तत्र सादृश्यान्तर्भावः (प्र० २. २६८)

The category of *viśeṣa* is not acceptable as a separate category as its purpose is served by the attributes *pṛthaktva.*

The Nyāyavaiśeṣikas have conceived *viśeṣa* to distinguish two *paramāṇus*. However, the Prābhākaras state that the attribute *pṛthaktva* i.e., distinctness, is sufficient to account for it.

This *pṛthaktva* is permanently present in *paramāṇu*. It has not arisen on the basis of *viśeṣa*. It is not a product of *viśeṣa*. Therefore, *viśeṣa* cannot be inferred as a cause of *pṛthaktva.*

विशेषाख्यं पदार्थं प्रमाणवादिनो नानुमन्यन्ते। स हि पृथक्त्वादतिरिक्तो नानुमातुं शक्यते। पृथक्त्वं हि परमाणूनां स्थूलद्रव्यारम्भलक्षणकार्योन्नेयम्। तदतिरेकिणि विशेषे न किञ्चित् प्रमाणम्। न च परमाणुपृथक्त्वमेव लिङ्गम्, नित्यत्वात् परमाणुपृथक्त्वस्य। कार्यं हि स्यात् कारणस्य लिङ्गम्। न च परमाण्वाश्रितं पृथक्त्वं कार्यमिति प्रमेयपारायणे निर्णीतम् । अतः पदार्थान्तरमेवेदं शक्तिवत् सङ्ख्यावच्चेति प्रमेयपारायण एवोक्तम् । (प्र०पं० २६८)

As *sādṛśya* cannot be included under one of the cetagories mentioned above, it has to be considered as a separate category.

Upamāna is a Separate Pramāṇa

Śālikanātha explains the grounds to consider it as a separate *pramāṇa* as under:

(1) *Upamāna* i.e., the knowledge of similarity cannot be categorized as perception since it is comprehended in an object that is not in contact with the eye.

(2) It cannot also be categorized as memory, since, it was not experienced at the time of first seeing the village cow by a person who had not yet seen the forest cow.

(3) It also cannot be categorized as inference as no *liṅga* i.e., *hetu*, is available to infer it, since the two, i.e. the similarity with the village cow and that with the forest cow have no relation, much less the invariable relation.

(i) **तदिदमुपमानं न प्रत्यक्षम् । तिरोहिते गवि चक्षुस्सन्निकर्षातिवर्तिनि जायमानत्वात् । न च स्मृतिः । गोदर्शनसमये अप्रतीतगवयस्य तत्सादृश्यानुभवाभावात् । नानुमानं लिङ्गाभावात् । एकदेशो हि लिङ्गम् । न गोर्गवयः तद्गतं सादृश्यं वा एकदेशः । ज्ञातसम्बन्धनियमश्च हेतुः । न गोगतेन सादृश्येन सह कश्चिदपि गवयवर्तिनः सादृश्यस्य सम्बन्धोऽस्तीति कुतस्तरां तस्य सम्बन्धनियमावगमः । (प्र०पं० २६९)**

It cannot be argued that on the basis of the presence of a large number of common features, the similarity can be inferred. It is not merely the presence of a large number of common features in an object that is the ground for the comprehension of similarity with the other, but it is the comprehension of the similarity with an object on the basis of the presence of the common features that leads to the comprehension of the similarity with the other. What is conceived as a *sāmagrī* for the inference of similarity viz., the presence of a large number of common features in one, is really not the *sāmagrī* to comprehend the similarity with the other but it is the similarity in one that is the *sāmagrī* to comprehend the similarity with the other. This *sāmagrī* is different from the *sāmagrī* envisaged for the inference.

Moreover, it is not mere presence of the *saṃbandhaniyama* of the common features that leads to the inference but it is *saṃbandhaniyama smaraṇa*. No such *saṃbandhaniyama smaraṇa* arises here.

ननु अवयवसामान्यबाहुल्याच्च अनुमानं सम्भवत्येव । गवयं हि गवयावयवसामान्यबाहुल्यभाजं प्रतीत्य एवमवधारणा जायते यो यदवयसामान्यबाहुल्यवान् स तत्सदृशः इति । तेन गां गवयावयवसामान्यबाहुल्ययोगिनं स्मरतः गवयसादृश्यविषयमनुमानमुपपन्नमेव । उच्यते । सम्बन्धनियमस्मरणमनुमानोदयकारणम् । न पुनः सम्बन्धनियमावधारणमेव । अत्र च अवयवसामान्यबाहुल्यभाजः गवयस्य सदृशतया प्रतीयमानस्यैव उपमानहेतुत्वमिति कारणभेदादुपमानमनुमानाद् भिन्नम् । (प्र०पं० २७०)

Rejection of Nyāya-Vaiśeṣika Analysis of Upamāna

Śālikanātha rejects the *Nyāya-Vaiśeṣika* explanation of *upamāna.* According to them the procedure of *upamāna* is as follows: A person who is told that the forest cow is similar to that of a village cow, on observing a forest cow comprehends that this is a forest cow as it is similar to village cow. Then, he comprehends that this is designated as *gavaya.* In this process the first step viz., the comprehension that the forest cow is similar to that of a village cow is a comprehension of the statement made by someone to him. The second step viz., his actually seeing the similarity with forest cow is a perception of similarity. The third step viz., his comprehending the forest cow as designated by the word *gavaya* is an inference. He infers that the word *gavaya* coneys this object since there is a usage of this word with reference to this object. Therefore, this analysis of the process of *upamāna* does not make any room for *upamāna* as a separate *pramāṇa* and hence it is not a proper way of analysing *upamāna.*

यत्तु प्रसिद्धसाधर्म्यात् साध्यसाधनमनुमानम् । (न्या०द० १-१-६) इत्युक्तं तदयुक्तम् । तथाहि यादृशो गौः तादृशः गवयः इति

श्रुतातिदेशवाक्यस्य वने गवयमुपलभामानस्य अयं गवयः इति प्रतीतिः उपमानफलमुच्यते ।

तत्र तावत् गो सदृशः गवयः इति प्रथमावगतिः पुरुषवाक्यमात्रप्रभवा नोपमानं भवति । यदपि वनं गतस्य गवये तद्गते च गोसादृश्यज्ञानं तदपि प्रत्यभिज्ञाप्रत्यक्षम् । या तु एतस्य गवयशब्दवाच्यताप्रतीतिः । सापि गवयशब्द प्रयोगादानुमानिकी । यस्य शब्दस्य यत्र प्रयोगः तस्य तद्वाचकतया सम्बन्धनियमः अवगतः ।

Purpose Served by the Different Clauses in the Definition of Upamāna

Finally Śālikanātha explains the purpose served by the various clauses in the definition of *upamāna*. The clause *sādṛśyadarśanottha* i.e., arising by the cognition of the similarity, excludes the similarity that is perceived by the eye from the scope of *upamāna*. The clause *sādṛśyaviṣayam jñānam* excludes the cognition of a large number of common features in the forest cow from the scope of *upamāna*. The cognition of merely the common feature is not *upamāna*.

Remembrance of a similar object on seeing an object is not *upamāna* since *smaraṇa* is not *pramāṇa* at all. Therefore, the clause *sādṛśya viṣayagrahaṇa* is not intended to exclude *smarāṇa*. The cognition of an object that is not really similar but taken as similar to that is also not an instance of *upamāna*.

(i) अत्र सादृश्यदर्शनोत्त्थमित्यनेन ऐन्द्रियकस्य सादृश्यज्ञानस्योपमानता निराकृता ।

(ii) सादृश्यविषयं ज्ञानमिति किं निराकृतम् ? उच्यते गोसदृशो गवय इति पुरुषवचनात् गोसादृश्यं गवयस्य प्रतीत्य यत्तदवयव-सामान्यबाहुल्यज्ञानं गवये जायते तन्नोपमानमित्युक्तम् ।

(iii) यत्तु सदृशदर्शनमात्रेण कस्मिंश्चिदर्थे तत्सदृशस्वरूपमात्रस्मरणं तस्योपमानत्वमेव न प्रसक्तम् । स्वरूपस्मरणं हि न प्रमाणम् । प्रमाणविषयस्य चेदं लक्षणमाख्यायते । तेन तन्निवृत्त्यर्थं सादृश्यविषयग्रहणमयुक्तम् ।

(iv) एतेनैव असदृशात् यत् तत्सदृशभ्रान्तिविषयात् तत्सदृशविषयज्ञानं तदप्युपमानं नाशङ्कनीयमेव । (प्र०प० २७०-२७१)

Arthāpatti

The Definition of Arthāpatti

Śālikanātha defines *Arthāpatti* in two ways:

(1) An observed fact leading to the envisaging of an unobserved fact in order to avoid the incompatibility with a known fact. For instance, the observed fact of the absence of a person at his residence leads to the envisaging of his presence outside in order to avoid the incompatibility of his being alive but still not being present at his residence.

विना कल्पनयाऽर्थेन दृष्टेनानुपपन्नताम् ।
नयत्यदृष्टमर्थं या सार्थापत्तिस्तु कल्पना ।।

दृष्टेन अर्थेन अदृष्टस्य अर्थस्य अर्थान्तरकल्पनायामसत्यामनुपपत्तिमापादयता या अर्थान्तरकल्पना सा अर्थापत्तिः । यथा जीवतो देवदत्तस्य गृहाभावदर्शनेन बहिर्भावस्य अदृष्टस्य कल्पना । (प्र०पं० २७२-७३)

(2) Envisaging something without which a known fact becomes doubtful is *arthāpatti*. For instance, the fact of a person being alive is made doubtful by his absence at his residence. Therefore, the very fact of being alive leads to the envisaging of his being outside.

यत्कल्पनां विना योऽर्थः प्रतीतोप्येति संशयम् ।
तेन तत्कल्पनामेकेत्वर्थापत्तिं प्रचक्षते ।।

यस्मिन् अकल्पिते योऽर्थः प्रमितोऽपि पूर्वप्रतिपन्नरूपात् रूपान्तरावगमेन संशयरूपामनुपपत्तिं भजते । सोऽर्थः स्वगतसन्देहव्युदासाय तस्य अर्थान्तरकल्पनां प्रसूते सा अर्थापत्तिः । (प्र०पं० २७५)

These two explanations are more clearly stated by Śālikanātha in his *Bhāṣyapariśiṣṭa*, as under:

(1) तत्र अर्थापत्तौ गृहाभावः बहिस्सत्तायामकल्पितायां देवदत्तसत्तामनुपपत्तिं नीत्वा तदुपपादनाय बहिर्देशसम्बन्धं तस्य अवबोधयति । (भा०प०)

(2) सत्तैव गृहाभावदर्शने सति बहिर्देशसम्बन्धमात्मनः उपपत्तये कल्पयति । (भा०प०)

The common point of both these explanations is the fact of a known fact becoming incompatible or doubtful. To resolve this incompatibility or doubt the process of envisaging the required fact is initiated by the observed fact in the first explanation and otherwise known fact in the second explanation. In both cases, it is the known that becomes incompatible or doubtful. The envisaged fact resolves this incompatibility or the doubt.

Arthapātti cannot be brought under the Anumāna

Those who hold the view that the *arthāpatti* could be included under *anumāna* propose the following syllogism.

Devadatta is outside his residence, since he is not at his residence but still alive. For instance, the very person who proposes this syllogism, when he is not present in his usual place, he is present somewhere else.

ननु एतद् गृहाभावदर्शनात् जीवतो बहिर्भावदर्शनं तदनुमानमेव । तथाहि यो जीवन् एकत्र नास्ति सोऽन्यत्रास्तीति सामान्येन प्रतीतम् ।

देवदत्तः बहिर्देशसंयोगी गृहाभावे सति विद्यमानत्वात्, यो यः गृहाभावे विद्यमानः सः सः ततोऽन्यत्रास्ति । यथा अहमेवेति प्रमातुः अनुमानमुत्पद्यते ।

For this syllogism there is *anumāna sāmagrī*. An important *sāmagrī of anumāna* is *ekadeśa saṃbandha niyama*. This is found between the absence at the residence and the presence outside both with reference to the time and the place. The presence at one place and the absence at another place at the same time are possible. Therefore, there is *ekadeśa saṃbandhaniyama* with reference to the time as in the case of the spate in the sea and the moon-rise. Similarly presence in one place and the absence in another also have *ekadeśa saṃbandhaniyama*. Therefore, there is *anumāna sāmagrī* in respect of the above syllogism.

(i) **एकत्र अन्यत्र च भावाभावौ एककालत्वलक्षणसम्बन्धयोगिनौ समुद्रवृद्धिचन्द्रोदयवदेकदेशभूतौ च कालस्य इत्यनुमानसामग्र्या यदा जीवन्नेव देवदत्तो गृहे नास्ति तदा बहिरस्तीत्यनुमानं भवति ।**

(ii) **तथा एकत्राभावे सति अन्यत्र विद्यमानत्वं देशान्तरसंयोगेन नियतैकार्थ समवायलक्षणसम्बन्धमेकदेशभूतं च देवदत्तस्येति अनुमान-सामग्रीसम्भवः । (प्र०पं० २७३)**

Śālikanātha points out the drawbacks of this syllogism by examining the *hetu* i.e., the ground of the inference. The ground (*hetu*) consists of two clauses viz., (i) Devadatta is alive (*vidyamāna*) (ii) He is not present at his residence (*gṛhe abhāva*). Out of these two the fact of being alive alone cannot be the ground to infer the fact of his being outside. Because, the fact of being alive is rendered doubtful by his absence at his residence. Those who are used to see him at his residence will have a doubt about the fact of his being alive though it might have been indicated by some other *pramāṇa*.

Even in respect of such facts that are broadly known, when these are not observed in their usual contexts in the usual way, a doubt arises. A fact that is doubtful cannot be the *liṅga* (*hetu*) for an inference.

अत्रोच्यते न तावत् विद्यमानत्वं लिङ्गं भवति । स्वयं संदेहास्पदीभूतत्वात् । विद्यमानता हि देवदत्तस्य गृहाधिकरणकैव येन नाम प्रतीता तस्य बहिर्देश

सम्बन्धे अप्रत्याकलिते गृहाभावदर्शनेन देवदत्तस्य विद्यमानता प्रमाणन्तरप्रतीतापि सन्देहमावहति 'गृहे देवदत्तः अविद्यमानः कथं विद्यमानः इति प्रतीतेऽपि हि वस्तुनि पूर्वप्रतीतरूपात् रूपान्तरावगमः संशयमापादयितुमलमेव । देवदत्तस्य विद्यमनता गृहसम्बद्धैव अवगतेति तदभावप्रतीतौ बहिर्देशसम्बन्धे च अनवगते सन्दिह्यते । तेन सा सन्देहग्रस्ता सति न लिङ्गत्तां गन्तुमलम् । (प्र०पं० २७४)

It cannot be argued that the doubt about the fact of Devadatta being alive will be eliminated by the realisation of his being outside. In this event what is proposed to be inferred is already realized and hence nothing remains to be inferred.

बहिर्देशसम्बन्धावगमादपगतसन्देहा भविष्यति लिङ्गमिति चेन्न । अनुमेयाभावात् । बहिर्देशसम्बन्ध एवहि देवदत्तादेरनुमित्सितः । स चेत् प्रतिपन्नः न प्रमेयमवशिष्यते । (प्र०पं० २७४)

The second clause viz., *gṛhābhāva* i.e., his absence at the residence itself is the *hetu* to infer the presence outside is also not tenable. Mere absence at the residence cannot prove his presence outside. Because, the absence can be explained by the death also. It has to be qualified by 'being alive' ie *jīvana.* It is already stated that it is doubtful. Hence, the two together also cannot be the *hetu.*

न च गृहाभावो बहिर्देशसम्बन्धावगमे लिङ्गमित्युपपन्नम् । तस्य हि न केवलस्य लिङ्गत्वमभ्युपगमनीयम् । किन्तु जीवनविशिष्टस्य । शुद्धस्य गृहाभावमात्रस्य मृतेषु जनिष्यमाणेषु च विनापि बहिर्भावमुपपत्तेः । तदुक्तम् ---

गेहाभावस्तु यः शुद्धः विद्यमानत्ववर्जितः ।
स मृतेष्वपि दृष्टत्वात् बहिर्वृत्तेः न साधकः ।।

जीवनं च विशेषणभूतं सन्दिग्धमिति न तद्विष्टस्य लिङ्गत्त्वम् । (प्र०पं० २७४)

Mere absence at the residence i.e., *gṛhābhāva* though cannot be a *hetu* to infer the presence outside, it can be a *gamaka*. An important distinction between *gamaka* and *hetu* is that the *gamaka* is that which makes room for doubt if the required fact is not envisaged to remove the doubt, while a *hetu* does not make any room for doubt nor leads to the envisaging of something to remove it. A *hetu* straight away proceeds to establish *sādhya*. The *gamaka* by itself is an observed fact. For instance, the *gamaka* i.e., *gṛhābhāva* i.e., absence at the residence, is definitely known. However, it creates a doubt about the very existence of the person if his presence is not envisaged outside.

तस्मात् केवलस्य अभावस्यैव स्वयं निस्सन्दिग्धस्य गमकत्वं युक्तम्। अर्थान्तरकल्पनायामनुत्पन्नायां यः संशयं कञ्चिदापादयितुमलं तस्य गमकत्वम्। तथाहि बहिर्देशकल्पनायामजातायां गृहाभावो देवदत्तस्य विद्यमानता-संशयमापादयन् बहिर्देशसम्बन्धस्य गमकः (प्र०पं० २७४)

However, *gṛhābhāva* will not be *gamaka* for the presence outside of a dead person or a person yet to be born since there is no doubt of their existence nor it is required to envisage their presence outside to remove any doubt. An important feature of *gamakatva* is giving room for doubt and the removal of it by envisaging a required fact.

ननु तस्य केवलस्य गमकत्वे मृतस्य जनिष्यामाणस्य वा बहिर्देशसम्बन्धावगतिः प्रसज्येत। उच्यते। अर्थान्तरकल्पनायामनुत्पन्नायां यः संशयं कञ्चिदापादयितुमलं तस्य गमकत्वम्। मृतजनिष्यामाणयोश्च अभावः न कञ्चिदपि संशयमापादयतीति न गमकः। अतो नातिप्रसङ्गः। तदेवचात्र गम्यं यत्कल्पनायामसत्यां संन्देहापत्तिः कल्पनायां च तद्विगमः। (प्र०पं० २७५)

The Sāmagrī of Anumāna and Arthāpatti are Distinct

The *sāmagrī* of *anumāna* and *arthāpatti* are altogether different in their nature. The method followed to yield the result is also different. In this respect the following positions may be noted.

1. (a) *Anumāna* arises from *ekadeśadarśana* (*hetujñāna*), supported by *saṃbandhianiyama smaraṇa.*

   (b) In *arthāpatti* the cognition of the absence of the person leads to the envisaging of his presence outside in order to remove the doubt about the very existence of the person. In other words, there is no *saṃbandhianiyama* between the absence at the residence and the presence outside until the doubt about the very existence is removed. There is no *ekadeśa* (*hetu*), and *ekadeśāntara* (*sādhya*) position on the part of the absence at the residence and the presence outside.

2. (a) In the case of *anumāna* the *liṅga* (*hetu*) is definite.

   (b) In the case of *arthāpatti* a part of the *hetu* (*liṅga*) proposed viz., *vidyamānatā* i.e., being alive is doubtful.

3. (a) In the case of *anumāna* the *hetu* is not confronted with any incompatibility or doubt in leading to the *sādhya.*

   (b) In the case of *arthāpatti* the absence at the residence is confronted with the incompatibility of the very existence and leads to the result of the presence outside only to resolve this incompatibility. The very incompatibility seeks its resolution by leading to the envisaging of the presence outside.

(1) **(अ) सम्बन्धनियमस्मरणोपकृतात् एकदेशदर्शनात् ज्ञानमनुमानम् ।**

(ब) गृहाभावस्तु बहिर्देशसम्बन्धकल्पनायामनुत्पन्नायां सत्यां विद्यमानतायां संशयमापाद्य संशयशमाय बहिर्देशसम्बन्धं कल्पयतीति नानुमानत्वसम्भवः

तत्सन्देहव्युदासाय कल्पना या प्रवर्तते ।
सन्देहापादकादर्थादर्थापत्तिरसौ स्मृता ॥

(2) **(अ) अनुमानस्य निश्चितं लिङ्गं जनकम् ।**
(ब) अर्थापत्तेः सन्देहग्रस्तमिति नास्ति विरोधः ।

(3) **(अ) निश्चित एव धूमः अग्नेः गमकः ।**

(ब) गृहाभावस्तु विद्यमानतायाः अनुपपत्तिमातनोति। तेन गृहाभावेन विद्यमानतैव बहिर्भावसम्बन्धकल्पनायामभूतायामनुपपत्तिमापादिता स्वात्मनो बहिर्देशसबन्धं कल्पयतीति भिन्ना अनुमानादर्थापत्तिः। (प्र०पं० २७५-७६)

It is already noticed that Śālikanātha explains the nature and the role of *arthāpatti* in two ways. He quotes a third way and rejects it.

The Anupapatti of Gṛhābhāva cannot be the Ground of Arthāpatti

Some suggest a third way for *arthāpatti.* According to the third way the very absence at the residence being untenable unless the presence outside is envisaged envisages the same. Śālikanātha rejects this third way.

यस्तु गृहाभाव एव अन्यथा अनुपपद्यमानः बहिर्भावस्य गमकः इति तदयुक्तम्। (प्र०पं० २७७)

Śālikanātha analyses the very nature of the untenability of the absence at the residence that is claimed to necessitate the envisaging of the presence outside. He reduces it to *vyatirekavyāpti.* Hence, this third way of analysing the instance of *arthāpatti* is not a correct approach. This analysis may be summarized as under.

The incompatibility of the absence at the residence of a living person is that it is not tenable unless the presence outside is accepted. This argument is of the nature of *vyatirekavyāpti.* The presence outside is *sādhya* here, its absence is *sādhyābhāva.* This should lead to the *hetu abhāva.* If *bahirbhāva* is not there, then, *gṛhābhāva abhāva* should be there. However, actually there is *gṛhābhāva* and hence *bahirbhāva* has to be accepted.

का गृहाभावस्य अन्यथा अनुपपद्यमानता? यदि तावद् बहिर्देशसम्बन्धेन विना नास्तिता जीवतो गृहाभावो बहिर्देशसम्बन्धं विना नास्तीति तर्हि साध्याभावे हेत्वभावलक्षणव्यक्तिरेकोऽयम्। (प्र०पं० २७७)

The *vyatireka* stated above could be ascertained only by ascertaining *anvaya* first. Without it *vyatireka* cannot be ascertained. There will be innumerable places of *sādhyābhāva*. It is difficult to ascertain *hetvabhāva* in all such places unless *saṃbandhaniyama* between the *hetu* and *sādhya* is ascertained. Once that is ascertained it is easy to ascertain the *saṃbandhaniyama* between *sādhyābhāva* and *hetvabhāva* by *arthāpatti*.

स च (व्यतिरेकश्च) हेतुसद्भावे साध्यसद्भावलक्षणेन अन्वयेन अवगम्यते। नान्यथा । नहि अनन्तेषु साध्याभाववत्सु विपक्षेषु हेत्वभावनियमोऽन्यथा अवधारयितुं शक्यते यावद्धेतुभावस्य साध्यभावेन सम्बन्धनियमो नावधार्यते । अवधारिते हि तस्मिन् अर्थापत्त्या साध्याभावे हेत्वभावनियमोऽवसीयते । (प्र०पं० २७७)

Śālikanātha further explains the process of ascertaining the *saṃbandhaniyama* between the *sadhyābhāva* and *hetvabhāva* by *arthāpatti* as under.

There are two possibilities viz., *hetubhāva* (presence of *hetu*) and *hetvabhāva* i.e., absence of *hetu*. In the first alternative when the *saṃbandhaniyama* between the *hetu* and *sādhya* is found, there is no scope for the *sādhyābhāva*. In the second alternative viz., *hetvabhāva* alternative, if the *sādhyābhāva* does not find room, then, it becomes incompatible. Therefore, it has to find a place there. This helps to ascertain the *saṃbandhaniyama* between *sadhyābhāva* and *hetvabhāva*.

द्वेहि कोटी हेतुभावः हेत्वभावश्चेति । तत्र हेतुभावकोटौ साध्यभावेन सम्बन्धनियमे सिद्धे साध्याभावः तत्र अवकाशं न लभते । स यदि हेत्वभावकोटावपि न स्यात् तदा नोपपद्यतैव । तेन हेतुभावकोटौ साध्यभावेन सम्बन्धनियमः अवगतः हेत्वभावकोट्यनुप्रवेशकल्पनायामनुपजातायां साध्याभावस्य अनुपपत्तिमापादयन् हेत्वभावकोटिनिवेशं कल्पयति । तथा सति हेत्वभावेन साध्याभावः नियतसम्बद्धः सम्पद्यते । तस्मात् साध्याभावे

अयं नास्त्येवेत्यवगम्य या प्रतीतिः सा सम्बन्धनियमावगमपूर्विकेत्यनुमानात् न भिद्यते ।

Anupapadyamānatva of *gṛhabhāva* cannot be taken in the sense that it is *sandigdha.* There is no doubt about the absence at the residence. Therefore, this third way of explaining *arthāpatti* instance is not proper. It is the fact of *jīvana* i.e., still living, that has become doubtful. Therefore, either *gṛhabhāva* that makes the *jīvana* dougtful or *jīvana* itself that has become doubtful on account of *gṛhabhāva* is the ground for *arthāpatti.*

(i) **नहि गृहाभावस्य संशयापत्तौ किञ्चित् कारणमस्ति**

(ii) **विद्यमानतायास्तु गृहसम्बन्धितयैव दर्शनात् गृहाभावेन संशयमापद्यत इत्युच्यते । अतः सन्देहापादकोऽर्थः तेनापादितसन्देहोऽर्थो वा अर्थापत्तिरिति स्थितम् । (प्र०पं० २७८)**

There is no Separate Category of Arthāpatti as Śrutārthāpatti

The Prābhākaras do not accept *śrutārthāpatti* as separate type of *arthāpatti.* Its instances are also included under *dṛṣṭārthāpatti.*

The example for *śrutārthāpatti* is pīno *devadatto divā na bhuṅkte* Devadatta is quite stout but does not eat during the day. Here, the fact of Devadatta being stout is found incompatible with his not eating during the day. This incompatibility is to be resolved by envisaging his eating during the night. Since the incompatibility arises out of a statement, the resolution of this incompatibility also has to be conveyed by the statement that he eats during the night. Since *śabdapramāṇa* is utilized for this *arthāpatti* the Bhāṭṭas name it as *śrutārthāpatti.*

अत्र केचित् 'पीनो देवदत्तः दिवा न भुंङ्क्ते इति वाक्येन देवदत्त-सम्बन्धितया अवगतस्य भोजनस्य दिवा निषिद्धस्य पीनत्वानुमितस्य रात्रौ भुंङ्क्ते इति कल्प्यते इति वदन्ति । (प्र०पं० २७९)

The above contention of the Bhāṭṭas is not acceptable to the Prābhākaras. They take the view that it is the very fact of eating during the night that has to be envisaged by *arthāpatti* but not mere statement about it. *Arthāpatti* should envisage that by which the incompatibility is resolved. Here, the incompatibility can be resolved by envisaging the fact of eating during the night. Mere statement about it shall not resolve the incompatibility.

तदयुक्तम् । अत्रापि अर्थस्यैव कल्पयितुमुचितत्वात् । यस्मिन् हि अकल्पिते अनुपपत्तिः तदर्थापत्त्या प्रतीयते रात्रिसम्बन्धे हि अनवगते भोजनस्य अनुपपत्तिः । कालसम्बन्धाभावेन हि एषा अनुपपत्तिः । सा कालान्तरसम्बन्धमेव कल्पयितुमलम् । (प्र०पं० २७९)

On this position of the Prābhākaras the Bhāṭṭas try to make a point. It is true that *arthāpatti* should envisage the fact only that resolves the incompatibility. However, the cognition of this fact is of the nature of *savikalpaka. Savikalpaka* cognition is always conveyed through words. Therefore, the statement about the fact to be envisaged is necessary to convey it. Such a statement is not necessary in the case of the perception and the inference. The senses and the *liṅga* are capable of conveying the facts at the *nirvikalpaka* stage without the words and these do so at the *savikalpaka* stage also. However, in the instance of *śrutārthāpatti*, since the incompatible facts are conveyed through a statement, the resolution of the incompatibility also has to be put in a statement only by *arthāpatti*. That is why it is designated as *śrutārthāpatti*. It is true that in *dṛstārthāpatti*, it is the fact only that is envisaged to resolve the incompatibility, but still the Bhāṭṭas insist that the statement is necessary in the case of *śrutārthāpatti* on the ground that in the case of *dṛṣṭārthāpatti* it is the envisaging of the fact that resolves the incompatibility while in the case of *śrutārthapatti* it is the statement that resolves the incompatibility.

(i) **अर्थसद्भावमेव कल्पयितुं अर्थापत्तिः प्रवर्तमाना तस्य अर्थस्य सविकल्पकज्ञानवेद्यत्वात् सविकल्पकज्ञानानां च शब्दपुरस्सरत्वात्**

पुरोवर्तिनि शब्दः एव अर्थापत्तिः पर्यवस्यति । स च शब्दः स्वार्थमुपस्थापयति।

(ii) नचेदमाशङ्कनीयम् । लौकिकं ऐन्द्रियकं च सर्वमेव सविकल्पकं शब्द एवानेन न्यायेन पर्यवस्येदिति । यतो निर्विकल्पकदशायामिन्द्रियस्य लिङ्गस्य च अर्थबोध एव सामर्थ्यं दृश्यते । तेन सविकल्पकावस्थायामप्यर्थ एव तयोः व्यापारः परिकल्प्यते । श्रुतार्थापत्तिबोधस्तु निर्विकल्पको न सम्भवति । शब्दव्युत्पत्तिपूर्वकत्वात् । व्युत्पन्नशब्द एव हि वाक्यस्यार्थमवबुध्य तदन्यथानुपपत्त्या अर्थान्तरमवबुभुत्सते । (प्र०पं० २४०)

Śālikanātha rejects the above contention of the Bhāṭṭas. He argues that the incompatibility is not resolved until the fact of eating during the night is known. Mere statement about it does not resolve the incompatibility unless its meaning is known. Therefore, it is the fact that is conveyed by *arthāpatti*. This is already agreed upon in the case of *dṛṣtārthāpatti* and the same holds good in *śrutāthāpatti* also.

अत्रोच्यते रात्रिसम्बन्धे हि भोजनस्य अनवगते अनुपपत्तिरापतति । सा तावत् शब्दस्वरूपमात्रे अवगतेपि न शाम्यति यावत् ततः शब्दात् रात्रिसम्बन्धो भोजनस्य नावगम्यते । नहि पीनो देवदत्तो दिवा न भुंङ्क्ते इति प्रयुज्य यदा पुनरेवमुच्यते यामिन्यामत्तीति तदा यामिनी शब्दे अत्तौ च अव्युत्पन्नस्य पूर्ववाक्यार्थविषया अनुपपत्तिः उपरमति अतोऽर्थस्यैव साक्षादुपपादकत्वं न शब्दस्य । उपपादकार्थविषया तु अर्थापत्तिः दृष्टार्थापत्तौ प्रतीतेति न क्वचिदुपपादकावबोधकशब्दो प्रमाणतामर्हति । (प्र०पं० २८०)

In conclusion Śālikanātha states that the words play a role in all *savikalpaka* cognitions by way of reminding the fact conveyed. Such a role may be assigned here also. However, since *smṛti* is not a *pramāṇa* according to the Prābhākaras this role assigned to *śabda* does not confer the status of *pramāṇa* in the context of *arthāpatti*.

Therefore, the so-called *śrutārthāpatti* instances also come under *dṛṣṭārthāpatti* only.

किञ्च अन्यत्र तावत् सविकल्पके शब्दस्य स्मृतिविषयता अङ्गीकरणीया । एवं चेदत्रापि स्मृतिविषय एव शब्दोऽस्तु । मा भूत् तस्य प्रमाणविषयता । अतः श्रुतार्थापत्तिरपि शब्दग्राहिणी न भवति । किन्तु उपपादकार्थग्राहिणी एवेति स्थितम् । (प्र०पं० २८१)

Rejection of Abhāva

The Prābhākaras do not accept the category of *abhāva*. Consequently they do not accept the *abhāvapramāṇa* also. Śālikanātha examines the arguments advanced to prove the *abhāvapramāṇa* and *abhāva* and rejects them.

Bhāṭṭas Accept Abhāva and Abhāvapramāṇa

The Bhāṭṭas who accept the category of *abhāva* and *abhāvapramāṇa* argue that a *pramāṇa* conveys its *prameya* by its very nature. For instance *pratyakṣa* conveys its *prameya* by its very nature. It does not require another *pramāṇa* to establish this fact. Similarly, *abhāvapramāṇa* conveys its *prameya* i.e., *abhāva* by its very nature. The cognition that there is no jar on the ground (*bhūtale ghato nāsti*), is the evidence to prove *abhāva*. This cognition is not about the ground, since, in that case, even when there is a jar on the ground such a cognition would have been possible. This is not possible. To overcome this difficulty if it is stated that this cognition refers to the ground alone (*kevala bhūtala*), then, the import of the very expression alone i.e., *kevala*, has to be examined. If it means nothing more than the very ground, then, the objection already raised will stand. If the expression 'alone' i.e., *kevala*, is an attribute of *bhūtala*, then, an additional content is introduced in this cognition. This additional content is *abhāva*.

(i) **सर्वमेव प्रमाणं स्वमहिम्नैव प्रमेयमुपस्थापयति । न खलु प्रत्यक्षस्यापि प्रमेयं प्रमाणान्तरव्यवस्थापनीयम् । किन्तु तत्प्रतीतिबलसिद्धम् । एवमभावाख्यमपि प्रमाणं शक्नोति स्वसामर्थ्येनैव प्रमेयमुपकल्पयितुम् ।**

(ii) तथाहि भूतले घटो नास्तीति तावदस्ति प्रतीतिः । सा तावत् भूतलमात्रविषया न भवति । सत्यपि घटे प्रसङ्गात् । अथ केवलभूतल विषयेत्युच्यते तत्रापि चिन्तनीयम् किमिदं कैवल्यम्? यदि तावद् भूतलस्वरूपमेव तदा सत्यपि घटे तस्य अनपायात् घटो नास्तीति धीः स्यात् । अथ भूतलधर्मः कैवल्यम् । तर्हि अस्ति तावत् प्रमेयान्तरं कैवल्यम् । (प्र०पं० २८३)

Abhāva cannot be Cognised by Pratyakṣa

Now the question is, how this additional content represented by the attributes *kaivalya* is cognised. It cannot be said that it is perceived, since, it has no contact with the sense i.e., the eye. It is true a person obtains the cognition 'there is no jar' when he employs his eye. However, the eye perceives only the ground but not the absence of the jar on it. The absence has to be in a certain place. The eye is employed to cognise that place. Then its role is over. There is no reason to say that it also cognises the absence of the jar, since the eye has no contact with the absence.

(i) तत्रेदं विचारणीयम् । किं तत् प्रत्यक्षादिबोध्यम् उत अभावप्रमाण प्रमेयम्? तत्र प्रत्यक्षप्रमेयं तावत् न भवति इन्द्रियव्यापारमन्तरेण प्रतीतेः।

(ii) ननु इदमयुक्तम् । व्यापृतेन्द्रिय एव हि इह भूतले घटो नास्तीत्यवबुध्यते । नान्धादिः । अत्रोच्यते । क्वचित् कस्यचिदभावः प्रतीयते । तेन यत्र अभावः प्रत्येतव्यः । तद्ग्रहणाय, इन्द्रियव्यापारापेक्षा न अभावग्रहणाय ।

Here a question may be raised. Since the *abhāva* is also present on the place towards which the eye is employed, how can it be said that only the place is cognised by the eye but not the *abhāva* present on it? In reply to this question Śālikanātha demonstrates the fact that the place alone is cognised but not the *abhāva* also' by quoting a situation wherein the place alone is cognised. For instance, when a person observes a place without cognising any particular *abhāva* and moves to another place, and then, tries to find what was not there at that place when he had observed it, he realizes the absence of the things that were not there. This is an instance of observing a place without observing the absence later realized. It cannot be said that this later realized absence was also cognised at that time, since no *pratiyogin* of this absence had come to his mind at that time. From this, it is clear that when the eye is employed towards a place where something is absent, it is merely the place that is cognized but not the absence of something also.

कथं पुनरयं विभागो अवसीयते? उच्यते भावग्रहणोपरतेन्द्रियस्यापि अभावप्रतीतिदर्शनात् भावग्रहणमात्र एव इन्द्रियव्यापारापेक्षा इति विज्ञायते । तथाहि स्वरूपमात्रेण गृहादिकं प्रतिपन्नवतः देशान्तरगतस्य तत्र भावान्तरसत्तां जिज्ञासमानस्य अभावावगमो जायते । न च शक्यते वक्तुं गृहीत एव तत्रापि प्रागेव अभाव इति । भावान्तरस्यैव तदानीं बुद्धावनारोहात् । तेन इन्द्रियव्यापारानपेक्षा अभावप्रतीतिः न ऐन्द्रियकीति न प्रत्यक्षप्रमेयं कैवल्यम् । (प्र०पं० २८४)

Further, the *pramāṇas* proceed to convey the *prameya* in two ways: (i) *pravṛtti* i.e., the application of the *pramāṇa* (ii) *nivṛtti* i.e., withdrawal of *pramāṇa.* The positive entities are cognised by the application of *pramāṇa*, and the withdrawal of *pramāṇa* is the ground for the cognition of the absence. The withdrawal of the *pramāṇa* itself is not the cognition of the absence. It generates the knowledge of the absence of *pramāṇapravṛtti* and then leads to the cognition of the absence. The knowledge of the absence of *pramāṇapravṛtti* is designated as *abhāvapramāṇa* and the absence cognised is *abhāva.*

(i) **न च वाच्यम्, प्रवृत्तिनिवृत्ती द्वे गती सर्वप्रमाणानाम् । तत्र प्रवर्तमानं प्रमाणं भावसाधकम्, निवर्तमानं तु अभावसिद्धिनिबन्धनम् ।**

(ii) **या निवृत्तिः प्रमाणस्य स्वतस्तावदवगतिरूपा न भवति सा कथमभावसिद्धिमाविर्भावयति । प्रवृत्तिस्तु प्रमाणानां अवगमात्मिकेति**

तां व्यवस्थापयितुमलम् । अथ प्रमाणनिवृत्तिः अवगत्यन्तरं जनयित्वा अभावं व्यवस्थापयति आयातं तर्हि प्रमाणान्तरम् ।

The Inference cannot Cognise Abhāva

Those who claim the cognition of the absence by the inference argue as under: the presence of a perceivable object is determined by its perception. If it is not perceived, then, its presence is not granted. Thus, from the absence of the perception of a perceivable object, its absence could be inferred. This line of argument is not tenable. For an inference, *vyaptijñāna* is necessary. For *vyaptijñāna* the knowledge of *vyāpya* and *vyāpaka* is required. Here, both *vyāpya* and *vyāpaka* viz., the absence of perceiving and the absence of the object to be perceived are negative. These cannot be cognised by the *pramāṇas* that cognise the positive entities. Therefore, no *vyāpti* relation could be ascertained between these two. Therefore, a separate *pramāṇa* has to be envisaged for the cognition of *abhāva*.

(i) भवतु प्रत्यक्षात् प्रमाणान्तरम् । अनुमानात्तु भेदो नास्ति । दृश्यस्य हि सत्ता दर्शनेन व्याप्ता दर्शनं निवर्तमानं दृश्यमपि निवर्तयति । व्यापकनिवृत्तिर्हि व्याप्यनिवृत्त्या व्याप्ता । व्याप्याच्च व्यापकावगतिरनुमानमेव भवति ।

(ii) तदिदमयुक्तम् । सर्वत्र हि व्याप्यं व्यापकं चावगम्य व्याप्तिरवसीयते । इह च व्याप्या व्यापिका च निवृत्तिरेव । सा च अभावात्मिका न भावग्राहकप्रमाणावसेया इति न व्यात्प्यवधारणं सम्भवतीति कथमनुमेयता । तस्मात् भावग्राहक प्रमाणाननुवृत्तिरेव अभावावगमं प्रसूते । तच्च अभावाख्यं प्रमाणम् ।

The Experience Confirms the Category of Abhāva

A separate category called *abhāva* is confirmed by the practical experience also. When a person moves on the ground without any fear of thorn etc., it is not on the basis of the cognition of the mere ground. In that case he would have walked equally freely on the ground with the thorn also. He makes an effort to ascertain the absence of the thorn etc., and then only moves. This means, along with cognising the ground he cognises the absence of the thorn etc., also and moves. This affirms the category *abhāva* and the *abhāvapramāṇa* to ascertain it. Otherwise his efforts would be in vain.

अपि च कण्टकादिविरहिणि भूतलादौ यः निश्शङ्कः पादविन्यासादिव्यवहारः प्रवर्तते स तावद् भूतलमात्रपरिच्छेदनिबन्धनः न अभ्युपगमनीयः । कण्टकादिसंयोगिन्यपि प्रसङ्गात् । भूतलमात्रपरिच्छेदे जाते सूक्ष्मेषु कीटकण्टकादिषु अनपगतेषु व्यवहारो यदि प्रवर्तते तदा सूक्ष्मकीटकण्टकजिज्ञासा निष्फला भवेत् । कैवल्य परिच्छेदस्य प्रयत्नमन्तरेण अवगन्तुमशक्यत्वात् युक्त एव प्रयत्नः । दृश्यादर्शनं हि अभावावगमे कारणम् । न च सूक्ष्माः कीटकण्टकादयः प्रयत्नमन्तरेण दृश्यतामापाद्यन्ते ।

Prābhākaras' Views on Abhāva

The Prābhākaras do not agree with the *Abhāvavādins.* According to the Prābhākaras the *abhāva* is not a separate category. In all instances of *abhāva* it is only the *adhikaraṇa* that is cognised but not any additional entity called *abhāva.* The positive entities are cognised in two ways:

1. Along with another positive entity.
2. Alone, i.e., without the other positive entity. The later also happens in two ways:

   (i) The other positive entity is seen elsewhere. (ii) It is not so seen.

In the instance, *bhūtale ghato nāsti* i.e there is no jar on the ground, the positive entity is the jar i.e., the jar elsewhere. The jar is called *pratiyogin.* The fact of seeing the ground only in such circumstances is called *abhāva* of the *pratiyogin* that is present elsewhere. Not seeing that which could be seen in a particular place, is the ground for envisaging *abhāva* in that place. Therefore, wherever the *abhāva* has to be thought of the cognition of the place has to be accepted. The *abhāva* of a *pratyogin* could be thought of only with reference to such places wherein the place alone is cognised. For instance, the *abhāva* of the jar could be thought of only when the ground alone is cognised. Therefore, it is better to consider the cognition of ground itself as the cognition of the so called *abhāva*. There is no need to posit a separate category as *abhāva* and a separate *pramāṇa* as *abhāvapramāṇa*.

The Prābhākaras' Concept of Sansṛṣṭa Buddhiḥ and Ekaviṣayābudhiḥ

To understand the Prābhākara's stand that the *abhāva* is not a separate category, their concept of *sansṛṣṭabuddhi* and *ekaviṣayābaddhi* need to be analysed. When two positive entities are cognised together it is *sansṛṣṭabuddhi* while cognising only one of them is *ekaviṣayābaddhi*. The latter serves the purpose of *abhāva*. The object which is present in *sansṛṣṭabuddhi* is not present in *ekaviṣayabuddhi*. *Bhutale ghaṭaḥ* is *sansṛṣṭabuddhi*, since both *bhūtala* and *ghaṭa* are cognised. When the *ghaṭa* is removed or destroyed it is *ekaviṣayābaddhi*. The absence of the jar is not a separate fact. Therefore, no separate *pramāṇa* is needed to cognise it. The jar that is removed or destroyed is designated as *dṛśyapratiyogin* i.e., *pratītiyogya* i.e., observable, if it ware there. Such observables characterize the absence conveyed by *ekaviṣayābaddhi* that serves the purpose of conveying the absence of the *pratiyogin*. There is no separate fact as *abhāva* (absence).

उच्यते भावानामवगतिः द्विविधा । एका तावत् भावान्तरसंसृष्टविषया । अपरा च तदेकविषया । यापि च तदेकविषया बुद्धिः सापि द्विविधा । प्रतियोगिनि दृश्ये अदृश्ये च । तत्र दृश्ये प्रतियोगिनि या तदेकविषया बुद्धिः सैव तस्य प्रतियोगिनः अभावः इति उच्यते ।

योऽपिहि प्रमेयमपरमभावमाह सोपि प्रतियोगिनि दृश्ये तदेकविषयां बुद्धिं तावदवश्यमभ्युपैति । नहि संसृष्टबुध्युदयेनापि अदृश्ये प्रतियोगिनि

अभावोऽवगम्यते । किञ्च दृश्यादर्शनमभावे प्रमाणम् । न च प्रमाणमन्तरेण प्रमेयसिद्धिरस्तीति । यत्राभावोऽभ्युपगमनीयः तत्र अवश्यं दृश्यादर्शन-माश्रयणीयम् । तुल्योपलम्भयोग्यार्थान्तरदर्शिनि दृश्यानुपलम्भोऽवधार्यते । अतो दृश्ये प्रतियोगिनि तदेकविषयोपलब्धिरेव वरमभावोऽस्तु ।

From the above discussion, it is clear that the Prābhākaras consider the cognition *bhūtale ghaṭaḥ* as *sansṛṣṭaviṣayabudhi* and *bhūtale ghato nasti* as *ekaviṣayabudhi*, and state that the latter serves the purpose of *abhāva*.

Three Objections Against Prābhākara's Explanation of Abhāva

On this *abhāvavādin* argues that this explanation does not work in the case of (i) *pradhvasābhāva* (ii) *ekabhāvaviṣayaka anumāna;* and (iii) *svarūpamātra pratīti*.

1. In the instance of *pradhvansābhāva*, such as *ghaṭo dhvastaḥ* ie the jar is destroyed, there has been *sansṛṣṭaviṣayabuddhi* when the jar was present on the ground. But when it is destroyed there is no *ekaviṣayabiddhi* with the background of *dṛśya pratiyogin* since the *pratiyogin* is destroyed. The *dṛśyapratiyogin* i.e., *ghata* is now the *pratiyogin* of *pradhvanasābhāva*. Here, *tadekaviṣayābuddhi*, i.e., *bhūtalaika viṣayābuddhi* can be managed only by accepting *pradhvansābhāva*. This amounts to the acceptance of *abhāva*.

ननु यद्यभावो नास्ति कथं तर्हि यत्र प्राक् संसृष्टबुद्धिरासीत् तत्र तदेकविषया बुद्धिराविर्भवति प्रध्वंसाभ्युपगमेतु सा स्यात् । (प्र०पं० २८७)

The objection referred to above could be resolved by examining the position of the *abhāvavādin* himself. *Abhāvavādin* has to explain as to how the *abhāva* of the jar occurred in the same place in which there was the *bhāva* of it without removing it. If he explains that because of certain causes such as hitting the jar by a stick, the absence of the jar arose in the same place, then, the Prābhākaras also will say that for the same reason *ekaviṣayābuddhi* arose in the same place where there was *sanṣṛṭabuddhi*. No additional factor called *pradhvasābhāva* need be accepted. Instead of the jar there are pieces of the jar. If these are taken into account there is *sanṣṛṭabuddhi*. But from the point of the view of the jar, there is *ekaviṣayabuddhi* i.e., *bhūtalamatṛabuddhi*. There is no need to introduce any additional factor i.e., *pradhvansābhāva*.

(i) **अत्राभिधीयते । यस्यापि मते प्रध्वंसाभावः स्वीक्रियते तमपि प्रति पर्यनुयोगोऽयं शक्यते दातुम् । यस्य यत्र भावः आसीत् कथं तस्य तत्र अभावः इति । स चेत् पर्यनुयुक्तो ब्रूते यत् करणोपनिपातेन तस्मिन्नेव अभावो जायते इति ततो वयमपि वदितुं शक्ताः कारणोपनिपातादेव तदेकविषया बुद्धिराविर्भवतीति । यथैव स वादी प्रध्वंसाभावस्य कारणमाह तथैव तदेकविषयायाः बुद्धेरपि वयं वदितुं क्षमाः ।**

(ii) **अथोच्येत मुद्गराभिघातादिः क्षणिकोऽभावस्य कारणम् स कथं कालान्तरे तदेकविषयां बुद्धिं जनयति इति हन्त तर्हि कपालमालाद्युत्पत्तिः तदेकबुद्धिविषयकारणमस्तु । (प्र०पं० २८७-८८)**

If the jar is taken to some other place, its presence in some other place itself is the basis for *tadaikaviṣayābuddhi* i.e., *bhūtalaikaviṣyābuddhi*.

एतेन देशान्तरानीते वस्तुनि तदेकविषया बुद्धिः व्याख्याता । अत्रापि देशान्तरं नीतस्य वस्तुनः तत्र स्थितिरेव तदेकविषयबुद्धिनिमित्तमाश्रयणीयम् । (प्र०पं० २८८)

(iii) **ननु भवतु स्वकारणोपनिपातात् तदेकविषया बुद्धिः संसृष्टविषयापि किमिति न स्यात्? तस्याः कारणविनाशात् सा न स्यादिति चेत् अङ्गीकृतः तर्हि नाशापरपर्यायो अभावः । उच्यते । न वयमपि संसृष्टबुद्धेः कारणं विनाशं ब्रूमः । किन्तु भावान्तरोदय एव कारणमिति । (प्र०पं० २८८)**

2. The second instance wherein the *abhāvavādins* claim that *ekabuddhi viṣayatva* cannot be worked out is that of certain inferences.

In the case of such entities that could be comprehended only by the inference, if the inference is not made, their absence is cognised. In such cases there is no other entity that could have been comprehended along with it. In other words there has been no *sanṣṛṭabuddhi* in respect of these. Therefore, no *ekaviṣayabiddhi* can be worked out in respect of these.

अपि च विनापि तदेकविषयां बुद्धिमभावावगतिरस्ति । अनुमानाद्येकविषयाणां भावानामनुमानाद्यभावे अभावो दृश्यते । तत्र तुल्योपलम्भयोग्यभावान्तरैकविषया बुद्धिर्नास्ति । अथ च अभावोऽवगम्यते इति तदेकबुद्धिव्यतिरेकेणापि अभावः अवगम्य इति । (प्र०पं० २८८)

The objection raised above is based on the assumption that *tadekaviṣayābuddhi* should always be of the nature of perception. Such an assumption is not correct. There can be *tadekaviṣayābuddhi* by the inference also. Therefore, there is no difficulty in working out *tadaikaviṣayābuddhi* in the above cases also.

यच्च तदैकबुद्धिव्यतिरेकेणापि अभावोऽवगम्यत इत्युक्तम् । अत्रोच्यते । न प्रत्यक्षरुपैव तदैकबुद्धिरभावरूपा इष्यते किन्तु अनुमानात्मिकापि तदेकविषया बुद्धिरुत्पद्यते । सैव अभाव इति व्यपदिश्यते ।

3. The third instance wherein *Abhāvavādins* claim that *ekaviṣaya-biddhitva* cannot be worked out is that of *svarūpamātrapratīti*. In the case of *buddhi* ie cognition that arises for a moment and ceases to be at the later moment, there is no second entity with it. Therefore, the very emergence of the second entity cannot be considered as the ground for *ekaviṣayābiddhi* as in the case *ghaṭavināśa*. This is a case of *niranvayavināśa*.

ननु निरन्वयविनाशिनीनां बुद्धियादीनां कस्य भावान्तरस्य उदयः विनाशः।

This objection is answered by pointing out that the presence of the very core nature of the object concerned is *bhāvāntarodaya* in such cases.

उच्यते । धर्मिणः स्वरूपमात्रेण अवस्थानमेव तत्र भावान्तरोदयः अवगन्तव्यः ।

The expression *svarūpamātra* does not mean the absence of the attributes and does not lead to the acceptance of *abhāva*. The positive categories are found in two ways: (i) together with some other positive entity (ii) as a single entity. The latter position is called *svarūpamātra.*

ननु किमिदं स्वरूपमात्रम् । न तावत् स्वरूपमेव तस्य धर्मोदयकालेपि अविनाशात् । तस्माद्धर्माभाव एव धर्मिणः स्वरूपमात्रमित्यङ्गीकरणीयम्। उच्यते । न भावातिरिक्तः अभावः अंङ्गीक्रियते । भाव एव तु एकाकी सद्वितीयश्चेति द्वयीमवस्यामनुभवति । एकाकी भावः स्वरूपमात्रमुच्यते । (प्र०पं० २८९)

In this context Śālikanātha points out that *Abhāvavādin* also has to state his *abhāva* by making a reference to a single positive category. For instance, when both *bhūtala* and jar are present the absence of the jar cannot be talked of. But when *bhūtala* alone is found then only he talks of *abhāva.* It is better to say that the *bhūtala* is singly present rather than introducing a separate category of the absence of the jar.

योऽपि च अभावाख्यं तत्त्वान्तरमभ्युपैति तेनापि तावदेकाकिभावोपलम्भनमाश्रित्य अभावप्रमितिराश्रयणीया । नहि अप्रतीते भावे अभावः प्रतीयते । (प्र०पं० २८९)

To cognise *abhāva* the *bhāva* to be referred to could be conceived in one of these three ways: (i) a *bhāva* together with another *bhāva*; (ii) a *bhāva* together with the *abhāva* that is proposed to be comprehended; (iii) a *bhāva* that is neither with another *bhāva* nor *abhāva.*

In the first alternative, since the two *bhāvas* are present, no *abhāva* of one of them could be conceived. For instance, the cognition of the ground and the jar together cannot lead to the cognition of the *abhāva* of the jar. The second alternative will result in the fallacy of *ātmāśraya*. For instance, taking *ghaṭābhāva viśiṣṭabhūtala* as the ground for the cognition of *ghaṭābhāva* is *ātmāśraya*. Therefore, the third alternative i.e., cognising *bhāva* alone i.e., *ekaviṣayābiddhi*, is the only possible way. The cognition of *bhāva* alone, that is to say, *bhūtala* alone takes place in such a situation. There is no such thing such as a *abhāva* as content of this cognition. It is the cognition of the *bhūtala* only. However, it is called *ghaṭābhāva*, because, the *ghaṭa* that is elsewhere is the *pratiyogin* for it.

(i) तत्र कीदृशस्य तावत् भावस्य प्रतीतिः अभावावगतौ निमित्तमिति चिन्तनीयम् । किं सद्वितीयस्य? अथवा अभावविशिष्टस्य? अथवा भावाभावानपेक्षस्य एकाकिनः इति । तत्र न तावत् सद्वितीयस्य भावस्य ज्ञानपुरस्सरमभावज्ञानं सम्भवति धटवति भूतले प्रतीते तदभावावगमप्रसङ्गात् । नापि अभावविशिष्टभावावसायनिमित्ता अभावावगतिः आत्माश्रयदोषप्रसङ्गात् । अभावं प्रतीत्य तद्विशिष्टं भावमवसाय अभावः प्रतिपत्तव्यः इत्यभावावगतिरेव अभावबोधोदये कारणमिति व्यक्तमात्माश्रयत्वम् । (प्र०पं० २८९)

(ii) किञ्च भावप्रतीत्यनुप्रवेशिन्यामभावावगतौ न अभावाख्यं प्रमाणान्तरं स्यात्

> स्वरूपमात्रं दृष्ट्वापि पश्चात् किञ्चित् स्मरन्नपि ।
> तत्रान्यनास्तितां पृष्टः तदैव प्रतिपद्यते ॥

इति अभावस्य प्रमाणान्तरत्वे युक्तिः । प्राक्तनभावस्वरूपावगतावेव चेदभावो प्रतीतः न प्रमेयमवशिष्यते । प्रमेयानवशेषे अभावो न प्रमाणान्तरमवकल्पते । तस्मादेकाकिनी भावप्रतीतिरेव अभावप्रतीतेः निमित्तमित्यास्थेयम् ।

(iii) ननु तदेकविषया बुद्धिः यदि अभावः कथं तर्हि घटाभावादिव्यवहारः। नहि तस्याः कश्चिदपि घटादिभिः सह सम्बधोऽस्ति। उच्यते। न तदेकविषयबुद्धिमात्रमभावः अभिधीयते। किन्तु दृश्ये प्रतियोगिनि या तदेकविषया बुद्धिः सा तदभावः इति व्यपदिश्यते। तेन यस्मिन् प्रतियोगिनि दृश्ये या तदेकविषया बुद्धिः सा तदभावः इति विशेषव्यपदेशः प्रवर्तते। तेन इह भूतले घटः नास्तीति किमुक्तं भवति? दृश्येपि घटे भूतलमात्रमुपलभ्यत इति। (प्र०पं० २८९)

The Concept of Abhāvapramāṇa Leads to Infinite Regress

The *abhāvapranāṇa* vādin who claims the *abhāva* to be a separate *pramāṇa* has to explain whether this *pramāṇa* conveys its *prameya* by mere presence or comprehended as *pramāṇābhāva*. In the case of perception it is well-known that the mere presence of the eye is sufficient to lead to the perception. The knowledge of the eye is not necessary. In the case of the inference, mere presence of *liṅga* is not sufficient. It has to be comprehended to lead to the inference. In the present case of *pramāṇābhāva* its comprehension is necessary. This is clear from the instance of the recollection of the cognition of *abhāva* in a place wherein it was observed earlier. Mere presence of *pramāṇābhāva* would not lead to such a recollection. The *pramāṇābhāva* that is comprehended earlier will only lead to such a recollection. Therefore, the *abhāvavādin* has to say that the *pramāṇābhāva* conveys *abhāva* when it is comprehended. Now, this *pramāṇābhāva* by itself being an abhāva needs another *pramāṇābhāva* to convey it. The second *pramāṇābhāva* needs a third one to convey it and so on. This leads to infinite regress. Such a contingency will not arise if *bhavāntarasaṃvitti* is taken as the ground for the cognition of so called *abhāva*. This *saṃvitti* is *svaprākāśa* and does not need anything else for its cognition.

किञ्च प्रमाणान्तरवादिनापि प्रमाणाभावः सत्त्वमात्रेण अभावबुद्धिजनको नाभ्युपगमनीयः। किन्तु विदितत्वेन। तथाहि कस्यचिद् वस्तुनः क्वचिददृष्टस्य

पुनस्तस्मिन्नेव दृश्यमानस्य अदर्शनकालभाविनमभावं प्रतिपद्यते 'नासीदयमिहेति'। तदा तत्र दर्शनाभावो निवृत्तः कथमभावावगमं जनयेत्? यदि सत्तया अवबोधः ततो न भवेत् । बुद्ध्युपारूढस्य हि जनकत्वे अतीतस्यापि सम्प्रति अनुसन्धीयमानस्य घटत एवाभावोपपादकत्वम् । (प्र०पं० २९१)

(ii) यथा चक्षुरादिकं स्वसत्तामात्रेण स्वकार्यकारि न च अतिवृत्तं स्वकार्यं जनयति । लिङ्गं च बुद्धिविषयापन्नं लैङ्गकबोधजनकम् स्मर्यमाणमतीतमपि सत् स्वकालवृत्तिलैङ्गिकमनुमापयति तथेति द्रष्टव्यम्। एवं चातीतस्यापि प्रमाणाभावस्य अभावावगमकत्वात् बुद्ध्यरूढस्य गमकत्वमङ्गीकरणीयम् ।

(iii) तत्र यदि प्रमाणाभवः यः सोऽभावरूपः तस्याप्यवगतिर्विदितादेव प्रमाणाभावादङ्गीकर्तव्येत्यनवस्था । यदि तु भावानामसंवित्तिरेव प्रमाणाभावोऽभ्युपगम्यते । ततः तस्याः स्वयं प्रकाशतया न अनवस्था आपाद्यते । तथा सति भावान्तरसंवित्तिरेव स्वयंप्रकाशा प्रमाणाभावरूपा प्रमेयाभावोऽस्तु किमपरेण प्रमेयाभावेन ।

(iv) घटो नास्तीति शब्दप्रयोगोपि तस्यामेव स्वयं प्रकाशायां भावान्तरोपलब्धौ युज्यते । न पुनः घटो नास्तीति बुद्ध्यन्तरमाविर्भवति । बोध्यन्तरानवभासात् । (प्र०पं० २९१-९२)

The Practical Experience does not Confirm Abhāva

The practical experience of moving on the ground by ascertaining the absence of thorns etc., also does not establish *abhāva*. This situation can be explained as due to *tadekaviṣayābuddhi* i.e., *bhūtalaikaviṣayabuddhi* without resorting to the category of *abhāva*. The effort to ascertain the thorns etc., is only a way of seeking *dṛśyapratiyogin*.

योपि पदन्यासादिव्यवहारः सोऽपि दृश्ये प्रतियोगिनि तदेकविषय-बुद्धिनिबन्धन इति दृश्यत्वोपपत्तये युक्तैव सूक्ष्मकण्टकादिजिज्ञासा । तथाविध

प्रतिपत्त्युदय एव अभावः । तेन तस्मिन् अनुमानं अभावसाधकं न प्रवर्तते । (प्र०पं० २९२)

Pramāṇa and Prameya are Distinct

Before concluding the discussion on *abhāva* Śālikanātha raises an interesting question viz., just as by the absence of *pramāṇa* the absence of *prameya* is presumed, the presence of *pramāṇa* has to be considered as the ground for the presence of the *prameya.* This gives room for the denial of the *prameya* itself outside *pramāṇa.*

ननु यथा प्रमाणाभावे एव अवश्यम्भावितया प्रमेयाभावोऽङ्गीक्रियते तथा प्रमाणसद्भाव एव तर्हि प्रमेयसद्भावः स्यात् । प्रमेयसद्भाववादिनापि हि प्रमाणसद्भावोऽवश्यमाश्रयणीयः इति प्राप्तो बाह्यार्थापलापः । (प्र०पं० २९२)

The above contention is rejected by Śālikanātha by pointing out that the *prameya* has its own distinct nature independent of *pramāṇa.* The cognition is comprehended as cognition while the objects are presented as blue etc., in the cognition distinctly. Hence, the objects cannot be denied. In the case *abhāva* no such distinct *prameya* is presented. No specific form of *abhāva* is comprehended, It is only a positive entity that is presented by way of *ekaviṣayabuddhi.* Therefore, there is no *prameya* called *abhāva* nor there is any need to conceive *abhāvapramāṇa* to cognise it.

नैतदेवम् । प्रमेयस्य हि बहिरर्थस्य प्रमाणस्वरूपातिरिक्तस्य स्वरूपप्रतिभासात् । प्रमितिर्हि प्रमित्येकरूपतयैव भासते । प्रमेयं नीलाद्याकारतया । अभावस्य तु स्वरूपावगतिर्नास्तीति न प्रमाणाभावादन्यः प्रमेयाभावः। प्रमाणाभावोपि च स्वरूपान्तरानवगमादेव न भावान्तरप्रमितेर्भिद्यते । भावान्तरप्रमितिश्च स्वयंप्रकाशा न प्रमेयतामनुभवतीति प्रमेयमभावाख्यस्य प्रमाणस्य नोपपद्यते । प्रमेयासद्भावाच्च न प्रमाणान्तरमवकल्पते इति स्थितम् । (प्र०पं० २९२)

Śālikanātha does not accept *saṃbhava*, *aitihya* and *pratibhā* as separate *pramāṇas*. He includes *saṃbhava* under *anumāna*, and rejects *pramāṇatva* to *aitihya* and *pratibhā*. He concludes the discussion on the *pramāṇas* affirming that there are only five *pramāṇas*.

CHAPTER VII

Vimalānjana

The Doctrine of the Natural Relation between the Word and the Meaning

The authority of the Vedas will be adversely affected if the relation between the word and the meaning is considered as fixed by human agency.

The human beings can fix the relation between the words and the meanings, only in such cases wherein they know the objects concerned by some other *pramāṇa*. The knowledge of the items like *kārya* i.e., *apūrva*, conveyed by Veda cannot be obtained by human beings by any other *pramāṇa*. This means that the relation between the Vedic injunctive suffix and its meaning viz., *kārya* i.e., *apūrva*, cannot be fixed by the human beings. Consequently, the Vedas will not be able to convey this meaning and cannot be the authorities to convey anything. It is this contingency that has made the Mīmāṃsakas to posit a natural and permanent relation between the word and the meaning.

यदि पौरुषेय एव शब्दानामर्थैः सह सम्बन्धः भवेत् तदा प्रमाणान्तरगोचरेष्वेव अर्थेषु पुरुषाणां सङ्केतकरणशक्तेः, अपूर्वकार्यात्मनि च वेदार्थे प्रमाणान्तराणामवकाशाभावेन तत्र सङ्केताभावात् असङ्केतिते च अवाचकत्वाभ्युपगमात् दुर्लभमेव वेदवाक्यानां प्रामाण्यमापद्येत इति अर्थवानेवायं अपौरुषेयशब्दार्थप्रतिपादनयत्नः।

अपौरुषये सम्बन्धे सिद्धे शब्दार्थयोः द्वयोः ।
प्रामाण्यं वेदवाक्यानामिति स प्रतिपाद्यते ॥ (प्र०पं० ३०१)

The relation between the word and the meaning is comprehended through the elders' conversation. The children who listen to the elders' conversation and observe the activity that follows, comprehend the relation between the words employed and the objects dealt with by the activity. For instance, on hearing the statement *gām ānaya* i.e., bring the cow, and observing the action of bringing the cow, the child comprehends the relation between the words concerned and the meaning conveyed. This process has been going on generation after generation. No generation has fixed the relation between a word and its meaning. Therefore, it is natural and permanent. It is beginningless.

अनादौ हि वृद्धव्यवहारपरम्परायां सत्यां वृद्धव्यवहारसिद्धो वाच्यवाचकभावः शब्दार्थयोः अपौरुषेयः प्रसिद्ध्येत् ।

तथाहि । वृद्धानां स्वार्थेन व्यवह्रियमाणानां वाक्यमुपश्रृण्वन्तो बालाः शब्दश्रवणसमनन्तरभाविना चेष्टाविशेषेण विशिष्टार्थविषयां मनीषामाकलयन्तो वाचकतां शब्दस्य अध्यवस्यन्ति । तेपि वृद्धाः यदा बालाः आसन् तदा तेप्यनयैव दिशा व्युत्पत्तिमलभन्त । तेपि अन्येभ्यः वृद्धेभ्यः इति विनापि सङ्केतयितारं पुरुषं उपपद्यत एव शब्दार्थयोः अनादिवृद्धव्यवहारसिद्धः सम्बन्धः । (प्र०पं०३०२)

This explanation of Mīmāṃsakas is contested by Vaiśeṣikas. They argue that the very human beings who speak have a beginning. Therefore, how can the language spoken by them be beginningless and the relation between the word and the meaning be beginningless.

In this connection Śālikanātha briefly narrates the Vaiśeṣika's position. All products have a beginning. These are produced from the *paramāṇus* by the process of the formation of *dvyaṇuka, tryṇuka* etc. The first step of two *paramāṇus* joining to produce *dvyaṇuka* is caused by *adṛṣṭa* of the persons who are going to utilize them. *Dharma* and *adharma* constitute this *adṛṣta*. The *adṛṣta* is non-sentient. Therefore, by itself it cannot initiate any activity. Hence, it has to be located in a sentient being i.e., *cetana jivātmā*. However, *jivātmā* will not be aware of it, though the *adṛṣṭa* is located in him. *Paramātmā* knows this. The *paramātmā* is conceived as omniscient and omnipotent by the very hypothesis by which he is established. It is he who fixes the relation between the word and the meaning. Therefore, this relation is of the nature of *īśvara saṅketa* i.e., a convention established by *īśvara.*

(i) न खलु अनादितैव वृद्धव्यवहारपरम्परायाः उपपत्तिमती । तथाहि । विदाङ्कुर्वन्तु भवन्तः तनुभवनादिकं सर्वं सावयवमवसीयते । यच्च नाम सावयवं तद् अवयवव्यतिषङ्गसमासादितात्मलाभम् । परमाण्वोश्च परस्परसंयोगः अन्यतरकर्मजः उभयकर्मजो वा अभ्युपगनीयः । कर्म च परमाणुषु अदृष्टवत्क्षेत्रज्ञसंयोगात् प्रतिज्ञायते । तदुक्तं 'अणुमनसोश्च आद्यं कर्मेत्यदृष्टकारितम्' (वै०द० ५-२-१३) । अन्यस्य कारणस्याभावात् ।

(ii) अदृष्टं अलब्धस्ववृत्ति कार्याय न पर्याप्तं अचेतनत्वात् । तदेवमदृष्टं क्षेत्रज्ञसमवायि चेतनाधिष्ठितं कार्याय पर्याप्तमिति दर्शनबलेन अभ्युपगमनीयम् । य एव क्षेत्रज्ञाः (अदृष्टाश्रयाः) त एव तेषामदृष्टानामधिष्ठातारः न भवेयुः । तेषामज्ञत्वात् । नहि ते स्वसमवायिनी अपि धर्माधर्मलक्षणे अदृष्टे स्वरूपतः कार्यतो वा वेदितुमीशते । य एव च यत् स्वरूपतः कार्यतः वेदितुमीष्टे स एव तस्य अधिष्ठाता । यथा तक्षा वास्याः । तस्मादन्यः क्षेत्रज्ञेभ्यः सकलक्षेत्रज्ञसमवायि धर्माधर्मलक्षणादृष्टसाक्षात्करण गोचराचिन्तनीय-शक्तिविभवः कोपि चेतनातिशयोऽभ्युपगन्तव्यः ।

(iii) यत एव प्रमाणात् तस्य सद्भावः अवगम्यते तत एव तस्य ज्ञानशक्तिरप्यवगम्यते इति अन्तर्भावितज्ञानशक्तिरेवासौ सामान्यतो दृष्टानुमानस्य गोचरः । तत्प्रभवस्य तनुभवनादेः आदिमत्त्वमुत्पत्तिमत्त्वं च । तथा आदिमत्तया विनाशित्वम्, कृतकाः हि भावाः ध्रुवभाविविनाशा इति न अनादित्वं वृद्धव्यहारपरम्परायाः । तेन पुरुषसङ्केतादेव शब्दस्यार्थप्रतिपत्तिहेतुत्वामास्थेयम् । (प्र०पं० ३०२-३०३)

The contention of Mīmāṃsakas that the relation between the word and meaning is comprehended through the elders' conversation does not hold good, because, in the case of the names of persons such as Devadatta and certain newly created objects, it is found that the convention to use these words with reference to these objects is fixed by the human beings, and this relation is *pauruṣeya.* On the anology of this, one can easily infer that the relation between the cow etc., objects, and the words that are used in elders' conversation is also fixed by a person. This person, naturally is *Īśvara* as already pointed out above. This *Īśvara* is omniscient and omnipotent. He can be easily conceived as the author of the Vedas and the Vedas can convey *apūrva* and be the authority for the same.

(i) अपि च देवदत्तादिपदेषु अविवादा तावत् पुरुषसङ्केतनिबन्धना वाचकता । तद्दर्शनात् गवादिशब्दानामपि तथाविधत्वमेव अनुमातुमुचितम् । देवदत्तादिपदेषु स्वाभाविकं स्वार्थबोधकत्वमित्यपि न समीचीनम् । प्रमाणाभावात् पुरुष सङ्केतानपेक्षत्वप्रसङ्गाच्च ।

(ii) गवादिष्वपि नियतार्थप्रतिपत्तिः पुरुषसङ्केतायत्तैव स्वाभाविकी स्वार्थप्रतिपादनशक्तिरनुपयोगिन्येव ।

(iii) किञ्च यथोदितप्रमाणबलसिद्धे भगवति तत्कर्तृकत्वेनापि सिद्ध्यति वेदानामपूर्वे अर्थे प्रामाण्यम् । (प्र०पं० ३०४)

This contention of the Vaiśeṣikas is rejected by the Mīmāṃsakas. The anology of the modern words like Devadatta needing someone to fix their respective meanings cannot be extended to all words that are employed all along in the elders' conversation. In these cases it is clear that the children comprehend the relation between these words and their meanings without bothering as to who has fixed their relation. The relation of these is comprehended generation after generation and the question who has fixed it is irrelevant for the comprehension of this relation.

In the cases of modern words like Devadatta, it is true that someone fixes the relation between the newly coined word and its meaning. However, it is the use of these words in these meanings that enables one to comprehend the relation between these words and the respective meanings but not merely fixing the relation by someone. These words are used after fixing the meaning while in the case of the words used for generations, no such fixing has been necessary. The important point to be noted is, in both the cases the relation is comprehended through conversation and the knowledge of fixing the relation is not relevant for the comprehension of the meaning.

(i) **यद्यपि देवदत्तादिशब्दानां पुरुषसङ्केतनिबन्धनं वाचकत्वम्, तथापि गवादिपदेष्वनुमानं न शक्यते कर्तुम् । अर्थप्रतिपत्तिलक्षणस्य कार्यस्य अन्यथापि उपपत्तेः । वृद्धव्यवहारनिबन्धनाद्धि स्वार्थे वाचकत्वशक्तिज्ञानादपि बालानां शब्दार्थप्रतिपत्तिः दृश्यते ।**

(ii) **अपि च शक्तिज्ञानमात्रनिबन्धना गवादिशब्दानामर्थप्रतिपत्तिरिति प्रत्यक्षमेवैतत् । देवदत्तादिपदेषु तु यस्य सङ्केतनिबन्धना अर्थप्रतिपत्तिः तस्य सङ्केत एव कारणम् । तेष्वपि ये व्यवहारदर्शनादेव वाचकतामवगम्य अर्थं प्रतिपद्यन्ते तेषां व्यवहारदर्शनप्रसूतं शक्तिज्ञानमेव अर्थप्रतिपत्तिकारणं न सङ्केतः । किन्तु तत्र सङ्केतपूर्वक एव व्यवहारः, अर्थप्रतिपत्तिश्च, तथा तत्पूर्वकमपि वाचकत्वज्ञानम् । गवादिपदेषु तु सर्वेषां शक्तिज्ञानादेव व्यवहारसम्भवादर्थावगतिरिति वैषम्यम् ।**

The contention of the Vaiśeṣikas that 'all products have a beginning and the very human beings who speak language have a beginning, therefore, elders' conversation generation after generation, must also have beginning and consequently the relation between the word and meaning also has a beginning' is not a valid contention. Even assuming that the products have a beginning and an end, it cannot be stated that all product arise together and all perish together. Beginning and the end of the products has a sequence and one need not envisage a situation of a total absence. This makes room for certain programmes to be all along.

भवतु सावयवं सर्वम् अवयवसंयोगारब्धसत्ताकम् अवयसंयोगापाये विनश्वरमिति च । तथापि एकदैव सकलस्य सम्भवः विनाशश्चेत्यत्र

नास्ति प्रमाणम् । प्रत्युत यथा दर्शनमिदमवसाययितुमुचितम् क्रमेण चोदयः क्रमेण विलयश्चेति । किञ्च यथा अद्यतनाः जनाः मातापितृसंयोग-निबन्धनात्मलाभाः तथा पूर्वेपि जनाः जनत्वात् इति शक्यमेव अनुमातुम् । (प्र०पं० ३०६)

The Vaiśeṣikas theory that the *adṛṣṭa* of the *kṣetrajña* i.e., *jīvātman*, is supervised and implemented by *Īśvara* is also not tenable. *Īśvara* has no *manas* and *indriyas*. Therefore, he cannot know the *adṛṣṭa* located in *kṣetrajña* i.e., *jīvātman*. It cannot also be claimed that the knowledge of *Īśvara* is eternal and therefore, he can supervise and implement the *adṛṣṭas* of *jīvātman*, since the very concept of eternal knowledge is untenable. To think of eternal knowledge to support the concept of *adhiṣṭhātṛtva* and to conceive *adhiṣṭhātṛtva* on the ground of the knowledge of *adṛṣṭa* cut each other.

(i) यच्चेदमुदितं धर्माधर्मौ चेतनातिशय (ईश्वर) अधिष्ठितौ इति, तदपि असिद्धमेव । यस्यैव तौ क्षेत्रज्ञस्य (जीवस्य), स एवाधिष्ठाताऽस्तु। अथ अज्ञत्वात् तस्य अधिष्ठातृत्वं नोपपद्यत इति चेत् तर्हि अन्यस्यापि कथमुपपद्यते । न हि तस्यापि परपुरुषवर्ति धर्माधर्मज्ञानमुपपद्यते । कारणाभावात् । नहि धर्माधर्मरहितस्य ईश्वरस्य इन्द्रियमनस्सम्बन्धो भवति । धर्माधर्मनिमित्तत्त्वात् तत्सम्बन्धस्य ।

(ii) अथ नित्यैव ईश्वरबुद्धिरिति चेत् । तदपि असुन्दरम् । बुद्धितत्त्वस्य नित्यत्वाभावात् ।

(iii) बुद्धिमता च अधिष्ठानं दृष्टं न अन्येन । अथ सिद्धे अधिष्ठातृत्त्वे ज्ञानमपि कल्प्यते इति तदयुक्तम् । ज्ञानाद्यननुबद्धस्य अधिष्ठातृत्वस्य कारणाभावात् प्रतिक्षिप्ते ज्ञाने सत्यनुमातुमशक्तेः । (प्र०पं० ३०७)

Further, what is meant by *adhiṣṭhātṛtva*? Is it the contact with the *adṛṣṭa* by *samyoga* or *samavāya*. The *samyoga* is not possible, because, *adṛṣṭa* which is of the nature *dharma* and *adharma* is a quality. It cannot be connected by *samyoga*. The quality that belongs to something else cannot be connected by *samavāya* also.

अपि च अधिष्ठानार्थोपि चिन्तनीयः । न तावत् संयोगः । गुणत्वेन धर्माधर्मयोः संयोगाभावात् । समवायोपि परपुरुषसमवायिनोः धर्माधर्मयोः ईश्वरं प्रत्यनुपपन्नः । (प्र०पं० ३०७)

The idea of implementation also cannot be properly explained. It is not action, since, *dharma* and *adharma* are qualities and cannot have any action. It is not providing the result, since, *dharma* and *adharma* can produce the result with the help of time, space etc., no other person is required to produce the result. Therefore, the very idea of *īśvara* to supervise and implement *adṛṣṭa* is uncalled for.

तथा प्रवृत्तिरपि कीदृशी । न तावत् क्रिया । गुणभूतयोः धर्माधर्मयोः क्रियाभावात् ।

फलदानमिति चेत् न । देशकालादि सहकारिसहिताभ्यां धर्माधर्माभ्यामेव फलम् । न चेतनव्यापारापेक्षम् । (प्र०पं० ३०७-८)

The Vaiśeṣika concept of *īśvara* to create a world also cannot be rationally explained. There is no basis to conceive *īśvara* as *adhiṣṭhāta* of *paramāṇus* and his desire to move the *paramāṇus* to form *dvyaṇuka* etc., products. In the case of human creation, the *dharma* and *adharma* of human beings are the basis. No *dharma* and *adharma* accrue in the case of *īśvara*. Further, no activity can take place by mere desire. There is no ground also for the emergence of the desire for the creation. If the desire is considered eternal, then, the creation also must take place all the time.

(i) **यदपि केचिदाहुः परमाणव एव ईश्वरेच्छावशेन प्रवर्तन्त इति । तदपि न युक्तम् । क्वचित् तथाविधस्य अधिष्ठानस्य अदर्शनात् । शरीरे तथा दर्शनमिति चेत् । न । तस्य क्षेत्रज्ञ धर्माधर्मपरिगृहीतत्वात् । न परमाणव एव ईश्वरधर्माधर्मपरिगृहीताः ।**

(ii) **न च तस्य इच्छामात्रेण प्रवृत्तिः किन्तु प्रयत्नवशात् । न च इच्छायामपि हेतुरस्ति । न च नित्यैवेच्छा नित्यं प्रवृत्तिप्रसङ्गात् । (प्र०पं० ३०८)**

Further, the *adhiṣṭhātā* is found to be a person with the body etc. This means that if *īśvara* is considered as *adhiṣṭhātā*, he also has to be considered as possessing body etc. This is not accepted by the Vaiśeṣikas. To envisage *adhiṣṭhātā*, a purpose to be served for him also has to be envisaged. However, no purpose of *Īśvara* is served by the creation. Since the very concept of *Īśvara* cannot be maintained, the question of *Īśvara* who is omniscient and who fixes the relation between the word and meaning does not arise.

(i) **यथा च चेतनो अधिष्ठाता इति प्रतीयते तथा विग्रहादिमानपि । तेन अनुमानं प्रवर्तमांन तथाविधमेव अनुमापयेत् ।**

(ii) **प्रयोजनाभावादपि अनधिष्ठानमिति ज्ञायते । (प्र०पं० ३०८)**

(iii) **तेन अनादिरेव वृद्धव्यवहारपरम्परा शब्दार्थावगमे हेतुः । (प्र०पं० ३०९)**

Therefore, the relation between the word and meaning is natural and is comprehended through elders' communication. *Śabda* is the only means to comprehend *dharma.* It is of the nature of *apūrva kārya* and conveyed by Vedas. The Vedas are *apaurṣeya* on the following grounds:

1. No author of Vedas is known and remembered.
2. *Kāṭhaka* etc., names are the names of the teachers of Vedas.
3. An author for the Vedas cannot be inferred also. No person can compose the work in respect of the subjects that are beyond the other *pramāṇas.*

कथमपौरुषेयत्वं वेदानाम्? उच्यते कर्तुरस्मरणात् । न च अनुमानमपि कर्तुरुपपद्यते । प्रमाणान्तरेण अप्रतीते अर्थे पुरुषाणाम् वाक्यस्य रचनायामशक्तेः । (प्र०पं० ३१०)

Therefore, the Vedas are *apauruṣeya.* The relation between the word and the meaning is *apauruṣeya.*

CHAPTER VIII

Tattvāloka

The light on the Tattva-ātmatattva

In this chapter Śālikanātha discusses the nature of *ātman* i.e., self. At the commencement he briefly states the views of various other systems of philosophy regarding the nature of *ātman* and then states his own view:

(i) Buddhi (*Vijñāna*), itself is *ātman*—The Vijñānavādins.

(ii) Senses are *ātman*—the Pourāṇikas

(iii) The body itself is *ātman*—the Cārvākas

(iv) It is distinct from *buddhi*, senses and body—the Prābhākaras

केचित् बुद्धिमेव आत्मानमवगच्छन्ति । अन्येतु पुनरिन्द्रियाण्येव । देहमपरे । तथा एके बुद्धीन्द्रियशरीरव्यतिरेकिणमनुमेयमाहुः । (प्र०पं० ३१५)

In respect of the cognition of *ātman* four views are current:

(i) It is known by inference—the Prābhākaras.

(ii) It is comprehended by *manas*—the Bhāṭṭas and Nyāya.

(iii) It is self revealed—Sāṃkhya.

(iv) It is comprehended in *kevalajñāna*—the Diagaṃbaras.

एके अनुमेयमाहुः । केचित्तु मानसप्रत्यक्षगम्यम् । स्वयं प्रकाशं च केचित् । सकलप्रतीतिसिद्धं तु अन्ये मन्यन्ते । (प्र०पं० ३१५)

In respect of its duration and the size, the following views are noted: (i) It is *kṣaṇika* (momentary)—Buddhist (ii) It is *kūtastha* (permanent)—All others.

(i) It is atomic (*aṇu parimāṇa*)

(ii) It is of the dimension of the body in which it is present—the Digaṃbara Jains

(iii) It is all pervasive—Nyāya, Bhāṭṭa etc. There are two views in respect of its number. There is a separate *ātman* in each body is one view; and there is only one in all bodies is another view.

क्षणिकं केचिदाहुः । कूटस्थमित्यपरे । अणुपरिमाणः, शरीरपरिमाणः, सर्वगतः इत्यादिवादिनो विवदन्ते तथा सर्वक्षेत्रेषु एकमित्येके नानाभूतमित्यपरे । (प्र०पं० ३१५-१६)

Stating the views of various other systems Śālikanātha presents the Prābhākara view as under:

बुद्धीन्द्रियशरीरेभ्यो भिन्न आत्मा विभुः ध्रुवः ।
नानाभूतः प्रतिक्षेत्रमर्थवित्तिषु भासते ॥

The *ātman* is distinct from *buddhi*, senses, and the body. It is all pervasive, permanent and is separate in each body. It is cognised in the cognitions of all objects as knower and the locus of the cognition.

The View of Vijñānavādin

Śālikanātha narrates the Vijñānavāda view of *ātman* in greater detail and rejects the same.

According to Vijñānavādins there is no knower distinct from the knowledge. The knower and the knowledge are always found together. The entities that are distinct are found separately sometime or the other. This is not the case in the case of the knower and the knowledge. The notion of the demarcation of the knower, known and the knowledge is an illusion like that of two moons or an object and its reflection. Such a difference is projected by the *vāsanā* of *buddhi* and *ātmā*.

ननु न बुद्धेः बोद्धुश्च भेदमुपलभामहे । कथम् । यतो घटमहं बुद्ध्ये इति बोद्धारो भिन्नमात्मानं प्रतिपद्यन्ते । सत्यम् । द्विचन्द्रादिबोधवत् बिम्बप्रतिबिम्बज्ञानवच्चायं भ्रमः इति प्रामाणिकाः । सहोपलम्भनियमेन च बुद्धेः बोद्धुश्च भेदो निराक्रियते । भेदस्य अनियमव्याप्तत्वात् । व्यापकविरुद्धोपलम्भेन बाध्यमानत्वात् । तदाहुः-

अविभागोहि बुद्ध्यात्मविपर्यासितदर्शनैः ।
ग्राह्यग्राहकसंवित्तिः भेदवानिव लक्ष्यते ॥
(प्र०वा० परि-२ श्लो० ३५४) (प्र०पं० ३१७)

Even those who accept a knower as distinct from the knowledge have to say that there will be a knower only when there is a knowledge. Therefore, let knowledge itself be the knower. The same is *ātmā*. It is self revealing. It is a continuous flux as cause and effect. It is present during the states of dream, deep sleep, infatuation etc.

This continuous flux is beginningless. Due to similar beginningless *vāsanā* the differences are projected. This leads to transmigration. One can overcome this by practising *mārga* i.e., right knowledge. The Tāyins i.e., wise men, continue in this flux in order to impart the right knowledge realized by them.

येपि बुद्धेरन्यं बोद्धारमिच्छन्ति तेपि सत्यामेव बुद्धौ तस्य विषये बोद्धृतामाहुः । एवं च सैव परं बोद्ध्री भवतु । कृतमन्येन बोद्ध्रा । बोद्ध्री च आत्मा भवतीति बुद्धिरेवात्मा । सा च स्वयं प्रकाशा कार्यकारणभावेन अनादिसन्तानवाहिनी स्वापमदमूर्छादिषु अभिभूततया पुनः पुनः अनुसन्धानपथं नायाति । वहति तु असौ तासु दशासु । अन्यथा जागृदादिषु बुद्ध्युदयासम्भवापत्तेः । स चायमनादिबुद्धिसन्तानः अनादिवासनानिबन्धनः संस्कार्यदर्शनाध्यवसितभेदः समुदयवशवर्ती संसरति । मार्गरूपसाक्षात्कारोन्मूलितसकलसत्त्वदृष्टिवासनानुबद्धस्तु उच्छिन्नः समुदयः प्रतिमुच्यते । तथा तायिनां च अङ्गीकृतसन्तानोच्छेदः ।

प्रदीपस्येव निर्वाणं विमोक्षः तस्य तायिनः । देशिकानां च अनेक जन्माभ्यासस्वात्मीभूत ब्रह्मादिस्तम्भपर्यन्त जगद्दयापि महाकरुणानां विशुद्धचित्तसन्तानोऽनन्त इति । (प्र०पं० ३१७-१८)

Rejection of Vijñānavāda View

The distinction between the knowledge and the knower cannot be denied. The comprehension of the two together invariably can happen even when these are distinct. Though the two are comprehended together, the knower is comprehended as the locus of the knowledge and the knowledge as located in it. This clearly shows that these are distinct. It is not correct to say that *buddhi* i.e., knowledge, can play the role of *boddhā* i.e., knower also. The knower is distinctly comprehended. It is also not correct to hold that the knowledge continues in deep sleep etc.

तदिदमसारम् । प्रतीतिसिद्धस्य बुद्धेः बोद्धुश्च भेदस्य निराकरणानर्हत्वात् । सहोपलम्भनियमस्तु यथा भेदेपि उपपद्यते तथा अत्रैव वक्ष्यामः । निराकृतश्च बाह्यार्थसिद्धौ ऋजुविमलायाम् । बुद्धिरेव परमस्तु अलं बोद्धा इति यदुक्तं तदपि काल्पनिके बोद्धरि वक्तुं युक्तम् । साक्षात् प्रतीतिसिद्धे तु न अवकाशः अस्य असत्प्रलापस्य । स्वापादिषु अपि बुद्धिः अनुवर्तते इति यदुक्तं तदपि प्रमाणाभावादसारम् । (प्र०पं० ३१८-१९)

Rejection of the View that the Senses are Ātmā

It is found that one and the same person undergoes the experiences through more than one sense. He who sees, also touches. If the senses are *ātman*, then, such an experience of the functions of more than one sense by one person would not be possible. Further, if one of the senses is defunct, then, there will be no memory of the function of that sense. Therefore, senses cannot be considered as *ātman*.

एवं तर्हि भवन्तु इन्द्रियाणि एव चेतनानि । एवं बुद्धेः बोद्धुश्च भेदावभासो घटिष्यते ।

भवेदेतदेवं यदि दर्शनस्पर्शनाभ्यामेकार्थप्रतिसन्धानं न स्यात् । यदहमद्राक्षं तदहं स्पृशामीति प्रतिसन्धाता एकः प्रतीयते ।

स्मरणं च इन्द्रियार्थानां तत्तदिन्द्रियाभावेपि यदुपलभ्यते तदिन्द्रियचैतन्ये नोपपद्यते । (प्र०पं० ३१९)

Rejection of the View that the Body is Ātman

The body also cannot be considered as *ātman. Ātman* is a knower. The body is not able to know. The body is an earthly object and non-sentient.

Here, it may be noted that the body is not the product of five or four elements the earth, etc., It is the product of only the earth. However, the other elements are joined to it. Therefore, it has the attributes of other elements also. Being the product of all elements is one thing, and to have association with other elements is quite another. The former position is not acceptable to the Prābhākaras. The latter is accepted to account for the presence of the attributes of other elements in the body.

अस्तु तर्हि देह एव आत्मा । न तत्र इमौ दोषौ प्रसज्येते । मैवम् । ज्ञाता हि आत्मा । न च देहस्य ज्ञातृता सम्भवति । तथाहि– देहो नाम पार्थिवो द्रव्यविशेषः । ननु पार्थिवत्वे तस्य भूतान्तरगुणानुपलम्भ आप द्येत । नेति ब्रूमः । भूतान्तरसहितस्य भूतान्तरस्य न कार्यारम्भकतेति वदामः । न पुनः मिथोपि भूतानि न संयुज्यन्त इत्याचक्ष्महे । अतः संयुक्तभूतान्तरगुणोपलम्भः नानुपपन्नः । (प्र०पं० ३२०)

The body cannot be taken as the product of five or four elements. The product of a combination of elements that could be perceived and those that cannot be perceived would not be perceptible. The *ākāśa* and *vāyu* are not perceptible. Therefore, if the body is taken as a product of five or four elements including these two then it can not be perceptible. The fact is that the body is perceptible. Therefore, it is a product of only the earth.

कथं पुनः आरम्भकत्वासम्भवः उच्यते । न तावत् पञ्चानां चतुर्णां वा सम्भूय आरम्भकत्वं सम्भवति । चाक्षुषाचक्षुषद्रव्यारब्धस्य तत्समवायिनः अचाक्षुषत्वापत्तेः । वायुवनस्पतिसंयोगवत् । चाक्षुषश्च देहः । अतः न पञ्चभिः चतुर्भिर्वा समारब्धः । आकाशानिलयोरचाक्षुषत्वात् । (प्र०पं० ३२०)

Imperceptibility of Ākāśa

According to Prābhākaras, *ākāśa* is imperceptible like *ātman*. This is because, it is a substance without colour. The impression that it is white or blue is erroneous. The white colour belongs to the *tejas* spread over the sky or it may be that of ice particles.

कथमचाक्षुषं । उच्यते । अचाक्षुषं नभः द्रव्यत्वे सति अरूपित्वात् आत्मवत् । ननु न अरूपं गगनम् । तद्धि धवलम् उत्पलपलाशशामलं वा उपलभ्यते । उच्यते । धवलिमा हि प्रायेण तैजस एव नीहारे तौहिनो वा । तदनपगमे तदनुपलम्भात् । (प्र०पं० ३२१)

As regards the impression of blue colour during the night, no such colour is really visible. The eye cannot comprehend it, because, without the light the eye cannot comprehend a colour. Since, such a colour does not exist, there is no question of its belonging to *ākāśa*. If such a colour was there, it would have been more clearly observed during the day. Moreover, an object that has colour will necessarily have the touch also. *Ākāśa* has no touch. Therefore, it has no colour.

यदयं निशि नीलिमेव अवलोक्यते नासौ नभसः । कस्य तर्हि ? न कस्यचित् । कथं पुनः गुणः न कस्यचित्? सत्यं गुण एवायमसिद्धः । ननु प्रतीतिबलेन सिद्ध एव । सत्यम् । सिद्ध्येत् यदि प्रतीतिः सिद्ध्येत् । सा तु कारणाभावात् न सिद्धा । ननु चक्षुरेव कारणम् । न । आलोकोपकारानपेक्षस्य चक्षुषः अप्रकाशकत्वात् । तेन अप्रतीतावेव अयं प्रतीतिभ्रमः मन्दानाम् । अतो दिवा तदनुपलम्भः । अन्यथा सौरीभिः भाभिः अनुगृहीतं चक्षुः स्फुटतरं व्योम्नि नीलिमानं प्रकाशयेत् ।

रूपं च स्पर्शसहचरितमिति स्पर्शवत्त्वं नभसः स्यात् । ततश्च सर्वमूर्तद्रव्यप्रतिघातप्रसङ्गः ।

Some hold that this blue-black colour belongs to *tamas* i.e., darkness, but it is taken as that of sky. However, the category *tamas* itself cannot be established. *Tamas* which is stated to have colour has to be made up of many constituents. No such constituents are found. If there were such constituents, the *tamas* would have been made even during the day.

केचित्तु तमसो नीलिमा गगनस्येवोपलभ्यते इत्याहुः । तदसदित्येके । तमसो निष्पत्त्यनवक्लृप्तः । रूपवत्त्वेन हि तमो द्रव्यं स्यात् । तच्च अनेकद्रव्यारब्धं चाक्षुषं भवेत् । न च तानि द्रव्याणि सन्ति । सन्ति चेत् दिवापि आरम्भेरन् । 'अतो अन्धानामिवासौ नीलिमाभिमानो नभसः' एवेति युक्तम् ।

Rejection of Tamas as a Separate Category

Some people hold that the shadow is *tamas*. It is a different category since it sometimes moves and sometimes is static, it is small and large, it is far and near. These attributes prove that it is a separate category.

This line of argument is not valid. When the light is withdrawn, the shadow is felt. This is nothing but the very area from which the light is withdrawn. The body prevents the light. Depending upon the movement of the body the light is withdrawn or spreads. This explains the movement felt as that of the shadow. The largeness and smallness arise from the number and the dimension. In the absence of these, the attributes small and large also cannot belong to the shadow.

यच्चेदमुच्यते छायैव तमः । सा च चलत्वाचलत्व-महत्त्वामहत्व-दूरत्वासन्नत्वादिगुणयोगिनी वस्तुभूतेति ।

तदप्यसारम् । निष्पत्त्यनवक्लृप्तेरेव । यच्च चलत्वाचलत्वादिकमुक्तं तदपि दूरदर्शितया । तथाहि आलोके अपवारिते छाया इष्यते ।

ततोऽपवारितालोकभूभागादिव्यतिरेकिणी न रूपान्तरवच्छाया दृश्यते । तेन मन्यामहे अपवारितालोकभूभागादिकमेव छायेति । एतेन चलत्वाचलत्व-महत्त्वामहत्व-दूरत्वासन्नत्वादीनि समर्थितानि ।

यत्तु तेजसः प्रतिरोधि द्रव्यम् तत् यथा यथा सञ्चरति तथा तथा आलोकः प्रतिमुच्यते प्रतिरुध्यते चेति चलतीव छाया प्रतिभाति । अन्यथा शरीरे चलति किमिति छायापि चलेत् । चलनहेत्वभावात् । एतेन अचलति शरीरे अचलत्वं व्याख्यातम् ।

संख्यापरिमाणयोगि महत्वम् । तदभावे कथमिव छायेयमुत्पत्स्यते इति अलमनया स्थूलदर्शिनः कथयाऽनवबुद्ध्या ।। (प्र०पं० ३२३)

The statement 'this is the shadow of that' refers to that by which the light is prevented. For instance, when the light is prevented by the body, the prevented area is called the shadow of the body. From this it is clear that the shadow is not a separate entity. The references to shadow in the *smṛti* and such other context be taken in this sense i.e., the area wherein the light is prevented but not in the sense of a separate entity.

ननु भूभागादेरेव छायात्वे कथं द्रव्यान्तरेण व्यपदेशः अस्य इयं छाया इति । उच्यते । अपवारितालोकभूभागादिरेव छायेत्युक्तम् । तत्र येन अपवारणं तदपेक्षया युज्यते तद्व्यपदेशः ।

एवं च स्मृतिकाराणामपि 'नाक्रामेत् कामतः छायाम्' इत्येवमादिको व्यवहारः उपपन्नः । योऽपि शास्त्रकाराणां व्यवहारः छत्रगृहादीनां तुल्यं छायालक्षणं कार्यमिति स आलोकापवारणाभिप्रायेण वर्णनीयः ।

There will be no such contingency as the total inability to see the area from which the light is removed, since, some particles of *tejas* still persist in that area. However, when there is a total absence of light it is deep darkness. This is only the inability to see the area but not seeing something else i.e., any separate entity called *tamas.*

ननु आलोकापवारणे भूभागादीनामदर्शनप्रसङ्गः । मैवम् । प्रचुरतरालोकावयवसंयोगः तत्र वार्यते । अल्पास्तु तेजोवयवाः समन्ततः

सञ्चरन्तः संयुज्यन्त एव । यत्र तु सर्वथा तेषामसंयोगः सः महानन्धकार इति निरवद्यम् । (प्र०पं० ३२३)

Establishment of Ākāśa as a Separate Element

Ākāśa is established on the ground that *śabda* is a quality and it needs a locus. *Śabda* has to be considered as a quality because it is cognised by one sense i.e., *śrotra* only. Though *vāyu* is also cognised by one sense i.e., touch, it is not considered as perceived. *Vayu* is inferred. If *vāyu* is taken as perceived, then, we add the clause that which is not perceived by touch but still perceived by only one sense i.e., *śrotra*. This quality of *śabda* does not belong to *pṛthvi, jala* etc. Therefore, a separate substance has to be thought of as the locus of *śabda*. This substance is *ākāśa*. The Prābhākaras do not consider *śabda* itself as a substance. It is only a quality.

नचैवं सति आकाशस्य असिद्धिरेव । शब्दलक्षणगुणानुमानसिद्धत्वात् । ननु गुणतैव शब्दस्य असिद्धा द्रव्यत्वेन वादिभिः अभ्युपेतत्वात्

यदाहुः-

वर्णात्मकाश्च ये शब्दाः नित्याः सर्वगतास्तथा ।
पृथाद्रव्यतया ये तु न गुणाः कस्य चिन्मताः ।। (स०द०कौ ६२ पृ)

तदिदमसारम् । एकेन्द्रियप्रत्यक्षतया रूपादिवत् गुणत्वसिद्धेः । न च वायुना अनैकान्तिकत्वम् । तस्य वायोः अतीन्द्रियतया अभ्युपेतत्वात् । येपि च ऐन्द्रियकं वायुमिच्छन्ति तेषामपि स्पर्शविरहे सतीति विशेषणोपादानाददोषः ।

एवं सिद्धगुणभावः शब्दः गुणिनमनुमास्यति । तस्य भूजलादिभावावगमे कारणाभावात् द्रव्यान्तरमेव तदवतिष्ठते । (प्र०पं० ३२४)

Śabda does not arise at the mouth of the speaker. *Śrotrendriya* has to perform its function of cognising the *śabda* by reaching *śabda*. Neither the ear can reach the mouth nor the mouth can reach the ear.

Therefore, it has to be envisaged that *śrotra* which is *ākāśa* cognises *śabda* present in it by *samavāya.* Therefore, there is no difficulty to cognise it by *śrotra* itself.

ननु मुखादिगतः शब्दः उपलभ्यते । नेत्युच्यते । श्रोत्रं प्राप्यकारि बहिरन्द्रियत्वात् । त्वगिन्द्रियवत् । तत्र न तावत् श्रोत्रं मुखादिदेशं गच्छति । प्रत्यक्षा हि कर्णशष्कुली स्वदेशस्था दृश्यते । नापि मुखं श्रोत्रदेशमुपसर्पति । तस्यापि स्वदेशे एवोपलम्भात् । अतः श्रोत्रगत एव शब्दः गृह्यते । भ्रान्तिस्तु एषा मुखे शब्द इति । समवायलक्षणैव तस्य प्राप्तिः । एवं च शब्दगुणत्वात् श्रोत्रस्य यत् शब्दगुणकं द्रव्यमाकाशपदवेदनीयं तदेव श्रोत्रम् । (प्र०पं० ३२५)

The Body is the Product of the Earth only

The body is not produced by the combination of the three viz., the earth, water and the *tejas.* In that case it would have had a touch different from cold, hot, and neither cold nor hot. These three touches belong to water, *tejas* and the earth respectively. Since, all the three are combined, the touch of the product of these three will have to be different from the touch of these three like a cloth made out of the threads of three colours being an object of variegated colour. For the same reason it cannot be the product of two also.

नापि त्र्यात्मकं शरीरं गुणान्तरप्रादुर्भावप्रसङ्गात् । भूजलतेजांसि हि यथाक्रममनुष्णाशीतशीतोष्णास्पर्शानि तैरारब्धं द्रव्यं एतत् त्रयविलक्षण स्पर्शमापद्येत चित्रपटवत् । यथा सितासितादितन्तुसमारब्धः पटः तन्तुरूपविलक्षणरूपः तथा शरीरमपि आरम्भकद्रव्यस्पर्शविलक्षणस्पर्शं भवेत् । अनुष्णाशीतस्पर्शं च एतदुपलभ्यते । एतेन द्व्यात्मकतापि निषिद्धा । (प्र०पं० ३२५)

Further, the fragrance which is a quality of earth alone, and is present in it by *samavāya* will not be able to produce the fragrance in the body which is a combined product of the three. Similarly, if the other two produce the body, their respective qualities cannot be brought about in the product. The *samavāya* relation between the respective quality and the element cannot extend to the combined product. Therefore, it has to be accepted that the body is the product of earth only. The others, of course, join it and bring about their features in the body. The point made here is that the other four or three elements are not *samavāya kāraṇa* for producing the body, though they may be present in it. It is only the earth that is *samavāya kāraṇa.*

किञ्च गन्धस्य पार्थिवद्रव्यसमवेतस्य एकाकिनो गन्धान्तरारम्भकत्वानुपपत्तेः अगन्धं शरीरं स्यात् । भूतेजसोः अप्तेजसोर्वा आरम्भकत्वे अगन्धत्वमरसत्वमेवं वेदितव्यम् । अतो रूप-रस-गन्ध-स्पर्शयोगि शरीरं पार्थिवमेव ॥ (प्र०पं० ३२६)

So far as knowledge is concerned, since, the *paramāṇus* of earth have no knowledge, the body which is a product of these also has no knowledge. Knowledge is a *viśeṣaguṇa.* A *viśeṣaguṇa* that is not present in the cause will not emerge into the effect.

ज्ञानं च विशेषगुणः । कार्यद्रव्ये च विशेषगुणः कारणगुणपूर्वक एव रूपादिवत् । न च कारणभूतेषु ज्ञानमस्ति । (प्र०पं० ३२६)

The Rejection of Cārvāka View

The *cārvākas* argue that just as the power of intoxication is present in the wine, even though it is not present in its causes, *caitanya* can be present in the body even though it is not present in its causes. This argument is rejected by pointing out that *śakti* is not a *viśeṣaguṇa.* Therefore, it can be present in the effect, though, it is not in the cause. But *jñāna* is a *viśeṣaguṇa.* Further, at *paramāṇu* level the intoxication can be brought about by the contact of other objects. In this way when it is introduced at the level of cause, it will naturally arise at the level of effect i.e., the wine.

स्यादेतत् मदशक्तिवत् चैतन्यमपीति । यथा मदशक्तिः पार्थिवेषु परमाणुषु असत्यपि तदारब्धे कार्यद्रव्ये सुराख्ये निष्पद्यते तथा चैतन्यमपि

निष्पत्स्यते इति । तन्न शक्तेरविशेषगुणत्वात् । शक्त्याख्यो हि गुणः सर्वद्रव्येषु तत्तत्कार्य विषयः कार्यसमधिगम्यः अभ्युपगम्यते । चैतन्यं तु न देहादन्यत्र विद्यत इति विशेषगुणोऽसौ । अपि च द्रव्यान्तरसंयोगादकार्यभूतेषु पार्थिवपरमाणुषु अकारणगुणपूर्वकोऽपि मदशक्त्याख्यो गुणो नानुपपन्नः। तदारब्धे कार्यद्रव्ये सुराख्ये कारणगुणपूर्वक एव । चैतन्यं तु न प्रत्येकं परमाणुषु अभ्युपगम्यते । तस्मात् शरीरदन्यस्य गुणो ज्ञानमिति देहव्यतिरिक्तपुरुषानुमानं द्रष्टव्यम् । (प्र०पं० ३२६-२७)

The objection that the *jñāna* is not a quality is answered by pointing out that it is a quality. This is established on two grounds: (i) It subsists in a substance (ii) By itself it has no qualities. Further, it is not a cause of conjunction and disjunction. As it is an effect, it has to be in a substance. The substance in which *jñāna* subsists is *ātman*. Similarly, as a ground of *sukha* etc., also *ātman* could be established.

स्यान्मतं गुणत्वमेव ज्ञानस्यासिद्धमिति । तन्न । द्रव्याश्रितत्वात् । निर्गुणतया संयोगविभागौ प्रति निरपेक्षकारणत्वाभावेन गुणत्वसिद्धेः ।

न च वाच्यं द्रव्याश्रितत्वमेव अप्रसिद्धमिति । कार्यत्वात् । नहि कार्यं किञ्चिदद्रव्याश्रितं आत्मानं लभते । एवं सुखादिभ्योपि देहातिरिक्तात्मानुमानं वेदितव्यम् । (प्र०पं० ३२७)

Rejection of the View that the Expression 'Aham' Refers to Body

In the statements 'I go' 'I am fat' etc., 'I' refers to the body only. Therefore, the body itself is knower. This is directly perceived. An inference that is contrary to the perception is not a valid inference.

Though *jñāna* is a *viśeṣa guṇa*, it is not necessary that it has to be at the cause level to emanate at the effect level. Hence, *jñāna* that is not at *paramāṇu* level may emerge at the body level.

घटमहं जानामीति ज्ञातुः अहङ्कारास्पदीभूतत्वात् 'अहं गच्छामि' 'अहं स्थूलः' इत्यादौ अहङ्कारस्य शरीर एव प्रवृत्त्यविवादात् शरीरमेव प्रत्यक्षं ज्ञातृ प्रतीयते । प्रत्यक्षविरोधे अनुमानं आत्मानं न लभते इति ।

वैशेषिकगुणोपि ज्ञानं न कारणगुणपूर्वकमिति पार्थिवपरमाणुषु अविद्यमानमपि ज्ञानं शरीरे सम्भविष्यतीति न शरीरादन्यस्य अनुमानम् । (प्र०पं० ३२७)

Though the consciousness belongs to the body, it is not found in the dead body as it has lost its vitality. The absence of consciousness in the dead body does not prove that the body is not a conscious entity at all.

The statement 'This is my body' also does not prove an *ātman* separate from the body. It is a secondary usage like that of a statement 'This is the body of a stone idol'. There is also a statement as *mama ātmā* i.e., the self of me. Just as this statement does not prove another self, the statement 'My body' does not prove a self separate from the body. The statements 'I am happy' etc., also do not prove a separate *ātmā.* These refer to the happiness of body only.

ननु शरीरस्य चैतन्ये मृतशरीरेपि तत् स्यात् । न । तस्य विगुणत्वात् । मरणेन शरीरं विगुणमित्यविवादम् ।

ननु ममेदं शरीरमिति देहातिरिक्तो अहङ्कारो निविशते । न । अभेदेऽपि भेदोपचारोऽयम् 'शिलापुत्रकस्य शरीरमितिवत् । अन्यथा मम आत्मा इति व्यपदेशात् आत्मान्तरमप्याश्रीयेत । येपि च सुखादयः ते च 'अहं सुखी' इति अहंकारविषयसम्बन्धितया अवगम्यमानाः शरीरसमवायिनः एव । अतो न तद्व्यतिरेकिणमात्मानमनुमापयितुमीशते । (प्र०पं० ३३६-३७)

Further, the knowledge, happiness etc., cause modification in the body such as a pleasant face, a serious face etc., for these the body is *samavāyi kāraṇa,* the knowledge, happiness etc., are *asamavāyikāraṇas*. It is natural to say that these *asamavāyikāraṇas* are present in the *samavāyikāraṇas* i.e., body, but not in a separate entity called *ātman*. There is no need to accept such an entity.

शरीरविकारहेतुत्वाच्च तेषां सुतरां शरीरगुणत्वम् । नहि अतद्गुणः तं गुणिनं विकर्तुमुत्सहते । विक्रियतेहि शरीरं नयनविकासमुखप्रसाद रोमहर्षादिभिः । सुखादिषु उत्पन्नेपु तत्र शरीरे विकार्ये विकारं प्रति समवायिकारणभूते तत्प्रत्यासन्नेनैव असमवायिकारणेन भवितुं युक्तम् । न च शक्यं वक्तुं सुखादिमदात्मसंयोग एव शरीरसमवेतेषु विकारेषु असमवायिकारणमस्तु इति । प्रमाणाभावात् । सिद्धे हि आत्मनि स्यादेषा कल्पना साध्ये तु अव्यवहितानामेव कारणता उचिता इति न देहातिरिक्तात्मानुमाने सुखादीनां सामर्थ्यम् । (प्र०पं० ३२८)

Rejection of the View 'There is no Ātman Apart from the Body'

In the experience 'I know the jar' a knower other than the body is comprehended. The experience 'I know the jar' etc., do not have any reference to the body. In all experiences the knower is necessarily comprehended. Otherwise, there will be no distinction between one's own experience and the other's experiences.

In the experience 'I go', there is a knower distinct from the body who comprehends the act of going on the part of the body. The reference to the body by the expression *aham* is secondary. In the statement *mama ātma* the expression secondarily applies to the body. The primary meaning of 'I' is a conscious being, not the body, since the body has no consciousness.

अत्रोच्यते । स्यादेतदेवं यदि देहातिरिक्तो नोपलभ्यते ज्ञाता । 'घटमहमुपलभे' इति घटस्य अनुभविता शरीरातिरिक्तः प्रतिभासते । शरीरं करचरणाद्यवयवयोगि । न च घटाद्यनुभवसमये तस्य अवभासोऽन्वयी । अवश्यं च ज्ञातुरवभासो मेयानुभवेष्वनुवर्तते इत्यास्थेयम् । अन्यथा स्वपरवेद्ययोरनतिशयप्रसङ्गात् ।

अहं गच्छामीति प्रतिपत्तिसमयेपि प्रतिपत्ता शरीरातिरिक्तः। प्रतिपत्तृस्वभावः गन्तारं देहं प्रतिपद्यमानः प्रतीयत एव। तत्र लाक्षणिकोऽहं शब्दानुविद्धस्तु शरीरे प्रत्ययः। 'मम आत्मा' इत्यत्रापि लाक्षणिकः शरीर एव ममकारः। यस्तु चेतनः तत्र अस्मच्छब्दः मुख्यः। न च शरीरं चेतनम्। चितिसमवायाभावात्। शरीरातिरिक्तवस्त्वन्तरसमवायिनी चेतना चकास्ति।

The question 'If the consciousness is an attribute of *ātman,* how is it that it covers the objects, since, it does not belong to them' is answered by pointing out that it is its very nature to cover different objects when it operates. However, it has no contact with the objects of the past and the future.

ननु आत्मधर्मभूता चेत् चितिः तर्हि विषयासंस्पर्शिनी कथं प्रतिविषयं विभज्यते। उच्यते। प्रतिभाससिद्धा तावत् चेतनसमवायिनी चितिः। अनागतातीतसंवेदने च व्यक्तमेव विषयानाश्रितत्वम्। प्रतिकर्मप्रविभागस्तु व्यवहारानुगुणस्वभावत्त्वात् चितेः। यद्व्यवहारानुगुणा या चितिः तदीयासौ व्यपदिश्यत इति। (प्र०पं० ३२९)

The permanent nature of *ātman* is established by the process of *pratyabhijña* i.e., recognition, through its *kartṛtva* and *bhoktṛva.* 'What I saw the other day I am seeing today' is the form of recognition. It is not only the recognition of the object seen, but it is the recognition of the knower himself. This means the same *ātman* is presented in both the experiences and he is permanent. If *ātman* is not parmanent his activities will be contingent. This affects the very *kartṛtva* and *bhoktṛtva.*

Though the *ātman* is permanent, his attribute i.e consciousness will not always be there. Some *asamavāyiākāraṇa* is necessary to give rise to it. The contact between *ātman* and *manas* is such *asamavāyikāraṇa.* The very moment of *manas* is for this contact. A further layer of *ātma manasānnikarṣa* initiates the effort for it and so on. This is a beginningless series of cause and effect like that of the seed and the sprout.

ननु एवं प्रथमदर्शनेपि देहाद् व्यतिरेके सिद्धे अन्येद्युः दृष्टे अपरेद्युः अहमिदमद्राक्षमिति प्रत्यभिज्ञोपन्यासो अनर्थकः । उच्यते–व्यतिरेकसिद्धावपि स्थिरतया क्रियावत्त्वसिद्धये प्रत्यभिज्ञा उपन्यास्ता । अस्थिरत्वे तत एव कादाचित्ककार्यसिद्धेः तत्सिद्धये न क्रियानुमानं क्रमते । अक्रियस्य कर्तृत्वं भोक्तृत्वं च काल्पनिकं स्यात् । कर्ता भोक्ता च यज्ञायुधिवाक्येन आक्षिप्तः समर्थयितव्यः इति युक्तः प्रत्यभिज्ञोपन्यासः ।

यदाचायमात्मा प्रत्यभिज्ञायते तदा योऽसौ चिदात्मा तस्य धर्मः नासौ तन्मात्रप्रभवः कदाचिदुदियात् । सदा सन्निहितकारणकं हि कार्यं न कादाचित्कं भवेत् । कारणासन्निधाननिबन्धनोहि कार्योदयव्याक्षेपः । तस्मादयमात्मा समवायिकारणभूतः किञ्चिदसमवायिकारणमपेक्षते ।

तच्च आत्ममनस्सन्निकर्षाख्यम् । तस्य च असमवायिकारणं मनसः परिस्पन्दः । तस्यापि आत्ममनस्सन्निकर्षान्तरमात्समवेतं प्रयत्नम् अदृष्टं वा अपेक्षमाणमसमवायिकारणम् । प्रयत्नादृष्टयोश्च आत्ममनस्सन्निकर्षान्तरमेवेति अनादिरेषा कार्यकारणपरम्परा बीजाङ्कुरवदिति वेदितव्यम् ।

Establishment of Manas and Senses

The nine *viśeṣa guṇas* of *ātman* viz., *buddhi, sukha, duḥkha,* etc., arise by the contact of *ātman* and *manas.* The very emergence of these qualities establishes *manas.* Among these *buddhi* is self revealing. *Sukha, duḥkha* etc., are perceived by *manas. Sukha* is not just the absence of *duḥkha.* The absence of *duḥkha* is the absence of its comprehension. The comprehension of mere *ātman* without *duḥkha* is the absence of the comprehension of *duḥkha. Sukha* is comprehended in addition to the comprehension of *ātman.*

मनसो अभ्युगमे च सकलात्मगुणोदय एव प्रमाणम् । बुद्धिसुखदुः खेच्छाद्वेषप्रयत्नादृष्टसंस्काराणां नवानामपि वैशेषिकात्मगुणानामात्ममनस्संयोगेनैवोत्पत्तेः ।

तत्र बुद्धिः स्वसंवेदनसिद्धा प्रमितिस्मृतिरूपा । सुखदुः खेच्छाद्वेषप्रयत्नास्तु मानसप्रत्यक्षवेद्याः । न च दुःखाभावमात्रं सुखम् ।

दुखाभावस्य दुःखानुपलम्भरूपत्वात् । तद्वियुक्तात्मोपलब्धेरेव दुःखानुपलम्भरूपत्वात् । आत्मोपलम्भातिरिक्तसुखोपलम्भाच्च । (प्र०पं० ३३०)

Sanskāra can be ascertained from its result viz., memory. The memory arises only in respect to those objects that are experienced earlier. Therefore, something that will lead to the memory has to be posited in *ātman*. This is *sanskāra*. *Dharma* and *adharma* constitute *adṛṣṭa*. This has to be ascertained from the scriptures. Mere contact between *ātman* and *manas* is not sufficient to produce the knowledge of outside objects. Therefore, five senses have to be posited. The body is the locus of these five senses and *manas*.

संस्कारस्य तु स्मृतिलक्षणमेव कार्यं गमकम् । अनुभूतविषय एव स्मृतिर्भवतीति अनुभवाधीनं कञ्चिदात्मनोऽतिशयमुपकल्पयति । अदृष्टं तु धर्माधर्मलक्षणमागमैकगम्यम् । न केवलमात्ममनःसन्निकर्षादेव रूपाद्यवगमः। अन्धादीनामभावादिति चक्षुरादीनि बहिरिन्द्रियाणि अङ्गीक्रियन्ते । मनः प्रभृतीनि षडिन्द्रियाणि यस्मिन्नायतन्ते तदिन्द्रियायतनं शरीरम् । (प्र०पं० ३३०)

Three Kinds of Bodies

Śālikanātha accepts only three kinds of bodies viz., *jarāyuja*, *aṇḍaja* and *svedaja*. He does not accept *udbhija* kind of bodies. Trees do not have senses, nor these experience joy or sorrow that are the grounds to have the body. Therefore, no *udbhija* kind of body exists. Certain *smṛti* statements such as *smaśāne jāyate vṛkṣah* which appear to suggest that even trees have life and hence constitute the body are not based on Vedic authority. Vedas convey only *kāryā* i.e., *apūrva*.

तच्च जरायुज-अण्डज-संस्वेदजभेदभिन्नं त्रिविधम् । उद्भिज्जं तु शरीरं न भवत्येव । भोगानुपलम्भात् । तदायतनं हि तत्प्रयोजकं वृक्षादिकस्य इन्द्रियायतनत्वे प्रमाणाभावात् ।

'यदपि श्मशाने जायते वृक्षः कङ्कगृध्रनिषेवितः' इति निषिद्धाचरणफलत्वस्मरणात् उद्भिज्जं शरीरमवभाति तदप्यनुपपन्नम् ।

तस्मिन्नंशे प्रमाणाभावात् । स्मृतेः निर्मूलतया मुख्यार्थत्वानुपपत्तेः । न च वेद एव मूलमवकल्पते । अकार्यार्थत्वात् । (प्र०पं० ३३१)

Further, birth as a tree cannot be taken as the result of a prohibited act. There are two opinions concerning the consequence of a prohibited act. One view is, it leads to *pratyavāya.* The other view is, there is no evidence to say so. But none holds the view that it will lead to the results like the birth as a tree in a cemetry. Therefore, the result mentioned in this *smṛiti* has no relevance. It is not valid.

नञ्विधेः निषिध्यमानार्थानुष्ठाने प्रत्यावाय इत्यत्र गमकाभावात् । शंव्याधिकरण (मी०द० ३-४-१०) सिद्धान्तपर्यालोचनया निषिद्धादपि कुतश्चित् प्रत्यवायोदयः तथापि वृक्षादिरूपशरीरफलताऽवसातुं न शक्यते । फलतया अन्वयायोग्यत्वात् ।

Such of the items that are incongruent cannot be taken as a part of the statement as in the instance 'sprinkle with the fire'.

Further, even in the Veda, such of the statements that do not enjoin but just state the facts have to be taken by way of *lakṣaṇā* or *gauṇi.*

यस्य हि अन्वययोग्यत्वमवधारितं तस्य वाक्यार्थानुप्रवेशित्वम् । यस्य तु अन्वययोग्यत्वासम्भवः तस्य वाक्यार्थानुप्रवेशितापि नास्ति 'वाह्निना सिञ्चेत्' इतिवत् ।

यस्तु वेदे तथाभूतार्थप्रयोगः स गौणः लाक्षणिको वा वर्णनीयः इति अत्रापि गौण्या लक्षणया वा वृत्त्या वर्णनीयम् । अतः त्रिविधमेव शरीरम् । (प्र०पं० ३३१)

Śālikanātha does not also accept *ayonija* bodies. These are stated to arise by religious power. However, since all bodies are found to be of earthly substance, it is difficult to accept this type of body.

यत् पुनः अपार्थिवं अयोनिजं शरीरं केवलधर्माधिपत्यनिबन्धनं कैश्चिदभ्युपगम्यते तत् सर्वशरीराणां पार्थिवत्वाव्यभिचारात् नानुमातुं शक्यते ।

The Nature and the Functions of Manas

Manas is within the body. It is of atomic size. It is a substance. The substances are of two types (i) single (ii) complex. *Manas* is a single substance. There is no need to consider it as complex. Its dimension is not of *paramamahat.* In that case the contact between *ātman* and *manas* will not be possible. Two *paramamahat* objects cannot have contact. Objects with *paramamahat* dimension have no parts, nor these can move. Therefore, *manas* is considered as atomic in size.

मनश्च अन्तःशरीरं परमाणुपरिमाणम् । द्रव्यं च द्विविधम् । अनेकद्रव्यम् अद्रव्यद्रव्यं चेति । अद्रव्यद्रव्यत्वेपि परममहत्वाभ्युपगमे आत्मना सह संयोगासम्भवः । नहि परममहतोः अपरिस्पन्दयोः अनवयवयोश्च संयोगोपपत्तिः । तस्मात् परमाणुपरिमाणमेव मनः । (प्र०पं० ३३२)

The *manas* is eternal. It is not caused. It moves quickly. Without the contact with the *manas* the senses are not able to cognise their respective objects. When the *manas* is entangled in something else, the sense is not able to do its task.

The *manas* gets contacted with *ātman* due to the *dharma* and *adharma.* It gets similar contact in the next birth also as a result of deeds performed.

तच्च सत्, अकारणत्वात् नित्यम् । आशुतरसञ्चारि च तत् । आशुतरेन्द्रियाधिष्ठानदर्शनात् । नहि तदनधिष्ठितमिन्द्रियं स्वविषयमवसाययितुमलम् । अन्यत्र व्यासक्तचित्तस्य विषयान्तराप्रतीतेः । तस्य मनसः अनादिधर्माधर्मसापेक्षः क्षेत्रज्ञेन संयोगः देहान्तरसंयोगश्च तस्माददृष्टापेक्षादात्ममनःसन्निकर्षादुत्पन्नस्य कर्मणः प्रसादेन ।

The *ātman* undergoes the experiences of the joy and sorrow. The body is the abode in which he undergoes these experiences. The senses are the means for these experiences. The external objects and the internal feelings like pain and pleasure are the objects of experience. Deriving the joy and the sorrow from these is enjoyment.

सोऽयमात्मा भोक्ता, भोगायतनं शरीरम्, भोगसाधनानि इन्द्रियाणि, भोग्याः सुखादयः आन्तराः, बाह्याश्च पृथिव्यादयः, भुक्तिश्च वित्तिः सुखानुभवः इति पञ्चसु विधासु सर्वं तत्त्वं परिसमाप्यते । (प्र०पं० ३३२)

The Mode of the Cognition of Ātman

Śālikanātha raises the question as to the means of the cognition of the *ātman*. He quotes the view that it is perceived by means of *manas* as in the case of joy, sorrow etc., and rejects it on the ground that one and the same cannot be both the agent and the object.

केन पुनः प्रमाणेन अस्य आत्मनः प्रमितिः? अप्रमीयमाणत्वे अस्य सत्तोपगमो निर्निबन्धनः ।

अत्र केचिदाहुः मानसं प्रत्यक्षं सुखादिष्विव आत्मनि प्रमाणमिति । तदयुक्तमिति प्राभाकराः । न हि एकस्य कर्तृत्वं कर्मत्वं च स्वापेक्षमुपपद्यते । स्वात्मनि क्रियावृत्तिविरोधात् । (प्र०पं० ३३३)

The cognition of *ātman* by himself through *manas* cannot be justified by quoting the experience as '*aham.*' This can be explained by considering it either as self revealed or as referred to in the cognition of the object. The latter explanation is justified by the fact that it is always cognised along with the object. The latter view is the Prābhākara view.

Śālikanātha just mentions a view that it may be taken as self revealed as in the case of *samvit* and takes up the question of the self revealing nature of *samvit* for detailed examination.

न च अहमिति संविद्दशेन अविरोधः । स्वयं प्रकाशत्वेन विषयप्रतीतिगोचरत्वेन वा तदुपपत्तेः । विषयैः सह सहोपलम्भनियमश्च एवं सति उपपन्नः ।

अन्ये मन्यन्ते स्वप्रकाशाय हि प्रमाणम् अप्रकाशस्वभावेषु विषयेषु अपेक्ष्यते । प्रकाशस्वरसे स्वात्मनि प्रकाशापेक्षा मुधैव संविद्वत् । (प्र०पं० ३३३)

Self Revealing Nature of Samvit

Samvit has to be accepted as self revealing. If it is not self revealing, then, the objects covered by it will not be known and no statement can be made that these are known. It cannot be argued that enabling to make the statement about the object itself is *samvit* and can be inferred from the statement about the object, because, no statement can be made before one is aware of the knowledge. *Mānasa pratyakṣatva* of *samvit* is also not acceptable.

प्रमाणफलभूता संवित्तिः अवश्यं स्वयंप्रकाशा अभ्युपगमनीया । अन्यथा उत्पन्नायामपि तस्यामप्रकाशमानायां विषयाणां विदितत्वावेदने विदितत्वव्यवहारो न स्यात् ।

न च वाच्यं व्यवहारयोग्यतैव विषयेषु पुरुषस्य संवित् सा व्यवहारे उत्पन्ने फलेन अनुमीयते । यतो व्यवहारप्रवृत्तेरपि पुरस्तात् विदितत्वं विषयाणामनुसन्धीयते इति सर्वजनसम्मतमेतत् नापि मानसप्रत्यक्षसमधिगम्या संवित् । स्वयंप्रकाशत्वेनाप्युपपत्तौ सत्यां तत्कल्पनायां प्रमाणाभावात् । (प्र०पं० ३३३)

So far as the objects are concerned, these cannot be accepted as self ravealing, because, permanent objects are always there and these would have been cognised even during the sleep. In the case of *samvit* such a difficulty does not arise, since, *samvit* does not arise during the sleep. On the other hand the permanent objects are present during the sleep. Their permanent nature can be ascertained by recognition. Therefore, the objects are not self revealing, while *samvit* is self revealing. This self revealing nature is mentioned here as an example in the context of claiming *ātman* as self-revealing. However, Śālikanātha does not accept the claim of self revelation for *ātman*, through self revealing nature of *samvit* is acceptable to him and it is one of his important doctrines.

विषयेषु हि स्थायिषु स्वयं प्रकाशेषु अभ्युपगम्यमानेषु स्वापादिदशाः पुरुषाणामनुपपन्नाः स्युः । संविदि तु स्वयं प्रकाशायां नैषः दोषः आपद्यते

स्वापादिषु तस्याः एव असत्त्वात् । विषयास्तु प्रत्यभिज्ञाबललब्धस्थेमानः पुरुषाणां स्वापादिदशायामपि न सन्तीति न वक्तुं शक्यमभिधातुम् । ततस्ते परायत्तप्रकाशाः । संवित्तिस्तु स्वयं प्रकाशेति सिद्धो नः दृष्टान्तः ।

Quoting the example of *samvit,* the claim of *ātman* to be self revealing and its advantages are further explained as under: Since *ātman* is self revealing, no separate evidence is necessary to establish it. It is revealed during the fourth state ie liberated state. This liberated state is the highest goal. If self revelation at that state is not accepted and only the absence of all other experience is stated, then, there will be no difference between the liberated and the sleep.

स्वयं प्रकाशस्य सत्तोपगमो न प्रमाणान्तरायत्तः । एवं च तुरीयेपि प्रकाशो नोपरमते । अत एव मोक्षस्य परमपुरुषार्थता । अन्यथा विच्छिन्नसकलोपलम्भानात् स्वापादविशिष्टः पुरुषैः नेष्यते ।

Stating the view of those who claim self-revealing nature for *ātman*, Śālikanātha rejects the same. If the *ātman* is self-revealing, then, it would have been revealed even during the deep sleep state and there would not have been any difference between this state and the waking state. A position that is natural will not stop or cannot be concealed.

एतदपि प्रामाणिकाग्रगण्याः न साधु इति आहुः । स्वरसप्रकाशत्वे पुरुषस्य जाग्रत्स्वप्न तुरीयेष्विव सुषुप्तावपि प्रकाशापत्तेः स्वापः तेभ्यो न भिद्यते । न हि स्वारसिकस्य उच्छेदः आवरणं वा सम्भवति ।

The argument that ‘the blackness of earthly particles which is natural is changed by the application of heat, similarly, in the case of *ātman* also the natural self-revealing nature may not be operative during the deep sleep state, is not a valid argument. Whatever is natural that cannot vanish and the blackness is claimed to be natural, therefore, it cannot change. Hence, on the basis of this example, the change in the self revealing nature of *ātman* during deep sleep cannot be justified.

In fact the blackness is not natural for earthly particles. It is brought about by the application of heat as the redness is sometimes brought about.

यत्तु इदं केनचित् प्रलप्यते स्वारसिकमपि पार्थिवानामणूनां श्यामत्वं पाकपदावेदनीयेन अग्निसंयोगेन निवर्तते इति । तदसत् । यदकृतकं तत् सर्वमविनाशि दिगादिवत् । अकृतकश्च श्यामिमा पार्थिवानामणूनामित्यनुमानग्रस्तत्वात् न आदरणीयम् । स्वारसिकता च पार्थिवानामणूनां श्यामता न सिद्धा । लौहित्यस्येव तस्यापि पाकजत्वोपगमात् ।

An object that exists but that is not caused is a permanent object. If that which is not caused (natural), is also considered as not permanent then, nothing will be permanent.

सद् अकारणवत्त्वमेव नित्यत्वम् । अकारणमपि चेदनित्यम्, न नित्यलक्षणं किञ्चिदवकल्पते ।

Prābhākaras View on the Cognition of Ātman

Neither the *ātman* i.e., knower is cognised without the cognition of the object, nor the object is cognised without the cognition of *ātman* i.e., knower. The *samvit* covers both the knower and the object. However, the knower is presented as the agent but not as the object though he shares the result of *samvit.* A person who walks, though gets the result of walking viz., reaching the destination, is considered only as an agent but not the object. An object is defined as that which gets the result of an action undertaken by someone else. The knower, the known and the *samvit* are comprehended together. Since, the *ātman* is cognized along with the cognition of the object, there will be no cognition of *ātman* during deep sleep, as there is no cognition of the object at that time. During the fourth state i.e., liberated state *ātman* remains in his basic state obtaining the knowledge of all.

तत्त्वविदः आचक्षते न आत्मा विषयाननुविद्धो अवभासते, न च विषयाः बोद्धरि अनवभासमने भासन्ते इति तावत् सिद्धम् । तत्र यदेतत्

विषयेषु प्रमाणम्, तज्जनितैव या संवित् सा पुरुषं स्वविषयांश्च विषयीकुर्वन्ती समुदीयते । तत्संवित्तिफलभागित्वेपि पुरुषस्य न कर्मता किन्तु कर्तृतैव गन्तृवत् । यथा गमनफलसंयोगयोगिनोपि गन्तुः न कर्मता किन्तुकर्तृतैव तथा बोद्धुरपि वेदितव्यम् । परसमवायिक्रियाफलयोगि हि कर्मेति कर्मज्ञाः ।

अत एव सहोपलम्भनियमोऽपि विषयवेत्तृसंवित्तीनामुपपन्नः । एवं च विषयवित्तिगोचरत्वादात्मनः विषयवेदनोपायोपरमात् स्वापादिषु अप्रकाशो युक्त एव । तुरीयेपि सम्भूतसकलोपलम्भाय आत्मा सन्मात्रावस्थ एव अवतिष्ठते । (प्र०पं० ३३४)

Prābhākara's Concept of Salvation

Cessation of all worldly miseries is salvation. It should not be argued that just as there is the cessation of miseries, there is the cessation of all happiness also in the so called liberated state. Therefore, it cannot be *puruṣārtha.* This argument does not hold good. The happiness enjoyed during the state of *sansāra* (transmigration), is also a kind of misery. It requires so much effort to secure and it is temporary also. Therefore, its cessation in salvation is as much welcome as the cessation of misery.

The plea that there will be highest bliss in the liberated state has no supporting evidence. *Śruti* does not convey mere fact. During the *sansāra* state no such bliss is experienced by anyone. It cannot be said that during *sansāra* it is veiled. The natural and self-revealing bliss cannot be veiled. It is also not convincing to hold that since everyone loves his self it is of the nature of bliss. It is not the love of *ātman* but it is an interest to avoid the perishing of the body that is mistaken to be the love for *ātman.*

Further, the so-called highest bliss is never experienced during *sansāra.* Therefore, how can one love *ātman* on that ground. Therefore, the correct position is that the joy derived from enjoying the objects during the *sansāra* is so called bliss and the cessation of worldly miseries is salvation.

न च मोक्षस्य अपुरुषार्थता । सांसारिकविविधदुःखोपशमरूपत्वात् मोक्षस्य । दुःखोपरमो हि पुरुषैः अर्थ्यते । न चेदं युक्तम्–यथा निखिलदुःखोपरमरूपत्वात् परमपुरुषार्थत्वम्, तथा सकलसुखोच्छेदरूपत्वात् अपुरुषार्थतापि इति । यतः सांसारिकं सुखं विवेकिनः साधनपरतन्त्रलक्षणतया क्षयितालक्षणतया च दुःखकवलितं दुःखमेवेति मन्यमानाः न अत्यन्तमाद्रियन्ते ।

अत एव मोक्षाय उत्तिष्ठन्ते । एवं च परमानन्दाभ्युपगमोपि मन्दफल एव । न च प्रमाणमपि तत्र अवकल्पते श्रुतीनां सिद्धवस्तुबोधकत्वाभावात् । प्रत्यक्षविरोधश्च । न च संसरन्तः तथाविधमानन्दमनुभवन्ति । न च अभिभूततया अननुभवः । स्वारसिकस्य स्वयं प्रकाशस्य आनन्दस्य अभिभावायोगात् ।

न च परमप्रेमास्पदतया आत्मनः आनन्दरूपतासिद्धिः । आत्मनि प्रेमासिद्धेः । शरीरोपघातेहि दुःखोदयात् तदुपघातपरिहारं सर्वे प्रार्थयन्त इति आत्मनि प्रेमाभिमानः । किञ्च संसारिणां स्वारसिकः परमानन्दः न अनुभूतपूर्व इति कथं तन्निबन्धनमात्मनि प्रेम । अतो विषयविशेषसम्भोगज एव आनन्द इति सुन्दरम् । मोक्षस्तु सांसारिकदुःखोपशमात् पुरुषार्थ इति पुष्कलम् । (प्र०पं० ३३५)

Review of the Advaita Concept of Liberation

Some say that the cessation of *avidyā* is liberation. The Brahman free from all adjuncts, all associations, and without second is *tatva.* Due to beginningless *avidyā,* it gets associated with the body etc., and as *jiva* it suffers bondage. In the light of this the association with the beginningless *avidyā* is bondage and the release from it by the knowledge of Brahman as free from all divisive attributes, is liberation.

कः पुनः एषः मोक्षः अविद्यास्तमयः इति केचित् । यत् एकमेव अद्वितीयमसंसृष्टं सकलोपाधिपरिशुद्धं ब्रह्मतत्त्वम्, तत् अनाद्यविद्यावशेन शरीरादि सद्वितीयमिव उपाधिकलुषितमिव अवभासमानं लब्धजीवव्यपदेशं

सत् बद्धमिव लक्ष्यते । अतो अनाद्यविद्यैव संसारः । निखिलविकल्पातीतपरिशुद्धविद्योदयात् तदस्तमय एव मोक्षः इति । (प्र०पं० ३३५)

The above theory of Advaita is not acceptable to the Prābhākaras. Advaita cannot be established by any *pramāṇa*. It is only a blind faith.

तदिदं श्रद्धामात्रविजृम्भितमिति प्रमाणपरतन्त्राः । स्यादेतदेवं यदि अद्वैतं कस्यचित् प्रमाणस्य गोचरः ।

Advaitins contend that *pratyakṣa* itself enables to cognise the one without the second. *Prātyakṣa's* purpose is served as soon as *sat* aspect is comprehended and it does not touch the divisive aspects.

This contention of *advaita* is not correct. It is true that the *pratyakṣa* cognises *sat* aspect of the objects but it also cognises the colour as colour, taste as taste and similar other aspects. It does not cognise all objects as one. If the cognition of the continuity of the colour in all coloured objects was continued in the objects with the taste also, then the *advaita* would have been cognised. This is not the case.

स्यान्मतम् प्रत्यक्षमेव विधिमात्रोपक्षीणव्यापारमपरिस्पृष्टान्योन्य-भेदमद्वितीयमेकं तत्त्वं साक्षात् करोतीति ।

सत्यं विधायकमेव प्रत्यक्षम् । विदधदपि रूपं रूपतया रसं रसतया विदधाति । न पुनः सर्वमेकतया । यथा रूपे धारावाहिनी बुद्धिः तथाभूतैश्च यदि रसेपि स्यात् तदा भवेदेव साक्षात् कृतमद्वैतम् । न तु एतदेवमिति सर्वप्रतिपत्तृस्वसंविदितम् ।

To establish that *sat* aspect alone is *vastu* (entity), and the other aspects are appearance, the very nature of *vastu* is analysed by Advaitin as under:

There are four possibilities: (i) *sāmānya* and *viśeṣa* are two different *vastus* (ii) These together constitute *vastu* (iii) *viśeṣa* alone is *vastu* (iv) *sāmānya* i.e., *mahāsāmānya* i.e., *sat,* alone is *vastu.*

Among these the last one constitutes *vastu*. That alone is real and the other aspects are appearances.

सामान्यविशेषौ किं वस्तुद्वयमथवा एकमेव सामान्यविशेषात्मकं वस्तु, अथवा विशेष एव वस्तु, अथवा सन्मात्रमेव वस्तु इति चतुर्धा विकल्प्य आद्यत्रयं दूषयित्वा सन्मात्रमेव स्वीकरणीयमिति मण्डनमिश्रः ब्रह्मसिद्धौ प्रतिपादयां बभूव ।

Prābhākaras do not accept this contention. They say both *sāmānya* and *viśeṣa* aspect closely knit constitute *vastu*. These two are comprehended by *pratyakṣa*. *Sāmānya* (*sat*) alone is not *vastu*. Therefore, *advaita* is not established by *pratyakṣa*.

Mere *viśeṣa* is not *vastu*, since *sāmānya* is also comprehended by the fact of continuity. *Sāmānya* and *viśeṣa* together do not constitute one *vastu*, since, these two are of different form. Therefore, *sāmānya* and *viśeṣa* have to be taken as two different *vastu* that are closely connected.

यच्च प्रमेयविकल्पेन सामान्यमेव वस्तु इति स्थापयित्वा सत्तायाः महासामान्यरूपत्वात् तावन्मात्रमेव सत्त्वमिति साधितम् । तदपि गगनग्रासकल्पम् । न विशेषमात्रं वस्तु, सर्वत्र अनुवृत्ति-प्रतिभासप्रवेदनीयस्य सामान्यस्य अपह्नोतुमशक्यत्वात् । नापि सामान्यविशेषात्मकमेकं वस्तु एकस्य द्वैरूप्यविरोधात् । सामान्यविशेषौतु परस्परसम्बद्धे द्वे वस्तुनी प्रत्यक्षमवगाहते । तथाच कुतः सत्ताद्वैतसिद्धिः । (प्र०पं० ३३६-७)

Advaita cannot be established by *śruti* also. *Śruti* conveys *kārya* only. It is not a *pramāṇa* in respect of *siddha*. Further, *āgama* consists of sentences. Since, a sentence consists of many words, many items are conveyed. Therefore, how can *āgama* convey *advaita*.

न च आगमादेव अद्वैतसाधनम् । आगमस्य कार्यैकविषयतया सिद्धे तत्त्वे प्रामाण्यानुपपत्तेः । अपि च वाक्यात्मा आगमः प्रमाणमिष्यते । तच्च अनेकपदात्मकमनेकपदार्थात्मनि वाक्यार्थे धियमुपजनयत् कथमद्वैतमवभासयेत् । प्र०पं० ३३७)

The *śruti* statements *neti, neti* etc., are claimed to establish *advaita* denying all other objects. However, no denial can be made with reference to *sat.* Such a denial will amount to say *sat* is *asat.* The *sat* cannot be syntactically connected with *asat.* This does not mean that the negative statements have no scope. The negative statements do not deny anything totally. These deny somethings in some places. However, Advaitin wants to deny all other entities. This results in predicating *asat* to *sat.* This goes against *advaita* itself.

An entity that exists somewhere is denied in some other place. An entity that is totally non-existent cannot be denied. Therefore, the so called *advaita śrutis* that contradict the *pratyakṣa* should be differently interpreted.

अथेदमुच्यते 'स एष आदेशो नेति नेतीति (बृ०उ० ३-६) सकलोपाधिनिषेधेन नानाभूतवस्त्वन्तरापाकरणादद्वैतमागमेन साध्यत इति । तदप्यसारम् । यः खलु एष इति सद्रूपतया अवमृष्टः पदार्थः सोऽसत्त्वापादकेन नञर्थेन सह सम्बद्धुमयोग्यः । अस्ति नास्तीतिवत् । अन्वयायोग्ययोश्च पदार्थयोरन्वयासम्भवात् न वाक्यार्थीभवनम् ।

एव तर्हि निराकृतानि सर्वाण्येव निषेधवाक्यानि । मन्द मैवं परिभावय । नहि निषेधवाक्येषु कस्यचिदात्यन्तिको निषेधः । किन्तु क्वचित् किञ्चित् निषिद्ध्यते । ब्रह्माद्वैताभिमानी तु भवानात्यन्तिकमेव निषेधमभिलषति तथाच सोऽयमात्मीय एव बाणो भवन्तं प्रहरति ।

लब्धरूपे क्वचित् किञ्चित् तादृगेव निषिध्यते ।
विधानमन्तरेणातो न निषेधस्य सम्भवः । (ब्र०सि०त०का० ३)

अतः प्रत्यक्षादिविरुद्धार्थत्वात् आम्नायो न यथाश्रुतो वर्णयितुं न्यायः । (प्र०प० ३३८)

The justification given in *advaita* to show that the *śruti* is superior to *pratyakṣa* and therefore, *śruti* be upheld rejecting *pratyakṣa* does not hold good. If *pratyakṣa* is given up, then, the very comprehension of the meaning of *śruti* becomes impossible.

Therefore, whenever there is conflict between *pratyakṣa* and *śruti*, the latter has to be liberally interpreted resorting to *gauṇī* or *lakṣaṇā* mode of communication.

यत्त्विदं प्रपञ्चेन प्रसाधितं प्रत्यक्षादिविरोधेऽपि आगमस्यैव बलीयस्त्वम्, तद्वशेन प्रत्यक्षादीनां भ्रान्तता कल्पनीयेति तदपि मनोरथमात्रम् । प्रत्याक्षादिविरोधे पदार्थानामन्वययोग्यताविरहात् आगमादर्थावबोधस्यैव तद्विरोधेऽनुदयात् । अतः प्रत्यक्षादिविरोधे आगमे गौणी लाक्षणिकी वा वृत्तिः आश्रयणीया ।

The *śrutis* that talk of bliss in the liberated state should be understood as saying the cessation of misery. The worldly pleasures are limited and affected by misery. Therefore, these are also not to be understood by *ānanda śrutis*. The *śrutis* that talk of one, should be understood in the sense that there is only one *ātman* in each body. The *śruti-Indro mayābhiḥ* etc., be understood in the sense that one *ātman* appears like distinct in each birth due to the attachment to the body in that birth. The *śruti* that denies the distinction should be understood as denying the distinction of *ātman* who assumes many bodies. The *sruti sa eṣaḥ neti* informs that the body etc., are not *ātman*. The śrutis that state consciousness of *ātman* are meant to distinguish the *ātman* from *ākāśa* etc.

The *śrutis* that state *sarvātmatva* convey that all things are meant for *ātman*. The *'śruti' ātmani vijñate sarvam vijñatam* 'conveys that since, the knowledge of *ātman* leads to liberation, that is most important and the knowledge of others is superfluous. In this way the *śrutis* have to be suitably interpreted.

तत्र आनन्दादिश्रुतयः स्वाभाविकदुःखाभावपरतया वर्णनीयाः । लौकिकानन्दस्याल्पतया दुःखानुषक्ततया च व्याख्येयाः । एकत्वश्रुतयश्च एकस्मिन्नायतने एकस्यैव स्वामित्वमित्येवंपराः । इन्द्रो मायाभिः पुरुरूप ईयते इति देहात्माभिमानेन जन्मनि जन्मनि भिन्न इव आभातीत्यर्थः । अनेकदेहपरिग्रहेपि एक एवात्मेति नानात्वनिषेधस्यार्थः ।

'स एष नेति एष नेति' इति च शरीरादीनामात्मत्वनिषेधः तद्व्यतिरिक्तप्रतिपत्तिपरः । सर्वात्मश्रुतयश्च सर्वस्यात्मार्थत्वात् तादर्थ्यनिमित्तोपचाराः । आत्मनि विज्ञाते सर्वमिदं विज्ञातं भवतीति (बृ०अ०४ मै०ब्रा) यदुच्यते तत् आत्मज्ञानस्य परमपुरुषार्थमोक्षफलत्वात् तस्मिन् विज्ञाते सर्वमेव ज्ञानं निष्कलमिति दर्शयितुमित्येषा दिक् । (प्र०पं० ३३८-३३९)

That which is distinct from the knowledge cannot be revealed. Whatever is revealed that is not distinct from the knowledge. Brahman is of the nature of knowledge. Therefore, everything that is revealed is identical with Brahman.

This contention of *advaita* goes against *advaita* itself. If the manifold objects are identical with the knowledge, then, the knowledge itself will be manifold. Consequently, Brahman who is of the nature of knowledge will have to be manifold.

अथोच्येत वित्तेः भिन्नस्य अप्रकाशात्मनः प्रकाश एव अनुपपन्नः इति यद्यत् प्रकाशते तत् तत् प्रकाशादभिन्नम् । प्रकाशात्मकश्च ब्रह्म । अतो ब्रह्मात्मकं जगदिति सिद्धमद्वैतमिति । तदिदं स्वपक्षविरुद्धम् । कथमेवं बुद्धिमन्तो अभिदधति । एवं हि नानाभूतानां आकाराणां प्रकाशाभेदे प्रकाशस्यापि नानाभावापत्तेः ।

Further, it is also not convincing to say that the world of manifold objects is a projection of *avidyā.* It is contradictory to say that *sat* which is of revealing nature and *asat* that is not so are identical. How can those that are of non-revealing nature reveal themselves. Moreover, it is already stated that those objects that are of non-revealing nature can only be revealed. This will land *Advaitin* into the fold of Māhāyanikas.

अथोच्येत विविधोऽयमाकारप्रपञ्चो अविद्याध्यासवशादवभासत इति । एतदपि स्ववचनविरुद्धम् । सदात्मा प्रकाशः तेन सह असदात्मानः आकाराः तावदभिन्ना इति न घटते । तथा सति अप्रकाशात्मानः ते कथमिव

प्रकाशेरन् । अपि च अप्रकाशात्मनः एव प्रकाशः सम्भवतीति बाह्यार्थसिद्धावुक्तम् । अतः एषोपि माहायानिकपक्षानुप्रवेशात् ब्रह्मवादिनां मोह एव ।

अपि च अत्यन्तमसन्तं प्रपञ्चं कथमिव अविद्या प्रकाशयितुमलम् । न खलु असत्ख्यातिरविद्या किन्तु अग्रहणरूपैवेति नयवीथ्यां साधितम् । अतः न अविद्यास्तमयो मोक्षः ।

Prābhākara's Concept of Salvation

Complete cessation of assuming bodies is the salvation. This is achieved by the cessation of *dharma* and *adharma. Jīva* undergoes transmigration on account of *dharma* and *adharma* practised by him. When he gets rid of these, he gets rid of the body and the worldly misery. This is liberation.

It should not be argued that since, one will have accumulated a large amount of *dharma* and *adharma* during his past births and the present, how can he get rid of these. If one makes up his mind to get liberated being disinterested in worldly pleasures and disgusted with worldly miseries and ceases to perform the prohibited acts, and acts that are meant for worldly benefits, then, he will get rid of *dharma* and *adharma.* Then he obtains the knowledge of *ātman* by practising *śama, dama* etc. and does not return to worldly life.

आत्यन्तिकस्तु देहोच्छेदो निश्शेषधर्माधर्मपरिक्षयनिबन्धनः मोक्षः इति युक्तम् । धर्माधर्मवशीकृतोहि जीवः तासु तासु योनिषु संसरति । सः तयोरेकान्तोच्छेदे व्यपगतदेहेन्द्रियसम्बन्धः समुत्खातनिखिलसांसारिक दुःखानुबन्धः मुक्तः इत्युच्यते ।

कथं पुनः अशेषधर्माधर्मपरिक्षयः । न तावदुपभोगेनैव । अनादिशरीरसन्ततिसञ्चितानां भोगसमयेपि सञ्चीयमानानामनन्तानां कर्माशयानां क्षेप्तुमशक्तेः । उच्यते । यः खलु सांसारिकेभ्यः दुःखेभ्यः उद्विग्नः, तदनुषङ्गशबलेभ्यः सुखेभ्योपि विगतस्पृहः मोक्षाय उत्तिष्ठते स तावद्बन्धहेतुभूतेभ्यः निषिद्धेभ्यः, प्रत्यवायहेतुभूतेभ्यः, कामेभ्यः

अभ्युदयसाधनेभ्यश्च निवर्तमानः समुत्पन्नपूर्वौ धमाधर्मौ भोगेन क्षयं नयन् शमदमब्रह्मचर्यादिकाङ्गोपबृंहितेन आत्मज्ञानेन 'न स पुनरावर्तते' इत्यपुनरावृत्तये चोदितेन निश्शेषकर्माशयं नाशयन् मुच्यते । (प्र०पं० ३४१)

The *apunarāvarti* (non-returning) to *sansāra* again, stated here, should not be taken as *arthavāda,* only in such instances wherein the item concerned is meant for something else, that is to say, when it is *parārtha,* the result stated is taken as *arthavāda.* The injunction to get knowledge is not meant for something else. Therefore, that is the ground for eligibility as in the case of *rātrisatra.*

It is not subordinate to the injunction of *karma.* There is no authority to say it is for something else. Mere *upakāratva* is not *śeṣatva, parārthatva* is *śeṣatva.*

न च अपुनरावृत्तेः अर्थवादतया वर्णनम् । आत्मज्ञानस्य अपरार्थत्वात् । परार्थत्वेहि न्यायेन फलश्रुतिरर्थवादतया वर्ण्येत । ज्ञानविधेः अपारार्थ्ये तु सैवाधिकारिविशेषणम् रात्रिसत्रवत् ।

न च कर्मविधिशेषभूतमात्मज्ञानम्, तस्य अपरार्थत्वात् । परार्थत्वे प्रमाणाभावात् । उपकारलक्षणशेषत्वनिराकरणात् । (प्र०पं० ३४२-४३)

The process of *ātmajñāna* itself being *puruṣārtha* is summed up as under:

He who desires to attain salvation should meditate upon the *ātman* is the injunction. He who desires to have salvation is *niyojya, ātmopāsānā,* i.e., acquiring *ātmajñāna* is *viṣaya.* Therefore, it is not meant for something else, that is to say, it is not *guṇa* i.e., *śeṣa* i.e., subordinate to any other *viṣaya.*

ब्रह्मवेद ब्रह्मैव भवति इति श्रुत्या ब्रह्मबुभूषुः - अमृतत्त्वकामः आत्मानमुपासीत इति विधिः कल्प्यते । अमृतत्वकामनियोज्यकमात्मोपासनाविषयकं कार्यमिति वाक्यार्थः । अतः आत्मज्ञानं न परार्थः । अपितु स्वातन्त्र्येण पुरुषार्थम् । (वि०टि० ३४३)

Eternity and all Pervasive Nature of Ātman

The Prābbhākaras hold that *ātman* is eternal. It is *sat* and it is not caused. Whatever is *sat* and not caused, that is eternal. In the librated state the *ātman* remains in its *sat* state.

ननु मुक्तस्यात्मनः सकलोपालम्भातीतस्य सन्मात्रावस्थितौ किं प्रमाणम् । उच्यते । सद् अकारणं च यत् तदविनाशि गगनवत् । सद् अकारणञ्च अयमात्मा इति अविनाशित्वाद् ध्रुवत्वसिद्धिः ।

The *ātman* is of the dimension of *paramamahat* as sky. Wherever the attributes of *ātman* are found, there, the presence of *ātman* has to be envisaged. The attributes of a substance shall not remain without the substance. The presence of *ātman* has to be envisaged either by the movement of *ātman* to the places wherein its attributes are found, or by its all-pervasive nature. In the first alternative, its movement as a*samavāyikāraṇa* for this movement have to be envisaged. Therefore, the alternative viz., it is all-pervasive, is a better way of envisaging the presence of *ātman*.

परममहत्वं च आत्मनः परिमाणं गगनवत् । यत्र यत्र आत्मनः गुणः उपलभ्यते तत्र तत्र तावद् आत्मा वर्तत इति प्रमाणसिद्धम् । गुणिनमन्तरेण गुणस्यावृत्तेः । तत्रहि एषः संशयः किमसौ गत्वा सन्निधीयते उत गतिनिरपेक्ष एवेति । तत्र गतिसव्यपेक्षत्वाश्रयणे गतेः तावत् कल्पना । तस्याश्च असमवायिकारणं कल्पनीयम् । न च तत्र किञ्चन प्रमाणमस्ति । अगच्छतोपि सन्निधानोपपत्तेः गगनवत् । (प्र०पं० ३४३)

Even if *ātman* is everywhere, the contingency of *ātmaguṇas* being found even in such places, where the body is not present will not arise. For *ātmaguṇas* will emerge only when there is the contact between the *ātman* and manas. The *manas* is present in the body only. The contact between *ātman* and *manas* can happen within the body only. Therefore, the *guṇas* will emerge in the body only.

अथोच्येत यत्रापि देहो न वर्तते तत्रापि चेदात्मा सन्निधीयते, तदा शरीर इव तत्रापि तद्गुणानामुपलब्धिः स्यादिति । तन्न । यतः

सर्वात्मगुणानामात्ममनःसन्निकर्षोऽसमवायिकारणम् । स च संयोगः द्विष्ठतया मनोविरहेण अन्यत्र न वर्तते । मनश्च शरीरस्यान्तः अवतिष्ठत इत्युक्तम् । यत्रैव च असमवायिकारणं तत्रैव कार्यमिति न बहिरात्मनो गुणोपलम्भः । (प्र०पं० ३४४)

It should not be argued that 'let the body also be not moving and be present everywhere'. Its movement is clearly visible. If the body were also all-pervasive, then, one would have observed it in the places where the body is not actually present. In the case of *ātman* by its very nature, it is not visible. Therefore, there is no difficulty in envisaging its presence everywhere.

ननु एवं शरीरस्यापि गतिकल्पनप्रमाणकमेव । तस्य एकत्र सतोऽन्यत्र दर्शनप्रसङ्गात् । आत्मनस्तु सतोऽपि सकलकारणपथातीतस्य दर्शनप्रसक्ति-रापादयितुं न शक्येति अगत्या सर्वसंयोगिभिः आत्मा संयुज्यते । (प्र०पं० ३४४)

The all-pervasive nature of *ātman* requires that it should be of the nature of *paramamahat* dimension. Therefore, it is neither of *aṇuparimāṇa*, nor of *śarīra parimāṇa.* If it is considered as *śarīra parimāṇa,* then, it has to have *avayavas* (parts). An object of *madhyama parimāṇa* is formed either by a number of parts or by loose contacts. None of these can be envisaged in the case of *ātman.*

तत्तु परममहत्वमन्तरेण न सम्भवतीति न अणुपरिमाणः शरीरपरिमाणो वा । शरीरपरिणामवत्त्वं च विना सावयवत्वमनुपपन्नम् । तादृशं हि महत्वम् अवयवबहुत्व महत्त्व-प्रचय विशेषाणामन्यतमस्मिन्नायत्तम् । न च अवयवकल्पना प्रमाणवती । (प्र०पं० ३४४)

This kind of arrangement is due to the *dharma* and *adharma* to the credit of each. The credit of *dharma* and *adharma* arises from one's own deeds. The *karmas* are performed through the body and senses. This chain of the body, deeds, *dharma* and *adharma* is a continuous process.

ननु सर्वगतत्वे पुरुषस्य शरीरान्तरेऽपि भोगप्रसङ्गः । मैवम् । यस्य यत् शरीरं तस्य तद् भोगायतनम् । यानि च यस्य इन्द्रियाणि तानि भोगसाधनानीति । न आयातानन्तरे भोगप्रसङ्गः ।

ननु शरीरेन्द्रियसम्बन्धव्यवस्थैव किं निबन्धना । उच्यते । धर्माधर्मसम्बन्धनिबन्धनेति भवान् बुद्ध्यताम् । यदीयाभ्यां धर्माधर्माभ्यां यानि शरीरेन्द्रियाणि उपात्तानि तस्यैव भोगायतनानीति । धर्माधर्मव्यवस्थैव किमायत्तेति चेत् । तदुपायभूतकर्मसम्बन्धायत्ता । कर्मसम्बन्धव्यवस्था तु तत्समवायिकारणभूत शरीरेन्द्रियसम्बन्धनिबन्धनेत्यनादितया शरीरेन्द्रिय धर्माधर्मसन्ततेः सर्वमुपपन्नम् । (प्र०पं० ३४४)

Rejection of the Theory of one Ātman

It should not be argued that 'If the *ātman* is all-pervasive, let there be only one *ātman* in all bodies like one sky being present in the house, jar etc., since, one can infer the presence of different *ātmans* in different bodies.

On the basis of the bodily functions of the other persons, as those of his own, one infers the presence of the *ātman* in others' bodies also. He comprehends the *ātman* in others' bodies not as his own but as the object of his comprehension. He does not comprehend them as himself. Thus, the difference between his *ātman* and those of others is vouchsafed by experience.

आह-विभुत्वं चेदात्मनः तदा सर्वशरीरेषु एक एव आत्मा अस्तु गगनवत् । यथा गगनमेकमेव घटमणिकादि तत्तदनेकसम्बन्धितया आत्मापि किं नाभ्युपेयते । किं प्रत्यायतनं भेदाभ्युपगमेन । उच्यते । यः तावत् प्रतिपत्ता परायतनस्वामिनं स्वप्रयत्नपूर्वकात्मीयशरीरसमवेतकर्मसमानचेष्टादर्शनात् अनुमानतः प्रत्येति प्रयत्नवत्तया नासौ ग्राहकैकरसतया किन्तु ग्राह्यकोटिनिविष्टमात्मभूतमेव । तेन प्रतीतिसिद्धत्वात् भेदस्य अलं भेदाभ्युपगमेनेति वचनमकिञ्चित्करम् । (प्र०पं० ३४५)

The *śruti agṛhyo na hi gṛhyate* etc., conveys that the *ātman* of one is not cognised by another as himself.

ननु एवमनुमानेन परमात्मप्रतीतौ कथमिदमुच्यते 'अगृह्यो नहि गृह्यते' इति । परेण न गृह्यते इत्येतदभिप्रायमेतद् भवतीत्युच्यते । ग्राहकैकरसतया परेण न गृह्यते इति तस्यार्थः । तस्मात् न विरोधः ।

The *dharma, adharma*, pleasures, pain etc., are different for different persons. If separate *ātman* is not accepted for each body, *dharma, adharma* committed by one will have to apply for all.

किञ्च नानाव्यवस्थानां नानाभूताः प्रतिक्षेत्रं पुरुषाः धर्माधर्म सुखदुःखादिव्यवस्थादर्शनात् । अन्यथा हि एकस्य धर्माधर्मादयः सर्वस्य भवेयुः । (प्र०पं० ३४५)

Those who talk of one *ātman* in all bodies explain their position as under: The difference felt in the pains and pleasures in different bodies is an illusion. Just as the pain felt in different parts of the body belongs to one and the same *ātman*, the pain felt in different bodies also belongs to one and the same *ātman*. The pain felt in the head is not felt in the foot and vice-versa. These pains do not pertain to these parts only. These belong to *ātman*. Similarly, the pains experienced in different bodies belong to one *ātman*.

अत्र कश्चित् पण्डितमानी प्राह काल्पनिकी सुखदुःखादिव्यवस्था भविष्यति यथा एकस्मिन्नेव शरीरे पादादिवेदनाव्यवस्था न व्यतिकीर्यते तथा नानाशरीरेषु न व्यतिकरिष्यत इति । नहि पादगता वेदना शिरसि न वा शिरोगतवेदना पादे । न च वेदना पादादिष्वेव समवैतीति शक्यते वक्तुम् । तेषाम् अज्ञत्वात् । ज्ञाता हि वेदनाभिः सह सम्बन्ध्यते । दुःखविशेषरूपत्वात् तासाम् । (प्र०पं० ३४५)

The example of the pain in different parts of the body does not support the concept of one *ātman* in many bodies. There is no pain in different parts of the body, there are only certain physical dislocations that cause the pain. This pain belongs to *ātman*. Therefore, a separate *ātman* is required in each body to suffer the pain in each body. Otherwise, the so called one *ātman* will have to suffer the pain through all the bodies which is against the experience.

'पादे मे वेदना' 'शिरसि मे वेदना' इति सर्ववेदनासु एको दुःखी प्रकाशते। पादादिषु सन्तापादिकं समवैति। तत्र सन्तापः तेजसा संयोगः। शूलस्तु वायुना सहेति वातपित्तश्लेष्मणां क्षोभजेषु सर्वेषु विकारेषु वेदितव्यम्। अचेतनानामपि पादादीनां पित्तादिसंयोगः न विरुध्यते। तज्जन्यं दुःखमात्मन्येव समवैति।

The parallel of *bimba-pratibimba* also cannot be utilized to explain one *ātman* in all bodies. In the instance of *bimba-pratibimba*, it is true that one and the same *bimba* assumes slightly different forms when reflected in different items such as mirror, sword, gem etc., but still its source *(bimba)*, is one and the same. However, the ground for these variations is, in these items, the variations belong to the reflections in these items. But in the case of pain and the pleasure, these belong to the very *ātman*. Consequently, if there is only one *ātman* in all bodies he has to suffer the pain and the pleasures through all bodies. In the case of *bimba-pratibimba*, the *dharmi* (*bimba*), is not affected by these changes, while in the case of *ātman* and bodies, the *ātman* will have to be affected, since pain and pleasure are the qualities of *ātman*.

Moreover, such explanations could be given only if the oneness of *ātman* is already established. There is no supporting evidence for oneness itself. The so called *advaita śrutis* are already explained.

अथोच्येत यथा प्रतिबिम्बभावे एकस्यैव बिम्बस्य मणिकृपाणदर्पणाद्युपाधिवशेन व्यवस्थितानि श्यामत्वादीनि तथा एकस्यात्मनो नानाशरीरोपाधिवशेन सुखादयः व्यवतिष्ठन्त इति। तदयुक्तम्- श्यामत्वादीनामौपाधिकानामुपाधिवशवर्तित्वात् बिम्बसम्बन्धाभावात्। तेन एकधर्मिधर्माणां सतामेषा व्यवस्था सम्भवति। सुखादयस्तु नौपाधिकाः किन्तु आत्मसमवायिनः एवेति एकात्मवर्तित्वेन व्यवस्थानुपपत्तिः।

किञ्च सिद्धे व्यक्तमेकत्वे स्यादपि एषा कल्पना । नचात्मैकत्वे प्रमाणमस्ति । एकपुरुषश्रुतयश्च प्रागेवोपवर्णितार्थाः इति सिद्धं प्रति क्षेत्रं नानाभूताः पुमांसः इति ।

नानाविवादसन्दर्भतमस्सङ्घातभेदनः ।
एषा शालिकनाथेन तत्त्वालोकः समर्थितः ।।

CHAPTER IX

Nyāyaśuddhi

The eternity of śabda

The Necessity of Accepting the Eternity of the Word

If the word vanishes as soon as it is uttered, then, its denotative power cannot be ascertained through the elders' conversation. The meaning of a word as distinct from the meaning of the other words can be ascertained only by observing its repeated use in the conversaton. If the word vanishes as soon as it is uttered, the observation of its repeated use will not be possible. Consequently, its denotative power and the meaning denoted by it cannot be ascertained. The words that do not convey the meaning cannot be the source of authority to convey the knowledge. Therefore, the Mīmāmsakas for whom the authority of verbal testimony is very vital have to establish the eternity of the word.

यदि उच्चरितमात्रविनाशी शब्दो भवेत् तदा तस्य वृद्धव्यवहारेण स्वाभाविकी स्वार्थाभिधानशक्तिः अवसातुमशक्या। भूयो भूयः प्रयोगदर्शने हि तत्तद् अस्वार्थपरिहारेण निष्कृष्य स्वार्थाभिधानसामर्थ्यमवधार्यते । न च उच्चरितमात्रापवर्गिणः शब्दस्य पुनः पुनः प्रयोगदर्शनमुपपद्यते । स्वार्थाभिधानसामर्थ्यानवधारणे च प्रथमश्रुत इव शब्दः न अर्थमवबोधयितुमलम् । अर्थं च अनवबोधयतः प्रामाण्यमयुक्तमिति शब्दस्य प्रामाण्यमिच्छता युक्तमभिधानस्य नित्यत्वस्थापनम् । (प्र०पं० ३५३)

The claim that even if the syllables *ga* etc., are perishable, the comprehension of their denotative power can be managed on the basis of the common characteristic *gatva* is not valid. Because, no common characteristic such as *gatva* could be envisaged for the syllables *ga* etc., that are distinct in each utterance. A common characteristic is envisaged in such instances wherein the difference is definitely known but still an identity is grasped. In the case of *gakāra* the identity could be wrongly comprehended as in the case of *śukti-rajata* without any real identity.

Those who accept the perishability of the syllables *gakāra* etc., do not comprehend the distinction of these in different utterances.

ननु क्षणिकत्वेपि वर्णानां गत्वादिविषयवृद्धव्यवहारपूर्वकमेव सम्बन्धाध्यवसानमुपपद्यते । किं नित्यत्वस्थापनयत्नेन । उच्यते । प्रत्युच्चारणं भिन्नेषु वर्णेषु न गत्वादिकं कल्पयितुं शक्यते । भेदाग्रहेणापि शुक्तिकारजतबोधवदभेदप्रत्ययाभिमानोपपत्तेः । यत्र भेदमध्यवस्यत एव अभेदज्ञानं तत्र अन्यथानुपपत्त्या सामान्याश्रयणं घटते । न च अनित्यत्ववादिनोपि वर्णेषु प्रत्युच्चारणं साक्षात् भेदाध्यवसानं सम्मतम् । (प्र०पं० ३५३)

Now, an attempt is made to point out a difference between the *śuktirajata* instance and the present case of *gakāras* uttered in different statements. In the instance of *śuktirajata* the identity between *śukti* and *rajata* is sublated later. No such sublation of the identity of the *gakāras* uttered in different statements takes place. Therefore, this case is different from *śuktirajata*. This argument does not help. The sublation is not the only ground to determine the error. The defective cause also leads to the error. In the present case the close similarity among the *gakāras* uttered in different statements is the ground for the erroneous knowledge of their identity. Therefore, the *gakāras* in different statements are not identical. Hence, no common characteristic such as *gatva* can be thought of.

ननु च युक्तं शुक्तिकारजतादिषु भेदाग्रहणादभेदव्यवहार इति सामान्यासम्भवः । नेदं रजतमिति बाधकप्रत्ययोदयात् । इह तु सामान्योपपत्तेः भ्रान्तिकल्पना निष्प्रमाणिकैव । नायं गकारः इति बाधकाभावात् । उच्यते । न बाधकमात्रायत्तैव भ्रान्तिकल्पना किन्तु कारणदोषायत्तापि । दृष्टं च अतिसादृश्यात् भेदाग्रहणात् भ्रान्तित्वमिति । साक्षादनुपजातेपि बाधके युक्तमेव भ्रमावधारणम् । अतो न गत्वादिः तत्र सम्भवति । (प्र०पं० ३५४)

Arguments against the Manifestation of Śabda

After disposing off the attempts of those who consider the syllable as perishable and try to manage a uniform presentation of the same on the ground of a common characteristic, Śālikanātha, takes up the question whether the syllables are produced or manifested. At the outset, he mentions the difficulties for considering the manifestation of the syllables.

1. It is not possible to envisage the manifestation for the *śabda.* Manifestation can be thought about in two ways: (i) by removing that which has veiled the object to be manifested or (ii) by close presence. The first way is not possible in the case of the manifestion of the *śabda.* The veiling can be made by preventing the contact between the *śabda* and the *śrotrendriya.* However, *śrotrendriya* is nothing but *ākaśa. Śabda* is a quality of *ākasa.* Therefore, these two are always in contact with each other. One cannot be veiled from the other. Therefore, the manifestation of the *śabda* by removing the veiling or obstruction is not possible. The second way of manifestation viz., by close presence is also not possible since the *śrotrendriya* i.e., *ākāśa,* and *śabda* are always close to each other and such closeness cannot be newly brought about to effect manifestation.

(i) तत्र न तावत् प्रयत्नस्य शब्दं प्रत्यभिव्यञ्जकत्वं सम्भवति । आवरणापायेन किञ्चिदभिव्यज्यते सन्निधानेन वा । न च शब्दस्य आवरणमुपपद्यते । इन्द्रियसम्बन्धप्रतिबन्धेन हि आवरणं कुडयादिना धटादेः उपलब्धम् । न च शब्दस्य इन्द्रियसम्बन्धः प्रतिबद्धुं शक्यते । नित्यत्वात् ।

(ii) आकाशश्च श्रोत्रेन्द्रियं तद्गुणश्च शब्दः तस्मिन् नित्यसमवेतः इति न तस्य आवरणसम्भवः । अतः तदपनयेन न अभिव्यक्तिः । अत एव सन्निधानस्य असम्भवः । नित्यसन्निधानात् ।

2. (i) Further, the manifestation of those things that are in the same place and are comprehended by the same sense organ is always simultaneous. For instance, the colour, size and the number of an object that are perceived by the eye are simultaneously revealed to the eye. On this analogy, if *śabda* is to be manifested to the ear, all *śabdas* that are on the *ākāśa* will have to be manifested simultaneously. This does not happen. It should also be possible for a person residing in Pāṭaliputra to listen to the *śabda* that is manifested in Srughna, since the *ākāśa* in both the places is one and the same.

(ii) It cannot also be said that *śabda* could be made to manifest by the *sanskāra* of the *śrotra*. The so called *sanskāra* cannot be of the nature of removing the veiling, since, the possibility of veiling is already rejected. It cannot be of the nature of assisting *śrotrendriya* by the internal air, like light assisting the eye, since, *ākāśa* has no parts for such a treatment. Even if it is possible, one *sanskāra* should be sufficient to manifest all *śabdas* to the ear.

(i) किञ्च अभिव्यञ्जकाः समानदेशस्थानेकेन्द्रियग्राह्यान् युगपदेव अभिव्यञ्जयन्ति रूपादीनिव प्रदीपादयः । रूपं परिमाणं संख्येति सर्वं सकृदेव प्रदीपादिभिः अभिव्यज्यते । अतः सर्वशब्दोपलम्भो

दुर्वारः एव । किञ्च आकाशविशेषगुणत्वात् शब्दस्य एकत्वादाकाशस्य स्रुघ्नस्थेन अभिव्यक्तः पाटलिपुत्रस्थेनाप्युपलभ्येत ।

(ii) अथ श्रोत्रेन्द्रियसंस्कार एव शब्दस्य अभिव्यक्तिरिष्यते न सोपि घटते । कः खलु इन्द्रियस्य संस्कारः । न तावत् उन्मीलनवत् आवरणापगमः । पूर्ववदावरणासम्भवात् । नापि आलोकेनेव आप्यायनं चाक्षुषस्य रश्मेः । कोष्ठ्यानां वायूनाम् आकाशस्य च अवयवसंयोगासम्भवात् ।

सकृच्च संस्कृतं श्रोत्रं सर्वशब्दान् प्रकाशयेत् ।
घटायोन्मीलितं चक्षुः पटं न हि न बुध्यते ।
(प्र०पं० ३५४-५५)(श्लो०वा०श०अ० ६०-६१)

The Theories of the Production of Śabda

Pointing out the above difficulties for the manifestation theory, the views of those who think of the production of *śabda*, instead of the manifestation are narrated as follows:

For producing *śabda*, men push the air within the body towards the vocal organs. Touching the vocal organs the air produces *śabda* and moves around. *Śabda* moves into the ear along with the air and it is heard by the ear. When the air ceases or withdrawn the *śabda* is not heard.

This view is not tenable. If *śabda* is produced by the air, then one should know it by touch. Consequently, even deaf persons should be able to hear the *śabda*. The contention that the quality of touch is veiled in the case of *śabda* or the air itself is not perceived through touch is not valid. If it is veiled, then, it would not have been comprehended even by the ear. The air is perceived by touch, since, the comprehension of the air arises by the touch. It is not correct to say that the touch only is comprehended but not the substance air, since, the substance air is also comprehended as distinct from the touch.

(i) पुरुषप्रयत्नेरितैः वाय्ववयवैः स्थानविशेषाभिधातसंस्कारसंस्कृतैः सर्वतोदिक्कैः संयोगाख्य असमवायिकारणानुगृहीतैः स्वसमवेतः शब्दः आरभ्यते । वायोश्च गतिमत्वात् तदारब्धशब्दोपि गतिमान् कर्णशाष्कुलीमण्डलावच्छिन्नेन नभसा श्रोत्रभावमापन्नेन संयुक्तः सन् उपलभ्यते । वेगाख्य संस्कारनिबन्धना च वायोः गतिरिति तदपगमे गतिविच्छेदात् दूरे यत् श्रोत्रं तत्र अप्रत्यासन्नत्वात् शब्दो न श्रूयते ।

(ii) न चैतद् उपपद्यते । वायवीयश्चेत् शब्दः स्पर्शनेन बधिरैरुपलभ्येत । अभिभूतत्वात् स्पर्शनेन अनुपलब्धिरिति । तन्न । प्रत्यक्षोपलब्ध्यर्हत्वात् । यदि हि असौ अभिभूतः तर्हि श्रोत्रेणापि नोपलभ्येत ।

(iii) न च वाच्यं न स्पर्शनेन्द्रियग्राह्यो वायुरिति । तदनुविधानेन तदवगतेः । अथ मतं स्पर्शमात्रं स्पर्शनेन्द्रियेणोपलम्यते न स्पर्शद्रव्यमिति । तन्न । स्पर्शव्यतिरेकेपि द्रव्यस्य प्रत्यभिज्ञायमानत्वात् ।

The production of *śabda* is explained in another way also. *Śabda* is produced by the contact between the air passing through the vocal organs and the *ākāṣa*. It is also produced from the separation of these. Further, *śabda* is produced in a series, the earlier *śabda* leading to the later. It is heard when it enters into the ear cavity. Since the efforts to produce the contact between the air and *ākaśa* through the vocal organs are varied, a variety of *śabdas* are produced. Such variation will not be possible in case of manifestation, since the basic *śabda* that is to be manifested is one. When more than one lamp is used to reveal an object, the object does not become many. On the other hand, different causes produce different objects. Therefore, on the basis of the variety of *śabda*, it has to be concluded that the *śabda* is produced. It is not manifested. This view of the production *śabda* by the efforts is held by Vaiśeṣikas.

(i) अन्येतु आहुः संयोगाद् विभागाद् वा आद्यः शब्दो निष्पद्यते। यथा ताल्वादिवायुसंयोगानुगृहीतात् वाय्वाकाशसंयोगात् आकाशे शब्दः सञ्जायते तथा ताल्वादिवायुविभागोपकृतात् वाय्वाकाश-विभागादाकाश एव शब्दः शब्दान्तरमारभते तदपि शब्दान्तरमिति कर्णशष्कुलीमण्डलावच्छिन्ने नभसि श्रोत्रभावमापन्ने तिष्पन्नः शब्दः श्रूयते। (प्र०पं० ३५६)

(ii) किञ्च अभिव्यङ्ग्यश्चेत् प्रयत्नेन शब्दः न प्रतियत्नं भेदेन उपलभ्येत। न खलु अभिव्यञ्जक प्रदीपभेदेपि नानाभावेन भावानामुपलम्भः। कारकभेदस्तु कार्यभेदहेतुरिति सम्प्रतीतः। अतः प्रयत्नः शब्दस्य जनयिता इति निश्चीयते।

नानाभावे प्रयत्नस्य नानाभावोपलम्भनात्।
वैलक्षण्ये च शब्दस्य वैलक्षण्येन कार्यता। (प्र०पं०१५६-५७)

Śālikanātha rejects these views of production of *śabda* and removes the difficulties stated above for the theory of the manifestation of *śabda.*

Replies to the Objections Raised against the Theory of the Manifestation of Śabda

1. Firstly, the difficulty that there could be no *sanskāra* of *śrotrendriya* that enables the manifestation of *śabda* is solved by explaining the nature and the process of *sanskāra.* The air within the body is moved by the effort of the inner self. It starts from the navel, moves through the eight places chest etc., reaches the *śrotrendriya* and provides the necessary *sanskāra* for the manifestation of *śabda.* The very contact of the air with *śrotrendriya* is its *sanskāra.* When this contact ceases, *śabda* is not heard.

श्रोत्रमेव संस्क्रियते। तत्संस्कारकता च तदभिव्यञ्जकता। कोष्ठ्यो हि वायुः प्रयत्नवदात्मसंयोगादुद्गच्छति। सः नाभेः उद्गच्छन्नुरःप्रभृतिषु अष्टसु स्थानेषु अभिघातेन संस्कृतः यावद्वेगमभिप्रतिष्ठमानः श्रोत्रमनुप्राप्तः

शब्दोपलम्भानुगुणं संस्कारमारभते । तत्संयोग एव श्रोत्रसंस्कारः । वेगवत्त्वाच्च वायोः कर्मोत्प तौ श्रोत्रविभागात् संयोगोपरमे शब्दस्यानन्तरमुपलम्भविच्छेदः । (प्र०पं० ३५७-५८)

2. The second difficulty of having a variety of *śabda* in different statements through the *abhivyaṅgya śabda* is one, is solved by pointing out that the difference in the effort put in, the movement of air, the variation in the contact at various levels of the movement of the air and vocal organs are responsible for the variety, though, *śabda* is one.

प्रयत्नभेदाच्च वायुकर्मभेदादुरःप्रभृतिस्थानसंयोगान्यत्वाद् व्यवस्थया शब्दश्रवणम् । शब्दोत्पत्तिवादी अपि उत्पादकभेदमनुमन्यत एव । अन्यथा कार्यभेदासम्भवात् । (प्र०पं० ३५८)

3. The third difficulty that, 'just as the eye grasps the object, its colour, size, number etc., in one revelation, let all the *śabdas* be manifested in one manifestion' is solved by pointing out that in the case of the eye there is only one *abhivyañjaka* while in the case of *śabda* there are many *abhivyañjakas*. Opening the eye is the only factor in the case of perception of the object, its colour etc., while in the case of hearing, several factors are involved for the *sanskāra* of the ear.

यत्तु उपवर्णितम् यथा उन्मीलनसंस्कृतं चक्षुः न समानदेशस्थान् उपलभ्यान् व्यवस्थया उपलम्भयतीति । तदयुक्तम् । तत्र एकत्वादभिव्यञ्जकस्य एकमेवहि उन्मीलनं सर्वोपालम्भानुगुणनेत्रसंस्कारारम्भकमिति कुतः उपलब्धिः व्यवतिष्ठताम् । इह तु एकत्वं संस्काराणामसिद्धम् । (प्र०पं० ३५८)

It is argued that when *abhivyaṅgya* i.e., that which is to be revealed, is comprehended by only one sense, then *abhivyañjaka* i.e., the revealer, will be one. For those that are comprehended by a common sense organ also the *abhivyañjaka* will be one only. For instance, the jar, its colour etc., are comprehended by the eye only and the *abhivyañjaka* for these viz., *āloka* i.e., the light, is only one. In the present instance viz., *śabda* also, it is comprehended by one sense organ i.e., *śrotrendriya*, hence, it has to have only one *abhivyañjaka*. This means that there cannot be any variety of *śabda*. Therefore, it is better to give up the idea of manifestation and accept its productions. This argument does not hold good since there can be many *abhivyañjakas* even when *abhivyaṅgya* is comprehended by one sense.

ननु अभिव्यङ्ग्यस्य एकेन्द्रियग्राह्यत्वे अभिव्यञ्जकस्य एकतैव आप्नोति। ये समानेन्द्रियग्राह्याः तेषामेक एव अभिव्यञ्जकः। यथा आलोको घटादीनाम्। एकत्वे च अभिव्यञ्जकस्य उपलब्धिव्यवस्था नोपपद्यते। अतोऽभिव्यञ्जकत्वा-सम्भवे कारकत्वे व्यवस्थिते भेदाग्रहणनिबन्धनैव प्रत्यभिज्ञेति न्याय्या कल्पना। अत्रोच्यते। एकेन्द्रियग्राह्यतापि भवेत् अभिव्यञ्जकभेदोऽपि भवेदिति किमनुप-पन्नम्। (प्र०पं० ३५८)

There is no invariable relation between *ekendriyagrāhyatva* i.e., being comprehended by only one sense, and *abhivyañjakaikya* i.e., there being only one *abhivyañjaka*. In the instance of the light and the jar, its colour etc., quoted above, the fact of there being only one *abhivyañjaka* may be due to *samavāya* relation between the jar and colour etc., or such a procedure may be applicable only to coloured objects.

इह तु न शक्यते निर्णेतुम् किमेकेन्द्रियग्राह्यतया घटादीनां तद्गतरूपादीनां च एको अभिव्यञ्जकः उत रूपिद्रव्यत्वात् तत्समवायित्वाच्चेति। अतो अनवधारितसम्बन्धव्याप्तिकमेकेन्द्रियग्राह्यत्वं न अभिव्यञ्जकैक्यानुमानसमर्थम्।

4. The objection that 'since the removal of the steady air is a *sanskāra*. When this air is removed all *śabdas* have to be heard' is also not a valid objection. The removal of the veil is not *abhivyañjaka*. The air cannot veil the *śabda*. The removal of the air is not the *sanskāra*. It is the contact with the air within the body that is *sanskāra*. This takes place first.

ननु स्थिरवाय्वपनय एव संस्कारः । अपनीते च तस्मिन् सर्वशब्दोपलब्धिः दुर्वारा । उच्यते । न आवरणापनयनं तस्य अभिव्यञ्जकम् । वायुना शब्दावरणासम्भवात् ।

अपि च न वयं स्थिरवाय्वपनयनं संस्कारमाचक्ष्महे किन्तु कोष्ठवायु-संयोगमेव । प्रथमभावित्वात् । (प्र०पं० ३५८)

The non-comprehension of all *śabda* at a stretch is due to the variation in the air within the body, and the variation of the *sanskāra*.

एवं च अपनेतृकोष्ठ्यवायुभेदात् स्थिरवायुविभागलक्षणसंस्कारभेदात् उपपन्नैव उपलब्धिव्यवस्था । (प्र०पं० ३५८)

5. The objection that 'since *śrotrendriyas* of all are of the nature of *ākāśa*, and since *ākāśa* is one, let all hear *śabda* when the *sanskāra* is effected for one ear, is not a valid objection, because, each person has a separate ear cavity, the *sanskāra* with the *śrotrendriya* with reference to each ear cavity is the ground for the manifestation *of śabda*. Since the air produced within the body can move to the ear cavity of the nearby persons supported by the outside air, the others also hear the *śabda*.

ननु चैकत्वादाकाशस्य, तस्य च श्रोत्रत्वात्, तत्संस्कारे सर्वपुरुषेन्द्रिय संस्कारात् सर्वेपि शब्दमुपलभेरन् । नैष दोषः । धर्माधर्मोपार्जित-कर्णशष्कुलीभेदात् । कर्णशष्कुलीसंस्कारो हि श्रोत्रसंस्कारः भिन्नाश्च प्रतिपुरुषं कर्णशष्कुल्यः इति असंस्कृतकर्णशष्कुलीको न शब्दं लभते । अनुवातं च दूरतः एव शब्दमुपलभते । बाह्यवायुनोदनानुगृहीतस्य कोष्ठवायुवेगस्य दूरगमनहेतुत्वात् । शब्दात् शब्दान्तरारम्भपक्षे तु न अनुवातस्य कश्चिदुप-योगः । (प्र०पं० ३५९)

6. When different persons speak the *śabda* is not different. These are different manifestations. The variations of short and long etc., of the syllable are also not the features of *śabda*, these are the features of manifestations. These arise out of the variations

in the contact of the air and also the opening or closing of the vocal organs of different persons.

अभिव्यञ्जकनानात्वात् शब्दो नानेव लक्ष्यते ।
नेत्रवृत्तिविभेदेन चन्द्रस्तैमिरिकैरिव ।

स्पष्टे तद्गृहे नानाभावोपलम्भः शब्दे तावदसिद्ध एव किन्तु परस्परनिरपेक्षैः अभिव्यञ्जकैः कोष्ठ्यवायुभिः नानावक्तृसमुत्थैः नानाभूतैः भिन्नं श्रोत्रसंस्कारमारभमाणैः नानाभूतशब्दबुद्धिं जनयद्भिः नानेव शब्दो बुद्ध्यते चन्द्र इव तिमिरविभिन्नाभिः नेत्रवृत्तिभिः । (प्र०पं० १५१)

The air arising within the body and moving through the vocal organs manifests *śabda.* Therefore, the mouth is also the place of manifestation. When the *śabda* is heard, the place of its manifestation is also brought to the mind in view of their invariable relation. Due to the variation of manifestations the notions of 'far' and 'near' are also envisaged. On the basis of the presence of the face in a certain direction, a direction for the manifestation is also envisaged. A person who is not able to realise all these makes a confusion between causes of manifestation and the place of comprehension. Since, the senses cannot comprehend their own experiences, the *śrotrendriya* does not realise that it is the place of the comprehension of *śabda.* Since, the place of its utterance is grasped it is taken as the place of comprehension.

Śabda is Heard at the Ear Cavity only

The *śabda* is comprehended at the ear cavity only. It is wrong to think that *śabda* is comprehended at many places. Such an erroneous notion is due to the mistaken notion of the *abhivyañjaka* place as the place of the comprehension.

भ्रान्तिरेषा नानादेशेषु शब्दः उपलभ्यते इति । किं निबन्धना भ्रान्तिः । अभिव्यञ्जकदेशनिबन्धना इति ब्रूमः । ताल्वादिस्थानाधातसापेक्षः कोष्ठ्यो

वायुरभिव्यनक्ति । अतो वक्त्रदेशोपि भवति अभिव्यञ्जकदेशः । तेन शब्दं शृण्वतः तदभिव्यञ्जकदेशोपि तदविनाभावोपकल्पितो बुद्धिस्थो भवति । शब्दाभिव्यक्तिविशेषेण च दूरासन्नत्वे तस्य कल्प्येते । प्रत्यक्षोपलभ्यमानवक्तृविषये च शब्दश्रुति विशेषे दिग्विशेषो नियममवधारितः अतः दिग्विशेषकल्पनापि ।

यस्तु न तथा विवेक्तुमलम् तस्य अभिव्यञ्जकदेशं प्रति व्यामोहो दृश्यत एव ।

एवं च इन्द्रियाणां स्वानुभवासमर्थत्वात् । श्रोत्रगतशब्दोपलम्भे तद्देशाग्रहणात् तदुच्चारणप्रदेशस्य प्रतीयमानत्वात् तद्गतत्वप्रतिपत्तेश्च तद्देशगतशब्दप्रतिपत्तिव्यवहारं प्रवर्तयतीति घटत एवेयं भ्रान्तिः ।

नानादेशोपलम्भे हि सर्वेषां भ्रान्तिसम्मतिः ।
कर्णच्छिद्रगतस्यैव शब्दस्य श्रवणं यतः ॥

The variations of the syllables as short, long etc., are not the features of *śabda*. These are the features of *abhivyañjakas*. When the effort to manifest *śabda* is greater, the air produced is stronger. It makes stronger impact. This creates the impression that the *śabda* itself is strong. Similarly, the features slow and speedy etc., are also not the features of *śabda*. The features of *abhivyañjaka* do not cause the corresponding features in *abhvyaṅgya*.

अभिव्यञ्जकवृद्धिह्रासयोश्च अभिव्यङ्ग्यवृद्धिह्रासहेतुत्वाभावात् न शब्दः वर्धते ह्रसते । किन्तु बलवति प्रयत्ने महान् वायुः उत्पद्यते । तस्य अवयवाः भूयांसः कर्णशष्कुलीमण्डलस्य नेमिभागैः बहुभिः सम्बध्यन्ते । ततश्च अभिव्यञ्जकसंयोगबहुत्वात् युगपदुपलम्भकबहुत्वात् तेषां विच्छेदाग्रहणात् महानिव शब्दोऽवभाति । तरूणामन्तरालाग्रहणादिव महद्वनम् । यदा ते वाय्ववयवाः सहसा विलम्बेन वा संयुज्यन्ते तदा उपलम्भोपि द्रुतः विलम्बितो वा । यदा तु एषामुच्चारणे ताल्वादीनां संवृतत्वं भवति तदा तदनुरोधेन वर्णोपलब्धिरपि एकमात्राकालैव भवतीति ह्रस्ववर्णव्यवहारसिद्धिः । यदा

विवृततरत्वं असंवृतत्वं वा ताल्वादीनामेव सम्पद्यते तदा वर्णप्रतीतेरपि मात्राकालवृद्ध्या दीर्घवर्णव्यवहारसिद्धिः । (प्र०पं०३६०)

वैलक्षण्यं स्वभावेन वर्णानां न च सम्मतम् ।
नादाल्पत्वमहत्वाभ्यां तथात्वभ्रान्तिसम्भवात् ।।

Recognition of Śabda is Possible though its Manifestation is Momentary

The manifestation of *śabda* is momentary. Therefore, its comprehension is not possible. Consequently, its recognition as this is the same *gakāra* is also not possible. Such a recognition arises from the *sanskāra* of previous experience. When there is no comprehension, there is no *sanskāra* and there is no recognition. This objection is answered by pointing out that *sanskāras* do not necessarily arise from the comprehension. These arise for other reasons also. Therefore, the *gakāra* etc., are recognised as such in the very first comprehension.

ननु क्षणिका शब्दस्य अभिव्यक्तिरिति कथं तद्ग्रहणसम्भवः । उपलब्धे हि घटादिभावे तद्वशेन पूर्वानुभवाहितसंस्कारप्रबोधेन 'स एवायमिति' प्रत्यभिज्ञा उदीयते । शब्दे पुनः उच्चरिततिरोहिते पुनरुत्तरकाले कथं प्रत्यभिज्ञोदयः । तत्राह—

नावश्यं तद्ग्रहेणैव तत्संस्कारप्रबोधनम् ।
तेन हेत्वन्तरोद्बुद्धात् संस्कारात् तद्ग्रहोदयः ।।

यदि हि अयं नियमः तदुपलम्भ एव तत्संस्कारोद्बोधहेतुरिति ततो नोपपद्यते शब्दे प्रत्यभिज्ञा । संस्कारास्तु अनियतोद्बोधहेतवः इति कारणान्तरवशेन उद्बुद्धात् संस्कारात् प्रथमसमागमसमय एव शब्दे प्रत्यभिज्ञा भविष्यति । (प्र०पं० ३६१)

Now, the question whether the comprehension 'This is the same *gakāra*' is due to the identity of *gakāras* in different statements or it is an erroneous notion of identity as in the case of *śukti-rajata* is raised again. It is made clear that in the case of *śukti-rajata* the difference is established by *pramāṇa* while no such *pramāṇa* is found in the instance of *gakāra* etc., syllables. The features i.e., short, and long etc., do not belong to the syllables. It is already stated that the difference among the *gakāras* is not comprehended. Therefore, on these grounds the *gakāras* cannot be considered as different.

ननु 'स एवायं गकारः' इति प्रतीतिः तद्ग्रहः । न पुनः भेदाग्रहणात् इति कथं निर्णयः ? दृष्टोहि शुक्तिकायां भेदाग्रहात् तदेवेदं रजतमिति प्रत्ययः इति । तत्राह—

भेदे मानं यदा नास्ति शुक्तिकारजतादिवत् ।
तदा प्रतीतिसंसिद्धः तद्ग्रहः केन वार्यते ।

स्पष्टे हि शुक्तिकारजतयोः भेदावभासिनि प्रमाणे सादृश्याद् भेदानवभासात् अभेदप्रतीतिरिति कल्प्यते । शब्दे तु न प्रत्यक्षसिद्धः प्रत्युच्चारणं भेदः । कथं न सिद्धः । ननु महत्वाल्पत्वाभ्यां विभिन्नो वर्णः उपलभ्यते । नैतदेवम् । महत्त्वाल्पत्वे प्रतीयतोपि वर्णप्रतीतेः महत्वाल्पत्व एव भिन्ने अवभातः । न वर्णाः ।

अतो भेदे प्रमाणाभावात् अभिन्न एवायं भिन्नावभासः इति साक्षात् प्रतीतिबलेनैव अवस्थापितम् ।

It may be noted here that the comprehension of identity is established by experience. The fact that it is not an erroneous notion of identity like *śuktirajata* is made clear by rejecting the inference to prove it. Therefore, there is no reciprocal dependency between the inference to reject the identity and the comprehension of identity.

ननु तद्ग्रहबलेनैव अनुमानं निरस्तम् । निरस्ते च अनुमाने तद्ग्रह इति इतरेतराश्रयमिति । तत्राह—

अनुमाननिरासेन तद्ग्रहत्वं न साध्यते ।
स्वयं प्रतीतिसिद्धत्वात् भ्रान्तिशङ्का तु वार्यते ।

भेदाग्रहनिबन्धनेयं भ्रान्तिरिति शङ्का केवलमनुमाननिरासेन अपनीयते । प्रतीतिबलसिद्धस्तु तद्ग्रहः न कारणान्तरमपेक्षते इति कथमितरेतराश्रयता । (प्र०पं० ३६१-६२)

The Analogy of Flames does not Suit here the Flames are Different

In the instance of 'flames' also the notion of identity of flames is erroneous. These are different. The flames are nothing but a group of fire particles. The flash of these fire particles is a quality and belongs to it. Each set of fire particles flashes and vanishes by the separation of particles. Each set is different from the others. As these occur in quick succession a notion of identity is wrongly projected.

ननु किमिति तद्बलात् ज्वालायामपि भेदानुमानं न निराक्रियते इत्यत आह—

ज्वालाभेदं विना भासां विततिर्नोपपद्यते ।
भेदाज्ञानेन सादृश्यात् प्रत्यभिज्ञा तु युज्यते ।

अवयवी ज्वाला । सर्वश्चावयवी स्वावयवसंयोगेन जातः तद्विनाशेन विनश्यति । न च द्रव्याश्रिताः रूपादयः द्रव्यं विरहय्य वर्तन्ते । तेन तैजसाः परमाणवः नित्यमभिभूतत्वादनुपलभ्यमाना अपि प्रत्यक्षतो यावत् प्रभातति सन्निधीयन्ते इत्यङ्गीकरणीयम् । एतेषां संयोगा विघटन्त इति विघटितेषु तेषु तदारब्धे द्रव्येपि नाशमुपेयुषि ज्वालादर्शनं ज्वालान्तरदर्शनमन्तरेण ।

The experiences of *śuktirajata, jvālā* etc., cannot be explained properly unless the difference is envisaged, while in the case of *śabda* the identity could be explained without resorting to the difference. Therefore the identity of *gakāra* etc., syllables is fully established.

विना तु शब्दभेदेन न किञ्चिन्नोपपद्यते ।
उक्तेन नीतिमार्गेण तद्ग्रहोऽतोऽत्र सम्मतः ।

प्रत्युच्चारणं भेदव्यतिरेकेणापि प्रयत्नानन्तरोपलभ्यमानत्वं यथा उपपद्यते तथा उक्तमेवेति अप्रतिपक्षा प्रत्यभिज्ञा—

सद् असत्कारणत्वेन तस्मात् शब्दस्य नित्यता ।
एतदेव हि नित्यत्वं व्योमादिष्वपि सम्मतम् ।
कारणरहितत्वे सति सत्त्वात् नित्यः शब्दः गगनादिवत् ।

CHAPTER X

Mīmāṃsā Jīvarakṣā

Refutation of Kṣaṇikavāda

The Buddhists hold that all the objects are momentary. However, this doctrine is not supported by any *pramāṇa.*

Pratyakṣa Does not Support the Theory of Momentariness

Pratyakṣa does not support the theory of the momentariness of objects. When the objects like a pole are observed their momentariness is not observed.

It is argued that the momentariness is a part and parcel of the nature of the objects and when object is observed its momentariness is also observed. It need not be separately observed.

This argument does not stand scrutiny. The nature of the objects is to be determined by the experience. The momentariness is never experienced. Therefore, the question of its being a part and parcel of the object and being cognised when the object is cognised does not arise.

अत्र सुगतमतानुसारिणः क्षणभङ्गिनः सर्वानेव भावानभिदधति ।

किं पुनः तेषां तत्र प्रमाणम्? न तावत् प्रत्यक्षं क्षणिकतामीक्षितुं क्षमते । स्तम्भादिभावं निपुणतरं निरीक्षमाणस्य क्षणिकत्वाध्यवसायाभावात् ।

स्यादेषा मनीषा न क्षणिकता नाम भावस्वभावबहिर्भाविनी । तेन भावानुभवादेव प्रत्यक्षं क्षणिकतामपि साक्षात् करोतीति ।

तदिदं मनोरथमात्रं मन्यन्ते मतिमन्तः । तथाहि—'संविन्निष्ठाः विषयव्यवस्थितयः' इति स्थितिरविवादा सर्ववादिनाम् । तदियमपि क्षणिकता भावस्य स्वभावभूता सती संवित्तिमधिरोहन्ती तदव्यतिरेकेण व्यवतिष्ठते नान्यथा । न च तथा संविदमुदीयमानामुदीक्ष्महे इति कुतः तस्याः भावस्वभावान्तर्भाविता । कुतस्तरां च तदवबोधेन बोधः । (प्र०पं० ३६५)

It is further argued that though the momentariness is perceived it does not assume the state of a definite cognition. Therefore, it is felt that it is not cognised.

अथ मन्वीरन्—क्षणिकता प्रत्यक्षमीक्षमाणापि न निश्चयपथमवतीर्णा । तेन अगृहीतेव अवभाति ।

The above argument also does not support the perception of the momentariness. According to Buddhists, *pratyakṣa* initially comprehends the object as devoid of all attributes. Then, there arises the cognition of attributes. This state is designated as perception. In the cases wherein the experience as 'seen' does not arise, it is not a perception.

तथापि न तस्यां प्रत्यक्षं प्रमाणम् । यत्रहि प्रत्यक्षस्य स्वभावतः विकल्पविरहिणः तत्पृष्ठभाविना सविकल्पकप्रत्ययेन व्यापारोऽनुगम्यते तत्र प्रत्यक्षं प्रमाणमिति सौगताः । यत्र च दृष्टमेतदिति प्रत्ययो नोदीयते न तत्प्रत्यक्षसमधिगतम् । (प्र०पं० ३६५)

It is further argued that the perception itself is momentary. Naturally it cognises the object during its presence. This means that the object cognised is also momentary.

यदपि केचिदूचिरे प्रत्यक्षं ज्ञानं क्षणिकम् । स्वकालकल्पितवस्तु विषयतया क्षणिकतां गमयति ।

The above argument does not help to establish the momentary nature of the object. The perception does not cognise the object as 'this is now only' setting aside its presence at other times. On the contrary the perception is of recognition type. It does refer to the past and the future. This removes the possibility of momentariness.

एकक्षणमात्रवर्तिता हि क्षणिकता । न तत् प्रत्यक्षेण इदानीमेव इदं वस्तु इति प्रतिपद्यते कालान्तरं प्रत्यौदासीन्यात् । प्रत्युत प्रत्यभिज्ञालक्षणं प्रत्यक्षमेव क्षणिकतां दूरमुपक्षिपति । पूर्वापरभावावकल्पितभावावकल्पनात् । (प्र०पं० ३६६)

The Inference Does not Support the Momentariness

The inference depends upon the comprehension of the relation between the *hetu* and *sādhya*. Since, nothing can have a relation with a momentary object, inference is not possible. There cannot be any cognition of the relation unless the objects to be related are known. Therefore, *anumāṇa* also does not help to establish *kṣanikatva.*

अनुमानमपि सम्बन्धानुसन्धाननिबन्धनं क्षणिकतां न पक्षीकर्तुं क्षमते । तया सह कस्यचित् लिङ्गस्य सम्बन्धबोधविरहात् । न खलु अप्रतीते सम्बन्धिनि सम्बन्धिबुद्धिः आविर्भवति । (प्र०पं० ३६६)

The Syllogism Proposed by the Buddhists to Establish the Momentariness viz., *yat Sat Tat Kṣaṇikaṃ*

However, the Buddhists do utilise *anumāna* to establish *kṣaṇikatva.* They put forward the following inference. Whatever is *sat* that is *kṣaṇika.* All objects are *sat.* Therefore, all objects are *kṣaṇika.* To be *kṣaṇika* is the very nature of a *sat* object. Just as *śiṃśapātva* proves *vṛkṣatva, satva* proves *kṣaṇikatva.*

तेहि स्वभावहेतुकानुमानसमधिगमनीयां क्षणिकतामाचक्षते । किं पुनस्तदनुमानम् । यत् सत् तत् क्षणिकम् । सन्तश्च सर्वे भावाः इति

भावमात्रनुबन्धिनि साध्ये स्वभावहेतुः भवति । यथा शिंशुपात्वं वृक्षत्वे । शिंशपामात्रानुबन्धि हि वृक्षत्वम् । तथा इहापि सत्तामात्रानुबन्धिनी क्षणिकता ।

This *vyāpti* i.e., invariable relation, between *sattā* and *kṣaṇikatva* is established on the ground that *sattā* is *arthakriyākāritā.* This is invariably associated with *krama* i.e., sequence, or *yaugapadya* i.e., simultaneity. These two features do not work unless the *sattā* is taken as *kṣaṇika.* Thus, *sattā* is governed by *krama* or *yaugapadya,* these are governed by *kṣaṇikatva.* Therefore, if an object is not considered as *kṣaṇika,* then, it will not have *krama* or *yaugapadya,* if it does not have these, then, it cannot have *sattā* itself. Therefore, the objects have to be considered as *kṣaṇika* in order to *sustain* their *sattva.* Just as there cannot be *śimśapātva* without *vṛkṣatva,* there cannot be *sattva* without *kṣaṇikatva.*

कथं पुनः तन्मात्रानुबन्धसिद्धिः? विपक्षे बाधकप्रमाणप्रवृत्तेः । अक्षणिकत्वे हि व्यापकानुपलब्धिः सत्तां बाधते । अर्थक्रियाकारिता हि सत्ता । न अपरा काचिदस्ति । सा च क्रमयौगपद्याभ्यां व्याप्ता । तृतीयकोटिविरहात् । अनयोः परस्परप्रतिपक्षतया एकप्रतिषेधस्य इतरविधिनान्तरीयकत्वात् । न च क्रमयौगपद्ये अक्षणिकेषु सम्भवतः । ते तु निवर्तमाने सत्तामपि निवर्तयतः वृक्षत्वं शिंशुपात्वमिव । (प्र०पं० ३६६)

The Inability of Enduring Object to Produce Arthakriyā

The Buddhists argue that unless a *sat* object is considered as *kṣaṇika* it will not be able to produce *arthakriyā.* In respect of *arthakriyākāritva* of an *akṣanika* ie non-momentary object, there are two possibilities, either producing the *arthakriyā* is its very nature or it is not its nature. In the first alternative, it should produce all *arthakriyā* during the very first moment. The next moment it will have no function left to it. Thus, it will become *asat.* It cannot go on producing the same thing again and again.

In the second alternative, that is to say, it is not its nature to produce *arthakriyā,* it will never do so and consequently it becomes *asat.*

कथमक्षणिकेषु क्रमयौगपद्याभ्यामर्थक्रियाविरहः? अत्राहुः— अक्षणिको हि भावो अर्थक्रियाजननस्वभावो वा भवेत् । अतत्स्वभावो वा । न अपरः प्रकारोऽस्ति । तत्र अग्रिमपक्षपरिग्रहे सर्वासामर्थक्रियाणामेकस्मिन्नेव क्षणे कृतत्वात्, कृतस्य पुनः करणानुपपत्तेः अनन्तरक्षणे अर्थक्रिया-समार्थ्यशून्यत्वात् असल्लक्षणत्वापत्तेः अक्षणिकत्वहानिः ।

द्वितीयकल्पावलम्बने तु कदाचिदपि ततो अर्थक्रिया नोदीयत इति । (प्र०पं० ३६७)

Now, an attempt is made to overcome the above difficulty. The object is capable of producing *arthakriyā*. However, it produces the same when the necessary aids are available, and does not do so when the same are not available.

स्यान्मतम्—समर्थोपि स्वभावतः भावः सहकारिसमवधानेन कदाचित् करोति । तदभावाच्च अन्यदा नेति ।

This attempt also does not help. Whether the so called aid causes something or not? If does not cause anything, then, such an aid is unnecessary. If it causes something, is it of the nature of the object or not? If it is of the nature of the object, then, it amounts to saying the object is also caused. The nature of an object cannot be caused, if the object itself is not caused, the uncaused cannot be of the nature of caused. The opposite attributes will result in the differentiation of the object itself. If the object is caused, then, its non-momentary nature is given up.

तदपि.। विमर्दं न क्षमते । सहि सहकारी किञ्चिदारभते न वा ? तेन आरभ्यमाणमपि । अर्थक्रियाकारित्वाभिमतभावस्वभावभूतम् उत अतत्स्वभावरूपं वेति विकल्पनीयम् । अनारम्भपक्षे अपेक्षार्थो अभिधातव्यः । न खलु अनुपकारकं प्रति अपेक्षा अर्थवती ।

अर्थक्रियासाधनत्वाभिमतभावस्वभावभूतस्यारम्भे च भावस्यापि उत्पत्तिरापतति । नहि अनुत्पद्यमानः उत्पद्यमानस्वभावः भवति ।

विरुद्धधर्माध्यासस्य भेदापादकत्वात् । भावोदयाङ्गीकारे च अक्षणिकत्वपक्षपरिक्षयः ।

If the aid is not of the nature of the object but still causes the *arthakriyā*, then, the object cannot cause the *arthakriyā* before the aid operates. A permanent object by itself cannot produce *arthakriyā* in a sequence. In fact the *arthakriyā* arises from the aid that is outside the object, since, the *arthakriya* takes place when the aid is present and it does not do so if the aid is not present.

अतत्स्वभावभूतस्य आरम्भाभ्युपगमे भावस्य प्रागसाधकत्वात् न अक्षणिकात् क्रमेण अर्थक्रियासिद्धिः । तत एव बाह्यादागन्तोरर्थक्रियोदयः । तद्भावे भावात् तदभावे च अभावात् । (प्र०पं० ३६७)

The Momentary Object can Produce Arthakriyā

The Buddhists argue that such a question cannot be raised in case *kṣaṇikatva* is accepted. The *kṣaṇika* is capable of producing *arthakriyā* by its very nature. It has *sahakārin* also. However, this *sahakārin* is not something that is brought separately. The *kṣaṇika* entity is never without it. It is not an outside aid. The earlier *kṣaṇas* assisting the *antyakṣaṇa* to produce *arthakriyā* is *sahakāritā*. It is the very nature of earlier *kṣaṇas* to be present earlier and assist the last *kṣaṇa* to lead to *arthyakriyā*. This is *sahakāritā*. Therefore, the questions raised in the case of *akṣaṇika* whether the *sahakārin* is of its very nature or different, cannot be raised in the case of *kṣaṇika*.

(i) ननु क्षणिकोपि भावः किमर्थक्रिया जननस्वभावः, अतत् स्वभावो वा?

तत्र अर्थक्रिया जननसमर्थस्वभावस्य सहकारिव्यपेक्षा न स्यात् । नहि असमर्थादर्थक्रिया उदीयते ।

(ii) श्रूयतां परमहस्यं सौगतानाम् । अन्त्यक्षणं प्राप्तः अर्थक्रियाजनन-समर्थस्वभावः एव भावः कार्यमप्येकमेवारभते ।

(iii) किमिति तर्हि सहकारिभिः विनापि न करोति ? अत्र वदामः । क्षणिको हि भावः न सहकारिभिः विना अस्ति । कथमसन् करिष्यति ?

(iv) सहकारिभिः विना किमिति न भवत्येव इति पर्यनुयोगे हेतुस्वभावैः उत्तरं वाच्यम् । ते तथा भवन्ति, भावयन्ति च । एककार्यकारिता च अन्त्यक्षणवर्तिनां सहकारिता । (प्र०पं० ३६८)

The questions as to why other *kṣaṇas* do not produce separate *arthakriyā* should not be raised. Our observation establishes only this much that whatever are produced, those only are produced. These are capable of producing those only.

ननु तेऽपि अन्यनिरपेक्षा एव जनकाः किमिति कार्यान्तरं नारभन्ते । अत्रापि वयमनीशाः । भावास्तु यदारम्भन्ते तदारम्भन्तामित्यनुमन्तुमेव वयं प्रभवामः । ते चामी जनका अपि सन्तः तदेव जनयन्तीति पश्यतामस्माकं तावत्येव अभ्युपगमः ।

The question 'when one *kṣaṇa* produces *arthakriyā* what remains to be done by other *kṣaṇas* would have been relevant if *arthakriyā* had to be produced one after the other. When all *kṣaṇas* produce *arthakriyā* together, there is no such a position as 'already produced.' The question 'when the purpose of producing *arthakriyā* is served by one *kṣaṇa*, why the other *kṣaṇas* participate in the same' is also not correct, since these are not aware of their role. These do not know that the other *kṣaṇas* can do this job without them. In short, the whole process of *antyakṣaṇa* producing the *arthakriyā* in co-operation with other *kṣaṇas* is a spontaneous and involuntary process. Therefore, the criteria that apply to the activities of a sentient being do not apply here.

ननु एकेन कृते अपरः किं करोतीति? भवेदेतदेवं पर्यायेणार्थक्रियायाम् । सह क्रियायां तु कृत इत्येव नास्ति । ननु एवमेकस्मादपि तत्सिद्धेः किमपरे कुर्वन्ति । नैतदेवम् । न प्रेक्षापूर्वकारिणः येन एवं पर्यालोचयेयुः । अन्योपि एवं कर्तुमस्माभिरपि विना समर्थः

इति । ते तु हेत्वधीनसन्निधानाः न भवितुं न क्षमन्ते इति का अनुपपत्तिः । (प्र०पं० ३६८)

Though different causes lead to different effects, different *sahakārins* do not lead to different effects. Therefore, the objection that 'how can one *arthakriyā* be produced by many *kṣaṇas* is not a sound objection.'

ननु कथमेकं कार्यमनेकस्मादुत्पद्यते । कारणभेद एव कार्यस्य भेदे हेतुः अन्यथा आकस्मिकत्वापत्तेः । उच्यते । नहि सहकारिकारणभेदात् भेदः कार्यस्य किन्तु सामग्रीभेदादिति हेतुबिन्दौ कृतपरिश्रमाणामनायाससमधिगम्यम् । तस्मात् न क्षणिकत्वेपि अक्षणिकत्वपक्षसदृक्षपर्यनुयोगावकाशः । (प्र०पं० ३६८)

In the instances of seed etc., a series of *kṣaṇas* will lead to such a *kṣaṇa* that produces the sprout. This *kṣaṇa* produces it without requiring any more *kṣaṇas*.

बीजादीनां हि क्षणपरम्परापरिणामेन तादृशः सञ्जायते यतो अपेक्षितहेत्वन्तरप्रवृत्तेरनन्तरमङ्कुरं प्रादुर्भवति । (प्र०पं० ३६८)

Arthakriyā is the Ground to Infer the Distinct Kṣaṇas

The objection that 'if the *kṣaṇas* function momentarily in a flux, there will be no recognition of the earlier and later *kṣaṇas*. Moreover, if there is recognition, the inference of distinct *kṣaṇas* is not possible' is not a valid objection. Though the *kṣaṇas* are radically distinct, these are similar. Therefore, the difference among them is not comprehended like that of *śukti-rajata*. This is the ground for the so called recognition. The inference in respect of the existence of these *kṣaṇas* leading to *arthakriyā* is made by means of the very *arthakriyā*.

ननु एवमपि परापरेषु बीजादिक्षणेषु तदेवेदमिति प्रत्यभिज्ञा नोपपद्यते । अपि च प्रत्यभिज्ञाप्रत्यक्षविरोधे कथमनुमानमात्मानं लभते इति वाच्यम् । समाधिरभिधीयते । ये ते क्षणाः तेषामात्यन्तिकं भेदं सुसदृशतया दृष्टमपि

प्रत्याकलयितुमनीशस्य भेदाग्रहणनिबन्धनः अभेदव्यवहारः प्रवर्तते शुक्तिकायामिव रजतव्यवहारः । न चानुमानोदयविरोधः अर्थक्रियायाः अन्यथानुपपत्तेः । प्रत्यभिज्ञा तु भेदाग्रहणेनाप्युपपद्यते ।

The wise scholars hold that the inference is superior to the perception. There is no ground to say that there will be a single knowledge as 'This is that.' The sense can comprehend the present only. It does not make any reference to the past time, nor it refers to the present as a continuation of the past. This is clear in the so called recognition of the flames.

अत एव च वृद्धा वदन्ति 'भवति च प्रत्यक्षादपि अनुमानं बलीयः' इति । युक्तं च इदं पश्यामः । तदेवेदमित्येकविज्ञानोदये कारणाभावात् । इन्द्रियं सन्निहिते व्याप्रियते । न पुनः पूर्वकालसम्बन्धितारूपां तत्तामुपस्पृशति । पूर्वानुभवभाविता च भावना नेदन्तामपरकालयोगात्मिकाम् । तदिदं ज्वालाप्रत्यभिज्ञानेन व्याख्यातम् । (प्र०पं० ३६९)

The Momentary Nature of Kṣaṇas could be Established by Their Perishable Nature

Created entities necessarily perish. Since the *kṣaṇas* perish these are created, and consequently are not enduring. From this it can be inferred that these are *kṣaṇikas*. Whatever necessarily happens, that does not require any separate cause. The perishing of the *kṣaṇas* necessarily happens. Therefore, the *kṣaṇas* perish on their own and do not need any other cause to make them perish.

अपि च कृतकानां भावानामवश्यं भावी विनाशः प्रतीयते । अतोपि शक्या क्षणभङ्गिता अनुमातुम् । तथाहि—यदि एषा ध्रुवभाविनी तत्र तेषां हेत्वन्तरापेक्षा नास्ति । ध्रुवभावी च कृतकानां विनाशः इति विरुद्धव्याप्तोपलब्धलिङ्गकमनुमानं विनाशस्य हेत्वन्तरापेक्षितां प्रतिक्षिपति । (प्र०पं० ३६९)

Those entities that need some other cause are not enduring. For instance, the colour of a cloth. The perishing of *kṣaṇa* does not need any other cause. That which perishes on its own, naturally perishes the very next moment of its rise. This establishes the *kṣaṇikatva* of *kṣaṇa*.

(i) ये हेत्वन्तरापेक्षाः ते ध्रुवभाविनो न भवन्ति । यथा वाससि रागादयः ।

(ii) स्वहेतोस्तु विनश्वरस्य उदये अनन्तरमेव अपवर्गः इति क्षणभङ्गुरत्वसिद्धिः। (प्र०पं० ३६९)

Further, the objects that are caused by their causes are either perishable by their nature, or enduring. In the former case the very next moment they have to perish. On the other hand, if these are of enduring nature, then, these will never perish. It cannot be said that these will perish by some other cause. In that case, the question arises whether, this perishing is different from the object or one with it. It cannot be said that it is one with it, since, it is caused by a different cause. If it is different from the object, then, object will have to be found as before. If it is said that the object is concealed by this, then, similar questions will be raised in respect of concealment itself.

अपि च इदं चिन्तनीयम् । किं कृतकाः भावाः स्वहेतुभ्यः समुपजायमानाः विनश्वरस्वभावा एव जायन्ते? अविनश्वरस्वभावा वा? विनश्वरस्वभावाः उदयानन्तरमेव लीयन्ते इति क्षणभङ्गिनः । अविनश्वरस्वभावास्तु न कदाचिद् विनश्येयुः । न च हेत्वन्तरात् तेषां विनाशः । विकल्पासहत्वात् । स हि जायमानो विनाशः भावादव्यतिरेकी व्यतिरेकी वा । न तावदव्यतिरेकी हेतुभेदात् । व्यतिरेकिणि तु जाते भावस्य प्राग्वदुपलब्ध्यादिप्रसङ्गः । तेन तिरोधीयते इति कल्पनायामपि तिरोधानं प्रत्येव विकल्पः वाच्यः इत्यलमतिप्रसङ्गेन । (प्र०पं० ३७०)

Refutation of Kṣaṇabhangavāda by some Mīmāmsakas

Some state that the experience 'that is this' refers to the presence of the object in the past and also at the present. These two together result in the cognition of one object for more than one moment. Consequently, the theory of *kṣaṇikatva* looses its ground.

अत्र केचिदेवं समादधति – तदेवेदमिति तत्तेदन्ते परस्परं संवलिते समाकलयदेकं प्रत्यभिज्ञासमाख्यातं प्रत्यक्षविज्ञानं क्षणभङ्गानुमानं निरुणद्धि इति । (प्र०पं० २७०)

It is not correct to say that these are two cognitions of experience and memory type. The memory relates to the past and the experience relates to the present. These two do not establish the fact that these relate to one and the same object.

It is against the experience to hold such a view of two experiences.

न चेदं समीचीनं द्वे एते विज्ञाने ग्रहणस्मरणरूपे यथायथं तत्तामात्रे इदंतामात्रे व्याप्रियमाणे नालमुभयानुभवसम्भवसमयवर्तितामर्थस्य अवभासयितुं । प्रतीतिविरोधात् । (प्र०पं० ३७०)

Just as an object that is present in a place and at a time is one object, an object that is in a different place and at a different time is also cognised as one. Such a cognition has to be one but not two as contended above. To justify an effect an appropriate cause has to be envisaged. It is not a right approach to change the nature of the effect to suit the cause.

Therefore, since, neither mere sense contact, nor mere *sanskāra* can give rise to the cognition 'That is this' i.e., *tadeva idam*. The two jointly give rise to such a cognition.

यथैव हि अभिन्नदेशकालं वस्तु एकतया चकास्ति तथा भिन्नदेशकालमप्येकतयैव परिस्फुरतीति तथाविधसंवेदनोदयश्च न एकविज्ञानोदयमन्तरेणेति एकमेवेदं विज्ञानमुररीकरणीयम् ।

कार्यसद्भावोपपादनाय अप्रतीतमपि कारणं कल्पनीयम् । न पुनः कारणमुखनिरीक्षणेन स्पष्टदृष्टकार्यविपर्ययः पर्यालोचनीयः ।

तेन यद्यपि केवलेन्द्रियात् केवलात् पूर्वानुभवसमासादितजन्मनो भावनाभिधानात् संस्काराद् वा नैवंविधमेकविज्ञानमुदेतुमर्हति । तथापि तयोरन्योन्यसमासादितदशान्तरयोरिदं कार्यमित्याचार्याः मेनिरे । (प्र०पं० ३७१)

It is also not correct to say that this cognition is not of the nature of perception. Though the *sanskāra* plays a role in it, it is generated by the sense contact, therefore, it has to be considered as perception. It cannot be claimed to be a *pramaṇābhāsa* i.e a distorted cognition, since no defect could be detected here.

The inference cannot detect any defect here, since, any inference to be made could be made only after this cognition is obtained. The point to be inferred has to be valid if the inference has to arise. One cannot infer coolness on the part of the fire.

न चेदमपि उचितम् । प्रत्यक्षमेवेदं न भवतीति । सत्यपि संस्कारोपयोगे इन्द्रियव्यापाराधीनजन्मतया अस्य प्रथमसमागमसमयभाविनः सकलवादिनामपहस्तितविवादानां प्रत्यक्षसंमतादविशेषात् ।

न चेदं प्रमाणाभासमित्यत्र किञ्चन प्रमाणमस्ति । बाधकारण-दोषविषयसंवेदनान्तरविरहात् । न चेदमेवानुमानं बाधकमिति चित्तमनुरज्यते । परस्पराश्रयदोषसमासक्तेः । यावत् खलु एतद्विज्ञानमबाधितम् । तावदनुमानमेव नोदितुं प्रभवति । सञ्जाते चानुमाने बाधितमिदं भवतीति विशदतरमितरेत-राश्रयत्वम् । अबाधितविषयता चापि कारणमनुमानोदये । अन्यथा हुतवहे शीतता किमिति नानुमीयते । (प्र०पं० ३७१)

On the above answer in respect of the inference, a point is raised that in the instance of flames the difference is established by the inference, though their unity is cognised by perception. This is answered by the Bhāṭṭas as in the instance of flames, the perception comprehends the general aspect and the inference points out the a particular aspect. According to the Bhāṭṭas all objects have a general as well as a particular aspect. Since the general aspect is cognised by perception and the particular by the inference, there is no conflict.

ननु एवं तर्हि कथं ज्वालादीनामेकत्वेन अवधारितानामनुमानतो भेदसिद्धिः । अत्र सिद्धान्तसारमुदीरयन्ति । सामान्यविशेषात्मकानि सर्ववस्तूनि । तत्र ज्वालादिषु प्रत्यक्षं सामान्यविषयम् । अनुमानं तु विशेषविषयमिति भिन्नगोचरप्रचारिणोः प्रत्यक्षानुमानयोः विरोधाभावात् । न प्रत्यक्षेणानुमानोदयविरोधः (प्र०पं० ३७१)

The Process of Enduring Objects Producing Arthakriyā

Reverting back to the question as to how *arthakriyā* is produced by the A*kṣaṇika* objects, it may be said that these produce *arthakriyā* in a sequence by a special capacity brought about by *sahakārins*. The difficulties raised in this connection viz., whether the special capacity is the very part of the nature of the object concerned or different etc., are solved by the Bhāṭṭas by the theory of the *sāmānya* and *viśeṣa* aspects of the objects.

कथं पुनः अक्षणिकस्य अर्थक्रियाकारिता? क्रमेणेति वदन्ति । स खलु सहकारिसमवधानोपहितविशेषो भावः तां तामर्थक्रियां क्रमेणैव सम्पादयति ।

ननु विकल्पितं सहकारिभिः किं व्यतिरिक्तः अव्यतिरिक्तो वा विशेष आधीयते इति, दूषणानि चेह विकल्पयुगले पूर्वमावेदितानि ।

अत्रापि त एव प्रक्रियामनुक्रमयन्ति । नेदमस्मन्मतमेकान्ततो भिन्नान्येव सर्ववस्तूनि । अभिन्नान्येव वेति । किन्तु सर्वभावेषु भेदाभेदौ सङ्गिरामहे । तत्र भेदमात्रविकल्पसम्भवीनि दोषाणि अभेदाश्रयेण परिहृतानि । अभेदमात्राश्रितानि भेदावलम्बनेनेति ।

There is no contradiction in accepting both difference and non-difference with reference to one and the same object. These are observed together, and these exist together. There would have been a contradiction if these did not exist together and were not observed together.

ननु एतौ भेदाभेदौ कथमेकत्र विरोधिनौ निविशेते । तत्राहुः— नेमौ विरोधिनौ सहदर्शनात् । सह अनवस्थानलक्षणो हि विरोधः । अनवस्थानं च अदर्शननिबन्धनम् । अतो नास्ति विरोधः । (प्र०पं० ३७२)

Rejection of the Theory of Bheda-abheda

The theory of *bheda-abheda* is not acceptable to the Prābhākaras. Seeing as one is *abheda.* Seeing as distinct is *bheda.* When there is the cognition as one there is no cognition as distinct and vice-versa. Therefore, difference and identity are not possible with reference to one and the same. Consequently, *arthakriyā* cannot be explained by resorting to this theory.

तदिदमविचारितरमणीयमिति प्रभाकरगुरोः नानुमतम् । स हि ददर्श— भेदाभेदावेव तावदेकत्र न सम्भवतः विरोधात् । न हि तयोः सहदर्शनमुपपद्यते । एकाकारप्रतीतिरेव खलु अभेददर्शनम् । विलक्षणाकारप्रतीतिश्च भेददर्शनम् । तत्र यदि एकाकारा प्रतीतिः तदा विलक्षणाकारप्रतीतिः नास्ति । विलक्षणाकारे प्रतीते एकाकारप्रतीतिरेव नास्ति । तेन भिन्नाभिन्नाश्रयणेन अर्थक्रियासमर्थनं न घटते इति । (प्र०पं० ३७३)

The View that Pratyabhijña Pratyakṣa Prevents Kṣaṇabhangavāda is Examined

Pratyabhijñā Pratyakṣa cannot negate the inference of the difference. The very *pratyabhijñā* needs to be examined. There is the cognition as 'It is the same *rajata*' in the case of *śukti-rajata.* Such a cognition arises by the absence of the cognition of the difference between *śukti* and *rajata*' due to similarity. Therefore, the question needs to be examined here.

Now, in order to justify the *arthakriyā,* the *kṣaṇikatva* of the object has to be accepted. Consequently, it has to be concluded that the so called *pratyabhijña* is the wrong cognition of the earlier and later *kṣaṇas* as one though these are distinct. Such a confusion is found in the instance of misunderstanding of the east-west quarters.

न च प्रत्यभिज्ञानेन अनुमानविरोधः । प्रत्यभिज्ञायाः एव परीक्षणीयत्वात् । दृष्टा शुक्तिकायां तदेवेदंरजतमिति मतिः । सा च साद्दश्यवशेन भेदाग्रहणनिबन्धनैवेति युक्ता अत्रापि परीक्षा ।

तत्र परीक्ष्यमाणस्य अर्थक्रियानुपपत्त्या क्षणिकत्वे निर्णीते सद्दशापरापरोत्पत्तिविप्रलम्भोऽयमिति निश्चीयते । भवति च दिङ्मोहादिषु अनुमानवशेन जातायाः अपि प्रतीतेः विपर्ययः । (प्र०पं० ३७३)

Prābhākara's Final Reply to Kṣaṇabhangavāda

Arthakriyā can be produced by the enduring objects also. The cognition 'That is this' arises in respect of pole etc., enduring objects that were seen earlier and seen again after sometime. Since *arthakriyā* is possible from such enduring objects there is no reason to envisage that this is a case of the cognition of oneness due to the absence of the cognition of the difference. The enduring objects are capable of producing *arthakriyā* and their enduring nature is cognised.

सम्प्रति समाधानमभिदधति—स्तम्भादिषु प्रथममनुभूतेषु पुनरन्तरा तिरोधानादिवशेन विच्छिन्नोपलम्भेषु पुनरनुभवतः 'स एवायमिति तावत् जायते' मतिः । तत्र यदि अर्थक्रिया स्थिरादपि कथञ्चिदुपपद्यते ततो भेदाग्रहणनिबन्धनोऽयमभेदव्यवहारः इति किमिति कलय । (प्र०पं० ३७३)

The enduring objects do produce *arthakriyā* in an order with their special capacity invested by the *sahakārins*. The special capacity is something additional to the object. This additional factor by itself does not produce *arthakriyā*. The object together with this special capacity is the means to produce *arthakriyā*. The object is not indifferent. But it produces *arthakriyā* invested with the special capacity by the *sahakārin*.

उपपद्यते स्थिरादपि भावात् सहकारिविशेषजातागन्तुक क्रियादिरूपविशेषभाजः क्रमेण अर्थक्रिया । स च विशेषो व्यतिरिक्त एव

भावादर्थक्रियाकारिणः । न च स एव अर्थक्रियाकारी भावस्तु उदास्ते इति चतुरस्रम् । तथाविधविशेषालीढतैव तस्य साधनता । यदनन्तरमर्थक्रियोदयः तद्विशेषयोगितयैव भावेषु साधनत्वव्यवहारः लौकिकानाम् । (प्र०प्रं० ३७४)

The special capacity has to be inferred as present in the object concerned, since, it has to assist the production of *arthakriyā* by that object. The object is not envisaged to be distinct at each moment since it is cognised as enduring. Just as the *arthakriyā* is recognised, the constant nature of the object is also cognised.

Now, it is established that the enduring objects can produce *arthakriyā* in an order or simultaneously. Therefore, one need not resort to *kṣaṇikatva* on the ground that the enduring objects are unable to produce *arthakriyā* in an order or simultaneously.

In this context it should be noted that *arthakriyākāritā* is not *sattā. Pramāṇa sambandha yogyatā* is *sattā.* In other words producing *arthakriyā* is not the ground of *sattā* but being comprehended by a *pramāṇa* is *sattā.* An object is *sat* even without producing *arthakriyā.*

कथं पुनरसौ विशेषः तस्येति व्यपदिश्यते? तदाश्रयतयैव अनुमानात् । कथं पुनः तदाश्रयतैव? स्वहेतुवशेनेति निवर्ततां भवान् ।

अथ कस्माद् भावस्यैव भेदो नानुमीयते । प्रत्यभिज्ञानुगुण्यादिति वदामः । दृष्टानुसारिच अनुमानमुचितम् । दृष्टोपपत्तिमुखत्वात् । यथा अर्थक्रिया दृश्यते तथा इदमपि दृश्यते स्थावरो भाव इति ।

स्थावरेपि अर्थक्रियाव्यापकक्रमयौगपद्यानिवृत्तेः असिद्धो व्यापकानुपलम्भः । तदसिद्धौ विपर्यये बाधकाभावात् । असिद्धतन्मात्रा-नुबन्धिनीं क्षणिकतां न सत्ता साधयितुमलम् ।

न च अर्थक्रियाकारितैव सत्ता किन्तु प्रमाणसम्बन्धयोग्यता । अतो अर्थक्रियामकुर्वन्नपि सन्निति न किञ्चिदनवद्यम् ।

Vināśa is not Pradhavansābhāva

In the context of the Buddhist's position that the objects perish on their own without requiring any other cause, the very concept of *vināśa* i.e., perishing, needs to be examined. What is meant by *vināśa*! *pradhvāmsābhāva!* It is already stated in the Amṛtakalā section that the statement 'there is no milk at the curd stage' does not convey the so called *abhāva*, it conveys only the curd. There is no negative element in it. The use of a negative particle is superfluous. The presence of the curd itself is the ground to say that there is no milk. There is no separate entity called the absence of milk.

यत्तु इदमुदितमनपेक्षा भावा विनाशं प्रति इति तदपि विमृश्यमानं दह्यमानं जातुषमिव आभरणं विलीयते । कं खलु भवन्तो विनाशमभिमन्यन्ते । प्रध्वांसाभावो विनाश इति चेत् – कः पुनः प्रध्वंसाभावः? दध्नि क्षीरं नास्तीत्येवमादिका अभावविषया संविदिति यद्युच्येत तदा अमृतकलायामुद्धृता नीतिः उद्धरणीया । न हि नास्तीति बुद्धिरस्ति । किन्तु दधिस्वरूपमात्रानुभव एव स्वयंप्रकाशे नञ् शब्दप्रयोगमात्रमेव । सैव पयसो नास्तिता या द्रष्येपि तस्मिन् दधिस्वरूपमात्रोपलब्धिः (प्र०पं० ३७४)

The presence of curd is not caused by mere milk, if other causes were not present milk would have been observed. It cannot be said that the milk that has resulted in curd is different from the one seen earlier, the recognition confirms it as the same.

It cannot be argued that 'if the curd requires another cause, in addition to the milk, then, its enduring nature cannot be maintained.' Just as its enduring nature is confirmed by observation, its requiring additional cause is also confirmed by the observation.

न च तां प्रति पयस एव निरपेक्षस्य हेतुता । अनुपनिपतिते हेत्वन्तरे पयसः एव उपलब्धेः । न चेदं पयोन्तरमुपलभ्यत इति शक्यं वक्तुम् । प्रत्यभिज्ञानस्य अभेदसाधकत्वात् ।

ननु च हेत्वन्तरापेक्षित्वे ध्रुवभाविता नोपपद्यते । ध्रुवभावितैव कुतोऽवगम्यते । दर्शनादिति चेत् हेत्वन्तरेण अवश्यं भवितव्यमिति दर्शनादेव अवगम्यताम् ।

The contention that 'if the objects are caused by their respective causes and these perish by some other cause, then, a contingency will arise that even after the arising of the perishment, the object has to be found intact since the causes of the two viz., the object and its destruction are different' is not a valid contention. It is already stated that the perishing is nothing more than the presence of another factor. This factor, of course, is found on the perishment of the object. The presence of this factor is the absence of the object. Therefore, there is no question of any re-emergence of the object perished.

यत्पुनरिदं स्वहेतुभ्यो भावानामपि नश्वराणामुत्पत्तौ हेत्वन्तरायत्ते विनाशे व्यतिरेकिणि जातेपि पूर्ववत् भावस्य उपलब्धिप्रसङ्गः इति ।

अत्रोच्यते—उक्तमस्माभिः यथा तन्मात्रोपलब्धिरेव विनाश इति । तेन तस्याः हेतुसद्भवात् तथैव भवितव्यम्, अनुपलब्धिरपि तस्य सैवेति अनुपलब्धिरेव तस्य न उपलब्धिः । तन्निबन्धनश्च अभावव्यवहार इति सर्वमनाकुलम् । (प्र०पं० ३७५)

Śālikanātha concludes this interesting discussion with the remark that the Mīmānsā was badly affected by the Buddhist theory of *kṣaṇabhaṅga* and he has restored the life of Mīmānsā in this chapter. That is why he has designated this chapter as Mīmānsā Jīvarakṣā.

सुगताशीविषविषमक्षणभङ्ग विषानलावलीढायाः ।
मीमांसायाः विहिता मर्ममयी जीवरक्षेयम् ॥

CHAPTER XI

Section – I

Vākyārthamātṛkā – I

The Anvitābhidhāna Theory of Sentence Meaning

The Theories of Sentence Meaning

Kārya is held to be the chief import of a sentence by *Vyākaraṇa*, Bhāṭṭa Mīmāṁsā and Prābhākara Mīmāṁsā. However, its exact nature is differently understood by these three. Vyākaraṇa understands it as *bhāva* i.e., *kriyā* i.e., *dhāthvartha* i.e., the action conveyed by the verbal root. Bhāṭṭa Mīmāṁsa understands it as *bhāvanā* i.e., *preraṇā* and *pravṛtti* the direction and the initiative conveyed by the injunctive suffix. Prābhākaras understand it as *apūrva* i.e., *niyoga, kārya* a unique sense of duty conveyed by a Vedic injunctive suffix which has to be accomplished by the performance of the action conveyed by the verbal root.

Among these three views Śālikanātha, naturally, proposes to expound the third view rejecting the other two. The basis of this view is the *anvitābhidhāna* theory of sentence meaning. Therefore, he takes up the consideration and the establishment of that theory before he expounds the concept of *kārya* of the Prābhākaras.

तत्र कार्यवाक्यार्थवादिनः एव भावम्, भावनाम्, अपूर्वं वाक्यार्थान् प्रतिजानते । तत्र अपूर्वमेव वाक्यार्थ इति साधनीयम् । तस्य मूलं पदानामन्विततार्थाभिधायितेति तामेव तावदादौ परिशोधयति ।

(प्र०पं० ३७६)

In connection with the procedure of the evolution of sentence meaning, three other views were current. These are:

(i) The sentence itself conveys the sentence meaning without any involvement of words separately.

(ii) It is the last syllable of a sentence accompanied by the impressions of the previous syllables that conveys the sentence meaning.

(iii) The words convey their meanings separately. These word meanings get connected with each other and result in sentence meaning.

These three views are not acceptable to Śālikanātha. He states his view that the words convey mutually connected meaning and give rise to the sentence meaning. In other words the sentence meaning is no more than the connected word meanings.

The denoting power of the words is exhausted by conveying their connected meaning. The comprehension of this connected meaning is the comprehension of the sentence meaning.

(i) अत्र ये प्रत्यस्तमितपदविभागं वाक्यमेव वाक्यार्थस्य वाचकमित्याचक्षते ।

(ii) ये च वाक्यान्त्यवर्ण एवेति

(iii) ये च पदैः अनन्विताः पदार्थाः अभिहिताः परस्परान्वयमात्मनोऽवगमयन्ति इति तन्निरासाय प्रतिजानीते—

पदेभ्य एव वाक्यार्थप्रत्ययो जायते यथा ।
तथा वयं निबध्नीमः प्रभाकरगुरोः मतम् ।

पदेभ्य एव, न वाक्यात्, नाप्यन्त्यवर्णात्, नापि पदार्थेभ्यः इत्यर्थः ।

(प्र०पं० ३७७)

Those who hold that the sentence itself conveys the sentence meaning have to explain as to how children acquire the language without the understanding of the words and word meanings. They have to understand these through the conversation of the elders identifying the words and meanings used in different sentences. If words and word meanings are not involved in the process of the comprehension of sentence meaning, the very process of understanding of sentence meaning through the understanding of the words and their meanings becomes difficult. It is not possible to say that while learning the language through the elders' conversation, the child understands the sentence meaning of each sentence as a unit by itself but not through the understanding of the words and word meanings. This is because, innumerable sentences are employed in the language in the course of conversation throughout the life. A child cannot go on learning the meaning of each sentence separately. Moreover, the Vedic sentences are not in day-to-day use. Therefore, the understanding of their import is not possible.

These difficulties are solved by those who take sentence itself as the unit of communication by explaining that though, really speaking, there are no separate words and word meanings, for practical purposes separate words and separate meanings are envisaged. These assist the comprehension of the sentence meaning through the elders' conversation.

वाक्यार्थप्रतिपत्तौ हि पदानामनुपायत्वे तदन्यथानुपपत्त्या वाक्यमेकं तदुपायभूतं कल्प्यते । यद्यपि व्युत्पत्त्यनपेक्षात् शब्दात् अर्थो नावगम्यते । यद्यपि च अनन्ताद् वाक्यानां तदर्थानां च वैदिकस्य च अर्थस्य अनन्योपायत्वात् व्युत्पत्तिरशक्या तथापि काल्पनिकपदपदार्थव्युत्पत्तिसंस्कृतात् वाक्याद् वाक्यार्थमवगच्छतीत्याश्रीयते । (प्र० पं० ३७७)

To envisage imaginary words and the imaginary word meanings is not a desirable procedure, therefore, another procedure is proposed by some others. They explain that there are no imaginary words and word meanings. Each syllable of a sentence is not able to convey the sentence meaning. Therefore, the last syllable of the sentence accompanied by the impression of the previous syllables conveys the sentence meaning. The comprehension of the words and their meanings that are real and that are comprehended at the time of learning the language assist the comprehension of the sentence meaning as explained above.

यदि काल्पनिकत्वे पदपदार्थानां प्रमाणाभावात्, एकैकवर्णोच्चारणेऽर्थानवबोधात्, क्रमेण उच्चरितानां च युगपत् श्रवणासम्भवात्, पूर्वपूर्ववर्णानुभव जनितसंस्कारसहितः अन्त्यो वर्णः प्रत्यायकः, तस्य च पारमार्थिकपदपदार्थव्युत्पत्तिः सहकारिणीति पक्षः स्वीक्रियते । (प्र०पं० ३७७)

The Bhāṭṭa Mīmāṁsakas reject the above two views and take the position that the words convey their meanings separately. These lead to the sentence meaning.

यद्वा पदैः सुकरव्युत्पत्तयः अनन्विताः एव स्वार्थाः अभिहिताः वाक्यार्थमवबोधयन्ति इत्यङ्गीक्रियते । (प्र०पं० ३७७)

Anvitābhidhāna Theory of Prābhākaras

The Prābhākaras reject the Bhāṭṭa's view also. According to the Prābhākaras the words convey the meanings connected with meaning of the relevant other words as main and subordinate. Such connected meanings of the words is the sentence meaning. Though the words are many and consequently the meanings are also many, these all get connected with the chief meaning and serve its purpose. Contributing to the evolution of the main meaning is the purpose of all other words. Therefore, these function as one sentence. All words in a sentence are employed to contribute to the evolution of the main meaning. That is the import of the whole sentence. Neither the individual words are the means of communication separately, nor the meanings of the individual words are intended to be communicated. This theory of sentence meaning is known as *anvitābhidhānavāda*.

यदि तु पदान्येव अन्वितान् स्वार्थान् अभिदधतीति शक्यते साधयितुं तदा वाक्यार्थस्य अवबुद्धत्वात् न एताः कल्पनाः आत्मानं लभन्ते ।

कथं पुनः पदानामन्वितस्वार्थमात्रबोधकत्वे वाक्यार्थावगतिः सिद्ध्यतीत्यत्राह—

प्रधानगुणभावेन लब्धान्योन्यसमन्वयान् ।
पदार्थानेव वाक्यार्थान् सङ्गिरन्ते विपश्चितः ।।३।।

ननु तेषां भूयस्त्वाद् भूयांसो वाक्यार्थाः वाक्यानिच स्युः इत्यत्राह–

भूयांसो यद्यपि स्वार्थाः पदानां ते पृथक् पृथक् ।
प्रयोजनतया त्वेकवाक्यार्थं सम्प्रचक्षते ।।४।।
कथं पुनः एकप्रयोजनत्वमित्यत आह–
प्रतिपत्तिर्गुणानांहि प्रधानैकप्रयोजना ।।५।।

यद्धि प्रधानभूतं तदेव कथं नाम विशिष्टं प्रतीयतामित्येवमर्थं गुणानां प्रतिपादनम्, तेन तत्रैव तात्पर्यम् । तदेव प्रमेयम् । तात्पर्यविषय एव शब्दस्य प्रमाण्याभ्युपगमात् । तस्य तथाभूतस्य प्रतिपत्तिर्नैकपदनिबन्धनेति वाक्यमेव तत्र प्रमाणम् ।

अत एव षष्ठाद्ये न पदं नाम किञ्चन वाक्ये न पदार्था नाम केचन वाक्यार्थे (बृ०टी० 6-1-1) इत्युक्तम् । प्रथग्भूताश्च पदार्था न प्रमेयाः सन्तीत्यर्थः । एतच्च तत्रैव स्पष्टमुक्तम् । (प्र०पं० ३७७-३७८)

Rejection of the View that the Sentence is a Unit of Communication Directly

There is no justification to envisage the sentence alone as a unit of communication ignoring the parts viz., syllables and words, that are actually observed. It is true that the communication takes place through the sentence only. It is also true that the elders' conversation through the sentences enables to learn the language. However, the denotative power of the words in a certain sense is identified by the use of the words in different sentences and the replacement of the same by other words. These words and word meanings lead to the sentence meaning. Therefore, it is not correct to hold that the sentence is directly a unit of communication ignoring the role of the words.

सम्प्रति वाक्यमेव वाचकं वाक्यार्थस्येति ये ब्रुवते । ये च वाक्यान्त्यवर्ण एवेति । तन्निराकरणायाह—

व्यवहारेषु वृद्धानां वाक्यश्रवणभाविषु ।
आवापोद्धारभेदेन पदानां शक्तिनिश्चयः ॥६॥

यद्यपि वृद्धव्यवहारपूर्विकैव सर्वा शब्दव्युत्पत्तिः । वाक्यैरेव च व्यवहारः । तथापि यत्पदावापे यस्यार्थस्यावापः, यदुद्धारे चोद्धारः तस्मिन्नेवार्थे तस्य पदस्य वाचकशक्तिरवसीयते । न च तथा सति वाक्यार्थप्रतिपत्तिर्नोपपद्यते वक्ष्यमाणत्वात् न्यायस्य । येन कार्यबलेन वाक्यमेकं प्रत्यक्षपरिदृश्यमानवर्णपदभेदापह्नवेन कल्प्येत । (प्र०पं० २७९)

Moreover, for the eight sentences (i) शिशो! गामानय (ii) शिशो गां बधान (iii) वत्स! गामानय (iv) वत्स! गां बधान (v) अर्भक! गामानय (vi) अर्भक! गां बधान (vii) डिम्भ! गामानय (viii) डिम्भ! गां बधान eight denotative powers will have to be envisaged if the sentence is considered to have the denotative power directly. However, if a word is taken as a unit of denotative power, since, these eight séntences contain only seven separate words, envisaging seven denotative powers will be sufficient.

वाक्यवादिनः वाक्यानामष्टौ शक्तयः कल्पनीयाः । पदवादिनस्तु सप्तानां पदानां सप्तैव शक्तयः इति कल्पनालाघवम् । Similarly, if one more word *Śuklam* is added to these sentences, eight more denotative powers have to be envisaged. For *Padavādin* one more only. The contention that the words and their meanings are not real, cuts the very basis of the learning the language.

According to those who hold the view that it is the last syllable of the sentence that communicates, the words are real, these assist the communication by the sentence.

It is true that it is only the last syllable that communicates. However, the other words and syllables are also the grounds for this final communication.

ये पुनः वाक्यान्त्यवर्णस्य वाचकतामाहुः, तन्मतेपि तावत् पदार्थविभागस्य पारमार्थिकत्वात् घटेतैव व्युत्पत्तिः । ननु वाच्यवाचकसम्बन्धग्रहणमेव व्यत्पत्तिरित्युच्यते । न च वाक्यान्त्यवर्ण वाचकत्ववादिनां पदं पदार्थस्य वाचकम् । अतस्तन्मतेपि निर्विषयैव व्युत्पत्तिः। उच्यते । न निर्विषया निमित्तिनैमित्तिकभावस्य अभ्युपगतत्वात् । (प्र०पं० ३७९)

The fact of other words also being the ground for the communication by the last syllable is explained as under: When a sentence containing certain words communicates certain meaning, the words in the sentence are the grounds for communicating that meaning:

केयमवाचकस्य निमित्तता? नैष दोषः । वाक्याद्धि यत्पदप्रयोगे सति यत्पदार्थान्वितो वाक्यार्थः प्रतीयते तत्पदं तस्य अर्थस्य अवाचकमपि भवति निमित्तम् । (प्र०पं० ३७९)

Explaining the **वाक्यान्त्यवर्णवाचकता** view as stated above, Śālikanātha rejects this view also on the same ground that this will also result in envisaging different denotative powers to different sentences and lands into **गौरव** ।

किन्तु तन्मतेपि शक्तिकल्पनागौरवं पूर्वोक्तन्यायेन तुल्यमेव (प्र०पं० ३७९)

Those who hold that the whole sentence itself is stored in the memory and communicates, are also not free from the drawback of the contingency of envisaging separate denotative power for each sentence. Bhāṣyakāra clearly states that the theory that the last syllable of sentence communicates has no scope.

येप्याहुः वाक्यमेव स्मृत्यारूढं वाक्यार्थं प्रतिपादयतीति, तेषामपि प्राच्यमेव शक्तिकल्पनागौरवलक्षणं दूषणमशक्यपरिहारम् । भाष्यकारव-

चनञ्च 'पूर्ववर्णसंस्कारसहितोऽन्त्यो वर्णः प्रत्यायकः' इति निर्विषयम् ।
(शा० भा० पृ० ४६)

Moreover, a long sentence cannot be remembered:

अशक्यं च महावाक्यस्य सकृत् स्मरणम् । तस्मात् पदानामेव वाचकशक्तिः आश्रयणीया । (प्र० पं० ३८०)

Anumāpakatva and Anuvādakatva of Śabda do not Come in the Way of Śaktigraha

While rejecting the view that the sentence itself is the conveyer of sentence meaning, the chief objection raised was 'How a child can learn the language through the conversation of the elders if the words and their meanings are not identified when used in different sentences.' In other words '*śaktigraha*' i.e., comprehension of the meaning of the words used in a sentence is a necessary requirement for comprehending the sentence meaning. The sentence itself cannot convey the sentence meaning without involving the words and their meanings.

Now, this point creates a problem for the Prābhākaras. According to the Prābhākaras the *śabda* is not a separate *pramāṇa.* It only helps to infer the speaker's knowledge of the things stated in his statement. The statement is merely an *anuvāda* i.e., a secondary presentation of the knowledge of the speaker inferred through his statement. This means that the words are not *vācaka* but are *anumāpaka* and *anuvādaka.* Hence, there is no question of *padaśakti* and *padaśaktigraha.* Therefore, the Prābhākaras are not entitled to raise an objection based on the ground that the absence of *padaśakti* and *padaśaktigraha* will hinder the view that the sentence itself conveys the sentence meaning.

अत्र केचित् चोदयन्ति ननु वृद्धव्यवहारप्रयुक्ते वाक्ये पदानां वाचकशक्त्यवधारणमेव नोपपद्यते । पुरुषवाक्यानामर्थं प्रति लिङ्गभावेन प्रमाणत्वाभ्युपगमात् । वाक्याद्धि कार्यभूतात् प्रतीतस्य वक्तुः तदर्थविषयं

पूर्वविज्ञानं कारणभूतमनुमीयते । तस्य च ज्ञानस्य ज्ञेयाव्यभिचारित्वात् । ज्ञेयभूतार्थनिश्चयः इति न वाचकशक्त्यवगमः । (प्र०पं० ३८०)

Śālikanātha takes up this question and reminds that it is already stated in 'Nītipatha' section that even according to the Prābhākaras the words are *vācaka* and have *vācakaśakti*. However, these are *anuvādakatayā vācaka*. A statement is a valid statement only if the knowledge of the speaker inferred through the statements is valid. The Prābhākaras consider all *pauruṣeya* statements as *anumāpaka* only.

To the extent to which the words are considered as *anuvādakatayā vācaka*, the process of *śaktigraha* is also worked out by the Prābhākaras at the time of learning the language through the elders' conversation. Śālikanātha quotes an instance of a sentence and points out as to how the child arrives at a proper *śaktigraha* and the proper sentence meaning.

(i) उच्यते— न नूनं भवान् नीतिपथोक्तमर्थं सम्यगाकलयति । परिहृतं हि तत्रेदम् ।

(ii) अनुवादकतया तस्यार्थस्य तद्वाक्यं वाचकमेव । (प्र०पं० ३८०)

The Objections Against Anvitābhidhāna

Before proceeding to give a full exposition on *anvitābhidhā-navāda*. Śālikanātha discusses the objections raised against it by *abhihitānvayavādins*. These are

1. According to *anvitābhidhāna* theory, each word is expected to convey its meaning as connected with the meaning of the relevant other word in the sentence. This connection is included in the scope of the meaning of the word. The other word will be different in different sentences. Consequently, the meaning of a word has to be as connected with the meaning of those many words. This means that each word will have an unlimited number of connections as its meanings. To have the *śaktigraha* of a word with reference to such a large number of meanings of other words is impossible.

अत्र केचिदाचक्षते भवतु पदानां पदार्थेषु शक्तिज्ञानम्, तथापि अन्विताभिधानं न सिद्ध्यति इति । तथाहि—प्रतियोगिनामनन्ततया अन्वयानामानन्त्यात्, तदानन्त्ये च अन्वितानामप्यानन्त्यात् सम्बन्धग्रहणं दुष्करम् ।

This difficulty cannot be solved by saying:

(i) The word conveys its meaning without *śaktigraha* in respect of all these meanings.

This solution does not work, since, in this case, one other word will be sufficient to convey the connection with all other words, as there is no need of *śaktigraha* in respect of each other word separately.

अगृहीतसम्बन्धस्य च पदस्य वाचकत्वे एकस्मात् शब्दात् सर्वार्थप्रतीति प्रसङ्गः ।

(ii) The word meaning is conveyed as connected with the meaning of the other word in a general way. This does not result in innumerable meaning for each word.

This solution also does not work since the sentence meaning has always a reference to the special connections only.

सामान्यान्वयाभिधानं च नाशङ्कनीयमेव वाक्येभ्यो विशेषान्वयावगमात् ।

Therefore, the word conveying its meaning as connected with the meaning of another word in the sentence does result in innumerable meanings being assigned to a word as it occurs along with different words in different sentences and such sentences are innumerable.

Since the purpose of obtaining the sentence meaning could be managed by words connecting their meaning without including the connection also in the scope of the word meaning, it is an unnecessary additional burden to include connection also in the scope of the word meaning.

स्वरूपमात्राभिधानेनापि वाक्यार्थप्रतिपत्त्युपपत्तौ अन्विताभिधानाश्रयणे शक्तिकल्पनागौरवम् । (प्र०पं० ३८०)

2. Further, when it is stated that a word conveys its meaning as connected with the meaning of the relevant other word, is the other word also has to be taken as conveying its meaning as connected with the meaning of thïs word or not? In the former case it will result in reciprocal dependency. X word needs the Y word to convey its meaning as connected with meaning of Y word, and the Y word needs X word to convey its meaning as connected with it. On the face of such a reciprocal dependency both X word and Y word fail to convey their meaning.

तथा पदेन अन्वित: स्वार्थ: अभिधीयमान: किमभिहितेन पदार्थान्तरेण अन्वितोऽभिधीयते? उत अनन्वितेनेति विकल्पनीयम् । अनभिहितेन चेत् पदान्तरप्रयोगवैयर्थ्यम् । एकस्माच्च सर्वान्वयप्रतीतिप्रसङ्गः । अभिहितेन चेत् तदपि तर्हि पदमन्विताभिधायितया पदान्तरोपात्तमर्थमभिधानाय अपेक्षते इति इतरेतराश्रय: प्राप्नोति ।

Mentioning these objections against *anvitābhidhānavāda*, it is concluded on behalf of the *abhihitānvayavādin* that the words in a sentence convey their meanings only. These word meanings aided by *ākāṅkṣā*, *yogyatā* and *sannidhi* lead to the sentence meaning. No relation is required to evolve such a sentence meaning, since, the relation is an attribute of words but not that of meanings.

तस्मात् पदान्तराभिधानानपेक्षस्वरूपमात्राभिधानमेव अर्थानां पदैः क्रियते । ते च तथा भूता: पदैः अभिहिता: । आकांक्षा सन्निधियोग्यतावन्त: वाक्यार्थमवगमयन्ति । न तेषां सम्बन्धग्रहणापेक्षा शङ्कनीया । यत: पदधर्मोऽयं नार्थधर्म: । तदाह भाष्यकार: पदानि हि स्वं स्वमर्थमभिधाय निवृत्तव्यापाराणि । अथेदानीमवगता: सन्त: वाक्यार्थमवगमयन्तीति । (पू०मी० १-१-२५) (प्र०पं० २८३)

The Language is Learnt through Elders' Conversation

Both the Prābhākaras and Bhāṭṭas are agreed on the point that the language is learnt through the elders' conversation and it is learnt by the process of identifying individual words and their meanings by the presence and the absence of these words in different sentences and the consequent changes in the import of the sentence. However, the Bhāṭṭas hold that the words and their meanings are identified in an isolated way and the Prābhākaras hold that the words are identified as conveying their meaning as connected with the meanings of the relevant other words. The Bhāṭṭas agree that the connection also has to be managed. But the question is whether this connection is to be included in the scope of the meaning of the words, or the word meanings themselves manage to get associated with the aid of *ākāṅkṣa*, *sannidhi* and *yogyatā*. The Bhāṭṭas go by the latter view.

ओप्यन्ते चोद्ध्रियन्ते च स्वार्थाः अन्वयशालिनः ।
अन्वितेष्वेव सामर्थ्यं पदानां तेन गम्यते ॥ ६ ॥

अत्राह—सत्यमन्वितपदार्थविषयावेव आवापोद्धारौ तथापि अन्विताभिधानमशक्यम् । पारम्पर्येणापि तदुपपत्तेः । तथाहि पदैरनन्वितोपि अभिहितः अर्थः अन्वितार्थप्रतिपत्तेः निमित्तं भवतीति पदानां पारम्पर्येण अन्वितेष्वपि हेतुत्वम् । तदाहुः वार्तिककारमिश्राः

न विमुञ्चन्ति सामर्थ्यं वाक्यार्थेपि पदानि नः ।
तन्मात्रावसितेष्वेव पदार्थेभ्यः स गम्यते ॥
(श्लो०वा०अधि० ७ श्लो २२६)

पदार्थप्रतिपादनं च वाक्यार्थ प्रतिपत्तये प्रयुक्तानां पदानामेव अवान्तर व्यापारः इति च तेषामेव व्यवहारः—

वाक्यार्थमितये तेषां प्रवृत्तौ नान्तरीयकम् ।
पाके ज्वालेव काष्ठानां पदार्थप्रतिपादनम् ॥
(श्लो०वा०अधि० ७ श्लोक ३४३)(प्र०पं० ३(३-४)

Analysis of the Statement 'Sveto Dhāvati'

To explain the possibility of *padārthas* getting associated by themselves, an interesting instance is quoted by the Bhāṭṭas. In the statement *svetaḥ aśāvaḥ dhāvati* (a white horse is coming running). The connection of different *padārthas* stated in the sentence is managed by the *padārthas* themselves. One who has made this statement obtains the knowledge of the various *padārthas* mentioned in this statement by different means. He obtains the knowledge of the white colour of the horse by perception, the knowledge of the presence of the horse through the inference by its peculiar voice, the fact of the coming running by the sound of the foot-steps. On the basis of such a knowledge of *padārthas* he makes the above statement. Here, the *padārthas* known from the different sources of knowledge are associated and put together in this statement. Their association is not conveyed by the words. From this, it is clear that for the evolution of the sentence meaning, it is the association of the *padārthas* that is more relevant. It is not necessary that such association should be conveyed by the words only.

स्यादेवम् यदि मानान्तरावसेयानां पदार्थानामन्योन्यान्वयावगमे सामर्थ्यं न स्यात् । अस्ति तु श्वैत्यस्य अनवधारिताश्रयविशेषस्य प्रत्यक्षदृष्टस्य, अश्वस्य अप्रतिपन्नगुणविशेषस्य प्रत्यक्षह्रेषाशब्दानुमितस्य पदनिक्षेपशब्दानुमितस्य अज्ञातकर्तृभेदस्य धावनस्य च श्वेतोऽश्वो धावतीत्यन्वयबोधकत्वदर्शनात् । तदाहुः वार्तिककारमिश्राः ।

पश्यतः श्वेतमारूपं ह्रेषाशब्दं च शृण्वतः ।
खुरनिक्षेपशब्दं च श्वेतोऽश्वो धावतीति धीः ॥

दृष्टा वाक्यविनिर्मुक्ता (श्लो०वा०वा०अधि० श्लो० ३५१) (प्र०पं० ३९२)

Śālikanātha analyses this statement and points out that the association of the *padārthas* that are comprehended by different other *pramāṇas* is conveyed here by *anumāna* or *arthāpatti*, but not by *śabdapramāṇa*. Such an association is not syntactical association. A person who has made the above statement has come to know all the facts and their association by *anumāna* and *arthāpatti*. It is wrong to say that the facts are known by the other *pramāṇas* and their association is communicated through the statement. Their association is also comprehended by other *pramāṇas* before the statement is made. Therefore, this example does not help to establish that the word meanings get connected on their own.

अत्रोच्यते—किं येनैव पुरुषेण श्वेत्यसमानाश्रयौ ह्रेषाध्वनि-पदनिक्षेपशब्दावगतौ तस्यैवेयं 'श्वेतोऽश्वो धावतीति धीः? उत यस्यापादानानध्यवसायः तस्यापीति? किमतः । यदि तावदप्रत्याकलितह्रेषाध्वनि पदविहार निर्घोषापादनस्येत्युच्यते तदा प्रतीतिविरोधः । सहि एवं प्रतिपद्यते भवितव्यमस्मिन् देशे नूनमश्वेन, भवितव्यं च केनचिद् धावतेति । अथ अश्वसम्बन्धिनमेव खुरपुटटङ्काररवमभ्यासपाटववशादवैति तदा असौ अश्ववर्तिनीमेव वेगवतीं गतिमनुमिनोतीति न पुनः केवलमेव अवगम्य तस्य अन्वयं पदार्थसामर्थ्येन अवबुद्ध्यते ।

योऽपि तस्मिन् देशे नास्त्यन्यो अश्वादिति निश्चित्य पारिशेष्या-दपादानाध्यवसायेपि ह्रेषाध्वनेः श्वैत्यसमानाधिकरणमश्वत्वमपि अध्यवस्यति तस्यापि गृहाभावदर्शनमिव बहिर्भावावगतौ अर्थापत्तिः 'योऽयं श्वेतः स एषोऽश्वः' इत्यत्र प्रमाणम् ।

यस्तु श्वैत्यसमानाधिकरणौ ह्रेषाध्वनि-खुरपुट टङ्कारौ अध्यवस्यति तस्यापि अश्वत्वे वेगवति गमने श्वेतवर्तिन्येवानुमानम् न स्वतन्त्रयोः । अतः प्रमाणान्तरेण असम्बद्धावभूतानां पदार्थानां न क्वचित् अन्योन्यसम्बन्धबोध-कत्वमनुमानार्थापत्तिव्यतिरेकेण प्रतीतम् । (प्र०पं० ३९६)

Further, if *padārthas* get connected on their own as soon as they are known, then, one has to say by which *pramāṇa* such an association is known. It cannot be *śabdapramāṇa*, because, it is the theory of the the Bhāṭṭas that the connection of only such *padārthas* that are communicated through the words is known as a part of verbal communication but not the connection of those *padārthas* that are known through the other *pramāṇas*. Now, if some other *pramāṇa* conveys such connection, let the same be the *pramāṇa* to comprehend the connection between the *padārthas* that are communicated by the words also. This means there will be no role left to *śabdapramāṇa*.

अपि च यदि पदार्थावगतिमात्रादेव परस्परान्वयावगमः तदा कस्मिन् प्रमाणे तस्यान्तर्भावः इति वाच्यम् । न तावत् शाब्दे शब्दाभावात् । पदार्थाभिधानावान्तरव्यापारेण हि यच्छब्दादन्वयज्ञानं तच्छाब्दमित्येष वो राद्धान्तः। तस्मात् नास्य शब्दे अन्तर्भावः । प्रमाणान्तराभ्युपगमे च शब्दस्योच्छेदः । शब्दावगतपदार्थविषयेपि तस्यैव प्रामाण्यप्रसङ्गात् । (प्र०पं० ३९३-९४)

The Contingency of a Three Tiered Denotative Power

The only way to effect a connection between the word meanings to evolve the sentence meaning is to invest the word meanings with a power to denote the connection and evolve the sentence meaning. This results in envisaging a three tiered denotative power viz., (i) A denatative power for the words to convey the word meaning (ii) A denotative power to the word meanings to convey the connection between different word meanings (iii) A power on the part of the words to invest the word meanings with the power to convey the connection. Instead of indulging in such a round about exercise, it is better to say that the words convey their meanings as connected with the meanings of the relevant other words in the sentence.

पदार्थानां हि शब्दादन्यतः प्रमाणात् प्रतीयमानानामन्योन्यान्वयबोधकत्वं न प्रतीतमिति शब्दाभिधेयानां तावदवगमशक्तिः कल्पयितव्या । तस्याः उत्पत्तौ शब्दसंस्पर्श एव हेतुरित्याश्रयणीयम् । शब्दो हि विशिष्टार्थप्रतिपत्तिपरतया लोकव्यवहारेषु प्रयुज्यमानो दृष्टः । न चासौ साक्षाद् वाक्यार्थप्रतिपादने समर्थ इति पदार्थानावन्तरव्यापारीकरोति । ते च यदि अन्योन्यान्वबोधने समर्थाः स्युः तदा तेषामवान्तरव्यापारता स्यात् न अन्यथेति विशिष्टार्थावबोधपर शब्दसंस्पर्शादिव तेषामेषा शक्तिराविर्भवतीति शब्दस्यापि पदार्थगतान्वयबोधकत्वशक्त्याधानशक्तिराश्रयणीया । (प्र०पं० ३९२)

शब्दाभिहितानां पदार्थानामन्यत्र अदृष्टं वाक्यार्थबोधनसामर्थ्यं कल्पयितव्यम् । तदाधानशक्तिश्च शब्दानामपीति, कल्पनालाघवात् शब्दानामेव अन्वितस्वार्थावबोधनशक्तिमात्रं कल्पयितुं न्याय्यम् । (प्र०पं० ३९४)

The Answers to the Objections Against Anvitābhidhānavāda

On the position of *anvitābhidhānavāda* an objection was raised earlier viz., considering the connection of the word meaning with the meaning of the relevant other word as the scope of the word meaning will result in envisaging innumerable denotative powers as there are innumerable words to be connected. This objection does not hold good if the way in which the connection is effected and ascertained is examined. The connection envisaged among the word meanings in a sentence is based on three criteria viz., *ākāṅkṣā*, *sannidhi* and *yogyatā*. Among these, *ākāṅkṣā* is very important. The words convey the meaning connected with the meaning of the relevant other word that has the *ākāṅkṣā*. This *ākāṅkṣā* in respect of different words in a sentence does not arise simultaneously or in a disorderly way. The import of the injunction viz., *kārya* i.e., *apūrva*, is the central meaning of a Vedic injunctive sentence. This needs a *viṣaya* i.e., *yāga*, it also needs a *niyojya* to perform the *yāga*. Then, the *karaṇopakārakas* are needed. All these have an *ākāṅkṣā* with the central meaning and convey the meaning connected with it in the respective order. In view of this orderly connection there is no room for any reciprocal dependency. Nor there is any need to envisage innumerable denotative powers to each word to convey the connection of its meaning with the meanings of different words in different sentences. Words have only one denotative power viz., its meaning connected with the meaning that satisfies the criterion of *ākāṅkṣā*, *yogyatā* and *sannidhi*. Such connection may differ in respect of different other words but the denotative power is common. Just as one can see many objects and their many attributes in one contact of the eye, similarly, one denotative power is sufficient to convey different connections with different other word meanings.

(i) ननु अनन्तप्रतियोग्यान्वितस्वार्थबोधनविषयाः अनन्ताः एव शब्दस्य शक्तयः कल्पिताः स्युः । अभिहितान्वयवादे तु एकस्मिन्नर्थे एकस्य शब्दस्य एकैव शक्तिरिति । तन्न । एकयैव आकांक्षित सन्निहितयोग्यार्थान्वित स्वार्थाभिधानशक्त्या प्रतियोगिभेदेन कार्यभेदोपपत्तेः चक्षुरादीनामिव । चक्षुः यथा एकया दर्शनशक्त्या घटादिप्रतियोगिसहायभेदात् ज्ञानानि भिन्नानि जनयति तथाशब्दोपि प्रतियोगिभेदादिति मन्तव्यम् । किञ्च पदार्थेष्वपि तुल्यमेतदिति न किञ्चिदेतत् । (प्र०पं० ३९४)

(ii) आकांक्षा सन्निधिप्राप्तयोग्यार्थान्तरसङ्गतान् ।
स्वार्थानाहुः पदानीति व्युत्पत्तिः संश्रिता यदा ।
आनन्त्यव्यभिचाराभ्यां तदा दोषो न कश्चन ॥

यत्तावदुक्तं आनन्त्यात् शब्दशक्त्यवधारणानुपपत्तिः । अगृहीतशक्तेश्च वाचकत्वे व्यभिचारप्रसङ्गः इति । तदनुपपन्नम् । उपलक्षणाश्रयणेनापि सम्बन्धबोधः सौकर्यादाकांक्षितेन योग्येन सन्निहितेन च अन्वितं स्वार्थं पदं वक्तीति व्युत्पत्तिराश्रियते । तेन

यद्यदाकांक्षितं योग्यं सन्निधानं प्रपद्यते ।
तदन्वितः पदेनार्थः स्वकीयः प्रतिपद्यते ॥ (प्र०पं० ३८४)

The Nature and the Role of Ākāṅkṣā

Those who have raised the objection of *ānantya* have raised it on the wrong understanding of the nature of *ākāṅkṣā*, therefore, Śālikanātha examines the very nature of *ākāṅkṣā* proposed by others, particularly, by the Nyāyavaiśeṣikas, and points out that their explanation of the nature of *ākāṅkṣā* is not correct. According to them, those that are invariably associated with each other have *ākāṅkṣā* for each other. For instance an action needs an instrument, and an instrument is meant for an action. Therefore, the words conveying these two have an *ākāṅkṣā* for each other.

This explanation of the nature of *ākāṅkṣā* is rejected by Śālikanātha on several grounds. (i) No limits can be fixed for such *ākāṅkṣā*. One who needs to know the instrument may also desire to know its size, colour, function and so on. This will result in an endless enquiry of associated things and the sentence will remain incomplete until all these are provided. (ii) If it is contended that since no purpose is served to accomplish the action by these attributes, the *ākāṅkṣā* will not extend to these, then, in the instances where the knowledge of action itself is sufficient, and no purpose is served by the *karaṇa* i.e., instrument, the *ākāṅkṣā* may not have to extend even to the *karaṇa* i.e., instrument. (iii) Further, in the instances where more than one *kāraka* i.e., *karma* and *karaṇa* are mentioned, and the *ākāṅkṣā* of the action is satisfied by one *kāraka*, the other *kāraka* will have to remain isolated in the absence of *ākāṅkṣā* for it. (iv) In the Vedic passages *aruṇayā ekahāyanyā piṅgākṣyā* etc., the words that do not indicate any *kāraka* will have to remain isolated in the absence of *ākāṅkṣā*. Finally, the action and the instruments talked of here are in the context of *laukika* statements. Such an *ākāṅkṣā* can be satisfied by any action and any instrument. Therefore, such a criterion does not help to bring out the import of the Vedic injunctions. The connection evolved by such *ākāṅkṣā* is not of any help to construct a Vedic injunction so as to organise a *prayogavidhi* consisting of *kārya* i.e., *niyoga*, *viṣaya* i.e., *yāga*, *niyojya*, *karaṇopakāra* etc. To obtain such a well organised import of a Vedic injunction, the nature of *ākāṅkṣā* has to be worked out differently. Śālikanātha works out the same from the Prābhākaras point of view as follows:

का पुनरियमाकांक्षा? प्रतिपत्तुः जिज्ञासा । किं निबन्धनाचासौ ? अविनाभावनिबन्धनेति केचित् । क्रिया हि कारकाविनाभाविनीति तां प्रतीत्य कारकं जिज्ञासते, एवं कारकमापि बुद्ध्वा क्रियामिति ।

तदयुक्तमिति मन्यामहे । (i) **जिज्ञासाविरामानुपपत्तेः । यदा तावत् कारकजिज्ञासा तदा तदीयजनक तद्गुणतत्क्रिया तत्कारकादि जिज्ञासाप्यापाद्यते ।** (ii) **अथ प्रयोजनाभावात् कारकातिरिक्तमन्यत् न जिज्ञास्यते तर्हि क्रियामात्रावगमेपि यत्र कारकज्ञानेन प्रयोजनं नास्ति तत्र जिज्ञासा न स्यात् ।**

The Nature of Ākāṅkṣā According to the Prābhākaras

Ākāṅkṣā arises under two circumstances viz., (i) *abhidhāna aparyavasāna* i.e., when the statement itself is incomplete (ii) *abhidheya aparyavasāna* i.e., when what is required to be conveyed is incomplete. The first may be illustrated by the statement *dvāram* the door. This statement is incomplete, because, the predicate part of it which is required to convey a connected meaning is missing. Therefore, there is *ākāṅkṣā* to seek it. This has to be conveyed by *adhyāhāra* i.e., supplementing. According to the Prābhākaras the supplementing is not of the nature of providing a word to convey the predicate. It is sufficient if the very act that has to be predicated viz., *samvriyatām* i.e., close or *vivriyatām* i.e., open, depending upon the context is brought to the mind.

अत्रोच्यतेअभिधानापर्यवसानम्, अभिधेयापर्यवसानं च जिज्ञासोदये निबन्धनम् । एकपदप्रयोगे हि द्वारमित्यादौ अभिधानमेव न पर्यवस्यति । नहि अनुच्चरिते प्रतियोगिसन्निधापके पदे अन्विताभिधानं शक्यते वक्तुम् । वृद्धव्यवहारवशेन अन्वितार्थप्रतिपादनपरता पदानामवधारितेति तदर्थं युक्तैव प्रतियोगिजिज्ञासा । यस्यापि अभिहितान्वय इति राद्धान्तः तन्मतेपि पदार्थस्य पदार्थान्तरमन्तरेणान्वयासामर्थ्यात् तदुपपत्तये युक्तैव प्रतियोगिजिज्ञासा । तस्यां च सत्यामपरिपूर्णवाक्यपरिपूरकतया लोके अध्याहारस्य विदितत्वात् प्रकरणादिवशेन योग्यप्रतियोग्यध्याहारः क्रियते ।

The second circumstance of *ākāṅkṣā* i.e., *abhidheya aparvyavasāna,* is explained by the example *visvajitā yajeta.* Here the *kārya* i.e., the import of the injunctive suffix, is stated. Its subject and the instrument i.e., *visvajid yāga* is stated. However, mentioning these, does not complete the requirements to accomplish the *kārya* that is the chief import of the statement.

To accomplish *kārya*, a *niyojya* is required. Such a *niyojya* must have the entitlement. In the present case, he who desires to have *svarga* is entitled to undertake *visvajid yāga.* Therefore, he is the *adhikārin* and consequently he is *niyojya* and *kartā* i.e., agent. Unless a *niyojya* is provided the accomplishment of *kārya* is not possible. Therefore, there is *niyojya ākāṅkṣā* here. However, in the case of *adhyayana vidhi*, since this injunction is to be implemented because of *adhyāpana vidhi*, no *niyojya* is necessary. Therefore, there is no *niyojyākāṅkṣā* in the case of *adhyayana vidhi*.

द्वितीयस्य उदाहरणं यथा—'विश्वजिता यजेत' इति अत्र अभिहितस्य अर्थस्य अपर्यवसानात् । लिङर्थः कार्यम् । धात्वर्थस्य विषयत्वकरणत्वाभ्यामन्वयात् विषयकरणान्वितस्य कार्यस्याभिधानं पर्यवसितम् । परन्तु तत्कार्यं नियोज्यविशेषमन्तरेण न पर्यवस्यति । न खलु कार्यमनुष्ठानं विनाऽवतिष्ठते । अनुष्ठानञ्च न अकर्तृकम् । न चानधिकृतः कर्ता भवति । न च अनियोज्योऽधिकृतः इति । विषयकरणान्वितस्य कार्यस्य पर्यवसानाय तदन्वययोग्य नियोज्यजिज्ञासा जायते । (प्र०पं०वि०टि० ३८६)

This is the usual example for *abhidheyāparyavasāna*. However, in *Prakaraṇa Pañcikā* the example of *piṇḍapitṛyajña* is given. In this example also *kārya* is stated but *niyojya* is not stated. Therefore, there is *niyojya jijñāsā*. Here also *svargakāmanā* is taken as the ground of *adhikāra*.

(i) **अमावास्यायमपराह्ने पिण्डपितृयज्ञेन चरन्ति (आ०श्रौ० १३-२ सू १) इत्यादिषु अनेकपदप्रयोगादन्विताभिधानेपि अभिहितस्य कार्यस्य अपूर्वात्मनः अनुष्ठानं विना कार्यत्वानुपपत्तेः, कर्त्रा च विना तदसम्भवात् अधिकाराद्दतेच तदयोगात् नियोज्यमन्तरेण च तस्यानवकल्पनात् तदुपपत्तये युक्तैव तदन्वययोग्यनियोज्यजिज्ञासा । (प्र०पं० ३८७)**

(ii) **सर्वकामिपुरुषव्यापि स्वर्गस्यैव नियोज्यविशेषणत्वयोग्यत्वात् स्वर्गकामो नियोज्योऽध्याह्रियते । (प्र०पं० ३८७)**

In the instance *sauryam charum nirvapet brahma varchasa kāmah*. The *kārya* and *niyojya* are stated. But *kārakas* are not stated.

Therefore, there is the *ākāṅkṣā* of *karaṇopakāra* in this case. These are the instances of *akanksa* due to *abhidheya aparyavasāna.*

(i) तथा अध्ययनविधौ अन्यप्रयुक्तानुष्ठान निर्वाहितकार्यभावे नियोज्यो नाध्याह्रियते ।

(ii) 'सौर्यं चरुं निर्वपेत् घृते शुक्लानां व्रीहीणाम् ब्रह्मवर्चसकामः' (मै.सं. २-२-२)

इत्यादौ करणोपकारमन्तरेण विधेः सिद्ध्यसम्भवात् तज्जिज्ञासा तज्जनकपदार्थजिज्ञासाच । अत एव तदभावे भाष्यकारो न्यूनतामाशङ्क्य परिहृतवान् । (प्र०पं० ३८६)

There are a few instances wherein to connect an adjective *ākāṅkṣā* is envisaged. In the instance *gām ānaya śuklām* ordinarily the *ākāṅkṣā* is satisfied by providing *gām* to *ānaya*. However, *śuklām* also has to form a part of the connected sentence meaning. Therefore, an *ākāṅkṣā* to elicit the connection of *śuklām* also is envisaged.

नन्वेवं तर्हि यत्र पदत्रयं प्रयुज्यते 'गामानय शुक्लामिति लोके । तत्र कारकद्वयस्य असम्भवात् न आकाङ्क्षा अस्तीति कथमन्विताभिधानम् । 'गामानय' इत्येतावतैव परिपूर्णत्वाद् वाक्यस्य । सत्यम् । पदान्तरानुच्चारणे एवम् । उच्चरिते तु तस्मिन् तस्यापि आनयति सन्निधानात्, एकवाक्यत्वावगमात्, आनयत्यन्वितस्वार्थाभिधायित्वात्, आकाङ्क्षां विना च तदसम्भवात् आनयतेः आकाङ्क्षा परिकल्प्यते । (प्र०पं० ३८७)

In the light of the above discussion Śālikanātha neatly states the grounds of *ākāṅkṣā.*

अन्वितस्याभिधानार्थमुक्तार्थ घटनाय च
प्रतियोगिनि जिज्ञासा या साऽऽकाङ्क्षेति गीयते । (प्र.पं. ३८६)

The *ākāṇkṣā* is an essential requirement to comprehend the import of a sentence cerrectly. The presence of the other two criteria viz., *sannidhi* and *yogyatā* are not sufficient. This is explained by an interesting example. In the statement *ayam eti putraḥ rājñaḥ puruṣo apasāryatām* though both the words *putra* and *puruṣa* have *sannidhi* and *yogyatā* to get connected with *rājñaḥ*, it is the word *putra* that gets connected with it but not the word *puruṣa*. Once *rājñaḥ* is connected with *putra* there is no further *ākāṅkṣā* to get connected with *puruṣa*. In such cases the *ākāṅkṣā* has to be settled on the basis of the propriety of evolving a suitable sentence meaning.

साचेयमाकांक्षा भवन्ती व्युत्पत्तौ उपलक्षणमाश्रियते । किमिति पुनः सन्निधियोग्यत्वे एव नाश्रीयेते । निराकाङ्क्षाणामन्विताभिधानादर्शनात् ।

अयमेति पुत्रः राज्ञः पुत्रोऽपनीयतामित्यादौ पुत्रपदसम्बन्धनिराकाङ्क्षो राजा न पुरुषेण अन्वीयते । कस्मात् पुनः अनयोः पुत्रपुरुषयोः सन्निधियोग्यत्वाविशेषेऽपि पुत्रेणैव राज्ञः सम्बन्धः न पुरुषेण । उच्यते— वाक्यात् वाक्यार्थप्रतिपत्तेः न्यायसापेक्षत्वात् । नित्यसापेक्षेण पुत्रेणैव राजा सम्बध्यते । तत्सम्बन्धनिराकांक्षश्च न पुरुषसम्बन्धमनुभवतीत्याकांक्षापि व्युत्पत्त्युपलक्षणमाश्रियते ।

परिपूर्णेन योग्यस्य समीपस्याप्यनन्वयः ।
व्युत्पत्तौ तेन शब्दानामाकङ्क्षाप्युपलक्षणम् ॥ (प्र०पं० ३८८)

The Nature and the Role of Sannidhi

After discussing *ākāṅkṣā*, Śālikanātha discusses *sannidhi* i.e., proximity. According to Prābhākara, *sannidhi* is not the proximity of the words concerned. It is the occurrence of the relevant other meaning to the mind which is to be connected as per the *ākāṅkṣā* and *yogyatā* with the meaning of the word that is heard earlier. Such occurrence of the other meaning is not necessarily through the word that conveys it. It may be by *adhyāhāra* i.e., supplementing. It is already stated that the *adhyāhāra* is not necessarily the *adhyāhāra* of the word. The *adhyāhāra*, in this context, is to be made by *arthāpatti pramāṇa*. The *arthāpatti pramāṇa* permits only the *adhyāhāra* of that much which is essentially required. It is only *arthādhyāhāra* that is necessarily required here.

The *sannidhi* is also not simultaneous or disorderly. It is as per the need of the connections to be developed. Just as *ākāṅkṣā* contributes to connect the various requirements to accomplish the main import of the injunction i.e., *kārya*, *sannidhi* also has to contribute to accomplish the same following the order of *ākāṅkṣā*.

अथ सन्निधिः कः? यस्य अर्थस्य श्रवणानन्तरमाकाङ्क्षा योग्यताभ्यामर्थान्तरे बुद्धिविपरिवृत्तिः । सा च न शब्दनिबन्धनैव केवलमन्विताभिधानव्युत्पत्तौ उपलक्षणम् । अध्याहृतेनापि लोकेऽन्विताभिधानदर्शनात् । न च वाच्यं शब्द एव अध्याह्रियते स च अर्थमुपस्थापयति इति, अनुपयोगात्, अप्रमाणिकत्वाच्च । यद्यपि अर्थापत्ति प्रमाणकोऽध्याहारः तथापि शब्दकल्पनमनुपपन्नम् । येन हि विना अनुपपत्तिः तदेव अर्थापत्तिप्रमेयम् । न च अर्थानां शब्दमन्तरेण अनुपपत्तिः । (प्र०पं० ३८९)

The Nature and the Role of Yogyatā

The nature of *yogyatā* is explained as the suitability to be connected. This creates a problem in working out *yogyatā* with reference to *kārya* i.e., *apūrva*. This *kārya* i.e., *apūrva* is not an action by itself, nor it is conveyed by the empirical evidence such as *pratyakṣa* or *anumāna*. It is conveyed only by a Vedic injunction. Therefore, it is difficult to explain the suitability of any connection or relation of the other items such as *yāga*, the agent etc., with this *kārya*. This difficulty is solved by pointing out that the suitability of connection of other items with the *kārya* has to be envisaged in a general way on the model of their connection with the actual action, and the particular relations have to be worked out in favour of the relations that the actual action i.e., the particular *yāga*, has with these items.

किं पुनरिदं योग्यत्वं नाम? उच्यते यत् सम्बन्धार्हम् । सम्बन्धार्हमिदमिति कथमवगम्यते । सम्बन्धित्वेन दृष्टत्वात् । ननु एवं तर्हि कथं अपूर्वे कार्ये अन्विताभिधानं वेदे तेन सह कस्यचित् सम्बन्धस्य अदर्शनात् । उच्यते— सामान्यतो योग्यतावधारणं विशेषप्रतिपत्तौ उपायः इत्यदोषः । यदपि तदपूर्वं तदपि कार्यमेवेति दृष्टचरकार्यसम्बन्धं यत् तद्योग्यमित्यवसीयते ।

सामान्येनैव योग्यत्वं लोके यदवधारितम् ।
तदन्विताभिधानस्य व्युत्पत्तावुपलक्षणम् ॥ (प्र० पं० ३९१)

Śālikanātha rejects a negative definition of *yogyatā* proposed by some to avoid the above difficulty. They define *yogyatā* as *ayogyatayā anavadhārita* the absence of unsuitability of connection is the suitability of connection. This does not help to solve the difficulty of working out a suitable connection in respect of *kārya*, because, if suitability cannot be ascertained, the unsuitability also cannot be ascertained.

अन्येतु यदयोग्यतया नावधारितं तद्योग्यम् । तेन अलौकिकेनापि विध्यर्थेन अन्विताभिधानं सिद्ध्यतीत्याहुः । तदिदमसारम् । यथा प्रमाणान्तरावेद्ये वस्तुनि कस्यचिद् योग्यता अवधारयितुं न शक्यते तथैव अयोग्यतापीति सर्वस्याप्रतीतेनापि सर्वप्रकारेण तस्मिन्नन्वयः स्यात् भावार्थस्यैव विषयत्वेन अन्वयः अनुपादेयविशेषणविशिष्टस्यैव स्वर्गकामादेः नियोज्यतया अन्वयः इति नियमः नोपपद्यत इत्यलमतिप्रसङ्गेन । (प्र० पं० ३९१)

Rejection of the View that Ākāṅkṣā, Sannidhi and Yogyatā Lead to Sentence Meaning. Therefore, there is no Need of Conveying Anvaya

A section of the *Abhihitānvayavādins* state that the word meanings connected by *ākāṅkṣā, sanndhi* and *yogyatā* constitute the sentence meaning. These do not convey the *anvaya* but form the very sentence meaning.

This is not satisfactory. If the word meanings also do not convey the *anvaya,* then, it will be without any cause. To say that 'when a verb or a *kāraka* word conveys its meaning that is in need of a relevant other meaning, it gets connected with that meaning' will not solve the problem. The question, by what the connection of these is conveyed still remains to be answered. since, neither the word nor the word meanings convey it as per this explanation.

अन्ये त्वाहुः आकाङ्क्षा सन्निधियोग्यतावन्तः पदार्थाः वाक्यार्थीभवन्ति न पुनः वाक्यार्थमेव बोधयन्तीति । तदिदमतिमन्दम् वाक्यार्थावगतेः कारणाभावप्रसङ्गात् । अनुपायत्वे पदानामन्वयप्रतीतौ पदार्था अपि चेत् न कारणम्, अकारणिकैव आपद्येत । स्यान्मतम् । क्रियापदेन, कारकपदेन वा साकाङ्क्षे अर्थे अभिहिते यदेव पदान्तरेण योग्यप्रतियोगिपदार्थान्तरं सन्निधाप्यते तदेव तस्य सम्बन्धित्वेन अवतिष्ठते इति । सत्यमेवम् । अवगतिस्तु तत्सम्बन्धस्य किं निबन्धनेति वाच्यम् । (प्र०पं० ३९४)

The Analogy of Prakriti and Pratyaya does not Help

Now, an attempt is made to get the *anvaya* conveyed on the anology of *pratyaya* conveying its meaning as connected with the meanings of the *prakṛti*. It is stated by the *grammarians* that *prakṛti* and *pratyaya* convey their meaning as connected. That is to say, *prakṛti* provides its meanings as an adjective of the meaning of the *pratyaya* while *pratyaya* conveys the meaning as *viśiṣṭa*. Similarly, when the meaning of an earlier word that is in need of a relevant other meaning is conveyed, the other word conveys its meaning as connected with that meaning.

This explanation amounts to accepting *anvitābhidhāna* for the second word. One cannot derive the satisfaction that at least the first word is *abhihita* only, because, there is nothing such as earlier word or later word in a sentence. The same word is sometimes used earlier, sometimes later.

(i) अथ पूर्वपदार्थे साकाङ्क्षे अभिहिते यत् पदान्तरमुच्चरितं तत् तत्सम्बन्धितयैव स्वार्थमुपनयति प्रत्ययवत् ।

यथा प्रकृत्यर्थे पूर्वप्रतीते प्रत्ययः उच्चार्यमाणः स्वार्थं तद्विशिष्टमेवाभिधत्ते तथा पदान्तरमपि । तदुक्तम्—'प्रकृतिप्रत्ययौ प्रत्ययार्थं सह ब्रूतः' इति । प्रकृतिः स्वार्थं प्रत्ययार्थविशेषणत्वेन उपनयतीति प्रत्ययेन तदर्थमाहेत्यर्थः । तथा चोक्तम्—

नित्यं विशिष्ट एवार्थे प्रत्ययो यत् प्रयुज्यते ।
तत्पूर्वतरविज्ञात प्रकृत्यर्थविशेषणात् । इति

(ii) अङ्गीकृतं तर्हि द्वितीयस्य पदस्य अन्विताभिधानम् । प्रथमस्य तथापि नास्तीति चेन्न । वाक्ये पदानां प्रयोगक्रमनियमाभावात् । यदेव कदाचित् प्रथमं तदेव कदाचित् द्वितीयमिति सर्वपदानामेव अन्विताभिधानमापतितम् । (प्र० पं० ३९४-९५)

Moreover, *Abhihitatānvayavādin* does not accept *anvitābhidhāna* for *pratyaya*. For him *prakṛti* and *pratyaya* convey their meaning separately. He accepts it by applying the criteria of *anvaya* and *vyatireka* i.c., positive and negative verifications.

अभिहितान्वयवादीच प्रकृतिप्रत्यययोरपि अन्वयव्यतिरेकावधारित-व्यतिरिक्तशक्तिकयोः अभिहितान्वयमेव पदमिच्छति। तथाच–

प्रकृतिप्रत्ययौ ब्रूतः प्रत्ययार्थं सहेति यत् ।
भेदेनैवाभिधानेपि प्राधान्येन तथोच्यते ।
पाकं तु पचिरेवाह कर्तारं प्रत्ययोप्यकः ।
पाकयुक्तः पुनः कर्ता वाच्यो नैकस्य कस्यचित् ।
इत्याह । (प्र०पं० ३९५)

Further, if Pratyaya could Convey Anvita Why not other Words?

It cannot be argued that if *prakṛti* and *pratyaya* have *anvitābhidhāna* there cannot be any incompleteness of *anvaya* in the instance of *dvāram*, since, there are two to get connected with each other viz., *prakṛti* and *pratyaya*. Hence, there is no need of any *adhyāhāra*. If *dvāram* is taken as *prathamā*, then, there will not be two. Both *prakṛti* and *pratyaya* will convey *prātipādika* only. However, when these two yield different meanings as in other case-suffixes, there is a need of a verb and *adhyāhāra* is necessary.

किञ्च प्रत्ययश्चेत् अन्विताभिधायी, तदा तदविशेषात् पदानामपि अन्विताभिधायिता किमिति नाभ्युपेयते । किमर्धवैशसेन ।

यदि प्रकृतिप्रत्यययोरपि अन्विताभिधानमस्ति, न तर्हि द्वारमित्यत्रान्वितानुपपत्तिनिबन्धनाकाङ्क्षया विव्रियतां संव्रियतां वेत्यध्याहारः । उच्यते । द्वारमिति प्रथमेयं प्रातिपदिकार्थाव्यतिरिक्तार्थाभिधायिनी । तेनात्र केन सह अन्विताभिधानम् । व्यतिरिक्तार्थे प्रत्यये प्रविशेत्यादौ योऽध्याहारः सोऽभिहितार्थानुपपत्त्यैव विश्वजिदादिवदित्यदोषः । (प्र०पं० ३९५)

The Review of Bhāṭṭa's View of Lakṣaṇā of Sentence Meaning

The *Abhihitānvayavādins* resort to *lakṣaṇā* to obtain the sentence meaning. Śālikanātha examines the feasibility of this procedure. According to *abhihitānvayavāda* procedure the words convey only their meaning. These word meanings lead to sentence meaning by way of *lakṣaṇā*. At the word meaning stage these are not syntactically connected. These get syntactically connected at the stage of the sentence by *lakṣaṇā*. Since, the formation of the sentence meaning could be managed in this way, there is no need to say that words convey the connection also as their meaning.

वार्तिककारमिश्रास्तु लाक्षणिकान् सर्ववाक्यार्थानिच्छन्तः पदार्थानामन्वयावबोधशक्तिकल्पनां निराकुर्वन्ति । अनन्वितावस्थो हि पदार्थोऽभिहितोऽन्वितावस्थां स्वसम्बन्धिनीं लक्षयति । अवस्थाऽवस्थावतोः सम्बन्धात् । अवस्थावति अभिहिते भवत्येवहि अवस्थापि बुद्धिस्था । सर्वत्र च सम्बन्धिनि दृष्टे सम्बन्ध्यन्तरे बुद्धिः भवतीति दृष्टमेव । तदाहुः— वाक्यार्थो लक्ष्यमाणो हि सर्वत्रैवेति नः स्थितिः । (प्र०पं० ३९०)

There are certain difficulties to accept *lakṣaṇā* here. In the standard instance of *lakṣaṇā* viz., *gaṅgāyām ghoṣaḥ* it is found that the primary meaning of the word *gaṅgā* is given up and the secondary meaning viz., *tīra* ie the bank, is developed. However, in the case of word meanings leading to the sentence meaning by way *lakṣaṇā*, the word meanings are retained.

Further, in the instance *gaṅgāyām ghoṣaḥ, lakṣaṇā* for the word *gaṅgā* is resorted, because, its primary meaning cannot be connected with the meaning of the other word. *Ghoṣaḥ* refers to the fisherman's village and *gaṅgā* refers to the river. There cannot be a village on the water of the river. Therefore, there is *anvayānupapatti*. To avoid this, the word *gaṅgā* which refers to the river in its primary sense is taken as referring to the bank of the river in the secondary sense by *lakṣaṇā*. The fisherman's village can be on of the bank of the river and there is no difficulty in connecting the bank and the village. In the present case of word meanings leading to the sentence meaning, there is no difficulty in connecting these meanings. Therefore, the very ground of *lakṣaṇā* viz., *anvayānupapatti* is not found in this case.

(i) **अत्र अपरे ब्रुवते—नेयं लक्षणा स्वार्थापरित्यागात् । स्वार्थपरित्यागेन हि गङ्गादिषु लक्षणा दृष्टा- इति ।**

(ii) **कथं पुनरियं लक्षणा ?**

वाच्यस्यार्थस्य वाक्यार्थे सम्बन्धानुपपत्तितः ।
तत्सम्बन्धवशप्राप्तस्यान्वयाल्लक्षणोच्यते ।

गङ्गायां घोषः इत्यादिषु श्रौतस्य गङ्गापदार्थस्य वाक्यार्थेऽन्वयासम्भवात् तं परित्यज्य तत्सम्बन्धात् लब्धबुद्धिसंनिधेः कूलाद्यर्थस्य वाक्यार्थान्वयिताऽध्यवसीयते । अत एवाहुः अनुपपत्त्या सम्बन्धेन च लक्षणा भवतीति । (प्र०पं० ३९९)

The first difficulty could be solved by saying that it is not necessary to give up the primary meaning in all cases of *lakṣaṇā*. The primary meaning may be retained and an additional secondary meaning may be developed. A number of *pūrvamīmāmsā* instances such as *sṛṣṭīrupa dadhāti paurṇamāsīm yajate* etc., are quoted to substantiate this claim.

लक्षणीयवशेन हि क्वचित् स्वार्थस्य त्यागः सङ्ग्रहो वा । 'सृष्टीरुपदधाति' इति लक्षणायाः स्वीकारः गुणिनां तद्गणपठितानां सृष्टिशब्दरहितानामपि लक्ष्यमाणत्वात् ।

In the instance of *paurṇamāsīṃ yajate* the word *paurṇamāṣī* is taken in the sense of the whole group of *darśapūrṇmāsa yāgas* by *lakṣaṇā* including *praurṇamāsa.* Here, *lakṣaṇā* is resorted without giving up *svārtha* i.e., *paurṇamāsi.* When a group is taken as a meaning, one of the member of the group is not given up.

In the instance of *itaretarayoga dvandva* also additional items are included in the meaning without giving up the one that is mentioned. In *niṣādasthapati adhikaraṇa, lakṣaṇā* is resorted in the sense of genetive case without giving up the sense of *prakṛti.* Similarly, in the instance of *rathaghoṣa* and the hymn of *meghapataye megham lakṣaṇā* is resorted without giving up *svārtha.*

तथा 'पौर्णमासीं यजते' इत्येकवचनानुपपत्त्या पौर्णमासीशब्दो यागवचनो यागसमुदायलक्षणार्थः । न च समुदायपरिग्रहे समुदायित्यागः तदाश्रयत्वात् तस्य । तथा इतरेतरयोगद्वन्द्वे द्विवचनबहुवचनानुपपत्तेः अर्थान्तरसहितावस्था लक्षणया आश्रियते । न च अवस्थावत्परित्यागः । तथा निषादस्थपत्यधिकरणे पूर्वपक्षे षष्ठ्यर्थलक्षणा स्यादित्युच्यते । न तत्र प्रकृत्यर्थस्य त्यागोप्यापद्यते । तथा रथघोषेणेत्यत्र रथस्यापरित्यागः। तथा 'मेघपतये मेघमित्येकवचनान्तस्य मन्त्रस्य लक्षणया प्रकृतौ निवेशः । न च गुणिनोः अग्निषोमयोः तत्र हानमिति स्वार्थापरित्यागेपि युक्तैव लक्षणा । (प्र०पं० ३९८)

As regards the second difficulty viz., the very ground of *lakṣaṇā* viz., *anvayānupapatti,* is not found in the case of word meanings leading to the sentence meaning by way of *lakṣaṇā,* an alternate suggestion is made. Let there not be *lakṣaṇā* however, when action is conveyed, it also conveys that it has to get connected with some object, since these two are invariably associated. This leads to the formation of the sentence meaning.

This solution is also not workable. In this case, the comprehension of the sentence meaning will be the result of a *sāmānyato dṛṣṭa anumāna* but not verbal communication. Moreover, by *sāmānyato dṛṣṭa anumāna* the *sāmānya anvaya* is conveyed but not the connection of a specific action with a specific object. Therefore, investing the words or the word meanings with the power to denote the connection cannot be avoided.

अथ माभूदेषा लक्षणा किन्तु क्रिया अवगता कारकान्वयिनीं आत्मनो दशामवगमयति । अविनाभावादिति । उच्यते—शाब्दत्वं तावदित्थमपह्नुतमन्वयावगमस्य किन्तु सामान्यतो दृष्टानुमानगोचरताऽभ्युपगता भवति । तथा विशिष्टावगतिरनुपपद्यमाना निर्मूला आपद्यते । (प्र०पं० ३९९)

To overcome the difficulty of not obtaining the connection between the specific action and the specific objects etc., it is argued that since, no activity can proceed without the comprehension of the connection between the specific action and the objects, the specific connections are also comprehended. This may be granted in the case of *laukika* sentences to some extent. However, in the case of Vedic sentences, the necessity of comprehending the meaning itself may not be necessary as these could be utilised for *japa, pārāyaṇa* etc. Even in the case of *laukika* sentences, these becoming purposeless if the specific connections are not comprehended is not sufficient ground to establish the comprehension of specific connections.

अथ विशेषान्वयं विना व्यवहारानवकल्पनात् अनर्थकं शब्दोच्चारणमिति तदाश्रयणम् । एवमपि प्रेक्षापूर्वकारिणां सार्थकवाक्यमात्रप्रयोगिणां वचनाद् विशेषावगमः । वेदेतु आनर्थक्येन न भवितव्यमिति प्रमाणाभावात् न शक्यते विशेषान्वयोऽवगन्तुम् । न च लोकेपि आनर्थक्यमापाद्यते इत्येतावता कारणेन न उपायाद् विना विशेषान्वयाध्यवसानं युक्तम् । काममानर्थक्यम् । न पुनः सामान्यतोदृष्टस्य विशेषान्वयावसायिता ।

The contention that the connection based on the *ākāṅkṣā* etc., is comprehended through the elders' conversation itself is also not correct, since, the ways and means for such a connection have to be found out at that level also.

अथ आकाङ्क्षितसन्निहितयोग्यान्वयपरता वृद्धव्यवहारे पदानामवगतेति व्युत्पत्त्यनुसारेण विशेषान्वयावगमः । तन्न । तत्र वृद्धव्यवहारे एव तत्परता पदानां पदार्थानां वा उपायाभावेन कथं नाम निर्वहति? चिन्ताहि सा पदानां पदार्थानां वा शक्तिकल्पनां विना अनुपपन्नेति मन्यामहे । (प्र.पं. ३९९-४००)

The Arguments in Favour of Anvitābhidhāna

Between the two alternatives viz., (i) Investing the power of conveying connected sentence meaning in the words, (ii) Investing it in the word meanings, the former is reasonable on the following grounds.

(i) The words occur first and then only the word meanings occur. There is no reason to wait for conveying the connection until the word meanings are conveyed.

(ii) The fact of the words conveying the meaning is accepted by all. The only question is to include the connection also in the scope of the word meaning. However, in the case of word meaning conveying the connection, the very capacity to convey the connection has to be assigned. It is better to extend the scope of the meaning of the words to include the conveying of the connection also, than assigning a special power to the word meanings to convey the connection.

(iii) Words are employed in a sentence ultimately to convey the sentence meaning. Therefore, there is no reason to think of two tier arrangement of words conveying the word meanings, and the word meanings leading to the sentence meaning. It is better to say that the words convey the connected sentence meaning.

Śālikanātha argues that on these grounds, one may safely conclude that the words convey the connected meaning.

प्राथम्यादभिधातृत्वात् तात्पर्यावगमादपि ।
पदानामेव सा शक्तिः वरमभ्युपगम्यताम् ॥ ११॥

(i) प्रथमभावीनि पदानि अतिलङ्घ्य न अर्थेषु वाक्यार्थबोधनशक्तिराश्रयितुं युक्ता ।

(ii) किञ्च पदानि तावदभिधायकानीति निर्विवादम् । तेन तेषामभिधानशक्तिः सम्प्रतिपन्नैवेति तस्या एव अन्वयपर्यन्तता कल्पयितुं सुकरा ।

(iii) पदार्थानां तु बोधनशक्तिरेव कल्प्या । तेन धर्मिकल्पनातो वरं धर्मकल्पना लघीयसी इत्यन्विताभिधानशक्तिः पदानामेव कल्पयितुमुचिता । (प्र० पं० ४००)

In this connection, Śālikanātha makes an interesting point. The words are stated to convey the meanings. This meaning cannot be the mere object. The mere object was already introduced while learning the language. That will be brought to the mind as soon as the word referring to it is heard. Therefore, conveying only this much is not verbal communication. If its connection with the meaning of the other relevant word is also conveyed by the word, then, that will be verbal communication. For this reason also the connection has to be included in the scope of the meaning of a word.

किञ्च पदानि अभिधायकानीष्यन्ते तत्र यदि स्वरूपमात्रविषयामेव पदार्थबुद्धिमादध्युः तदाप्यभिधायकता हीयेत । तस्याः बुद्धेः सम्बन्धग्रहणसमयजातपदार्थबोधकसंस्कारोन्मेषप्रभवत्वात् । अवश्यं हि सम्बन्धस्मरणसिद्ध्यर्थं सम्बन्धिभूतार्थस्मरणसंस्कारोद्बोधोऽङ्गीकरणीयः । तस्मात् सम्बन्धग्रहणसमयानधिगतान्वितार्थप्रतिपादनाभ्युपगम एव शब्दानामभिधायकतेति तामङ्गीकुर्वता पदानामन्विताभिधायकता आश्रयणीया । (प्र०पं० ४००-१)

Some hold that the word only reminds the object referred to and does not communicate it. However, the object so reminded has to be connected with similarly reminded other objects, actions etc., by other words and therefore, the connection of these has to be conveyed by the words concerned only. This ultimately results in the communication of the connected sentence meaning by the words.

यस्तु 'पदमभ्यधिकाभावात् स्मारकात् न विशिष्यते' (श्लो०वा० अधि० ६ श्लो० १०७)

तथा—'भावनावचनस्तावत् तां स्मारयति लोकवत्' (श्लो०वा० अधि० ७ श्लो० २४८)

इति च आचार्यवचनदर्शनात् स्मारकतामेव पदानामभिधायकत्वमाह तं प्रत्याह तात्पर्योपगमादपीति ।

येनापि वादिना पदानां स्मारकत्वमेव पदार्थेषु अङ्गीकृतम् सोपि वाक्यार्थप्रतिपत्तिपरतां पदानामभ्युपेत्यैव । अन्यथा वाक्यार्थस्य अशाब्दत्वप्रसङ्गः । एवं चेत् पदानामेव साक्षात् वाक्यार्थबोधनशक्तिरस्तु किं परम्पराश्रयणेन । (प्र०पं० ४०१)

As stated earlier, those who state that the words convey the meaning and the meanings lead to the sentence meaning have to think of a three tier arrangement of denotative power viz., (i) A denotative power for the words to convey their meanings. (ii) Investing the word meanings with a power to convey the connection (iii) A denotative power that actually conveys the connection. Those who hold that the words only remind the objects referred to, have a two tier arrangement of the powers consisting of the second and the third power stated above. However, if we go by *anvitābhidhānavāda* viz., the words convey the connected meaning, to convey the sentence meaning only one denotative power is sufficient. In this case mere word meanings are not conveyed, nor they are pressed into service a second time to evolve the sentence meaning. In the very first instance the word in a sentence conveys the connected sentence meaning.

तेन पदार्थेषु पदानां स्मारकत्वातिरिक्तं येऽभिधायकत्वमाहुः तेषां शक्तित्रयकल्पना । (i) एका तावत् पदानामभिधायकत्वशक्तिः,

(ii) अपरा च पदार्थगतान्वयबोधनशक्त्याधानशक्तिः, (iii) पदार्थानां च अन्वयज्ञापनशक्तिरिति । स्मारकत्ववादिनस्तु अभिधानशक्तिं हित्वा शक्तिद्वयलाघवात् उक्तेनैव न्यायेन पदानामेव शक्तिकल्पनायाः उचितत्वात् अन्विताभिधायीनि पदानीतिस्थापितम् । प्र०पं० ४०१)

The Procedure of the Communication of Sentence Meaning According to Prābhākaras

The procedure of the communication of the sentence meaning is as follows: As soon as the words of a sentence are heard, the objects, action etc., referred to by these words are reminded. Then, he sorts out that the object, action etc., reminded by a certain word is suitable to be connected with the object, action etc., reminded by certain other word. This leads to his comprehension to the connected meaning. It is the connected meaning that is the meaning of a word but not merely the reminded object. The reminding of the object referred to is necessary as a first step, because, those who will not have learnt certain words and their references while learning the language, or have forgotten that certain words refer to certain objects will not be able to understand a sentence that contains such words, getting introduced to the fact that certain word refers to certain object, while learning the language and remembering it when this word is used in a sentence is a precondition for the comprehension of verbal communication. But merely remembering it, is not its comprehension by verbal communication. Comprehending it as a part of the structure of a sentence with the comprehension of the relevant other object similarly presented by another word is verbal communication. The presentation of the other object or action by the other word is a *sahakārin*. Before this *sahakārin* plays its role, the object referred to by the earlier word is just remembering of it. Its presentation as connected with the other is the meaning of it. Mere hearing of one word and remembering the object referred to by it, is not verbal comprehension.

पदजातं श्रुतं सर्वं स्मारिताऽनन्विवितार्थकम् ।
न्यायसम्पादितव्यक्ति पश्चाद् वाक्यार्थबोधकम् ।। १२।।

यस्तावदगृहीतसम्बन्धः यस्य च सम्बन्धग्रहणसंस्कारो नोत्पन्नः प्रध्वस्तो वा सः वाक्यार्थप्रतिपत्तौ नाधिक्रियते । यस्तु अनपभ्रष्टसम्बन्धग्रहणसंस्कारः स पदं श्रुत्वा नूनं तावदिदं स्मरति—इदमस्य आकाङ्क्षितसन्निहितयोग्यप्रतियोग्यन्वयस्य वाचकमिति । एवञ्च स्मरता स्मृतमेव अनन्वितमपि स्वरूपमन्वयभाजाम् । न चैकपदश्रवणे वाक्यार्थावगतिरिति कश्चित् मन्यते । (प्र०पं० ४०२)

In the procedure adopted by *Abhihitānvayavādins* also, each word separately communicates the meaning concerned, remembering the isolated meanings so communicated to evolve a connected meaning is inevitable. Therefore, the presentation of the objects referred to by the words to the mind and evolving the connection is common to both. The real question is, whether mere presentation of the object to the mind be considered as the meaning of the word without reference to its particular position and connection in the structure of the sentence, or the scope of the meaning is inclusive of its position and the connection in the structure of the sentence. The Prābhākaras go by the latter view.

अभिहितान्वयवादिनोपि हि यावत् पदान्तरमर्थान्तरं नोपस्थापयति तावदन्वयावगमो नास्ति । पदार्थस्य अन्वयावबोधिनः पदार्थान्तरापेक्षत्वात् । प्रतियोगिसापेक्षत्वादन्वयस्य । अतस्तन्मतेपि सर्वपदैः अनन्वितस्वार्थाः अभिधानीयाः । पश्चात् तेभ्यः सर्वेभ्यः स्मृत्यारूढेभ्यः वाक्यार्थप्रतिपत्तिः अङ्गीकरणीया । तदाहुः वार्तिककारमिश्राः

तेऽपि नैवास्मृता यस्माद् वाक्यार्थं गमयन्ति नः ।
तस्मात् तत्स्मरणेष्वेव संहतेषु प्रमाणता ।। (बृहट्टीका)

अत एव तत्र भवतः आचार्यस्य वाक्यलक्षणम् 'संहत्या अर्थमभिदधति पदानि वाक्यमिति' (शा०भा०बला-अधि पृ०२४ प्र०पं० ४०२)

Another point to be noted in connection with the *anvitābhidhāna* is that it is not only one word in a sentence that yields the connected sentence meaning but all words in a sentence duly connected with each other that yield a connected sentence meaning.

In case one insists that one word can do the job, he has to say which is that word. It cannot be the first word or a word that is considered as a central word. For instance in the passage *aruṇayā ekahāyanyā piṅgākṣyā somam krīṇāti* the word *aruṇayā* is the first word and the *somam* is the central word but still the entire sentence structure or sentence meaning cannot be managed merely by the meaning of one of these words.

येपि वादिनः एवमाहुः— एकमेव पदमन्विताभिधायकमस्तु । इतराणि पदानि प्रतियोगिसन्निधापनमात्र एव व्याप्रियन्ताम् । न चागृह्यमाणविशेषता प्राथम्येन प्रधानपदत्वेन वा विशेषग्रहणात् । अत एव चाहुः 'पदमाद्यं वा वाक्यम् प्रधानपदं वा वाक्यमिति । (वा०प०कां० 2 श्लो 2) तान् प्रत्याह सर्वमिति । प्रथमस्यैव स्याद् वाक्यता यदि सर्वपदार्थानां प्रथमपदार्थान्वितता स्यात् । न चायं नियमः । अरुणया एकहायन्या पिङ्गाक्ष्या सोमं क्रीणाति। (तै०स ६-१-९) इति क्रयमात्रान्वयित्वादारुण्यस्य । वाक्ये पदानामानुपूर्व्यनियमाभावात् । कदाचित् तदेव सदन्विताभिधायकम्, अन्यदा नेति न युक्तम् । तथा प्रधानपदस्यापि वाक्यत्वमयुक्तम् । सोमपदार्थेन सह सर्वेषामनन्वयात् । यद्यपि आरुण्यादीनां सर्वेषां सोमं प्रति ऐदमर्थ्यमस्ति तथापि अस्मिन् वाक्ये क्रय एव आरुण्यादीनामैदमर्थ्येन क्रियाकारकभावेन चान्वयः । क्रयद्वारेण सोमं प्रति ऐदमर्थ्यमात्रम् ।

It cannot also be said that the word that conveys the central item is the central word, because, it goes on changing in different sentences. In the instance *agnihotram juhoti* the *homa* conveyed by the verb is intended to be enjoined. In the sentence *dadhnā juhoti* it is a subordinate item i.e., *dadhi,* that is intended to be enjoined, therefore, no particular word can be picked up uniformly as central word to yield the sentence meaning. Therefore, all the words in a sentence connected with each other in a suitable way yield the sentence meaning.

अथ यत्प्रतिपादनपरं वाक्यं तत् प्रधानमित्युच्यते । इह तु क्रय एव सर्वकर्मकरणावच्छिन्नः प्रतिपाद्यते । तेन क्रीणातीत्येव प्रधानं पदम् तदन्वयिताच सर्वेषामारुण्यादीनामिति ।

अत्रोच्यते वाक्यस्य यत् तावत् तात्पर्यं तन्न व्यवस्थितम् । क्वचिदाख्यातपरत्वमेव 'अग्निहोत्रं जुहोतीति' । क्वचिद् गुणविधिपरत्वं 'दध्ना जुहोतीति' । तेन प्रधानपदत्वस्यापि सर्वेषां पदानां सम्भवात् सर्वेषामेव अन्विताभिधानशक्तिराश्रयणीया । तथा सति यत्रापि गुणपरत्वं तत्रापि क्लृप्तशक्तिकतया तदन्विताभिधायकत्वमविरुद्धम् । पदार्थेष्वपि च एतत् तुल्यमेव । (प्र०पं० ४०३)

Two Other Objections Against Anvitābhidhāna are Cleared

Two more objections are raised against *anvitābhidhāna* and answered. These are: (1) If each word conveys its meaning as connected with the meaning of the other relevant word, then, it amounts to saying that two words connected with each other convey the same meaning. For instance, in the sentence *gām ānaya* the word *gām* conveys *ānayanāvita gau* and the word *gau* conveys *gavānvita ānayana,* in effect the two words convey one and the same, and consequently have to be treated as synonyms. This objection is not valid. The two items stated viz., *ānayanvita gau* and *gavānvita ānayana* are not one and the same.

नन्वेवं गामानयेत्यादौ परस्परपर्यायता शब्दानां स्यात् । यथा गामित्यनेन आनयत्यन्विताभिधानम् तथा 'आनय' इत्यनेनापि गवान्विताभिधान-मिति । उच्यते– द्वावेतावर्थौ यदानयनान्वितं गोत्वम्, गवान्वितञ्च आनायन-मिति । तेन एकैकेन एकैकस्यार्थस्याभिधानात् कुतः पर्यायत्वप्रसङ्गः । पदार्थेष्वपि च एतत् समानम् ।

The second objection is, in the passage *Aruṇayā* ekahāyanyā etc., each word *aruṇā, ekahāyani* etc., have to get connected with *krīṇāti* separately, this results in taking this passage as split into many sentences. Splitting one sentence into many sentences is not desirable. This objection is answered by saying that the technique of *tantra* is utilised in organising this sentence. *Anekoddeśena sakridanusthāna* is *tantra*. Here, *aruṇā, ekahāyani* etc., merely get connected with *krināti* through *gau* in one sentence.

ननु क्रीणात्यर्थस्य आरुण्याद्यनेकार्थान्विताभिधानात् आवृत्तिलक्षणो वाक्यभेदः स्यात् । न । तन्त्रोच्चारणात् । वैरूप्ये च तन्त्रतानुपपत्तेः वाक्यभेदः स्यात् ।

Utilisation of Worldly Experience to Determine the Role of Words in Anvitābhidhāna

Another important point to be noted in connection with *anvitābhidhāna* is, the role of various words in a sentence as subject, predicate, principal, subordinate etc., has to be determined by worldly experience and the guidelines. It is with the help of that the roles played by the objects referred to by the words have to be identified and then, the suitable connection among them has to be comprehended as the meaning conveyed by these words. That is why the Mīmāmsā śāstra that codified these guidelines is considered as an aid to understand the import of Vedic passages. It is true that in the day-to day use of the language, one will not take the trouble of identifying the role etc., to comprehend the meaning of the sentences. This is, because, they do not need to go into these subtlities for understanding the sentences in day-to-day usage. However, those who have to analyse the *śāstric* discourse do need it.

न्यायसम्पादितव्यक्तीति किमिदम् ? यावत् न्यायेन वचनव्यक्तिः न सम्पाद्यते तावत् पदजातं वाक्यार्थसम्पादकं न भवति । लोकव्यवहारवर्तिभिः न्यायैः यावत् इदं विधेयम्, इदमनुवाद्यम्, इदं प्रधानम्, इदं गुणभूतम्, इदं विवक्षितम्, इदमविवक्षितमित्यादि न सम्प्रधार्यते तावद् न क्वचिद् वेदवाक्यार्थोऽवबुध्यते । तदुक्तं वार्तिककारमिश्रैः

तावदेवहि सन्देहो वेदवाक्ये श्रुतेः भवेत् ।
यावन्नवचनव्यक्तिः तस्य स्पष्टाऽवधार्यते
ज्ञात्वा तु वचनव्यक्तिं मीमांसान्यायकातराः ।
प्रलीयन्ते समस्ताश्च वेदवाक्यार्थसंशयाः । (इति)

अत एव मीमांसायाः वेदवाक्यार्थप्रतिपत्तौ इतिकर्तव्यतात्वम् । तदुक्तं तैरेव

धर्मे प्रमीयमाणेहि वेदेन करणात्मना ।
इतिकर्तव्यताभागं मीमांसा पूरयिष्यति ।। (बृहट्टीका)

ननु लोके द्रागेव वाक्यार्थावगतिः अत्यन्ताभ्यस्तेषु वाक्येषु स्यादेवम् । अदृष्टार्थेषु स्मृत्यादिवाक्येषु लोकेपि नानाविधविवादोत्त्थानात् कुतो द्रागेवार्थनिश्चयः ।

अपि च कारणाभावेनापि लोकस्यायं विवेको नास्ति । तदुक्तम्–

बहुजातिगुणद्रव्यकर्मभेदावलम्बिनः ।
प्रत्ययान् सहसा जातान् श्रौतलाक्षणिकात्मकान् ।
न लोकः कारणाभावान्निर्धारयितुमर्हति ।
बलाबलादिसिद्ध्यर्थं वाक्यज्ञास्तु विचिन्वते ।

A point to be noted in respect of *gauṇa* and *lākṣaṇika* meanings is that the *gauṇa* or *lākṣaṇika* words such as *simḥa* and *tīra* are not *anvitābhidhāyaka* but the very *vācaka* word whose *vācyārtha* is given up and *gauṇārtha* or *lākṣyārtha* is taken up is *anvitābhidhāyaka.* This word does not convey its *vācyārtha* that is remembered but conveys the *gauṇa* or *lākṣaṇika* meaning as connected with the meaning of the relevant other word. All words shall not be *lākṣaṇika* or *gauṇa* in a sentence.

यच्चेदं सर्वपदानामन्विताभिधायित्वमुच्यते तत् सर्वेषु श्रौतार्थेषु पदेषु । लाक्षणिकगौणार्थपदप्रयोगे तु यदेव तत्र श्रौतार्थं पदम्, तदेव अन्विताभिधायकम्, इतरत्तु पदं प्रतियोगिसन्निधापनपरमेव । तत्र वाचकत्व

शक्त्यनवधारणात् स्वार्थस्यापि तत् तदानीमवाचकम् । अन्वयायोग्यत्वात् । किन्तु तदर्थेन स्मृतेन यत् स्वसम्बन्धि स्वसदृशं वा स्वयमन्वययोग्यमुपस्थाप्यते तेन अन्वितं श्रौतार्थमेव पदं स्वार्थमभिधत्ते इति दर्शनरहस्यमिदम् । न च सर्वपदान्येव लाक्षणिकानि गौणानि वा वाक्ये सम्भवन्तीति निरवद्यम् । (प्र०पं० ४०५)

Presentation of the Object to the Mind when the word is heard

In respect of the procedure of the comprehension of *anvita* meaning it was stated earlier that as soon as a word is heard the object referred to by it is presented to the mind, then its connection with the meaning of the relevant other word is conveyed as its meaning. Just as by seeing an object the word that refers to it is reminded, when a word is heard, the object referred by it is reminded. This reminded object along with the connection it has with the meaning of the other word forms the meaning of this word. There is no difficulty in the core object being reminded when the word referring to it is heard. Just as the core object is presented in the *nirvikalpaka* experience, here also the core object is presented to the mind. The Bhāṭṭas also have to agree to it.

कथं पुनः अन्विताभिधायिना पदेन स्वरूपमात्रं स्मारयितुं शक्यमित्याह–

अन्वितस्याभिधानेपि स्वरूपं विद्यते सदा ।
तेन स्वरूपमात्रेपि शब्दो जनयति स्मृतिम् ।

एवं तावत् सम्बन्धगहणान्तर्गतस्वरूपमुक्तम् । सम्प्रति स्वरूपमात्रमपि पदादेव नानुपपन्नमित्याह–

यथार्थेना प्रमाणेन स्वपदं स्मार्यते क्वचित् ।
पदेनाप्यप्रमाणेन तथार्थस्मृतिरिष्यते ॥ २४॥

नहि यत् प्रमाणं तदेव स्मरणकारणम् । अप्रमाणमेव तत् । यस्य तु येन सह कदाचित् प्रत्यासत्तिः प्रतीतपूर्वा सा तत्र संस्कारोब्दोधद्वारेण शक्नोत्येव स्मृतिं जनयितुम् । अस्ति च स्वरूपस्यापि तदभिधेयान्तर्गत्या शब्देन प्रतीतिरिति शक्नोति तत्रापि शब्दस्मृतिं जनयितुम्, अर्थवत् । यथानिर्विकल्पकदशाप्रतीतमर्थस्वरूपमात्रमनभिधेयमपि शब्दं स्मारयति तथा शब्दोपि अर्थमिति किमनुपपन्नम् । एतेन पदोच्चारणानन्तरं पदार्थस्वरूप प्रतीतिः समर्थिता । अभिहितान्वयवादिनोऽपि सा न प्रमाणम् । अभ्यधिकार्थपरिच्छेदाभावात् । अनधिगतार्थगन्तृ प्रमाणमिति सिद्धान्ताभ्युपगमात् । तदुक्तम्–

सर्वस्यानुपलब्धेऽर्थे प्रामाण्यं स्मृतिरन्यथा (श्लो०वा० औ०सू०श्लो० 11)

अत एव स्मृतिरियम् । यदि पुनः स्मृतिरेषा नाभ्युपेयेत तदा प्रमाणस्मृति-संशय-विपर्ययेभ्यः प्रतिपत्त्यन्तरानभ्युपगमात् पदात् पदार्थप्रतीतिः क्वान्तर्भाव्यतामिति वाच्यम् । अत एव अभिहितान्वयवादेपि स्मारकत्वमेव अस्मभ्यं रोचते । (प्रं०पं० ४०६)

Rejection of the Contingency of Vākyabheda

Here a question is raised. When a word is heard not only the object referred to by it is reminded but many other associated aspects of the object are also likely to be reminded. This means that in *anvitābhidhāna* not only that object is to be involved but one or more of these aspects also may have to be involved. Consequently, the very sentence meaning will be distorted. This objection is not valid. When a word is heard only that object or aspect of the object referred to by it is reminded which is relevant to be connected in the present sentence. If the other associated aspects are brought into the structure and the meaning of the sentence, it will result in more than one sentence or splitting of a sentence into many sentences i.e., *vākyabheda*, which is not desirable.

Śālikanātha rejects this objection by pointing out that according to *anvitābhidhāna* theory the meaning of a word gets connected with only that meaning of a relevant other word with which it is intended to get connected. It does not seek connection with any other meaning or aspect of meaning of that word. Therefore, there is no room for *vākyabheda*. He quotes a number of Vedic instances to show how *vākyabhedha* is carefully avoided in interpreting Vedic passages.

अत्र कश्चिदाह–यदि स्मृतिसन्निहितमाश्रित्यान्विताभिधानं पदैः क्रियते तदा स्मरणस्य प्रत्यासत्तिनिबन्धनत्वात् अनेकेषां च अर्थानां प्रत्यासत्तिसम्भावात् तेषु स्मृतिसन्निहितेषु अगृह्यमाण विशेषत्वात् 'उखायां पचतीति नोखा पचत्यर्थान्वितैव केवला अभिधीयेत। साहि कुलालाद्यन्वितापि प्रतिपन्नैवेति स्मरणात् तदन्वितापि उखा अभिधीयेत । तथा पचत्यर्थोऽपि पिष्टकादिकरणकोऽवगतः इति तत्स्मरणात् न ओदनान्वित एवाभिधीयेत । अभिहितान्वयवादेतु नायं दोषः एकैकस्यार्थस्य अभिधेयत्वादिति । (प्र० पं० ४०७)

(ii) **अपि च अन्वितार्थवादिन एवेदं प्रतिनियतान्वयित्वमुपपद्यते यत्पदार्थान्तरान्वयिताभिधायकतया स्मार्यते। तदन्वितस्यैव वृद्धव्यवहारे वाच्यत्वदर्शनात् । (प्र० पं० ४०७-८)**

(iii) **अपि च ज्ञातं तावदेतत् यदनेन पदेन अयमर्थो वाच्य इति । यदि अन्येनापि अन्विताभिधानं स्यात् तदा वाक्यभेदो भवेत् । न चासौ एकवाक्यत्वसम्भवे न्याय्यः । तदुक्तम्– सम्भवत्येकवाक्यत्वे वाक्यभेदस्तु नेष्यते। (श्लो० वा० प्र० सू० श्लो ९) (प्र० पं० ४०८)**

Further, among the objects or the aspects of the object reminded when the relevant one is connected, the *ākāṅkṣā* is satisfied. Then, the others have to be ignored.

In spite of all these clarifications, if it is insisted that the word conveys the object referred to by it not by reminding it but by verbal communication only, then we will not hesitate to assign two denotative powers to the word, one to convey the object, the other to convey its connection with the meaning of the relevant other word. What the Prābhākaras insist upon is, it is the word that conveys connection, that is to say, the connected sentence meaning but not the isolated word meanings.

Śālikanātha explains the remark in the *Ṣābarabhāṣya* viz., *padani svam svam artham abhidhāya nivṛttavyāpārāṇi* etc., in favour of *anvitābhidhāna.* According to him, this passage informs us that the words convey the connected meaning. These do not convey the connection separately, since the connection is already included in the word meaning. When the connected meaning is conveyed, the connection is conveyed without any additional denotative power to convey the connection. He illustrates this by the example of *jāti* and *vyakti.* The words convey *jāti*, since without the comprehension of *vyakti*, the *jāti* cannot be comprehended the *vyakti* is also comprehended. No separate denotative power is required to convey the *vyakti.* In the present case also, since *anvita* cannot be comprehended without the comprehension of *anvaya* the *anvaya* is also comprehended when *anvita* is conveyed. However, the denotative power of the word conveys *anvita* making *anvaya* an integral part of it. There is an important difference between the example of *jāti* and *vyakti*, and *anvita* and *anvaya.* The *jāti* and *vyakti* are separate. But the *anvaya* and *anvita* are not totally separate. Therefore, the example should be taken into account only for the purpose of comprehension of a related object on the comprehension of an object that is conveyed by a word.

कथं तर्हीदं भाष्यम् 'पदानिही' त्यादि । तत्राह--

अन्वितेषु पदैरेवं बोध्यमानेषु शक्तिभिः ।
अन्वयार्थोगृहीतत्वात् नान्यां शक्तिमपेक्षते ॥ १६ ॥

आशङ्कितोत्तरमिदं भाष्यम् । किमाशङ्कितम्? यद्यन्विताभिधायीनि पदानि तर्हि नान्वयाभिधायीनि । तत्सिद्ध्यर्थं पदानां शक्त्यन्तरं कल्पनीयमिति । अत्रेदमुत्तरम्–यत् पदमन्विताभिधायकं तदन्वयाभिधायकमेव । अन्वितएवासौ नाभिहितः स्यात् । अन्वितरूपेण अर्थेन अन्वयः स्वीकृतः तं विना तदसम्भवादिति नापरा पदानां तद्विषया शक्तिः कल्पनीया ।

Śālikanātha discusses another question before he closes his presentation of *anvitābhidhānavāda.* The question whether the *anvita* meaning conveyed is *sāmānyānvitā* or *viśeṣānvitā* is raised. He favours *viśeṣānvita* procedure, for the reasons: (1) Mere *sāmānyānvaya* cannot yield the specific sentence meaning (2) *ākāṅkṣa, sannidhi,* and *yogyatā* convey only the *viśeṣānvyaya,* since these can be only with reference to specific items.

He concludes his discussion compactly summarising the points made by him as follows:

(i) A sentence by itself cannot convey the sentence meaning without involving a reference to words, word meanings, connection etc.

(ii) The last syllable of sentence accompanied by the impression of previous syllable also cannot convey the sentence meaning.

(iii) Merely a group of words not connected mutually, the first word or the central word, mere verb, or isolated word meanings, cannot convey the sentence meaning.

(iv) *Sāmanya anvita* words also cannot convey the sentence meaning.

(v) The words that convey the connected meanings with the meaning of the relevant other word specifically convey the sentence meaning. In fact such connected word meanings constitute the sentence meaning.

वाक्यमेकं न निर्भागं वाक्यान्त्यो वर्ण एव वा ।
पदवृन्दं स्मृतिस्थंवा प्रथमं पदमेव वा ।।
आख्यातपदमात्रं वा पदार्थां वाप्यनन्विताः ।
सामान्यान्वयबोधे वा हेतुर्वाक्यार्थबोधने ।।
पदान्येव समर्थानि वाक्यार्थस्यावबोधने ।
विशेषान्वयवादीनि भागशो भागशालिनः ।।

Section – II

Vākyārthamātṛkā – II

Kārya - The Import of Vedic Injunction

After establishing *anvitābhidhāna*, the central theme viz., *kārya*, is the import of a Vedic injunction, is taken up for discussion.

An Objection Against the Theory that the Vedic Injunction Conveys the Kārya

Right at the start, this concept of *kārya* i.e., *apūrva*, has to overcome a serious difficulty. To comprehend the *kārya i.e., apūrva*, as conveyed by the Vedic injunction, the *vācya-vācaka bhāva* relation between the Vedic injunction and the *kārya* has to be grasped. The *vācya-vācaka bhāva* relation is normally grasped through the elders' conversation. However, *kārya i.e., apūrva,* is conveyed only by the Vedic injunction. In the absence of the knowledge of *kārya* before it is conveyed by the Vedic injunction, it is not brought into the elders' conversation and no *vācya-vācakabhāva* relation between the Vedic injunction and *kārya* is understood. Therefore, it cannot be comprehended as the import of the Vedic injunction.

उपोद्धातभूतमन्विताभिधानं प्रसाध्य अपूर्वं कार्यं वेदवाक्यानामर्थः इति साधयितुकामः पूर्वपक्षं तावदाह—

ननु व्युत्पत्त्यपेक्षेषु शब्देष्वर्थाभिधायिषु ।
कथं मानान्तरावेद्यं कार्यमाहुः लिङादयः ॥

अपूर्वाधिकरणे (मी०द० २-१-२) लिङ्गाद्यर्थो अपूर्वमित्युक्तम् । प्रमाणान्तरायोग्यं च अपूर्वमिष्यते । यच्च प्रमाणान्तरायोग्यं तत्र सम्बन्धग्रहणमशक्यम् । सम्बन्धिग्रहणपूर्वकत्वात् तस्य । विशिष्टार्थव्यवहारदर्शनेन हि तद्विषया शक्तिरनुमीयते । तदेव च सम्बन्धग्रहणम् । यच्च न प्रतीयते न तद्विषयो व्यवहारोऽवसीयते । तदनवसाये च न तद्विषया बुद्धिरनुमीयते । तदननुमाने च कुतः शब्दस्य शक्तिः कल्प्यते । अपूर्वं च न प्रमाणान्तरगोचरः । (प्र०पं० ४१७)

It cannot be argued that the very Vedic injunction conveys the *vācyavācakabhāva* relation also between itself and its import i.e., *kārya*. This will result in reciprocal dependency. The fact of *kārya* being the import of the Vedic injunction can be granted if the denotative power to convey it is granted to Vedic injunction, and the power to denote *kārya* can be granted if the *kārya* is granted to be the import.

न च शब्दादेव तदवगम्य सम्बन्धावधारणम्, इतरेतराश्रयप्रसङ्गात् । अवसितशक्तेः अवबोधकत्वात् । अवबोधकत्वादेव शक्त्यवगमात् । (प्र०पं० ४१७)

It cannot also be argued that the Vedic injunctions have such a special capacity. The normal procedure of conveying an action by an injunction can be worked out in the case of Vedic injunction also. Hence, the so-called special concept of *kārya i.e., apūrva*, is merely a wishful thinking. Since the very concept of *kārya* is not tenable, the question of all other words in the sentence conveying the meaning as connected with it does not arise.

स्यान्मतम् । लिङादेः शब्दस्य अयं महिमा, यदनवसितशक्तिरपि स्वार्थमवगमयतीति । तदिदमप्रमाणम् । क्रियामात्रावबोधकत्वाङ्गीकारेण लिङादेः लोकतो व्युत्पत्तिसम्भवे शब्दान्तरवैलक्षण्येन अगृहीतसम्बन्धस्यैव वाचकत्वकल्पनानुपपत्तेः ।

वेदवाक्यादपूर्वकार्यावगतेः एवं कल्प्यते इति चेत् । न । तस्या एव असिद्धत्वात् । क्रियैव कार्यतया वेदवाक्येभ्यः अवगम्यते इति व्युत्पत्तिबलेन अप्रामाणिकं मनोरथमात्रविजृम्भितं तु अपूर्वं कार्यं प्रतीयत इति । तथा च कथं तद्वाक्यार्थः । अभिधेय एवार्थो भवति वाक्यार्थः ॥

एवं च–

शब्दान्तराण्यपि कथं तेन अदृष्टेन कुत्रचित् ।
वदिष्यन्त्यन्वितं स्वार्थं व्युत्पत्तिपथदूरगम् ।

तस्मिन्न प्रतीयमाने तदन्वितस्य अप्रतीतेः । तत्र सम्बन्धावधारणानुपपत्तेः दूरनिरस्तं शब्दान्तराणां तदन्वितस्वार्थबोधकत्वमिति । (प्र०पं०४१७-१८)

The Fact of a Vedic Injunction Conveying Kārya could be Established through Elders' Conversation

The above objection against the concept of *kārya* is answered by fully analysing the process of *śaktigraha* through the elders' conversation.

When a young boy listens to the statement of the eldest person to an elder person 'O, Chaitra! bring water' and the elder person proceeds to bring it, the boy understands that the elder person proceeded to bring water by comprehending the import of the statement made by the eldest person. He further understands that the elder person understood that which led him to proceed to act. He understood this through the statement. I sometimes understand what prompts me to act by other means also. However, when one proceeds to act on hearing a statement, it is the statement that prompts to act. Therefore, the statements have the capacity to prompt. This is *kārya* and this is conveyed by the injunction. Thus, the *śaktigraha* of *kārya* arises from the elders' conversation by a reflection on the very process of *śaktigraha*. Therefore, the objection raised above against *kārya* to be the import of the Vedic injunction does not hold good. It is *kārya* that is conveyed by the Vedic injunction and it prompts the *niyojya* to accomplish it.

राद्धान्तमुपक्रमते—

(i) अत्रोच्यते यदा नाम वृद्धेनैकेन भाषिते ।
जलं चैत्राहरस्वेति चैत्र आहरते जलम् ॥ ३ ॥
तदा व्युत्पित्समानोऽन्यः तत्रैवमवगच्छति ।
बुद्धिपूर्वा ममैवास्य प्रवृत्तिरियमीदृशी ॥

(ii) लिङादियुक्तवाक्यश्रवणानन्तरं वृद्धस्य विशिष्टार्थविषयां प्रवृत्तिं दृष्ट्वा व्युत्पित्समानो बालः एवमाकलयति-

(a) 'अस्य प्रवृत्तिः मद्वद् बुद्धिपूर्विका' इति (b) 'मम मानान्तरेण यद्विषया सा बुद्धिः प्रवृत्तिहेतुभूता तद्वस्तु अनेन शब्देन बोध्यते ।

इति शब्दस्य प्रवृत्तिहेतुभूतार्थावबोधकतामवधारयति । (प्र०पं० ४१८)

The points stated above are put in syllogistic form as follows:

1. वृद्धस्य स्वतन्त्रा प्रवृत्तिः बुद्धिपूर्विका स्वतन्त्रप्रवृत्तित्वात् मदीयस्वतन्त्रप्रवृत्तिवत् ।

2. वृद्धस्य प्रवृत्तिहेतुभूता बुद्धिः यद्विषया मम प्रवृत्तिहेतुभूता तद्विषयैव प्रवृत्तिहेतुभूतबुद्धित्वात् मदीयप्रवृत्तिहेतुभूतबुद्धिवत् । (प्र०पं० ४१८)

Rejection of the Bhāṭṭa's Scheme of the Import of a Vedic Injunction

After setting his view in favour of *kārya*, śālikanātha reviews the view of the Bhāṭṭas viz., *śābdībhāvana* is the import of an injunction.

Before this he disposes two other views as insignificant. These are: (i) The view that the very injunctive suffix prompts action but not its import, (ii) An intermediary power of the injunctive suffix prompts action. Both these views are not correct, since, the learner does not envisage these as the prompting factors.

तेन शब्द एव प्रवृत्तिहेतुभूतो विधिः, तद्व्यापारो वेति निरस्तम् । तयोः बालेन आत्मनि प्रवृत्तिकारणत्वेन अदर्शनात् । (प्र०पं० ४१९)

These two views are quite childish. Therefore, do not deserve a detailed review. If the very injunctive suffix were to prompt without the comprehension of its import, then every one who hears it would have proceeded to act. This does not happen. Those who think of an intermediary power for the injunctive suffix will have to be convinced of its stupidity by the God alone.

अतिमन्दतया च इमौ पक्षौ न साक्षादुपन्यस्य निरस्तौ । तथाहि— लिङादि शब्दस्वरूपस्य प्रवर्तकत्वे सर्व एव तच्छ्राविणो नियमेन प्रवर्तेरन् । न चैवं दृश्यते कस्यचित् कदाचित् प्रवृत्तेः ।

लिङादिव्यापारस्य प्रवृत्तिहेतुत्वाश्रयणं देवाः प्रतिपद्यन्ताम् । पिशितचक्षुषो मानुषा वयं न इयतीं प्रमाणभूमिमवगाहितुं क्षमाः । (प्र०पं० ४१९)

The Bhāṭṭas hold the view that a Vedic injunctive suffix conveys *śābdībhāvanā.* This is also called *pravartanā* or *preraṇā.* Its knowledge leads to *ārthībhāvanā* i.e., *pravṛtti.* The knowledge of *śābdībhāvanā* is *karaṇa* i.e., the instrument, while *ārthībhāvanā* is *bhāvya* i.e., the result. *Prāśastyajñāna conveyed* by *arthavāda* is an aid. *Śābdībhāvanā* is of the nature of prompting for the action and *ārthībhāvanā* is the initiative. The injunction *svādhyāyo adhyetavyaḥ* prompts to undertake initiative to implement all Vedic injunctions in a general way, and all other Vedic injunctions prompt to undertake the specific items enjoined. Thus, it is *śābdībhāvanā* that is the import of the Vedic injunction.

The *ārthībhāvanā* is also conveyed by the injunctive suffix. *Yāga* is its *karaṇa, svarga* is *bhāvya,* and the other sacrificial details are *itikartavyatā.*

केयं शब्दभावना? उच्यते—लिङादिव्यापाररूपा पुरुषप्रवृत्तिभ-वनानुकूला स्वज्ञानकरणिका अर्थवादोदितप्राशस्त्यलक्षणेतिकर्तव्यता योगिनी प्रेरणात्मिका कल्प्यते ।

स्वाध्यायाध्ययनविधिना हि सर्वे विधायकाः स्वाध्यायपदोपात्तश्चात्मा नियुज्यन्ते भावयेदिति (त०वा०पृ० १४४) तत्र किमित्यपेक्षायां पुरुषप्रवृत्तिः सम्बद्ध्यते । केनेत्याकाङ्क्षायां विधिज्ञानमेव योग्यतया करणत्वेन अङ्गीक्रियते । ज्ञाता हि शाब्दभावना प्रवृत्तिं प्रसूते । योग्यतयैव अर्थवादसमुत्त्थप्राशस्त्य ज्ञानमितिकर्तव्यतांशे निविशते । अवसीदन्ती हि विधिशक्तिः प्राशस्त्यज्ञानेन उत्तम्यते । तस्याश्च पुरूषव्यापाररूपा स्वर्गादिभाव्यावच्छिन्नभावार्थकरणिका श्रौतस्मार्ताचारप्राप्तपदार्थ जनितकरणोपकारवती अर्थभावना समानप्रत्ययवाच्या विषयभूता । (प्र०पं० ४२०)

The view of the Bhāṭṭas is not acceptable to the Prābhākaras. The Prābhākaras argue that there is no evidence to hold that the injunctive suffix conveys *preraṇā* or *pravartanā.* The *pravṛtti* that follows the comprehension of injunction cannot be the ground to say that the *pravartanā* is conveyed by the injunctive suffix, since, *pravṛtti* does not follow *pravartanā* in other instances. The injunctive suffix itself cannot be the evidence since the *vācyavācakabhāva* between the injunctive suffix and *preraṇā* is yet to be established.

तन्न । लिङादेः तादृशो व्यापारो विद्यत इत्यत्र न किञ्चन प्रमाणम् । लिङादिशब्दानन्तरभाविनी पुरुषप्रवृत्तिरेव प्रमाणमिति चेत् । न । तन्निबन्धनत्वेन प्रवृत्तेरन्यत्र अदृष्टत्वात् । यन्निबन्धनाहि प्रवृत्तिः दृष्टा तदेव तां दृष्ट्वा शक्यमनुमातुम् न पुनः अप्रतिपन्न पूर्वकारणभावः शब्दव्यापार विशेषः ।

अथ लिङादिशब्द एव प्रमाणमिति साहसम् । अगृहीतसम्बन्धस्य अवाचकत्वात् । अनवधारिते सम्बन्धिनि सम्बन्धबोधवैधुर्यात् । (प्र०पं० ४२०)

The idea that *svādhyāya vidhi* prompts to undertake the initiative to implement all other Vedic injunctions also does not hold good. The persons only can be prompted to take the initiative but not the injunctions.

Further, *śābdabhāvanā* proceeds on its own. Therefore, the very idea of prompting or not prompting does not work in its case. It cannot also be said that the persons are not prompted for initiative but only enabled to comprehend the import of the *śābdibhāvanā.*

कथं च तत्र स्वाध्यायाध्ययनविधिना सर्वे विधायकाः स्वात्मा च विनियुज्यन्ते । पुरुषं विधिः अर्थभावनायां प्रेरयति । यश्च येन प्रेर्यते स तेन नियुज्यते । न च अचेतनानां विधीनां नियोजकत्वमपि सम्भवति ।

अथ न नियोज्यन्ते तदप्यनुपपन्नम् । शब्दभावनासु सर्वशब्दानां स्वत एव कर्तृत्वात् विनियोगानपेक्षणात् । अथ न पुरुषाः प्रेरणे विनियुज्यन्ते किन्तु अर्थावबोधने तदपि न घटते तत्रापि नियोज्यानपेक्षायाः तुल्यत्वात् (प्र०पं० ४२०-२१)

Further, *adhyayana vidhi* is only a *samskāravidhi.* A *samskāravidhi* will not prompt any initiative or action on the part of a *samskārya.*

अध्ययनविधेश्च अक्षर संस्काररूपाध्ययनविधायकत्वाभ्युपगमात् । संस्कारविधिश्च न संस्कारं विनियुङ्क्ते (प्र०पं० ४२१)

The idea that *ārthībhāvanā* is the *bhāvya* of *śābdibhāvanā*, is also not acceptable to the Prābhākaras. It cannot be a *bhāvya* merely on the ground that it follows *śābdībhāvanā.* In this case it will not require any *karaṇa. Vidhijñāna* will cease to be its karaṇa.

कथं पुरुषप्रवृत्तिः तस्याः भाव्यम् । न तावदनन्तरनिष्पत्तेः । विधिज्ञानस्य करणत्वाभावप्रसङ्गात् । (प्र०पं० ४२१)

In case *ārthībhāvanā* is considered the result of *śābdībhāvanā*, it amounts to saying that it is a result of an action. No action needs a *karaṇa* to lead to its result.

क्रियाफलं हि तदा पुरुषप्रवृत्तिः स्यात् न च क्रिया स्वफलप्रसवाय करणमपेक्षते । (प्र०पं० ४२१)

It cannot be said that the injunctive suffix produces comprehension of its import, takes it as *karaṇa* and then conveys *preraṇā.* This is beyond common experience. No entity is produced by its own knowledge.

स्यान्मतम् । लिङ्गादिशब्दो विधिज्ञानं जनयित्वा करणानुगृहीतः प्रेरणारूपं स्वव्यापारमारभते इति । तदिदमलौकिकम् । न हि कस्यचिद् वस्तुनः स्वज्ञानमुत्पादहेतुः प्रतीतम् ।

The Prābhākaras do not accept *prāśastyajñāna as itikartavyatā.* The *prāśastyajñāna* cannot be an aid to the *preraṇā* conveyed by the word, it can be an aid to the initiatives of the persons. It cannot be argued that since the persons will not take any initiative for an activity that is not *praśasta,* no *preraṇā* will arise unless it is aided by *prāśastyajñāna,* because, according to the Prābhākaras, the undertaking of an activity does not depend upon its possible results. It is the result that follows and depends upon the activity. This is clear from the fact that the initiative is prompted even in respect of the activities that have no result. It cannot be further argued that even the result is an aid, in that case, let the result alone be the aid but not the *prāśastyajñāna* also. If it is contended that the *prāśastyajñāna* will also be taken into account whenever it is available, then, the trouble taken to work out *karaṇa* itself serving the purpose of *itikartavyatā* in the instance *darvīhoma* will be unnecessary.

एवमर्थवादोदितप्राशस्त्यस्यापि इतिकर्तव्यतात्वं विध्वस्तम् । योग्यतया हि तस्य तथाभावः । न च प्रेरणोत्पत्तौ शब्दकर्तृकायां करणीभूतज्ञानानुग्रहयोग्यता तस्य शक्यते अवगन्तुम् । पुरुषकर्तृकायां तु प्रवृत्तौ स्यात् तस्य योग्यतावगमः प्रशस्ते पुरुषप्रवृत्तिदर्शनात् ।

स्यान्मतम् । अप्रशस्ते पुरुषप्रवृत्त्यसम्भवे प्रेरणैव नोपपद्यते । तदसत् । न फलसम्भवायत्ता क्रियानिष्पत्तिः क्रियानिष्पत्त्यायत्तैव तु फलसिद्धिरिति लोके प्रतीतम् । अत एव तस्मिन् पक्षे निष्फलेपि प्रेरणासिद्धेः प्रवृत्तिः स्यात् ।

अथ फलमपि इतिकर्तव्यतापदनिवेशि प्राशस्त्यवत् । अतः तदभावे न प्रेरणा निष्पद्यते इति । तर्हि फलमेवास्तु इतिकर्तव्यतांशपरिपूरकं किं प्राशस्त्येन ।

सत्यमेतद् । अस्ति तावत् तदपीति न त्यज्यते । एवं तर्हि अश्रुते प्राशस्त्ये तदपेक्षा माभूत् । ततश्च तदतिदेशादिकल्पनमघटमानं केवलस्य विधेः दर्विहोमवत् करणेतिकर्तव्यता कल्पनापि कल्पनामात्रमेव । (प्र०पं० ४२२)

(ii) दर्विहोमाः अपूर्वाः अश्रुतेतिकर्तव्याश्च । यथा तत्रोत्पन्ना कथम्भावापरपर्यायेतिकर्तव्यताकाङ्क्षा यथाश्रुतकर्मस्वरूप-मात्रानुष्ठानेन निवर्तते तत्र स्वरूपनिष्पादनातिरिक्तस्य व्यापारस्याश्रवणात् । (प्र०पं० वि०टि० ४२३)

Incidently, Śālikanātha also notes that *darvihoma* has certain *itikartavyatā.* Therefore, it cannot serve as an instance.

दर्विहोमवदिति च असिद्धो दृष्टान्तः । तत्रापि श्रौतद्रव्य-देवता-स्मृत्याचारप्राप्ताचमनादीतिकर्तव्यतामात्रेणोपकारक्लृप्तेः अभिमतत्वात् । (प्र०पं० ४२२-२३)

Finally, *śabda* is a quality of *ākāśa.* A quality cannot have a *vyāpāra,* only a *dravya* can have a *vyāpāra.* In the case of *abhidhāna vyāpāra,* the procedure is as follows:

As soon as a word is heard the object referred to by it is known. *Śabdā* is the agent to make it known. This is called *abhidhāna.* This is not the *vyāpāra* of *śabda* in the strict sense.

Thus, the Prābhākaras reject the very scheme of *vidhyartha* of Bhāṭṭas viz., the *śābdībhāvanā* is the import of the injunctive suffix, the comprehension of this is the *karaṇa, prāśastyajñāna* is *itikartavyatā* and *ārthībhāvanā* is the *bhāvya.*

किञ्च शब्दः अम्बरगुणः इति प्राप्यकारीन्द्रियवादिना अभ्युपेयम् । अन्यथा नभसः श्रोत्रभूतस्य शब्दस्य च प्रात्यसम्भवात् । संयोगसमवाययोः अन्यतरस्य प्राप्तिरूपत्वात् ।

संयोगस्य अन्यतरकर्मजस्य उभयकर्मजस्य संयोगजस्य च शब्दस्य द्रव्यत्वे नभसा सह असम्भवात् पारिशेष्यात् समवायप्राप्तिरिति आकाशगुणः शब्दः । न च तस्य व्यापारसम्भवः द्रव्याश्रितत्वात् व्यापाराणाम् ।

कथं तर्हि शब्दस्य अभिधानलक्षणः व्यापारः आश्रियते । यथा तत्तथा श्रूयताम् । यत्तावत् आत्मनि अर्थविषयज्ञानं शब्दविषयज्ञानानन्तरं जायते तत् शब्दकर्तृकतया यदा विवक्ष्यते तदा तदाभिधानिकमित्युच्यते परस्थेपि व्यापारे भवत्येव कर्तृता परिस्पन्द इव आत्मनः इति न कश्चिद्दोषः ॥

All Verbal Terminations Do not Convey Bhāvanā

After pointing out the untenability of the Bhāṭṭa scheme of *śābdībhāvanā* as the import of the injunctive suffix, Sālikanātha takes the question whether all verbal suffixes convey *bhāvanā* i.e., *kṛti*, or only the injunctive suffix. Those who hold the view that all verbal suffixes convey the *bhāvanā* argue that the implications of all verbal terminations is explained in terms of performing action. For instance *kim karoti, pacati, kim akārṣīt apacat,* and so on. This means that performing action is implied by all verbal terminations. Sālikanātha states that this is not a correct analysis of these statements. Here, the questions do not seek the action conveyed by the verbal terminations but seek the specific form of the act performed that is to be supplied by the verbal root. Therefore these instances do not prove that the verbal terminations convey the action in general apart from the specific action conveyed by the root. The verbal terminations only convey the number, person etc., and do not convey the action. No reference to any action as an import of a verbal termination is found while learning the language through elders' conversation. This is the position in respect of all other verbal terminations excepting the injunctive suffix.

ननु सर्वाख्यातानां भावनावचनता करोतिसामानाधिकरण्यादवसीयते । तथाहि भवत्यर्थस्य कर्तुः प्रयोजकव्यापारो भावना । सैव कृतिः । भाव्यमानस्यैव क्रियमाणत्वात् । तस्य च कृतिकर्मत्वात् । किमकार्षीत् ?

अपाक्षीत् । किं करोति ? पचति । किं करिष्यति पक्ष्यति इति प्रश्नोत्तरदर्शनात् करोत्यर्थः सर्वाख्यातैरभिधीयते इति गम्यते । अन्यथा करोत्यर्थप्रश्ने तदुत्तरानुपपत्तिः । तत्र सत्यामपि प्रकृतौ घञन्तादिषु करोत्यर्थानवबोधात् आख्यातप्रत्ययसन्निधाने च तदवगमात् आख्यातानामेव सोऽर्थः इति निश्चीयते । (प्र० पं० ४२४)

तदसत् । किं करोति इति प्रश्नस्य यदि अयमर्थः 'यत् करोति तत् किमिति?' तत्र चेत् पचतीत्युत्तरं स्यात् तदा पाकं करोतीत्यस्मिन् अर्थे पचतीति वर्तते तथा च सिद्ध्येदाख्यातानां करोत्यर्थता । न चैवम् ।

अनवगतेहि धातुवाच्ये व्यापारविशेषे तद्विशेष एव एवं पृच्छ्यते तत्र पचतीत्युत्तरम् । तथा च न सिद्ध्यति धात्वर्थातिरिक्तकरोत्यर्थवचनता आख्यातानाम् । सर्वे धात्वर्थाः कस्य चिदभूतस्य भवने अनुकूलतां भजन्तः करोत्यर्थतामापन्नाः करोतिना प्रष्टुं निर्देष्टुं च शक्यन्त इति तद्विशेषप्रश्नोत्तर एव एते । किञ्च धातुवाच्यव्यापारविशेषविषयत्वेनापि प्रश्नोत्तरोपपत्तौ तदतिरिक्त करोत्यर्थवाचकता आख्यातानां न शक्यते वक्तुम् । (प्र० पं० ४२४)

अपि च वृद्धव्यवहारात् शब्दार्थनिर्णयः । न च आख्यातानां भावनावचनत्वमन्तरेण कस्यचिद् वृद्धव्यवहारस्य अनुपपत्तिः । प्रश्नोत्तरे तु सम्बन्धज्ञानोत्तरकालभाविनी । अतो न तद्वशेन सम्बन्धिनिरूपणा । कर्त्रादि संख्यामात्रवाचितया अख्यातप्रयोगोपपत्तौ नाधिकं वाच्यं शक्यं कल्पयितुम् । (प्र० पं० ४२६)

Injunctive Suffix Conveys both Kārya i.e., Apūrva, and Kṛti i.e., Bhāvanā

In the case of Vedic injunctive suffixes, these convey the *kārya* and also *kṛti* i.e., *bhāvanā.* The accomplishment of *kārya* is intimately connected with the *kṛti.* Therefore, both these are conveyed by the Vedic injunctive suffix.

The conveying of *kṛti* cannot be managed either by *daṇḍinyāya* or by the *ākṣepa* of *kṛti* by the *kriyā* conveyed by the verbal root. In the instance of *daṇḍi* the holding of *daṇḍa* is conveyed by the suffix 'in' because of the presence of the word *daṇḍa* as *prakṛti*. In its absence such a meaning cannot be obtained. Here *kṛti* is not conveyed by the verbal root. Even if it is taken as conveyed by the verbal root by way of *ākṣepa*, it will not be verbal communication. Further, the fact of such a *kṛti* accomplishing *kārya* will not be brought out if it is outside the import of the injunctive suffix. Therefore, it is necessary to say that the Vedic injunctive suffix conveys *kṛti* i.e., *bhāvanā* and *apūrva*.

न सर्वाख्यातप्रत्ययानां भावनावचनत्वमभ्युपेमः । किन्तु कार्याभिधायिनः लिङादयः कार्यस्य अन्यथा अनभिधानात् कृत्यभिधायिनः इष्यन्ते । कृतिसम्बन्धिहि कार्यं कृत्यनभिधाने नाभिहितं स्यात् । नहि अस्ति सम्भवः कृतिः नाभिधीयते कार्यञ्चाभिधीयते इति ।

अथ मतं दण्डी इत्यत्र प्रत्ययेन दण्डो नाभिधीयते अथ च तद्विशिष्टपुरुषप्रतीतिः एवमिहापि भवेदिति । तन्न । तत्र अप्रतीते दण्डे न तद्वति प्रत्ययः । अस्ति च तत्र प्रकृतिभूतो दण्डशब्दः सच तस्य प्रत्याययिता । न चेह तथा सम्भवति । प्रकृतीनां पुरुष व्यापाराभिधानानियमात् । पुरुषोहि चेतनः कार्यं लिङादिभिः अवबुध्यते। न चासौ परकृतिसम्बन्धि स्वयं कार्यं बोद्धुमलमिति तदीयकृत्यभिधानमेषितव्यम् । कृतिः प्रयत्नरूपा । तदननुभवे न सर्वथा तदभिधायिनः इति न दण्डिन्यायस्य अयं विषयः ।

स्यान्मतम् । यथा लिङं कर्त्रादिसङ्ख्यामात्रवचनता । क्रियाक्षेपेण च कर्त्रादीनां प्रतीतिः तथा इहापि क्रिया प्रयत्नमाक्षिपति माभूत् तस्य लिङ्वाच्यता इति तदसत् । यद्यपि प्रकृत्यर्थभूतया क्रियया प्रयत्नः आक्षिप्यते तथापि तदायत्तसिद्धिकतया कथमपूर्वं गम्यते । प्रयत्नाभिधाने तदवच्छिन्नतया प्रतीयमानं तदायत्तसिद्धिकमवगम्यते नान्यथा । न च कृत्यनवच्छिन्नस्वरूप-मात्रेणापूर्वमभिहितं कृतिमाक्षेप्तुमलम् । अवगतसम्बन्धं हि वस्तु आक्षिप्यते । न च शब्दमन्तरेण अपूर्वस्य प्रयत्नसम्बन्धावगमे कारणमस्ति

अथ कथं तत् प्रयत्नमाक्षिपेत् । तस्मात् अपूर्वकार्याभिधायिनां प्रयत्नमवश्यमाश्रयणीयमिति विषयकरणीये निपुणतरमुपपादितम् । (प्र०पं० ४२७)

The fact of the comprehension of *kārya* being the basis of *kṛti* i.e., *pravṛtti,* is clear from the process by which one undertakes initiative. A person does not proceed to undertake initiative merely by the knowledge of the activity or its result. Not even by the knowledge of the intention of the person who has made the statement. He only proceeds to undertake the initiative by understanding that it is his *kārya.* A person undertakes initiative in respect of all day-to-day activities and even such activities that satisfy one's hunger and thirst by realizing that it is his *kārya.* Therefore, *kārya* that is to be accomplished by *kṛti* is the import of an injunction.

तत्र न क्रियामात्रं बुद्ध्वा अहं प्रवृत्तः, नापि फलमात्रम्, क्रियाफलसम्बन्धमात्रं वा । क्रियाफलयोः साध्यसाधनतावगमेपि न प्रवृत्तिरुपपद्यते । तृप्तिहेतौ भोजने अतीते वर्तमाने वा अप्रवृत्तेः । भविष्यत्यपि तत्साधने सामुद्रविदाख्यात इव अनुष्ठानाभावात् । पुरुषाशयावगमस्तु प्रवृत्तिहेतुत्वे नाशङ्कितोपि । स्वतन्त्रप्रवृतौ व्युत्पित्सोः दूरोत्सारितत्वात् ।

किन्तु कार्यतां बुद्ध्वा प्रवृत्तोहं ममेदं कार्यमिति प्रतीत्य अहं सर्वत्र प्रवृत्तः

आस्तां तावत् क्रिया लोके गमनागमनादिका ।
अन्ततस्तन्यपानादिः तृप्तिकारिण्यपि क्रिया ।
सा तावन्ममकार्येयमिति नैवावधार्यते ।
तावत् कदापि मे तत्र प्रवृत्तिरभवन्नहि ।

Rejection of the View of Brahmasiddhi

However, the author of *Brahmasiddhi* holds the view that this *kāryatā* is nothing but *iṣṭasādhanatā.* It is *iṣṭasādhanatā* that prompts one to undertake initiative. Therefore, *iṣṭasādhanatā* is the import of an injunction. Since the comprehension of *iṣṭasādhanatā* prompts a person to undertake initiative it is called *pravartanā*.

अत्र अपर आह—सत्यं कार्यावगमादेव प्रवृत्तिः । इष्टसाधनतैव कार्यता न परा काचित् । सैव प्रवृत्तिहेतुः विधिरुच्यते । तदाह—

अपेक्षितोपायतैव विधिरिष्टो मनीषिभिः ।
अतोऽध्यवसायादिः नाकस्मान्नाभिधानतः ॥
(ब्र०सि०का० ३-१०३)

पुंसो नेष्टाभ्युपायत्वात् क्रियास्वन्यः प्रवर्तकः ।
प्रवृत्तिहेतुं धर्मं च प्रवदन्ति प्रवर्तनाम् । (वि०वि० ३६)
कर्तुरिष्टाभ्युपायेहि कर्तव्यमिति लोकधीः ।
विपरीतेत्वकर्तव्यमिति तद्विषये ततः ॥ (वि०वि० ३०)

This view is not acceptable to Śālikanātha. He makes a distinction between *kāryatā* and *iṣṭasādhanatā* on the ground that *kāryatā* is that which is to be accomplished by *kṛti* without seeking any outside result while *iṣṭasādhanatā* is an instrument to achieve a desired result. It is true that ordinarily *iṣṭasādhanatā* and *kāryatā* exist in the same. However, these two are not identical. *Iṣṭasādhanatā* indicates the *kāryatā*. Ordinarily one proceeds to take initiative for such activity that is *iṣṭasādhana*. Therefore, it is a convenient basis to comprehend *kāryatā*. But by itself it is not *kāryatā*. A person proceeds to undertake initiative transcending this notion of *iṣṭasādhanatā* with a realisation of *kāryatā*. *Iṣṭasādhanatā* is only a stepping stone.

(i) **तत्र तावदिदमेव वक्तव्यम् । अतीतस्य वर्तमानस्य च इष्टसाधनता अस्ति । न च तत्कार्यतया अवसीयते । तेन च अन्या कार्यता अन्या इष्टसाधनता इति । फलसाधनता-कार्यतयोः भेदं निर्दिशति—**

फलसाधनता नाम या सा नैव च कार्यता ।

कार्यता कृतिसाध्यत्वं फलसाधनता पुनः ॥ ६ ॥
करणत्वं फलोत्पादे भिद्येते ते परस्परम्

यद्यपि एकवस्तु निवेशिता द्वयोः तथापि स्वरूपभेदोऽस्त्येव । तदेव हि वस्तु फलं प्रत्युपायभावात् फलसाधनमित्युच्यते कृत्यधीनात्मलाभतया च कार्यमिति । प्र०पं० ४२८)

(ii) किमिति इष्टाभ्युपायेष्वेव कर्तव्यत्वावगमः अन्यत्र न इत्यत्राह—

किन्तु स्वयं क्लेशरूपं कर्म यत् कार्यतां व्रजेत् ।
फलसाधनता तत्र कारणं तेन कार्यता ।
तद्भावभाविनी नित्यं तदात्मेव प्रकाशते ॥ ९ ॥

(iii) कर्मसु कार्यत्वावगमः फलसाधनतावगमनिबन्धनः इति ज्ञापककोटिनिविष्टा फलसाधनता कार्यतामनुरुध्यते । न तु असौ तदात्मैव । तथा च असाधनस्यापि सुखस्यैव अस्ति कार्यता । सुखं हि सर्वः कार्यतया अवैति । न तस्य फलसाधनतामपेक्षते । तेन फलसाधनतोत्तीर्णकार्यतावगमेन मे प्रवृत्तिरिति निश्चित्य व्युत्पत्स्यमानः चैत्रं दृष्ढवा अनुमिनोति चैत्रोपि कार्यबोधात् प्रवर्तत इति । (प्र०पं० ४३०)

Kārya is Comprehended by Elders' Conversation by Mānasapratyakṣa, and by Inference

The fact that the *kārya* is the import of injunctive suffix is comprehended in the same way in which the import of the other words is comprehended. This is by way of *āvāpa* and *udvāpa*. From the statements that contain a verb with an injunctive suffix *kārya* is comprehended and from the statements that do not contain such an injunctive suffix *kārya* is not comprehended. From this it is clear that *kārya* is the import of an injunctive suffix. It is to be noted here that though *praiṣa* etc., certain other meanings are assigned to an injunctive suffix, these are all special forms of *kārya*. The *kāryata* is commonly present in all of them. *Kārya* conveyed by an elderly person is *praiṣa*, by an equal is *āmantraṇa* and by a person of a lesser status is *adhyeṣaṇa*. However, *kāryatā* is common in all these.

(i) ननु एवमपि कथं लिङादीनां कार्ये व्युत्पत्तिरित्यत्राह—

शब्दान्तराणि स्वार्थेषु व्युत्पद्यन्ते यथैवहि ।
आवापोद्वापभेदेन तथा कार्ये लिङादयः ॥

लिङादियुक्तवाक्यश्रवणे तद्भावभाविन्या प्रवृत्त्या विशिष्टकार्यावगतिमनुमाय वाक्यस्य हेतुतामध्यवस्यति । तत्रापि कोऽर्थः केन शब्देन अभिहितः इतिविवेचने लिङाद्यावापे कार्यावगतिदर्शनात् तदुद्धारे च अदर्शनात् त एव कार्यावगतिं कुर्वन्तीति शब्दान्तरवत् लिङादीनां कार्यवाचकत्वव्युत्पत्तिसिद्धिः ।

(ii) ननु लोकव्यवहारात् लिङादयो वाचकतया व्युत्पाद्यमानाः प्रैषादिष्वेव वाचकतया व्युत्पत्तिमर्हन्ति । तत्रैव तेषां प्रयोगदर्शनात् इत्याशङ्क्याह—

कार्यमेवहि वक्तॄणां ज्यायः समकनीयसाम् ।
प्रवर्त्त्यापेक्षया भेदात् प्रैषादिव्यपदेशभाक् ॥ ११ ॥

प्रवर्त्त्यपुरुषापेक्षया ज्यायसा वक्त्रा प्रतिपाद्यमानं कार्यं प्रैष इति व्यपदिश्यते । समेन आमन्त्रणं हीनेन अध्येषणमिति प्रैषादिप्रतिपादका अपि लिङादयः कार्यमेव प्रतिपादयन्ति न अर्थान्तरम् ॥ ११ ॥

This *kārya* though conveyed by a Vedic injunction and comprehended as its import, it could be ascertained by certain other means also. *Kārya* can be accomplished by *kṛti* only and it is the objective of *kṛti*. *Kṛti* which is of the nature of *prayatna* could be perceived by the mind. Therefore, its objective viz., *kārya* could also be perceived by the mind. Further, *kārya* can be accomplished if there is *kṛti* and it cannot be accomplished if there is no *Kṛti*. Therefore, it can be ascertained by the inference as something that is to be achieved by *kṛti*.

केन पुनः प्रमाणेन बालः स्वयं कार्यमवगच्छति । यतः प्रवर्तते इत्यत आह—

कृतिसाध्यं प्रधानं यत् तत्कार्यमभिधीयते ।
तच्च मानान्तरेणापि वेद्यमोदनपाकवत् ॥

कृतौ सत्यां भावात् असत्यां च अभावात् अनुमानतः कृतिसाध्यता तावदवगम्यते । यदधिकृत्य कृतिः प्रवर्तते तत् कृतेः प्रधानम् । प्रयत्नश्च कृतिः । स च मानसप्रत्यक्षवेद्य इति विशिष्टप्रयोजनतापि प्रयत्नस्य प्रत्यक्षवेद्यैव । तेन प्रत्यक्षानुमानाभ्यां कार्यमवगम्यते । यथा च ओदनपाकयोरिति न किञ्चिदनुपपन्नम् । उपसंहरति—

एवं कार्यात्मकेप्यर्थे व्युत्पद्यन्ते लिङादयः ।
तदन्वितेषु स्वार्थेषु तथा शब्दान्तराण्यपि ॥ (प्र०पं० ४३१-४३२)

This *kārya* is conveyed by the injunctive suffix as already stated and all other words in the sentence convey their respective meanings as connected with it.

Kārya is Distinct from Kriyā

For the correct understanding of the nature and role of *kārya* it is necessary to understand the distinction between the *kriyā* and *kārya.* On hearing the *laukika* statements containing injunctive suffixes, a person proceeds to undertake the activity conveyed by the verbal root. Therefore, it is natural to consider that as *kārya.* On this analogy one is inclined to consider the action conveyed by the root in the Vedic injunction also a *kārya.* However, this approach is not satisfactory in the case of Vedic injunctions. The distinct role of a Vedic injunction is explained in the next section.

(1) सम्प्रधार्यं त्विदन्त्वत्र तत् कार्यं किं क्रियात्मकम् ।
यद्वा तद्व्यतिरेकीति..........
को नु निर्णयः इत्यत्राह—तत्र लोकानुसारतः ।

प्रमाणान्तरविज्ञेया क्रिया कार्येति यद्यपि ॥

लोकेहि लिङादियुक्तवाक्यश्रवणे विशिष्ट क्रियानुष्ठानदर्शनात् तद्विषया कार्यावगतिः लिङादिभिः क्रियते इति युक्तम् । अवगतिप्रवृत्त्योः एकविषयत्वात् । नहि अन्यत् कार्यतया अवगम्य अन्यत्र बालः प्रवर्तते । किञ्च क्रियायां कार्यभूतायामभ्युपगम्यमानायां शक्तिकल्पना लाघवं स्यादेव । इति क्रियैव कार्यतया वेदेपि अवगम्यत इति यद्यपि विवेकासमर्थानामवगतिर्भवति ।

तथापि वेदे षष्ठाद्ये सिद्धान्तेऽवस्थिते सति ॥ १६ ॥
स्वर्गकामादयः कार्ये नियोज्यत्वेन सम्मताः ।
स्वर्गकामादिभिः शब्दैः वक्तव्या इत्यवस्थितम् ॥ १७ ॥

It is agreed by those who consider *kriyā* as *kārya* that *kārya* is conveyed by an injunction. This *kārya* has to be accomplished by kṛti i.e., initiative. An initiative can be undertaken by an agent only. An agent undertakes an initiative for something only which he understands it as his *kārya.* The adjective *svargakāma* mentioned in the context indicates that a person who desires to have *svarga* is one who understands it as his *kārya.* His desire to obtain *svarga* is the ground for his entitlement to undertake this activity as his *kārya.* This *kārya* is also called *niyoga.* Therefore, the person entitled to perform this activity on the ground of his desire to obtain *svarga* is *niyojya.* He has to accomplish the *kārya* conveyed by the injunction by performing the activity concerned. It is the accomplishment of *kārya* that provides the *svarga.* It is not the *kriyā* i.e., activity that provides *svarga* but it is *kārya* that is accomplished by the performance of *kriyā* that provides it. This is because, the *kriyā* i.e., activity, is perishable. It cannot remain until one attains *svarga.* Since *kriyā* cannot provide the desired result it cannot be taken as *kārya* by the *niyojya* who is *svargakāma* and the very relation between the *kārya* and *niyojya* as *niyoga* and *niyojya* will be broken down. Therefore, *kārya* is distinct from *kriyā.* The *kriya* is only an instrument and a subject i.e., *karaṇa*, and *viṣaya* of the *kārya* and accomplishes *kārya*.

षष्ठाद्येहि एतदुक्तम्—लिङादिप्रयोगे तावत् कार्यावगतिरस्तीति निर्विवादम् । कृतिसाध्यं च कार्यं भवति । सति कर्तरि तस्य आत्मलाभः । कर्तृलाभश्च स्वसम्बन्धिकार्यावबोधे सति भवति नान्यथा । तेन यद्यपि लोकानुसारेण क्रियाया एव कार्यतया बोध्यमानायाः वाक्यार्थत्वात् तदन्वयित्वाच्चेतरेषामपि पदार्थानाम् । कारकत्वाद् ऋते अन्यस्य क्रियान्वयित्वासम्भवात् लोहितोष्णीषन्यायेन विशेषणीभूतस्वर्गकामना समर्पणपरतया कर्तृविशेषणत्वेन स्वर्गकामस्य अन्वयोऽगम्यते । तथापि स्वसम्बन्धिकार्यबोद्धृत्वेनैव अन्वयो वर्णनीय इति नियोज्यसमर्पकत्वमेव आश्रियते ।

नियोज्यः स च कार्यं यः स्वकीयत्वेन बुध्यते ।
स्वर्गादिः कामयोगाच्च साध्यत्वेनैव गम्यते ॥ १८ ॥

साध्यविषयैवहि सर्वत्र कामना भवति । तेन तत्सम्बन्धात् साध्यभूतं स्वर्गादि काम्यमानतया पुरुषं विशनष्टि—

तेन साध्यत्वपर्यन्तस्वर्गादीच्छाविशेषितः ।
तदेव शक्नुयात् कार्यं बोद्धुं यत् काम्यसाधनम् ॥ १९ ॥

(ii) स्वर्गादिकं कामयमानस्य तदेव कार्यतया बोद्धुमवकल्पते यदेव तस्य काम्यमानस्य सिद्ध्यनुगुणम् । अन्यथाहि तत्कामिना सता तत्कार्यतया अनवबुद्धं स्यात् । अपरित्यक्ततत्कामनासम्बन्धोहि तत्साधनं कार्यतया अवबुद्ध्यते । तस्मात् यत्कामिनो यत् कार्यतया उपादिश्यते तत् तत्काम्यस्य साधनमिति नियोज्यकार्यान्वयानुपपत्त्यैव गम्यते ।

एवं सति किं फलमित्याह—

लिङादिस्तत्र कार्यं चेत् क्रियामेवावबोधयेत् ।
समन्वयो नियोज्येन तदानीमेव हीयते ॥ २० ॥

तत् कथमित्याह—

क्रिया हि क्षणिकत्वेन न कालान्तरभाविनः ।
स्वर्गादेः काम्यमानस्य समर्था जननं प्रति ॥ २१ ॥
इष्टस्याजनिका सा च नियोज्येन फलार्थिना
कार्यत्वेन न सम्बन्धमर्हति क्षणभङ्गिनी ॥ २२ ॥ (प्र०पं० ४३३)

(iii) तस्मान्नियोज्यसम्बन्धसमर्थं विधिवाचिभिः ।
कार्यं कालान्तरस्थायि क्रियातो भिन्नमुच्यते ॥ २३ ॥ (प्र०पं० ४३६)

Rejection of Maṇḍana Miśra's View in Respect of Svarga

Śālikanātha rejects Maṇḍana Miśra's view that the expression *svarga* does not refer to the heaven but it only refers to happiness.

The expression *svarga* mentioned in the context of *jyotiṣṭoma* cannot be taken in the sense of ordinary joy or happiness. This is clear from the *arthavāda* statement in this connection. It has to be taken in the sense of a special happiness that could be obtained in another world. This means it cannot be realized immediately after the *yāga*. Hence, mere *kriyā* is not its means.

(i) ननु प्रीतिमात्रवचनः स्वर्गः इति षष्ठाद्ये साधितम् । प्रीतिसाधनेषु द्रव्येषु स्वर्गशब्दप्रयोगात् । न च तेषु स्वरूपनिबन्धन एव तत्प्रयोगः प्रीत्यपगमे तदभावात् । न च तत्साधनवचनता तदनभिधाने घटते तदभिधानाभ्युपगमे तद्वाचकतैव । तत्र शक्तिकल्पनापरिक्षयात् ।

(ii) उच्यते—न प्रीतिमात्रवचनतया ज्योतिष्टोमादिचोदनासु स्वर्गशब्दस्य प्रयोगोऽवकल्पते । अर्थवादेषु दुःखासम्भिन्न चिरतरोपभोग्याभिलाषोपनेयप्रीतिश्रवणात् । तत्र यदि विध्युद्देशगतः स्वर्गशब्दः तथा विधप्रीतिपरतया न वर्ण्यते तदाऽतिपरोक्षार्थवादपदानां वृत्तिराद्ता न भवेदिति तदानुगुण्येन तादृश्यामेव प्रीतौ स्वर्गशब्दः प्रयुक्त इति निश्चीयते । तथा भूता च सा नियतमेव देशान्तरभोग्या । अतो न कर्मानन्तरभाविनीति न तत्र कर्मणः आशुतरविनाशिनः साधनता अवकल्पते । (प्र०पं० ४३५)

Kriyā cannot Remain Until Svarga is Achieved

An attempt is made by some to manage the connection between the *kriyā* and the *svarga* in two ways: (i) considering *kṛiyā* itself as continuing in some way until *svarga* is realised (ii) envisaging a power of *kriyā* that will continue until *svarga* is realized though *kriyā* as such vanishes.

Śālikanātha points out that both these explanations are not tenable. Firstly, the fact of *kriyā* being perishable is obvious. Therefore, no continuity of it in someway after it vanishes can be thought of. It is against our experience.

(ii) Envisaging some power of *kriyā* that can continue until the *svarga* is realized does not help to solve the problem. When that which possesses the power vanishes, the power also vanishes. When the locus of the power ceases to exist where can the power exist. It cannot exist on the self of the performer of *kriyā*. The power of one entity cannot remain in another entity. Further, it is the entity that has the power is the means of the result to be achieved by it, but not mere power separated from the entity.

ननु क्रियैव कार्यता उच्यताम् । अस्तु सैव फलसाधनम् । तेन तस्या अपि नियोज्यसम्बन्धो घटत एव ।

ननु असौ क्षणभङ्गिनी देहान्तरोपभोग्यफलसाधनतां कथमवलम्बते ? उच्यते—वरं तस्या एव तदनुपपत्त्या चिरतरावस्थायिता कल्पना । न पुनः अदृष्टस्य अश्रुतस्य तदतिरेकिणोऽर्थस्य कल्पना ।

यद्वा कर्मण एव शक्तिरवस्थायिनीत्यभ्युपगम्यताम् । तदिदमुभयमपि प्रमाणान्तरविरोधात् न कल्पनामर्हति ।

शक्तिमति च अतीते शक्तिरपि अतीतेति प्रमाणान्तरसिद्धमिति न सापि स्थायिनि कल्पयितुं शक्या । अपि चाश्रये निवृत्ते किमाश्रया शक्तिरवतिष्ठताम् । आत्माश्रितेति चेत् न अन्यदीया शक्तिः अन्यत्र

वर्तते प्रमाणान्तरविरोधादेव । किञ्च शक्तिमति असति शक्तेः फलं न युक्तम् । शक्तिमद्धि साधनम् न शक्तिः केवला । अन्यथा शक्तित्वं न स्यात् । (प्र०पं० ४३६)

Sacrifice is not Worship of Deities

Śālikanātha refutes the view that *yāga* is of the nature of worship of deities and provides the *svarga* through the grace of the deities. He argues that there is no authority to say that the *yāgas* are of the nature of the worship of deities. Further, the deities have no form and therefore, cannot comprehend the worship offered to them. This rules out the possibility of their grace. The deities are *gauṇa* in the sacrifice. It is the accomplishment of *kriyā* that is the primary object.

ननु यागादिक्रिया देवताराधनोपायभूता सती कार्यतया उच्यताम् । सा तत्प्रत्त्यासत्तिद्वारेण कालान्तरेपि फलं जनयितुमलमेव । देवता फलदानसमर्था कर्मभिराराध्यते । सा आराधिता प्रसीदति । प्रसन्नाच कर्तॄन् कालान्तरेपि फलेन योजयत्येव इति ।

नैतदेवं यागादीनां देवताराधनहेतुत्वे प्रमाणाभावात् । नहि देवताराधनोपायभूतो याग इत्यत्र किञ्चित् प्रमाणमस्ति । ननु देवपूजार्थएव यजिः स्मर्यते । पूजा च सर्वा पूज्यमानाराधनार्थेत्यवगतम् । उच्यते—न स्मृतिः प्रमाणं स्मृतित्वादेव । प्रमाणान्तरापेक्षयाच स्मृतीनामर्थवर्णनम् । तदनुवर्तित्वात् तासाम् । न च प्रमाणान्तरेण देवताराधनोपायता यागस्यावगम्यत इत्युक्तम् । अतो देवतोद्देशेन द्रव्यत्यागो यागः इति गौणं देवतापूजात्मकत्वमित्यवगन्तव्यम् । पूजापि पूज्योद्देशेनैव प्रवर्तते इति ।

अपि च सा कर्मभिः आराध्यते या आराधनं प्रतिपद्यते । नानादेशगामिना पुरुषेण अनुष्ठीयमानयागात्मकपूजावगमश्च देवताया इति प्रमाणविरुद्धमेव । विग्रहवतश्च प्रतिपत्तियोगिता । तस्य च वेदेन अनादिना आराध्यतया

प्रतिपादनमपि प्रमाणान्तरविरूद्धमेव । तस्यानादित्वानुपपत्तेः । देवताधिकरणे च (९-१-४) प्रपञ्चेनायमर्थो निरस्तः । (प्र०पं० ४३९)

Bhāṭṭa's Concept of Apūrva Does not Help to Relate Yāga and Svarga

It cannot be insisted that let *kriyā* itself be the means of *svarga*, let an intermediary that remains until the *svarga* is realized be envisaged to establish a link between the *yāga* and *svarga*. This intermediary is *apūrva*. This *apūrva* can remain on the self of the sacrificer until he attains *svarga*.

This claim is not tenable. If another entity between *yāga* and *svarga* is envisaged to produce *svarga*, then *yāga* ceases to be means of *svarga*. It will be the means of *apūrva* only which is now the means of *svarga*. The *apūrva* cannot be treated merely as a *vyāpāra* or the power of *yāga*. That which is not present in *yāga* but is present on the self cannot be considered as *vyāpāra* or *śakti* of *yāga*. Therefore, to think of *apūrva as* an intermediary by *arthāpatti pramāṇa* does not help to retain the position that the *yāga* is the means of *svarga*. The best way is to consider *kārya* which is permanent as providing *svarga*. Keeping this role of *kārya* in mind it is also called *apūrva*.

ननु क्रियैव कार्यतया उच्यताम् । फलसाधनताच तस्या एव आश्रियताम् । तदन्यथानुपपत्त्या तु किञ्चिदप्यपरं तज्जन्यं फलोदयानुगुणं कालान्तरस्थायि आत्माश्रयं परिकल्प्यताम् । माभूत्तस्य लिङादिवाच्यता इति ।

उच्यते—तद्धि तदनुपपत्त्या कलप्यते यद् यस्योपपादकम् । न च क्रियाजन्येन अन्येन फलजनकेन कल्पितेन क्रियायाः फलसाधनता उपपादिता भवति । नहि साधनसाधनं तस्य साधनं भवति । अवान्तरव्यापारो वा शक्तिर्वा तत्साधनतां निर्वाहयति । व्यापारोपयोगितयैव शक्तिमतां साधनता यतः ।

न च आत्मसमवायि अर्थान्तरं कर्मणामवान्तरव्यापार:, नापि शक्तिरिति न तस्य अर्थान्तरगम्यता युक्ता । किन्तु अन्विताभिधाने स्थिते नियोज्यानुगुण्यात् शब्दवाच्यतैव उचिता इति सूक्तम् नियोज्यसम्बन्धसमर्थं कालान्तरस्थायि कार्यं क्रियातिरिक्तं लिङादिभि: उच्यते । (प्र०पं० ४४०)

Jaiminīya Sūtras and Adhikaraṇas that are the Sources of the Concept of Kārya

Śālikanātha neatly sums up the Prābhākara's position in respect of *kārya* quoting the relevant *adhikaraṇas* of Pūrvamīmāmsā sūtras as follows:

1. *Kārya* is stated as the import of an injunction in *codanā sūtra.*
2. *Svargakāma* is stated as *niyojya* of this *kārya* in the first *adhikaraṇa* of the sixth chapter.
3. *Svargakāmana* is stated as the qualification of *niyojya* in the first *adhikaraṇa* of the eleventh chapter.
4. The fact that the *kārya* produces the result i.e., *svarga,* desired by *niyojya* is stated in *bādari adhikaraṇa. Kṛiyā* is not *kārya,* since, it cannot produce the result.
5. The fact that the *yāga* does not lead to *svarga* through the worship of deities is stated in *devatā-adhikaraṇa.* It does not lead to *svarga* through *puruṣasanskāra* is stated under *karmani ārambha-bhāvyatvāt.*
6. The *yāga* or its power does not remain until the *svarga* is obtained is stated in *apūrvādhikaraṇa.*
7. The *kārya* ie *apūrva,* when accomplished remains on the self of *niyojya.* This *kārya* is conveyed by the Vedic injunction.
8. *Kārya* can be accomplished by the *kṛti* only. *Kṛti* is human initiative. This cannot operate without being connected with *kṛiyā.* Therefore it is conveyed as connected with *kṛiyā.* This is stated in *bhāvārthādhikaraṇa.* It is also stated in *śabdāntarādhikaraṇa* that the *kṛiyā* gives a form to it.

9. The fact that *kṛiyā* i.e., *yāga* is both *viṣaya* and *karaṇa* is stated in *bādari adhikaraṇa.*

10. Finally, in *bādari adhikaraṇa,* it is stated that the *niyojya* will accomplish the *kāryā* through *kṛiyā* i.e., *yāga.*

The above sketch of the *Prābhākaras'* position clearly brings out the role of *niyojya, yāga* and *kārya* in implementing the import of a Vedic injunction.

अत्रैषा प्रक्रिया—

(i) **चादनासूत्रे कार्यार्थता प्रतिपादिता**

(ii) **षष्ठाद्ये तस्यैव कार्यस्य स्वसम्बन्धितया बोध्यः स्वर्गकामादिः नियोज्य इति व्युत्पादितम् ।**

(iii) **स्वर्गकामनाच नियोगविशेषणमित्येकादशाद्ये (११-१-१) व्युत्पादितम् ।**

(iv) **तस्य च कार्यस्य नियोज्य विशेषणीभूतकाम्योत्पत्तिहेतुत्वमिति बादर्यधिकरणे राद्धान्तितम् । (३-१-३)**
तच्च तथाभूतं कार्यं क्रियाभूतं न भवति तस्याः फलसाधनत्वायोगात् ।

(v) **देवताराधनमुखेन तावत् फलसाधनता नास्तीति देवताधिकरणे व्युत्पादितम् (९-१-४) । पुरुषसंस्कारमुखेन नास्तीति कर्मण्यारम्भभाव्यत्वादित्यत्रोक्तम् । कालान्तरस्थायिनः कार्यस्य नियोज्यान्वययोग्यतामाह—**

(vi) **कर्मणः तच्छक्तेर्वा स्थायिता नेति च अपूर्वाधिकरणे (२-९-२) प्रतिपादितम् ।**

(vii) **अतो नियोज्यान्वयमुखेन मानान्तरापूर्वमात्मसमवायि कार्यं लिङादिभिरभिधीयत इति अनेकन्यायसाध्यम् ।**

(viii) **कार्यं च कृतिसाध्यम् । कृतिश्च पुंसां प्रयत्न एव । न चासौ भावार्थमन्तरेण अस्तीति तत्सम्बद्ध एवोच्यत इति भावार्थाधिकरणे (२-१-१)**

स्थितम् । स च भावार्थः सम्बध्यमानः तमवच्छिनतीति शब्दान्तराधिकरणे (२-२-१) निर्णीतम् ।

(ix) विषयभूतश्च भावार्थः करणीभवतीति बादर्यधिकरणे एवोक्तम् । स्वकार्यसाधने भावार्थे पुरुषस्यैश्वर्यमिति तत्रैवोक्तम् ।

तच्च कालान्तरस्थानात् शक्तं स्वर्गादिसिद्धये ।
सम्बन्धोप्युपपद्येत नियोज्येनास्य कामिना ॥ २४ ॥ (प्र० पं० ४४०)

The Designations Apūrva and Niyoga for Kārya

The *kārya* is called *apūrva* in the sense that it is not conveyed by any other *pramāṇa* than a Vedic injunctive suffix. As it remains permanently i.e., until *svarga* is obtained, it is located on the self of *niyojya* who desired to realize *svarga*.

क्रियादिभिन्नं यत्कार्यं वेद्यं मानान्तरैः न तत् ।
अतो मानान्तरापूर्वमपूर्वमिति गीयते ॥ २५ ॥

This *kārya* is called *niyoga* as it commands the *niyojya* to accomplish it. Since *kārya* is the chief import of an injunction it is the import of an injunctive sentence associated with *niyojya* and *viṣaya* i.e., *yāga*.

ननु एवमप्यपूर्वं वाक्यार्थः स्यात् न नियोगः । नियोगश्च वाक्यार्थ इति प्राभाकरणामुल्लापः इत्यत्राह—

कार्यत्वेन नियोज्यं च स्वात्मनि प्रेरयन्नसौ ।
नियोग इति मीमांसा निष्णातैरभिधीयते ॥ २६ ॥

एवमपि कथं तस्य वाक्यार्थत्वमित्याह—

कार्यस्यैव प्रधानत्वात् वाक्यार्थत्वं च युज्यते ।
वाक्यं तदेव हि प्राह नियोज्यविषयान्वितम् ॥ २७ ॥

उक्तं हि एतत् यत् प्रधानतया प्रतिपद्यते तद्वाक्यार्थः इति कार्यं च प्रधानतया उच्यत इति तस्यैव वाक्यार्थत्वम् । (प्र०पं० ४४१)

The Instances Where no Separate Niyojya is Required

The association of *niyojya* with the *kārya* is a general rule. However, there are a few exceptions.

In the case of *agnyādhāna, adhyayana, aṅga- pradhāna, utpatti niyoga* etc., there is no need of a *niyojya.* A *niyojya* is required for *anuṣṭhāna* i.e., performance. In the case of *agnyādhāna* its performance is done for the purpose of the sacrifices to be undertaken. Therefore, no separate *niyojya* is necessary. In the case of *adhyayana,* it is undertaken to implement *adhyāpanavidhi,* therefore, here also no separate *niyojya* is necessary. Similarly, the *pradhāna utpatti niyogas* are implemented by the *anuṣṭhāna* on account of *adhikāraniyoga.* Same is the case with *aṅgotpatti niyoga.*

नियोज्यान्विताभिधानं च प्रायिकम् । आधानाध्ययनाङ्गप्रधानोत्पत्तिनियोगानाम् नियोज्यशून्यानामभिधानात् ।

(i) विवरणकारा हि आधानविषयमपि नियोगान्तरमिच्छन्ति क्रतुनियोगप्रत्यभिज्ञानाभावात् । असन्निधाने तन्नियोगप्रत्यभिज्ञानं नोपपद्यते ।

(ii) उच्यते—नियोग एव अत्रापि प्रधानं साध्यम् । अनीप्सितकर्मता तु अग्नीनाम् । अनीप्सितकर्मत्वेपि यत्तदाधानजन्यं फलमग्निसमवायि तद्योगिनि आहवनीयादिशब्दप्रयोगात् आहवनीयदीनां च क्रतूपयोगित्वात् तत्सिद्ध्यर्थतयैव पुरुषप्रवृत्त्युपपत्तेः अनुष्ठानलाभादलं नियोज्यन्विताभिधानेन इति ।

(iii) तथा अध्ययन विधावपि आचार्यकरणविधिप्रयुक्तैयव अनुष्ठानलाभात् नियोज्यशून्याभिधानमिति स्थितम् । प्रधानोत्पत्तिनियोगा अपि अधिकार नियोगाक्षिप्त स्वविषयानुष्ठानेनैव लब्धसिद्धय इति न तत्र नियोज्यान्विताभिधानान्वेषणम् । (प्र०पं० ४४२)

The Result is only a side Product. Niyoga i.e., Kārya is the Primary Import

It is stated above that the *niyoga* leads to the result i.e., *svarga.* Therefore, it appears that the result has to be the chief import of the injunctive sentence. However, such a position is not acceptable to the Prābhākaras. The *niyoga* leads to the result not so much as its objective but to accomplish itself. This is clear if we observe the sequence of its operation. It is as follows:

Kārya needs the association of a *niyojya* for its accomplishment. *Niyojya* has to accomplish it by the performance of *kriyā* i.e., *yāga.* This needs an agent. An agent is one who has entitlement. One will not have entitlement unless he is *a niyojya.* One who desires something will not be the *niyojya* for that which does not fulfil that desire. Therefore, *niyoga* .that has to attract a *niyojya* has to provide the desired result i.e., *svarga,* for him. Hence, the *niyoga* to play its very function has to be the means of the desired result i.e., *svarga.* It is something like a master maintaining a servant to serve his own interest. In view of this though *niyoga* provides the result i.e., *svarga,* it is the *niyoga* that is the chief import of the injunction but not the result provided by it.

ननु नियोगस्य काम्यमानफलसाधनत्वाभ्युपगमात्, फलस्यैव प्राधान्यात् तस्यैव वाक्यार्थत्वं युक्तमित्यत आह ।

आत्मसिद्ध्यनुकूलस्य प्रयोज्यस्य च सिद्धये ।
कुर्वत् स्वर्गादिकमपि प्रधानं कार्यमेव नः ॥ २८ ॥

यत्तदपूर्वं कार्यं तस्य नियोज्यान्वयं विना कार्यत्वानुपपत्तेः अनुष्ठानं विना तदसम्भवात् कर्त्रा च विना तदनुपपत्तेः, अधिकारेण च विना कर्तुः अभावात् नियोज्यत्वं विना तदयोगात् अकामसाधने च कामिनो नियोगानवगमादिति आत्मसिद्ध्यर्थमेव नियोगः काम्यमानफलसिद्धिहेतुत्वमवलम्बते स्वामिवत् । यथा आत्मनः एव संविदधानः स्वामी गर्भदासस्योपकरोति तथा नियोगोपि नियोज्यस्येति न प्राधान्यप्रच्युतिः ।

Here, a point has to be clarified. Though *niyoga* is accomplished by the performance of *yāga*, it does not produce the result immediately. This is because, it needs a *sahakārin*. Waiting for a *sahakārin* does not take away *karaṇatva* of a *karaṇa*. For producing the result both *apūrva* and *puruṣakāra* are necessary. The process of the emergence of *apūrva* is as under:

(i) The *utpattiniyogas* of *pradhāna* and *aṅgas* are accomplished by the performance of the concerned items and their *sannipatyopāraka aṅgas*. The *aṅga apūrvas* emerging from these contribute to the emergence of *pradhāna utpatti apūrva*. Finally, *paramāpūrva* emerges. Similarly, the emergence of *apūrva* in respect of *ārādupakārakas* also has to be worked out.

ननु नियोगस्य फलसाधनत्वात्, तस्य च सेति कर्तव्यताककरणनिबन्धन सिद्धित्वात् तदनुष्ठानानन्तरं नियोगसिद्धेः फलसिद्धिः स्यात् । अनन्तरं नियोगो न निष्पद्यते तर्हि क्रियायामतीतायां कुतः तत्सिद्धिरित्याह—

विषयानुष्ठितौ सत्यां सिद्धो नहि विधिः फलम् ।
तदानीमेव कुरुते सहकारिव्यपेक्षया ।। २९ ।।

एषा अत्रदर्शनस्थितिः प्रधानोत्पत्तिनियोगाः अङ्गोत्पत्तिनियोगाश्च यथायथं संनिपत्योपकारकाङ्गयुक्तस्वविषयमात्रानुष्ठानेनैव सिद्ध्यन्ति । तत्र यान्यङ्गपूर्वाणि तानि सम्भूय प्रधानोत्पत्त्यपूर्वेषु उपकुर्वन्ति तस्माच्च परमापूर्वं निष्पद्यते ।

यान्यपि चाङ्गपूर्वाणि दीक्षणीयादीनां तेषामपि आरादुपकारकातिदेशि-काङ्गभाजामेकमुत्पत्त्यपूर्वम्, अपरमङ्गापूर्वं प्रधानवद् वेदितव्यम् इति । अनया दिशा सर्वत्रापि ऊहनीयम् । इत्थं यद्यपि कर्मानुष्ठानानन्तरमेव नियोगसिद्धिः तथापि यत् फलस्यानन्तराभवनम् तत् उपपत्त्या कल्प्यते इति । २९ ।।

बाध्येतेत्यत्राह—

सहकारिव्यपेक्षा च करणत्वं न बाधते ।
मा बाधिष्ठेति सर्वत्रानुग्रहकल्पना ।। ३० ।।

तथेत्यर्थः 'अतः पुरुषकारश्च दैवं च फलसाधनमित्याचार्याः । दैवम्—अपूर्वम्, अपक्षेणीयं सहकारि पुरुषकारपदवेद्यम् ।

(प्र०पं० ४४३-४४४)

The Nature of Niyojya in Respect of Nityakarmas

So far the fact that the *kārya* is the import of injunctive suffix is discussed with reference to the injunctions in respect of *kāmya karmas*. Now, it has to be worked out with reference to *nitya* and *naimittika karmas,* and *niṣedhas* ie prohibitions. In these cases there is no result i.e., *svarga.* Therefore, it appears that it is difficult to get *adhikārin* and *niyojya* for the *kārya* i.e., *niyoga,* in these cases. However, the statement *yāvad jīvam agnihotram juhuyāt* states that *jīvana* is the ground for the *adhikāra* here. Hence, *adhikārin* and *niyojya* are available here without any reference to the result. It is made clear more than once that the result is not the ground for *pravṛtti* i.e., initiative, but it is the comprehension of *kārya.* Therefore, in the case of *nitya karmas* since the *adhikārin* and *niyojya* comprehends the *kārya* without needing the qualification of *phalakāmanā* to be an *adhikārin* and *niyojya,* there is no difficulty in undertaking initiative by him. He comprehends *kārya* from the Vedic injunction without the need of a result.

It is a trivial argument to say that in the absence of result he may infer *akāryatva* as well. Such arguments cannot take away the comprehension of *kārya* conveyed by the Vedic injunction.

It is true that the fact of *kārya* being the import of Vedic injunction is first worked out with reference to *kāmyakarma* injunctions. However, the same holds good in the case of *nityakarma* injunctions also.

ननु एवं भवतु काम्येषु अपूर्वकार्याभिधानं लिङादीनाम्, नित्यनैमित्तिकनिषेधाधिकारेषु कथम् ?

नहि तेषु फलोदयं प्राभाकराः अनुमन्यन्ते । नहि फलं फलतया अन्वीयते किन्तु अधिकारिविशेषणतया । लब्धे तु जीवनादौ अधिकारिविशेषणे किं फलान्वेषणेन । न च फलमन्तरेण प्रवृत्त्यसम्भवः स्वसम्बन्धिका-

र्यावगममात्रायत्तत्वात् प्रवृत्तेः । निरपेक्षात् शब्दात् फलमन्तरेणापि स्वसम्बन्धिकार्यावगमः । तावन्मात्रस्य लोके प्रवृत्तिहेतुत्वावगमात् । कार्यावगमोत्पादनायैव फलमुपयुज्यत इत्युक्तम् ।

ननु यथा शब्दात् कार्यावगतिः तथा निष्फलत्वादनुमानेन अकार्यताप्रतीतिरपीति कथं प्रवृत्त्युपपत्तिः ? न । आगमविरोधेन अनुमानस्य आत्मलाभाभावात् एतावानेव प्रमाणव्यापारः यत् प्रवृत्तियोग्यार्थोपदर्शनम् । अन्यथा यदि कश्चित् कल्पिते फले न प्रवर्तते तदा किं कर्तव्यम् ॥ ३० ॥

ननु फलोदयानभ्युपगमे च प्राच्यमार्गासम्भवात् नित्यादिषु अपूर्वकार्याभिधानमप्रमाणं स्यात् तत्राह—

एवं कामाधिकारार्थपर्यालोचनयोत्थिता ।
व्युत्पत्तिः सर्ववाक्यार्थप्रतिपत्तिनिबन्धनम् । ३१ ॥

उक्तमिदमन्याय्यं च अनेकार्थमिति । तेन कामाधिकारे सिद्धे अपूर्वकार्याभिधायकत्वे नित्यादिष्वपि स एवार्थो विरोधाभावादाश्रियते । नित्याधिकारानुगुण्येन तु क्रियाकार्यत्वाभिधानं काम्येषु अनुपपन्नमिति सर्वत्र अपूर्वमेव वाक्यार्थः इति ॥ ३१ ॥ (प्र०पं० ४४६)

The Import of Vedic Expression is Comprehended by Prasiddhapada Samabhivyavahāra also

In this context a point needs to be clarified. The import of a word in a Vedic passage is not only comprehended through its use in the conversation of the elders but also by the association of another word whose meaning is well known. This guideline is demonstrated in *yavavarāha adhikaraṇa.* The import of the words like *trivṛt, yūpa, āhavanīya* etc., is comprehended in this way also. Now, in the case of *kārya* i.e., *niyoga,* also its import is comprehended on the basis of its association with *niyojya.* Thus the import of an injunction as *kārya* could be ascertained both by elders' conversation and *prasiddhārtha padasamabhi vyāvahāra* i.e., occurrence along with a word of well known meaning.

There is a subtle distinction in the comprehension of the *kārya* as the chief import of an injunctive sentence and its special nature as *apūrva*. The *kārya* aspect is comprehended through elders' conversation while the *apūrva* aspect is known only by the Vedic injunctive suffix. That is why it is called *apūrva*.

(i) तत्र एतदेव तावद् वक्तव्यम्— न केवलं वेदे लोकव्यवहारादेव शब्दार्थावधारणं किन्तु प्रसिद्धार्थपदसम्बन्धादपि पदार्थान्तरान्वययोग्यार्थाभिधायकतेति स्थिते तदनुरूपार्थविधायकता निर्णीयत एव । एतच्च यववराहाधिकरणे व्युत्पादितम् । (१-३-५)

व्यवहारत एव सम्बन्धावधारणात् उभयथापि व्यवहारदर्शनात् समा विप्रतिपत्तिरिति पूर्वः पक्षः ।

पदान्तरसम्बन्धादपि पदान्तरार्थाध्यवसानं भवत्येव तेन वैदिकवाक्यशेषान्वयार्हतापर्यालोचनेन दीर्घशूकाद्यर्थत्वमेवेति राद्धान्तः ।

(ii) तथा त्रिवृत् शब्दे यूपाहवनीयादिषु शक्त्यवधारणात् । लोकेपि चायं व्यवहारो विपुलमुपलभ्यते । तथा सति वैदिकनियोज्यान्वययोग्यतया लिङादीनामपूर्वकार्याभिधायकत्वनिर्णयः न अनुपपन्नः ।

(iii) अयं च अपरो विशेषः यत् लिङादियुक्तानां वाक्यानां कार्यार्थत्वं तावद् वृद्धव्यवहारादेव सिद्धम् । किन्तु लिङादिप्रत्ययानां यद् वाच्यं कार्यम् तच्च अपूर्वपदमित्येतावन्मात्रं वैदिकपदसम्बन्धादवसीयते इति ।। ३१ ।। (प्र.पं. ४४६)

Kārya cannot be Comprehended by Laukika Vyavahāra

Śālikanātha quotes the view of a section of the Prābhākaras who insist that the *kārya* is comprehended by *laukika vyavahāra* also. It is found that when one hears an injunctive sentence he takes initiative. The initiative is always taken on the comprehension of *kārya* as distinct from *kriyā*. The comprehension of *kriyā* only cannot lead to initiative. Thus, one understands *kārya* by *vyavahāra*. This does not mean that such *vyavahāra* is necessarily *vaidika vākyavyavahāra*. The *kārya* is understood by *laukika vyavahāra* also. However, its *kāryatva* nature is understood by reflecting on Vedic injunctive sentences.

Śālikanātha does not agree with this view. *Kārya* cannot be known by any other means than Vedic injunction. Therefore, one cannot comprehend the denotative power of an injunctive suffix through *laukika vyavahāra.* In *laukika* injunctive sentences, the *kārya* is comprehended through *kriya* only. Just as *ākṛti* is comprehended through *vyakti, kārya is* comprehended through *kriyā* in *laukika* injunctions. *Kārya* as distinct from *kriyā* is not clearly understood in *laukika* injunctions. Since, *kārya* is not known by any other *pramāṇa* earlier, it cannot be communicated through *laukika vyavahāra.* The initiative is taken on the basis of *kriyā* only in the case of *laukika* statement. *Kriya* itself is taken as *kārya.* That is why it is called *kriyākārya.*

(i) एकदेशिमतमधुना निराकर्तुमुपन्यस्यति—

व्यवहारत एवाहुर्व्युत्पत्तिमपरे पुनः ।
कार्ये मानान्तरावेद्ये क्रियादिव्यतिरेकिणि ॥ ३१ ॥

अस्यार्थः—केचिदेवमाहुः लिङादियुक्तवाक्यश्रवणे प्रवृत्तिदर्शनात् कार्यावगतिनिबन्धनत्वात् प्रवृत्तेः कार्यमात्रमेव तेषामर्थः न क्रिया । ननु एवं वेदादेव व्युत्पत्तिरास्थिता स्यादित्याशङ्क्याह—

व्युत्पत्तिरपि कार्याऽर्थे व्यवहारानुसारिणी
किन्तु निर्धारणामात्रं वेदवाक्यविमर्शजम् ॥

तस्यां शब्दस्य प्रवृत्त्यनुपयोगित्वादिति क्रियानिष्कृष्टकार्याभिधायिता लौकिकव्यवहारादेव निर्णीयत इति ।

(i) तदिदमयुक्तमिति प्रतिजानीते ।

सितेतर इवत्वेष पक्षश्चित्तं न कर्षति ।
चन्द्रातपामलन्यायप्रवासमलिनीकृतः ॥ ३४ ॥

कथमित्याह—

कार्ये मानान्तरावेद्ये पार्श्वस्थः तन्निबन्धनम् ।
व्यवहारं कथं कारं शब्दात् प्रागवबुद्ध्यताम् ॥ ३५ ॥

व्यवहारमविज्ञाय तन्निबन्धनतद्गता ।
प्रतिपत्तिः कथं ज्ञेया शब्दशक्तिः कथंतराम् ॥ ३६ ॥

इदमत्राकूतम् । यद्यपि कार्यमात्रमेव प्रवृत्त्युपयोगीति तावन्मात्रमेव शब्दार्थः तथापि लोके तस्य क्रियागतस्यैव प्रवृत्तिदर्शनात् शक्यते क्रियाश्रितता प्रत्येतुम् । यथा आकृतिमात्रस्य शब्दार्थत्वेपि व्यक्त्याश्रिततापि न प्रतिक्षिप्यते तथा क्रियाश्रितत्वं प्रमाणान्तरप्रमितं न प्रतिक्षेपमर्हति । तेन क्रियातिरिक्तकार्याभिधायकत्वमसिद्धम् । यदि परं तन्निबन्धनव्यवहार एव स्यात् तद्दर्शनात् तद्धेतुभूतप्रतिपत्त्यन्यथानुपपत्त्या अनुमानेन शब्दस्य वाचकत्वाध्यवसानं भवेत् । न चैतदस्ति, तस्य शब्दादन्यतः प्रागनवगमात् तन्निबन्धनव्यवहाराप्रतीतिः । तदप्रतिपत्तौ च तद्धेतुभूतप्रतिपत्त्यनुमानात् न शक्तिकल्पनोपपत्तिः ॥ ३४-३६ ॥

तत्राकूतं विवृणोति—

कार्यप्रतीतिमात्रं च प्रवृत्तेरनुमीयताम् ।
किन्तु कार्या क्रियैवेति लोकदृष्ट्या अवसीयते ।

(प्र०पं० ४४६-४७)

लोकप्रतीतं क्रियारूपत्वं च न शक्यते अपह्नोतुं इति कार्यमात्रार्थत्वे क्रियैव कार्यतया लिङाद्यर्थ इति निश्चीयते । न पुनः प्रमाणान्तरादपूर्वम् ॥ ३७॥

The Concepts of Kriyākārya and Apūrvakārya

Some people argue that since, pupils proceed to undertake the performance of morning and evening prayers etc., on the words of their teachers, they comprehend *kārya* as distinct from *kriyā* through *laukika* sentence also. They would not have undertaken to perform these if they had not comprehended *kārya*. Performance of these is a strenuous activity and does not give any pleasure. In case, it is understood as *kārya*, its performance can be justified. Therefore, the *laukika* statement of the teacher also conveys *kārya*. Śālikanātha does not agree with this view. He points out that the pupil comprehends *kriya kārya* only from the statement of the teacher. They take initiative on this basis only. If necessary, a result also may be envisaged to induce it. However, the *apūrvatā* nature of *kārya* is understood only through the Vedic injunctive suffix. To distinguish the *kārya* conveyed through *kriya* by *laukika* injunctions and *kārya* conveyed by Vedic injunctions, Śālikanātha uses the expressions *kriyakārya* for the former and *apūrvakārya* for the latter. These are not opposed to each other. The expression *apūrvakārya* conveys the primary sense.of the term *kārya* while the expression *kriyākārya* expresses the secondary sense. An average person cannot comprehend this subtle distinction and therefore, he takes *kriyā* itself as *kārya* in the *laukika* usage. To conclude, a Vedic injunctive sentence conveys *kārya* connected with the meanings of the other relevant words in the sentence. This *kārya* is conveyed only by a Vedic injunction.

(i) अन्ये पुनः वेदार्थबोधकाचार्यवचननिबन्धनप्रवृत्तिदर्शनेन अतीन्द्रिये कार्ये लिङादयो व्युत्पद्यन्त इत्याहुः । यदि आचार्यवचनादपि क्रियैव कार्यतया अवगम्यते तदा तस्याः स्वयं दुःखरूपत्वात् पुरुषार्थान्तरानुबन्धनं विना प्रवृत्त्यसम्भवात् नियमेन सुखार्थिनः प्रवृत्तिः न स्यात् । न च सन्ध्योपासनादौ पुरुषार्थोऽस्ति । तस्मात् क्रियातिरिक्तकार्यमाचार्यवचनेभ्यो अवगम्यते ।

(ii) तान् प्रत्याह–

वेदार्थाचार्य वाक्येषु प्रवृत्तिर्यापि दृश्यते ।
तत्रापि एषैव सम्बन्धपरिज्ञानविधा भवेत् ॥ ३८ ॥

आचार्यवाक्यश्रवणादपि शिष्याणां या सन्ध्योपासनादौ प्रवृत्तिः तत्रापि बालः स्वविषयनिरूपितं क्रियाकार्य विषयत्वावगममेव कारणत्वेन

परिकल्पयेत्। फलं विना च तदनुपपत्तेः फलागममपि सम्भावयेत्। लोकव्युत्पत्त्यनुसारेण वेदार्थमपि प्रतिपद्यमानः नित्यनैमित्तिक निषेधाधिकारेष्वपि फलं कल्पयेत्। स एव बाल्यदशायां व्युत्पन्नः स्वयमाचार्यपदवीमारूढः वेदार्थं प्रतीत्य शिष्येभ्यः उपदिशन् क्रियामेव कार्यतया प्रतिपादयेत्। नापूर्वं कार्यमिति।

उपसंहरति—

तस्मात् लोकानुसारेण व्युत्पत्तिः कार्यमात्रके।
तस्य तु अपूर्वरूपत्वं वेदवाक्यानुसारतः॥ ३९॥

(iii) एवमपूर्वकार्याभिधायित्वे सिद्धे चोदयति—

ननु लोकविरोधित्वं पक्षेऽस्मिन्नपि दृश्यते।
सर्वथैव यतो लोके क्रिया कार्यैव गम्यते॥ ४०॥

परिहरति—

भवेदेवं विरुध्येते कार्यापूर्वेपि, लौकिकौ।
प्रतिपत्तिप्रयोगौ चेत् क्रियाकार्यत्वगौचरौ॥

यदि क्रियाकार्यत्वगोचरौ लौकिकौ प्रतिपत्तिप्रयोगौ अपूर्वकार्यत्वाङ्गीकारे विरुध्येते ततो लोकविरुद्धत्वं स्यादस्मत् पक्षस्य। न चैतदस्तीत्याह—

अपूर्वं हि क्रियासाध्यं साधिता साधनं क्रिया।
तस्मादपूर्वकार्यत्वं क्रियाकार्यत्वसङ्गतम्।
प्रमाणान्तरगम्यं हि लोकः शब्दैः विवक्षति।
क्रियाकार्यत्व एवातः प्रयोगो लक्षणान्वितः।

प्रतिपत्तिप्रयोगौहि न अवश्यं श्रौतवृत्त्यनुसारिणावेव, लक्षणयापि लोके तद्दर्शनात्। तेन यद्यपि उक्तेन न्यायेन अपूर्वमेव कार्यं लिङादीनामभिधेयम्, तथापि तस्य क्रियाकार्यत्वाव्यभिचारात् तत्र लक्षणया तयोर्नानुपपत्तिः।

यत्तु श्रौतपदार्थे कार्ये लोके लिङादि न प्रयुज्यते इति तत् तस्यापूर्वात्मनः प्रमाणान्तराप्रतीतत्वात् प्रतितिविषयत्वाच्च लौकिकप्रयोगस्य। क्रिया साध्यं तु अपूर्वम्, साधिता च सती क्रिया साधनं भवति इति अपूर्वेण सह क्रियाकार्यत्वं नित्यसम्बद्धमिति शक्यते तल्लक्षयितुम् ।। ४२-४३।।

(iv) यद्येषा लक्षणा किमिति तर्हि लोको नावगच्छतीत्याह—

लक्षणानभिमानस्तु मुखयार्थानवधारणात् ।
ये तु मुखयार्थकुशलाः तेषां लाक्षणिकत्वधीः ।

मुखयमर्थमविदित्वा लाक्षणिकमपि अर्थं श्रौतमिव मन्यन्ते म्लेच्छा इव यववराहाद्यर्थम्। मुखयार्थविवेकिनो तु परीक्षकाणां लाक्षणिकत्वधीः इति ।। ४४ ।।

उपसंहरति—

तस्मान्मानान्तरावेद्यं कार्यमर्थान्तरान्वितम् ।
वेदवाक्यं ब्रवीतीति संक्षेपोऽयमुदहृतः ।।
४५ ।। (प्र०पं० ४४८-४९)

In the context of the development of the concepts of *kriyā kārya* and *apūrva kārya*, a clarification is necessary. There is no conflict between *kriyā kārya* and *apūrva kārya*. These two concepts are utilized in their respective areas of *laukika* injunction and Vedic injunction. In fact *apūrva kārya is* accomplished by *kriya. Kriya* is the means and the accomplishment of *apūrva kārya* is the result. Hence, the use of the expression *kārya* for *apūrva* is primary while its use for *kriya* is secondary. The former is conveyed by Vedic injunction and the latter by *laukika* injunction.

CHAPTER XII

Viṣaya Karaṇīyam

Yāga is both Viṣaya and Karaṇa

It is already stated that the injunctive suffix conveys *kārya*. The same suffix conveys *kṛti* also. *Kṛti* is of the nature of initiative. It is an activity of the self and comprehended by the mind. Self is the agent for *kārya*. He accomplishes *kārya* by his *kṛti* through the activity i.e., *yāga*. As it is an activity of the agent i.e., *bhavituḥ*, who accomplishes *kārya* i.e., *bhāvya*, it is called *bhāvanā*. It is conveyed by the injunctive suffix as subordinate while *kārya* is conveyed as main. There can be no objection for these two being conveyed by one and the same injunctive suffix, since, these two are not conveyed on equal basis.

The *kṛti* i.e., initiative, is invariably connected with an action. The initiative is undertaken to accomplish *kārya* conveyed by the injunctive suffix. Therefore, the initiative accomplishes the *kārya* through the action i.e., *yāga*.

1. कार्यञ्च कृतीप्सितमुच्यते । कृतिः—आत्मव्यपारः पुरुषव्यापारः इत्यनर्थान्तरम् । चेतनश्च आत्मा कार्ये बोद्धृतया अन्वयमुपैति । न च अन्यव्यापाराभिनिर्वर्त्यमन्यः स्वसम्बन्धितया कार्यत्वेन संवेदयितुमलमिति आत्मनः मानसप्रत्यक्षसमधिगमनीयः प्रयत्नः स्वव्यापारः । अतः तन्निर्वर्त्यमेव अपूर्वं कार्यमात्मा मन्यते ।

प्रयत्न एव भवितव्ये अपूर्वे प्रयोजकीभूतस्य भावयितुः आत्मनः व्यापारः इति भावना शब्देन उच्यते । न च कार्याभिधानं कृतिमनभिदधतां

लिङादीनामुपपद्यत इति ते कृतिमपि अभिदधति अपूर्वञ्च । न च युगपदनेकाभिधानं दोषः । तथा अवगमात् आनुगुण्याच्च । अवगताहि प्रमाणेन लिङादीनां कार्याभिधायिता । आनुगुण्यात् कृतिः गुणभूता प्रधानपदवर्तिनि अपूर्वात्मनि कार्ये । अविवादाच कर्त्रादिगतसङ्ख्यावाचिता लिङादीनां कार्याभिधायिनामपि । न च अभिधेयतामात्रेण भावनाया एव वाक्यार्थत्वम् । भाव्यमपूर्वं प्रति गुणभावेन अभिधानात् । प्रधानभावेन अपूर्वस्य अभिधानात् तदेव वाक्यार्थ इति न किञ्चिदनुपपन्नम् । अत एव भगवतो भाष्यकारस्य तत्र तत्र व्यवहारः—पुरुषप्रयत्नः करणमपूर्वस्य भावना उच्यते इति । (प्र०पं० ४५२)

Yāga is both Viṣaya and Karaṇa

The action performed by the initiative gives a form to the *kārya* and in a way becomes its content. In fact the *kārya* is observed through the action only. The performance of *yāga* is such an action and therefore, *yāga* is the *viṣaya* of the *kārya* conveyed by a Vedic injunctive suffix.

तस्य तथाविधस्य कार्यस्य नूनं केनचित् भावार्थेन अवच्छेदः । नहि प्रयत्नो भावार्थमन्तरेणास्ति । सर्वोहि पुरुषप्रयत्नः कश्चिद् भावार्थमवश्यमाश्रयते तेन विना तदभावात् । तेन प्रयत्नाविनाभावी भावार्थः प्रयत्नाभिनिर्वर्त्यमपूर्वमवच्छिनत्ति ।

अवच्छेदकतयैव विषयभावः । यत्रैव यो भवति नान्यत्र स तस्य विषयः इति विषयविदः । अनन्यत्र भावो विषयशब्दार्थः इति च । अतः भाव्य एवार्थो विषयः भाव्यस्यैव पुरुषप्रयत्नगोचरत्वात् । तेन कार्याभिधायिभिः सह विषयबोधकतयैव भावार्थः कर्मशब्दः समभिव्याहारं प्रथममर्हति । तस्य प्रतिपत्त्यनुबन्धत्वात् । अविषयं हि अपूर्वं कार्यं प्रत्येतुमशक्यम् ।

प्रतीतस्य हि कार्यस्य साधनाकाङ्क्षा तेन न जघन्यया साधनतया भावार्थानामपूर्वेण सह अन्वयः । किन्तु प्रतीत्युपायतामेव मन्यमानः भगवान् ब्रूते न हि अविषयात् नियोगात् नियोगज्ञानमुत्पद्यते । (प्र०पं० ४५३)

The *kārya* also needs a *karaṇa*. Ordinarily, that which is connected with the initiative undertaken to achieve certain result is *karaṇa*. In the present context, initiative is connected with the action i.e., *yāga*. Therefore, *yāga* itself serves the purpose of *karaṇa* also. Just as an axe associated with the rise and the fall to cut a piece of wood is the *karaṇa*, the action i.e., *yāga*, associated with the initiative to accomplish *kārya* is the *karaṇa* for that *kārya*. Though the performance of *yāga* is the result of the initiative, it is not *bhāvya*. It is only *karaṇa*. It is through the *yāga* that the *kṛti* i.e., *bhāvanā*, accomplishes *kārya* i.e., *apūrva*, therefore, it is designated as *apūrva bhāvanā*. This status of *apūrvabhāvanātva* is due to the performance of *yāga*. It is in this sense that the *yāga* is *karaṇa* but not in the sense ot causing the *kṛti* or *kārya*, since the *yāga* is *karaṇa* the statements such as *udbhīdā yajeta* are justified.

1. **स च विषयीभूतभावार्थावच्छिन्नो विध्यर्थः कार्यात्मा प्रतीतः करणम् इतिकर्तव्यतां च अपेक्षते । अन्यत्रापि साध्ये तथा दर्शनात् । तत्र स एव भावार्थः विषयीभूतः करणमित्यवसीयते कृतिव्याप्यत्वात् । यो हि यया कृत्या अन्यार्थप्रवृत्तया विषयीक्रियते स एव तत्र करणम् । यथा परशुः उद्यमननिपतनाभ्यां काष्ठगतद्वैधीभावलक्षणकार्ये प्रवृत्ताभ्यां व्याप्यमानः तयोरेव द्विधाभवनलक्षण फलावच्छेदलब्ध-द्वैधीकरणव्यपदेश्ययोः छिदिधातुवाच्ययोः करणम् तथा इहापि अपूर्वार्थप्रवृत्तपुरुषप्रयत्नव्याप्यमानो भावार्थः तस्मिन्नेव प्रयत्ने अपूर्वभावनारूपे करणम् ।**

ननु कथं प्रयत्नलब्धात्मा भावार्थः भावनायां करणम् । भाव्यमानतया कर्मेव स्यात् । उच्यते । तत्र धात्वर्थो न कर्म अपूर्वार्थकृतिविषयत्वात् । सर्वाणि एव हि कारकाणि कर्तृव्यतिरिक्तानि तद्व्यापारव्याप्यानि । न चैतावता तानि कर्मतां भजन्ते । अनीप्सितत्वात् । क्वचिच्च अनीप्सिते कर्मता दृश्यत एव । यथा 'अग्निहोत्रं जुहोति' इति ।

करणं तु यद्यपि स्वरूपनिवृत्तौ न सम्भवति तथापि अपूर्वभावनारूपता तदधीनेति अनुपपन्नम् । यथा परशोरेव ।

नहि परशुः कर्म, करणं तु भवति । अनीप्सितत्वात् । उद्यमन निपातनयोः द्वैधीकरणरूपतायाः तदधीनत्वात् । परशुसम्बन्धप्रभावेन हि उद्यमननिपातने द्वेधाभवनफलनिष्पादकतया द्वेधाभवने करणतां भजेते ।

अतः उद्भिदा यजेत (ता०ब्रा० १९.७.२.३) इति तृतीया निर्देशोपपत्तिः । अपूर्वभावनायां करणत्वाद् यागस्य तन्नामत्वाच्च उद्भिद् शब्दस्य । एवं च अपूर्वफलयोः एकैव भावना एकत्वात् पुरुषप्रयत्नस्य । एकमेव च करणम् । तद्भावनाव्याप्यत्वात् एकैव भाव्यता । अत एव च साध्यविवृद्धिरियमिति प्राभाकराः । (प्र०पं० ४५४)

The position of one and the same i.e., *yāga* being treated both as *viṣaya* and *karaṇa* appears to create some problems in the instance of *darśapūrṇamāsa* which consists of *āgneya* etc., six *yāgas*. While these *yāgas* together constitute one *viṣaya*, these are considered as *karaṇa* separately. This means that the oneness of *viṣaya* and *karaṇa* is given up here. Therefore, a clarification is needed to explain the nature of oneness of *viṣaya* and *karaṇa*. By oneness it is not meant that the *viṣaya* and *karaṇa* should have one to one agreement. But it is meant that whatever constitutes *viṣaya* the same is *karaṇa*. In this instance wherein more than one *yāga* constitutes a unit, they are together *viṣaya*, because, these accomplish the *kārya* together. However, these are separately *karaṇa*, because, each item has to be separately performed. But the content of both *viṣaya* and *karaṇa* are the same. A point to be noted here is that though the *karaṇas* are separately performed one and the same *niyoga* is accomplished. The *utpatti apūrvas* of these are different while *paramāpūrva* is one.

यदि विषयीभूतस्य करणता हन्त तर्हि दर्शपूर्णमासाभ्यामित्यत्र तन्त्राभिहितानां तन्त्रेणैव प्रतिपत्यनुबन्धत्वात् । विषयभावस्यैकत्वादेकमेव करणं स्यात् ततश्च भेदेन इतिकर्तव्यता सम्बन्धो न स्यात् ।

उच्यते—न सम्यगवधृतमायुष्मता श्रुतिशालिनां वचः । यदेव विषयीभूतं तदेव करणं नान्यदिति तस्यार्थः । प्रतीत्यनुबन्धतयाच विषयभावः स यथाभिधानमवकल्पते । प्रतिपत्त्युपायत्वादभिधानस्य । अतः तन्त्राभिधानात् सहितानां विषयभावः, करणं तु सिद्ध्यनुबन्धी नियोगस्य तच्च यथास्वभावं वेदितव्यम् । स्वभावाधीना हि साधनानां साधकता इति स्वभावभेदे भिन्ना साधकता । साधकत्वे च कृतिविषयत्वात् करणतेति भेदेन करणभावः ।

ननु एवं प्रत्येकं करणाश्रयणे करणान्तरनिरपेक्षाणां किमिति नियोगसिद्धिहेतुता न भवति ? नैवं यथाश्रुतकरणाधीनसिद्धित्वात् नियोगस्य । तत्र बहूनि करणानि श्रूयन्त इति तथैव तस्य सिद्धिः । अनेककारणसम्पाद्यतापि एकस्य दृष्टा । यथा गमनस्य अश्वेन शिबिकया रथेन वा गच्छतीति । भिन्नस्तत्र कारणावान्तरव्यापारः इति यद्युच्येत अत्रापि उत्पत्त्यपूर्वाणि अवान्तरव्यापारभूतानि भिन्नानि सङ्गिरामहे एव । अत एव तद्भेदेन भिन्नत्वात् करणभावस्य परमापूर्वप्रयुक्तत्वेपि आज्यौषधसान्नायधर्माणामसङ्करः । अपूर्वसाधननिवेशित्वात् धर्माणाम् तस्य च भेदात् ।

Those who do not accept *bhāvanā* i.e., *kṛti*, to connect *yāga* with *apūrva* i.e., *kārya*, will not be able to assign the status of *karaṇatva* to *yāga*. *Karaṇatva* is due to a *vyāpāra*. *Apūrva* by itself is not a *vyāpāra*. Therefore, *kṛti* is required to bring about the *karaṇatva* of *yāga*.

ये पुनः यागादीनां अपूर्वं च अन्तरा भावनां न अनुमन्यन्ते तेषां यागादीनां करणभावो दुर्घटः । अव्यापाररूपत्वादपूर्वस्य व्यापारसम्बन्ध प्रभवत्वाच्च करणभावस्य ।

गौणं करणत्वमिति चेत् । कथं तर्हि इतिकर्तव्यता सम्बन्धः ? करणं हि इतिकर्तव्यतया सम्बध्यते गौणञ्च न करणम् । न हि गौणे मुखयधर्मः सम्भवति ।

Śalikanātha rejects the view that all verbal terminations convey *bhāvanā*.

येपि सर्वाख्यातेषु भावनाभिधानमाहुः तेषामपि मतमस्मभ्यं न रोचते। नहि कार्यानभिधायिषु लडादिषु भावनाभिधाने प्रमाणमस्ति ।

यदपि किं करोति पचतीत्युत्तरदर्शनं प्रमाणमुपन्यस्तम् तदपि न साधकम् । व्यापारविशेषप्रश्नोऽयं किं करोतीति । तत्र पचतीत्युत्तरेणापि तदेव निर्दिश्यते । अत एव अचेतनव्यापारे वर्तमानापदेशादीनां प्रयोगः । लिङादयस्तु चेतनमेव अधिकृत्य प्रयुज्यन्ते । (प्र०पं० ४५६)

CHAPTER XIII

Aṅgapārāyaṇa – I
Exposition of Aṅgas – I

Sannipatyopakārakas

In this chapter the nature and role of *sannipatyopakāraka aṅgas* is described. The *sannipatyopakāraka* is of four types viz., *utpatti* i.e., origination, *prāpti* i.e., obtaining, *vikṛti* i.e., change, and *sanskṛti* i.e., refinement. The ritualistic instances of these are-a rice ball is prepared, the milk is obtained from the cow, the ghee is melted and the paddy is sprinkled with the water. A *sannipatyopakāraka* is defined as that which produces the result by the operation on the agent, object, instruments etc., *kārakas*. For instance *tīrthe snāti* (bathes in the holy water) is a *sanskāra* for the agent, *vrihin āvahanti* (pounds the paddy) is a *sanskāra* for the object, *Tapte payasi dadhi ānayati* i.e., puts the curd in the heated milk is a *sanskāra* for the locus etc. These are all *sannipatyopakārakas* of *sanskāra* type.

इह चतुर्विधमङ्गजातम्—जातिगुणद्रव्यभावार्थात्मकम् । तत्र भावार्थात्मकमपि द्विविधम्—सन्निपत्योपकारकम्, आरादुपकारकञ्चेति । तत्र सन्निपत्योपकारकं चतुर्विधम् । साध्यभूतोत्पत्ति-प्राप्ति-विकृति—संस्कृति भेदात् । यथाक्रमं संयवन दोहनविलापन-प्रोक्षणादिरूपम् । तत्र संयवनेन प्रागभूतं पिण्डमुत्पद्यते । सदेव क्षीरं दोहनेन प्राप्यते । विलापनेन प्राचीं संहतामवस्थामपबाध्य इतरा द्रवावस्था आज्यस्य उत्पद्यते ।

किं पुनरेतेषां सन्निपत्योपकारिणां लक्षणम्? यत् कारकविध्यपेक्षं फलं जनयति तत् सन्निपत्योपकारकम् । यथा कर्तरि स्नानम्, कर्मणि अवघातादि, अधिकरणे दध्यानयनमित्याद्यूह्यम् । (प्र० पं० ४५८)

No Separate Injunctions for Aṅgas

Here, Śālikanātha raises the question whether *avaghāta* etc., *sannipatyopakārakas* have their own separate injunctions or these are connected with the ultimate *kārya*. The Bhāṭṭas hold the view that these have their own separate injunctions. They argue that if separate injunctions are not envisaged these cannot be considered as *aṅgas*. These cannot be treated as *aṅgas* through their association with *dravya*, because, the words *vrīhi* etc., convey only *vrīhitva* etc., universal, but not the *vrīhi-vyakti*. The *vyakti* is comprehended by *lakṣaṇā*. Its status as a means of *apūrva* is not comprehended. This status cannot be conveyed by further *lakṣaṇā*, because, indulging in double *lakṣaṇā* is not permissible. Without the comprehension of *apūrvasādhanatva*, the *aṅgatva* of these cannot be comprehended. If these are not *aṅgas*, then, these need not be performed. On the other hand, if *utpattividhi* type of injunctions are accepted for these *aṅgas*, the *adhikāra* to perform these will have to be envisaged. Since, no separate *adhikāra* is mentioned in this context, he who is entitled to perform the main sacrifice will have to be considered as *adhikārin* to perform the *prayāja* etc., *aṅgas* also. In this way the *aṅgatva* of these could be worked out.

तत्र सन्निपत्योपकारकाङ्गवाक्येषु केचित् पृथग् विधीन् अभ्युपगच्छन्ति । तेहि मन्यन्ते यद्यत्र पृथग् विधयो नाभ्युपेयेरन् तदा अधिकृताधिकारादङ्गतैव अवघातादीनां न स्यात् । न च द्रव्यसम्बन्धमुखेन प्रकृताधिकारापूर्व-सम्बन्धाङ्गतासिद्धिः व्रीह्यादिशब्दानामाकृतिवचनत्वात् । यद्यपि कार्यप्रत्यासन्नतया व्यक्तीनां तल्लक्षणार्थो जातिशब्दः तथापि व्यक्तिमात्रं लक्ष्यते न अपूर्वविशेषसम्बद्धा व्यक्तिः ।

न च प्रकृततया आग्नेयीवत् तदपूर्वसाधनव्यक्तिलक्षणावशेन अपूर्वसम्बन्धः । यद्यपि आग्नेयीन्यायेन सन्निहितव्यक्तिपरिग्रहः तथापि

स्वरूपेणैव तासाम् अप्रकृतव्यक्तिपरिहारेण प्रतीतिः । न पुनः अपूर्वविशेषसाधनतया, तस्य स्वरूपस्य लाक्षणिकत्वात् ।

न च लक्षितलक्षणायां कारणमस्ति । जात्या व्यक्तिः लक्ष्यते, व्यक्त्या च साधनविशेषः इति लक्षितलक्षणा कारणाभावात् अयुक्ता ।

एवञ्च स्वरूपमात्रेणैव अवधातादीनां सम्बन्धात् न अपूर्वविशेषसम्बन्धसिद्धिः ।

ततश्चाधिकारापूर्वं प्रति अवधातादीनामङ्गता न स्यात् । तदनङ्गत्वे च तत्प्रयुक्त्यभावात् अवघातादीनामनुष्ठानं न स्यात् । अतः अवघातादिषु उत्पत्त्यपूर्वो अङ्गीकरणीयः । तस्मिन् खलु आश्रिते अधिकाराभावे तस्य अननुष्ठानापत्तेः अधिकारिणि कल्पयितव्ये प्रकृताधिकारापूर्वे अधिकृत एव प्रयाजादिष्वपि अधिक्रियत इति । (प्र०पं० ४५८-५९)

This approach to work out *aṅgatva* is not acceptable to the Prābhākaras. They point out that if a separate injunction is envisaged in respect of *avaghāta* etc., there arise two *kāryas* to be accomplished. The *kārya* comprehended through the main injunction and the *kārya* comprehended through the intermediary injunction. This is not desirable. In respect of main injunction also, no doubt, two results are achieved viz., accomplishment of *kārya* and providing of svarga. However, in this case, one of the results viz., *svarga* gets connected with *niyojya* as his qualification, but here the *avaghāta* etc., are not connected in that way. The result of *niyoga* only is the qualification of *niyojya.*

तदिदं तत्र भवानुपाध्यायो न मृष्यति । तदाह अनभिज्ञो भवान् विषयनियोज्यानामित्यत्र । (बृ०टी० ३-१-३)

अवघातादिषु शब्दतः वस्तुस्वभावतश्च तुषकणविमोचनादि दृष्टम् । प्रोक्षणादिषु शब्दतः एव अदृष्टञ्च कार्यमङ्गीक्रियते । तत्र यदि नियोगोपि अपरः आश्रीयेत कार्यभूतः तदा कार्यद्वयमेकस्मिन् वाक्ये अन्वीयते । न च यथा स्वर्गादिकं फलं तथाभूतमेतद् भवितुमर्हति । तस्य नियोज्यविशेषणत्वेन

अन्वीयमानत्वात् न च तुषकणविमोचनादिनियोज्यविशेषणम् । क्रियाफलत्वात् । यदेव नियोगफलं तदेव नियोज्यविशेषणतामनुभवति ।

साध्यविशिष्टो हि नियोज्यः तदेव कार्यतया प्रतिपत्तुमर्हति यदेव तस्य साध्यं साधयतीति नियोज्यविशेषणस्य सिद्धिरवसीयते । यच्च क्रियाफलं न तन्नियोगात् सिद्ध्यतीति न तद्विशिष्टो नियोगे नियुज्यतामश्नुते । न च प्रतीततुषकणविमोचनकार्यत्यागो युक्तः प्रतीतहानादेव ।

The injunctions stated in connection with *avaghāta* etc., are not to be taken as separate injunctions. If *avaghāta* etc., could not be included in the subject-matter of the main injunction, then, there would have been a case to cover these by separate injunctions. These are related with the main injunction only. Mere *vrīhi* etc., cannot be related with the injunction, *avaghāta* has to be taken into account. If *avaghāta* is not related with the injunction, then, the other alternatives of removing the husk could not be ruled out. Since, *avaghāta* etc., are connected with the main injunction, the statement of separate injunctions in respect of these should be taken as *anuvāda* but not as separate injunctions.

१. सन्निहिते विधौ विधिरवगम्यमानः स एव तावदवगन्तुमुचितः । तत्र यदि तद्विषयानुप्रवेशिता न स्यात् तर्हि भवेद् विध्यन्तरम् । अनुप्रविशति च अवधातादि तद्विषयं तदर्थव्रीह्यादिसम्बन्धात् ।

२. यदि स्वरूपमात्रावस्थितैः व्रीह्यादिभिः सह सम्बन्धः स्यात् तदा तदधिकारसम्बन्धो न स्यादिति तदीयसाधनविशेषलक्षणया व्रीह्यादिपदैः उपस्थापितः अवधातादिभिः अन्वीयते । न स्वरूपमात्रम् ।

३. अत एव अवधातादयो नियोगसाधनतया अप्राप्ता एव विधीयन्ते । नियमस्तु प्रयोजनम् । यदि नियोगाङ्गतया अवधातादयो न विधीयेरन् तदा पुरोडाशमात्रसिद्ध्यर्थतया नखविदलनाद्यप्याक्षिप्येत ।

४. नियोगाङ्गत्वाच्च अवधातादीनां नियोगसम्बन्धः प्राप्तः सः लिङादिभिः अनूद्यते । (प्र०पं० ४६०)

It should be noted here that *avaghāta* etc., are not the subject-matter of the injunction in the full sense. These are only related with the injunction. That which accomplishes the injunction is only its subject but not that which is merely related. A*vaghāta* etc., carry out only an intermediary activity viz., removing the husk. This does not entitle it to be the subject-matter of the injunction. However, these are related with the injunction since these are utilised to accomplish the injunction. On this ground these are considered as *aṅga*. However, these are not *viṣaya*.

ननु यदि अवधातादीनां नियोगसम्बन्धोऽस्ति कथं तर्हि तेषां नियोगाविषयत्वमुच्यते । इत्थमुच्यते—न नियोगसम्बन्धितामात्रमुच्यते यस्य नियोगसिद्धिरेव कार्यं स विषयः । अवधातादीनां च तुषकणविमोचनाद्य-वान्तरं कार्यं कुर्वतां नियोगाविषयत्वम् । तेन नियोगाविषयत्वम्, अङ्गता चेतिसिद्धम् ।

विधेयास्तु अवधातादयः नियोगसिद्ध्यर्थतया उपादीयमानत्वात् । तदुक्तम्- यत्तु तत्सिद्ध्यर्थ—मुपादीयते तद्विधेयमिति तन्त्रे व्यवहारः । (सू०२-बृ०टी०पृ० ३६) तदेवं प्रत्यभिज्ञामात्रोपबृंहितसन्निधानमात्रेणैव अवधातादीनां नियोगाङ्गता न पदार्थान्वयमुखेन । (प्र०पं० ४६०)

A*vaghāta* etc., are not to be considered as related with the injunction through the connection with the *vrīhi* etc., items. In this case, *pāñcadaśya* and *sāptadaśya* will also have to be considered as connected through *sāmadheni*. This means both of these will belong to *prakṛti* only and will have to be performed alternately. This is not desirable. On the other hand, if these are taken as connected by their proximity to the injunction, *pāñcadaśya* will have precedence and gets connected with *prakṛti*. The *sāptadaśya* will naturally get connected with *vikṛti* and *vikalpa* will be avoided.

येषां पुनः पदार्थान्वयमुखेन अनुप्रवेशः अभिमतः तेषां प्रकरणाधीतस्य पाञ्चदश्यस्य अनारभ्याधीतस्य साप्तदश्यस्य सामधेनीमुखेन अनुप्रवेशिनोः अविशेषात् उभयोरपि प्रकृतावेव निवेशः विकल्पश्च स्यात् । सन्निधानमात्रेण

तु प्रकरणाधीतस्य ग्रहणे शीघ्रं पाञ्चदश्यमधिकारानुप्रविष्टमिति तदवरुद्धे साप्तदश्यमधिकारविधौ नानुप्रविशति । तेन विकृतावेव तस्य निवेशः । (प्र०प० ४६१)

In the instance *yasya parṇamayī juhūḥ bhavati* juhū is invariably associated with the sacrifice, *Parṇatā* is related with it. Therefore, *parṇatā* is related with sacrifice through *juhū,* though it is not stated in the context of any injunction.

यदि सन्निधानतो अधिकारविधौ अनुप्रवेशः तर्हि पर्णतादीनामनारभ्याधीतानां कथमनुप्रवेशः? उच्यते जुह्वादयो अव्यभिचरितक्रतुसम्बन्धा इति तत्सम्बन्धमुखेन क्रतुसम्बन्धसिद्धिः तत्सम्बद्धेष्वेव च जुह्वादिषु पर्णतादिसम्बन्धात् । (प्र०पं० ४६१)

In connection with the explanation of the nature of *sannipatyopakārakas*, Śālikanātha clarifies a statement of *Bhāṣyakāra* viz., *na avihitam aṅgam bhavati.* The remark applies to *ārādupakārakas* but not *sannipatyopakārakas.* Therefore, the stand taken by the Prābhākaras viz., 'The *aṅgatva* of *sannipatyopakārakas,* could be managed by their connection with the main injunction only. These are not enjoined by separate injunctions. The separate injunctive sentences found in respect of *aṅgas* are merely the *anuvāda* i.e., restatements of the main injunction' is quite in order.

The Role of Śruti, Liṅga etc.

From the above discussion, it is clear that the fact of *avaghāta* etc., *sannipatyopakārakas,* being the *aṅgas* is determined by their very connection with the *kārya* i.e., *niyoga,* through *vrīhi* etc. Therefore, the question arises as to what is the role of *śruti, lṅga* etc., that are stated to be the criteria to point out the *aṅgatva.* Śālikanātha explains the role of *śruti, liṅga* etc., as under:

In the statement *vrīhin avahanti* the *dvitiyaśruti* i.e., accusative suffix, does not determine that the *vrīhi* is *aṅgi* and *avaghāta* is *aṅga.* The *aṅgatva* of *vrīhi* as well as that of *avaghāta* is determined by their association with *kārya*. It is only restated by the case suffix. The fact of *vrīhi* being the *aṅga* and also its being the medium to the *avaghāta* is restated by the accusative suffix. The *aṅgitva* i.e., *śeṣitva*, is not the import of accusative suffix. Its import viz., *karmatva*, has to be explained as *kriyājanyaphala bhāgitva*.

किं पुन: अवधातस्य व्रीह्यादिशेषत्वे प्रमाणम्? कार्यमिति ब्रूम: । तथाहि न कार्यमन्यार्थं भवति कार्यत्वादेव । तेन यत् कार्येण सम्बद्धम् तत् तदर्थम् । यदपि च कार्यैदमर्थ्यापन्नेन सम्बद्धं तेनापि सह यस्य साध्यसाधनभाव: तदपि तदर्थमेव । कार्यैदमर्थ्यापन्नस्य अन्यैदमर्थ्ये प्रमाणाभावात् । एवं सर्वेषु शेषशेषित्वं वेदितव्यम् ।

यदि कार्यतयैव ऐदमर्थ्यावगम:, कथं तर्हि श्रुत्यादीनां विनियोगकारणत्वम्? द्वारविशेषसमर्पकतया । कार्यविशेषकरतया च शेष: शेषिणि शेषतामापद्यते नान्यथा । अकिञ्चित्करस्य शेषत्वानुपपत्ते: । तत्रहि श्रुति: व्रीहीनवहन्तीति द्वितीयात्मिका व्रीह्यादिगतं तुषकणविमोचना-दिसमभिव्याहृतक्रियासाध्यभूतं समर्पयन्ती नियोगकरणतामनुवदति । न पुन: द्वितीयैव शेषितां व्रीह्यादीनां अवधातस्य च शेषतामाह । गां ददातीत्यादिषु व्यभिचारात् । क्रियाजन्यफलभागिता हि सर्वत्र अव्यभिचारिणी द्वितीयावाच्या । न शेषिता व्यभिचारित्वात् । (प्र०पं० ४६४)

Similarly, *liṅga* also indicates the *aṅgatva* through the medium of some or the other *kāraka* that are associated with the *kārya*. For instance, *snāna* i.e., bath, by its very nature is *kartṛsanskāra* and consequ-ently is the *aṅga* through the *kartā* who is associated with the *kārya*.

स्नानादिषु वस्तुस्वभावपर्यालोचनया लिङ्गात् कर्तृसंस्काररूप कार्याङ्गीकार: । तेन कर्तरि शेषता स्नानादीनाम् सामर्थ्यात् । सामर्थ्यमात्रञ्चलिङ्गम्, न अभिधानसामर्थ्यम् । (प्र०पं० ४६५)

In the instance *abhikrāmam juhoti* the *aṅgatva* of *abhikrāma* through *homa* is indicated by *vākya*.

अभिक्रामं जुहोति (तै०सं० २-६-६-१) इत्यादिषु वाक्यादभिक्रमणस्य होमः कार्यतया प्रतीयत इति वाक्येन अयं विनियोगः । (प्र०पं० ४६५)

Prakaraṇa, Sthāna and Samākhyā do not Indicate Aṅgatva

So far as *prakaraṇa* is concerned it does not provide any medium for *sannipatyopakārakas* and therefore, does not indicate their *aṅgatva.* Similarly *sthāna* and *samākhyā* also do not indicate *aṅgatva* of *sannipatyopakārakas.*

The important point to be noted in respect of *aṅgatva* of *sannipatyopakārakas* are:

(i) The role of *sannipatyopakārakas* serving the purpose of *niyoga* is expressly stated by the *niyoga* aspect of injunctive suffix.

(ii) The role of *sannipatyopakārakas* serving the purpose of *kārakas* i.e., operating on *kārakas,* is indicated by *viniyoga* aspect of the injunctive suffix.

(iii) The role of *sannipatyopakārakas* serving the purpose of *yāga* is indicated by *upādāna* aspect.

These three roles are known as *grāhakatva, viniyojakatva* and *prayojakatva* respectively.

सन्निपत्योपकारकाणां तु न प्रकरणेन विनियोगः सम्भवति । येषां प्रकरणं द्वारं कल्पयति तेषां प्रकरणाधीनो विनियोगः ।

इतिकर्तव्यताकाङ्क्षा प्रकरणम् । तया च करणोपकारः कार्यभूतः कल्प्यते । न चासौ सन्निपत्योपकारिणां द्वारमिति न तेषां प्रकरणेन विनियोगः । स्थानसमाख्ययोरपि सन्निपत्योपकारकाणि प्रति न कार्यकल्पकतेति न विनियोगकारणत्वम् ।

एवं सन्निपत्योपकारकाणां नियोगैदमर्थ्यमभिधानतः, विनियोगतश्च कार्यैदमर्थ्यम्, उपादानतश्च अधिकारनियोगकरणीभूतयागाद्यैदमर्थ्यम् । (प्र०पं० ४६६)

नियोगापरपर्यायस्य अधिकारापूर्वस्य ग्राहकत्व-विनियोजकत्व-प्रयोजकत्वाख्याः तिस्रः अवस्थाः क्रमेण भवन्ति । (प्र०पं०वि०टि० ४६६)

The Concept of Upādāna

The concept of *upādāna* is especially envisaged to connect the *prokṣaṅa* etc., *sanskāras* with the *yāga*. *Upādāna* is that which is brought in by the *niyoga* itself to make it a requirement of *yāga*. For instance, *prokṣaṇa* i.e., sprinkling the paddy with the water to serve the purpose of *yāga* is brought in as a requirement by the *niyoga* itself as it is connected with the *niyoga*. Such items are known as brought by *upādana.*

नियोगाक्षेपोहि उपादानम् तत्कृतं प्रोक्षणादेः क्रत्वर्थत्वम् । यदि तदीयकरणोपकारकता प्रोक्षणादेः न स्यात् तदा केन अपरेण प्रकारेण तदन्वितनियोगप्रतीतिः निर्वहतीति नियोग एव तदन्वितः प्रतिपन्नः तस्य करणोपकारकतां कल्पयन् करणैदमर्थ्यमाक्षिपतीति तत्कृतमेव प्रोक्षणादेः क्रत्वर्थत्वम् । विनियोगात् पुनः कारकैदमर्थ्यमेव । (प्र०पं० ४६६)

Lastly, though both *avaghāta etc., sannipatyopakārakas* and *prayāja* etc., *ārādupakārakas* are attracted by *itikartavyatākāṅkṣā* there is an important difference between the two. The former aids the *yāga* by operating on *kārakas* while the latter aids separately. Further, *sannipatyopakārakas* do not require separate *niyoga* while *ārādupakārakas* need a separate *uptattiniyoga.*

कस्मात् पुनः प्रयाजादिवदवधातादयोपि उपकारका न अभ्युपेयन्ते?

प्रकृताधिकारनियोगप्रत्यभिज्ञानात् । सम्भवतिचात्र नियोगैक्यं तदीयव्रीहिसंस्कारमुखेनेत्युक्तम् ।

प्रयाजादितुल्यत्वे हि अवघातादीनामङ्गीक्रियमाणे उत्पत्तिनियोगान्तरमाश्रयणीयमिति वक्ष्यामः । (प्र०पं० ४६७)

सन्निधानवशोत्पन्ना प्रकृतापूर्वगामिनी ।
मा बाधि प्रत्यभिज्ञेति तदनुग्रहकाङ्क्षया ॥

अवहन्त्यादिभिः शब्दैः कार्यान्वितपदार्थकैः ।
प्रकृतापूर्वसम्बद्ध एव स्वार्थोऽभिधीयते ।। (प्र० पं० ४६७)

In the light of the above discussion the position of *sannipatyopa-kārakas* may be stated as under:

The *avaghāta* etc., *sannipatyopakārakas* convey their meaning as connected with *apūrva*. This is based on the ground that these are stated in closeness with the *kārya* and are intended for it. In order to serve the purpose of *kārya* these are connected with *vrīhi* etc., that are the media for the operation of these.

Aṅgapārāyaṇa – II
Exposition of Aṅgas – II

The Review of Bhāṭṭas' View of Āradupakāraka

Before Śālikanātha proceeds to give Prābhākaras' view on the nature and the role of *āradupakārakas,* he reviews the view of Bhāṭṭas'. According to Bhāṭṭas 'He who has the *adhikāra* to perform *darśapūrṇamāsa* will have to be thought of as having *adhikāra* for the performance of *prayāja* etc., *āradupakārakas.* The statement *samidho yajati* etc., contain *uttpatiniyoga.* Therefore, these require a *niyojya.* If such a *niyojya* is separately envisaged for these *niyogas,* the *itikartavyatākāṅkṣā* of the main injunction will not be satisfied. If the *niyojya* of *paramāpūrva* and the *avāntarāpūrva* are different, then, the one being the means of the other cannot be sustained. On the other hand, if he who has *adhikāra* for *darśapūrṇamāsa* is considered as also has *adhikāra* for *prayāja,* the fact of *prayāja* etc., being the aids of *paramāpūrva* will be clear. This process is known as *grāhaka grahaṇa.* The nature of these aids will be *itikaravyatā* type, since the *āgneya* etc., are already spelt out as *karaṇa.*

तत्र केचित् अधिकारापूर्वं प्रति अङ्गतासिद्ध्यर्थम् एषाम् अधिकृताधिकारमिच्छन्ति ते हि मन्यन्ते—उत्पत्तिनियोगाः तावत् समिदादिषु निर्विवादं सम्मताः । न च नियोगो नियोज्यमन्तरेणाभिधीयते । तथा सति विश्वजिदादिषु नियोज्यपरिकल्पना न स्यात् । तत्र नियोज्ये कल्पयितव्ये यदि अनुषङ्गः फलपदस्य कल्प्येत, यद्वा विश्वजिन्न्यायेन अधिकारः कल्प्येत तदा अधिकारापूर्वस्य इतिकर्तव्यताकाङ्क्षा न परिपूर्यते ।

परमापूर्वाधिकृते तु अधिकारिणि सति उपायोपेयभावो गम्यते । नहि अन्यथा अधिकृताधिकारभावः उपपद्यते ।

यस्य हि परमापूर्वं साध्यम् स परमापूर्वाधिकारी । तेन यथा 'दर्शपूर्णमासाभ्यां स्वर्गकामो यजेत' इत्यादौ स्वर्गकामे साध्यस्वर्गविशिष्टे अधिकारिणि स्वर्गयागयोरुपायोपेयभावः तथा इहापि समिदादिपरमापूर्वयोः ।

तत्र न च कार्यमन्यार्थमिति न्यायेन अधिकारनियोगैदमर्थ्यमेव समिदादीनामवसीयते । तदिदं ग्राहकग्रहणमिति गीयते । तत्र उत्पत्तिशिष्टाग्नेयादिकरणावरुद्धे परमापूर्वे प्रकारान्तरेण ऐदमर्थ्यानुपपत्तेः इति कर्तव्यतत्वेनैव सम्बन्धः इति । (प्र०पं० ४६८-६९)

This contention of the Bhāṭṭas is not acceptable to the Prābhākaras. Śālikanātha points out that this contention is based on the assumption that every *niyoga* needs a *niyojya*. However, this does not hold good in the case of *videvana* etc., connected with the *rājasūya* sacrifices. Just as in the case of *videvana*, no *niyojya* is thought of since their performance could be managed by the need of *paramāpūrva* only, no *niyojya* is required for the *viniyoga* of *prayāja* etc., since it is managed by *prakaraṇa*. These are intended to serve the purpose of the main *niyoga*. Therefore, the connection of these with the *niyojya* of the main *niyoga* is already known. The *prakaraṇa* makes it explicit.

तदिदमनुपपन्नमिति प्राभाकाराः । तथाहि—यदि सर्वस्य नियोगस्य नियोज्यान्विताभिधानमाश्रियते तर्हि राजसूयकानामिज्याविशेषाणामुत्पत्ति नियोगानामपि साधिकारत्वं स्यात् । ततोऽभिषेचनीयतन्त्रमध्ये पठितानां विदेवनादीनामभिषेचनीयावान्तरापूर्वप्रकरणेन तदङ्गत्तैव स्यात् ।

अथोच्येत—न अदृष्टार्थो नियोगः नियोज्यान्वितः अभिधीयते किन्तु अनुष्ठानलब्धये । अभिषेचनीयादयश्च परमापूर्वप्रयुक्त्यैव लब्धानुष्ठानाः परमापूर्वस्यापि तद्विषयत्वात् तेनैव स्वसिद्ध्यर्थं विषयीभूतासु इज्यासु प्रयुज्यमानासु तद्विषयोत्पत्तिनियोगा अपि लब्धसिद्धयो न स्वसिद्धये

नियोज्यान्तरमाकाङ्क्षन्ति इति । तर्हि प्रयाजादिविनियोगा अपि विनियुक्तविषयत्वात् न अधिकारान्तरमपेक्षेरन् । (प्र०पं० ४६९)

The Prābhākaras' Explanation of the Role and the Nature of Ārādupakārakas

The statement *samidho yajati* etc., are found stated in closeness with the *darśapūrṇamāsa* injunction. No separate result or a separate performance is stated for these. Therefore, these are conveyed as connected with the main injunction. Since these statements make a reference to *dravya, devatā*, these convey some minor rituals connected with the main *niyoga* through the major ritual. Thus these constitute the aids of *karaṇa* and through the medium of *karaṇa* contribute to the accomplishment of *paramāpūrva.*

स्यान्मतम् विनियोग एव तेषामधिकृताधिकारमन्तरेण अनुपपन्नः इति । तदसत्—नियोगैदमर्थ्यमात्रेण प्रथमं शब्देनावगताधिकारसम्बन्धानां प्रकरणेन इतिकर्तव्यतात्वेन विनियोगात् । तथाहि अधिकारविधिसन्निधौसमिधो यजतीत्यादयो निरधिकाराः एव तावदाम्नायन्ते । तत्र योऽसावधिकारविधिः स एव प्रयोजनीभूतो निरधिकारैः समिदादिभिः स्वयमप्रयोजनभूतैः अन्वितः स्वशब्देन अभिधीयते । समिदादिवाक्यानि च द्रव्यदेवताविशिष्टानि यागस्वरूपमेव सन्निधापयन्ति । सन्निधानमात्रेण तैः सह अधिकारनियोगस्य अन्वयः । यदि च सन्निधानं नाद्रीयेत तदा समिदादिष्वपि किमिति परमापूर्वाधिकारी कल्प्यते ।

तदेवं सन्निधानमात्रतः सिद्धमधिकारैदमर्थ्यं कथं भवतीत्यपेक्षा । तथा साध्यभूतस्य अधिकारापूर्वस्य च कथमित्याकाङ्क्षा । तेन करणोपकार एव तेषां द्वारमाश्रीयते । तत्र यदैदमर्थ्येन अन्विताभिधानं तद् ग्राहकग्रहणम् । यच्च तेषां करणोपकारद्वारकल्पनम् स एव प्रकरणविनियोगः इति । (प्र०पं० ४७०)

This way of *prayāja* etc., contributing does not mean that the *avāntara apūrvas* are dispensed with. Since the *ārādupakāraka aṅgas* are not permanent, these cannot contribute to the accomplishment of *paramāpūrva* without *avāntarāpūrva.* Therefore, the *avāntarāpūrvas* do accrue. But these are also conveyed by the main injunctive suffix that conveys *parmāpūrva.* Just as the *viniyoga* of *avaghāta* etc., is conveyed by the main injunctive suffix and it is only restated by *vrīhin āvahanti* etc., statements, similarly, the *avāntarāpūrva* accomplished by these is also conveyed by the main injunctive suffix only. In this context, it has to be noted that in *dīkṣanīya,* no separate *avāntarāpūrva* accrues from the item *vāṅniyama,* because, this item is intended to give rise to the very form of *dīkṣaṇīya* and is connected with its *avāntarāpūrva.*

ननु एवमवान्तरापूर्वाणि अपह्नुतानि । न अपह्नेष्यामहे । यद्यपि लिङादयो प्रथमे न व्यतिरिक्तं नियोगं प्रतिपादयितुमीशते व्रीहीनवहन्तीत्यादिषु इव शङ्क्यमानाधिकारानुवादकत्वात् तथापि अधिकारं नियोगं प्रति एषां क्षणभङ्गिनां अवान्तरापूर्वमजनयतामङ्गता नोपपद्यते इति पश्चात् यदधिकारापूर्वाङ्ग भावोपपादनाय आश्रयणीयानि अवान्तरापूर्वाणि लिङा अभिधेयान्युपादीयन्ते ।

यानिच अवान्तरापूर्वाणि तानि शब्देन अङ्गभूतानि अधिकारापूर्वं प्रति उपनीयन्ते ।

तदेवं स्वयमङ्गत्वात् लब्धानुष्ठानेषु प्रयाजादिषु न अधिकार-कल्पनावकाशः । (प्र०पं० ४७०)

(a) **ननु एवं तर्हि दीक्षणीयादिषु वाङ् नियमस्य अवान्तरापूर्वप्रयुक्तता न स्यात् । न तस्य स्वरूपनिष्पत्त्यर्थत्वात् । यद्यपि अवान्तरापूर्वाणां परमापूर्वाङ्गभावः तथापि तेषु स्वरूपनिष्पत्यर्थ एव वाङ्नियमादिको धर्मः । (प्र०पं० ४७०)**

Rejection of the Concept of Avāntaraprakaraṇa

Continuing his discussion on *ā.ādupakārakas*, Śālikanātha rejects the Bhāṭṭas' concept of *avāntaraprakaraṇa.* This concept is envisaged by the Bhāṭṭas to explain the *prayājaṅgatva* of *abhikramaṇa*. Śālikanātha points out that this can be managed by *vākya* only.

1. न अवान्तरप्रकरणं नाम प्रमाणमस्ति प्रमेयाभावे प्रमाणानुपपत्तेः । यावदेव तानि अवान्तरापूर्वाणि नावगम्यन्ते तावदेव सर्वस्यारादुपकारकस्य पदार्थजातस्य अविशेषेण प्रधानविधिपरिगृहीतत्वात् । पश्चात्तु सर्वेषामधिकारनुप्रवेशाविशेषात् अन्योन्यं तादर्थ्यमस्तीति न अवान्तरप्रकरणविनियोज्यत्वसम्भवः ।

2. यानि तु वाक्यादिभिः तानि तत्र प्रतिष्ठितानि न परमापूर्वं सङ्क्रमिष्यन्ति (प्र०पं० ४७२)

3. अयं भावः अभिक्रामन् जुहोति इत्यत्र प्रयाजसन्निधौ विहितस्य अभिक्रमणादेः वाक्यात् प्रयाजाङ्गत्वम् । यदर्थमवान्तरप्रकरणं स्वीकृतं तस्य प्रकारान्तरेण अङ्गत्वोपपत्तेः अवान्तरप्रकरणविनियोज्यस्य अङ्गस्य असम्भवात् अवान्तरप्रकरणं नाम विनियोगप्रमाणं नेषितव्यमिति । (प्र०पं०टि० ४७२)

The Nature and the Role of Itikartavyatā Ākāṅkṣā and Avāntara Apūrva

In respect of *itikartavyatākāṅkṣā* and *avāntara apūrva*, the Prābhākaras' position is quite different from that of the Bhāṭṭas. the Prābhākaras envisage two types of *itikartavyatākāṅkṣā* viz., (i) *svārasikī* (ii) *liṅgabalotthāpaniyā*. The *itikartavyatākāṅkṣā* that arises for the purpose of accomplishing *kārya* is *svārasikī*, while that which is required to connect the *aṅgas* is *liṅgabalatthāpaniyā*. The *ārādupakārakas* first get connected with the *niyoga* to serve its purpose. This is by *svārasikī itikartavyatākāṅkṣā*. Then, the *aṅgas* that have to serve the purpose of *karaṇa* get connected with *karaṇa* to serve the purpose of *karaṇa*. This is by *liṅgabalotthāpanīyā ākāṅkṣā*. Since these *aṅgas* are not durable, the *avāntarāpūrvas* are envisaged to lead to *paramāpūrva*.

1. ननु एवं प्रयाजादिषु सौमिकविध्यन्तप्रसङ्गः । नायं दोषः । यदि निरधिकाराणामपि साधिकाराणामिव स्वारसिकी आकाङ्क्षा भवेत् भवेदेवम् । अननुष्ठेयत्वात् न स्वाभाविकी इतिकर्तव्यताकाङ्क्षा ।

2. कथं पुनः कार्यता अननुष्ठेयता च । नूनं भवान् अश्रुतपूर्वसप्तमाद्यः। विविक्तं हि तत्रेदं गुरूणा यदेव हि पुरुषेण ममेदं कार्यमिति निरपेक्षमवगम्यते तदनुष्ठेयम् । यत्तु तत्सिद्ध्यर्थं प्रागसिद्धं विनियुज्यते तत् कार्यम् ।

3. यदेव च अनुष्ठेयं तत्रैव कथमित्याकांक्षा न कार्यमात्रे । अयं हि नो राद्धन्तः—स्वारसिकी इतिकर्तव्यताकाङ्क्षा निरधिकाराणां नास्ति । कारणान्तरसमुत्था तु नापह्नूयते ।

तत्र दीक्षणीयादिषु प्रयाजादि दर्शनेन इति कर्तव्यताकाङ्क्षा कल्प्यते ।

प्रयाजादिषु न किञ्चिदाकाङ्क्षोत्त्थापने कारणमस्ति इति न सौमिकधर्मातिदेशः । सिद्धश्च दीक्षणीयादिषु ऐष्टिक विध्यन्तलाभः । (प्र०पं० ४७३)

The Concept of Āśrayikarma

In respect of *āśrayikarma* also the Bhāṭṭas and the Prābhākaras have different views. Śālikanātha explains these differences.

ननु एवमाश्रयिकर्मेषु द्रव्यदेवता संस्कारमुखेन करणोपकारजननसिद्धिरिति न अपूर्वसमाश्रयणे किञ्चन प्रमाणम् ।

किं भवान् ऋजुविमलायामनवहितः । दर्शितं हि तत्रेदं चतुर्थे—न साक्षात् द्रव्यदेवतोपकारो यागे किन्तु स्वाङ्गभूतमन्त्राद्यंशमुखेन । न च यागे अधिकाराऽननु प्रविष्टे तयोः तत्र विनियोगोपपत्तिः । न च अपूर्वमन्तरेण यागस्य अधिकारानुप्रवेशः इति अवश्यमाश्रयणीयमवान्तरापूर्वम् । तेषां च अदृष्टतया न प्रयोजकत्वम् । दृष्टतया च द्रव्यदेवतासंस्कार एव प्रयोजकः ।

तत्रापि द्रव्यदेवता संस्कारयोः द्रव्यप्रतिपत्तिरेव प्रयोजिका यागे द्रव्यस्य साक्षाद् व्यापारादिति मन्तव्यम् । (प्र०पं० ४७७)

In respect of the mode of the application of the numbers in the instances like *paśunā yajeta* the Prābhākaras differ from the Bhāṭṭas. They hold the view that the number has to be taken into account by way of *upādāna.*

The Procedure of Viniyoga of Dravya, Guṇa etc.

The relation of *dravya* with *yāga* is not conveyed by *śruti* nor it is conveyed by *prakaraṇa.* It is conveyed by *liṅga, vākya, sthāna* or *samākhyā.* It is related with *bhāvārtha* i.e., *yāga,* as its producer. The relation of qualities and the universal is conveyed by *vākya.*

द्रव्यस्य तु न श्रुतिविनियोगः । न क्वचिद् द्रव्यस्य द्वारं श्रुतिः समर्पयति । न च प्राकरणिकोपि द्रव्यस्य विनियोगः साक्षात् करणोपकारजनकत्वाभावात् । तस्य हि लिङ्गेन, वाक्येन, स्थानेन समाख्यया वा भावार्थ एव जनकतया सम्बन्धः ।

गुणजात्योस्तु वाक्येन विनियोगः नानाव्यापारत्वात् करणानाम् अतः साधनभूतद्रव्योपादाने तदवच्छेदकतया अस्त्येव तयोरुपयोग इति न कारकतया विनियोगो विरुद्ध्यते ।

The Position of Number in Connection with an Injunction

To ascertain whether the number is also to be enjoined or not, it has to be ascertained whether the number is stated while enjoining the very *karma* or later i.e., whether it is *utpanna karma samavāyi* or *utpadyamānakarmasamaveta.* In the former case the number is enjoined as associated with the *karma* and in the latter case it is not enjoined. However, in the latter case it qualifies the *karma.* In the instance of *ekādaśa prayājān yajati* the number is stated while enjoining *karma.* Therefore, it is enjoined as associated with *karma.* Since the number qualifying the *uddeśa* is not to be taken into account to avoid *vākyabheda,* the eleven *prayājas* cannot be taken as one unit of eleven. These can be taken as a group. To form such a group of eleven the *prayāja* has to be repeated.

यातु सङ्ख्या उत्पन्नकर्मसावायिनी यथा—'एकादश प्रयाजान् यजति' (श०ब्रा० ३-६-५-१) सा उत्पन्नानां कर्मणां विधानासम्भवात् कर्माश्रितो विधीयते। यद्यपि च उद्देशगतं विशेषणं वाक्यभेदभयेन विवक्षां नार्हतीति प्रयाजादीनां साहित्यं न विवक्षितम् तथापि तस्याः पृथक्त्वनिवेशित्वात् न प्रत्येकमभिसम्बन्धः किन्तु समुदायेनैव। न च अभ्यासं विना तस्याः परिपूर्तिरिति अर्थादभ्यासाश्रयणे प्रकृतग्रहणात् स्वस्थानविवृद्ध्यैव परिपूरणम्।

So far as the *utpadyamānakarmasamaveta* number is concerned, it is not enjoined. It only qualifies the *karmas* that are already enjoined. Though it is not enjoined it bifurcates the *karmas*. When it is stated with separate words as in the case of *aruṇayā ekahayanyā* etc., it enjoins the *kārakas* with reference to the *karma*.

यः पुनः उत्पद्यमानकर्मसमवेतः सङ्ख्याख्यो गुणः नासौ विधेयः। सहि विधीयमानानि कर्माणि अवच्छिनत्ति। न च तस्य विधेयत्वसम्भवः। बहुषु विहितेषु प्रचयो लक्ष्यत एवेति न पृथग् विधेयत्वमवलम्बते। अविधेयभूतोपि चासौ भावार्थं भिन्दन् विधौ उपकरोतीति सोऽन्वयी। यस्तु भिन्नप्रातिपदिकाभिधेयः सोऽरुणिमादिवत् कर्मणि कारकतया विधीयते (प्र०पं० ४७८)

The Procedure of Connecting the Number of Paśu with the Injunction

In the instance *'paśunā yajeta' paśutva, liṅga, saṁkhyā* are first solicited by the injunction i.e., *grāhaka. Paśu* serves the purpose of the injunction as an aṅga of *yāga. Liṅga, saṁkhyā* etc., serve the purpose of the injunction through *paśu.* This process is known as *upādāna* i.e., *ākṣepa* by the injunction. Both *paśu* and *saṁkhyā* are solicited by the injunction. *Paśu* cannot get connected with the injunction through *yāga* without the indication of its number and the number cannot get connected without an *āśraya.* Therefore, the injunction solicits them in an associated state. Ordinarily, the *saṁkhyā* etc., that are conveyed by the suffix get connected with the import of the stem. However, this does not bring out their connection with the injunction. But the context demands their connection with the injunction.

(i) यः पुनरयं विभक्त्यभिधेयः तस्य यद्यपि शक्त्या प्रातिपदिकार्थसम्बन्धः तथापि तस्य तन्मात्रसम्बन्धे प्रकरणसमाम्नापादितो ग्राहकसम्बन्धो नोपपद्यत इति ग्राहकीयावस्थासम्बन्धितयैव औपादानकीति निर्णीयते । विनियुक्तस्य पश्वादेः उपादानमनवच्छिन्नस्य न सम्भवतीति अस्ति तदवच्छेदकीभूतसंख्यापेक्षा, संख्यायाश्च प्रतीतग्राहकान्वयनिर्वाहाय आश्रयापेक्षा इति तदवस्था सम्बन्धितां विधिः कल्पयति । सङ्ख्यान्वितश्च विध्यर्थः प्रतीतः तदन्वयोपपत्तये ग्राहकीयदशा सम्बन्धितामापादयति । (प्र०पं० ४७९)

(ii) पशुना यजेत इत्यत्र प्रशुत्व-लिङ्ग सङ्ख्या सम्बन्धानामन्योन्यमनन्वितानामेव प्रथमं ग्राहकग्रहणे सति पश्चात् पशुनेति तृतीयाविभक्त्या प्रातिपदिकार्थगतानां लिङ्गसंख्या करणत्वादीनाममभिधानेपि प्रथमं तृतीयाश्रुत्या पशोः यागशेषत्वेन ग्राहकैदमर्थ्यस्य निर्वाहो भवति । लिङ्गसंखययोश्च करणत्वेन अनभिधानात् साक्षाद् यागान्वयासम्भवात् पश्चाद् पशुद्वारा ग्राहकैदमर्थ्य निर्वाहो वक्तव्यः । तयोः पशुमात्रान्वयेपि तदनिर्वाहात् उपादानाखयेन विधिव्यापारेण ग्राहकीयपशुशेषत्वसिद्धेः निर्वाहः । (वि०टि० ४७८)

The Areas of Upādāna

According to Prābhākaras the *śeṣatva* (*aṅgatva*) is indicated in two ways (i) By *viniyoga* conveyed by *śruti*, *liṅga* etc., six criteria (ii) By *upādāna*. Soliciting by the injunction is *upādāna* (*ākṣepa*) by *vidhi*. Such an *upādāna* will operate in the areas of *utpatti*, *viniyoga*, *adhikāra* and *prayoga*. The instances of these are briefly noted by Śālikanātha.

(i) उपादानलक्षणो विधिव्यापारः आक्षेपापरपर्यायो मीमांसकैः प्रतिपन्नः उत्पत्ति-विनियोग-अधिकार-प्रयोगविषयः प्रतिज्ञायते तस्य यथाप्रतीतविध्यनुपपत्तिरेव बीजम् । (प्र०पं० ४७९)

(ii) प्राभाकरमते शेषत्वं द्विविधम् । वैनियोगिकम् औपादानिकं चेति । तत्र वैनियोगिकं शेषत्वं श्रुत्यादिषट्क प्रमाण सहकृतं तृतीयाध्याये निरूपितम् । औपादानिकं चतुर्थाध्याये निरूप्यते । इदं च उपादानं विध्याक्षेपरूप विधिव्यापारात्मकं शब्दप्रमाणान्तर्गतमेव । (वि०टि० ४७९)

The Sequence is Necessary to Organize the Sacrifices

Śālikanātha quotes the views of *Vivaraṇa* and *Nibandhana* the two important works of Prabhākara Guru in respect of *krama* i.e., sequence, and states that *krama* cannot be neglected, since, it has to be taken into account to implement *prayogavidhi.* He also states that though it is conveyed by the injunction, it has to be taken as conveyed by *codanālakṣaṇa.*

In the course of narrating the views of *Vivaraṇa* and *Nibandhana* the position of the *krama* stated in the third chapter and the fifth chapter are duly explained. It is also made clear that *artha, pāṭha, sthāna,* etc., criteria of *krama* do not expressly state *krama.*

क्रमस्याऽनङ्गभावेपि नैवादरणीयता ।
तदभावे विशिष्टस्य प्रयोगस्याप्रसिद्धितः ।। (वि०टि० ४८२)

The Implementation of Aṅgas Does not Depend upon the Adhikāra

All the *aṅgas* that are required for the accomplishment of injunction have to be implemented. One cannot plead his inability. The *adhikāra* i.e., entitlement, depends upon the capacity to implement *aṅgas* i.e., *viniyoga.* The implementation of these does not depend upon the capacity of the entitled person. If he is not able to implement all the *viniyogas,* then, he fails in accomplishing the injunction. That is why it is made clear that the blind, lame etc., are declared as not eligible.

In the case of *kāmyakarma* the performance of all the details is necessary. Otherwise one will miss the result. However, in the case of *nitya,* the core part has to be performed. Such of the *aṅgas* that cannot be observed by a person may be dropped. The *naimittikas* depend upon *nimitta.*

(i) तत्र न यथाधिकारं विनियुज्यते अपितु यथा विनियोगमधिकारः ।

(ii) स्वर्गकामादौ अधिकारिणि लब्धे साधिकारत्वे सम्पन्ने ग्राहकग्रहणे संवृत्ते विनियुक्तेषु अङ्गेषु तदवच्छिन्ने विध्यर्थे कार्यात्मनि तदनुष्ठानसमर्थस्य स्वर्गकामिनो अधिकारः ।

(iii) अत एव अन्ध बधिरपङ्ग्वादीनामवेक्षण-आश्रवण-अभिक्रमणाद्यङ्गवति अनधिकारः ।

(iv) आहवनीयादि योगिनिच अनाहिताग्नीनाम् अनधिकारः ।

(v) निमित्तवतश्च केवलभावार्थविषय एवाधिकारः इत्याङ्गानुपसंहारेपि विषयाप्रमोषात् न अधिकारापगमः । (प्र०पं० ४८२-८३)

The Arrangement of Aṅgas in Relation to Apūrva

The *aṅgas* are stated in the context of each *apūrva.* These are solicited by *apūrva* and their implementation is indicated. These *aṅgas* are connected with *apūrva* to serve the purpose of its accomplishment. These serve the same through assisting the *karaṇa* i.e., *yāga.* These are enabled to do so by the function of *upādāna* of the injunction. The expression *kārya* means *upakāra* in this context.

(i) कार्यनिबन्धनं किञ्चिदङ्गं मीमांसका मन्यन्ते । उपदेशोहि प्रतिप्रकरणमङ्गानां व्यवस्थित एव । अपूर्वग्रहणप्रयुक्तत्वाद् विनियोगस्य ।

(ii) तत्र अङ्गानामपूर्वेण सह तादर्थ्येनापि अन्विताभिधानम् । प्रकरणेन च करणोपकारलक्षणद्वारपरिकल्पनम् । तत्र उपादानलक्षणेन विधिव्यापारेण अङ्गानां समुदितानामुपकारकल्पनमिति प्रतिप्रकरणमङ्गव्यवस्था । (प्र०पं० ४८४-८५)

Prākṛta Upakāras are brought to Vikṛti by Upadeśa

The *apūrva* of *vikṛti* solicits the *prākṛta upakāras* only. These *upakāras* solicit the *prākṛta aṅgas* by *atideśa*, and also the substitutes i.e., *ūha*. These *prākṛtopakāras* are brought by the *vikṛti* injunction itself.

(i) क्व पुनः केषां कार्यं निबन्धनमङ्गत्वम्? प्राकृतानां वैकृतापूर्वेषु, तदीयकरणत्वेच यमतिदेशमाचक्षते, प्राकृतानां प्राकृतस्थानपतिते अर्थान्तरे यमूहमभिदधति ।

(ii) वैकृतापूर्वस्य साध्यभूतस्य सेतिकर्तव्यताककरणाङ्क्षस्य विषयभूते भावार्थे लब्धे प्राकृते तु उपकारे स्वीकृते तन्मुखेन द्विविधप्राकृत पदार्थोपस्थापनात् आकाङ्क्षा परिपूर्यत इति प्राकृतमेव उपकारं स्वीकरोति ।

(iii) य एवासौ नियोगाभिधायी लिङादिशब्दः स एव प्राकृतोपकारान्वितं स्वार्थमभिदधति ।

(iv) उपकारलक्षणकार्योपस्थापितप्राकृतपदार्थजन्यज्ञानं विकृत्यपूर्वकार्यजं शाब्दमित्युच्यते । (प्र०पं० ४८६-८७)

Ūha, Bādha, Tantra and Āvapa

In respect of *ūha*, *bādha* etc., also, the *padārtha* affected by these get associated with *apūrva* through the respective *upakāra* and therefore are covered by the injunction.

(i) प्राकृतद्रव्यस्थानपतितपदार्थ सम्बन्धनिश्चयः ऊहापरनामापि कार्यज एव शाब्दः ।

(ii) एवं कृष्णलादिषु अवधातादिषु ऊहितेषु द्वारभूतकार्याभावेन यो बाधनिश्चयः सोऽपि कार्यज एव ।

(iii) तेषामौपदेशिकानां कार्यसम्बद्धानां च अङ्गनामनेकप्रधानसम्बन्धे प्रयुक्तिविशेषः तन्त्रमनुष्ठानस्य ।

नाना भ्रमविषयाणां विधिसिन्धौ निमज्जताङ्गनाम् ।
प्रविततगम्भीराणां पारायणमेतदाचरितम् ॥ (प्र०पं० ४८७-८८)

CHAPTER XIV

Atideśa Pārāyaṇa

In this chapter Śālikanātha discusses the procedure of *atideśa* and *upadeśa* of *aṅgas* i.e., *padārthas*, and *upakāra* from *prakṛtiyāga* to *vikṛti yāga*.

According to the Prābhākaras *upakāra* is brought in from *prakṛti* to *vikṛti* by *upadeśa* while *aṅgas* are brought by *atideśa*. A Vedic injunction conveys its import i.e., *kārya*, associated with the requirements that are necessary to accomplish it. These requirements are solicited by *ākāṅkṣā*, *yogyatā* and *sannidhi*. The *upakāra* provided by various aṅgas in *prakṛti* are also required in *vikṛti* to accomplish *kārya*. Therefore, these are brought by *vikṛti* injunction itself from *prakṛti*. That which is brought by the injunction is called *upadeśa*. Hence, *upakāras* to be provided by various *aṅgas* are stated as brought by *upadeśa* from *prakṛti* to *vikṛti*. The *aṅgas* i.e., *padārthas*, come by *atideśa* to provide these *upakāras*.

प्राकृतेनोपकारेण पदार्थैश्चैव वैकृतः ।
प्रयोगविधिना स्वेन विधिरन्वित उच्यते ।।
यद्यदाकाङ्क्षितं योग्यं सन्निधानं प्रपद्यते ।
तेनान्वितो हि विध्यर्थः स्वशब्देनैव वर्ण्यते ।
साध्यभूतश्च विध्यर्थः उपकारमपेक्षते ।
वाक्यादिभिः प्राकृतश्च स योग्यः सन्निधाप्यते ।

(श्लो. २-५, प्र० पं० ४९२)

The procedure to be followed to connect the *upakāras* and *aṅgas* with the *kārya* is quite reverse in *vikṛti*. The *upakāra* is connected first and then the required *aṅgas* are connected through these *upakāras*. In *prakṛti*, *padārthas* are first connected and then, *upakāra* is envisaged. In the case of *vikṛti*, since the *upakāras* were already envisaged in *prakṛti* and readily available for *vikṛti*, these are connected first and then the required *aṅgas* are taken into account as providing these *upakāras*. This connection of *aṅgas* i.e., *padārthas*, is by way of atideśa as already stated.

प्रकृतौ तु स्वशब्दत्वात् पदार्थानां पुरोऽन्वयः ।
उपकारस्य कल्प्यस्य पश्चादिति परं भिदा ॥ ११ ॥
व्युत्क्रमेणोपकारेण पदार्थैश्चैव वैकृतः ।
प्राकृतैः विधिरन्वेति सोऽतिदेशश्च सम्मतः ॥ १२ ॥ (प्र०पं०४९३)

Though the *upakāras* are brought by *upadeśa*, these can also be called as *atideśa* since the ground of *atideśa* viz., bringing from *prakṛti* to *vikṛti* is found in the case of these *upakāras* also.

यस्य देशे विधिर्यस्मिन् ततोऽन्यत्रापि तद्गतिः ।
अतिदेशः प्रकारस्य धर्माणां चैव युज्यते ॥ १३ ॥
अन्यत्रत्यो यथान्यत्र प्रकारोऽन्वयमृच्छति ।
तथा धर्मा अपीष्यन्ते तेषामप्यतिदेश्यता ॥ १४ ॥

Here, a ticklish question is raised. At the commencement of tenth chapter it is stated that the *padārthas* will not come to *vikṛti* by *atideśa*. This statement will be violated if these are stated as brought by *atideśa in vikṛti*. This objection is answered by pointing out that it is only stated that the *aṅgas* will not come by *atideśa* on their own but only to provide *upakāra*. If no *upakāra* is to be provided by certain *aṅga* it will not come by *atideśa*. There is no total rejection of *aṅgātideśa* by that remark.

नन्वेवं दशमाद्येन विरोधस्ते प्रसज्यते ।

नैवं कार्यानपेक्षोऽसावतिदेशो निवारितः ॥ १५ ॥

An objection is raised that if the two units of *Mīmāmsadarśana* arranged in six chapters are designated as *upadeśa ṣatka* and *atideśa ṣatka,* this scheme will be violated. This objection is answered by pointing out that the correct way of designating these units is *upadeśa* and *kārya.* The designations *upadeśa* and *atideśa* do not suit since *bādha* and *tantra* that are of the nature of *upadeśa* are discussed in the latter *ṣatka.*

उपदेशकार्यरूपप्रमाणद्वयसंश्रयौ ।
षट्कावुभौ नोपदेशमतिदेशं च संश्रितौ ।
अतिदेशाश्रयत्वेहि बाधे तन्त्रे च भूयसी
उपादिष्टार्थविषया चिन्ता नैवोपपद्यते ॥ (६०-६१) (प्र०पं० ४९८)

The Important Differences Between Bhāṭṭas and Prābhākaras

	Bhāṭṭas		Prābhākaras
1.	*Preraṇā* or *iṣṭasādhanatā* is the import of the Vedic injunction.	1.	*Kārya* or *niyoga* is the import of Vedic injunction.
2.	*Pauruṣeya vākya* also comes under *śabdapramāṇa*.	2.	*Pauruṣeya vākya* only helps to infer the knowledge of the speaker. It does not come under *śabdapramāṇa*.
3.	Bhāṭṭas accept *abhihitānvaya*.	3.	Prābhākaras accept *anvitābhidhāna*.
4.	Bhāṭṭas accept the category of *abhāva* and *anupalabdhi pramāṇa*.	4.	Prābhākaras do not accept the category of *abhāva*. Consequently, they do not accept *anupalabdhi pramāṅa* i.e., *abhāva pramāṇa*.
5.	Bhāṭṭas accept both *śrutārthāpatti* and *dṛṣṭārthāpatti*.	5.	Prābhākaras accept only *dṛṣṭārthāpatti*.
6.	According to Bhāttas the knowledge is inferred.	6.	According to Prābhākaras the knowledge is self revealing.
7.	Bhāṭṭas accept *viprita khyāti* for perceptual error.	7.	Prābhākaras accept *akhyāti*.

8. The categories are five viz., substance, attributes, motion and universal.	8. The categories are eight viz., substance, attributes, motion. universal, potency, similarity, number and inherence.
9. *Śabda* and *tamas* are accepted as additional substances.	9. Not accepted.
10. *Vāyu* and *karma* are perceived.	10. *Vāyu* and *karma* are inferred.
11. The injunction to study Veda is a separate injunction.	11. The injunction to study Veda is consequential of the injunction to teach Veda.
12. The relation between jāti and vyakti is bhedā-abheda.	12. The relation between jāti and vyakti is bhedā. The bheda i.e., difference, is an internal attribute of the object (dharmisvarūpa)

These are important differences. They also differ in many details. Particularly, in the process of organizing the sacrifices and the injunctive sentence that conveys it.

Glossary of Technical Words

अङ्गम्: A subsidiary item.

अख्याति: Prābhākara's theory of error.

अतिदेश: Borrowing from *prakṛti* to *vikṛti*.

अधिकार: Entitlement to perform sacrifice.

अध्ययनविधि: The injunction to study the Veda.

अध्यापनविधि: The injunction to teach the Veda.

अध्याहार: Supplementing to complete the meaning of a sentence. (Bhāṭṭas hold that the necessary word has to be supplemented while Prābhākaras say that the meaning has to be supplemented.)

अन्वय: Syntactical connection.

अन्विताभिधानवाद: (i) The theory that the Vedic injunction conveys the *kāryānvita* meaning.

(ii) According to this theory the connected word meanings constitute the sentence meaning. The connection is included in the scope of the word meaning. Isolated words do not communicate.

अन्वयव्यतिरेकौ: Positive and negative verification.

अनुपलब्धि: (अभावप्रमाण) It is considered as a *separate pramāṇa* to cognise *abhāva* by Bhāṭṭas. Absence of cognition is the means of cognising *abhāva* i.e., the absence of an entity.

अनुव्यवसाय: Awareness of the knowledge obtained, the knowledge of the knowledge. (This concept of Nyāyavaiśeṣikas is not acceptable to Prābhākaras. They accept self-revealing nature of the knowledge.)

अन्यथाख्याति: Nyāyavaiśeṣika theory of error. According to this theory one entity is mistaken to be another.

अपूर्वम्: (मानान्तरापूर्वम्) The import of Vedic injunction. It is conveyed by Vedic injunction only. Therefore, it is called *apūrva*. It is also called *kārya* and *niyoga*. (This is Prābhākara meaning.)

अपूर्वम्: (यागेन फलप्राप्तौ द्वारम्) A potency produced by *yāga* that leads to its result. A link between the *yāga* and *svarga* (This is Bhāṭṭa meaning.)

अभिधा: Denotative power of a word, denotation of a word.

अभाव: One of the seven categories according to Nyāyavaiśeṣikas. It is a negative category as against other positive categories (*abhāva* versus *bhāva*). It is of the nature of the absence of an entity. Prābhākaras do not accept this category.

अभ्यास: Repetition, it is one of the criterion to decide whether the sacrifices or rituals concerned are distinct.

अर्थवाद: A praise of the sacrifice or an item connected with it to impress upon the need of its performance. It provides *prāśastyajñāna*. In some cases, it also censures some item to indicate that this should be avoided. In this role it is called *nindārthavāda*.

अर्थापत्ति: One of the *pramāṇas* accepted by both Bhāṭṭas and Prābhākaras. Nyāyavaiśeṣikas include it in *anumāna*. It is utilized to resolve the conflict between two known facts by presuming the third fact.

अर्थसंस्पर्श: Meaning of a word agreeing with the fact conveyed by it.

अर्थासंस्पर्श: (अर्थव्यभिचारिता) Meaning of a word not agreeing with the fact conveyed by it.

अव्यपदेश्यम्: A perception stated in words is not a perception. *Vyapadeśya* means stated in words. For instance, after perceiving a colour, the statement made viz., This is colour, is not a perception. It is only a statement of perceptual cognition of colour.

आकाङ्क्षा: The injunction i.e., *niyoga*, seeking a *niyojya, viṣaya, karaṇa* etc., to accomplish *kārya* is *ākāṅkṣā* according to Prabhākāras. Ordinarily this term is translated as expectancy. The nature of this expectancy is differently explained by *Anvitābhidhānavādins* and Abihitānvayavādins. The injunction seeking the agent, object, instrument etc., is *ākāṅkṣa* in the former while the reciprocal expectancy of different word meanings to lead to the formation of the sentence meaning is *ākāṅkṣa* in the latter.

आर्थीभावना: The meaning of the injunctive suffix in its general capacity as a verbal suffix. It conveys *pravṛtti* i.e., proceeding to undertake the sacrifice.

आरादुपकारकम्: The *aṅgas* that assist the chief sacrifice without operating on other sacrificial items. *Prayāja* etc., rituals come under this category. The other category of *aṅgas* viz., *sannipatyopakārakas* assist the chief sacrifice by operating on other items. *Prokṣaṇa, avaghāta* etc., come under this category.

इतिकर्तव्यता: The manner or the process of performing a sacrifice. Performance of *prayāja* etc., *aṅgas* constitutes this process.

उपादानम्: The process of *niyoga* getting connected with certain items by *ākṣepa*. In these cases direct expressions to connect these with the *niyoga* will not be available.

उपदेश: Directly stated by Vedic injunction.

उपमानम्: A *pramāṇa* that is utilized to cognise the similarity.

ऊह: Substitution. In the course of borrowing from *prakṛti* to *vikṛti* the substitution made to suit the requirements of *vikṛti* in respect of *mantra, sanskāra* etc., is called *ūha*.

एकदेश: A term used to refer to *hetu* in Prābhākara system.

एकदेशान्तरम्: A term used to refer to *sādhya* in Prābhākara system. These terms are used in *Śābarabhāṣya* also.

औत्पत्तिक: सम्बन्ध: Natural relation between the word and meaning.

कार्यम्: The import of the Vedic injunction. It is also called *apūrva* and *niyoga*. It is of the nature of accomplishment of a task i.e., *yāga*.

कृति: (भावना) Initiative generated by the Vedic injunction in the mind of the person who has to undertake the sacrifice. *Kārya* is the chief import of Vedic injunction. Since, *kārya* has to be accomplished by *kṛti*, it is also included in the import of injunction. It is called *bhāvanā*. This is Prābhākara view of *kṛti* and *bhāvaṇā*. The Bhāṭṭas have a different scheme of *śabdibhāvanā* and *ārthībhāvana*.

क्रिया: (यागक्रिया) The programme of the sacrifice.

क्रत्वर्थ: The items that serve the purpose of *yāga*. These are in contrast with *puruṣārtha* that serve the requirement of the person who undertakes the sacrifice.

करण: The means to produce certain result. In the context of Pūrvamīmānsā, *yāga* is *karaṇa*. According to Prābhākaras it is both *viṣaya* i.e., the subject, and *karaṇa* i.e., the instrument of *kārya*.

क्रियाकार्य: Ordinary injunctions convey *kriyākārya* while Vedic injunctions convey *apūrvakārya*.

कार्यैदमर्थ्यम्: Serving the purpose of *kārya*.

कारकैदमर्थ्यम्: Serving the purpose of *kārakas*.

(i) **गुण:** Quality, attribute.

(ii) **गुण:** Subordinate, in the Pūrvamīmānsā context.

(iii) **गुण:** One of the criterion to distinguish the sacrifices or rituals in Pūrvamīmānsā usage.

ग्राहकग्रहणम्: Solicited by the vedic injunction.

चोदना: The Vedic injunction.

जाति: Universal.

तत्ताप्रमोष: Deletion of the reference to the time in the memory when *rajata* is remembered on seeing *sūkti.*

त्रिपुटीकरणम्: The formula of perceptual cognition evolved by Prābhākaras. The perceptual cognition covers the three i.e., knower, the object known, and the knowledge. Out of these three, the knowledge is self-revealing *(svaprakāśa),* while the object is comprehended through the knowledge. The cognition of the knower and the knowledge is perception. Prābhākaras do not confine the scope of perception to sense perception only. The knower and the knowledge are covered in all cognitions. The cognition of these is perception. This concept is closer to the *sākṣī* concept of Dvaita Vedanta. It despenses with the need of *anuvyavasāya* of Nyāyavaiśeṣikas

तन्त्र: Performance of a ritual item once only as applicable to many. For instance, *yūpāhuti* is performed only once for eleven *yūpas.*

नियोग: Direction, command. This is the import of Vedic injunction according to Prābhākaras. It generates the urge that 'This is my task'.

नियोज्य: A person who is directed by *niyoga* to undertake its accomplishment.

नियमविधि: Mandatory injunction.

नियतसम्बन्ध: Invariable association.

पुरुषार्थ: The sacrificial items that serve the person who has undertaken the sacrifice.

प्रकृति: The original sacrifice.

प्राकृतोपकार: The assistance rendered in *prakṛti yāga.*

प्रत्यक्षम्: Perception. This is not confined to sense perception only.

प्रधानम् The main sacrifice.

(i) **प्रमाणम् (भावसाधनम्):** Valid knowledge.

(ii) **प्रमाणम् (करणसाधनम्):** The means of valid knowledge.

प्रतियोगिन्: A counter correlative. Ordinarily it is used in the sense of a counter correlative to *abhāva.* However, in several other contexts also the expressions *anuyogin* and *pratiyogin* are used to indicate an entity and its counter correlative. The contexts specify the roles played.

प्रवर्तना (प्रेरणा): Impelling, directing. It is taken as the import of Vedic injunction in a section of Bhāṭṭa tradition.

बाध: Sublation.

बाध: Not implementing the *prakṛti yāga* items in *vikṛtiyāga* under certain circumstances. This is Pūrvamīmānsā usage.

भ्रम: Perceptual error.

प्रसङ्ग: When a ritual item performed with reference to one also serves another, it is called *prasaṅga.*

Serving more than one is involved both in *tantra* and *prasaṅga.* However, in *tantra* the purpose of serving more is the aim while in *prasaṅga* it is incidental.

यथार्थज्ञानम्: The cognition the content of which agrees with the fact conveyed.

यथार्थख्याति: The theory that even in the so called error the object cognised is true.

योग्यता: Compatibility of words to get syntactically connected.

यागः *Dravya* and *devatā* give a form to *yāga.*

यागैदमर्थ्यम्: Serving the purpose of *yāga*, connected with *yāga.*

लिङ्गम् (हेतुः) Middle term in a syllogism.

लिङ्गम् (वस्तुसामर्थ्यम्) : One of the criterion to decide the *aṅga* status in Pūrvamīmānsā usage.

विकृतिः A derivatory sacrifice or ritual.

विधिः Injunction. This is conveyed by *liṅ* i.e., optative suffix and also by *tavya* suffix.

विवेकाग्रहणम्: Non-realization of the difference between the two cognitions *idam* and *rajatam* in the error. This is also termed as *bheda-agraha.*

वेद्यः The object of a cognition.

शेषः Subordinate.

शास्त्रप्रमाणम्: (शब्दप्रमाणम्) The Veda only is *śabda-pramāṇa.* The statement of men are not *śabdapramāṇa* according to Prābhākaras. Therefore, *śabdapramāṇa* is called *śastrapramāṇa.* For Bhāṭṭas both Veda and the statements of reliable persons are *śabdapramāṇa.*

विश्वजिन्न्यायः A ruling given in respect of *viśvajid-yāga* that the result i.e., *svarga*, has to be envisaged even if it is not stated. This ruling is adopted in similar cases.

रात्रिसत्रन्यायः A ruling given in the case of *rātrisatra* that the result stated in *arthavāda* be taken as the result of the sacrifice. This ruling is adopted in similar cases.

शक्तिः Potency. Every object has its own potency. This is called *śakti.* It is considered as a separate category by Prābhākaras.

शक्तिः The power of a word to convey its primary meaning.

सन्निधिः Proximity. It is not necessary that the proximity is that of a required word only. If the object concerned is brought to the mind that is sufficient. That is Prābhākara view of *sannidhi.*

स्वलक्षणम्ः The core nature of an object.

समवायः The relation of inherence.

स्वप्रकाशत्वम्ः Self revealing nature.

सादृश्यम्ः Similarity. This is considered as a separate category by Prābhākaras.

सन्निपत्योपकारकम्ः The *aṅgas* that assist the sacrifice by operating on *kārakas. Prokṣaṇa, avaghāta* etc., come under this category.

सविकल्पकज्ञानम्ः The perceptual cognition in which the object and its attributes are presented organized as *viśeṣya* and *viśeṣaṇa.*

संस्कारः Impressions of previous cognition.

संस्कारः Purification, refinement.

ज्ञाततः The fact of an object being known. This fact is utilized by Bhāṭṭas to infer the knowledge.

Bibliography

Sanskrit Texts

Bhāṭṭamīmānsā			Authors
1.	*Śabarabhāṣya*	-	Śabaraswamin
2.	*Ślokavārtika*	-	Kumārilabhaṭṭa
3.	*Tantravārtika*	-	do
4.	*Bhāvanāviveka*	-	Maṇḍana Miśra
5.	*Vibhramaviveka*	-	do
6.	*Vidhiviveka*	-	do
7.	*Tattvakaṇika* (Commentary on Vidhiviveka)	-	Vācaspati Miśra
8.	*Śāstradīpikā* (Tarkapāda)	-	Pārthasārathi Miśra
9.	*Nyāyaratnamālā*	-	do
10.	*Nyāyakaratna* (Commentary on Nyāyaratnamāla)	-	Rāmānuja
11.	*Tattvabindu*	-	Vācaspati Miśra
12.	*Bhāṭṭarahasya*	-	Khaṇḍadeva
13.	*Bhāṭṭasaṅgraha*	-	Rāghavedra Tīrtha
14.	*Mānameyodaya*	-	Nārāyaṇa
15.	*Mīmāṃsā Kośa*	-	Kevalānanda Sarasvati

16. *Mīmāṃsāmañjarī* - Thangaswamy

Prābhākara Mīmāmsā

17. *Bṛhati* - Prabhākara Miśra

18. *Ṛjuvimalā* (Commentary on Bṛhati) - Śālikanātha

19. *Bhāṣyadīpa* - do

20. *Prakaraṇa Pañcikā* - do

21. *Nayaviveka* - Bhavanātha Miśra

22. *Vivekatattva* (Commentary or Nayaviveka) - Ravideva

23. *Nayavivekadīpikā* (Commentary) - Varada Rāja

24. *Tantrarahasya* - Rāmānuja

25. *Prabhākara Vijaya* - Nandīśvara

Nyāya

26. *Nyāyamañjarī* - Jayanta Bhāṭṭa

27. *Nyāyakusumāñjali* - Udayana

28. *Tatvacintāmaṇī* - Gaṅgeśa

29. *Siddhantamuktāvalī* - Viśvanātha

Vedānta (Advaita)

30. *Iṣṭasiddhi* - Vimuktātmā

31. *Vivaraṇaprameyasaṅgraha* - Vidyāraṇya

32.	*Khyātitattvasamīkṣā*	-	Vepatturu Subramanya Shastry

Vedānta (Viśiṣṭādvaita)

33.	*Śrī Bhāṣya*	-	Rāmānujacārya
34.	*Nayadyumaṇi*	-	Meghanandāri Suri
35.	*Yatindra Matadīpikā*	-	Śrīnivāsadāsa
36.	*Yathārthakhyatibhūṣaṇam*	-	Rāmānuja Tātācārya

Vedānta (Dvaita)

37.	*Nyāyasudhā*	-	Jayatīrtha
38.	*Pramāṇa Paddhati*	-	Jayatīrtha
39.	*Tarkatāṇḍava*	-	Vyāsatīrtha
40.	*Nyāyāmṛtam*	-	"

Studies in English

1. Pūrvamīmānsā in its sources - Ganganath Jha
2. The Prābhākara school of Pūrvamīmānsā - Ganganath Jha
3. Introduction to the Pūrvamīmānsā - Paśupatinātha Shastry
4. Introduction to Tantrarahasya - K.S. Ramaswamy
5. The theories of error in Indian Philosophy - Bijayananda Kar
6. A critique of the theories of Viparyaya - Nanilal Sen
7. Perceptual errors Indian theories - Srinivasa Rao
8. Thinking ritually - Francis X Clooney

Articles

1. Prābhākaras Old and new - M. Hiriyanna
2. The doctrine of Niyoga (Indian Philosophical Studies Vol. II) - M. Hiriyanna
3. Prābhākara school of Pūrvamīmānsā (Commemoration Vol. 1981) - Kuppuswamy Shastry
4. Problem of categorical imperative in the Philosophy of Prābhākaras school - Hajme Nakamura